September 4–7, 2012
Paris, France

**Association for
Computing Machinery**

Advancing Computing as a Science & Profession

DocEng 2012

Proceedings of the 2012 ACM Symposium on
Document Engineering

Sponsored by:
ACM SIGWEB

In cooperation with:
ACM SIGDOC

Supporters:
Adobe, Hewlett Packard, & Telecom ParisTech

Association for Computing Machinery

Advancing Computing as a Science & Profession

Symposium and PC Chairs' Welcome

It is our great pleasure to welcome you to the *2012 ACM Symposium on Document Engineering – DocEng 2012*, which is being held September 4–7, 2012, in Paris, France. This year's symposium continues its tradition of being the premier forum for presentation of research results and experience reports on leading edge issues of document presentation and adaptation, analysis, modeling, transformation, systems, theory, and applications. The mission of the symposium is to share significant results, to evaluate novel approaches and models, and to identify promising directions for future research and development. DocEng gives researchers and practitioners a unique opportunity to share their perspectives with others interested in the various aspects of document engineering.

The call for papers attracted 89 submissions from Asia, Australia, Canada, Europe, the Russian Federation, and the United States. The program committee accepted 14 of 42 full paper submissions (33%), plus another 20 short papers, and 5 demos and posters, for a combined acceptance rate of 44%. The papers cover a variety of topics, including Layout and Presentation Control, Document Analysis, OCR and Visual Analysis, Multimedia and Hypermedia, XML and Related Tools, Architecture and Document Management, Search and Sense-making, and Digital Humanities. In addition, the program includes workshops on authoring issues, and on education models and curricula for Document Engineering. DocEng 2012 features keynote speeches by Bruno Bachimont of the Institut National de l'Audiovisuel, and Université de Technologie de Compiègne, and by Thierry Delprat of Nuxeo. We hope that these proceedings will serve as a valuable reference for document engineering researchers and developers.

We want to thank the authors for contributing the high quality papers that made for a very competitive submission pool. We are very grateful to the program committee and the additional reviewers, who prepared nearly 300 thoughtful and thorough reviews, comments, and feedback to the authors.

We must also thank Telecom ParisTech for hosting DocEng 2012, and to our colleagues and those who "volunteered" to help with the organization, and local arrangements. We are also very grateful to the Steering Committee Chair Peter King for his support. Special thanks go to Lisa Tolles of Sheridan Printing Company for her care and patience in preparing the proceedings. Finally, we thank our sponsor, ACM SIGWEB, and our generous corporate supporters, Adobe and Hewlett-Packard.

We hope that you will find this program interesting and thought-provoking and that the symposium will provide you with a valuable opportunity to share ideas with other researchers and practitioners from institutions around the world.

Patrick Schmitz
DocEng 2012 Program Chair
University of California, Berkeley

Cyril Concolato
DocEng 2012 Symposium Chair
Telecom ParisTech

Table of Contents

Keynote Address I
Session Chair: Peter King *(University of Manitoba)*

Session 1: Layout and Presentation Generation
Session Chair: David Brailsford *(University of Nottingham)*

Session 2: Document Analysis
Session Chair: Simone Marinai *(University of Florence)*

Session 3: Multimedia and Hypermedia
Session Chair: Cyril Concolato *(Telecom ParisTech)*

Keynote Address II

Session Chair: Patrick Schmitz *(University of California, Berkeley)*

Session 4: XML and Related Tools

Session Chair: Matthew Hardy *(Adobe Systems Inc.)*

Session 5: OCR and Visual Analysis

Session Chair: Laurence Likforman-Sulem *(Telecom ParisTech)*

Session 6: Demonstrations and Posters

Session Chair: Kim Marriott *(Monash University)*

Session 7: Search and Sensemaking

Session Chair: Charles Nicholas *(University of Maryland, Baltimore County)*

Session 8: Digital Humanities

Session Chair: Patrick Schmitz *(University of California, Berkeley)*

Session 9: Architecture and Document Management

Session Chair: Anthony Wiley *(Hewlett-Packard)*

Author Index

DocEng 2012 Symposium Organization

Symposium Chair: Cyril Concolato *(Telecom ParisTech, France)*

Program Chair: Patrick Schmitz *(University of California, Berkeley, USA)*

Local Arrangements Chairs: Jean-Claude Dufourd *(Telecom ParisTech, France)*
Jean-Claude Moissinac *(Telecom ParisTech, France)*

Steering Committee Chair: Peter King *(University of Manitoba, Canada)*

Steering Committee: David Brailsford *(University of Nottingham, UK)*
Dick Bulterman *(CWI, The Netherlands)*
Rolf Ingold *(University of Fribourg, Switzerland)*
Michael Gormish *(Ricoh Innovations, USA)*
Ethan Munson *(University of Wisconsin-Milwaukee, USA)*
Charles Nicholas *(University of Maryland, Baltimore County, USA)*
Maria da Graca C. Pimentel *(Universidade de Sao Paulo, Brazil)*
Cécile Roisin *(Université Pierre Mendes-France and INRIA, France)*
Steven Simske *(HP Laboratories, Palo Alto, USA)*
Jean-Yves Vion-Dury *(Xerox Research Centre Europe, France)*
Anthony Wiley *(HP Laboratories, Bristol, UK)*

Program Committee: Apostolos Antonacopoulos *(University of Salford, UK)*
Steven Bagley *(University of Nottingham, UK)*
Helen Balinsky *(Hewlett Packard Laboratories, UK)*
Uwe Borghoff *(Universität der Bundeswehr, Munich, Germany)*
David Brailsford *(University of Nottingham, UK)*
Dick Bulterman *(Centrum Wiskunde & Informatica, The Netherlands)*
Pablo Cesar *(Centrum Wiskunde & Informatica, The Netherlands)*
Boris Chidlovskii *(Xerox Research Centre Europe, France)*
Michael Collard *(The University of Akron, USA)*
Cyril Concolato *(Telecom ParisTech, France)*
Pierre Genevès *(INRIA, France)*
Gersende Georg *(French National Authority for Health (HAS), Paris, France)*
Bob Glushko *(University of California, USA)*
Luiz Fernando Gomes Soares *(PUC-Rio, Brazil)*
Michael Gormish *(Ricoh Innovations, Inc., USA)*
Matthew Hardy *(Adobe Systems, Inc. , USA)*
Nathan Hurst *(Adobe Systems, Inc. , USA)*
Rolf Ingold *(University of Fribourg, Switzerland)*
Min-Yen Kan *(National University of Singapore, Singapore)*

Program Committee (continued):

Peter King *(University of Manitoba, Canada)*
Alberto Laender *(Federal University of Minas Gerais, Brazil)*
Nabil Layaïda *(INRIA, France)*
Baoli Li *(Henan University of Technology, China)*
John Lumley *(Independent, UK)*
Simone Marinai *(University of Florence, Italy)*
Kim Marriott *(Monash University, Australia)*
Mirella Moro *(Univ. Federal de Minas Gerais, Brazil)*
Ethan Munson *(University of Wisconsin-Milwaukee, USA)*
Charles Nicholas *(University of Maryland, Baltimore County, USA)*
Moira Norrie *(ETH Zurich, Switzerland)*
Maria Da Graça Pimentel *(Universidade de Sao Paulo, Brazil)*
Stefan Pletschacher *(University of Salford, UK)*
Steve Probets *(Loughborough University, UK)*
Cécile Roisin *(Université Pierre Mendes-France and INRIA, France)*
Sebastian Rönnau *(HQ 38th Command and Support Regiment, Germany)*
Ryan Shaw *(University of North Carolina, Chapel Hill, USA)*
Steven Simske *(Hewlett-Packard Laboratories, USA)*
Margaret Sturgill *(Hewlett-Packard Laboratories, USA)*
Frank Tompa *(University of Waterloo, Canada)*
Jean-Yves Vion-Dury *(Xerox Research Centre Europe, France)*
Anthony Wiley *(Hewlett-Packard Laboratories, USA)*
Raymond Wong *(University of New South Wales, UK)*

Additional reviewers:

Roberto Gerson Azevedo
Carlos Batista
Thomas Bohne
Michael Decker
Laurence Likforman-Sulem
Diogo Martins
Carlos Soares Neto
Ricardo Rios
Thiago Salles
Fengming Shi
Alexander Uherek

DocEng 2012 Sponsors & Supporters

Sponsor:

In cooperation with:

SIGDOC

Special Interest Group on
Design of Communication

Supporters:

Adobe

TELECOM
ParisTech

Document and Archive: Editing the Past

Bruno Bachimont

Université de Technologie de Compiègne

UMR CNRS 7253 Heudiasyc

BP 20259 60205 Compiègne cedex

bruno.bachimont@utc.fr

ABSTRACT

Document engineering has a difficult task: to propose tools and methods to manipulate contents and make sense of them. This task is still harder when dealing with archive, insofar as document engineering has not only to provide tools for expressing sense but above all tools and methods to keep contents accessible in their integrity and intelligible according to their meaning. However, these objectives may be contradictory: access implies to transform contents to make them accessible through networks, tools and devices. Intelligibility may imply to adapt contents to the current state of knowledge and capacity of understanding. But, by doing that, can we still speak of authenticity, integrity, or even the identity of documents?

Document engineering has provided powerful means to express meaning and to turn an intention into a semiotic expression. Document repurposing has become a usual way for exploiting libraries, archives, etc. By enabling to reuse a specific part of a given content, repurposing techniques allow to entirely renegotiate the meaning of this part by changing its context, its interactivity, in short the way people can consider this piece of content and interpret it.

Put in this way, there could be an antinomy between archiving and document engineering. However, transforming document, editing content is an efficient way to keep them alive and compelling for people. Preserving contents does not consist in simply storing them but in actively transforming them to adapt them technically and keep them intelligible. Editing the past is then a new challenge, merging a content deontology with a document technology.

This challenge implies to redefine some classical notions as authenticity and highlight the needs for new concepts and methods. Especially in a digital world, documents are permanently reconfigured by technical tools that produce variants, similar contents calling into question the usual definition the identity of documents. Editing the past calls for a new critics of variants.

Categories and Subject Descriptors

H.3.7 [**Information Storage and Retrieval**]: Digital Libraries – *systems issues*

Keywords

Archive, Digital Preservation, Document Engineering.

Bio

Bruno Bachimont is Professor at the Université de Technologie de Compiègne where he teaches computer science, logics and philosophy. More precisely, he is Head of research of UTC since 2006. A graduate of the Ecole des Mines de Nancy, Prof. Bachimont received a PhD in Computer Science from the Paris 6 University in 1990 as well as a PhD in Philosophy from the Ecole Polytechnique in 1996.

Prof. Bachimont has published widely in the fields of artificial intelligence, knowledge-based systems, indexation, and document engineering and is the author of "knowledge and content engineering: Documents and ontologies" (in french, Paris: Hermès, 2007) and of « Le sens de la technique: le numérique et le calcul » (in french, Paris : Les Belles Lettres, 2010).

Prof. Bachimont is currently involved in projects related to digital preservation, audiovisual/multimedia indexing, using formalisms and theories drawn from the knowledge representation paradigm (ontologies, conceptual graphs, logic), the document paradigm and the audiovisual world. The projects are undertaken within a general conceptual framework on the philosophy of knowledge and technology to explore the mutual influence of mind and the digital.

DocEng'12, September 4–7, 2012, Paris, France.
ACM 978-1-4503-1116-8/12/09.

Ad Insertion in Automatically Composed Documents

Niranjan Damera-Venkata
Hewlett-Packard Laboratories
1501 Page Mill Road
Palo Alto, CA 94304
damera@hpl.hp.com

José Bento
Stanford University
Dept. of Electrical Engineering
Stanford, CA 94305
jbento@stanford.edu

ABSTRACT

We consider the problem of automatically inserting advertisements (*ads*) into machine composed documents. We explicitly analyze the fundamental tradeoff between expected revenue due to *ad* insertion and the quality of the corresponding composed documents. We show that the optimal tradeoff a publisher can expect may be expressed as an *efficient-frontier* in the revenue-quality space. We develop algorithms to compose documents that lie on this optimal tradeoff frontier. These algorithms can automatically choose distributions of *ad* sizes and *ad* placement locations to optimize revenue for a given quality or optimize quality for given revenue. Such automation allows a market maker to accept highly personalized content from publishers who have no design or *ad* inventory management capability and distribute formatted documents to end users with aesthetic *ad* placement. The *ad* density/coverage may be controlled by the publisher or the end user on a per document basis by simply sliding along the tradeoff frontier. Business models where *ad* sales precede (*ad-pull*) or follow (*ad-push*) document composition are analyzed from a document engineering perspective.

Categories and Subject Descriptors

I.7.4 [**Computing Methodologies**]: Document and Text Processing:Electronic Publishing

General Terms

Algorithms, Design

Keywords

automated publishing, advertisement insertion, document composition, layout synthesis

1. INTRODUCTION

In traditional publishing every subscriber gets the same copy of a newspaper/magazine, and design costs are amortized over the subscriber base. While professional graphic design works well for the traditional publishing industry where a single high quality document may be distributed to an audience of millions, it is not economically viable (due to its high marginal cost) for the creation of highly personalized documents that change per subscriber and by device form factor. Publishers want to deliver targeted personalized content not only because it is much more engaging and relevant to their subscribers but also because of the potential advertisement (*ad*) revenue boost when content and advertisements are accurately targeted.

Automated document composition attempts to transform personalized content automatically (without per-copy manual graphic design) into documents with high aesthetic value. This has been a topic of much research [8] [6]. However, the problem of automated advertisement insertion into machine composed documents has not received attention from the document engineering community. In this paper we analyze the problem of automated advertisement insertion into machine composed documents from a document engineering perspective.

A key insight is that if content is to be formatted for a particular page count then the specific sizes of *ads* and their placement affect the overall aesthetics of a document composition. For example, consider the case where we are trying to place a large *ad* in a single page document with a lot of content. An automated document composition algorithm may deal with this by shrinking images (*ads* cannot be shrunk of course), reducing whitespace, reducing font sizes or line spacing. These changes may have undesirable effects on the quality of the resulting formatted document. On the other hand an *ad* insertion may also have a beneficial impact on document composition quality. Consider the case where the inserted *ad* fills an undesirable whitespace or void in the composition. The preceding examples illustrate that in general there is a fundamental tradeoff between revenue due to *ad* insertion and the quality of machine composed documents. The notion of quality could be expanded to include relevance of the *ads* to the target audience. For example, in internet advertising where pages are scrollable and *ads* are not integrated into the content (but instead appear in their own to one side in reserved area of the page) the tradeoff is between revenue and the relevance of an *ad* measured by its click-through-rate.

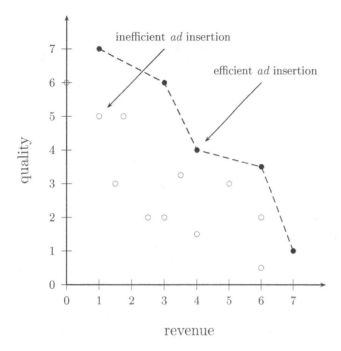

Figure 1: The *efficient-frontier*. Each dot represents a document composition of the given content with advertisements. The number of *ads*, *ad*-size distribution and the specific placement of *ads* is allowed to vary across compositions. Efficient documents are those for which we cannot find another document with at least the same revenue and better quality, or at least the same quality and better revenue. The discrete set of efficient points (represented here with the filled discs, connected with dashed lines) is called the *efficient-frontier*. This frontier represents the *optimal* tradeoff between revenue and quality when advertisements are inserted.

Fig. 1 illustrates the tradeoff between revenue and quality for a document with given content composed automatically with different *ad* size distributions and placements. Each point represents a document with a specific distribution of *ad* sizes with the *ads* placed at specific locations within the document. Note that many points (labeled *inefficient*) are not sensible document compositions since we can find other documents that have at least the same revenue and better quality or that have at least the same quality and better revenue. Note also that there are a set of points (labeled *efficient*) that represent a valid tradeoff between revenue and quality. There are no other documents that have at least the same revenue and better quality or have at least the same quality and better revenue. The set of *efficient* points is called the *efficient-frontier* and represents an optimal way to tradeoff revenue and document quality for *ad* insertion. The dashed connecting line in Fig. 1 simply serves as a visual aid to help judge the relative positions of points. The *efficient-frontier* is a discrete set.

In this paper we analyze algorithms that attempt to efficiently compute documents that are points on the *efficient-frontier*. The business model for *ad*-sales impacts problem formulation and hence the specific algorithms we develop. We consider two business models. In the *ad-pull* business model, *ad* sales precede document composition. Advertiser bidding creates a pool of *ads* (with associated bid-prices) for each publication. The goal is to select or *pull* specific *ads* from the pool and compose documents with *ad* placement that represents documents on the *efficient-frontier*. In the *ad-push* business model the *ad* sales come after the document composition. Here, the algorithm uses expected revenues of *ads* of particular sizes and automatically chooses *ad* size distributions and placement to generate documents with empty *ad* slots on an expected *efficient-frontier*. The *ad* slots (a.k.a. *ad* inventory) are then *pushed* to the market for sale. Note that with this model it is possible that an *ad* slot may be unsold and so may need to be filled with filler content. However, over time, the expected market value of *ads* of particular sizes will be more accurately estimated by the publisher. Adjusting his templates and/or *ad* reserve prices accordingly, over time, the publisher is less likely to have unsold *ads* slots in his documents.

The paper is organized as follows. Section 2 reviews related work. Section 3 reviews a structured probabilistic model of document quality used in developing the algorithms in this paper. Section 4 develops and analyzes algorithms for determining the discrete *efficient-frontier* for both the *ad-pull* and *ad-push* business models. Section 5 analyzes inter-subscriber tradeoffs that naturally gives rise to the concept of a continuous *stochastic efficient-frontier* that is the convex-envelope of the discrete *efficient-frontier*. Algorithms that allow us to produce documents on the *stochastic* frontier are presented. Finally Section 6 concludes the paper by summarizing the contributions and indicating future directions. We also provide an Appendix of mathematical complements.

2. RELATED WORK

The concept (and term) *efficient-frontier* (a.k.a. the *Pareto set*) was first introduced in finance by Harry Markowitz [9] in the context of selecting portfolios of securities that trade off risk (portfolio variance) versus expected return (portfolio mean). An investor seeks portfolios on the *efficient-frontier* risk-return space. Efficient portfolios are those where additional expected return cannot be gained without increasing the risk of the portfolio. This seminal work lead the 1990 Nobel prize in economics and forms the basis for modern portfolio theory. The *efficient-frontier* has also found several applications in pricing and revenue management [11] in the tradeoff analysis of competing goals like revenue and profit, short-term price discounting vs. lifetime customer value, optimization of airline booking classes etc. In the internet advertising space companies like Efficient Frontier[1] trade cost of keywords vs. expected return on investment (ROI) to manage their clients keyword marketing campaigns.

The computational task of determining the *efficient-frontier* efficiently from a discrete set of candidate points has also been studied in computer science [7, 4] where the problem is called the maximal vector computation or Skyline algorithm. However, in many cases (such as the problems discussed in this paper) the number of possible candidate points could be very large and each point itself corresponds to significant computational effort. So the naive method of generating all possible candidate points (documents in our case) and using the Skyline algorithm to compute the frontier is not viable.

---

[1]http://www.efrontier.com

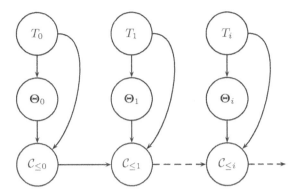

Figure 2: PDM as a graphical model.

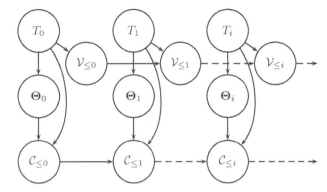

Figure 3: PDM with ordered Ad Insertion.

3. MODELING DOCUMENT QUALITY

In this section we review a structured model for document aesthetics based on a probabilistic modeling of designer choice in document design. This model will be used in developing efficient *ad* insertion algorithms. We represent the given set of all the units of content to be composed (ex: images, units of text, sidebars etc.) by a finite set $\mathcal{C}$. Text units could be words, sentences, lines of text or whole paragraphs. We denote by $\mathcal{C}'$ a set comprising all sets of discrete content allocation possibilities over one or more pages starting with and including the first page. For example, if there are 3 lines of text and 1 floating figure, $\mathcal{C} = \{l_1, l_2, l_3, f_1\}$ while $\mathcal{C}' = \{\{l_1\}, \{l_1, l_2\}, \{l_1, l_2, l_3\}, \{f_1\}, \{l_1, f_1\}, \{l_1, l_2, f_1\}, \{l_1, l_2, l_3, f_1\}\} \cup \{\emptyset\}$. Note that the specific order of elements within an allocation set is not important since $\{l_1, l_2, f_1\}$ and $\{l_1, f_1, l_2\}$ refer to an allocation of the same content. However allocation $\{l_1, l_3, f_1\} \notin \mathcal{C}'$ since lines 1 and 3 cannot be in the same allocation without including line 2. $\mathcal{C}'$ includes the empty set to allow the possibility of a null allocation.

In order to compose documents, one must make aesthetic decisions on how to paginate content, how to arrange page elements (text, images, graphics, sidebars etc.) on each page, how much to crop/scale images, how to manage whitespace etc. These decision variables are *not* mutually exclusive, making the aesthetic graphic design of documents a hard problem often requiring an expert design professional. The probabilistic document model (PDM) [2] explicitly models the dependency between key design choices including pagination, choice of relative arrangements for page elements, and page edits (including image re-targeting and whitespace adjustment). The coupling between these design variables is explicitly modeled as a Bayesian network shown in Fig. 2. A probability distribution can be associated with the network by multiplying the conditional probability distributions of each node conditioned only on its parents [10].

$$\mathbb{P}(D, I) = \prod_{i=0}^{I-1} \mathbb{P}(\mathcal{C}_{\leq i} | \mathcal{C}_{\leq i-1}, \mathbf{\Theta}_i, T_i) \mathbb{P}(\mathbf{\Theta}_i | T_i) \mathbb{P}(T_i) \quad (1)$$

Random variable T_i represents choice of a relative arrangement of page elements for the ith page from a library of page templates representing different possible relative arrangements of content. Random vector $\mathbf{\Theta}_i$ encodes template parameters representing possible edits to the chosen

template. Possible choices for variable template parameters Θ include figure dimensions, whitespace between page elements, margins etc. Random set $\mathcal{C}_{\leq i}$ represents choice of a content allocation to the first i pages from the set of possible allocations $\mathcal{C}'$. Note that content allocation to the ith page (i.e. pagination) is computed as $\mathcal{C}_i = \mathcal{C}_{\leq i} - \mathcal{C}_{\leq i-1}$. In this paper we treat the page count I as a given constant. More generally we could treat page count as a random variable also. See [2] for details.

PDM is in fact a *micro* model for document quality that associates a probability (or quality score) with each *conditional* design choice made on each page. The overall probability of a document is the product of these *micro* probability scores. A document $\mathcal{D}$ of I pages is defined by a triplet $\mathcal{D} = \{\{\mathcal{C}_{\leq i}\}_{i=0}^{I-1}, \{\mathbf{\Theta}_i\}_{i=0}^{I-1}, \{T_i\}_{i=0}^{I-1}\}$ of random variables representing the various design choices made in the document creation process. The overall quality $\mathbb{P}(D, I)$ of a document $\mathcal{D}$ of I pages is the product of the conditional probabilities of all design choices made. PDM contrasts with *macro* models for document quality [1, 5] that attempt to quantify abstract aesthetic notions such as harmony, balance, regularity etc.

In equation (1) probability distribution $\mathbb{P}(T_i)$ governs relative preference of template T_i from a set Ω of possible templates. The conditional multi-variate probability distribution $\mathbb{P}(\mathbf{\Theta}_i | T_i)$ may be regarded as a *prior* probability distribution that determines the *prior* preference (before seeing content) for template parameters. Finally the probability distribution $\mathbb{P}(\mathcal{C}_{\leq i} | \mathcal{C}_{\leq i-1}, \mathbf{\Theta}_i, T_i)$ reflects how well the content allocated to the current page fits template T_i when template parameters are set to $\mathbf{\Theta}_i$.

Once the probability distributions in equation (1) are defined we can simply calculate $\mathbb{P}(\mathcal{D}, I)$ as a measure of document quality. We may also use $L(\mathcal{D}, I) = \log \mathbb{P}(\mathcal{D}, I)$ as the quality measure in practice, since taking the logarithm converts products to summations that are often easier to work with. A logarithmic transformation (in fact any monotonic function) of the quality axis does not change the *efficient-frontier* set.

In this paper, we choose $\mathbb{P}(T_i)$ to be the uniform over all templates in the template library, indicating no *a priori* preference for a particular template. Human design knowledge regarding parameter preferences may be used in specifying $\mathbb{P}(\mathbf{\Theta}_i | T_i)$ (ex: by designer input of mean, variance, min and max of the parameter values) [2]. $\mathbb{P}(\mathcal{C}_{\leq i} | \mathcal{C}_{\leq i-1}, \mathbf{\Theta}_i, T_i)$ is simply a goodness of fit function and is calculated based on a specific parameterization of a template as a graph introduced in [2]. Fit is assessed by how well content fills the page along all paths in the graph from top to bottom and left to right. Please see [2] for more details on these probabilistic template parameterizations.

4. EFFICIENT-FRONTIER COMPUTATION

This section analyzes algorithms for the automated composition of documents with optimal *ad* insertion. Section 4.1 analyzes the case when *ad* sales precede document composition (*ad-pull*) while Section 4.2 analyzes the case when document composition precedes *ad* sales (*ad-push*).

4.1 Ad-Pull

In the *ad-pull* scenario advertisers bid on *ad* placements in documents based on several factors that may include demographics of the target audience, *ad*-size, *ad*-position etc. Business logic then creates an *ad*-pool for each document that selects candidate *ads* that are good matches for the documents target audience. Since more than one advertiser may bid on a particular size of *ad*, each bid is treated as a different *ad*-placement opportunity. The *ad*-pool thus has a specific distribution of *ad*-sizes and associated bid prices. The goal is to derive the *efficient-frontier* tradeoff over all subsets that meet certain constraints (ex: At least one *ad* per page must be inserted). The revenue of a subset is defined as the sum of all bid prices of *ads* in that subset.

For an *ad*-pool with M *ads*, there are $\sum_{k=0}^{M} \binom{M}{k}$ ways of choosing a subset of *ads* to be composed. For each of the subsets of size k there are $k!$ possible orderings of the *ads*. Thus, in general there are at least $\sum_{k=0}^{M} \binom{M}{M-k}$ possible *ad* insertions to be considered. Of course, a particular *ad* order may still correspond to several different possible *ad*-insertion points and hence *ad* positions within a document. So composing all possible documents and then using the skyline algorithm [7, 4] (see Appendix for pseudocode) to compute the *efficient-frontier* is not feasible.

While there is no optimal way (one may always resort to sub-optimal heuristics in practice) to simplify the subset selection and *ad* ordering problems, we may develop efficient algorithms to compose a document that is optimal given a particular ordering of *ads* to be inserted. To do this we extend the *ad*-free PDM model for document quality to include *ads*. The Bayesian network representation of this extended model is given in Figure 3. The resulting document probability becomes:

$$\mathbb{P}(D, I) = \prod_{i=0}^{I-1} \mathbb{P}(\mathcal{C}_{\leq i} | \mathcal{C}_{\leq i-1}, \mathbf{\Theta}_i, T_i) \mathbb{P}(\mathbf{\Theta}_i | T_i) \cdots$$
$$\mathbb{P}(\mathcal{V}_{\leq i} | \mathcal{V}_{\leq i-1}, T_i) \mathbb{P}(T_i) \quad (2)$$

where the newly introduced random set $\mathcal{V}_{\leq i}$ refers to an allocation of *ads* to the first i pages of the document from the set $\mathcal{V}'$ of all possible *ad* allocations. The probability $\mathbb{P}(\mathcal{V}_{\leq i} | \mathcal{V}_{\leq i-1}, T_i)$ is defined as

$$\mathbb{P}(\mathcal{V}_{\leq i} | \mathcal{V}_{\leq i-1}, T_i) = \begin{cases} 1 & \mathcal{V}_{\leq i} - \mathcal{V}_{\leq i-1} \text{ matches } T_i \\ 0 & else \end{cases} \quad (3)$$

This filters cases where template T_i does not have *ad* slots that match the allocation $\mathcal{V}_{\leq i} - \mathcal{V}_{\leq i-1}$ of *ads* to page i.

The optimal document $\mathcal{D}^*$ is defined by the quadruple sequence $\mathcal{D}^* = \{\{\mathcal{C}_{\leq i}^*\}_{i=0}^{I-1}, \{\{\mathcal{V}_{\leq i}^*\}_{i=0}^{I-1}, \{\mathbf{\Theta}_i^*\}_{i=0}^{I-1}, \{T_i^*\}_{i=0}^{I-1}$

that maximizes equation (2). The maximization (optimal document *inference*) algorithm is very similar to the dynamic programming algorithm derived in some detail in[2] for the maximization of equation (1) and is succinctly summarized in Algorithms 1 and 2 below.

Algorithm 1 Pull-based *ad* insertion: Forward pass

1: $\Psi(\mathcal{A}_c, \mathcal{B}_c, T) = \max_{\mathbf{\Theta}} \mathbb{P}(\mathcal{A}_c, |\mathcal{B}_c, \mathbf{\Theta}, T) \mathbb{P}(\mathbf{\Theta}|T)$
2: $\Phi(\mathcal{A}_c, \mathcal{B}_c, \mathcal{A}_a, \mathcal{B}_a) = \max_{T \in \Omega} \Psi(\mathcal{A}_c, \mathcal{B}_c, T) \mathbb{P}(\mathcal{A}_a|\mathcal{B}_a, T) \mathbb{P}(T)$
3: $\tau_0(\mathcal{A}_c, \mathcal{A}_a) \leftarrow \Phi(\mathcal{A}_c, \emptyset, \mathcal{A}_a, \emptyset)$
4: $\tau_i(\mathcal{A}_c, \mathcal{A}_a) = \max_{\mathcal{B}_c, \mathcal{B}_a} \Phi(\mathcal{A}_c, \mathcal{B}_c, \mathcal{A}_a, \mathcal{B}_a) \tau_{i-1}(\mathcal{B}_c, \mathcal{B}_a), i \geq 1$

Algorithm 2 Pull-based *ad* insertion: Backward pass

$i \leftarrow I - 1, \mathcal{A}_c \leftarrow \mathcal{C}, \mathcal{A}_a \leftarrow \mathcal{V}$
while $i \geq 0$ **do**
    $\mathcal{C}_{\leq i}^* \leftarrow \mathcal{A}_c, \mathcal{V}_{\leq i}^* \leftarrow \mathcal{A}_a$
    $\mathcal{B}_c^*, \mathcal{B}_a^* = \arg\max_{\mathcal{B}_c, \mathcal{B}_a} \Phi(\mathcal{A}_c, \mathcal{B}_c, \mathcal{A}_a, \mathcal{B}_a) \tau_{i-1}(\mathcal{B}_c, \mathcal{B}_a)$
    $T_i^* = \arg\max_{T \in \Omega} \Psi(\mathcal{C}_{\leq i}^*, \mathcal{B}_c^*, T) \mathbb{P}(\mathcal{V}_{\leq i}^*|\mathcal{B}_a^*, T) \mathbb{P}(T)$
    $\mathbf{\Theta}_i^* = \arg\max_{\mathbf{\Theta}} \mathbb{P}(\mathcal{C}_{\leq i}^*, |\mathcal{B}_c^*, \mathbf{\Theta}, T_i^*) \mathbb{P}(\mathbf{\Theta}|T_i^*)$
    $\mathcal{A}_c \leftarrow \mathcal{B}_c^*, \mathcal{A}_a \leftarrow \mathcal{B}_a^*$
    $i \leftarrow i - 1$
end while

The algorithm consists of two passes. In the *forward pass* we successively eliminate each variable by first grouping terms in equation (2) involving the variable and then finding the maxima of these terms with respect to that variable. This gives us functions of the remaining variables. These functions (dynamic programming tables) are then propagated to the next maximization step for further grouping and variable elimination. $\mathcal{A}_c$ refers to an allocation of content to all pages upto the current page. $\mathcal{A}_a$ refers to an allocation of *ads* to all pages upto the current page. $\mathcal{B}_c$ refers to an allocation of content to all previous pages. $\mathcal{B}_a$ refers to an allocation of *ads* to all previous pages. Table entries are computed for all valid content allocation sets $\mathcal{A}_c, \mathcal{B}_c \in \mathcal{C}'$ with $\mathcal{A}_c \supseteq \mathcal{B}_c$ and advertisement allocations $\mathcal{A}_a, \mathcal{B}_a \in \mathcal{V}'$ with $\mathcal{A}_a \supseteq \mathcal{B}_a{}^2$. The continuous variable maximization in Step 1 of algorithm 1 may be performed efficiently as a quadratic programming problem with bound constraints for appropriate probability parameterization [2].

In the *backward pass* we traverse the tables backward starting from the term $\tau_{I-1}(\mathcal{C}, \mathcal{V})$ that equals the global maximum of equation (2) over all the content and *ads*. The backward pass successively infers the allocations of content and *ads* to the previous pages along with templates and template parameters that are on the path to achieving the global maximum.

4.1.1 Example

Table 1 illustrates an example *ad*-pool of four *ads* to be inserted into a given sample two-page Lorem Ipsum content with two figures.

---
[2]This embedding of previous page allocations inside the current allocation ensures that the *ad* order is never violated

(a) $(r, \log q) = (7.0, -0.20)$

(b) $(r, \log q) = (11.0, -0.27)$

(c) $(r, \log q) = (5.5, -0.33)$

(d) $(r, \log q) = (11.0, -1.47)$

Figure 4: *ad-pull* example results obtained using algorithms 1 and 2 on sample content with *ad-pool* given in Table 1. (a) and (b) are *efficient-frontier* document compositions representing a sensible tradeoff between revenue and quality. (c) and (d) show examples of inefficient document compositions since they are dominated by a frontier-composition which has at least the same revenue and better quality or at least the same quality and better revenue. The red areas indicate *ad* placement slots.

Sample *ad*-pool for *ad-pull* Insertion				
	V_1	V_2	V_3	V_4
ads	(2,1/6)	(1, 1/6)	(1, 1/6)	(3,1/4)
Bids	2	3.5	5	6

Table 1: Example *ad*-pool. The first index in *ad* category $(\cdot, \cdot)$ refers to the column span while the second index refers to approximate fractional page area covered.

The template library used for document composition consisted of 16 templates including *ads* of various sizes placed at different positions. All templates had exactly one *ad*-slot. Each *ad* slot is characterized by columns spanned and *ad*-area. For example $(1, 1/6)$ refers to an *ad* that spans one column and has an area of roughly a sixth of the page. Note that the *ad*-pool has two *ads* of the same size with different bid prices (*ads* V_2 and V_3). We further require that all document compositions have exactly two *ads* and take up two pages. There are 12 possible *ad* orderings of 2 *ads* selected from the pool of 4 *ads*.

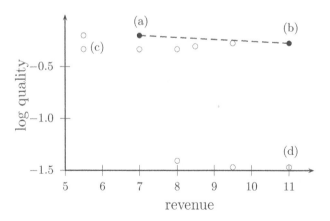

Figure 5: *efficient-frontier* for *ad-pull* example. The labeled points correspond to document compositions shown in Figure 4.

Figures 4(a)-(b) show the frontier compositions while Figures 4(c)-(d) show some examples of inefficient compositions. Figure 5 shows the revenue-quality points and the corresponding computed *efficient-frontier*. Note that as we move along the frontier from left to right, revenue increases while quality drops. Figure 4(c) is inefficient because it has lower revenue and quality (notice column mis-alignment on page 2) than Figure 4(a). Figure 4(d) is inefficient because although it has the same revenue as Figure 4(b) it has lower quality (both images have more distortion).

Notice also that the points at $(5.5, -.20)$ and $(7.0, -.20)$ have the same quality but the one with higher revenue is on the frontier. In fact these are exactly the same composition with the same *ad* slot sizes. This is because there are 2 bids for the same size of *ad* in the *ad* pool (*ads* V_2 and V_3). The *ad* with the higher bid (V_3) is used in the frontier composition. There are two compositions at point $(8.5, -0.3)$. Both use *ads* V_2 and V_3 but in different order. This results in two compositions with the exact same revenue and quality.

4.1.2 Complexity

We may analyze asymptotic complexity of this algorithm in a similar manner to the analysis presented in [2]. For a given set of *ads* with a specific order the complexity of document composition with *ad*-insertion is thus $O(|\mathcal{C}||\mathcal{V}||\Omega|)$ assuming linear content ordering, bounded page capacity and bounded number of *ads* on a page. This is still significantly better than the naive approach of considering all possible document compositions (document compositions for all $\{\{\mathcal{C}_{\leq i}\}_{i=0}^{I-1}, \{\{\mathcal{V}_{\leq i}\}_{i=0}^{I-1}, \{\Theta_i\}_{i=0}^{I-1}, \{T_i\}_{i=0}^{I-1}\}$) and choosing the best scoring document. The efficiency stems from the fact that possibilities are eliminated in the maximizations at a given step do not propagate to the successive steps in algorithm 1. This feature is a direct consequence of the structured probabilistic model in which direct dependencies between variables are limited (so conditional probability terms can be grouped without having to maximize over all variables at once). However, if we consider the overall problem of *efficient-frontier* computation, the complexity grows combinatorially in terms of the size of the *ad*-pool. Hence this is a viable method only for small *ad*-pools.

4.2 Ad-Push

In the *ad-push* scenario document composition takes place before *ad* sales and the inserted *ad*-slots in a document are *pushed* to the market for sale. Unsold *ad* inventory is often replaced by filler content. Since the *ads* are not yet bid on at the time of composition, the publisher must estimate the price of each *ad* size. Over time, the expected market value of *ads* of particular sizes will be more accurately estimated by the publisher. Adjusting his templates and/or *ad* reserve prices accordingly, over time, the publisher is less likely to have unsold *ads* slots in his documents. The publisher has an *ad*-matrix of *ad*-sizes and corresponding expected prices. Since there are no specific *ads* to be inserted the algorithm is free to determine the size, distribution and placement of advertising in the document.

The *ad*-free model of document quality introduced in section 3 of document quality can be used in this case without any explicit treatment of *ad* allocations to pages, with the additional understanding that the templates in the library already have designed *ad*-slots. The revenue of a template is simply the sum of the *ad* prices of all *ad*-slots in the template. Thus, when content is allocated to a template, each template may be associated with a revenue and a quality. The algorithm although similar in spirit to *ad*-free PDM inference algorithm developed in [2] operates directly on

efficient-frontiers in the revenue-quality space. Algorithms 3 and 4 summarize the method for efficiently computing the *efficient-frontier* document compositions.

Algorithm 3 Push-based *ad* insertion: Forward pass

1: $\Psi(\mathcal{A}, \mathcal{B}, T) = \max_{\Theta} \mathbb{P}(\mathcal{A}, |\mathcal{B}, \Theta, T)\mathbb{P}(\Theta|T)$

2: $\mathcal{F}(\mathcal{A}, \mathcal{B}) = \underset{T \in \Omega}{\text{eff}} \left\{ \left(\underbrace{r(T)}_{r(T)}, \underbrace{\log(\Psi(\mathcal{A}, \mathcal{B}, T)\mathbb{P}(T))}_{l(\mathcal{A},\mathcal{B},T) = \log q(\mathcal{A},\mathcal{B},T)} \right) \right\}$

3: $\mathcal{T}_0(\mathcal{A}) \leftarrow \mathcal{F}(\mathcal{A}, \emptyset)$

4: $\mathcal{T}_i(\mathcal{A}) = \underset{\mathcal{B}}{\text{eff}} \left[\text{eff} \left\{ \mathcal{F}(\mathcal{A}, \mathcal{B}) \oplus \mathcal{T}_{i-1}(\mathcal{B}) \right\} \right], i \geq 1$

Algorithm 4 Push-based *ad* insertion: Backward pass

1: $i \leftarrow I - 1, \mathcal{A} \leftarrow \mathcal{C}$
2: select $(r^*, l^*) \in \mathcal{T}_{I-1}(\mathcal{C})$
3: **while** $i \geq 0$ **do**
4: $\quad \mathcal{C}_{\leq i}^* \leftarrow \mathcal{A}$
5: $\quad T_i^{*}, \mathcal{B}^* = T, \mathcal{B} : (r^* - r(T), l^* - l(\mathcal{A}, \mathcal{B}, T)) \in \mathcal{T}_{i-1}(\mathcal{B})$

6: $\quad \Theta_i^* = \arg\max_{\Theta} \mathbb{P}(\mathcal{C}_{\leq i}^*, |\mathcal{B}^*, \Theta, T_i^*)\mathbb{P}(\Theta|T_i^*)$
7: $\quad r^* \leftarrow r^* - r(T_i^*), l^* \leftarrow l^* - l(\mathcal{C}_{\leq i}^*, \mathcal{B}^*, T_i^*)$
8: $\quad \mathcal{A} \leftarrow \mathcal{B}^*$
9: $\quad i \leftarrow i - 1$
10: **end while**

The *forward pass* algorithm 3 computes dynamic programming tables as before, but table entries are now sets instead of scalar values. $\mathcal{A}$ refers to an allocation of content to all pages upto the current page while $\mathcal{B}$ refers to an allocation of content to all previous pages. Table entries are computed for all valid content allocation sets $\mathcal{A}, \mathcal{B} \in \mathcal{C}'$ with $\mathcal{A} \supseteq \mathcal{B}$. Note that we have dropped the subscript in $\mathcal{A}_c$ that explicitly indicates a content allocation vs. an *ad* allocation, since we do not need to deal with *ad* allocations.

Step 1 is unchanged from PDM inference and essentially computes and stores a table of scores of how well content in the set $\mathcal{A} - \mathcal{B}$ is suited for template T. This step may be performed efficiently as a quadratic programming problem with bound constraints for appropriate template probability parameterization [2]. Table entries for the case when $\mathcal{A} - \mathcal{B}$ does not match template T may be set to zero without requiring any further computation.

Step 2 loops over templates in the library (only templates matching content in the set $\mathcal{A} - \mathcal{B}$ need be considered) and computes a revenue $r(T)$ and a log quality $l(\mathcal{A}, \mathcal{B}, T) = \log q(\mathcal{A}, \mathcal{B}, T)$ score for each template. Then an *efficient-frontier* $\mathcal{F}(\mathcal{A}, \mathcal{B})$ for the allocation $\mathcal{A}, \mathcal{B}$ with respect to the template library is computed using the skyline algorithm on all candidate revenue-quality points. This *efficient-frontier* is propagated for consideration in future steps.

Step 4 sets up a recursion to successively compute the efficient-frontiers $\mathcal{T}_i(\mathcal{A})$ for the allocation of content $\mathcal{A}$ to the first i pages of the document. First the intermediate *efficient-frontier* $\mathcal{F}(\mathcal{A}, \mathcal{B})$ from the previous step is *summed* with the *efficient-frontier* $\mathcal{T}_{i-1}(\mathcal{B})$ for an allocation $\mathcal{B}$ to the previous pages. By sum we mean the Minkowski sum [3] of two sets in Euclidean space represented by the operator $\oplus$ which is essentially the set formed by adding every element of the first set to every element of the second set. The pseudocode for this operation is given in algorithm 8 in the

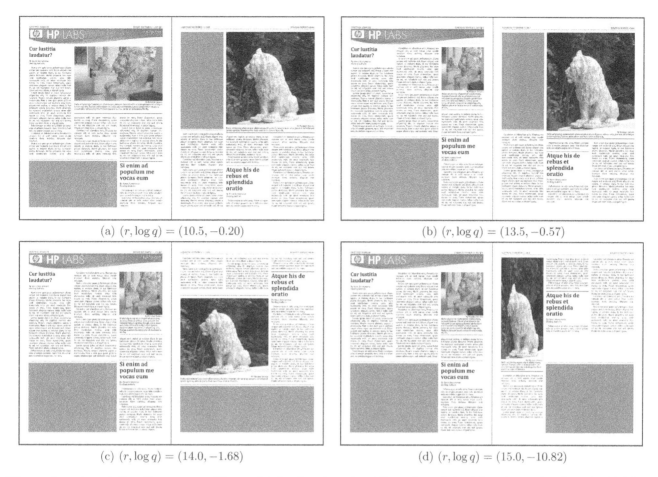

(a) $(r, \log q) = (10.5, -0.20)$

(b) $(r, \log q) = (13.5, -0.57)$

(c) $(r, \log q) = (14.0, -1.68)$

(d) $(r, \log q) = (15.0, -10.82)$

Figure 6: *ad-push* frontier compositions obtained using algorithms 3 and 4 with *ad*-matrix given in Table 2. The red areas indicate *ad* placement slots. Note how quality degrades along the *efficient-frontier* as revenue is increased from (a)-(d). Fig. 7 shows the corresponding frontier.

Appendix. An *efficient-frontier* is computed over the points in the Minkowski sum and over all possible previous allocations $\mathcal{B}$ to obtain the *efficient-frontier* $\mathcal{T}_i(\mathcal{A})$. Step 3 seeds the recursion with initial values.

The recursion terminates when we have the final *efficient-frontier* $\mathcal{T}_{I-1}(\mathcal{C})$ which may be regarded as the *efficient-frontier* for the whole document when all content $\mathcal{C}$ has been allocated. A publisher must choose an operating point on this frontier set to actually produce a document with a certain revenue and log quality. Once a point (r^*, l^*) is chosen the *backward pass* algorithm 4 traverses the dynamic programming tables built during the forward pass to compute the optimal document that achieves the desired tradeoff. Note that instead of explicitly choosing a point the publisher may simply indicate a revenue or quality target. In the case of a quality target the maximal revenue frontier point whose quality is greater than or equal to the quality target is automatically chosen. In the case of a revenue target the maximal quality frontier point whose revenue is greater than or equal to the revenue target is automatically chosen.

Step 5 searches over previous page frontiers for a partial document with revenue $r^* - r(T)$ and log quality $l^* - l(\mathcal{A}, \mathcal{B}, T)$. The template T_i^* and previous allocation $\mathcal{B}^*$ that resulted in the desired partial document are identified

as the optimal template for the current page and the best previous allocation of content to previous pages. From these optimal values the best template parameters Θ_i^* to compose the current page are computed. This process recurses from the last page to the first to sequentially compose all pages of the optimal document.

4.2.1 Example

Expected Revenue Matrix for *ad-push* Insertion			
	1 column	2 column	3 column
Twelfth of a page	1	-	-
Sixth of a page	3.5	3.5	3
Quarter of a page	4.5	5	4

Table 2: *ad*-matrix for *ad-push* example

Table 2 shows an example *ad*-matrix for *ad-push* insertion. It lists *ads* of various sizes and their expected revenue potential. We also assume (to make the example more interesting) that first page *ads* are expected to receive twice the expected revenues shown. The goal is to compute the *efficient-frontier* document compositions when *ads* are inserted into the same two page content as in the *ad-pull* example in Section 4.1.1.

Figure 6 shows the *efficient-frontier* document compositions computed by our algorithm. Figure 7 shows the corre-

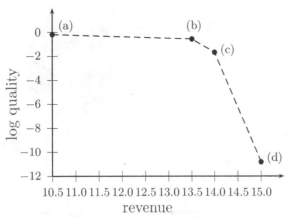

Figure 7: *efficient-frontier* for *ad-push* example. The labeled points correspond to document compositions shown in Figure 6.

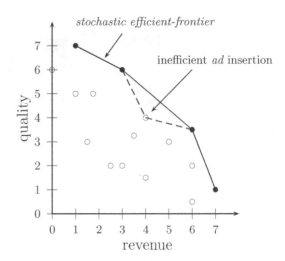

Figure 8: The *stochastic efficient-frontier*. This frontier allows the notion of a continuous tradeoff between revenue and quality by stochastically varying the documents over subscribers and considering average revenue and quality. Since any point between two frontier points is also on the frontier, this frontier is in fact the convex-envelope of the discrete *efficient-frontier* developed earlier.

sponding *efficient-frontier*. A publisher may choose to publish document 6(b) or 6(c) since quality only drops moderately for substantial increase in revenue. Note however that just because a document composition is on the *efficient-frontier* it does not imply that it is a good quality composition. For example the composition 6(d) corresponds to a significant drop in quality that is clearly visible and also reflected in the graph of Figure 7.

In general a publisher may set a quality threshold and seek to publish at a point on the frontier that maximizes revenue, subject to this threshold. Alternatively, a publisher (or end user) can have a slider that increases revenue (or *ad* coverage) by sliding along the *efficient-frontier*. This may also allow new business models where each user may substitute increased *ad* coverage (subject to publisher quality thresholds) for lower subscription cost according to his/her preference.

4.2.2 Complexity

Asymptotic complexity of *ad-push* algorithm for *efficient-frontier* computation is $O(|\mathcal{C}||\Omega|)$ assuming linear content ordering, bounded page capacity [2]. This is the same as asymptotic complexity of *ad*-free document composition using PDM inference [2]. It is important to note that unlike the *ad-pull* case, asymptotic complexity does not grow with the number of *ads* to be inserted. Although *efficient-frontier* computations involve more work than simple maxima computations, they do not grow with the number of *ads* inserted. The algorithms efficiency stems from the fact that possibilities that are eliminated in the *efficient-frontier* computations at a given step do not propagate to successive frontiers in algorithm 3.

5. INTER-SUBSCRIBER TRADEOFFS

The *efficient-frontier* is a discrete set representing tradeoffs for a single document for a single subscriber. This means that we must choose one of the frontier points to compose a single document. However, a publisher armed with automated composition technology may produce different document compositions for different subscribers using the exact same content (ex: by demographic group). The publisher may choose for example, to produce a first fraction of the documents for part of the subscriber base at one frontier point and a second fraction of documents for another part of the subscriber base at a different frontier point. We call this

stochastic document composition. If the notion of revenue and quality of a document could be extended to the notion of *average* revenue and *average* quality of a document collection, then all points on the dashed lines between frontier points now become possible *continuous* tradeoff possibilities.

We see from Figure 1 that the set of points connecting *adjacent* discrete *efficient-frontier* points may be non-convex. However, since we now consider the set of all points connecting any two discrete *efficient-frontier* points, we see that this set is convex. This is illustrated by the bold line in Figure 8 which shows the effect of considering *stochastic* compositions between any two discrete frontier compositions of Figure 1. In fact, the *stochastic efficient-frontier* is exactly the *convex-envelope* of the discrete *efficient-frontier*. Note from Figure 8 that there may now be points on the discrete frontier that are not on its convex-envelope and are hence inefficient from a *stochastic* document composition perspective. We call the points on both the discrete and continuous (*stochastic*) frontiers as *key points*. Any revenue-quality combination on the *stochastic* frontier may be realized by stochastically composing key point documents.

The notion of a *stochastic* frontier must be used with care. When two frontier points are far apart in quality, the *average* quality may not be a good indicator of quality since a publisher would definitely not want to send a bad quality document to a fraction of his subscriber base. This case may be mitigated by pruning discrete frontier points below a quality threshold before the convex envelope is calculated. Note also that a *stochastic* frontier exists strictly only in the revenue-quality space and not in the revenue-log(quality) space since averaging log(quality) is not meaningful. However, the revenue-log(quality) space may still be used to locate key points.

In the case of *ad-pull* insertion the computation of the key points on the *stochastic* frontier simply amounts to computing the discrete *efficient-frontier* and deleting vertices that are dominated by line segments connecting any two other points. A point (r_0, q_0) is said to be dominated by a line segment between points (r_1, q_1) and (r_2, q_2) if any point $(\alpha r_1 + (1 - \alpha) r_2, \alpha q_1 + (1 - \alpha) q_2)$, $\alpha \in [0, 1]$ on the line segment has a greater revenue for the same quality or a greater quality for the same revenue. This translates to the following two conditions respectively.

$$\frac{q_0 - q_2}{q_1 - q_2} r_1 + \frac{q_1 - q_0}{q_1 - q_2} r_2 > r_0 , \; \frac{q_0 - q_2}{q_1 - q_2} \in [0, 1] \quad (4)$$

$$\frac{r_0 - r_2}{r_1 - r_2} q_1 + \frac{r_1 - r_0}{r_1 - r_2} q_2 > q_0 , \; \frac{r_0 - r_2}{r_1 - r_2} \in [0, 1] \quad (5)$$

In the case of *ad-push* insertion one may derive an algorithm that directly optimizes the parametric convex envelope. A key-point document $\mathcal{D}_\alpha$ that is on the convex envelope must be a solution to the problem:

$$\mathcal{D}_\alpha = \arg\max_{\mathcal{D}} \alpha \, r(\mathcal{D}, I) + (1 - \alpha) \, \log Q(D, I) \quad (6)$$

where $Q(D, I)$ is given by equation (1). We can easily modify the *ad*-free PDM algorithm [2] to the task of computing $\mathcal{D}_\alpha$ for a given $\alpha \in [0, 1]$. Algorithms 5 and 6 summarize this approach. Note that other than Step 2 of the forward pass algorithm 5 and the taking of logarithms (converting products into sums), this approach is identical to the *ad*-free PDM algorithm[3].

Algorithm 5 Computing Document $\mathcal{D}_\alpha$: Forward pass
---
1: $\Psi(\mathcal{A}, \mathcal{B}, T) = \max_{\Theta} \mathbb{P}(\mathcal{A}, |\mathcal{B}, \Theta, T) \mathbb{P}(\Theta | T)$
2: $\Psi_\alpha(\mathcal{A}, \mathcal{B}, T) = \alpha \, r(T) + (1 - \alpha) \log \Psi(\mathcal{A}, \mathcal{B}, T)$
3: $\Phi(\mathcal{A}, \mathcal{B}) = \max_{T \in \Omega} (\Psi_\alpha(\mathcal{A}, \mathcal{B}, T) + \log \mathbb{P}(T))$
4: $\tau_0(\mathcal{A}) \leftarrow \Phi(\mathcal{A}, \emptyset)$
5: $\tau_i(\mathcal{A})) = \max_{\mathcal{B}} (\Phi(\mathcal{A}, \mathcal{B}) + \tau_{i-1}(\mathcal{B}))$, $i \geq 1$

Algorithm 6 Computing Document $\mathcal{D}_\alpha$: Backward pass
---
$i \leftarrow I - 1, \mathcal{A} \leftarrow \mathcal{C}$
while $i \geq 0$ **do**
$\quad \mathcal{C}^*_{\leq i} \leftarrow \mathcal{A}$
$\quad \mathcal{B}^* = \arg\max_{\mathcal{B}} (\Phi(\mathcal{A}, \mathcal{B}) + \tau_{i-1}(\mathcal{B}))$
$\quad T^*_i = \arg\max_{T \in \Omega} (\Psi_\alpha(\mathcal{C}^*_{\leq i}, \mathcal{B}^*, T) + \log \mathbb{P}(T))$
$\quad \Theta^*_i = \arg\max_{\Theta} \mathbb{P}(\mathcal{C}^*_{\leq i}, |\mathcal{B}^*, \Theta, T^*_i) \mathbb{P}(\Theta | T^*_i)$
$\quad \mathcal{A} \leftarrow \mathcal{B}^*$
$\quad i \leftarrow i - 1$
end while

To compute the key-points of the *stochastic efficient-frontier* we sweep α through its range $[0, 1]$ and store the resulting compositions (ignoring duplicate compositions). While this approach requires minimal modifications to the *ad*-free PDM algorithm and may be massively parallelized (documents for different α values may be computed independently) it is not an efficient way to compute the key points of the *stochastic* frontier. However, we have included it for completeness.

A much better approach for computing key points of the *stochastic efficient-frontier* is to modify the efficient algorithm for *ad-push* insertion given in Section 4.2 that operates directly on frontiers. In fact all we need to do is to use the key-points of the convex-envelope of the efficient frontiers computed in the intermediate steps 2 and 4 of the for-

---

[3]where templates are assumed to have pre-designed *ad*-slots

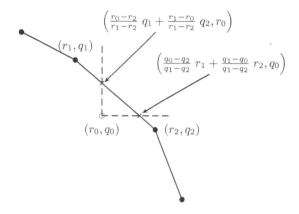

Figure 9: Constructing the convex envelope of a discrete *efficient-frontier*. We prune points on the discrete frontier that are dominated by line segments between any two other frontier points when one of the conditions in equations (4) or (5) is met.

ward pass algorithm 3. The convex-envelope of an *efficient-frontier* is obtained as outlined earlier by applying conditions (4) and (5) to prune points that will be inefficient when we consider the *stochastic efficient-frontier*. Figure 9 illustrates the pruning criteria graphically.

In fact another aspect of algorithm 3 is benefited by the forced convexity of the efficient frontiers. The Minkowski sums $\oplus$ computed in step 4 of the forward pass become $O(m + n)$ instead of $O(mn)$ where m and n denote the number of points in the two summed frontiers respectively. This is because we may treat each frontier as a convex polygon (by linking the first and last points). It is well known that the Minkowski sum of two convex polygons of m and n vertices can be performed as an $O(m + n)$ operation [3]. See Appendix for pseudocode.

6. CONCLUSIONS

In this paper we showed that a fundamental tradeoff exists between revenue and document composition quality. The optimal tradeoff can be represented in terms of a set of *efficient* points called the *efficient-frontier*. We developed algorithms that can compute the frontier compositions, automatically determining how many *ads* of each size to place and how to best arrange them on the page. The user or the publisher may control *ad* density and the algorithms will produce compositions that slide along the frontier while avoiding *in-efficient* compositions. Our complexity analysis of *ad*-insertion business models in Section 4.1.2 and Section 4.2.2 reveals that both *ad-pull* and *ad-push* business models scale linearly with content size for a given ad-set size or ad-density (in the best case). However, for a given content size, as the ad-set size is increased, the optimal *ad-pull* algorithm grows combinatorially with ad-set size while the *ad-push* algorithm is not influenced by ad-density (the typical complexity of the skyline algorithm is dependent only on the expected number of *efficient* points [4]). Thus from a document composition perspective it is much more efficient to compose documents with *ad*-slots (*ad-push*) and then sell the resulting *ad* inventory than to first conduct *ad* sales and then compose documents that consider the bid prices of particular *ads* ((*ad-pull*). The downside of the *ad-push* model is that the demand for *ad*-slots must be forecast in advance and there is the possibility of unsold inventory. Finally, we considered inter-subscriber tradeoffs and introduced the concept of a continuous and convex *stochastic efficient-frontier* and developed *ad*-insertion algorithms that exploited convexity.

While the complexity of optimal *ad-pull* insertion may be prohibitive, heuristic algorithms that work well in practice may exist. Also, we may expand the notion of quality to include keyword relevance enabling dynamic ad-insertion based on keyword proximity. This would allow advertisers to bid on keywords used in a document much like they do today for internet advertising. These are topics we intend to pursue in future work.

7. ACKNOWLEDGMENTS

The authors would like to thank Eamonn O'Brien-Strain, Jerry Liu and Qian Lin at HP Labs Palo Alto for their support of this research. Jose Bento was supported by the AFOSR grant FA9550-10-1-0360.

8. REFERENCES

[1] H. Y. Balinsky, A. J. Wiley, and M. C. Roberts. Aesthetic measure of alignment and regularity. In *DocEng '09: Proceedings of the 9th ACM symposium on Document engineering*, pages 56–65, New York, NY, USA, 2009. ACM.

[2] N. Damera-Venkata, J. Bento, and E. O'Brien-Strain. Probabilistic document model for automated document composition. In *Proceedings of the 11th ACM symposium on Document engineering*, DocEng '11, pages 3–12, New York, NY, USA, 2011. ACM.

[3] M. de Berg, O. Cheong, and M. van Kreveld, Marc. Overmars. *Computational Geometry: Algorithms and Applications*. Springer-Verlag, Berlin/Heidelberg, 2010.

[4] P. Godfrey, R. Shipley, and J. Gryz. Algorithms and analyses for maximal vector computation. *The VLDB Journal*, 16(1):5–28, jan 2007.

[5] S. J. Harrington, J. F. Naveda, R. P. Jones, P. Roetling, and N. Thakkar. Aesthetic measures for automated document layout. In *DocEng '04: Proceedings of the 2004 ACM symposium on Document engineering*, pages 109–111, New York, NY, USA, 2004. ACM.

[6] N. Hurst, W. Li, and K. Marriott. Review of automatic document formatting. In *DocEng '09: Proceedings of the 9th ACM symposium on Document engineering*, pages 99–108, New York, NY, USA, 2009. ACM.

[7] H. T. Kung, F. Luccio, and F. P. Preparata. On finding the maxima of a set of vectors. *J. ACM*, 22(4):469–476, oct 1975.

[8] S. Lok and S. Feiner. A survey of automated layout techniques for information presentations. In *SmartGraphics '01: Proceedings of SmartGraphics Symposium '01*, pages 61–68, New York, NY, USA, 2001. ACM.

[9] H. Markowitz. Portfolio selection. *Journal of Finance*, 7(1):77–91, March 1952.

[10] J. Pearl. *Probabilistic reasoning in intelligent systems: networks of plausible inference*. Morgan Kaufmann Publishers Inc., San Francisco, CA, USA, 1988.

[11] R. Phillips. Efficient frontiers in revenue management. *Journal of Revenue and Pricing Management*, pages 1–15, September 2011.

APPENDIX

Algorithm 7 Skyline algorithm [4] $\mathcal{F} = \text{eff } \mathcal{S}$.

1:    $\mathcal{S} = \{\mathbf{p}_1, \mathbf{p}_2, \ldots, \mathbf{p}_N\}$
2:    **function** eff($\mathcal{S}$)
3:      $\mathcal{F} \leftarrow \emptyset$
4:      **while** ($\mathcal{S}$ is not empty) **do**
5:        $\mathbf{p} \leftarrow shift(\mathcal{S})$ // Get the first.
6:        **for all** $\mathbf{q} \in \mathcal{S}$ **do**   // Find a max.
7:          **if** $(\mathbf{p} \succ \mathbf{q})^4$ **then**
8:            remove $\mathbf{q}$ from $\mathcal{S}$
9:          **else if** $\mathbf{q} \succ \mathbf{p}$ **then**
10:           remove $\mathbf{q}$ from $\mathcal{S}$
11:           $\mathbf{p} \leftarrow \mathbf{q}$
12:          **end if**
13:        **end for**
14:        $\mathcal{F} \leftarrow \mathcal{F} \bigcup \mathbf{p}$
15:        **for all** $\mathbf{q} \in \mathcal{S}$ **do**   // Clean up.
16:          **if** $(\mathbf{p} \succ \mathbf{q})$ **then**
17:            remove $\mathbf{q}$ from $\mathcal{S}$
18:          **end if**
19:        **end for**
20:      **end while**
21: **end function**

Algorithm 8 General Minkowski sum $\mathcal{F}_3 = \mathcal{F}_1 \oplus \mathcal{F}_2$

1:    $\mathcal{F}_1 = \{\mathbf{p}_1, \mathbf{p}_2, \ldots, \mathbf{p}_M\}$
2:    $\mathcal{F}_2 = \{\mathbf{q}_1, \mathbf{q}_2, \ldots, \mathbf{q}_N\}$
3:    **function** $\oplus(\mathcal{F}_1, \mathcal{F}_2)$
4:      $\mathcal{F}_3 \leftarrow \emptyset$
5:      **for** i = 1,M **do**
6:        **for** j = 1,N **do**
7:          $\mathbf{z} = \mathbf{p}_i + \mathbf{q}_j$
8:          $\mathcal{F}_3 \leftarrow \mathcal{F}_3 \bigcup \mathbf{z}$
9:        **end for**
10:      **end for**
11: **end function**

Algorithm 9 $\mathcal{F}_3 = \mathcal{F}_1 \oplus \mathcal{F}_2$, $\mathcal{F}_1, \mathcal{F}_2$ are convex polygons.

1:    $\mathcal{F}_1 = \{\mathbf{p}_1, \mathbf{p}_2, \ldots, \mathbf{p}_M\}$, ordered clockwise
2:    $\mathcal{F}_2 = \{\mathbf{q}_1, \mathbf{q}_2, \ldots, \mathbf{q}_N\}$ ordered clockwise
3:    **function** $\oplus(\mathcal{F}_1, \mathcal{F}_2)$
4:      $\mathcal{F}_3 \leftarrow \emptyset$
5:      Locate extreme $\mathbf{p}_i$ and $\mathbf{q}_j$ in -Y direction.
6:      $\mathbf{z}_1 = \mathbf{p}_i + \mathbf{q}_j$, $F_3 \leftarrow \mathcal{F}_3 \bigcup \mathbf{z}_1$
7:      Make parallel lines at $\mathbf{p}_i, \mathbf{q}_j$ so $\mathcal{F}_1, \mathcal{F}_2$ lie to the right.
8:      **for** k = 2, M+N **do**
9:        Determine angles θ_i and ϕ_j at $\mathbf{p}_i$ and $\mathbf{q}_j$
10:     $\mathbf{z}_k = \begin{cases} \mathbf{p}_{i+1} + \mathbf{q}_j & \theta_i < \phi_j \\ \mathbf{p}_i + \mathbf{q}_{j+1} & \theta_i > \phi_j \\ \mathbf{p}_{i+1} + \mathbf{q}_{j+1} & \theta_i = \phi_j \end{cases}$ // i,j circular.
11:        $\mathcal{F}_3 \leftarrow \mathcal{F}_3 \bigcup \mathbf{z}_k$
12:        Rotate parallel lines to get next $\mathbf{p}_i$ and $\mathbf{q}_j$.
13:      **end for**
14: **end function**

---

[4] $\mathbf{p} \succ \mathbf{q}$ means $(\mathbf{p}(1) \geq \mathbf{q}(1)$ and $\mathbf{p}(2) > \mathbf{q}(2))$ **or** $(\mathbf{p}(1) > \mathbf{q}(1)$ and $\mathbf{p}(2) \geq \mathbf{q}(2))$

Optimal Guillotine Layout

Graeme Gange
Dept of CSSE
University of Melbourne
Vic. 3010, Australia
ggange@cs.mu.oz.au

Kim Marriott
Clayton School of IT
Monash University
Vic. 3800, Australia
kim.marriott@monash.edu

Peter Stuckey
Dept of CSSE
University of Melbourne
Vic. 3010, Australia
pjs@cs.mu.oz.au

ABSTRACT

Guillotine-based page layout is a method for document layout commonly used by newspapers and magazines, where each region of the page either contains a single article, or is recursively split either vertically or horizontally. Suprisingly there appears to be little research into algorithms for automatic guillotine-based document layout. In this paper we give efficient algorithms to find optimal solutions to guillotine layout problems of two forms. Fixed-cut layout is where the structure of the guillotining is given and we only have to determine the best configuration for each individual article to give the optimal total configuration. Free layout is where we also have to search for the optimal structure. We give bottom-up and top-down dynamic programming algorithms to solve these problems, and propose a novel interaction model for documents on electronic media. Experiments show that our algorithms are effective for realistic layout problems.

Categories and Subject Descriptors

I.7.2 [**Document and Text Processing**]: Document Preparation—*Format and notation, Photocomposition/typesetting*

General Terms

Algorithms

Keywords

guillotine-based document layout, constrained optimization, dynamic programming, typography

1. INTRODUCTION

Guillotine-based page layout is a method for document layout, commonly used by newspapers and magazines, where each region of the page either contains a single article, or is recursively split either vertically or horizontally. The newspaper page shown in Figure 1(a) is an example of a

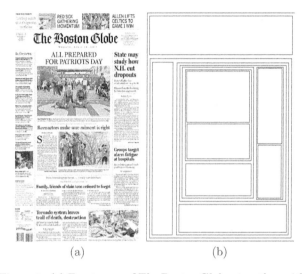

(a)   (b)

Figure 1: (a) Front page of The Boston Globe, together with (b) the series of cuts used in laying out the page. Note how the layout uses fixed width columns.

guillotine-based layout where Figure 1(b) shows the series of cuts used to construct this layout.

Surprisingly, there appears to have been relatively little research into algorithms for automatic guillotine-based document layout. We assume that we are given a sequence of articles $A_1, A_2, \ldots, A_n$ to layout. The precise problem depends upon the page layout model [10].

- The first model is vertical scroll layout in which layout is performed on a single page of fixed width but unbounded height: this is the standard model for viewing HTML and most web documents. Here the layout problem is to find guillotine layout for the articles which minimises the height for a fixed width.

- The second model is horizontal scroll layout in which there is a single page of fixed height but unbounded width. This model is well suited to multicolumn layout on electronic media. Here the layout problem is to find guillotine layout for the articles which minimises the width for a fixed height.

- The final model is layout for a sequence of articles in fixed height and width pages. Here the problem is to find a guillotine layout which maximises the prefix of the sequence of articles $A_1, A_2, \ldots, A_k$ that fit on the (first) page (and then subsequently for the second, third, ... page).

We are interested in two variants of these problems. The easier variant is *fixed-cut* guillotine layout. Here we are given a guillotining of the page and an assignment of articles to the rectangular regions on the page. The problem is to determine how to best layout each article so as to minimise the overall height or width. The much harder variant is *free* guillotine layout. In this case we need to determine the guillotining, article assignment and the layout for each article so as to minimise overall height or width.

The main contribution of this paper is to give polynomial-time algorithms for optimally solving the fixed-cut guillotine layout problem and a dynamic programming based algorithm for optimally solving the free guillotine layout. While our algorithm for free guillotine layout is exponential (which is probably unavoidable since the free guillotine layout problem is NP-Hard (see Section 2), it can layout up to 13 articles in a few seconds (up to 18 if the articles must use columns of a fixed width).

Our automatic layout algorithms support a novel interaction model for viewing documents such as newspapers or magazines on electronic media. In this model we use free guillotine layout to determine the initial layout. We can fine tune this layout using fixed-cut guillotine layout in response to user interaction such as changing the font size or viewing window size. Using the same choice of guillotining ensures the basic relative position of articles remains the same and so the layout does not change unnecessarily and disorient the reader. An example of this is shown in Figure 2. However, if at some point the choice of guillotining leads to a very bad layout, such as articles that are too wide or narrow or too much wasted space, then we can find a new guillotining that is close to the original guillotining, and re-layout using this new choice.

Guillotine-based constructions have been considered for a variety of document composition problems. Photo album composition approaches [3] have a fixed document size, and must construct an aesthetically pleasing layout while maintaining the aspect ratio of images to be composed.

A number of heuristics have been developed for automated newspaper composition [8, 13] which also focus on constructing layouts for a fixed page-width. The first approach [8] considers only a single one column configuration per article, and lays out all articles to minimize height in a fixed number of columns. The second approach [13] breaks the page into a grid and considers up to 8 configurations on grid boundaries per article, It focuses on choosing which articles to place in a fixed page size, using a complex objective based on coverage. Both approaches make use of local search and do not find optimal solutions.

Hurst [9] suggested solving the fixed-cut guillotine layout problem by solving a sequence of one-dimensional minimisation problems to determine a good layout recursively. This approach was fast but not guaranteed to find an optimal layout. A genetic algorithm was also proposed for guillotine layout, using a linear approximation for content [7].

A closely related problem to these is the guillotine stock-cutting problem. Given an initial rectangle, and a (multi-)set S of smaller rectangles with associated values, the objective is to find a cutting pattern which gives the set $S' \subseteq S$ with maximum value. This in some sense a harder form of the third model we discuss above. A number of exact [5, 4]

and heuristic [2] methods have been proposed for the guillotine stock-cutting problem. This differs from the guillotine layout problem in that each leaf region has a single configuration, rather than a (possibly large sized) disjoint set of possible configurations. It does not appear that these approaches scale to the size of problem we consider.

2. PROBLEM STATEMENT

In the rest of the paper will focus on finding a guillotine layout which minimises the height for a fixed width. It is straightforward to modify our algorithms to find a guillotine layout which minimises the width for a fixed height: we simply swap height and widths in the input to the algorithms.

We can also use algorithms for minimising height to find a guillotine layout maximising the number of articles in a fixed size page. For a particular subsequence $A_1, .., A_k$ we can use the algorithm to compute the minimum height h_k for laying them out in the page width. We simply perform a linear or binary search to find the maximum k for which h_k is less than the fixed page height. We can use the area of the articles' content to provide an initial upper bound on k.

The main decision in the fixed-cut guillotine layout is how to break the lines of text in each article. Different choices give rise to different width/height configurations. Each article has a number of *minimal configurations* where a minimal configuration is a pair (w, h) s.t. the content in the article can be laid out in a rectangle with width w and height h but there is no smaller rectangle for which this is true. That is, for all $w' \leq w$ and $h' \leq h$ either $h = h'$ and $w = w'$, or the content does not fit in a rectangle with width w' and height h'.

Typically we would like the article to be laid out with multiple columns. One way of doing this is to allow the configuration to take any width and to compute the number of columns and their width based on the width of the configuration. We call this *article dependent* column layout. In this case for text with uniform height with W words (or more exactly, $W - 1$ possible line breaks), there are up to W minimal configurations, each of which has a different number of lines. In the case of non-uniform height text, there can be no more than $O(W^2)$ minimal configurations.

The other way of computing the columns is to compute the width and number of columns based on the page width and then each article is laid out in a configuration of one, two, three etc column widths. This is, for instance, the approach used in Figure 1. We call this *page dependent* column layout. In this case the number of different configurations is much less and is simply the number of columns on the page.

We assume the minimal configurations for an article A are given as a discrete list of allowed configurations $C(A) = [(w_0, h_0), \ldots, (w_k, h_k)]$, ordered by increasing width (and decreasing height). In the algorithms described in the following sections, we refer to the ith entry of an ordered list L with $L[i]$ (adopting the convention that indices start at 0), and concatenate lists with ++. For a configuration c, we use $\mathsf{w}(c)$ to indicate the width, and $\mathsf{h}(c)$ for the height. Note that we can choose to not include configurations that are too narrow or too wide.

A guillotine cut is represented by a tree of cuts, where each node has a given height/width configuration. A leaf node CELL(A) in the tree holds an article A. An internal node is either: VERT(X, Y), where X and Y are its child nodes, representing a vertical split with articles in X to the left

(a)   (b)

Figure 2: Example of (a) a possible guillotine layout, and
(b) the same layout adapted to a narrower display width.

and articles in Y to the right; or $\text{HORIZ}(X, Y)$, representing
a horizontal split with articles in X above and articles in Y
below. Given a chosen configuration for each leaf node we
can determine the configuration of each internal nodes as
follows:

If $c(X) = (w_x, h_x)$ is the chosen configuration for X and
$c(Y) = (w_y, h_y)$ is the chosen configuration for Y, then define

$$\text{vert}((w_x, h_x), (w_y, h_y)) = (w_x + w_y, \max(h_x, h_y))$$
$$\text{horiz}((w_x, h_x), (w_y, h_y)) = (\max(w_x, w_y), h_x + h_y)$$

and let

$$c(\text{VERT}(X, Y)) = \text{vert}(c(X), c(Y))$$
$$c(\text{HORIZ}(X, Y)) = \text{horiz}(c(X), c(Y)).$$

The *fixed-cut guillotine layout problem* for fixed width w
is given a fixed tree T, determine the configuration of leaf
nodes (and internal nodes) such that $c(T) = (w_r, h_r)$ where
$w_r < w$ and h_r is minimized.

The *free guillotine layout problem* for fixed width w is
given a set of articles S determine the guillotine cut T for
S and configurations of leaf nodes (and internal nodes) such
that $c(T) = (w_r, h_r)$ where $w_r < w$ and h_r is minimized.

We note that the free guillotine layout problem is NP-
hard, by reduction from PARTITION [6]. Consider an instance
$\{n_1, \ldots, n_k\}$ of PARTITION. We construct a free guillotine
layout instance with $w = 2$, and leaves $L_1 \ldots L_n$ with configurations $C(L_k) = \{(1, n_k)\}$. The PARTITION instance is
satisfiable iff the minimum height is $\frac{\sum_k L_k}{2}$.

3. FIXED-CUT GUILLOTINE LAYOUT

We will first look at solving the fixed-cut guillotine layout problem. This is a restricted form of guillotine layout,
where the tree of cuts is specified, and the algorithm must
pick a configuration for each article which leads to the minimum height layout. Fixed-cut guillotine layout is useful in
circumstances such as online newspapers, where the layout
should remain consistent, but must adapt to changes in display area. An example of this is given in Figure 2. It might
also be useful in semi-automatic document authoring tools
that support guillotine layout.

3.1 Bottom-up construction

Dynamic programming is a natural approach to tackle
minimum height guillotine layout problems since each sub
problem of the guillotine layout is again a (smaller) minimum height guillotine layout problem. The only real choices

that arise in fixed-cut layout are where to place the vertical
split between X and Y in a vertical cut $\text{VERT}(X, Y)$ in order
to obtain the minimal height. Rather than searching for a
best vertical cut, we solve this problem in the bottom-up
construction by computing the *list* of minimal configurations, $C(X)$ for each subtree X of T.

Consider a node $\text{VERT}(X, Y)$, where $C(X)$ is the list of
minimal configurations for X and $C(Y)$ is the list of minimal configurations for Y. To construct the list of minimal
configurations for $\text{VERT}(X, Y)$ we iterate across the configurations $C(X)$ and $C(Y)$. Given a minimal configuration
$\text{vert}(C(X)[i], C(Y)[j])$, we want to find the next minimal
configuration that is wider (and shorter). If $C(X)[i]$ is taller
than $C(Y)[j]$, we can only construct a shorter configuration
by picking a shorter configuration for X. In fact, the next
minimal configuration is exactly $\text{vert}(C(X)[i + 1], C(Y)[j])$.
We can use similar reasoning for the cases where $C(X)[i]$ is
shorter than $C(Y)[j]$. Since $\text{VERT}(C(X)[0], C(Y)[0])$ is the
narrowest minimal configuration, we can construct all minimal configurations by performing a linear scan over $C(X)$
and $C(Y)$. Pseudo-code for this is given in Figure 3.

```
vert_configs(CX,CY,w)
    C := ∅
    i := 0
    j := 0
    while (i ≤ |CX| ∧ j ≤ |CY|)
        (wₓ,hₓ) := CX[i]
        (w_y,h_y) := CY[j]
        if(wₓ + w_y > w) break
        C := C ++[ vert(CX[i], CY[j]) ]
        if(hₓ > h_y) i := i + 1
        else if(hₓ < h_y) j := j + 1
        else
            i := i + 1
            j := j + 1
    return C
```

Figure 3: Algorithm for constructing minimal configurations
for a vertical split from minimal configurations for the child
nodes.

EXAMPLE 3.1. *Consider a problem with 3 articles* $\{X, Y, Z\}$
having configurations $C(X) = C(Y) = [(1, 2), (2, 1)]$, $C(Z) =
[(1, 3), (2, 2), (3, 1)]$, *and the tree of cuts shown in Figure
4.*

Consider finding the optimal layout for $w = 3$. *First
we must construct the minimal configurations for the node
marked* H_1. *We start by picking the narrowest configurations for* X *and* Y, *giving* $C(H_1) = [(1, 4)]$. *We then need
to select the next narrowest configuration from either* X *or*

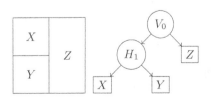

Figure 4: Cut-tree for Example 3.1.

15

```
horiz_configs(CX,CY,w)
    C := ∅
    minW := max(w(CX[0]), w(CY[0]))
    i := arg max_{i'} w(CX[i']) s.t. w(CX[i']) ≤ minW
    j := arg max_{j'} w(CY[j']) s.t. w(CY[j']) ≤ minW
    while (i ≤ |CX| ∨ j ≤ |CY|)
        C := C ++ [ horiz(CX[i], CY[j]) ]
        (w_x, h_x) := CX[i + 1]
        (w_y, h_y) := CY[j + 1]
        if(j + 1 = |CY| ∨ w_x > w_y) i := i + 1
        else if(i + 1 = |CX| ∨ w_x < w_y) j := j + 1
        else
            i := i + 1
            j := j + 1
    return C
```

Figure 5: Algorithm for producing minimal configurations for a horizontal split from child configurations. While the maximum width is included as an argument for consistency, we don't need to test any of the generated configurations, since the width of the node is bounded by the width of the input configurations.

```
layout_set(T,w)
    switch (T)
        case CELL(A):
            return C(A)
        case VERT(T_1, T_2):
            return vert_configs(layout_set(T_1, w),
                                layout_set(T_2, w), w))
        case HORIZ(T_1, T_2):
            return horiz_configs(layout_set(T_1, w),
                                 layout_set(T_2, w), w))
    endswitch
```

Figure 6: Algorithm for constructing the list of minimal configurations for a fixed set of cuts.

Y. Since both have the same width, we then join both $(2, 1)$ configurations, to give $C(H_1) = [(1, 4), (2, 2)]$.

We then construct the configurations for V_0. We again select the narrowest configurations, $C(H_1)[0]$ and $C(Z)[0]$, giving $C(V_0) = [(2, 4)]$. Since $C(H_1)[0]$ is taller, we select the next configuration from H_1. Combining $C(H_1)[1]$ with $C(Z)[0]$ gives us $C(V_0) = [(2, 4), (3, 3)]$. Since $w = 3$, we can terminate at this point, giving $(3, 3)$ as the minimal configuration. If w were instead 4, we would combine $C(H_1)[1]$ with $C(Z)[1]$, giving the new configuration $(4, 2)$. □

Constructing the minimal configurations for HORIZ(X, Y) is exactly the dual of the vertical case. From a minimal configuration constructed from $C(X)[i]$ and $C(Y)[j]$, we can construct a new minimal configuration by picking the narrowest of $C(X)[i + 1]$ and $C(Y)[j + 1]$. The only additional complexity is that (a) HORIZ$(C(X)[0], C(Y)[0])$ is not guaranteed to be a minimal configuration, and (b) we must keep producing configurations until both children have no more successors, rather than just one. Pseudo-code for this is given in Figure 5, and the overall algorithm is in Figure 6.

Consider a cut VERT(X, Y) with children X and Y. Given $C(X)$ and $C(Y)$, the algorithm described in Figures 3 to 6 computes the configurations for $C(\text{VERT}(X, Y))$ in O($|C(X)|+$

```
layout(T,w)
    c := lookup(T,w)
    if c ≠ NOTFOUND return c
    switch (T)
    case CELL(A):
        c := C(A)[i] where i is maximal s.t. w(C(A)[i]) ≤ w
    case HORIZ(T_1, T_2):
        c := horiz(layout(T_1, w), layout(T_2, w))
    case VERT(T_1, T_2):
        c := (0, ∞)
        for w' = 0..w
            c' := vert(layout(T_1, w'), layout(T_2, w − w'))
            if (h(c') < h(c)) c := c'
        endfor
    endswitch
    cache(T,w,c)
    return c
```

Figure 7: Pseudo-code for the basic top-down dynamic programming approach, returning the minimal height configuration $c = (w_r, h_r)$ for tree T such that $w_r ≤ w$.

$|C(Y)|)$, yielding at most $|C(X)| + |C(Y)|$ configurations (and similarly for HORIZ(X, Y)). Given a set of leaf nodes S, we construct at most $\sum_{A \in S} |C(A)|$ configurations at any node. As we perform this step $|S| - 1$ times, this gives a worst-case time complexity of O($|S| \sum_{A \in S} |C(A)|$) for the bottom-up construction.

An advantage of the bottom-up construction method is that, if we record the lists of constructed configurations, we can update the layout for a new width in O($\log |C| + |T|$) time by performing a binary search on configurations of the root node using the new width, then follow the tree of child configurations (or O($|T|$) time if we use O(w) space to construct a lookup table).

3.2 Top-down dynamic programming

We also consider a top-down dynamic programming approach, where subproblems are expanded only when required for computing the optimal solution. Consider a subproblem layout(HORIZ(X, Y), w). Using a top-down method, we need only to calculate subproblems layout(X, w) and layout(Y, w), rather than all configurations for the current node. The difficulty is in the case of vertical cuts, as we cannot determine directly how much of the available width should be allocated to X or Y. As such, we must compute layout(X, w') and layout(Y, $w - w'$) for the set of possible cut positions w'.

A top down dynamic programming solution is almost a direct statement of the Bellman equations as a functional program, with caching to avoid repeated computation. The main difficulty is the requirement to examine every possible width when determining the best vertical split. Psuedocode is given in Figure 7, where lookup(T, w) looks in the cache to see if there is an entry $(T, w) \mapsto c$ and returns c is so, or NOTFOUND if not; and cache(T, w, c) adds an entry $(T, w) \mapsto c$ to the cache.

This algorithm is outlined in Figure 7. Note that for simplicity we ignore the case where there is no layout of tree T with width $\leq w$. This can be easily avoided by adding an artificial configuration $(0, \infty)$ to the start of the list of configurations for each article A.

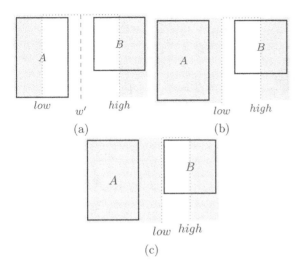

low $\quad w' \quad$ high $\qquad$ low $\qquad$ high

(a) $\hspace{4cm}$ (b)

low high

(c)

Figure 8: Illustration of using a binary chop to improve search for the optimal cut position. If $h_A^{w'} > h_B^{w-w'}$ as shown in (a), we cannot improve the solution by moving the cut to the left. Hence we can update (b) $low = w'$. Since B will retain the same configuration until the cut position exceeds $w - w_B^{w-w'}$, we can (c) set $low = w - w_B^{w-w'}$.

While the algorithm finds the optimal solutions quite quickly for fixed trees, there are a number of improvements to this basic algorithm which will also be useful for the free layout problem (Section 4).

3.2.1 Restricting vertical split positions

The algorithm given in Figure 7, on a vertical split, must iterate over all possible values of w' to find the optimal cut position. Let w_{min}^T indicate the narrowest possible configuration for T. Since we are only interested in feasible layouts, for a node $\text{VERT}(T_1, T_2)$ we need only consider cut positions in $[w_{min}^{T_1}, w - w_{min}^{T_2}]$. We can improve this by using a binary cut to eliminate regions that cannot contain the optimal solution, keeping track of the range $low..high$ where the optimal cut is.

Consider the cut show in Figure 8(a). Let $h_A^{w'} = \mathsf{layout}(A, w')$ and $h_B^{w-w'} = \mathsf{layout}(B, w - w')$. In this case, $h_A^{w'} > h_B^{w-w'}$. As the resulting configuration has height $\mathbf{max}(h_A^{w'}, h_B^{w-w'})$, the only way we can reduce the overall height is by adopting a shorter configuration for A – by moving w' further to the right. Normally we would set $low = w'$ as shown in Figure 8(b). In fact, we can move low to $\mathbf{max}(w', w - w_B^{w-w'})$ as shown in Figure 8(c), since moving w' right cannot increase the overall height until B shifts to a narrower configuration.

We can improve this further by observing that, if configurations are sparse, we may end up trying multiple cuts corresponding to the same configuration. If we construct a layout for A with cut position w', but A does not fill all the available space (so $w_A^{w'} < w'$), we can use that additional space to lay out B. If B is still taller than A (as shown in Figure 9), we know that the cut can be shifted to the left of $w_A^{w'}$, rather than just w'.

The case for $\text{VERT}(T_1, T_2)$ in Figure 7 can then be replaced with the following:

```
c := (0, ∞)
low := w_min^{T_1}
high := w − w_min^{T_2}
while (low ≤ high)
    w' := ⌊(low+high)/2⌋
    c_1 := layout(T_1, w')
    c_2 := layout(T_2, w − w(c_1))
    c' := vert(c_1, c_2)
    if (h(c') < h(c)) c := c'
    if (h(c_1) ≤ h(c_2)) high := w(c_1) − 1
    if (h(c_1) ≥ h(c_2)) low := max(w' + 1, w − w(c_2))
```

EXAMPLE 3.2. *Consider again the problem described in Example 3.1. The root node is a vertical cut, so we must pick a cut position. Since $w_{min}^{H_1} = w_{min}^Z = 1$, the cut must be in the range $[1, 2]$.*

We choose the initial cut as $w' = 1$. The sequence of calls made is as follows:

$$
\begin{aligned}
&f(V_0, 3) \\
&\quad w' = 1 \\
&\quad f(H_1, 1) \\
&\quad\quad f(X, 1) \\
&\quad\quad\quad \to (1, 2) \\
&\quad\quad f(Y, 1) \\
&\quad\quad\quad \to (1, 2) \\
&\quad\quad \to (1, 4) \\
&\quad f(Z, 2) \\
&\quad\quad \to (2, 2) \\
&\quad \to (3, 4)
\end{aligned}
$$

The best solution found so far is $(3, 4)$. Since the height of H_1 is greater than the height of Z, we know an improved solution can only be to the right of the current cut. We update $low := 2$, and continue:

$$
\begin{aligned}
&\quad w' = 2 \\
&\quad f(H_1, 2) \\
&\quad\quad f(X, 2) \\
&\quad\quad\quad \to (2, 1) \\
&\quad\quad f(Y, 2) \\
&\quad\quad\quad \to (2, 1) \\
&\quad\quad \to (2, 2) \\
&\quad f(Z, 1) \\
&\quad\quad \to (1, 3) \\
&\quad \to (3, 3) \\
&\to (3, 3)
\end{aligned}
$$

Finding the optimal solution at $w' = 2$, giving configuration $(3, 3)$. $\qquad\square$

4. FREE GUILLOTINE LAYOUT

In this section we consider the more difficult problem of free guillotine layout. Given a set of leaves (say, newspaper articles), we want to construct the optimal tree of cuts such that all leaves are used, and the overall height is minimized. Both the top-down and bottom-up construction methods given in the last section for fixed-cut guillotine layout can be readily adapted to solving the free layout problem.

The structure of the bottom-up algorithm remains largely the same. To compute the minimal configurations for a set S', we try all binary partitionings of S' into S'' and $S' \setminus S''$. We then generate the configurations for $\text{VERT}(S' \setminus S'', S'')$

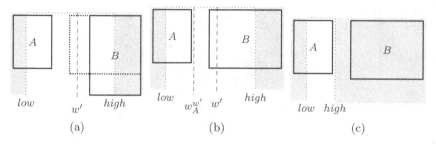

Figure 9: If the optimal layout for layout(A, w') has width smaller than w', then we may lay out B in all the available space, using $w - w_A^{w'}$, rather than $w - w'$. If B is still taller than A, we know the cut must be moved to the left of $w_A^{w'}$ to find a better solution.

and HORIZ($S' \setminus S''$, S'') as for the fixed problem. However, we must then eliminate any non-minimal configurations that have been generated. This is done by merge, which merges two sets of minimal configurations. Pseudo-code for this process is given in Figure 10. As we need to generate all configurations for all $2^{|S|}$ subsets of S, we construct the results for subsets in order of increasing size.

For the top-down method, at each node we want to find the optimal layout for a given set S and width w. To construct the solution, we try all binary partitions of S. Consider a partitioning into sets S' and S''. As there are a large number of symmetric partitionings, we enforce that the minimal element of S must be in S'. We then try laying out both VERT(S', S'') and HORIZ(S', S''), picking the best result.

Pseudo-code for the top-down dynamic programming approach is given in Figure 11. The structure of the algorithm is very similar to that for the fixed layout problem, except it now includes additional branching to choose binary partitions of S and try both cut directions. As before, w_{min}^S indicates narrowest feasible width for laying out S. This is calculated by taking the the widest minimum configuration width for any node in S.

4.1 Bounding

The dynamic program as formulated has a very large search space. We would like to reduce this by avoiding exploring branches containing strictly inferior solutions. We can improve this if we can calculate a lower bounds lb(S, w) on the height of any configuration for S in width w. If h_{max} is the best height so far and lb(S, w) $\geq h_{max}$, we know the current state cannot be part of any improved optimal solution, so we can simply cut-off search early with the current bound. This is a form of bounded dynamic programming [12].

For the minimum-height guillotine layout problem, we compute the minimum area used by some configuration of each leaf. This allows us to determine a lower bound on the area required for laying out the set of articles S. Since any valid layout must occupy at least area(S), a layout with a fixed width of w will have a height of at least $\lceil \frac{\text{area}(S)}{w} \rceil$.

We can also use the area approximation to reduce the set of vertical splits that must be explored. If we have a current best height h_{max}, any cut for VERT(X, Y) where $w' \leq \lceil \frac{\text{area}(X)}{h_{max}} \rceil$ or $w' \geq w - \lceil \frac{\text{area}(Y)}{h_{max}} \rceil$ cannot give an improved solution. Pseudo-code for the bounded dynamic programming approach is given in Figure 12. Note that configurations are now given as a triple (w_i, h_i, e_i), where $e_i \in \{\text{true}, \text{false}\}$ in-

```
layout_free_bu(S,w)
    for(c ∈ {2, ..., |S|})
        for(S' ⊆ S, |S'| = c)
            C(S) := ∅
            e := min i ∈ S'
            for(S'' ⊂ S' \ {e})
                C(S') := merge(C(S'),
                        horiz_configs(C(S' \ S''), C(S''), w))
                C(S') := merge(C(S'),
                        vert_configs(C(S' \ S''), C(S''), w))
    return C(S)[|C(S)| − 1]

merge(CX, CY)
    C := []
    i := 0
    j := 0
    while (i ≤ |CX| ∧ j ≤ |CY|)
        (wx, hx) := CX[i]
        (wy, hy) := CY[j]
        if(wx < wy)
            if(hx > hy)
                C := C ++[ CX[i] ]
                i := i + 1
            else j := j + 1
        else if(wx > wy)
            if(hx < hy)
                C := C ++[ CY[j] ]
                j := j + 1
            else i := i + 1
        else % wx = wy
            if(hx ≤ hy) j := j + 1
            else i := i + 1
    while (i ≤ |CX|)
        C := C ++[ CX[i] ]
        i := i + 1
    while (j ≤ |CY|)
        C := C ++[ CY[j] ]
        j := j + 1
    return C
```

Figure 10: Pseudo-code for a bottom-up construction approach for the free guillotine-layout problem for articles S. The configurations $C(S')$ for $S' \subseteq S$ are constructed from those of $C(S' \setminus S'')$ and $C(S'')$ where $S' \setminus S''$ and S'' are non empty and the first set is lexicographically smaller than the second.

```
layout_free(S,w)
    c := lookup(S,w)
    if c ≠ NotFound return c
    if (S = {A})
        c := C(A)[i] where i is maximal s.t. w(C(A)[i]) ≤ w
    else
        e := min(S)
        c := (0,∞)
        for S' ⊂ S \ {e}
            L := {e} ∪ S'
            R := S \ L
            % Try a horizontal split
            c' := horiz(layout_free(L,w), layout_free(R,w))
            if(h(c') ≤ h(c)) c := c'
            % Find the optimal vertical split
            low := w^L_min
            high := w - w^R_min
            while(low ≤ high)
                w' := ⌊(low+high)/2⌋
                c_l := layout_free(L,w')
                c_r = layout_free(R, w - w(c_l))
                c' := vert(c_l,c_r)
                if(h(c') ≤ h(c)) c := c'
                if(h(c_l) ≤ h(c_r)) high := w(c_l) - 1
                if(h(c_l) ≥ h(c_r))
                    low := max(w' + 1, w - w(c_r))
    cache(S,w,c)
    return c
```

Figure 11: Basic top-down dynamic programming for the free guillotine layout problem.

```
layout_free_bnd(S,w,h_max)
    c := lookup(S,w)
    if(c ≠ NotFound)
        if(e(c) ∨ h(c) ≥ h_max)
            return c
    % If the bound is greater than
    % h_max, we can stop early
    if (⌈area(S)/w⌉ ≥ h_max)
        c := (w, ⌈area(S)/w⌉, false)
    if (S = {A})
        i := maximal i' s.t. w(C(A)[i']) ≤ w
        c := (w(c'), h(c'), h(c') ≤ h_max) where c' = C(A)[i]
    else
        e := min(S)
        c := (0,∞)
        for S' ⊂ S \ {e}
            L := {e} ∪ S'
            R := S \ L
            A_l := area(L)
            A_r := area(R)
            % Try a horizontal split
            c_l := layout_free_bnd(L, w, h_max - ⌈A_r/w⌉)
            c_r := layout_free_bnd(R, w, h_max - h(c_l))
            if(h(c_l) + h(c_r) ≤ h(c))
                c := (max(w(c_l), w(c_r)), h(c_l) + h(c_r), e(c_l) ∧ e(c_r))
                if(h(c) = ⌈area(S)/w⌉) break
            % Ensure a vertical split is feasible
            if(w^L_min + w^R_min > w)
                continue
            h^vert_min := max(⌈A_l/(w - w^R_min)⌉, ⌈A_r/(w - w^L_min)⌉)
            if(h^vert_min > h_max)
                if (h^vert_min < hc) c := (w, h^vert_min, false)
                continue
            % Find the optimal vertical split
            low := max(w^L_min, ⌈A_l/h_max⌉)
            high := w - max(w^R_min, ⌈A_r/h_max⌉) + 1
            while(low < high)
                w' := ⌊(low+high)/2⌋
                c_l := layout_free_bnd(L, w', h_max)
                if(h(c_l) ≥ h_max)
                    c_r := (w - w(c_l), ⌈A_r/(w - w(c_l))⌉, false)
                else
                    c_r := layout_free_bnd(R, w - w(c_l), h_max)
                if(max(h(c_l), h(c_r)) ≤ h(c))
                    c := (w(c_l) + w(c_r), max(h(c_l), h(c_r)), e(c_l) ∧ e(c_r))
                    if(h(c) ≤ h_max) h_max := h(c)
                if(h(c_l) ≤ h(c_r)) high := h(c_l) - 1
                if(h(c_l) ≥ h(c_r))
                    low := max(w' + 1, w - w(c_r))
                if(h(c) = ⌈area(S)/w⌉) break for
    cache(S,w,c)
    return c
```

dicates whether the configuration is exact ($e_i = \mathsf{true}$), or a lower bound ($e_i = \mathsf{false}$). We use $\mathsf{e}(c)$ to extract the third component of a configuration.

A final optimization is to note that if we find a configuration c which has height equal to the lower bound ($\mathsf{h}(c) = \left\lceil \frac{\mathrm{area}(S)}{w} \right\rceil$) we can immediately return this solution.

5. UPDATING LAYOUTS

In the interaction model proposed in the introduction, we suggested using a fixed-cut layout to relayout an article during user interaction, until the current fixed-cut leads to a very bad layout. Bad layout can be for two reasons. The first reason is that current choice of guillotining does not allow a layout for the desired width while a different choice of guillotining will. The second reason is that the choice of guillotine leads to quite un-compact layout and so to a page height that is unnecessarily large. We note that un-compact layout is typically more of a problem for page dependent column layout. In the case that the current fixed-cut leads to bad layout we wish to modify the guillotining to give a layout close to the current layout.

First, we must determine how bad a layout can be before we relayout the document.

Given a set of articles S, we can precompute the optimal layout for a set of given widths W using `layout_free_bu` or `layout_free`. We can then build a piecewise linear approximation `approx_height`(S,w) to the minimal height for free layout of S for width w for all possible widths. However, since the optimal layout is generally close to the area bound,

Figure 12: Pseudo-code for the bounded top-down dynamic programming approach. Note that while bounding generally reduces search, if a previously expanded state is called again with a more relaxed bound, we may end up partially expanding a state multiple times.

```
interact(T,w)
    c := layout(T,w)
    S := articles in T
    k := 1
    while(h(c) > α × approx_height(S,w))
        c := relayout(T,w,k)
        k := k + 1
    return c

relayout(T,w,k)
    c := lookup(T,w)
    if(c ≠ NotFound) return c
    if(theight(T) ≤ k)
        S := set of articles appearing in T
        return layout_free(S,w)
    switch (T)
    case CELL(A):
        c := C(A)[i] where i is maximal s.t. w(C(A)[i]) ≤ w
    case HORIZ(T₁, T₂):
        c := horiz(relayout(T₁, w, k), relayout(T₂, w, k))
    case VERT(T₁, T₂):
        c := (0, ∞)
        for w' = 0..w
            c' := vert(relayout(T₁, w', k), relayout(T₂, w − w', k))
            if (h(c') < h(c)) c := c'
        endfor
    endswitch
    cache(T,w,c)
    return c
```

Figure 13: Pseudo-code for the basic top-down dynamic programming relayout, where we can change configuration for subtrees with tree height less than or equal to k.

we can use the simpler approximation $\mathsf{approx\_height}(S,w) = \left\lceil \frac{\mathsf{area}(S)}{w} \right\rceil$. We use this function to determine when to change guillotine cuts during user interaction. Assume the current layout of S is T, then if $\mathsf{layout}(T,w) > \alpha \times \mathsf{approx\_height}(S,w)$ we know that the fixed-cut is giving poor layout. We use $\alpha = 1.1$.

When we are generating a new guillotine cut for S, we want to ensure that the new layout is "close" to the current cut T. Our approach is to try and change the guillotining only at the bottom of the current cut T. Define the tree height of a tree T as follows: $\mathsf{theight}(\mathrm{CELL}(A)) = 0$, $\mathsf{theight}(\mathrm{VERT}(T_1,T_2)) = \max(\mathsf{theight}(T_1), \mathsf{theight}(T_1)) + 1$, $\mathsf{theight}(\mathrm{HORIZ}(T_1,T_2)) = \max(\mathsf{theight}(T_1), \mathsf{theight}(T_1)) + 1$. We first try to modify only subtrees with tree height 1 (that is parents of leaf nodes). If that fails to improve the current layout enough we modify subtrees of tree height 2, etc. Psuedo-code for the interactive layout problem is given in Figure 13.

6. EXPERIMENTAL RESULTS

To evaluate the methods described in Sections 3 to 4, we required a set of documents suitable for guillotine layout. To construct this data-set, we randomly select a set of n of articles from the REUTERS-21578 news corpus [1], then use a modified version of the binary search described in [11] to determine the set of available configurations for each article. All times are given in seconds, and all experiments are run

n	td	td+b	BU
10	< 0.01	< 0.01	< 0.01
20	< 0.01	< 0.01	< 0.01
30	0.02	0.01	< 0.01
40	0.03	0.02	< 0.01
50	0.06	0.05	< 0.01
60	0.13	0.10	< 0.01
70	0.18	0.14	< 0.01
80	0.29	0.22	< 0.01
90	0.41	0.33	< 0.01

Table 1: Results for the fixed-cut minimum-height guillotine layout problem with $w = w_{min} + 0.1(w_{max} - w_{min})$.

n	td	td+b	BU
10	< 0.01	< 0.01	< 0.01
20	< 0.01	< 0.01	< 0.01
30	0.01	< 0.01	< 0.01
40	0.01	< 0.01	< 0.01
50	0.02	0.01	< 0.01
60	0.03	0.01	< 0.01
70	0.03	0.01	< 0.01
80	0.04	0.01	< 0.01
90	0.05	0.02	< 0.01

Table 2: Results for the fixed-cut minimum-height guillotine layout problem with $w = w_{min} + 300$.

with a time limit of 600 seconds. Times given are averages over 10 instances of each problem size. Bold entries indicate the best result for each problem size.

For convenience in generating the dataset, we assume the use of a fixed-width font. While A-series page sizes have a $1 : \sqrt{2}$ aspect ratio, fixed-width fonts fit approximately equal number of lines as characters per line.

All experiments were conducted on a 3.00Ghz Core2 Duo with 2 Gb of RAM running Ubuntu GNU/Linux 8.10. td denotes the top-down dynamic programming approach, and td+b is top-down dynamic programming with bounding. bu denotes bottom-up construction.

6.1 Fixed-Cut Layout

Instances for fixed-cut guillotine layout were constructed with a random tree of cuts, selecting horizontal and vertical cuts with equal probability. Initially, we selected the instance width as a linear combination of the minimum and maximum width configurations for the instance. Results given Table 1 are constructed with $w = w_{min} + 0.1(w_{max} - w_{min})$, where w_{min} is the overall width when each article takes the narrowest feasible configuration (and similarly for w_{max}). Clearly, the top-down methods degrade quite rapidly compared to the bottom-up method. This appears to be due more to the rapidly increasing width than the increasing number of articles; the instances with 90 articles are laid out on a page that is 3000 to 5000 characters wide. This is illustrated in Table 2, where we calculated $w = w_{min} + 300$. Although the top-down methods are still distinctly slower than the bottom-up approach, they now scale far more gracefully.

n	td	td+b	bu
4	< 0.01	< 0.01	< 0.01
5	< 0.01	< 0.01	< 0.01
6	0.01	< 0.01	< 0.01
7	0.03	< 0.01	0.01
8	0.12	**0.01**	0.04
9	0.42	**0.03**	0.15
10	1.62	**0.11**	0.50
11	5.81	**0.41**	1.64
12	22.33	**1.50**	5.02
13	106.46	**6.09**	17.51
14	413.63	**24.43**	53.11
15	—	**74.84**	143.83

Table 3: Results for the free minimum-height guillotine layout problem. Times (in seconds) are averages of 10 randomly generated instances with n articles.

n	td	td+b	bu
4	< 0.01	< 0.01	< 0.01
5	< 0.01	< 0.01	< 0.01
6	< 0.01	< 0.01	< 0.01
7	< 0.01	< 0.01	< 0.01
8	< 0.01	< 0.01	< 0.01
9	0.01	< 0.01	0.01
10	0.04	< 0.01	0.05
11	0.12	< 0.01	0.16
12	0.39	**0.01**	0.47
13	1.23	**0.04**	1.53
14	3.85	**0.10**	4.38
15	13.10	**0.37**	15.50
16	41.65	**0.50**	48.32
17	168.19	**1.17**	157.96
18	590.76	**3.80**	442.19

Table 4: Results for the free minimum-height guillotine layout problem using page dependent column-based layout. Times (in seconds) are averages of 10 randomly generated instances with n articles.

6.2 Free Layout

For the free layout problem, we constructed instances for each size between 4 and 15. The instance width was selected as $\left\lceil \sqrt{(1+\alpha)\mathsf{area}(S)} \right\rceil$, to approximate a layout on an A-series style page with α additional space. For these experiments, we selected $\alpha = 0.2$. Times given in Table 3 denote the average time for solving the 10 instance of the indicated size.

As before, td performs significantly worse than the other methods. Unlike the fixed layout problem, these instances have much narrower page widths, and the search space arises largely from the selection of binary partitions. As a result, bounding provides a substantial improvement – td+b is consistently around twice as fast as bu on these instances.

In this first experiment we did not use column-based layout. However, in practice column-based layout is preferable so as to avoid long text measures. We generated test data for page dependent column-based layouts in a similar manner to the other guillotine layouts; having selected a column width, we calculate the number of lines required for the article body, and use this to determine the dimensions given

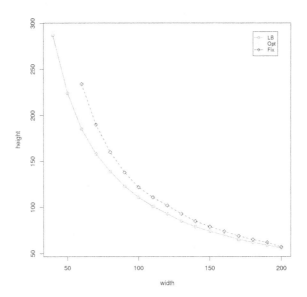

Figure 14: Layout heights for a 13-article document used in Section 6. LB the lower bound at the given width, and OPT is the minimum height given by layout_free_bnd. For FIX, we computed the optimal layout for $w = 200$, and adjusted the layout to the desired with using layout.

a varying number of columns. This is combined with the layout for the article title (calculated as before).

We select a column width of 38 characters, chosen as being typical of print newspapers. Page width is selected as before, then rounded up to the nearest number of columns. Results for this dataset are given in Table 4. The results for this case differ substantially to those for the non column-based instances – since the number of possible vertical cuts is much smaller (even the large instances generally have only 4 columns) fewer subproblems need to be expanded at each node during the execution of the dynamic programming approaches. In this case, td actually slightly outperforms bu, but td+b is substantially faster than both.

6.3 Updating Layouts

In practice, for non page dependent column-based layouts, a fixed optimal cutting remains near-optimal over a wide range of width values. To illustrate this, we took a document with 13 articles from the set used in Section 6, and computed the optimal cutting for $w = 200$. Figure 14 shows the height given by laying out this fixed cutting using layout with widths between 40 and 200. We compare this with the height given by the area bound and the optimal layout for each width. While the fixed layout is quite close to the optimal height over a wide range of values, it begins to deviate as we decrease the viewport width. For widths 40 and 50, this fixed layout is infeasible, and we are forced to compute a new tree of cuts.

To test the performance of the relayout algorithm, we consider again the set of 13-article documents used in the previous experiment. We computed the optimal layout for page widths between 40 and 200 characters, in 5 character intervals. We compared this with adapting the fixed layout computed for $w = 40$, and progressively used relayout

21

at each width. relayout was implemented with the bounded top-down methods for both the fixed and free components.

The average runtime for layout_free_bnd over the varying documents and widths was 7.48s. Runtime for layout was less than 0.01s in all cases, but deviated from the minimal height by up to 40%. Average runtime for relayout (with $\alpha = 1.1$) was 0.02s, and deviated from the minimal height by at most 10%. Results for page dependent column-based layout are similar. For documents with 16 articles, layout generated layouts up to 32% taller than the optimum; layout_free_bnd took 0.48s on average, compared to less than 0.01 for relayout (and $\alpha = 1.1$).

7. CONCLUSION

Guillotine-based layouts are widely used in newspaper and magazine layout. We have given algorithms to solve two variants of the automatic guillotine layout problem: the fixed cut guillotine layout problem in which the choice of guillotine cuts is fixed and the free guillotine layout problem in which the algorithm must choose the guillotining. We have shown that the fixed guillotine layout problem is solvable in polynomial time while the free guillotine layout problem is NP-Hard.

We have presented bottom-up and top-down methods for the minimum-height guillotine layout problem. For fixed-cut guillotine layout, the bottom-up method is far superior, as complexity is dependent only on the number of leaf configurations, rather than the page width; the bottom-up method can optimally layout reasonable sized graphs in real-time.

For the free guillotine layout problem, which has smaller width and larger search space, the bounded top-down method was substantially faster than the other methods. On instances with arbitrary cut positions, the bounded top-down method could solve instances with up to 13 articles in a few seconds; when restricted to page dependent column-based layouts, we can quickly produce layouts for at least 18 articles.

We have also suggested a novel interaction model for viewing on-line documents with a guillotine-based layout in which we solve the free guillotine layout problem to find an initial layout and then use the fixed cut guillotine layout to adjust the layout in response to user interaction such as changing the font size or viewing window size.

Currently our implementation only handles text. Future work will be to incorporate images.

8. ACKNOWLEDGEMENTS

The authors acknowledge the support of the ARC through Discovery Project Grant DP0987168.

9. REFERENCES

[1] Reuters-21578, Distribution 1.0. http://www.daviddlewis.com/resources/testcollections/reuters21578.

[2] R. Alvarez-Valdés, A. Parajón, and J. M. Tamarit. A tabu search algorithm for large-scale guillotine (un)constrained two-dimensional cutting problems. *Computers & OR*, 29(7):925–947, 2002.

[3] C. B. Atkins. Blocked recursive image composition. In *Proceedings of the 16th International Conference on Multimedia 2008*, pages 821–824, 2008.

[4] N. Christofides and E. Hadjiconstantinou. An exact algorithm for orthogonal 2-d cutting problems using guillotine cuts. *European Journal of Operational Research*, 83(1):21–38, 1995.

[5] N. Christofides and C. Whitlock. An algorithm for two-dimensional cutting problems. *Operations Research*, pages 30–44, 1977.

[6] M. Garey and D. Johnson. *Computers and intractability*. W. H. Freeman, 1979.

[7] E. Goldenberg. Automatic layout of variable-content print data. Master's thesis, School of Cognitive & Computing Sciences, University of Sussex, 2002.

[8] J. González, J. Merelo, P. Castillo, V. Rivas, and G. Romero. Optimizing web newspaper layout using simulated annealing. In J. Mira and J. Sanchez-Andres, editors, *Engineering Applications of Bio-Inspired Artificial Neural Networks*, volume 1607 of *Lecture Notes in Computer Science*, pages 759–768. Springer Berlin / Heidelberg, 1999.

[9] N. Hurst. *Better Automatic Layout of Documents*. PhD thesis, Monash University, Department of Computer Science, May 2009.

[10] N. Hurst, W. Li, and K. Marriott. Review of automatic document formatting. In *Proceedings of the 9th ACM symposium on Document engineering*, pages 99–108. ACM, 2009.

[11] N. Hurst, K. Marriott, and P. Moulder. Minimum sized text containment shapes. In *DocEng '06: Proceedings of the 2006 ACM symposium on Document engineering*, pages 3–12, New York, NY, USA, 2006. ACM.

[12] J. Puchinger and P. Stuckey. Automating branch-and-bound for dynamic programs. In R. Glück and O. de Moor, editors, *Proceedings of the ACM SIGPLAN 2008 Workshop on Partial Evaluation and Program Manipulation (PEPM '08)*, pages 81–89. ACM, 2008.

[13] T. Strecker and L. Hennig. Automatic layouting of personalized newspaper pages. In B. Fleischmann, K.-H. Borgwardt, R. Klein, and A. Tuma, editors, *Operations Research Proceedings 2008*, pages 469–474. Springer Berlin Heidelberg, 2009.

ALMcss: A JavaScript Implementation of the CSS Template Layout Module

César Acebal
Departamento de Informática
Universidad de Oviedo
c/ Calvo Sotelo s/n
33007 Oviedo, Spain
acebal@uniovi.es

Bert Bos
W3C/ERCIM
2004, Route des Lucioles, B.P. 93
06902 Sophia Antipolis Cedex, France
bert@w3.org

María Rodríguez[*]
Departamento de Informática
Universidad de Oviedo
c/ Calvo Sotelo s/n
33007 Oviedo, Spain
rodriguezfmaria@uniovi.es

Juan Manuel Cueva
Departamento de Informática
Universidad de Oviedo
c/ Calvo Sotelo s/n
33007 Oviedo, Spain
cueva@uniovi.es

ABSTRACT

Traditionally, web standards in general and Cascading Style Sheets (CSS) in particular take a long time from when they are defined by the W3C until they are implemented by browser vendors. This has been a limitation not only for authors, who had to wait even years before they could use certain CSS properties in their web pages, but also for the creators of the specification itself, who were not able to test their proposals in practice.

In this paper we present ALMcss, a JavaScript prototype that implements the CSS Template Layout Module, a proposal for an addition to CSS to make it a more capable layout language, which has been developed inside the W3C CSS Working Group by two of the authors of this paper. We present the rationale of the module and an introduction to its syntax, before discussing the design of our prototype.

ALMcss has served us as a proof of concept that the Template Layout Module is not only feasible, but it can be in fact implemented in current web browsers using just JavaScript and the Document Object Model (DOM). In addition, ALMcss allows web designers to start to use today the new layout capabilities of CSS that the module provides, even before it becomes an official W3C specification.

---

[*]This author was formerly a researcher at CTIC Foundation, Asturias (Spain), where she developed the initial version of ALMcss.

Categories and Subject Descriptors

H.5.2 [**Information Interfaces and Presentation**]: User Interfaces; I.7.2 [**Document and Text Processing**]: Document Preparation; H.4.3 [**Information Systems Applications**]: Communications Applications—*Information browsers*

General Terms

Design, Standardization, Experimentation

Keywords

Browsers, CSS, CSS3, layout, web standards, W3C, JavaScript

1. INTRODUCTION

The standardisation process of the various parts of Cascading Style Sheets (CSS) usually takes several years. There are good reasons for that, but the fact is that there is a considerable time between the moment the W3C CSS Working Group decides to publish a new *Working Draft* and when it reaches the *Recommendation* status and is implemented by major web browsers. (The last part sometimes happens even later.) There are two main consequences of this:

- For people involved in the standardisation of the language (**editors** of the specification, **contributors** to the W3C public mailing lists, etcetera), it means that they are usually only able to test and discuss their proposals theoretically, writing CSS code on a whiteboard or in an email message and trying to draw or explain what that code is supposed to do.

- For **web designers** and **authors** in general, it prevents them to use the new features of the language.

In this paper we describe an approach that, although it cannot solve the whole problem—in the end, browsers must still implement the new features natively, like they do with the rest of CSS specification—can certainly *alleviate* it. The approach is to use JavaScript to provide an experimental implementation of new CSS features.

2. IMPLEMENTATION ALTERNATIVES

JavaScript was neither the first nor the most obvious approach to follow in order to implement the CSS3 module of which we were editors. As in any other research project, the first task was to study the different alternatives for implementing our proposal. We concluded that these were the three main possible choices:

- Modifying the code of an open-source existing browser, such as Mozilla Firefox or Webkit.

- Implementing a prototype from scratch.

- Developing a browser plugin.

Probably the most evident option was developing a prototype from scratch that implemented only the Template Layout Module and none of the other stylistic information (otherwise, it would not be a prototype, but a whole browser, which was out of the scope of the project). This is to what has been done by other authors to demonstrate certain research results in layout and document formatting [3, 8]. This option had, however, the disadvantage of being able to show only modest visible results: the web pages rendered by the prototype would necessarily have to be very simple, no real examples of HTML/CSS could have been used.

On the contrary, modifying an existing browser would have allowed us to reuse most of its rendering engine. Nevertheless, this task is far from simple, and it would have required much time trying to decipher the intricate C++ code that deals with layout before we could begin to actually work on it.

Finally, the solution that better fit our needs (when considering the balance between results and cost of development) and also fulfilled most of the desirable requirements for the prototype (browser, operating system, and platform independency) turned out to be developing a plugin for existing browsers. In order to accomplish these goals, it has been implemented in JavaScript, so that it can work on any modern browser. After all, that approach, although not very common when we started its development, had already been tried before, either to improve the CSS support of certain browsers [5] or to implement experimentally new CSS3 modules [11].

3. THE TEMPLATE LAYOUT MODULE

The Template Layout Module [2] is an attempt to supersede the limitations of current CSS layout mechanisms (namely, floats, tables and absolute positioning) that prevent a true separation between content and presentation, thus making it a true layout language [6].

It adds a new value to the `display` property of CSS, which allows to define a *grid* of rows and columns for the element it is applied to. To a certain extent, this property lets us specify the layout of an element or the entire page in a similar way to what we used to do with tables in HTML, but without their drawbacks (fixed order of elements, limited influence over their size). The proposed syntax (at this moment still a working draft) consists of a string for each row in the grid, in which each character represents a column and multiple repeated characters in adjacent rows and columns form a single slot in the overall grid that spans that number of rows and columns. The available space is automatically distributed over the columns and rows, but it is also possible

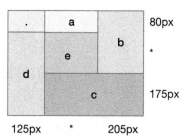

Figure 1: Schema of the layout generated by the CSS template in the first example.

to set an explicit width and height for columns and rows, or let them be determined by their content. This is combined with a new value for the `position` property that specifies where the content of an element is placed in the grid (that is, into which slot it goes). Although this is not the focus of this paper, the following provides a brief introduction to the syntax of the Template Layout Module.

3.1 Introduction to the Template Layout Module

The positioning is based on templates. You can think of the template as a two-dimensional matrix in which the contents are distributed. This example shows all parts of the syntax (in practice, many parts can be omitted):

```
body {
  display: ".ab" /80px
           "deb" /*
           "dcc" /175px
           125px * 205px;
}
```

For readability, we inserted line breaks into the value; it could also have been typed all on one line. The above will define the grid shown in Figure 1.

3.2 Template Definition

The template is specified as one or more text strings on the `display` property. Each string defines one row and is composed of characters, one character per column. Each character thus represents a position in the matrix.

The characters can be:

letter
> slot for content

@ (at sign)
> default slot

. (period)
> empty slot

A group of identical letters in adjacent rows or columns forms a single slot that spans those rows and columns. Non-rectangular slots are illegal.

Each row can optionally be followed by a value which sets the height of the preceding row. The default is *. The values are as follows:

length
> An explicit height for that row, e.g., '80px'.

:   The height of the row is determined by its contents.

* (asterisk)
:   All rows with an asterisk will be of equal height.

It is also possible to specify the width of each column. This can be done after the last row has been defined. Each value sets the width of one column. If there are fewer values than columns, the missing ones are assumed to be *. Some of the possible values for the width are the following:

length
:   An explicit width for that column, e.g., '125px'.

* (asterisk)
:   All columns with a * have the same width.

max-content, min-content
:   The height of the row is determined by its contents. (These keywords are defined elsewhere in CSS.)

If no widths are specified, then all columns will have the same width.

3.3 Mapping

Once the template has been defined, it can be used to specify the position of the elements of the page. The mapping of elements to slots is done with the position property. The possible values are:

letter
:   The element is taken out of the flow of its parent and put into the specified slot in its template ancestor.

same
:   Computes to the same letter as the most recent element with a letter as position.

For example:

```
#header { position: a; }
```

There are some examples of document fragments using these CSS properties in the following sections.

4. ALMCSS

ALMcss is a relatively complex piece of JavaScript, with near two thousand lines of code. Since it is not possible to directly manipulate the internal layout engine of the browser, all the work must be done through the Document Object Model (DOM), which is probably one of the most intricate parts of JavaScript programming: "if there is a DOM method, there is probably a problem with it somewhere, in some capacity" [9]. In addition, there is much tedious work to do to actually perform the layout algorithm itself. A great portion of the code is devoted to retrieve and parse the styles applied to the document, something that is usually performed by the browser but that in this case was not possible, because the new values defined by the Template Layout Module are not yet supported by current browsers. Finally, and although the situation has improved a lot during last years, JavaScript still suffers from a lack of development environments, debugging tools, automated testing frameworks, or logging libraries of the same quality as that of mainstream programming languages like Java, C++, or C#.

4.1 Architecture of ALMcss

The rendering process in ALMcss is divided into four sequential processing steps, thus following a Pipes and Filters architectural pattern [4]. The four phases of the rendering process are enumerated and briefly described below:

1. **Parsing the style sheet.** First, all the style rules that are applied to the document are parsed, to obtain those rules that contain a template definition, a slot position, or a vertical alignment property. Those are the rules (and the elements retrieved by their selectors) that should be processed by the prototype, since they are not yet understood by browsers.

2. **Decorating the DOM.** Browsers do not store information about the CSS declarations that use any of the values defined in the Template Layout Module for the display or position properties, since they are not yet officially part of CSS. In fact, they make style rules illegal and must be ignored, according to the CSS 2.1 specification. The approach followed in ALMcss to retain them until they are processed in subsequent steps is to store them in the Document Object Model itself. It is what we have called "decorating the DOM".

3. **Parsing the templates and creating the object structure.** The previously annotated template properties are retrieved from the DOM and parsed, creating an object structure that represents the templates defined in the style sheet: how many rows and columns they have, what slots they contain, the position of each slot and how many rows and columns it spans, etcetera.

4. **Computing the dimensions of templates and slots.** During this phase, for each template, the dimensions of their slots and the template itself are computed, according to the rules defined by the Template Layout Module (as we described in the previous section).

5. **Positioning the elements into slots.** The final stage consists on actually moving each element that is positioned in a template into the appropriate slot. Templates and slots are absolute positioned according to the dimensions calculated in the previous step and they are rendered by the browser.

The whole process is shown in Figure 2, which depicts the overall architecture of the prototype. Following sections describe the design of each phase in more detail.

4.2 Design of ALMcss

4.2.1 Parsing the Style Sheet

In this first stage, all the style rules applied to the document must be parsed. This is needed to retrieve the style declarations that use the properties and values defined by the Template Layout Module. Although it reuses the existing properties display and position, those properties are augmented with new values specific of the Template Layout Module, and for this reason they can not be accessed through the DOM. (Until they are actually standardized, the values are officially illegal). Therefore, all the styles applied to the document must be manually fetched and then

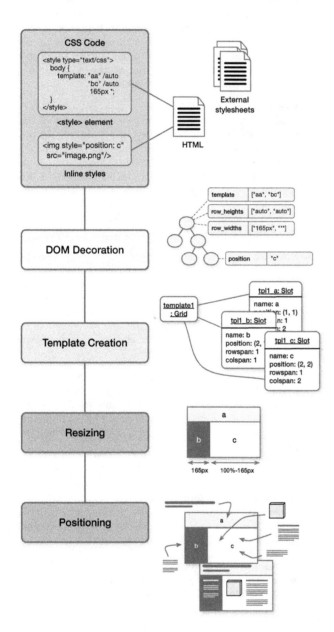

Figure 2: ALMcss architecture consists on four sequential phases that implement the rendering process.

parsed to retrieve only those declarations in which we are interested: template definitions, elements positioned into a slot of some template, etcetera. The process is outlined below:

1. First, style sheets are traversed. Note that this require to fetch the CSS code of:

    (a) Inline styles

    (b) Styles embedded in the `style` element

    (c) External style sheets

2. Once all the CSS rules have been compiled, the resultant code is parsed, looking for the following declarations:

    (a) a `display` property that has a template definition as a value

    (b) a `position` property with a *letter*, `@`, or `same` value

    (c) a `vertical-align` property

    (d) `::slot(x)` pseudo-elements

4.2.2 Decorating the DOM

Once all the style rules have been obtained and parsed, they must be stored in some place, so that they can be accessed by other modules of the prototype. Making an analogy, we could say that we need something like the symbol table of any compiler or interpreter [1]. Given the high number of searches that are going to be done in subsequent phases of the rendering process, some associative structure, like a hash map would be desirable. JavaScript arrays can perfectly emulate it, since they allow to use strings for the index of the array. In our case, the access key will be the selector of the style rule, for which an object with information about the template properties of such rule will be stored in the corresponding position of the array.

4.2.3 Creation of the Structure

The next phase consists of processing the CSS rules that are using some of the template positioning properties—which have been previously stored in the DOM in the previous phase—to create the object structure that represents the templates and their slots. Note that this phase does not do any actual layout process: it simply recreates in memory the same structure of templates that have been defined by the user in the style sheet.

This phase is divided into two steps:

1. First, the previously decorated DOM is parsed to identify all the templates defined in the style sheet, and structures of JavaScript and DOM objects are created for representing such templates.

2. A second step actually moves the elements of the original HTML document into their corresponding slot (one of the DOM objects created in the previous step).

To understand how this process works, let us consider the following template definition in CSS (the spaces inside the template are optional and for readability only):

```
display: ". a b" /165px
         "d e b" /auto
         "d c c" /220px
         180px * 12em;
```

A template can be represented with a two-dimensional array. Once the raw data of the template definition (the value of the `display` property) has been copied into the array, the next step is to identify the slots that compose the template. First, a `Grid` object is created and associated to the actual HTML element where the template is defined (a `DOM HTMLElement` object). Then, the array that contains the template definition is traversed, according to the following algorithm:

1. The template is traversed, starting in the position (1, 1) (first row, first column), and following from left to right and from top to bottom ((1, 2), (1, 3), (2, 1)...).

2. A `Slot` object is created and assigned to the template (the `Grid` object) with the current position.

3. While the slot identifier matches that of the last position, the `colspan` or `rowspan` properties of the current slot are incremented accordingly.

4. When a different slot identifier is found, a new `Slot` object is created.

   As for the creation of the templates themselves, it deserves more explanation, because each `Grid` object is not isolated, but it must know its ancestors (in compiler construction terms, its *scope*). This is needed for the case of nested templates. The pseudocode is as follows:

```
if (current DOM element is a template)
  // Creates a new Grid object with no
  // position and width and height
  // equal to 0
  var grid = new Grid()
  grid.makeGrid() // Creates the slots
                  // of the template
  if (the element does not have any ancestor)
    add it to the list of containers
  else
    add it to the ancestor
  end_if
end_if
// Parse the children of the current element
// passing this element as ancestor
foreach (child: element.getChildren())
  child.parse(element)
end_foreach
```

The whole process is shown in the UML sequence diagram of Figure 3, where the interactions at execution time among the different objects are outlined for an imaginary template definition like "aaab", "aaac"...

Another step consists of creating an HTML element for each slot in the template. This is done through the DOM. These `HTMLElement` nodes act as placeholders to contain the actual elements of the HTML document that are positioned into slots, which will be done in the next phase of the rendering algorithm. Note that this step would not be necessary if we were implementing the Template Layout Module natively in a browser. In that case, *boxes*, rather than new elements, would be created to represent the slots. But, since this is not possible from JavaScript, the internal boxes of the layout

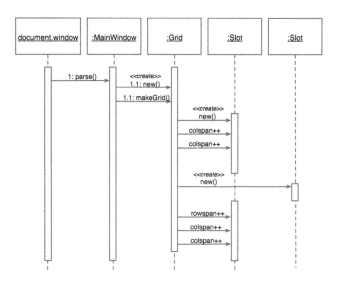

Figure 3: UML sequence diagram showing a possible scenario of creation of a grid. First, the a slot is created, and since it spans three columns, its colspan property is incremented. Then, in position (1,4) a new slot identifier is found: b, which does not span any columns. After the first row is processed, comes the second one. The a letter appears again in the position (2,1) of the template, so the rowspan property of the previously created slot must be incremented. The process continues until the last position of the template definition has been reached.

engine are emulated by inserting *artificial* HTML elements into the Document Object Model.

Since this is the basis for what will come later, and a fundamental piece in the design of ALMcss, it will be explained with a *real* example. Let it be the following markup:

```
div id="header">...</div>
<div id="content">
  <div id="nav">...</div>
  <div id="mainContent">...</div>
</div>
<div id="footer">...</div>
```

And the CSS code below, which creates two nested templates[1]:

```
body {
  display: "a"
          "b"
          "c";
}
#header { position: a; }
#content {
  position: b;
  display: "de";
}
#footer { position: c; }
```

---

[1] Note that although the example, for clarity, uses different letters for the nested template, this is not required, and implementations must be aware of the context of the element (its ancestor templates, that is, the *scope* where it is defined).

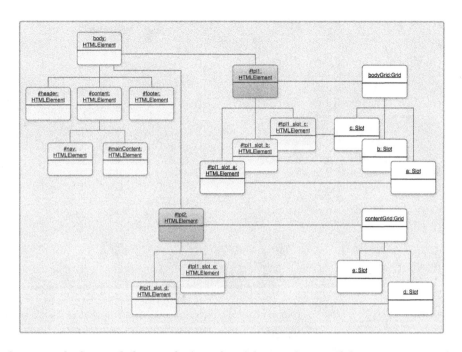

Figure 4: When the second phase of the rendering algorithm ends, an object structure of grids, slots, and HTML elements represents all the templates defined in the style sheets for a given document. The figure shows the object diagram for the above HTML and CSS code, where green boxes represent the DOM nodes (HTMLElement objects) of the original HTML document (they are created by the browser when the document is loaded), whereas blue ones are those HTMLElements that have been created and inserted in the DOM by ALMcss to represent each slot. As it can be seen, each Slot object has an associated HTMLElement. It is in these artificially created elements where the DOM nodes that represent actual content of the document will be moved in the last phase of the rendering process. No elements are created for grids, but they are associated instead with the existing DOM node corresponding to the element for which they are defined.

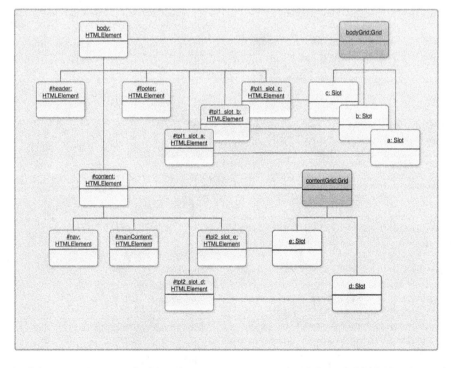

Figure 5: The final object structure of this phase, once every positioned HTML element in the original document has been moved, manipulating the DOM, into their corresponding slot.

Then, the result of this step for that example is the creation of the structure of templates (*grids*) and slots shown in Figure 4, where each grid has a reference to the HTML element where it has been defined and each slot points to the newly created HTML element. At this point, the DOM for the current example would be as follows:

```
<div id="header">...</div>
<div id="content">
  <div id="nav">...</div>
  <div id="mainContent">...</div>
  <div id="tpl2_slot_d">...</div>
  <div id="tpl2_slot_e">...</div>
</div>
<div id="footer">...</div>
<div id="tpl1_slot_a">...</div>
<div id="tpl1_slot_b">...</div>
<div id="tpl1_slot_c">...</div>
```

The final step of this phase consists of actually moving each element in the original HTML document to the slot where it has been positioned (that is, to one of the `HTMLElement` nodes inserted in the DOM in the last step). The resultant structure of DOM (`HTMLElement`) and ALMcss (`Grid` and `Slot`) objects is shown in Figure 5 and is represented below:

```
<div id="tpl1_slot_a">
  <div id="header">...</div>
</div>
<div id="tpl1_slot_b">
  <div id="content">
    <div id="tpl2_slot_d">
      <div id="nav">...</div>
    </div>
    <div id="tpl2_slot_e">
      <div id="mainContent">...</div>
    </div>
  </div>
</div>
<div id="tpl1_slot_c">
  <div id="footer">...</div>
</div>
```

After finishing the creation of all the templates defined in the style sheet, a structure of `Grid` and `Slot` objects is created in memory for each template of the document. When modelling the representation of the templates, the issue of nested templates arose. Basically, it means that a template can contain not only slots, but also other templates. One of the premises of ALMcss (and of any piece of software) is that it should have the conditional logic reduced to a minimum. In particular, we did not want to have to check, every time an element is rendered, whether it is a template (a grid) or a slot. Fortunately, this is a well-known software design problem, as is its solution: the Composite design pattern [7]:

> Compose objects into tree structures to represent part-whole hierarchies. Composite lets clients treat individual objects and compositions of objects uniformly.

Figure 6 shows all the classes that participate in the template representation. Specifically, the Composite design pattern is implemented by `Element`, `Slot`, and `Grid`, which play

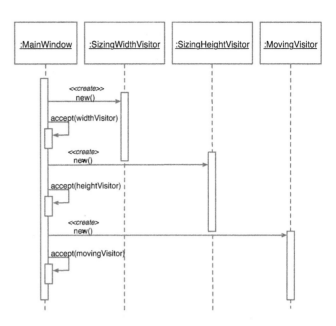

Figure 7: A simplified UML sequence diagram which depicts the sizing and positioning phases of the rendering process done by ALMcss. It is simplified because it does not show, for clarity reasons, how the actual object structure of a template is traversed by visitors.

the roles of Component, Leaf, and Composite in the pattern, respectively. Note also how each element (slot or grid) created by ALMcss keeps a one-to-one relationship with the actual DOM HTML element to which it belongs.

4.2.4 Resizing

The third of the four phases of the rendering process is responsible for computing the dimensions of the templates and slots created in the preceding phase. This process has necessarily to be done in two steps: first, the widths are computed, and then the heights. This is so because of the *flexible* widths introduced in the Template Layout Module with values like `max-content`, `min-content` and `*` (asterisk), which were not present in early drafts of the module, where only fixed widths were allowed.

With these new values, the width of a slot may depend on its contents; and so do its height, if a value of `*` or `auto` has been specified for some row. For this reason, the dimensions of the slots (and, therefore, of the templates themselves) can not be computed in a single-pass algorithm, but the two passes above mentioned are needed.

For computing the size of the slots and templates, the Visitor design pattern [7] has been applied. Thus, the following two visitors traverse the object structure of each template (its slots and nested templates, if any), computing their widths and heights, respectively:

- `SizingWidthVisitor`

- `SizingHeightVisitor`

Once all the templates, slots, and their associated HTML elements, have been created, inserted in the right place in the DOM, and their dimensions have been computed, we can actually place the elements on the screen. This is what the

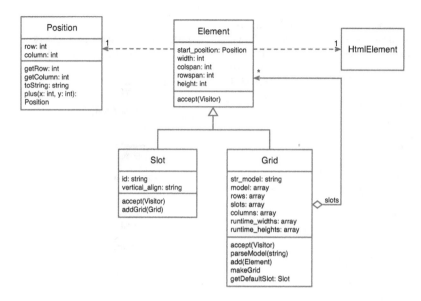

Figure 6: Class diagram showing the template structure as it is represented in ALMcss.

last phase of the prototype does, the arrangement of the elements in their right position on the screen. In other words, it is in this phase that the actual layout of the document is created.

This phase relies on the values that have been computed in the preceding phases, specially the dimensions of the templates and slots. Therefore, this final procedure is relatively simple, since it only has to access the DOM elements that define a template and, for each, traverse the slots it contains and read their dimensions. As the slots of each template are being traversed, their horizontal and vertical offsets are computed based on the position and size of the preceding slot. Finally, slots are *absolutely positioned* using these computed coordinates.

As it was done in the previous phase, positioning of the elements is implemented following the Visitor design pattern, by the `MovingVisitor` class. See Figure 7, which shows a very simplified sequence diagram of the last two phases of the algorithm.

4.3 Usage

Using ALMcss to achieve the benefits of the CSS Template Layout Module in current browsers is as simple as to include the following line in the HTML document:

```
<script src="ALM.js"type="text/javascript"></script>
```

Then we will be able to use (to a certain extent) the new properties and values defined by the Template Layout Module, as if they were actually supported by the browser.

5. DEMONSTRATION

For demonstrating both the benefits of the Template Layout Module and the way of working of our prototype, we will use both of them to achieve any number of columns of equal height in any order, just like the One True Layout technique does, [10], but much more easily. Let the following HTML code:

```
<div id="content">
```

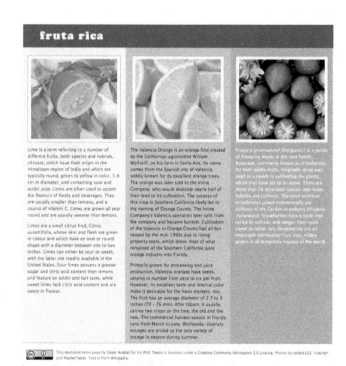

Figure 8: A 3-1-2 layout as is shown in a browser using the Template Layout Module and ALMcss.

```
<div class="fruit" id="orange">...</div>
<div class="fruit" id="strawberry">...</div>
<div class="fruit" id="lime">...</div>
</div>
```

Using the Template Layout Module, a 3-1-2 layout would be as simple as:

```
#content {
  display: "312";
}
#orange     { position: 1; }
#strawberry { position: 2; }
#lime       { position: 3; }
```

With just those properties we are achieving the desired order and equal-height columns, using a liquid layout (the result is shown in in Figure 8). But, unlike One True Layout, we can obtain hybrid layouts that mix fixed-width with liquid columns, using as many different length units as we want. For example, the following template would create a three-column layout where the first two columns have a width of 120 pixels and 18 em, while the third one is liquid:

```
#content {
  display: "312";
          120px 18em max-content;
```

Bun the major strength of template layout comes when more drastic changes are required. Thus, it is possible to get the layout of Figure 9 with only using this template:

```
#content {
  display: "332"
          "111";
}
```

6. ACKNOWLEDGEMENTS

A preliminary version of this work was part of the research project *Extensión del estándar CSS3 que permita la adaptación multidispositivo de contenidos Web*, funded by CTIC Foundation (Centre for the Development of Information and Communication Technologies in Asturias).

7. CONCLUSIONS

Although ALMcss is just a prototype, and it has several bugs, it has already served several purposes.

First, having an earlier implementation, even a not fully compliant one, has allowed us to present the Template Layout Module using "real" examples and to show them working in current browsers, which has been helpful to promote the proposed solution among the web designer community.

That, in turn, has allowed web designers to try the proposed features and give feedback (on syntax, on required features, etcetera), which many of them would otherwise not have been able to do.

In addition, it has showed that, since it is possible to implement the Template Layout Module in a current browser using just JavaScript and the DOM, without having access to the underlying layout engine, it should be feasible to implement it natively by browser vendors.

Finally, it has proved that JavaScript can be used as a rapid prototyping tool for adding support for experimental CSS modules to current browsers, even years before those features are present in a native way.

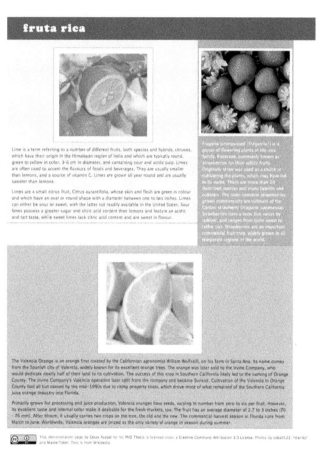

Figure 9: Any variation of the original One True Layout technique can be achieved just with a simple change of letters in the template, even if it involves several rows, or different number of columns. The figure shows how the template below is rendered in a real browser using ALMcss.

8. REFERENCES

[1] A. V. Aho and J. D. Ullman. *Principles of Compiler Design*. Addison-Wesley Longman Publishing Co., Inc., Boston, MA, USA, 1977.

[2] B. Bos and C. Acebal. CSS Template Layout Module. W3C Working Draft 29 April 2010, 2010. http://www.w3.org/TR/2010/WD-css3-layout-20100429/.

[3] C. Braganza, K. Marriott, P. Moulder, M. Wybrow, and T. Dwyer. Scrolling behaviour with single- and multi-column layout. In *Proceedings of the 18th international conference on World wide web - WWW '09*, page 831, New York, NY, USA, Apr. 2009. ACM Press.

[4] F. Buschmann, R. Meunier, H. Rohnert, P. Sommerlad, and M. Stal. *Pattern-oriented software architecture: a system of patterns*. John Wiley & Sons, Inc., New York, NY, USA, 1996.

[5] D. Edwards. IE7, 2008. http://dean.edwards.name/IE7/.

[6] C. Fernández Acebal. *ALMcss : separación de estructura y presentación en la Web mediante posicionamiento avanzado en CSS (ALMcss: Separation between Structure and Presentation on the Web with CSS Advanced Layout)*. Phd thesis, Universidad de Oviedo, 2010.

[7] E. Gamma, R. Helm, R. Johnson, and J. Vlissides. *Design patterns: elements of reusable object-oriented software*. Addison-Wesley Longman Publishing Co., Inc., Boston, MA, USA, 1995.

[8] C. Jacobs, W. Li, E. Schrier, D. Bargeron, and D. Salesin. Adaptive grid-based document layout. *ACM Transactions on Graphics*, 22(3):838, July 2003.

[9] J. Resig. The DOM Is a Mess, 2009. http://yuilibrary.com/theater/john-resig/resig-dom/.

[10] A. Robinson. In search of the One True Layout, 2005. http://www.positioniseverything.net/articles/onetruelayout/.

[11] C. Savarese. Introducing the CSS3 Multi-Column Module. *A List Apart*, 2005. http://www.alistapart.com/articles/css3multicolumn.

Learning How to Trade Off Aesthetic Criteria in Layout

Peter Moulder
Clayton School of IT
Monash University
Vic. 3800, Australia
peter.moulder@monash.edu

Kim Marriott
Clayton School of IT
Monash University
Vic. 3800, Australia
kim.marriott@monash.edu

ABSTRACT

Typesetting software is often faced with conflicting aesthetic goals. For example, choosing where to break lines in text might involve aiming to minimize hyphenation, variation in word spacing, and consecutive lines starting with the same word. Typically, automatic layout is modelled as an optimization problem in which the goal is to minimize a complex objective function that combines various penalty functions each of which corresponds to a particular bad feature. Determining how to combine these penalty functions is difficult and very time consuming, becoming harder each time we add another penalty. Here we present a machine-learning approach to do this, and test it in the context of line-breaking. Our approach repeatedly queries the expert typographer as to which one of a pair of layouts is better, and accordingly refines the estimate of how best to weight the penalties in a linear combination. It chooses layout pair queries by a heuristic to maximize the amount that can be learnt from them so as to reduce the number of combinations that must be considered by the typographer.

Categories and Subject Descriptors

I.7.2 [**Document and Text Processing**]: Document Preparation—*Format and notation, Photocomposition/typesetting*

General Terms

Algorithms

Keywords

typography, line-breaking, progressive articulation of preference, multi-objective optimization

1. INTRODUCTION

Typesetting software is often faced with conflicting aesthetic goals. One example is line breaking in justified text: choosing where to end one line and start the next. This is

a difficult problem because of the need to trade off a large number of conflicting desires such as keeping word spacing fairly consistent between lines, using hyphenation sparingly, or not starting consecutive lines with the same phrase. Automatic line breaking is provided in several document formatting systems in which the problem is modelled as an optimization problem in which the goal is to minimize a linear objective function that combines various penalty functions each of which corresponds to a particular bad feature. However, automatic line breaking is still not as good as can be done by hand, and experienced typographers will tweak the results of automatic line-breaking. One of the reasons that automatic line-breaking is still not optimal is that it only takes account of a subset of the features that typographers consider.

Another example of layout with conflicting aesthetic goals is float placement in documents in which floats should be close to their references but placed in an aesthetically pleasing manner: not too many floats on a page, not too close together. Float placement is even more difficult if text can wrap around floats since this means that float placement interacts with line breaking. This was in fact the problem that motivated this research. We wished to extend the objective function used in line-breaking to include more penalty functions and also to take into account float placement.

Unfortunately, we found that determining how to combine and appropriately weight these penalty functions was difficult and time consuming, growing harder each time we added a new penalty function. As a result, we decided to automate the process of learning how to weight the penalty functions. Here we present a supervised machine learning based approach to do this.

Our approach repeatedly queries the expert typographer by showing them two possible layouts for the same content and asking if one is better than the other. We treat each of these judgements as a mathematical constraint on the aggregate objective function (and hence on the weights): a constraint that the aggregate objective function value for one of the layouts is less than that for the other. One can then use a support vector machine [9] to give a representative weight vector that is consistent with these constraints. One difficulty is that we do not wish to bore or annoy our captive typographer by asking them to make too many comparisons. Thus we automatically generate a huge number of different layouts. It refines this objective function by asking queries that heuristically maximize the amount that can be learnt from them so as to reduce the number of combinations that must be considered by the typographer.

2. RELATED WORK

Automatic text layout algorithms and software are discussed more fully in [3]. The seminal paper on line breaking is due to Knuth and Plass [4], who formulated line breaking as an optimization problem and gave an efficient dynamic programming algorithm to solve it that is used in the TeX document layout system.

Holkner [2] addresses the problem of an unknown aggregate objective function by presenting multiple Pareto-optimal solutions along a specified trade-off direction.

So far as we are aware we are the first to suggest the use of machine learning techniques to learn how best to combine the penalties for line breaking and other kinds of document layout. However machine learning has been used to identify other kinds of aesthetic criteria, for instance facial beauty [1]. Machine learning techniques have been used previously to determine how to analyze the layout of a document [5].

The main work on determining how to weight different criteria is in the field of multi-criteria decision analysis.

One notable approach here to determining weights is the Analytic Hierarchy Process [7], which constructs a matrix of pairwise comparisons of the relative importance of different criteria; and proposes both a way of combining this matrix of relative weights into a single vector, and a measure of inconsistency in the matrix, as a means of detecting anomalies that warrant revisiting the pairwise comparisons.

3. THE BASIC APPROACH

We wish to form an aggregate objective function that comprises various component features of a layout (such as number of hyphenations, variation in word spacing, and so on). More specifically, we assume that the aggregate objective function is a weighted linear sum of component penalty functions $P_1, \ldots, P_n$ that together correspond to the layout features we wish to consider; such that the question of "which of two layouts is better" can be answered by finding which layout L has the lower aggregate objective function value

$$\sum_{j=1}^{n} w_j P_j(L)$$

where $w_j > 0$ $(j = 1, \ldots, n)$ are the weights that we wish to learn.

There doesn't have to be a one-to-one correspondence between component penalty function and what one might think of as a layout feature: if there is interaction between abstract features (for example two consecutive hyphens being considered worse than two hyphens on distant lines) then there might be a distinct penalty component to represent that interaction.

What is important is that the component penalty functions are written to be additive: for example that returning a value twice as large should correspond to twice as much impact on the overall value or badness of the layout. This is because we wish to make inferences of the form "if a layout L whose penalty vector $p = \langle P_1(L), \ldots, P_n(L) \rangle$ is considered preferable to a layout with penalty vector p' (that is, if $p \prec p'$), and if $q \prec q'$, then it follows that $2p+3q \prec 2p'+3q'$": such inferences reduce the number of questions we need to ask the human typographer.

Our approach repeatedly queries the expert typographer by showing them two ways of laying out the same content

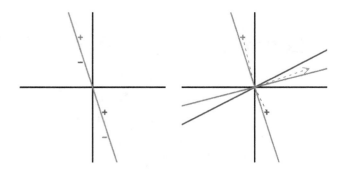

Figure 1: Left: Example showing how learning the weighting for the objective function is equivalent to learning a hyperplane that separates positive and negative instances.
Right: An alternative visualization of the same example. This time the solution is considered a point bounded by input hyperplanes.

and asking if one is better than the other. Given these comparisons an SVM-like approach determines how best to weight the penalties in a linear combination. Each iteration of the above process provides a revised estimated weight vector, so that the process can be stopped at any time. (Otherwise, the process stops once each input paragraph has a known-optimal layout. This occurs after a finite number of iterations, as each iteration rules out at least one possible better layout.)

There are two sub-problems: (i) estimating a vector of weights from the comparison results that are available to us so far; and (ii) choosing a pair of layouts to present to the typographer to get our next comparison result.

3.1 Weight vector estimation

We wish to learn the weights given a set of layout pairs (L, M) where L and M are layouts of the same content and our expert typographer has said that they prefer layout L over M. We let $p = (P_1(L), \ldots, P_n(L))$ and $q = (P_1(M), \ldots, P_n(M))$. The layout pair gives a positive tuple $d = q - p$ and a corresponding negative tuple $-d = p - q$. Determining suitable values for the weights w can be re-couched as finding a hyperplane $w \cdot x = 0$ that represents the "indifference curve", separating the positive tuples from the negative tuples; i.e. finding a w s.t. $w \cdot d \geq 0$ for all positive difference vectors d that the typographer has expressed (including a d for each component vector, corresponding to the initial assumptions that $\forall j. w_j \geq 0$). This is because $w \cdot d \geq 0$ iff

$$\sum_{j=1}^{n} w_j (P_j(M) - P_j(L)) \geq 0$$

for layout pair (L, M).

An example should make this clearer. Suppose that we have just two types of badness that we're trading against each other when determining our objective function for line breaking. For concreteness, suppose that one of them is number of hyphens, and the other is a measure of variation in whitespace between lines (which might be measured as the standard deviation of the amount of unused space per line, measured in ems).

We ask a typographer to compare two layouts, where one layout has one more hyphen than the other, but in exchange has two units less whitespace variation than the other. The human says that this layout (with the extra hyphen) is worse, i.e. that the hyphen is more costly than two units of whitespace variation.

We then ask the typographer to compare another two layouts, where one layout has one more hyphen than the other, but this time it's allowed a reduction of four units in whitespace variation. The human says that in this case, the layout with less whitespace variation is better.

The example gives rise to the positive and negative data points shown in the left half of Figure 1. The two blue points are from the first comparison, and the two green points are from the second comparison. Recall that each pair is simply the negation of each other: the minus signs in the diagram are for the direction where a tradeoff in this direction makes the layout better (lower penalty), while the plus signs represent the direction where it's a change for the worse.

The red line is one possible separating line (hyperplane) whose normal is a vector in the direction $(1, 3)$, indicating that one hyphen is worth about 3 units of whitespace variation.

This separating hyperplane (red line) represents the set of difference vectors that would have zero net penalty.

Finding a hyperplane that separates positive and negative examples is, of course, a well-studied problem in machine learning. Here we describe an SVM approach, and a simplification of it.

We require the separating hyperplane to pass through the origin, so that a difference vector of zero (no change) is considered to have zero net penalty change. (Put another way, having it pass through the origin makes it "half way between the positive points and the negative points", since the origin is half way between each positive point and its corresponding negative point.)

In SVM terminology, this corresponds to finding an unbiased hyperplane.

The usual initial visualization of an SVM problem is with the input represented as points (our d) that define a dividing hyperplane (our w), as shown in the left half of Figure 1. However, the relation $d \cdot w \geq 0$ is symmetrical between d and w, and so can equally be visualized as a hyperplane for each d that represents a constraint on a point w. This is shown in the right half of the figure.

Standard unbiased SVM for our problem would be to choose w to minimize $|w|$ subject to $w \cdot d \geq 1$ for each input d. Our implementation instead solves the simpler problem of minimizing $\sum_j w_j$ subject to those constraints, taking advantage of the fact that we constrain $\forall j. w_j \geq 0$ as part of our set of d vectors.

The approach used to guess a coefficient vector from aesthetic judgements is independent of the approach used to choose layout comparisons to present to the typographer. One could replace the above with something that also used estimates supplied by the typographer rather than just hard bounds. See [8] for some possibilities.

3.2 Choice of layout pair

One difficulty is that we do not wish to bore or annoy our captive typographer by asking them to make too many comparisons.

In our first implementation, we chose one of the two layouts to be optimal according to the current best *guess* of the weights, and the other layout to be a layout that might

be better than that layout for some different weight vector that's consistent with our existing comparisons; more specifically, the layout that's the best possible improvement (in the sense described below) on that guessed best layout.

Depending on the computational characteristics of the component penalty functions, finding the optimal layout for a given weight vector might use a dynamic programming algorithm (such as the shortest path algorithm used in [4] and in fact in our evaluation implementation), or $A^\star$ [6], or a combination where a shortest-path algorithm provides lower bounds for $A^\star$. In any of these algorithms, the search proceeds by a sequence of comparisons: "which of these two partial layouts is better, which of these partial routes is shorter?". The comparison itself is performed according to the aggregate objective function with our guessed weight vector. However, for each such comparison, we also calculate a *utility* value for revisiting this guess as to which partial layout is better. Each node in the search tree records not only a shortest-path predecessor node and corresponding total distance of that path as in a normal shortest-path search, but also the most promising comparison to revisit (along with its corresponding utility value).

Calculating the utility function for revisiting a guess that an attribute difference vector $\tilde{d}$ is a change for the worse proceeds as follows.

We return a measure of how useful it is to ask the human which is better. In our current implementation, we use a measure of "how wrong we might be": an upper bound on how much the true penalty might increase, if the weight vector is normalized to a unit vector, and if the true penalty function is consistent with the comparisons given so far.

More precisely: let $D = w \cdot \tilde{d}$ be the penalty function for the pair, where w is the unknown weight vector. (It follows that $D \geq 0$ if $w = \tilde{w}$.)

We use linear programming to determine the minimum value that D can take while still satisfying $w \cdot d \geq 0$ for all previous comparisons d.

4. EXPERIENCE IN PRACTICE

The initial runs often present two bad layouts, which is frustrating: one wants to tell it how it most needs to improve, rather than answering a question about an unimportant direction. Accordingly, we changed the software so that the typographer can also specify a direction DW to try to move from the current guessed weight vector. For example, if both layouts have too many hyphens compared to what the typographer thinks the optimal layout for that paragraph would have, then the typographer might give a DW direction of increased weight for the hyphen component. We implement this with an additional metric on comparison difference vectors encountered in the search. Let C be the comparison difference vector with sign chosen in the direction that our existing guessed weights consider a change for the worse. Then the DW metric is $(DW \cdot C)/|C|$. This is in effect a metric on the cosine of the angle between DW and C: we want to reward direction rather than magnitude. If the typographer has supplied a (non-zero) DW, then we require this DW metric to be positive for this comparison to have a positive utility value. If both the how-wrong-we-could-be metric and the DW metric are positive, then the final utility value is the product of the how-wrong-we-could-be metric and the DW metric. (If one or both are negative, then we similarly assign a non-positive utility value, and this comparison will not be revisited for this iteration of the process.) A typographer cannot in general be sure that a better layout exists with fewer hyphens (or whatever the suggested direction); therefore, this suggested direction only affects the choice of comparison, it doesn't directly affect the set of constraints used to estimate a weight vector. If in fact no layout in the suggested direction for any of the input paragraphs is even feasible, then the typographer is informed, and the typographer can either proceed without a suggested direction, or can suggest a different suggested direction.

We also found that some typographical penalty components are slower to be noticed than others, such that it is useful to draw the typographer's attention to these differences. The obvious approach would be to annotate such differences graphically, but a simpler and surprisingly effective approach is just to list for each layout which penalty components are bigger for that layout. (We present these lists in order of decreasing importance according to the current guessed weights; though this doesn't actually make much difference to the typographer in efficiency.)

A final observation is that we have found that some layout pairs of similar overall quality are hard to compare because they differ in too many respects, and it is difficult to weigh one combination of features against another combination of features. We haven't considered in detail how to estimate the difficulty a comparison will present to the typographer, but an obvious starting point is the number of non-zero components in the difference vector. One approach would be to divide a comparison's utility value by this number of non-zero components. However, since some components have very little effect on the comparison, we modify this count by first multiplying each component by the guessed weight vector, then squaring each resulting component, then dividing by the maximum such square, then summing the resulting divided squares. The resulting number can be thought of as like a count of non-zero components, but where near-zero components behave nearly like zero components.

5. DISCUSSION

We have given a machine learning based approach to determine how to combine penalties when determining what makes a layout aesthetically pleasing. While our approach is reasonably general and could be applied to a wide variety of document and diagram layout problems, it does have a number of limitations. The first of these is the assumption that the objective function is a weighted linear sum of the penalty functions. While weighted linear sums are commonly used to combine penalty functions, this is not always true. Furthermore, we do not know if this provides a reasonable approximation to what typographers do.

A more serious limitation is that it assumes that the positive and negative instances are actually separable by a hyperplane. This may not always be true as the answers provided by the typographer might be inconsistent. This could be because: (1) the assumption that there is a single objective function that is a weighted linear combination of the penalties is incorrect; or (2) the typographer has made an error.

If an inconsistency arises, it is relatively easy to determine from a linear constraint solver a subset of comparisons that are causing the inconsistency. A first step is to confirm with the typographer that they have not made an error in any

of these comparisons, thus ruling out cause (2). In the case of (1) this means we can either try and find better penalty functions or try a non-linear weighting. Knowing where the inconsistency occurs should help with this. However if this proves too difficult then a fallback approach would be to find the hyperplane that separates as many as possible: this is straightforward to do with an SVM. Essentially this means that we are trying to find the weighted linear combination of the penalties that best approximates the answers of the typographer. In this scenario, we can no longer use the utility function given above for the proposed layout pair (L, M). Instead we might compare the effect on the weight estimate assuming L is preferred to M against the converse and use the difference in weight estimates as the utility function taking into account the estimated probability of each using the current weight estimate.

It is worth pointing out that our approach was designed for determining the preferences of a single typographer. One would expect that different typographers would share some core aesthetic judgments but might well vary in how they trade off different aesthetic criteria. While one could lump the comparisons from different typographers together (almost certainly leading to inconsistencies), we think there is value in keeping them separate so as for instance to determine if they can be clustered into a few different objective functions, perhaps reflecting different schools of typography. This is something we plan to investigate.

Acknowledgements

We acknowledge the support of the ARC through Discovery Project Grant DP0987168.

6. REFERENCES

[1] H. Gunes and M. Piccardi. Assessing facial beauty through proportion analysis by image processing and supervised learning. *International journal of human-computer studies*, 64(12):1184–1199, 2006.

[2] A. Holkner. Global multiple objective line breaking. Honours thesis, RMIT University, Australia, 2006.

[3] N. Hurst, W. Li, and K. Marriott. Review of automatic document formatting. In *Proceedings of the 9th ACM symposium on Document engineering*, pages 99–108. ACM, 2009.

[4] D. E. Knuth and M. F. Plass. Breaking paragraphs into lines. In *Software—Practice and Experience, 11(11)*, pages 1119–1184, Nov. 1982.

[5] D. Malerba, F. Esposito, O. Altamura, M. Ceci, and M. Berardi. Correcting the document layout: A machine learning approach. In *Document Analysis and Recognition, 2003. Proceedings. Seventh International Conference on*, pages 97–102. IEEE, 2003.

[6] S. Russell and P. Norvig. *Artificial Intelligence: a Modern Approach*. Prentice Hall, 2nd edition, 2002.

[7] T. Saaty. *The Analytic Hierarchy Process*. McGraw-Hill, New York, 1980.

[8] B. Schölkopf and A. Smola. *Single-Class Problems: Quantile Estimation and Novelty Detection*, chapter 8. MIT Press, 2002.

[9] I. Steinwart and A. Christmann. *Support Vector Machines*. Springer-Verlag, New York, 2008.

Challenges in Generating Bookmarks from TOC Entries in e-Books

Chandrashekar Ramanathan
International Institute of Information
Technology Bangalore
India
rc@iiitb.ac.in

Yogalakshmi Jayabal
International Institute of Information
Technology Bangalore
India
j.yogalakshmi@iiitb.org

Mehul Sheth
International Institute of Information
Technology Bangalore
India
mehulkumarjayprakash.sheth
@iiitb.net

Categories and Subject Descriptors

I.7.4 [**Document And Text Processing**]: Electronic Publishing.

General Terms

Documentation

Keywords

PDF, bookmarks, structure analysis, table of contents, TOC.

1. INTRODUCTION

The document structure extraction and hierarchy detection is an active area of ongoing research. In view of that, Table of contents (TOC) is important, as it provides the index into the various portions of books, journals, magazines, reports and so on. TOC contains references to the different parts of the book and reflects the natural and the logical structure of the book. Automatic extraction of the table of contents (TOC) is of importance as any further processing of the document content is made easier as it eases the way to obtain the appropriate division information from the TOC. The task of adding bookmarks, document categorization, and document content analysis can also be carried out using the TOC of the books. Specifically, extraction of TOC is an important pre-requisite for the task of adding bookmarks automatically. Most of the PDF based e-books come with built in bookmarks which points to just the page in which that content is present rather than pointing to exact location of the content within a page which helps us to identify structure later on. In our approach we have considered a case where in PDF based e-books are of single column based PDF. Once we identify correct location of each of the TOC entry in a page, we can then use this information to extract structure by referring to the content as a section or chapter content between two subsequent section and chapter entry within a page. Earlier, there has been work done on the extraction of TOC from digital documents, but they were more focused on scanned images. Also work on bookmark creation was targeted only for e-book readers. Our goal is to add bookmarks automatically using the information extracted from the TOC for any PDF based e-book. Also, the bookmarks are placed at the exact location of the text inside the book as opposed to

merely linking it to the beginning of the page. Also, bookmarks are not present for all section & subsections always. Since TOC is used, bookmarks are created for all sections & subsections in our approach.

The task of adding bookmarks automatically is divided into two major sub-tasks. 1) Extraction of TOC content 2) Adding Bookmarks (links).

2. RELATED WORK

A number of methods exist for TOC extraction, which is widely reported. Mandal et al [1] proposed to extract the TOC from the scanned documents. Their approach is primarily based on optical character recognition (OCR), page heuristics and related techniques. Kwon and Park [2] proposed a segmentation algorithm to extract the author information, title and page number from the table of contents of journals. From the images, the segmentation algorithm identifies regions of interest with some threshold and extracts table of contents without the use of character recognition technique. Liangcai et al, [3] propose to extract the table of contents by generating a statistical model for the same and using the model to analyze the other TOC entries with the use of clustering algorithms. This paper also gives a brief analysis of the existing attempts on the extraction of the TOC and categorizes the same. Sarkar and Saund [4] extensively study the structure and styles of TOC. Here, they propose a framework for understanding TOC of books, journals and magazines. They propose a universal logical structure for the entries in the TOC as a combination of the descriptor with its locator. They explain the triplets that could be obtained from the TOC entries and about the hierarchal tree generation from the same. They also have proposed possible methods to retrieve the book's contents based on the retrieved TOC. Belaid [6] proposes the recognition of TOC with part-of-speech tagging. Bourgeois et al [5] propose a stochastic model based on the text attributes and the spatial relations. Lovegrove et al, [11] proposed to extract the logical structure / reading order using geometric layout of the content in the document. This is mainly addresses document classification and understanding. This approach will help in identification of the TOC pages but, still requires additional logic, as it mainly identifies: Text, Titles, Images, Header, Footer, Caption, and Unknown. In order to retrieve the actual title from the TOC pages, additional parsing of the content is required to identify them appropriately. Marinai et al, [12] propose heuristic approaches to retrieve TOC pages. The titles corresponding to a page number are built by working backwards, till the previous page number is reached. This works fine in bookmark creation, only when the potential title built has title alone without any division number and separator that separate title from page number. No information on, whether any more processing is done on the potential title is not clearly available on the paper. The approach used to match these titles with the ones inside the content of the book is using word similarity with tri-gram indexing and Title's Bounding box numbers, which is different from our proposed approach below. Déjean and Meunier [7] proposed a functional approach that relies on the functional properties of a TOC. These properties are: Contiguity, Textual similarity, Ordering, Optional elements, No self-reference. Their hypothesis is that these five properties are sufficient for the entire characterization of a TOC, independently of the document class and language. Attempts have been made to create bookmarks in e-books but none of them is targeting automatic creation of bookmarks. They are either device oriented or require manual activities. Schöning et al. [9] have proposed bookmark creation for e-reader. Yoon et al [10] propose bookmark creation for Touch based device. Steimle et al [8] propose bookmark creation using electronic pen and physical color coded paper. Automatic bookmark creation is not widely reported partly due to the fact that the most of the e-books come with the bookmarks at least at the chapter level. Even those existing bookmarks are only at the page level.

3. PROPOSED APPROACH

Adding automatic bookmarks to e-books is a 2-step process. The first step involves the process of extracting the table of content (TOC) entries. The second step involves using them to create the bookmarks. Here, we describe these tasks in detail.

3.1 Extraction of TOC Entries

Automatic parsing of TOC will be of great use to extract the structure of the document, document recognition etc. To extract TOC entries, actually poses a big challenge, since TOC appears in wide variety of styles and structures. Parsing TOC of a particular known structure and style is less challenging, than parsing any given TOC in a systematic way. An entry in TOC can be characterized by a triplet that is comprised of <division, title, page number>. For example, <"Chapter 1", "Introduction", 5> is an example of a TOC triplet. The extraction of these triplets can be subdivided into the following tasks: 1) Identification of the start of the TOC page. 2) Identification of the end of the TOC page 3) Parsing the TOC entries to construct triplets. All the books need not necessarily contain the triplets; instead it could contain just the <"Introduction", 5> and not having any division number, or a combination of these. We rely mainly on title and page number for bookmarks creation.

3.1.1 Challenges in extraction of TOC entries

The challenges are described below:

1. **Identification of beginning of TOC**: The words "Contents" or "Table of Contents" in a single line, indicates the potential start of the table of contents. To confirm the same, the occurrence of <division, title, page number> triplet throughout that page is checked. This shows that a particular page contains the TOC entries.

2. **Identification of end of TOC**: The first line item of the TOC is stored as the "End Indicator" for TOC entries. For example, if the first TOC entry is "Chapter 1. Introduction", then all the content until the next occurrence of "Chapter 1. Introduction" is treated as the full table of contents. As this is not always true, identification of the pattern between title and page number in the TOC entry is also important.

3. **Identification of TOC triplet**: The TOC entries are parsed to separate the page number, title and the division names and numbers into a separate data structure. The parsing makes use of regular expressions to populate the triplets. **(i)** Separation of Roman and Arabic numerals for division number is comparatively easier and regular expressions are created accordingly to distinguish these two. **(ii)** Appearance of alphanumeric in division part like "**Chapter 1: Introduction ....5**" is little trickier. This is also handled in tool through regular expression with some additional constraints.

4. **Identification of separator between title and page number**: The catch here is appearance of separator should be unambiguously distinguished from any special character that appears as part of the title. The regular expression comes handy, to distinguish these ambiguous situations. For example, TOC entry like "**Java 1.1 and Earlier ....305**" is parsed and results in <"Java 1.1 and Earlier", 305>. Here, the period(".") in the title (i.e., "Java 1.1") needs to be distinguished from the actual separator "...." that appears later in the line before the page number.

5. **Identification of roman and Arabic numerals for page numbers**: The page numbers could be roman numerals or Arabic numerals. Regular expressions are used to differentiate these.

6. **Identification of TOC triplets in multi-line entries**: Most TOC entries are single line, but some could span more than a single line. An additional constraint validates the same. A check is made for the presence of the separator pattern. If a separator pattern is not found, parser assumes that it could be potential candidate for a multi-line TOC entry and therefore expects immediate next line to have separator pattern. If found, then these two lines are concatenated to form a single line TOC entry. From this, the actual triplet is extracted. Point to be noted is that, when a separator pattern is not found, there could be two possibilities: (a) the line could be page header i.e. something like the "Part I" as it indicates beginning of "Part I". Or (b) the line is actually the multi-line TOC entry.

7. **Identification of Non-TOC entry**: Non-TOC entries such as Header / Footer / decorative elements etc. can appear in between TOC entries at the start of the page and at end of the page respectively. Regular expressions are used to identify these and remove them.

3.2 Adding Bookmarks

Once table of content is extracted in the form of triplets, it is used to create bookmarks. It might be possible that source file already has bookmarks in which case bookmark's creation will be ignored. Or, existing bookmarks can be deleted and this approach could be used to create bookmarks for the entire TOC. Bookmarks are placed at the exact location of the text inside the document.

3.2.1 Challenges in bookmark creation

Bookmark creation starts by first matching exact text followed by finding page that has matching text and position of matching entry. The challenges faced are summarized below:

1. **Identification of physical page number based on page number from triplet**: The page number extracted from TOC

as a part of triplet, might not be the exact page number, as physical page number might be different from logical page number. So we cannot rely only on the page number to look for the exact match. It requires intelligently finding out the page with matching text.

2. **Extracting meaningful content from PDF**: In PDF format, content is stored in the form of glyph and there is no notion of line, paragraph etc. In order to match content of TOC title within the page content, we need to extract contents, one line at a time which helps in identifying entries spanned across multiple lines. iText API, which we used in our implementation, extracts text but not in line formats. We use positional information of text extracted to form lines in our algorithm.

3. **Variations in TOC entries and corresponding actual entries in a page**: Apart from the exact matches, there are other cases which are quite interesting. **(i)** In some cases, only chapters are associated with the division numbers, while the subsections are not associated with the division numbers. **(ii)** There are cases, where the actual entry corresponding to the TOC, spans across multiple lines. For e.g.: "Introducing AWT, Windows…" could actually span two or more lines which needs to be matched exactly.

4. **Discarding entries which are not candidates for bookmarks:** Sometimes, TOC title may appear multiple times inside the document. For example, in many books page header contains chapter title which exactly matches with TOC title (of an entry) for a chapter. Obviously, all those occurrences are not candidates for the bookmark target for that TOC entry.

5. **Finding exact position of a matching entry**: Once we find an exact match, next step is to find position of matching entry in a page. If actual content is present in multiline then we need to get the position of the first match of the substring of TOC title. Once we have found exact match as well as position for the same, we can create bookmarks that link to specific position within a page.

4. IMPLEMENTATION DETAILS

4.1 System Architecture

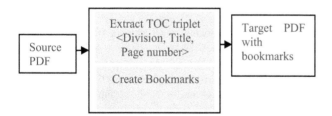

Figure 1: System Architecture of BOOKY

It consists of two modules: 1) Extract TOC Triplets 2) Create Bookmarks. The input to tool and output from tool is both PDF documents. Tool is implemented in Java. Open source library iText [http://itextpdf.com] is used to extract text from PDF. It is an open source library, with good documentation. Any other tool can be used to extract the text. iText retrieves the text and the images as per the order present in the PDF, which is useful during

both the extraction of TOC and the creation of bookmarks. The proposed algorithm is presented in plain English.

Table 1. Proposed Algorithm in English

Extract TOC Entries:
1.   Extract content of a book one page at a time
2.   For each page, extract content line by line: Forming a line: iText gives glyph information for extracted text. For PDF, co-ordinates are like graph where origin is at left-bottom corner. We form line by concatenating content having same y-co-ordinate.
3.   To check start of TOC, check if line contains:
 a. Matching regex pattern for TOC like "Content"
 b. If it matches, then find out if it has other pattern like "table", "of" only and not something else.
 c. It could be detailed TOC, if it satisfies the condition.
  • Has the Triplet pattern throughout the page
 d. Store the first item of the TOC in a global variable
 e. For TOC candidate, divide line in the group of 3 -- <Division no; Title; Page No>. If division no; is not present it is left blank;
 f. Add triplet entry into a file
4.   The end of TOC is identified when matching entry of the global variable is encountered. An Enhancement, to check for pattern in subsequent pages is on. If subsequent page do not have pattern (dots, spaces, dash) which is available in TOC then assume end of TOC.
5.   Stop, when the condition in line 4 satisfies.

Create Bookmarks:
1.   Retrieve triplets one by one formed from above step.
2.   Retrieve title from triplet and page no
3.   Start search from the given page no if it's a proper numeric entry or else from page 1. Search for matching entry for 'title' in triple by searching line by line.
4.   Check for multiline title while matching TOC entry: If entire line is part of triple 'title' then check for subsequent line for remaining part of TOC 'title', continue until we get full match or we get unmatched entry. Also during this process store position of the first matching entry which will be used for creating bookmarks that links to particular position.
5.   If it is a single line entry keep track of position of it.
6.   Use bookmark creation feature with stored positions.

The output is a PDF with bookmarks pointing to exact location of titles present in TOC. Challenges involved in extraction of TOC entries and in creation of bookmarks are discussed in detail in section 4; are implemented in Booky. There are a few open issues in this context, which will be discussed in section 5. Tool was tested with over 2000 bookmarks spanning across several books in PDF format. The results are tabulated in Table 1.

The results indicate that almost 98% of the bookmarks were created correctly using this approach. However, there are a few open issues, which are discussed in next section. An analysis shows that failures were caused by erroneous extraction of TOC triplets. In our assessment, if we are able to increase the reliability of TOC triplet extraction, then automatic creation of bookmark will have even fewer errors.

Table 2. Results of bookmark creation using TOC entries

Book	No.of TOC entries	Correctly extracted TOC entries	Correctly created bookmarks	Errors
Book 1	781	696	696	**5 (0.6%)**
Book 2	398	393	393	**5 (1.2%)**
Book 3	279	278	278	**1 (0.3%)**
Book 4	72	71	71	**1 (1.3%)**
Book 5	375	373	373	**2 (0.5%)**
Book 6	178	166	166	**12 (6.7%)**
Total	2083	2057	2057	**26 (1.2%)**

5. OPEN ISSUES

There are some issues which are still open, are discussed here:

1. **Disambiguation Issue**: Discriminating headings [main headings like PART I etc.] from the actual TOC line items is tricky. Such headings are characterized by lack of any page number information, and must be distinguished from a decorative element. This is an issue that is yet to be fully addressed in our solution.

2. **Identification of Multi-pattern TOC entries**: While extracting TOC entries, if TOC contains more than one type of separator, then they must be matched accordingly.

3. **Matching of Symbols**: PDF may contain symbols like α, β, Ω etc. as a part of TOC entry and should be matched with the actual entry in a page. We have used iText API for our implementation which does not extract symbols. While this is an open issue in our solution, it might be possible that some other API supports extraction of symbols along with text.

4. **Identification of cases where division or title might be in the form of an image**: There are cases where division from TOC triplet appears as an image in actual entry. For e.g. "Chapter 1" might appear as an image. Sometimes TOC title along with division appears as an image. Our current implementation relies only on text entries and not images. Along with basic text matching we might require to perform OCR for such cases but bookmark in that case will link to an image rather than text.

5. **Discarding matching entries that are not candidates for bookmarks**: As discussed in challenges, we are able to discard matching entries which appear as header. If the same entry appears somewhere else apart from running text and header then some intelligence is required to discard those entries (e.g., as a part of decorative element).

6. SUMMARY AND CONCLUSION

The automatic bookmark creation in e-books using the TOC entries are discussed at length in this paper. The approach here is novel and has significant advantages, that the extracted TOC entries could be used for extracting different parts of the book with the use of bookmarks. Bookmarks will give the exact location of the content, which could be used in the extraction of a particular Chapter / Section / Sub-section of an e-book.

Apart from this, these could be guide to extract the structure information and extraction of hierarchy in e-books (e.g., Chapter→Section→Sub-section). Various challenges involved are discussed at detail. Solutions to the challenges identified were demonstrated using a PDF-specific tool named Booky. The solution however could be generalized for any digital format. Some relatively minor issues still are still open. However, we have been able to achieve about 98% success rate in the accurate extraction and linking of bookmarks automatically.

7. REFERENCES

[1] S. Mandal, et al. "Automated detection and segmentation of table of contents", page from document images. In ICDAR '03, page 398, Washington, DC, USA, 2003.

[2] Young-Bin Kwon; Jaehwa Park. "Implementation of Content Analysis System for Recognition of Journals' Table of Contents", ICDAR'2007, page: 1018-1022.

[3] Liangcai Gao; Zhi Tang; Xiaofan Lin; Xin Tao; Yimin Chu. "Analysis of Book Documents' Table of Content Based on Clustering", ICDAR'2009, page: 911-915.

[4] Prateek Sarkar and Eric Saund "On the Reading of Table of Contents", the Eighth IAPR Workshop on Document Analysis Systems, 2008, pp-386-393.

[5] A. Belaïd. "Recognition of table of contents for electronic library consulting". IJDAR, 4(1):35–45, 2001.

[6] Le Bourgeois et al, "Document understanding using probabilistic relaxation: Application on tables of contents of periodicals." In ICDAR '2001, page 508, Washington, DC, USA, 2001. IEEE Computer Society.

[7] Hervé Déjean, Jean-Luc Meunier, "Structuring Documents According to Their Table of Contents", In Proc. of DocEng 2005, pp. 2-9.

[8] Jürgen Steimle et al, "Digital Paper Bookmarks: Collaborative Structuring, Indexing and Tagging of Paper Documents", In CHI EA'2008, pp. 2895-2900.

[9] Johannes Schöning et al, "iBookmark: Locative Texts and Placebased Authoring", In CHI EA'2009, pp. 3775-3780.

[10] Dongwook Yoon et al, "Touch-Bookmark: A Lightweight Navigation and Bookmarking Technique for E-Books", In CHI EA '2011, pp. 1189-1194.

[11] William S. Lovegrove et al, "Document analysis of PDF files: methods, results and implications", Electronic Publishing, Vol. 8 (2 and 3), 227-220, (June & September 1995).

[12] S. Marinai et al, "Table of contents Recognition for converting PDF Documents in E-book formats", In Proc. of DocEng '2010, pp.73-76.

A Section Title Authoring Tool for Clinical Guidelines

Mark Truran
School of Computing
Teesside University
United Kingdom
m.a.truran@tees.ac.uk

Marc Cavazza
School of Computing
Teesside University
United Kingdom
m.cavazza@tees.ac.uk

Gersende Georg
Haute Autorité de Santé
Saint-Denis La Plaine Cedex
France
g.georg@has-sante.fr

Dong Zhou
Hunan University of Science
and Technology
China
dongzhou1979@hotmail.com

ABSTRACT

Professional users of medical information often report difficulties when attempting to locate specific information in lengthy documents. Sometimes these difficulties can be attributed to poorly specified section titles which fail to advertise relevant content. In this paper we describe preliminary work on a software plug-in for a document engineering environment that will assist authors when they formulate section-level headings. We describe two different algorithms which can be used to generate section titles. We compare the performance of these algorithms and correlate our experimental results with an evaluation of title quality performed by domain experts.

Categories and Subject Descriptors

J.3 [**Life and Medical Sciences**]: Medical information systems; I.7.2 [**Document and Text Processing**]: Document Preparation

General Terms

Documentation, Measurement, Human Factors

Keywords

Clinical guideline, section, title, content, quality

1. INTRODUCTION

Clinical guidelines are expert-level documents which describe best practices for the diagnosis and treatment of specific conditions. They are produced by groups of experts under the auspices of health regulatory bodies. Accessing the contents of these documents can be a challenging task for health professionals, who often have to hunt for specific

information within a lengthy guideline. As a result, online access to a complete guideline in PDF format frequently proves unproductive [8]. Furthermore, due to the regulatory nature of the information concerned, arbitrary content summarisation (as a possible solution to the document access problem) is simply not feasible. There is a genuine risk that important medical information relevant to patient health and safety may be omitted from auto-generated summaries.

Within HAS (the French National Authority for Health), guidelines are authored using G-DEE, a purpose built document engineering environment [4]. Recently, HAS has begun supplementing each PDF guideline it releases with a limited depth hypertext containing a subset of the same information (in French: *recommandations cliquables*, or reco2clics[1]). Experience with this new document format has reinforced the *vital* importance of section titles as signposts for readers interested in specific sub-topics within a guideline. Poorly specified section titles confuse or mislead guideline readers, thereby reducing the usefulness of the document as a whole.

In this paper we present preliminary work on an authoring tool for clinical guidelines which addresses the problem of poorly specified section titles. This tool will function in an unobtrusive manner, suggesting possible title words to G-DEE users as they author new guidelines. The novel contributions of this work include (1) a contrastive experiment which exports two techniques popular in article-level title generation to the sectional level and (2) an evaluation of title quality, performed by domain experts, correlated against our experimental results.

2. RELATED WORK

Most recent work on the automatic generation of titles has concentrated on *article-level* title generation. For example, Witbrock and Mittal [10] generated titles for a large collection of news-wire articles using a technique inspired by statistical translation (see also [1]). Processing the text of each article in turn, they built a statistical model describing the relationship between the occurrence of a specific term in the document and the occurrence of the same term in

---

[1]HAS currently host 12 reco2clics guidelines on their web site, each attracting 150-200 downloads per week. In a recent survey, 68% of respondents agreed that the new document format facilitates document access.

the document title. This allowed the authors to estimate the conditional probability of any given term t appearing in the title by calculating $P(t \text{ in title} \mid t \text{ in document})$. Having trained their model using a corpus of 8000 articles, they generated titles for 1000 unseen documents, achieving a respectable overlap with the 'actual' titles.

In [5], Jin and Hauptmann compared the Naïve Bayesian approach described above with three alternative techniques for generating titles:

1. A model based on concepts drawn from the field of Information Retrieval (IR), which included various term weighting measures (see §3.1).

2. An approach that utilised the K-Nearest Neighbour (KNN) algorithm, as applied to topic classification.

3. An algorithm exploiting Expectation-Maximisation (E-M), which was used to build a statistical translation model between the 'concise' language of the title and the 'verbose' language of the document.

In an experiment involving over 50,000 document and title pairs, the IR approach to the title word selection problem was declared the most effective, followed closely by the Naïve Bayesian model and KNN.

In a slightly different context, Chakrabarti et al. used a statistical model that exploited multiple sources of information to create link-titles for result URLs [2]. In addition to the content of the the web page indicated by the URL, the authors utilised del.icio.us tags, anchor tags and queries associated with the web page via click-through logs to generate 'quicklinks'. In an empirical evaluation, their statistical model outperformed various competing approaches, including the technique described by Banko et al. [1] (see above).

2.1 Evaluation of generated titles

Systems that generate title words are often evaluated using the F1 score [7]. Assuming you have a human specified title T_{human} and an auto-generated title T_{auto}, the F1 score for T_{auto} is:

$$F1 = 2 \cdot \frac{\text{precision} \cdot \text{recall}}{\text{precision} + \text{recall}}$$

where *precision* is the number of words in T_{auto} that match words appearing in T_{human} divided by the count of words in T_{auto}, and *recall* is the number of correctly generated words in T_{auto} divided by the number of words in T_{human}. This calculation produces a value in the range of [0-1], a value of 1 being the best score and 0 the worst. Providing a useful baseline for title generation algorithms, Jin and Hauptmann recorded F1 scores of 0.226 using the IR model and 0.201 for the Bayesian model in [5].

3. METHODOLOGY

The data used in this experiment was taken from 28 clinical guidelines published in PDF format by the French Health Authority between January 2008 and December 2011. Each guideline was processed in the following way:

1. All of the text in each guideline was extracted using Apache PDFBOX[2] (a Java class library for manipulating PDF documents).

2. A *stop list*[3] was used to remove words with little informational value e.g. determiners, conjunctions, prepositions and pronouns [9].

3. All inflected words were reduced to their root stem e.g. 'mountaineering' and 'mountaineer' were reduced to 'mountain'. We used a stemming algorithm[4] based on Porter's SNOWBALL project [6].

4. We extracted all of the sections from the document using the section titles as delimiters. We saved each section to a separate file.

5. We removed all of the sections with *generic* titles (e.g. 'Sommaire', 'Recommandations', 'Introduction', 'Appendix') to isolate the *ideational* section headings i.e. titles that indicate the content of the section [3].

At the end of this process we had 435 sections (avg. 15.5 sections per guideline) containing 7429 unique terms.

3.1 Algorithms

We used two different techniques when generating title words. The first technique, which is known as TF*IDF, belongs to the field of information retrieval. It involves calculating the number of times a particular word has appeared in a document (TF, or *term frequency*). This value is balanced against the popularity of the word across all of the documents (IDF, or *inverse document frequency*). As shown in Algorithm 1, we make minor modifications to this statistic to generate title words from document *sections*.

Algorithm 1 Generating title words using TF * IDF

Require: s, a stemmed section with stop words removed
Require: n, the number of title words required
  create empty map m (string → integer)
  calculate number of sections in the corpus as c
  for all unique words w in s as $w_1, w_2 \ldots w_n$ **do**
    calculate tf as count of $w \in s$
    count sections in corpus that contain w as df
    calculate idf as LOG (c / df)
    put s, $(idf * tf)$ in m
  end for
  order m by $(idf * tf)$, in descending order
  select n topmost entries in m as title words

So, where a section s has 100 terms in total, and a term x is mentioned 7 times, the term frequency of $x \in s = 0.07$. If that term occurs in 25 out of 90 sections in the corpus, its final weight is LOG(90/25) = 0.55 * 0.07 = 0.038. Note that inverse document frequency diminishes the importance of terms that are common across the corpus.

The second technique we used when generating title words was based on a Naïve Bayesian approach. We followed the approach of Witbrock and Mittal [10], creating a limited vocabulary statistical model that described the relationship between source text units in the section and target text units in the title. Generating title words using this approach involved two distinct stages. In the first stage, we trained the model (see Algorithm 2). In the second stage, we used the model to generate title words (see Algorithm 3). Assume a

---

[2] http://pdfbox.apache.org/

[3] http://members.unine.ch/jacques.savoy/clef/frenchST.txt
[4] http://morphadorner.northwestern.edu/morphadorner/

term x appears in 9 sections, and 4 of those sections have titles that also contain x. According to our algorithm, the conditional probability $P(x \text{ in title} \mid x \text{ in section})$ would be $= 4/9 = 0.44$.

Algorithm 2 Training the model

Require: c, a corpus of sections
  create empty map m (string $\rightarrow$ integer)
  for all sections s in c as $s_1, s_2 \ldots s_n$ **do**
    for all unique words w in the section $w_1, w_2 \ldots w_n$ **do**
      if $w \notin m$ **then**
        put $(w, 0)$ in m
      end if
      if $w \in$ title of s **then**
        increment w in m
      end if
    end for
  end for

3.2 Training corpus and experimental corpus

In this experiment we separated the data into two parts. The *training corpus* was made up from sections extracted from 27 clinical guidelines (approx. 420 sections). We used this corpus to train the statistical model described in Algorithm 2 and to generate the document frequency statistics needed in Algorithm 1. The *experimental corpus* was made up from sections extracted from just 1 clinical guideline (approx. 15 sections). We used this corpus to test the performance of our title generation algorithms. We iterated through the experimental corpus, generating title words for every section using both algorithms. We evaluated the performance of the two algorithms using the precision measure described in §2.1. We repeated this procedure 28 times, rotating the data so that each guideline in the collection 'took its turn' as the experimental corpus.

Algorithm 3 Generating title words using the model

Require: s, a stemmed section with stop words removed
Require: n, the number of title words required
Require: $alg2$, the map from Algorithm 2
  create empty map m (string $\rightarrow$ integer)
  for all unique words w in s as $w_1, w_2 \ldots w_n$ **do**
    retrieve value for w in $alg2$ as $hits$
    count sections in corpus that contain w as df
    put $(s, hits/df)$ in m
  end for
  order m by $hits/df$, in descending order
  select n topmost entries in m as title words

Here is a worked example that describes our evaluation technique. The original section title for guideline 55 §3.1 is 'Quelles sont les situations pouvant faire l'objet d'une prescription médicamenteuse par téléphone lors de la régulation médicale?', *trans*: 'In which situations can drug prescriptions be made over the telephone by medical staff in charge of emergency helpline and dispatching?' Following the application of a stop list and a stemming algorithm, this is reduced to 'situat pouv fair l'objet d'une prescript médic téléphon lor régul'. We pass the text for this section to the title generation algorithms with the parameter n arbitrarily set to the length of the pre-processed title (i.e.,

	TF*IDF	NBL
MINIMUM	0.07	0.0
LOWER QUARTILE	0.10	0.004
MEDIAN	0.20	0.06
UPPER QUARTILE	0.23	0.11
MAXIMUM	0.347	0.306

Table 1: Precision of TF*IDF and NBL algorithms across 28 iterations of experiment

10 terms). The algorithm exploiting TF*IDF produces 5 matching terms (régul, médic, prescript, situat, téléphon) and 5 non-matching terms, thereby achieving a precision score of 0.5. The NBL algorithm produces two matching terms (régul, médic) and 8 non-matching terms, achieving a lower precision score of 0.2. Note that since n is equal to the length of the pre-processed title, the precision measure is equivalent to both recall and F1.

4. RESULTS AND ANALYSIS

The results of the experiment are described in Table 1. As illustrated, the algorithm exploiting TF*IDF produced the best performance, achieving an average precision of 0.18 i.e., it accurately predicted 18% of the title words used by authors. By comparison, title generation based on a Naïve Bayesian model with limited vocabulary (NBL) was inferior, achieving an average precision of 0.07. This was the result we expected. The two techniques used in this experiment, and in particular the technique reliant on a Naïve Bayesian model, generally produce results which are positively related to the size and quality of the training corpus. Our training corpus had less than 500 sections. Researchers developing models to predict the title of articles commonly use tens of thousands of documents [5, 1]. Given the above, we consider these to be satisfactory scores. More importantly, the fundamental aim of the experiment - i.e. proof of concept for section level title generation - was comfortably achieved.

4.1 Expert evaluation

Most studies of this type will score the generated title words against the original title, thereby implicitly assuming that the original title was a 'good' one (see §2.1). We decided to challenge this assumption. We asked a panel of 20 domain experts to evaluate 20 section titles randomly selected from the corpus. The judges scored each section title using a 5-point Likert scale which described the relevance of the title to the section text. The highest ranked section title was an extremely specific heading taken from guideline 55 §5.4 (in French: 'Comment assurer la traçabilité de l'entretien téléphonique?', *trans*: 'How to log and trace calls made to emergency helplines', average human score 3.9/4). The lowest ranked section title, extracted from guideline 78 §5.1 (in French 'Aspects physiques', *trans*: 'Physical aspects', average human score 1.5/4) was perhaps too generic for the panel given the context.

When we correlated the human scores with our experimental results, we noticed a possible *inverse relationship* between human satisfaction and the performance of the TF*IDF algorithm. As described in Table 2 and illustrated in Figure 1, the TF*IDF score for the bottom 10 section titles (as ranked by humans) was 0.31, which is approximately 3 times higher than the same score for the top 10 titles. A

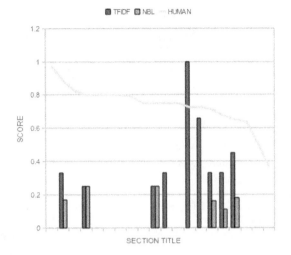

Figure 1: Comparison of title generation performance with human judgements. Human judgements have been transformed from [0,4] to [0,1] range. Zero values indicate that TF*IDF/NBL algorithm matched zero title words.

RANK ASSIGNED BY EXPERTS	1-10	11-20
AVERAGE TF*IDF SCORE	0.083	0.310

Table 2: Correlation of average TF*IDF scores with the rank assigned by the human judges. Titles were sorted in descending order by human rating and split into two equal sized groups, 1-10 and 11-20.

(very tentative) hypothesis given the limited data - algorithms exploiting TF*IDF may have a tendency to produce title words that are unpopular with humans! This is an intriguing finding because a number of popular title generation algorithms rely heavily on TF*IDF (see §2). If this inverse relationship is replicated in a larger study, it may prompt a re-evaluation of these techniques in favour of algorithms exploiting other sources of information (e.g. [2]).

5. FURTHER WORK

Given the understated performance of the Naïve Bayesian model in this experiment, further work should include an attempt to expand the training resources used to generate section-title representations. Possible repositories of useful training data include the French Wikipedia medical portal and CISMeF[5]. Future work could also include the use of a domain specific ontology or French medical thesaurus to enrich the suggestions made by the TF*IDF algorithm.

6. CONCLUSION

In this paper we have described preliminary work on a software plug-in for the G-DEE document engineering environment that will assist authors as they formulate section-level headings. These titles are vitally important to readers as signposts marking the position of specific sub-topics within a clinical guideline. Our work exports two techniques popular in article-level title generation to the sec-

---

[5]http://www.chu-rouen.fr/cismef/

tional level. Our primary findings indicate that an algorithm based on TF*IDF will outperform a Naïve Bayesian model when training resources are meagre. This is not surprising. Our secondary findings, which disclose a possible inverse relationship between human satisfaction and weighted term frequency analysis, are more interesting. An extensive follow up study featuring qualitative survey questions (e.g. what makes this a good/bad section title?) is indicated.

7. ACKNOWLEDGEMENTS

Many thanks to HAS staff from SBPP/SEESP units who participated in this study. The authors would also like to thank the anonymous reviewers for their valuable comments.

8. REFERENCES

[1] M. Banko, V. O. Mittal, and M. J. Witbrock. Headline generation based on statistical translation. In *Proceedings of the 38th Annual Meeting on Association for Computational Linguistics*, ACL '00, pages 318–325, Stroudsburg, PA, USA, 2000. ACL.

[2] D. Chakrabarti, R. Kumar, and K. Punera. Generating succinct titles for web urls. In *Proceedings of the 14th ACM SIGKDD international conference on Knowledge discovery and data mining*, KDD '08, pages 79–87, New York, NY, USA, 2008. ACM.

[3] S. Gardner and J. Holmes. From section headings to assignment macrostructures in undergraduate student writing. In *Thresholds and Potentialities of Systemic Functional Linguistics: Multilingual, Multimodal and Other Specialised Discourses*, pages 268–290. Edizioni Universita di Trieste, 2010.

[4] G. Georg and M.-C. Jaulent. A document engineering environment for clinical guidelines. In *Proceedings of the 2007 ACM symposium on Document engineering*, DocEng '07, pages 69–78, New York, NY, USA, 2007. ACM.

[5] R. Jin and A. G. Hauptmann. Learning to select good title words: An new approach based on reverse information retrieval. In *Proceedings of the Eighteenth International Conference on Machine Learning*, ICML '01, pages 242–249, San Francisco, CA, USA, 2001. Morgan Kaufmann Publishers Inc.

[6] M. F. Porter. Readings in information retrieval. chapter An algorithm for suffix stripping, pages 313–316. Morgan Kaufmann Publishers Inc., San Francisco, CA, USA, 1997.

[7] C. J. V. Rijsbergen. *Information Retrieval*. Butterworth-Heinemann, Newton, MA, USA, 2nd edition, 1979.

[8] A. H. Rø svik and H. P. Fosseng. Usability testing of clinical guidelines. Guidelines International Network Conference 2011, Korea University, Seoul, Korea, 2011.

[9] J. Savoy. A stemming procedure and stopword list for general french corpora. *Journal of the American Society for Information Science*, 50:944–952, 1999.

[10] M. J. Witbrock and V. O. Mittal. Ultra-summarization (poster abstract): a statistical approach to generating highly condensed non-extractive summaries. In *Proceedings of the 22nd annual international ACM SIGIR conference*, SIGIR '99, pages 315–316, New York, NY, USA, 1999. ACM.

A Methodology for Evaluating Algorithms for Table Understanding in PDF Documents

Max Göbel
Tamir Hassan
PRIP, Technische Universität Wien
goebel@prip.tuwien.ac.at
tam@prip.tuwien.ac.at

Ermelinda Oro
ICAR - CNR
Università della Calabria
oro@icar.cnr.it

Giorgio Orsi
Dept. of Computer Science
University of Oxford
giorgio.orsi@cs.ox.ac.uk

ABSTRACT

This paper presents a methodology for the evaluation of table understanding algorithms for PDF documents. The evaluation takes into account three major tasks: table detection, table structure recognition and functional analysis. We provide a general and flexible output model for each task along with corresponding evaluation metrics and methods. We also present a methodology for collecting and ground-truthing PDF documents based on consensus-reaching principles and provide a publicly available ground-truthed dataset.

Categories and Subject Descriptors: I.7.5 [**Document and Text Processing**]: Document Capture—*document analysis*; H.3.4 [**Information Storage and Retrieval**]: Systems and Software—*performance evaluation*

Keywords: Table processing, metrics, ground-truth dataset, performance evaluation, document analysis, document understanding

1. INTRODUCTION

The problem of *table understanding* has attracted much interest in previous years from the database as well as the document engineering communities. On the Web, discovering structured data is a tremendous challenge [1] and PDF documents represent the most common document format after HTML. It is commonly recognized that table understanding consists of three tasks of increasing complexity:

- *table detection:* locating the regions of a document with tabular content;
- *table structure recognition:* reconstructing the cellular structure of a table;
- *table interpretation:* rediscovering the meaning of the tabular structure. This includes:
  - (a) *functional analysis:* determining the function of cells and their abstract logical relationships;
  - (b) *semantic interpretation:* understanding the semantics of the table in terms of the entities represented in the table, their attributes, and the mutual relationships between such entities.

The comparative evaluation of different table understanding algorithms is a non-trivial matter. Currently available datasets for table understanding algorithms suffer from the following limitations: *(i)* the documents in these datasets are scanned images, not natively digital PDF (*PDF Normal* or *Formatted Text and Graphics*) documents; *(ii)* in such cases where ground truth is provided, only the tabular regions are present; *(iii)* custom performance measures make it very difficult to appreciate fine differences between the algorithms being compared.

In order to overcome the limitations of existing datasets and evaluation approaches, we provide:

- a model and corresponding evaluation metric for each output of the three stages of table understanding. At the interpretation stage, we address only functional analysis because the semantic interpretation of a table is domain specific, and we believe it is premature to include it in a generic benchmarking dataset;
- a consensus-based methodology for collecting and ground-truthing natively digital PDF documents;
- an initial open-access and extensible ground-truthed dataset of PDF documents containing tables.

2. RELATED WORK

Common problems in the comparative evaluation of different table understanding algorithms are the lack of standardized datasets, benchmarking procedures and measures in experimental evaluation. This section discusses previous work in the: *(i)* creation of ground-truthed datasets, *(ii)* modelling of tabular information and *(iii)* definition of evaluation metrics.

Ground-truthed datasets. The lack of availability of ground truth datasets has proved to be a major hindrance to the comparative evaluation of table recognition algorithms.

Publicly available datasets containing tabular content in monochrome page images, such as the UW datasets [11], and UNLV[1], have long been available in the OCR community. The ground truth has been generated interactively by using visual tools [4, 12]. However, only the tabular regions, and no higher-level information, is provided.

The first publicly-available dataset containing natively digital PDF documents was used to test the PDF-TREX system [10]. However, it contains mostly Italian financial tables and does not include ground-truth information. As our goal was to create a multi-domain database in the En-

---

[1]UNLV dataset originally at http://www.isri.unlv.edu/ISRI/OCRtk. No longer available; accessed at web.archive.org

glish language, we decided to begin the document collection process from scratch.

Table models. There are a number of different levels at which table understanding can operate, a fact that is reflected in a variety of table models. In particular, we can distinguish between *structural models*, used for representing region and cell structures of tables, and *conceptual models*, enabling the abstraction of content from presentation.

Interesting structural models have been proposed in [5, 7, 12]. In particular Hu et al. [5] modelled a table as a directed acyclic attributed graph (table DAG) where columns, rows, cells and relations among them are represented. Hurst [7] presents an approach to deriving an abstract geometric model of a table from a physical representation based on spatial relations among cells named *proto-links*, which exist between immediate neighbouring cells. Shahab et al. [12] use an image-based representation to describe the cell structure, adopting different colour channels to represent different row and column positions. As discussed in Section 3.2, for comparing two cell structures of a table we use a model inspired by Hurst's proto-links, which enables an effective and simple evaluation measure to be defined.

Possibly the most well-known and cited conceptual model has been proposed by Wang [13] and extended by Hurst [6]. Wang defines a table divided into four main regions: *(i)* the *stub* that contains the row headings; *(ii)* the *boxhead* that contains the column headings; *(iii)* the *stub head* that contains the index sets in the stub and *(iv)* the *body* that contains entries (also named data cells). At the lowest level, a table can be seen as being composed of two types of cell: the *data cell*, and the *access cell* (or label). The data cells comprise the core of the table, whereas the access cells occur within headers and are further classified into *categories* that are organized hierarchically. In Section 3.3 we use many of these concepts in defining our functional model.

Evaluation metrics. In order to evaluate the results of table understanding algorithms, several metrics for table structure recognition have been proposed. However, well defined evaluation metrics do not yet exist for the results of table interpretation.

Performance measures from the information retrieval domain such as recall, precision [9] and combined F-measure have also found their way into evaluating table recognition algorithms [8, 10]. Results of the PDF-TREX system [10] were given using separate precision and recall values for table areas and cell structures. In [2] the concepts of *completeness* and *purity*, based on the definitions of recall and precision, were introduced as well-defined evaluation metrics for any segmentation task. Whereas these measures can intuitively be adopted for the table (region) recognition phase, they are not so applicable for table (cell) structure recognition. In table structure recognition, a variety of errors can occur that need to be considered separately (e.g. cells can be split in one direction, merged in another; entire blank columns can appear) and classifying these errors can lead to ambiguities [3]. An alternative approach, which uses several precision and recall measures at several levels, including cell, row, column and region, is proposed in [12].

Hurst [7] sidestepped these problems by evaluating precision and recall at the proto-link level.

3. MODELLING THE GROUND TRUTH

The ground-truth enables a fair comparison between different approaches to the table understanding problem. In order to be considered in our dataset, a table must have a meaningful representation in each of the output models of the three understanding tasks: (1) the *region model* for table detection, (2) the *cell structure model* for table structure recognition, (3) and the *functional model* for functional analysis. More precisely, a table in our dataset has the following characteristics:

(i) it consists of (rectangular) cells belonging to an unambiguous two-dimensional row-and-column structure. Cells may span more than one row or column;

(ii) the contents of the table must fit within a rectangular bounding box that must not contain any further textual content (titles, captions and footnotes are not considered to be part of the table);

(iii) it has a clear *functional model* based on clearly defined *access cells* and *data cells*. Each data cell must be accessed by at least two access dimensions.

3.1 Table regions

Region model. Table regions are defined as rectangular areas of a given page by their coordinates. Since a table can span more than one page, several regions can belong to the same table. For each region, we store the textual *operator* (and, if necessary, *operand*) *ID*s of their originating PDF text instructions (i.e. Tj and TJ), which point back to the particular point in the PDF file where the text was drawn. Each region in the ground truth is set to the minimal bounding box that bounds all textual objects within.

Comparing regions. In order to compare a table region against the ground truth, we can use two methods:

(i) if comparing algorithms that can be adapted to return the internal PDF operators, we can compare each character with reference to the particular operator responsible for drawing the text on the page;

(ii) for other (e.g. "black-box") algorithms, bounding boxes and content are used. A region is correct if it contains the minimal bounding box of the ground truth without intersecting additional content.

For comparing tabular regions, we use the measures *completeness* and *purity* [2] as they are well defined in the context of segmentation. In order to obtain the best mapping between two sets of regions, which may also differ from each other, a correspondence matrix [12] is used.

3.2 Cell structure

Cell structure model. The cell structure of a table is defined as a matrix of cells. The ground truth provides its textual content and its start and end column and row positions. Blank cells are not represented in the grid. A benefit of such a representation is that each cell is independent from what has previously occurred in the table definition.

Comparing cell structures. For comparing two cell structures, we use a method inspired by Hurst's proto-links [6]: for each table region we generate a list of *adjacency relations* between each content cell and its nearest neighbour in horizontal and vertical directions. No adjacency relations are generated between blank cells or a blank cell and a content cell. This 1-D list of adjacency relations can be compared to the ground truth by using precision and recall measures, as shown in Figure 1. If both cells are identical and the

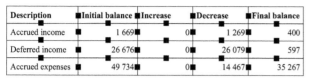

Description	■Initial balance	■Increase	■Decrease	■Final balance
Accrued income ■	1 669■	0■	1 269■	400
Deferred income ■	26 676■	0■	26 079■	597
Accrued expenses ■	49 734■	0■	14 467■	35 267

(a) Original table as in ground truth

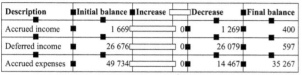

Description	■Initial balance	■Increase	☐Decrease	■Final balance
Accrued income ■	1 669☐	0■	1 269■	400
Deferred income ■	26 676☐	0■	26 079■	597
Accrued expenses ■	49 734☐	0■	14 467■	35 267

(b) Incorrectly recognized cell structure with split column

■ Correct adjacency relations ☐ Incorrect adjacency relations

$$\text{Recall} = \frac{\text{correct adjacency relations}}{\text{total adjacency relations}} = \frac{24}{31} = 77.4\%$$

$$\text{Precision} = \frac{\text{correct adjacency relations}}{\text{detected adjacency relations}} = \frac{24}{28} = 85.7\%$$

Figure 1: Comparison of an incorrectly detected cell structure with the ground truth

direction matches, then it is marked as correctly retrieved; otherwise it is marked as incorrect. Using neighbourhoods makes the comparison invariant to the absolute position of the table (e.g. if everything is shifted by one cell) and also avoids ambiguities arising with dealing with different types of errors (merged/split cells, inserted empty column, etc.).

3.3 Table interpretation

Functional model. Our functional model focuses on expressing the most important relations of a table, which reflect the way a naïve human reader would use the table to look up information. As in [13, 6], our functional model consists of a set of access relations defined as follows: Let $I = \{I_1, \ldots, I_n\}$ be a collection of *access dimensions* and E the set of *data cells*. An *access function* $f : \bigotimes I \to E$ maps the unordered cartesian product of access dimension sets to the set of entry values. Given a set of access cells as input, an access function returns a data cell.

A table's functional representation cannot usually be fully rediscovered from the layout alone. For example, in Figure 2 domain-specific knowledge is required to discover that the cell Nationality of parent: is a heading for the cells below it, and not the cells to its right. Dot notation is used to represent access cells arranged hierarchically. Although the *physical* structure of a table is 2-D, often more dimensions are projected into this 2-D space. For instance, in Figure 2 there are three dimensions that allows for describing a data cell: years, nations and the set given by the cells Activity, Passivity and Net position (which are repeated for each year).

It is not always clear which cells serve as access cells and which cells are the data cells in a table. For instance, in Figure 3 both the airline name and airline code could be used to look up the airline's turnover; thus both columns serve simultaneously as access cells to the figures. A further example is that of a conversion table between e.g. metric and imperial units, which could be read in either direction.

It is worth nothing that, in contrast to the cell structure model which is purely physical, in the functional model it is important to represent blank *data* cells. For instance, the table in Figure 3 includes a blank data cell that represents a null value.

Comparing functional representations. As with the cell structure model, we compute precision and recall measures for all the access relations within the functional representa-

INTERNATIONAL ASSETS AND LIABILITIES OF BIS REPORTING BANKS BY NATIONALITY OF PARENT
(outstanding amounts in billions of dollars)

Nationality of parent:	1997			1998		
	Activity	Passivity	Net position	Activity	Passivity	Net position
USA	961.9	1 008.4	−46.5	1 105.3	1 173.0	−67.7
Canada	211.5	219.5	−8.0	239.1	237.3	1.8
Japan	2 045.1	1 598.0	447.1	1 758.2	1 312.1	446.1
Europe	5 025.7	5 218.3	−192.6	5 789.3	6 064.1	−184.8
of which: Germany	1 346.9	1 345.1	1.8	1 630.3	1 638.2	−7.9
France	903.6	968.7	−65.1	1 021.7	1 060.1	−38.4
United Kingdom	478.8	539.1	−60.3	558.8	632.3	−73.5
Italy	419.0	416.8	2.2	443.1	434.0	9.1
Switzerland	709.4	706.0	3.4	836.5	836.5	9.6
Other regions	539.0	522.7	16.3	626.7	515.1	111.6
Total	8 783.2	8 566.9	216.3	9 518.6	9 301.6	217.0

Source: BIS

Source: Adapted from the PDF-TREX dataset [10]

Functional representation:
[Nationality of parent.USA],[1997],[Activity] → [961.9],
[Nationality of parent.USA],[1997],[Passivity] → [1 008.4],
[Nationality of parent.USA],[1997],[Net position] → [−46.5],
[Nationality of parent.USA],[1998],[Activity] → [1 105.3],
. . . ,

Figure 2: A financial table and its functional model

		Turnover ($bn)		
		2008	2009	2010
AA	American Airlines	17.5	18.1	17.2
AF	Air France	11.6	10.8	11.9
KL	KLM Royal Dutch Airlines	8.3	9.5	9.4
LH	Lufthansa	12.8	14.1	13.8
NA	New Airline		2.1	2.4

Functional representation:
[AA],[Turnover ($bn).2008] → [17.5],
[American Airlines],[Turnover ($bn).2008] → [17.5],
[AA],[Turnover ($bn).2009] → [18.1],
[American Airlines],[Turnover ($bn).2009] → [18.1],
. . . ,
[NA],[Turnover ($bn).2008] → [],
. . . ,

Figure 3: A table with two alternative access paths

tion of a table. An access relation is marked as correctly detected if it is identical to the ground truth, i.e. all levels of each access path are present. However, in cases where the heading structure has only been partly recovered but the lowest level access cells have all been correctly detected, the relation is marked as *partially detected*. If we consider an algorithm that analyses a table with multiple-level headings correctly, but misses some of the higher-level headings, the result is still likely to be useful. Thus, our evaluation measure better reflects the usefulness of the result.

Precision and recall can be calculated from the number of *correctly detected* access relations, the *total number of correct* access relations and the number of *incorrectly detected* (or false positive) access relations.

For an access relation that has had all of its lowest-level access cells and its data cell correctly recognized, the number of correctly detected access relations is incremented by the following fraction:

$$\frac{\text{number of correctly detected entities}}{\text{total number of entities}}$$

where *entity* refers to access or data cell. Access cells

are counted as having been correctly detected if the access path from the *lowest level upwards* is identical to the ground truth; otherwise they are considered as false positives, even if they are pointing to the correct cell.

Likewise, for an access relation that has had all of its lowest-level access cells and its data cell correctly recognized, the number of incorrectly detected (false positive) access relations is incremented by the following fraction:

$$\frac{\text{number of incorrectly detected entities}}{\text{total number of entities}}$$

Here, any incorrectly detected access cells above the lowest level are counted as incorrectly detected entities. If the data cell or any access cell at the lowest level is incorrect, the number of incorrectly detected access relations is incremented by 1.

4. THE DATASET

In order to build an objective dataset of freely distributable PDF documents from several domains, we performed a Google search and inspected each returned document in sequence. We used the following search terms in order to obtain documents from government sites whose publications are known to be in the public domain: (a) `filetype:pdf site:europa.eu` (b) `filetype:pdf site:*.gov`

The size of documents and the number of tables contained within the documents varied greatly. For longer documents (more than 5 pages), *excerpts* of pages containing tables were extracted, with approximately 2 pages of non-tabular content before and after the tables of interest. Thus, we also include non-tabular pages, giving the opportunity to also test each algorithm against its resistance to false positives.

Core dataset. Our core dataset, which is freely downloadable at `http://www.tamirhassan.com/dataset/`, contains 59 excerpts as individual PDF files, with a total of 117 tables, with ground truth information corresponding to all three tasks defined in Section 3. Each of these files has a domain-generic model, specified as an XML Schema Definition (XSD), enabling the output of existing systems to easily be converted for comparison with the ground truth. Table 1 gives overall statistics on the tables we have gathered.

The ground truth has been created interactively using a visual tool for annotating table regions and cells. Since the nature and the content of tables is often a subjective matter, the construction of the ground truth has followed a strict consensus-reaching methodology. Document excerpts have been collected and ground truth has been generated independently and then validated by a group of three experts. If it was not possible to reach consensus on any aspect of the ground truth or the representation in any of the models was considered ambiguous by at least one expert, the excerpt was excluded from our dataset. Because of the difficulties and increased ambiguity in the functional analysis of "one-dimensional" tables such as conversion tables, and tables with two "primary keys" (Figure 3), we decided not to include to such typologies of tables in our dataset.

5. CONCLUSION

In this paper we have presented an evaluation methodology for table understanding algorithms. Although we have focused on PDF documents, we believe that the same models can be easily adapted and applied to other formats such as scanned images and web documents (e.g. HTML). We invite researchers and practitioners from the web data management and document engineering communities to join our initiative and collaborate on the enrichment of the initial dataset that we provided. In addition, our models have been defined to be extensible and we expect them to be adapted to embrace more cases than those defined in this paper.

Acknowledgements: This work was funded in part by the DIADEM Project (EC FP7 Programme Grant No. 246858), the Oxford Martin School (Grant No. LC0910-019) and the Austrian Federal Ministry of Transport, Innovation and Technology (Grant No. 829602).

Data source	EU	US Gov.
Number of documents containing:	12	15
single-column layout	12	11
multi-column or complex layout	0	4
Number of excerpts	34	28
Number of pages	101	74
Number of tables of which:	74	38
are split across more than one page	0	5
contain indentations	9	1
are partly ruled	45	17
are fully ruled	19	34
are laid out using monospaced text	0	0

Table 1: Summary of the tables in the core dataset

6. REFERENCES

[1] M. J. Cafarella, A. Halevy, and J. Madhavan. Structured data on the web. *Commun. ACM*, 54(2):72–79, 2011.

[2] A. C. e Silva. Metrics for evaluating performance in document analysis: application to tables. *IJDAR*, 14(1):101–109, 2011.

[3] T. Hassan. Towards a common evaluation strategy for table structure recognition algorithms. In *Proc. of DocEng*, 2010.

[4] J. Hu, R. Kashi, D. Lopresti, and G. Wilfong. Evaluating the performance of table processing algorithms. *IJDAR*, 4(3):140–153, 2002.

[5] J. Hu, R. Kashi, D. Lopresti, G. Wilfong, and G. Nagy. Why table ground-truthing is hard. In *Proc. of ICDAR*, pages 129–133, 2001.

[6] M. Hurst. *The Interpretation of Tables in Texts*. PhD thesis, University of Edinburgh, 2000.

[7] M. Hurst. A constraint-based approach to table structure derivation. In *Proc. of ICDAR*, pages 911–915, 2003.

[8] T. Kieninger and A. Dengel. An approach towards benchmarking of table structure recognition results. In *Proc. of ICDAR*, pages 1232–1236, 2005.

[9] D. D. Lewis. Evaluating and optimizing autonomous text classification systems. In *Proc. of SIGIR*, pages 246–254, 1995.

[10] E. Oro and M. Ruffolo. PDF-TREX: An approach for recognizing and extracting tables from PDF documents. In *Proc. of ICDAR*, pages 906–910, 2009.

[11] I. T. Phillips. User's reference manual for the uw english/technical document image database III. Technical report, Seattle University, 1996.

[12] A. Shahab, F. Shafait, T. Kieninger, and A. Dengel. An open approach towards the benchmarking of table structure recognition systems. In *Proc. of DAS*, pages 113–120, 2010.

[13] X. Wang. *Tabular Abstraction, Editing and Formatting*. PhD thesis, University of Waterloo, 1996.

Interactive Non-linear Video: Definition and XML Structure

Britta Meixner
Chair of Distributed Information Systems
University of Passau
Innstraße 43, 94032 Passau, Germany
meixner@fim.uni-passau.de

Harald Kosch
Chair of Distributed Information Systems
University of Passau
Innstraße 43, 94032 Passau, Germany
harald.kosch@uni-passau.de

ABSTRACT

A literature review on the term "interactive video" and "interactive non-linear video" revealed different levels of interaction in varying definitions. We give a formal definition of the term "interactive non-linear video" to clarify the elements and possible relations between elements contained in such videos. Furthermore, we introduce a new event-based XML format consisting of four required and two optional elements to describe this form of video. A scene graph consisting of scenes with triggers for annotations builds the core of the format. Formal definition and XML format are both illustrated by a real world example.

Categories and Subject Descriptors

I.7 [**Document and Text Processing**]: Document Preparation—*Hypertext/hypermedia, Multi/mixed media, Standards*

General Terms

Design, Languages

Keywords

Interactive Video, Non-linear Video, Video Annotations, Multimedia Document

1. INTRODUCTION

Several definitions of interactive (non-linear) video can be found in the literature. An early definition of interactivity in videos is presented by Stenzler and Eckert: *"A video application is interactive if the user affects the flow of the video and that influence, in turn, affects the user's future choices."*[17]. About ten years later Hammoud draws the following definition: *"Interactive video is a digitally enriched form of the original raw video sequence, allowing viewers attractive and powerful interactivity forms and navigational possibilities."* and extends it in the following way: *"Interactive video presentation is a form of interactive video document that is centered on enriched video but is not exclusively video."*[6]. We

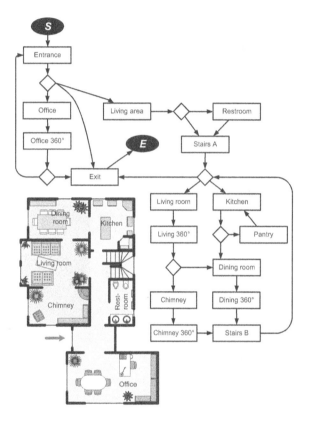

Figure 1: Scene graph with one scene in detail

extended this definition to: *"Contrary to linear videos, an interactive non-linear video is a digitally enriched form of video materials arranged for an overall concept. It presents additional information beyond the original content. Furthermore, it offers new forms of influence and navigation in the video and additional contents."*[12]. Interactive non-linear videos can be classified somewhere between multimedia presentations and simple clickable videos. They are based on videos and thus more restrictive than multimedia presentations, but in addition they provide a wider range of interactivity. Clickable videos are mainly linear and provide less interactivity compared to interactive non-linear videos.

Interactivity and additional information provided with interactive non-linear videos can be used in different scenarios and areas like e-learning, e-commerce, tourism and knowledge management. For example, a tour through a building can be implemented as an interactive non-linear video. Real-estate agents can film the different parts of a house. People interested in buying it can take a virtual walk through the house to get a first expression. Figure 1 shows an exemplary structure representing a tour through the ground floor of a house. The lower left part of the figure illustrates the layout of the ground floor. The video scenes are paths from one door to another. Viewers are asked where they want to go at certain points and are able to choose their own unique way through the house. The structure of the scenes defines a scene graph. The 16 scenes of the video are represented as labeled rectangles. The rhombus symbolizes a fork in the flow where the viewer can select a scene. Possible targets of a scene are another scene, a fork, or the end of the video. The decision which path is selected depends on the click of the respective button. The scene graph has a source (start) and a sink (end). Additional information for the different rooms can be provided with the videos. Images can show detailed views of furniture, flooring, or lamps. Texts provide information about the size or the characteristics of a room. Music files can be added to create a certain mood while watching the video. The potential buyer of the house is asked what adjacent room he wants to watch after a scene and can chose his own way through the house. If he wants to jump to a certain room, he can do this by picking the room in a table of contents or searching for it with a search function.

1.1 Problem Statement

According to the authors knowledge of this work, no formal definition of interactive non-linear video exists so far. A formalism would help to make clear what an interactive non-linear video is, of which elements it consists and which rules apply. Different possibilities exist to bring the structure and contents of the interactive non-linear video to the player. The first way is to save it to a database. Another way is to save it in a file and the contents in a folder structure. The video is then downloadable to a device and can be played without Internet connection, but contents may be stored more than once. The file must have a well defined file structure in order to make the processing effective at player side. Different standards like SMIL, NCL and HTML5 exist. These standards have to be extended or a new XML structure has to be created. According to the structure of interactive non-linear videos, it should fulfill the following requirements:

- It is based on a scene graph.

- Annotations are triggered by scenes or users.

- Local and global annotations exist.

- Different kinds of annotation exist.

- A table of contents can be used as an overlying navigation structure.

- A keyword search can be used to jump to scenes or annotations.

- Annotations may have influence on the main video.

- The flow-control is event-based.

- Each annotation can be positioned in relation to the video canvas.

- Timing issues should be kept as local as possible.

- Status information can be stored and evaluated.

1.2 Research Contributions

We give a *formal definition* of the term "interactive non-linear video" in Section 3. A conceptual model is used to make the definition evident. This is needed to outline relationships between the elements of an interactive non-linear video. Furthermore, rules are needed to define interactions and display of scenes and annotations. After all we propose an *XML file specification* to bring the model into a transferable form for internal use in Section 4.

2. RELATED WORK

Requirements for a XML data structure for interactive non-linear videos are the feasibility to define temporal and spatial relationships between videos and annotations. Elements needed at a fork in the video flow like button panels or quizzes need to be defined in the structure as well. Constructs for a table of contents and a keyword reference list are required to implement the extended navigation characteristical for interactive non-linear videos. The structure has to be extensible in case of new ways of interaction that should be mapped into the model. An event-based timing model is preferred to a structured timing model. Timing issues should be kept as local as possible.

Many of the tasks related to interactive non-linear video can be implemented with the **Synchronized Multimedia Integration Language 3.0 (SMIL 3.0)** ([20]). *"Using SMIL, an author may describe the temporal behavior of a multimedia presentation, associate hyperlinks with media objects and describe the layout of the presentation on a screen"* [20]. All basic navigation issues and the attachment of annotations to scenes can be implemented straightforward. However, a search functionality for keywords is not provided in SMIL. The `metadata`-element of SMIL 3.0 could be used to add keywords to scenes and annotations. This non intended use of the element has to be implemented in the search function in players. No structure for a table of contents is provided by SMIL. It is possible to arrange `text`-elements in form of a static tree-based structure. But by this mechanism, branches of the tree cannot get collapsed because no basic function is implemented in SMIL players therefore. Our future work includes a quiz as a decision module at a fork. One page of a quiz can be modeled with `text`-elements similar to the table of contents, the current score can be saved in a `state`-element for later usage. The player has to implement this functionality accordingly.

Vaisenberg et al. [19] introduce the SMPL framework which is able to add a table of contents, a search function, and a bookmark function to SMIL presentations. Thereby a semantic layer is added to SMIL presentations. It is not possible to implement a quiz, which is part of our future work. Pihkala and Vuorimaa describe "nine methods to extend SMIL for multimedia applications" (like for example multimedia consoles) in [15]. Thereby, SMIL 2.0 is extended with "location information, tactile output, forms, telephoning, and scripting." A generic, document-oriented way to publish multimedia documents on the web using HTML5, CSS, and SMIL Timesheets is called Timesheets.js which is presented by Cazenave et al. [4]. The combination of the different standards allows to combine logical and temporal structures. Additional libraries provide a table of contents and other forms of navigation.

Several other extensions and investigations for and on different versions of SMIL exist. Some extensions of one version of SMIL became part of the subsequent version of the standard. Bulterman examines SMIL 2.0 for document-related requirements of interactive peer-level annotations in [3]. An extension to XLink 1.0 called XConnector is proposed by Muchaluat-Saade et al. in [14]. Reaction to user inputs of different forms is integrated into XML documents and evaluated with real time programming by King et al. in [10]. Both extensions are applicable to SMIL 2.0 documents. An extension for SMIL 2.1 called SMIL State is proposed by Jansen and Bulterman in [7] and [8]. It allows to add variables to a multimedia presentation enabling dynamic adaptation to user interactions. SMIL State became part of SMIL 3.0. A temporal editing model for SMIL 3.0 is described by Jansen et al. in [9]. Thereby different forms of document transformations are analyzed.

The **Nested Context Model (NCM)** [16] is a model underlying the **Nested Context Language (NCL 3.0)** ([16], [1]). Parts five to ten of the NCM specify the NCL. Part five defines the full profile of NCL thereby. The same as for SMIL, NCL does not provide native structures to define a table of contents or a list of keywords and associated scenes or annotations. Furthermore, the construction of quizzes is not possible as well. A live editing solution for NCL is proposed by de Resende Costa et al. in [5].

Hypertext Markup Language (HTML5) [21] is able to describe the layout of a multimedia representation. The scope of this markup language is not multimedia documents. With the new version of the standard, video and audio files are taken into account to integrate media into a website. It is necessary to write functions in a scripting language like Java script. These for example invoke the display of an element at a certain time or realize a keyword search.

Descriptive XML standards like MPEG-7 [13] and similar standards are not suitable for the definition of interactive non-linear video, because no advanced mechanism for the linking of elements to parallel storylines, cycles in the storyline, or synchronization issues is available. Concepts dealing with semantic-based interaction in video content (for example NCL [18]) show some similar concepts to ours. However no open standard evolved from this research area.

The shortcomings of the previously proposed standards and their extensions can be summarized as follows:

- No specific XML format for the definition of interactive non-linear videos exists. The format should be restrictive enough to be read flawlessly by players and at the same time extensive enough to define interactive videos for a wide variety of scenarios.

- Existing formats need to be restricted on the one hand and extended on the other hand to be able to implement all requirements for interactive non-linear videos.

- An event-based model with a simple time synchronization is needed because of the high level of interactivity.

- An XSD is preferred to a DTD, because it is more restrictive. Less errors are possible in consequence.

- Keyword search and table of contents should be provided by the XML format natively for a seamless integration of the whole concept.

Contrary to the previously described formats, our XML format provides small structures for extended navigation like a keyword search or a table of contents. Timing issues are kept locally because the counter for the time starts new with each scene. The annotations are triggered at specific points in time related to the timing information of the scene. Intelligence for buffering and caching of elements is implemented in the player logic to make the specifications in the XML file (and thus provided by the user) as few as possible.

3. INTERACTIVE NON-LINEAR VIDEO

In this section, a formal definition of interactive non-linear video as well as rules for playback and interaction with scenes and annotations are given. A similar definition can be found in [11]. This definition narrows down the structures, constraints and functions needed in the XML file and in authoring tools and players. It defines precisely which structures are describable with an authoring tool. Furthermore, it is possible to detail a specific interactive non-linear video with the elements of this definition in a formal way. This section is divided into three parts. First basic functions are determined in order to enable a clear definition of interactive non-linear video. Then the term interactive non-linear video and incidental transition rules are defined and explained on the basis of a conceptual model. The section ends with a formal description of the house scenario.

3.1 Basic Functions

A projection function is needed to get a specific value from a tuple. This basic function is defined in function 1. It can be assigned to each element $\mathcal{E}_\mathcal{V}$ of the video.

$$\pi_i : \mathcal{E}_\mathcal{V}^k \mapsto \mathcal{E}_\mathcal{V}, k \in \mathbb{N}^+, (e_1, \ldots, e_k) \mapsto \pi_i(e_1, \ldots, e_k) := e_i \tag{1}$$

It may be necessary to pause the main video when the display of an annotation is triggered. This might be the case if the author wants to draw the viewers attention to an important information provided in the annotation. Therefore, a pause function is defined in function 2. It determines whether the main video is paused when an annotation is displayed or not. Returning $false$, the annotation is displayed at a given point in time and the video is not paused. Returning $true$, the video is paused. If the annotation which causes the pause of the scene is a continuous annotation, the video starts playback again when the duration of the annotation is over. Dealing with a static annotation, the user has to start the video when he is ready viewing the annotation.

$$pause : \mathcal{P}_\mathcal{V} \mapsto \{true, false\}, p_i \mapsto pause(p_i)$$

$$pause(p_i) := \begin{cases} false, & \text{Scene } p_i \text{ is not paused} \\ true, & \text{Scene } p_i \text{ is paused} \end{cases} \tag{2}$$

Another important feature is the possibility to mute the sound of the main video. This can be useful if the video material is provided with sound, but music should be played instead. Another use case is a second sound track, for example a text spoken in another language that has to be played instead of the original soundtrack. The mute function works similar to the pause function. It is defined in function 3. An annotation with sound like an audio or video file is able to mute the main video. The main video is unmuted again when the duration of the annotation is over.

$$mute : \mathcal{P}_\mathcal{V} \mapsto \{0, 1\}, p_i \mapsto mute(p_i)$$

$$mute(p_i) := \begin{cases} false, & \text{Scene } p_i \text{ is not muted} \\ true, & \text{Scene } p_i \text{ is muted} \end{cases} \quad (3)$$

Each annotation must have a point in time where it is displayed and where it is hidden at. This may be a fixed frame in both cases. If the annotation is displayed because of a user interaction, no fixed point in time can be set as start point. In this case, a duration for displaying the information will be set, the annotation is hidden when it is passed. These facts are expressed by equation 4. The first case describes a fixed start and end frame, the second case describes a user interaction and the duration.

$$dh_j := \begin{cases} (f_{i,m}, f_{i,n}), & \text{static trigger, } f_{i,m}, f_{i,n} \in \mathcal{F}_\mathcal{V}, \\ & 1 \leq m < n \leq j_i, \\ (null, dur_{a_o}), & \text{user interaction} \end{cases} \quad (4)$$

Each additional element that is displayed with the main video has to be positioned on the player canvas. The size of the element has to be stated as well. If the element should be moving as an overlay over the main video, a combination of time, position, and size is needed for each change of position or size. Each element has at least a position information $pos_i := (x_i, y_i)$. The dimensions of the surrounding rectangle $dim_i := (sx_i, sy_i)$ have to be defined if the size of the element is not given by its natural form (for example for texts). A time information t_i is needed if the element changes its position. It states the position of the element at a given fixed point in time t_i. This leads to the definition of an $area_i$ as stated in equation 5.

$$area_i := \begin{cases} (null, pos_i, null), & \text{displaying a (standard)} \\ & \text{button or an element} \\ & \text{with a fixed size at a} \\ & \text{fixed position} \\ (t_i, pos_i, null), & \text{displaying a moving} \\ & \text{(standard) button or} \\ & \text{an element with a} \\ & \text{fixed size} \\ (null, pos_i, dim_i), & \text{displaying an area} \\ & \text{with a given} \\ & \text{rectangular outline} \\ & \text{at a fixed position} \\ (t_i, pos_i, dim_i), & \text{displaying a moving} \\ & \text{area with a given} \\ & \text{rectangular outline} \end{cases} \quad (5)$$

Elements have a set of positions $\mathcal{POS}_i$ as defined in equation 6. This set must not be empty. The set contains one $area_i$ if the element is displayed in one place. It contains more than one $area_i$ if the element is moving. Thereby, each element has a time information.

$$\mathcal{POS}_i := \{area_1, \ldots, area_n\} \neq \emptyset \quad (6)$$

The size of an element is designed in size function 7. It returns the size of an element (annotation or frame) in kByte. This function is relevant for download and buffer management at player side.

$$s : \mathcal{E}_\mathcal{V} \mapsto \mathbb{N}^+, e_i \mapsto s(e_i) := \pi_s(e_i) \quad (7)$$

3.2 Definition of Interactive Non-linear Video

After defining the functions and sets above, a definition of an interactive non-linear video with additional information can be determined. The conceptual model illustrated in Figure 2 shows two ways of navigation in the video. The first one called "basic navigation" is based on the structure of the video respectively its scene graph. The second one called "extended navigation" is independent from the basic navigation.

An interactive non-linear video $\mathcal{V} = (\mathcal{P}_\mathcal{V}, \mathcal{F}_\mathcal{V}, \mathcal{A}_\mathcal{V}, \mathcal{C}_\mathcal{V}, \mathcal{N}_\mathcal{V}, \sigma, \epsilon, \mathcal{TOC}_\mathcal{V}, \mathcal{S}_\mathcal{V})$ can be defined as a set $\mathcal{P}_\mathcal{V}$ of x scenes:

$$\mathcal{P}_\mathcal{V} = \{p_1, \ldots, p_x\}, p_i := (\mathcal{F}_{p_i}, \mathcal{POS}_i) \quad (8)$$

The conceptual model in Figure 2 shows them in green color. Each scene in the graph consists of a **set of frames** $\mathcal{F}_\mathcal{V}$

$$\mathcal{F}_\mathcal{V} = \{f_{1,1}, \ldots, f_{1,j_1}, f_{2,1}, \ldots, f_{2,j_2}, \ldots, f_{x,1}, \ldots, f_{x,j_x}\},$$

$$f_{i,m} := (\zeta_{i,m}, s) \text{ with } s \in \mathbb{N}^+,$$

$$f_{i,m} \subset p_i, \ p_i \in \mathcal{P}_\mathcal{V}, \ 1 \leq m \leq j_i, \ 1 \leq i \leq x \quad (9)$$

where each $\{f_{i,1}, \ldots, f_{i,j_i}\}$ represents a scene. Each $f_{i,m}$ is defined by a two-tuple $(\zeta_{i,m}, s)$ consisting of the content of a frame $\zeta_{i,m}$ and the size s of this content. The scene has a reference to the video resource (blue color in Figure 2). The linkage of a scene with its video content makes it easy to exchange the content, for example to implement multi-lingualism, to provide different levels of quality, or to make different video formats available for different end user devices (more precisely for different display sizes and different bandwidths).

Scenes are linked with each other to a **scene graph** by the definition of **transition constraints** (black arrows in Figure 2). Transition constraints tc_j form a set $\mathcal{N}_\mathcal{V}$

$$\mathcal{N}_\mathcal{V} = \{tc_1, \ldots, tc_n\}, \ tc_j := (p_m, p_n, u), \ u \in \{bexpr, null\}$$

$$p_m, p_n \in \mathcal{P}_\mathcal{V}, \ 1 \leq m, n \leq x \quad (10)$$

Each transition constraint tc_j of the set implies that scene p_n is successor of scene p_m. The last value of the tuple tc_j, defines the constraint for selecting the follow-up scene. If u is null, no constraint is given ($p_i \overset{null}{\longmapsto} p_j$), for example at a sequential arrangement of scenes. The Boolean expression $bexpr$ defines conditions which are linked by a disjunction. If an expression is true, the according scene is selected ($p_i \overset{bexpr}{\longmapsto} p_j$).

Each scene graph has a **beginning**

$$\sigma : \exists!k, (\sigma, p_k, null) \in N_\mathcal{V} \wedge \nexists k, (p_k, \sigma, null) \in N_\mathcal{V}, \ 1 \leq k \leq x \quad (11)$$

The first scene is always connected in series with the start of the video, this can be expressed as $\sigma \overset{null}{\longmapsto} p_j$. The **end** of the video

$$\epsilon : \exists k, (p_k, \epsilon, u) \in N_\mathcal{V} \wedge \nexists k, (\epsilon, p_k, null) \in N_\mathcal{V}, \ 1 \leq k \leq x \quad (12)$$

can be reached serially after a scene ($p_i \overset{null}{\longmapsto} \epsilon$) or after the Boolean expression is evaluated as true ($p_i \overset{bexpr}{\longmapsto} \epsilon$). Each scene of the scene graph must have a path to the end ϵ and, if the edges are reversed, to the beginning σ of the scene graph. The start (source) and the end (sink) of the graph are illustrated in UML notation in Figure 2.

Annotations (purple color in Figure 2) form a self-contained set, because the same annotation can be displayed more than once in the whole video. A set $\mathcal{A}_\mathcal{V}$ of annotations

$$\mathcal{A}_\mathcal{V} = \{a_1, \ldots, a_k\}, a_o := (\alpha_o, s) \text{ with } s \in \mathbb{N}^+, \ 1 \leq o \leq k \quad (13)$$

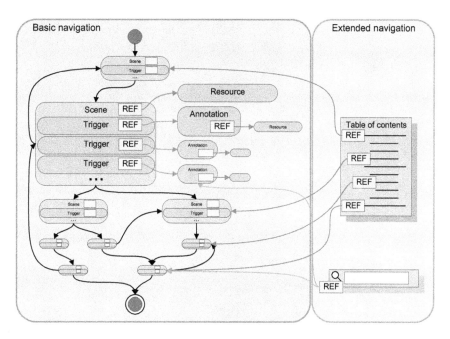

Figure 2: Conceptual model of an interactive non-linear video as defined in this work

contains only the annotation itself. Each a_o is defined by a two-tuple (α_o, s) consisting of the content of an annotation α_o and the size s of this content.

The link of an annotation with a scene is accomplished by an **annotation constraint** (trigger). All triggers are implicitly assigned to a scene by the specification of a start and an end frame. Both of them belong to the same scene (except in case of a so called global annotation which is displayed during the whole playback of the video). The annotation constraints form a set $\mathcal{C}_\mathcal{V}$,

$$\mathcal{C}_\mathcal{V} = \{c_1, \ldots, c_n\}, c_j := \begin{cases} (dh_j, a_o, \mathcal{POS}_{a_o}, pause(p_i), \\ mute(p_i), null), \\ \quad a_o \text{ is a standard annotation} \\ (dh_j, a_o, \mathcal{POS}_{a_o}, pause(p_i), \\ mute(p_i), \mu), \\ \quad a_o \text{ is an interactive annotation} \end{cases}$$

$$a_o \in \mathcal{A}_\mathcal{V}, \ 1 \leq o \leq k, \ 1 \leq i \leq x, \ 1 \leq j \leq n \quad (14)$$

It contains two different types of annotation. The "standard annotation" is displayed without any user interaction. It is displayed at frame $f_{i,m}$ and hidden at frame $f_{i,n}$. The position is defined by the set $\mathcal{POS}_{a_o}$. If the annotation should attract the attention of the viewer, the scene can be paused by setting $pause(p_i)$ to *true*. If the scene and other annotations should be muted, $mute(p_i)$ is set to *true*. The other type is called "interactive annotation". It is defined in the same way as the standard annotation but has a $\mu := \{area_1, \ldots, area_n\}$ as a last value of the tuple. It represents a clickable area, for example a rectangle marking, an object in the video, or a button on a button panel. In this case $dh_j = (null, dur_{a_o})$ is used to indicate when the invoked annotation has to be hidden.

The following five transition rules describe the interaction between scene and annotation and between user and annotation more precisely:

- $p_i \xrightarrow{\pi_1(\pi_1(c_j))} \pi_2(c_j) \to \pi_3(c_j)$

describes the case in which an annotation is displayed at a point in time at a given position on the player canvas as defined by a trigger.

- $\pi_2(c_j) \xrightarrow{\pi_2(\pi_1(c_j))} p_i$

defines the hiding of an annotation. Either a trigger can cause the hiding of the annotation or the annotation is hidden after a timeout is reached.

- $\pi_7(c_j) \xrightarrow{click} \pi_2(c_j)$

describes an annotation initiating the display of another annotation. This scenario occurs when an object in the video is marked, the viewer clicks on that mark, then another annotation is displayed.

- $p_i.a_j \xrightarrow{\pi_4(c_j)} p_{i_{paused}}$

describes the pause of the main video triggered by the annotation. The main video pauses when the annotation is displayed and the attention of the viewer is drawn to the annotation. If the annotation is a static annotation, the user has to press the start button to resume the video. The video resumes automatically after continuous annotations.

- $p_i.a_j \xrightarrow{\pi_5(c_j)} p_{i_{muted}}$

mutes the main video. It can only be triggered by annotations with sound, namely video and audio files.

One optional element of an interactive non-linear video is a **table of contents** $\mathcal{TOC}_\mathcal{V}$,

$$\begin{aligned} \mathcal{TOC}_\mathcal{V} &:= (\mathcal{I}, \mathcal{E}) \\ \mathcal{I} &:= \{item_1, \ldots, item_n\} \\ \mathcal{E} &:= \{(item_i, item_j) | item_j \text{ is subcategory of } item_i\} \end{aligned}$$

$$(15)$$

The two sets form a tree structure, where $\mathcal{I}$ are the nodes of the tree and $\mathcal{E}$ defines the relationships between the items of $\mathcal{I}$. If both, $\mathcal{I}$ and $\mathcal{E}$ are empty sets, $\mathcal{I} = \emptyset$ and $\mathcal{E} = \emptyset$, no table of contents is provided. An item $item_i$

$$item_i := \begin{cases} (descr, p_i), & \text{scene } p_i \text{ is linked with } descr \\ (descr, null), & \text{no scene is linked with } descr \end{cases} \tag{16}$$

consists of a caption $descr$ which is displayed to the user. If the tuple contains a scene p_i as second value, it points to a scene and the viewer can jump directly to that scene $(\perp \xrightarrow{\text{tocentry}} p_j)$. If the second value of the tuple is $null$, no interactivity is provided by the caption. The conceptual model (Figure 2) shows the table of contents in red color. It contains references to four different scenes of the video indicated by red arrows. The second optional element is a **keyword search** $\mathcal{S_V}$,

$$\mathcal{S_V} := \{word_1, \ldots, word_x\},$$

$$word_i := (string, \{target_1, \ldots, target_i\}) \tag{17}$$

The set $\mathcal{S_V}$ describing the keyword search consists of $word$-elements or is an empty set $(\mathcal{S_V} = \emptyset)$. It contains a search string and a set of one or more targets $target_j$ with:

$$target_j := \begin{cases} (p_i, f_{i,1}), & \text{the target is the} \\ & \text{start of a scene} \\ (p_i, \pi_1(\pi_1(c_j))), & \text{the target is the} \\ & \text{start of an annotation} \end{cases} \tag{18}$$

A target can point to the start of a scene $(p_i, f_{i,1})$, $\perp \xrightarrow{\text{keyword}} p_i$ or to the start of the display of an annotation in a scene $(p_i, \pi_1(\pi_1(c_j)))$, $\perp \xrightarrow{\text{keyword}} \pi_1(\pi_1(c_j))$. The element for the keyword search is depicted in orange color in Figure 2, the inserted word would match for a scene and an annotation indicated by orange arrows.

3.3 Example Scenario

An interactive non-linear video consists of seven sets, a start and an end element $\mathcal{V} = (\mathcal{P_V}, \mathcal{F_V}, \mathcal{A_V}, \mathcal{C_V}, \mathcal{N_V}, \sigma, \epsilon, TOC_\mathcal{V}, \mathcal{S_V})$. The sets are specified as follows:

- The **set of scenes** is defined as $\mathcal{P_V} = \{p_1, \ldots, p_{16}\}$. It consists of 16 scenes.

- The **set of frames** $\mathcal{F_V}$ is $\{f_{1,1}, \ldots, f_{1,710}, f_{2,1}, \ldots, f_{2,363}, f_{3,1}, \ldots, f_{3,684}, f_{4,1}, \ldots, f_{4,656}, f_{5,1}, \ldots, f_{5,229}, f_{6,1}, \ldots, f_{6,554}, f_{7,1}, \ldots, f_{7,333}, f_{8,1}, \ldots, f_{8,225}, f_{9,1}, \ldots, f_{9,511}, f_{10,1}, \ldots, f_{10,530}, f_{11,1}, \ldots, f_{11,649}, f_{12,1}, \ldots, f_{12,603}, f_{13,1}, \ldots, f_{13,362}, f_{14,1}, \ldots, f_{14,319}, f_{15,1}, \ldots, f_{15,353}, f_{16,1}, \ldots, f_{16,383}\}$. It consists of 7464 frames. These frames are split into the 16 scenes in unequal shares. The average frame size is 141 kByte for each frame in each scene.

- The **set of annotations** $\mathcal{A_V}$ is $\{a_1 = (I1, 35), a_2 = (I2, 48), a_3 = (I3, 23), a_4 = (I4, 47), a_5 = (I5, 47), a_6 = (I6, 32), a_7 = (I7, 34), a_8 = (I8, 24), a_9 = (I9, 47), a_{10} = (I10, 53), a_{11} = (I11, 23), a_{12} = (I12, 48), a_{13} = (I13, 371), a_{14} = (I14, 402), a_{15} = (I15, 128), a_{16} = (I16, 322), a_{17} = (I17, 228), a_{18} = (I18, 319), a_{19} = (P1, 37), a_{20} = (P2, 125), a_{21} = (T1, 3), a_{22} = (T2, 5), a_{23} = (T3, 4), a_{24} = (T4, 3), a_{25} = (T5, 2), a_{26} = (T6, 1), a_{27} = (T7, 1), a_{28} = (T8, 2), a_{29} = (I8, 265), a_{30} = (T9, 3)\}$. The sizes of the annotations are given in kByte.

- The **set of annotation constraints** $\mathcal{C_V}$ can be found in Table 1.

- The **set of transition constraints** $\mathcal{N_V}$ can be found in Table 1. Nine of the tuples describe serial transitions, 15 of them contain conditions for the attainment of the next scene.

- The entrance scene p_1 is the **start scene** as defined in $(\sigma, p_1, null)$.

- The **end of the scene graph** ϵ can be reached from scene p_4 as defined in $(p_4, \epsilon, null)$.

- Further definitions:

  - **Four areas** are defined for displaying annotations, namely
    $area_l = (null, (0, 0), (150, 600))$,
    $area_r = (null, (650, 0), (150, 600))$,
    $area_t = (null, (150, 500), (500, 100))$ and
    $area_b = (null, (150, 0), (500, 100))$
    assuming that the origin of the coordinate system is in the lower left corner. The values are set in pixels.

  - **Global annotations** which are displayed for the whole duration of the video are
    $(f_{1,1}, f_{4,656}, a_{29}, \{area_{right}\}, false, false, 1, null)$
    and
    $(f_{1,1}, f_{4,656}, a_{30}, \{area_{right}\}, false, false, 1, null)$

4. XML FORMAT FOR INTERACTIVE NON-LINEAR VIDEO

We followed the design principles of SMIL [20], which are the maintenance of a declarative XML format, the separation of content and structure, and the support of a flexible architecture [2]. However, our format shows several differences in its internal structure compared to SMIL. Our goal was the design of a minimal, restrictive, modular and event-based data exchange format for interactive non-linear videos with annotations which provides a clearly specified set of functions for the player. We chose the XSD instead of the DTD for the definition of the structure of our files to ensure the internal correctness of references and data types. Using the XSD allows to define constraints which ensure a consistent definition of keys and references.

The XML file compliant to our XSD can be divided into the following six parts: the project information, a scene list, resources, actions, a table of contents, and a list of keywords linked to annotations or scenes. We chose to separate structure and contents in the XML format itself. The scene graph defines the primary structure of the video. Each scene contains triggers for actions which may show annotations or invoke interactive elements. The synchronization issues are limited to the scene, which makes it easy to schedule downloads and deal with intra scene user interaction. All internal and external resources are defined in a particular section which makes it easy to maintain the files in several languages. Additional sections for a table of contents and a keyword search enhance the modularity and with that maintainability and expandability.

The scene graph (scene list) is explained after the resources and the actions part because both are referenced

Table 1: Elements of the House Scenario

Scene	$\mathcal{C}_\nu$	$\mathcal{N}_\nu$
Entrance	$\{((f_{1,1}, f_{1,239}), a_1, \{area_l\}, false, false, 1, null),$ $((f_{1,100}, f_{1,199}), a_{19}, \{area_r\}, false, false, 1, null),$ $((f_{1,200}, f_{1,710}), a_{20}, \{area_r\}, false, false, 1, null),$ $((f_{1,1}, f_{1,149}), a_{21}, \{area_t\}, false, false, 1, null),$ $((f_{1,170}, f_{1,710}), a_{22}, \{area_b\}, false, false, 1, null),$ $((f_{1,60}, f_{1,269}), a_{23}, \{area_t\}, false, false, 1, null),$	$\{(p_1, p_2, b_{Office} == true),$ $(p_1, p_4, b_{Exit} == true),$ $(p_1, p_5, b_{Living\ area} == true),$
Office	$((f_{2,1}, f_{2,363}), a_2, \{area_l\}, false, false, 1, null),$	$(p_2, p_3, null),$
Office 360	$((f_{3,1}, f_{3,342}), a_3, \{area_l\}, false, false, 1, null),$ $((f_{3,342}, f_{3,684}), a_{15}, \{area_l\}, false, false, 1, null),$	$(p_3, p_1, b_{Entrance} == true),$ $(p_3, p_4, b_{Exit} == true),$
Exit	$((f_{4,1}, f_{4,300}), a_1, \{area_l\}, false, false, 1, null),$ $((f_{4,1}, f_{4,656}), a_{17}, \{area_l\}, false, false, 1, null),$ $((f_{4,301}, f_{4,656}), a_{28}, \{area_b\}, false, false, 1, null),$	$(p_4, \epsilon, null),$
Living area	$((f_{5,1}, f_{5,229}), a_4, \{area_l\}, false, false, 1, null),$	$(p_5, p_6, b_{Restroom} == true), (p_5, p_7, b_{Stairs\ A} == true),$
Restroom	$((f_{6,1}, f_{6,400}), a_5, \{area_l\}, false, false, 1, null),$	$(p_6, p_7, null),$
Stairs A		$(p_7, p_8, b_{Living} == true), (p_7, p_{10}, b_{Kitchen} == true),$
Living room	$((f_{8,1}, f_{8,225}), a_6, \{area_l\}, false, false, 1, null),$	$(p_8, p_9, null),$
Living 360	$((f_{9,1}, f_{9,511}), a_7, \{area_l\}, false, false, 1, null),$ $((f_{9,1}, f_{9,511}), a_{24}, \{area_b\}, false, false, 1, null),$	$(p_9, p_{12}, b_{Chimney} == true),$ $(p_9, p_{14}, b_{Dining} == true),$
Kitchen	$((f_{10,105}, f_{10,530}), a_8, \{area_l\}, false, false, 1, null),$ $((f_{10,1}, f_{10,418}), a_{14}, \{area_l\}, false, false, 1, null),$	$(p_{10}, p_{11}, b_{Pantry} == true),$ $(p_{10}, p_{14}, b_{Dining} == true),$
Pantry	$((f_{11,301}, f_{11,649}), a_9, \{area_l\}, false, false, 1, null),$	$(p_{11}, p_{10}, null),$
Chimney	$((f_{12,102}, f_{12,498}), a_7, \{area_l\}, false, false, 1, null),$	$(p_{12}, p_{13}, null),$
Chimney 360	$((f_{13,1}, f_{13,362}), a_{11}, \{area_l\}, false, false, 1, null),$ $((f_{13,1}, f_{13,362}), a_{13}, \{area_l\}, false, false, 1, null),$	$(p_{13}, p_{16}, null),$
Dining room	$((f_{14,1}, f_{14,319}), a_{25}, \{area_b\}, false, false, 1, null),$ $((f_{14,1}, f_{14,319}), a_{26}, \{area_t\}, false, false, 1, null),$	$(p_{14}, p_{15}, null),$
Dining 360	$((f_{15,1}, f_{15,353}), a_{10}, \{area_l\}, false, false, 1, null),$ $((f_{15,98}, f_{15,353}), a_{13}, \{area_l\}, false, false, 1, null),$	$(p_{15}, p_{16}, null),$
Stairs B	$((f_{16,1}, f_{16,383}), a_{27}, \{area_b\}, false, false, 1, null)\}$	$(p_{16}, p_8, b_{Living} == true), (p_{16}, p_{10}, b_{Kitchen} == true)\}$

by the scene list. The structure of the XML file is illustrated for a walk through a house[1]. All line-numbers in this section refer to Listing 1 which is explained in the following subsections.

```
1  <?xml version="1.0" encoding="UTF-8" standalone="no"?>
2  <siva xmlns:xsi="http://www.w3.org/2001/XMLSchema-instance"
3      xsi:noNamespaceSchemaLocation="sivaPlayer.xsd">
4  <projectInformation>
5    <languages defaultLangCode="de-de">
6      <language langCode="de-de"/>
7      <language langCode="en-us"/>
8    </languages>
9    <settings name="startmode" value="full"/>
10   <settings name="size_width" value="800"/>
11   <settings name="size_height" value="600"/>
12   <settings name="area_left_width" value="0.2"/>
13   <settings name="area_top_height" value="0.2"/>
14   <settings name="area_bottom_height" value="0.0"/>
15   <settings name="area_right_width" value="0.2"/>
16   <projectResources REFactionID="s-NAPic_1"/>
17   <projectResources REFactionID="s-NARtxt_1"/>
18 </projectInformation>
19 <sceneList REFsceneIDstart="NSc_1">
20   <scene REFresID="v_Sc_1" name="Entrance" sceneID="NSc_1"
21       xPos="0.063" yPos="0.101">
22     <storyBoard REFactionIDend="select-NSel_1">
23       <trigger REFactionID="s-NAa_1" endTime="00:00:07.211"
24           startTime="00:00:03.230" triggerID="t-NAa_1"/>
25       <trigger REFactionID="s-NAa_2" endTime="00:00:13.440"
26           startTime="00:00:07.236" triggerID="t-NAa_2"/>
27       <trigger REFactionID="s-NAPic_2" endTime="00:00:09.304"
28           startTime="00:00:00.000" triggerID="t-NAPic_2"/>
29       <trigger REFactionID="s-NARtxt_2" endTime="00:00:03.799"
30           startTime="00:00:00.000" triggerID="t-NARtxt_2"/>
31       <trigger REFactionID="s-NARtxt_3" endTime="00:00:13.440"
32           startTime="00:00:04.781" triggerID="t-NARtxt_3"/>
33       <trigger REFactionID="s-NARtxt_4" endTime="00:00:10.183"
34           startTime="00:00:01.912" triggerID="t-NARtxt_4"/>
35     </storyBoard>
36   </scene>
37 <!-- ... -->
38 <scene REFresID="v_Sc_4" name="Exit" sceneID="NSc_9"
39     xPos="0.31" yPos="0.43">
40   <storyBoard REFactionIDend="end-siva">
41     <trigger REFactionID="s-NAPic_4" endTime="00:00:13.640"
42         startTime="00:00:00.000" triggerID="t-NAPic_4"/>
43   </storyBoard>
44 </scene>
45 <!-- ... -->
46 <scene REFresID="v_Sc_5" name="Living room" sceneID="NSc_6"
47     xPos="0.525" yPos="0.652">
48   <storyBoard REFactionIDend="load-NSc_10">
49     <trigger REFactionID="s-NAPic_5" endTime="00:00:20.440"
50         startTime="00:00:00.000" triggerID="t-NAPic_5"/>
51   </storyBoard>
52 </scene>
53 </sceneList>
54 <resources>
55   <videoStream resID="v_Sc_1">
56     <content href="videos/v_Sc_1-de_DE.flv" langCode="de-de"/>
57   </videoStream>
58 <!-- ... -->
59   <audioStream resID="a_NAa_1">
60     <content href="audios/Audio_1-de_DE.mp3" langCode="de-de"/>
61   </audioStream>
62 <!-- ... -->
63   <richPage resID="rp_NARtxt_1">
64     <content href="richpages/RT_1-de_DE.html" langCode="de-de"/>
65   </richPage>
66 <!-- ... -->
67   <image resID="i_NAPic_1">
68     <content href="pix/Pic_1-de_DE.jpg" langCode="de-de"/>
69   </image>
70 <!-- ... -->
71   <label resID="l_t_TI_1">
72     <content langCode="de-de">House</content>
73   </label>
74 <!-- ... -->
75 </resources>
76 <actions>
77   <showImage REFresID="i_NAPic_1" actionID="s-NAPic_1"
78       pauseVideo="false">
79     <area screenArea="right"/>
80   </showImage>
81 <!-- ... -->
82   <showRichPage REFresID="rp_NARtxt_1" actionID="s-NARtxt_1"
83       pauseVideo="false">
```

[1] The XSD file can be downloaded from http://siva.uni-passau.de/sites/default/files/downloads/sivaPlayer.xsd, the example used in this work can be downloaded from http://siva.uni-passau.de/sites/default/files/downloads/export.xml.

```
84      <area screenArea="right"/>
85    </showRichPage>
86    <!-- ... -->
87    <showRichPage REFresID="rp_NARtxt_4" actionID="s-NARtxt_4"
88          pauseVideo="false">
89      <path>
90        <point time="00:00:09.618" xPos="0.248" xSize="0.497"
91              yPos="0.326" ySize="0.32"/>
92        <point time="00:00:10.138" xPos="0.32" xSize="0.497"
93              yPos="0.27" ySize="0.32"/>
94      </path>
95    </showRichPage>
96    <!-- ... -->
97    <playAudio REFresID="a_NAa_1" actionID="s-NAa_1"
98          muteVideo="true" pauseVideo="false"/>
99    <!-- ... -->
100   <showSelectionControl REFcontrolIDdefault="NSelCtrl_1"
101         REFresID="l_t_NSel_1" actionID="select-NSel_1"
102         timeout="00:00:00" type="default">
103     <path>
104       <point time="00:00:00.000" xSize="-1.0" ySize="-1.0"/>
105     </path>
106     <controls REFactionID="load-NSc_2" REFresID="l_t_NSelCtrl_1"
107           controlID="NSelCtrl_1"/>
108     <controls REFactionID="load-NSc_3" REFresID="l_t_NSelCtrl_2"
109           controlID="NSelCtrl_2"/>
110   </showSelectionControl>
111   <!-- ... -->
112   <showMarkControl REFactionID="i_NAPic_6" actionID="SMC_1"
113         duration="00:00:15.000">
114     <ellipse>
115       <ellipsePath time="00:00:01.010" xPos="0.013333334"
116             yPos="0.024" lengthA="0.27666667" lengthB="0.192"/>
117       <!-- ... -->
118       <ellipsePath time="00:00:24.120" xPos="0.8333334"
119             yPos="0.0" lengthA="0.14333333" lengthB="0.1"/>
120     </ellipse>
121   </showMarkControl>
122   <!-- ... -->
123   <loadVideoScene REFsceneID="NSc_1" actionID="load-NSc_1"/>
124   <!-- ... -->
125   <endSiva actionID="end-siva"/>
126 </actions>
127 </siva>
```

Listing 1: Example XML

4.1 Project Information

The first part of the XML file is the project information part, see lines 4-18. It defines the languages available for the interactive non-linear video (lines 5-8). This is not explicitly part of our definition in Section 3.2, but it may be useful in videos watched by people of different nationalities. The conceptual model in Figure 2 shows resources colored blue. These can contain contents in different languages. Different settings are possible according to the capabilities of the player implementation. They are described in settings elements

<settings name=``...'' value=``...''/>

(lines 9-15) where a value can be assigned to a name. The settings in the example are defined for the SIVA Desktop Player. Four static areas are defined in this player and can easily be set to a size (lines 12-15) as stated in function 5. The project resources defined in lines 16-17 are shown during the whole interactive non-linear video in the right annotation area. Project resources usually do not pause the main video and in this case they do not mute it.

4.2 Resources

Resources state the content of an annotation (lines 54-75) or a scene. Resources are defined by the set of annotations $\mathcal{A}_v$ in function 13 and the set of frames $\mathcal{F}_v$ in function 9.

It is possible to compile them in different languages. Each resource has an ID to be identified by the action causing the display of the annotation. Labels and subtitles are defined inline, because they mostly consist of only a few words and are commonly styled by a player. Examples of an inline definition of resources can be found in line 72. All other resources - images, rich texts, video, and audio files - are defined as links in the XML file, see lines 56, 60, 64 and 68.

4.3 Actions

Actions are triggered at certain points in time in the video or by a user interaction. They are described in lines 76-126. Actions cause the display of a resource, a selection panel, a marked object in the video, load a scene, or indicate the end of a video.

4.3.1 Display of additional information ("standard annotations")

All actions causing the display of an annotation are formalized as annotation constraints in set $\mathcal{C}_v$ in function 14. Each of them has a reference REFresID to one of the resources (lines 77, 82, 87 and 97). No action is able to pause the video when it is displayed, which is stated in the pauseVideo-attribute in lines 78, 83, 88 and 98. Actions starting a video or an audio file are able to mute all other annotations and the main video, as defined in the optional muteVideo-attribute. The playAudio-element (lines 97-99) is the only one which mutes the video. The actions have a positioning information. They are either displayed in one of the areas (lines 79 and 84) defined in the project information part of the XML file (lines 12-15), or they are displayed as an overlay having a time-based position and size information (lines 90-93). The referenced annotation a_o, the positioning information $\mathcal{POS}_{a_o}$, the pause information for the main video $pause(p_i)$, and the mute information $mute(p_i)$ are defined in an annotation constraint c_i according to function 14. The related transition rules are $p_i.a_j \xmapsto{\pi_4(c_j)} p_{i_{paused}}$ and $p_i.a_j \xmapsto{\pi_5(c_j)} p_{i_{muted}}$.

4.3.2 Action to load a new scene

A new scene can be loaded with a loadVideoScene-action (line 123). The element consists of a reference to a scene from the scene list (REFsceneID) and an actionID. This action can be found implicitly in transition rules $p_i \xrightarrow{\text{null}} p_j$ and $p_i \xrightarrow{\text{bexpr}} p_j$ described in Section 3.2

4.3.3 Button panel

A button panel is defined in the showSelectionControl-element in lines 100-110. It consists of two or more buttons (two in our example) as stated in the controls-elements. Each button has a controlID for a unique identification, a reference REFresID to a label, and a reference to load a scene or another showSelectionControl-element (not in this example), which is loaded after a click on the button. This part of the XML file can be found in bexpr in function 10 and more precisely in transition rules $p_i \xrightarrow{\text{bexpr}} p_j$ and $p_i \xrightarrow{\text{bexpr}} \epsilon$ in Section 3.2. The button panel also has a reference to a label REFresID and an actionID to be referenced at the end of a scene. One of the controls can be defined as default control in REFcontrolIDdefault (line 100). It is selected after the period of time set in the timeout-attribute (line

102). A positioning information is set similar to the position of an action displaying a resource. The button panel will be displayed as a centered overlay over the video area, because of the negative coordinates in line 104.

4.3.4 Marked object in the Video

Clickable objects are expressed by a `showMarkControl`-action as shown in lines 112-121. After the user has clicked on a marked object in the video, a referenced resource by the action set in the `REFactionID`-attribute in line 112 is loaded. An object can be marked with an elliptic outline, a polygon outline, or a labeled button which can be placed near the object. The example shows the definition of an elliptic outline (lines 114-120). A `duration` is set to determine how long the referenced annotation has to be shown. In our example it will be shown for 15 seconds (line 113). This can not be solved by a trigger, because it depends on the time of the user interaction. This form of user interaction is stated in the second case of c_j in function 14 and in transition rule $p_i.a_j \xrightarrow{\text{click}} p_i.a_k$.

4.4 Scene List

The most important part of the XML file is the scene list (see lines 19-53). It links scenes with the video contents and defines the structure of the whole video (a scene graph). Triggers for displaying and hiding of annotations are set with each scene.

4.4.1 Action at the end of a scene

The start scene of the video is defined as

```
<sceneList REFsceneIDstart=''NSc_1''>
```

according to function 11 and transition rule $\sigma \xrightarrow{\text{null}} p_j$ in line 19.

Each scene has a storyboard which defines what happens during the scene and when the scene is over. This is defined in `REFactionIDend` in the `storyBoard`-element in lines 22, 40 and 48. The example shows all possible end actions after a scene. A linear transition between two scenes is defined with

```
<storyBoard REFactionIDend=''load-NSc_10''>
```

in line 48. The according transition constraint in $\mathcal{N}_\mathcal{V}$ (function 10) is defined as $(p_m, p_n, null)$, the transition rule is $p_i \xrightarrow{\text{null}} p_j$.

```
<storyBoard REFactionIDend=''end-siva''>
```

in line 40 references the end action of the video as defined in function 12 and in transition rule $p_i \xrightarrow{\text{null}} \epsilon$. A button panel is shown after scene 1 as defined in line 22. This kind of action is defined as a subset $\mathcal{N}_i \subset \mathcal{N}_\mathcal{V}$, $|\mathcal{N}_i| \geq 2$ consisting of elements $(p_m, p_n, bexpr)$ having the same source scene p_m. The appropriate transition rules are $p_i \xrightarrow{\text{bexpr}} p_j$ and $p_i \xrightarrow{\text{bexpr}} \epsilon$.

4.4.2 Triggers during a scene

The points in time where annotations are shown and hidden are also defined in the storyboard of a scene. A `trigger`-element (see lines 23-34, 41-42 and 49-50) consists of an action to show an annotation, the start time where the action is performed, the end time where the annotation is hidden again, and an ID of the trigger like:

```
<trigger REFactionID=''s-NARtxt_3''
endTime=''00:00:13.440'' startTime=''00:00:04.781''
triggerID=''t-NARtxt_3''/>
```

This element implements a subpart of $C_\mathcal{V}$ (function 14). The first three elements of tuple c_j, namely $f_{i,m}$, $f_{i,n}$ and a_o are stated in the trigger-element. Displaying an annotation is defined by transition rules $p_i \xmapsto{\pi_1(\pi_1(c_j))} \pi_2(c_j) \rightarrow \pi_3(c_j)$ and $\pi_2(c_j) \xmapsto{\pi_2(\pi_1(c_j))} p_i$.

4.5 Table of Contents

The table of contents is defined in the form of an adjacency list. An entry with no link to a scene is defined with a reference to a label `REFresID` and a `contentsNodeID`. An entry with a link to a scene is defined in a similar way:

```
<contents REFactionID=''load-NSc_4''
REFresID=''l_t_TI_6'' contentsNodeID=''TI_6''/>
```

Only the reference to an action-ID is added to refer to the scene which has to be loaded. If an entry is a leaf of the tree structure, no further lines are added. Sub-nodes are added with a reference to another node if the entry is an internal node. The definition of the table of contents can be found in the set $\mathcal{TOC}_\mathcal{V}$ in function 15. The labels of the entries are defined as set $\mathcal{I}$ in function 15. The adjacency list of a node is defined as a subset of $\mathcal{E}$. Entries without a link to a scene are defined as $(descr, null)$, entries with a link are defined as $(descr, p_i)$.

4.6 Keyword Search

Keywords listed in the `index`-element are arranged in a list structure where every entry of the main list has a sub-list. The main list consists of keyword-elements `<keyword word=...>`. Each of the keywords has a sub-list with elements of the video matching the keyword. The scene is loaded and played from the beginning, if the user selects the entry in the search results page. If an annotation matches the keyword, the player starts at the point in time of a scene where the annotation is displayed. The formal definition can be found in set $\mathcal{S}_\mathcal{V}$ in function 17.

4.7 Reflection

Our approach was to define "interactive non-linear video" formally first and then derive an XML format from this definition. We think this approach is valid, because the formality leads to a precise specification of the structure and possible forms of interaction in interactive non-linear videos. The formalisms narrow down the definition of XML formats and player functions. Algorithms for download and cache management can be defined using the same formalism [11]. The XML format is event-based and provides simple time synchronization. Furthermore it is defined as XSD, which supports accuracy by the definition of constraints. The format itself is easy to extend because of its high level of modularity. Because of the locality of the elements, single XML files are easy to extend, too (for example in case of collaborative editing functions in a player).

5. CONCLUSION

We introduced a formal definition of interactive non-linear video with additional information in this work. In order to be able to transform this formal definition into practice, we defined an XML schema for interactive non-linear videos. The formal definition is stated and explained. Instead of describing the XML schema, an example is shown with all elements that can be used in it. The elements from the XML file are linked to the formal definition.

Future work includes the extension of definition and XML schema for quizzes that may replace a simple button panel. This kind of extension is useful for the control of the learning progress in e-learning. It may also be necessary to invoke interactive annotations with sounds of other input devices (not only by clicking a button) in new usage scenarios. The evaluation of Boolean expressions consisting of parts of a history of user interactions are taken into account for further navigation in the video. This will be refined by the definition of priorities for annotations. A future goal is the implementation of collaborative elements.

6. ACKNOWLEDGMENTS

This work was partially supported by European Social Fonds and the Bayrisches Staatsministerium für Wissenschaft, Forschung und Kunst (Bavarian State Ministry of Sciences, Research and the Arts) under project names "iVi-Pro" and "iVi-Pro 2.0". We thank Martin Schmettow and Beate Siegel for their contributions to this work.

7. REFERENCES

[1] M. Antonacci, D. Muchaluat-Saade, R. Rodrigues, and S. L.F.G. Improving the expressiveness of xml-based hypermedia authoring languages. In *Proc. of the Multimedia Modeling Conference 2000*, pages 71–88, Nagano, Japan, 2000.

[2] D. C. Bulterman and L. W. Rutledge. *SMIL 3.0: Flexible Multimedia for Web, Mobile Devices and Daisy Talking Books.* Springer Publishing Company, Incorporated, 2nd ed. edition, 2008.

[3] D. C. A. Bulterman. Using smil to encode interactive, peer-level multimedia annotations. In *Proc. of the 2003 ACM Symp. on Document Engineering*, DocEng '03, pages 32–41, New York, NY, USA, 2003. ACM.

[4] F. Cazenave, V. Quint, and C. Roisin. Timesheets.js: when smil meets html5 and css3. In *Proc. of the 11th ACM Symposium on Document Engineering*, DocEng '11, pages 43–52, New York, NY, USA, 2011. ACM.

[5] R. M. de Resende Costa, M. F. Moreno, R. F. Rodrigues, and L. F. G. Soares. Live editing of hypermedia documents. In *Proceedings of the 2006 ACM Symposium on Document Engineering*, DocEng '06, pages 165–172, New York, NY, USA, 2006. ACM.

[6] R. Hammoud. Introduction to interactive video. In R. Hammoud, editor, *Interactive video: algorithms and technologies*, Signals and communication technology, pages 3–25. Springer, 2006.

[7] J. Jansen and D. C. Bulterman. Enabling adaptive time-based web applications with smil state. In *Proceedings of the eighth ACM Symposium on Document Engineering*, DocEng '08, pages 18–27, New York, NY, USA, 2008. ACM.

[8] J. Jansen and D. C. Bulterman. Smil state: an architecture and implementation for adaptive time-based web applications. *Multimedia Tools Appl.*, 43(3):203–224, July 2009.

[9] J. Jansen, P. Cesar, and D. C. Bulterman. A model for editing operations on active temporal multimedia documents. In *Proceedings of the 10th ACM Symposium on Document Engineering*, DocEng '10, pages 87–96, New York, NY, USA, 2010. ACM.

[10] P. King, P. Schmitz, and S. Thompson. Behavioral reactivity and real time programming in xml: functional programming meets smil animation. In *Proceedings of the 2004 ACM Symposium on Document Engineering*, DocEng '04, pages 57–66, New York, NY, USA, 2004. ACM.

[11] B. Meixner and J. Hoffmann. Intelligent download and cache management for interactive non-linear video. *Multimedia Tools and Applications*, 2012. to appear.

[12] B. Meixner, B. Siegel, G. Hölbling, F. Lehner, and H. Kosch. Siva suite: authoring system and player for interactive non-linear videos. In *Proceedings of the International Conference on Multimedia*, MM '10, pages 1563–1566, New York, NY, USA, 2010. ACM.

[13] Moving Picture Experts Group. Mpeg-7 overview. Website, October 2004. (accessed January 14, 2012).

[14] D. C. Muchaluat-Saade, R. F. Rodrigues, and L. F. G. Soares. Xconnector: extending xlink to provide multimedia synchronization. In *Proc. of the 2002 ACM Symposium on Document Engineering*, DocEng '02, pages 49–56, New York, NY, USA, 2002. ACM.

[15] K. Pihkala and P. Vuorimaa. Nine methods to extend smil for multimedia applications. *Multimedia Tools Appl.*, 28(1):51–67, Jan. 2006.

[16] L. F. G. Soares and R. F. Rodrigues. Nested context model 3.0: Part 1 - ncm core. Website/Technical Report, 2005. (accessed January 15, 2012).

[17] M. K. Stenzler and R. R. Eckert. Interactive video. *SIGCHI Bull.*, 28:76–81, April 1996.

[18] M. F. Ursu, J. J. Cook, V. Zsombori, R. Zimmer, I. Kegel, D. Williams, M. Thomas, J. Wyver, and H. Mayer. Conceiving shapeshifting tv: a computational language for truly-interactive tv. In *Proceedings of the 5th European Conference on Interactive TV: a shared experience*, EuroITV'07, pages 96–106, Berlin, Heidelberg, 2007. Springer-Verlag.

[19] R. Vaisenberg, R. Jain, and S. Mehrotra. Smpl, a specification based framework for the semantic structure, annotation and control of smil documents. In *Multimedia, 2009. ISM '09. 11th IEEE Intl. Symposium on*, pages 533 –539, dec. 2009.

[20] W3C. Synchronized Multimedia Integration Language (SMIL 3.0). Website, December 2008. (accessed January 14, 2012).

[21] W3C. Html5: A vocabulary and associated apis for html and xhtml, w3c working draft 25 may 2011. Website, May 2011. (accessed January 15, 2012).

Just-in-Time Personalized Video Presentations

Jack Jansen[1], Pablo Cesar[1], Rodrigo Laiola Guimaraes[1,2], Dick C.A. Bulterman[1,2]

[1]CWI: Centrum Wiskunde & Informatica, Amsterdam, NL   [2]VU University, Amsterdam, NL

jack.jansen@cwi.nl, p.s.cesar@cwi.nl, rlaiola@cwi.nl, dick.bulterman@cwi.nl

ABSTRACT

Using high-quality video cameras on mobile devices, it is relatively easy to capture a significant volume of video content for community events such as local concerts or sporting events. A more difficult problem is selecting and sequencing individual media fragments that meet the personal interests of a viewer of such content. In this paper, we consider an infrastructure that supports the just-in-time delivery of personalized content. Based on user profiles and interests, tailored video mash-ups can be created at view-time and then further tailored to user interests via simple end-user interaction. Unlike other mash-up research, our system focuses on client-side compilation based on personal (rather than aggregate) interests. This paper concentrates on a discussion of language and infrastructure issues required to support just-in-time video composition and delivery. Using a high school concert as an example, we provide a set of requirements for dynamic content delivery. We then provide an architecture and infrastructure that meets these requirements. We conclude with a technical and user analysis of the just-in-time personalized video approach.

Categories and Subject Descriptors

D.3.2 [**Language Classifications**]: Specialized application languages; I.7.2 [**Document and Text Processing**] Document Preparation - Languages and systems.

General Terms

Design, Experimentation, Standardization, Languages.

Keywords

Video mashups, late binding of media, seamless playback.

1. INTRODUCTION

When considered as a document, a video is distributed as a compressed, read-only object. During production, the video is assembled from available source content during the editing phase. It is then compressed for storage and transfer efficiency, and made available as an on-line community video as a block downloadable media item, or incrementally as a streaming media object. The nature of video shifts any significant amount of content

personalization to the creation phase: if viewer A and viewer B are interested in different content aspects, they traditionally require separate video objects.

One approach to providing more personalized presentations of a single event is to supply a few video feeds in parallel, giving the viewer an opportunity to select a vantage point of interest. This is an approach already in use for live sports events, and it could be applied to other public events, both live and pre-recorded, such as popular concerts. Given an appropriate user interface, a viewer could take on the role of a director and select the shot of greatest personal interest. This approach is limited by the number of cameras used and the transfer bandwidth available.

Our work considers another approach to video personalization. We examine a model in which many cameras are available as sources (which may cover only short sections of the event, and more than feasibly could be broadcast in parallel) and in which a viewer is offered the ability to select a particular view based on not only camera positioning, but also on personal affinity with the content of the video. We consider a high school music concert in which parents record fragments of the event. By combining all of the media objects captured and then analyzing the contents, we allow an interested viewer to obtain a personalized presentation that focuses on individual performers or instruments. The main motivation to watch this content is not the musical quality of the event, but the strong personal bonds that exist with the performers. These bonds are highly partitioned: in general, the family and friends of, say, the trombone player will be interested primarily in content related to this person, while other performers (such as the clarinet player) may have an essentially disjoint community of interested viewers. This means that for each sub-community, separate personalized presentations will be required. Even within a sub-community, viewers will have different interests (and tolerances) to the concert content: some will want to see all of the footage involving their performer of interest, while others will be more than satisfied with a few key fragments. In essence, this shifts content selection within a video object to the consumption phase of video viewing. We refer to this approach as *just-in-time content personalization,* since the media content to be shown is determined by the context of the viewer and his/her interaction while viewing the media.

This paper focuses on the language and real-time processing required to support dynamic just-in-time content personalization. We consider a video to be an incremental electronic document in which follow-on fragments are determined dynamically. While other work describes the selection of appropriate source material based on user preferences and media annotations [23] or the general application of dynamic video selection [8], this paper concentrates on the infrastructure needed to dynamically assemble and render the presentation as a seamless video document.

The contribution of this paper is an architecture that enables the presentation of dynamic just-in-time media content. We describe the requirements for such a system, the processing architecture needed for client-side selectivity, and our implementation experience. We also summarize the results of user tests that help determine the viability of our approach.

This paper is structured as follows: section 2 provides an overview of our user-case scenario and the requirements for our work. Section 3 gives a brief overview of approaches that enable end-user customization of video content. Sections 4 and 5 describe the design and implementation for our approach. Section 6 describes the results of our work, including both a technical and user analysis of our results. Section 7 concludes with thoughts for broader applicability and future work.

2. SCENARIO AND REQUIREMENTS

During the past decade, the wide introduction of video capture devices has enabled video to become a ubiquitous method for documenting shared events. At the same time, any one video has not really become a ubiquitous method of presenting a shared events because it provides only a single point of view: that of its creator.

2.1 Classifying Community Events

In this paper, we focus on support for relatively personal events. In particular, we study asynchronous communication and scenarios in which groups of people are motivated to edit and share audiovisual material over extended time periods. Unlike many collaborative editing systems, the primary purpose of the content sharing is not the publishing of a collective common work, but the provision of highlighting the roles of individuals within a shared event.

Our use case, which we call *MyVideos[1]*, centers around a musical performance of young high school students. At the concert the audience consists of parents and friends of the performers, many of whom capture the event using video. After the concert, all video material is collected, preprocessed for temporal alignment, analyzed for appearance of performers, instruments and shot types and stored in a database called the *Vault*. Once this has been done, the material is made available to the interested parties for browsing, sharing and viewing through a specialized MyVideos web application, shown in Figure 1. The MyVideos application allows access to recorded material in a number of different ways, ranging from a rather traditional browse and assemble interface to having a presentation generated fully automatically by the system.

In this article we are interested in the latter view option, called the *Interactive Narrative*. The system provides an initial baseline presentation based on the viewer's preferences and relationship to the performers. This baseline presentation can then be altered - while watching - based on user input.

A viewing sequence starts with an initialization phase in which a particular viewing session contacts the *Narrative Engine*, requesting an initial playlist of video fragments and audios. The design and implementation of the narrative engine are out of the scope for this article, they can be found in [23], here we provide a summary useful for understanding the contribution of this paper. The Narrative Engine has access to metadata for all available clips, including performers and instruments featuring in each clip,

esthetically pleasing in and out points and cinematographic shot type such as wide angle or closeup. In addition, the Narrative Engine has a profile for the user, so it knows which performers or instruments the viewer is interested in. This data is fed into a rule-based engine which compiles a story from the relevant clips. The resultant compilation is sent back to the client application, which is in charge of rendering it to the viewer.

2.2 Requirements for Just-In-Time Videos

The narrative engine provides the web-based user client with a dynamic playlist of video clips that are refined continuously based on user feedback. From this perspective of this paper, our problem can be formulated as: *can we enable an external agent to do late composition of audio and video material while still maintaining a seamless playback experience for the viewer?* This problem can be broken down into two distinct requirements:

- combining audio and video material from multiple sources in such as way that it plays back identical as it would have done had the combination been done statically, and

- ensuring that the material for the next shot is available sufficiently in advance so that we can satisfy the previous requirement.

There is also a key interaction requirement:

- Through a series of user evaluations and user studies, we have determined that most viewer want a *lean-back* control experience, in which they provide broad guidance on interests rather than a *lean-forward* experience, where the user actively browses and selects individual items.

To maintain the lean-back experience within the context of the first two requirements, the interactions will not have an immediate effect (such as a channel change or switching to a different YouTube video would have), but they will influence the material selected in the near future. Figure 2 shows a screenshot of video playback, with two interaction buttons. Note that having the buttons on-screen is a choice made for this implementation. In a production system it would be better to have the buttons on a secondary screen, or at least make them less intrusive. This is purely a presentation choice, it makes no difference to the structure of the application.

3. BACKGROUND AND RELATED

Figure 1. MyVideos web application user interface.

---

[1] MyVideos is a use case with the FP7 Project TA2: Together Any- where, Together Anytime. See: http://ta2project.eu

WORK

The contribution of this paper is a document model and a design that allows for just-in-time video presentations. In a sense, this work on be video as an on-demand instance of a *video mash-up*: a custom video projection of a shared event based on community assets. The primary difference of our approach is that we shift the customization phase of the mash-up production to the client side at viewing time, rather than to a source side at production time. In order to provide a general context for our work, this section reviews related research in the areas of community-based mashups and rich multimedia document models.

3.1 Community-Based Storytelling

Research on community-based video mashups has primarily focused on content analysis for searching purposes. Kennedy and Naaman [11] describe a system for synchronizing and organizing user-contributed content from live music events, creating an improved representation of the event that builds on the automatic content match. Shrestha et al. [17], report on an application for creating mashup videos from YouTube recordings of concerts. They present a number of content management mechanisms (e.g., temporal alignment and content quality assessment) that then are used for creating a multi-camera mashup. Results indicate that the final videos are perceived almost as if created from a professional video editor. Unlike our work, however, the resulting mashup is not dynamic but a static conventional media object. (Multiple objects are required to capture alternative story lines.) Shaw et el. [16], explore the creation of videos by remixing existing assets in a database, focusing on the human aspects and reporting on how final videos were created. More recent work has proposed a media sharing application that takes into account the interpersonal ties. This tool is capable of producing presentations shows based on events, people, locations, and time [18]. In comparison to our work, these applications do not use a client-side facility for compiling stories during viewing.

Various AI approaches for interactive storytelling have been suggested in the past decade. One representative example is Vox Populi [1], in which rhetorical documentaries are created from a pool of media fragments. More recently, a system capable of creating different story variants from a baseline video was presented and evaluated [14]. In comparison to our work, these articles only focused on the quality of the final story (in narrative terms), without taking into consideration the underlying document model, the performance, and the rendering issues. Based on our design guidelines, the work reported in this article is applicable to any third-party narrative engine, enabling a robust delivering and rendering environment.

Figure 2. Video Playback, with interaction

3.2 Mashups in Multimedia Documents

Structured multimedia documents provide support for mashups, as the composition of sequential video fragments with an external audio track. Such models were traditional rather static, in which the media items to be included were known in advance not meeting the requirements impose by our problem space. Recently, additions to the standards are intended for extending the flexibility and dynamism of the models, as we will detail in this section.

NCL (Nested Context Language) [19] is the standard XML-based application language for defining interactive multimedia presentations in the Brazilian Terrestrial Digital TV System (SBTVD-T). In NCL, authors can take advantage of its high-level constructs to describe, in a declarative manner, the temporal behavior of a multimedia presentation. Authors can as well associate hyperlinks with media objects, define alternatives for presentation, and describe the layout of the presentation on multiple devices. Moreover, NCL provides support for imperative scripts in order to extend its computational power [20]. Unlike HTML and Flash, NCL has a strict separation between the document's content and structure, and it provides non-invasive control of presentation linking and layout. This means that an NCL player can be used to render (portions of) videos in the context of a video mash-up, and to control the timing and rendering properties of in such a way that potentially the videos can be displayed seamlessly.

While some investigations have been reported on dynamic content insertion, support for generalized dynamic modifications of a running presentation are restricted. Some works target for dynamism by allowing commenting and annotating user generated videos [5], but without changing the actual video being played. Other works [4] propose a method for live editing of NCL programs, preserving not only the presentation semantics but also the logical structure semantics defined by a professional author. In their solution a void media placeholder was inserted in the presentation, which then could be modified in real-time by a third party. We follow a similar method in our work, but go one step further since in our case we cannot predict the time at which the presentation ought to be modified, nor the number of elements and their duration.

SMIL (Synchronized Multimedia Integration Language) [2] is another example of a structured multimedia document model that can be used a content container within our scenario. Similarly to NCL, SMIL provides temporal and synchronization constructs for the creation (and adaptation) of complex multimedia presentations. The inclusion of SMIL State [9,10] provided support for dynamic variables in running multimedia presentations. In our work we take advantage of such functionality showing it usefulness for rather complex scenarios.

Document engineering research has investigated the problem of dynamically generating and adapting documents. The terminologies come in different flavors depending on the target domain: just-in-time, real time, live editing etc. For example, King et al. [12] presented a set of document extensions that may dynamically react to continuously varying inputs, both in a continuous way and by triggering discrete, user-defined, events. Such extensions are discussed and realized in the context of SMIL Animation and SVG, but could be applied to many XML-based languages. Our work differs from the one described in [12], whose main target is animation. Also related to our work, Zhang et al. [22] provided a general solution to supplementing virtual documents from third party applications with just-in-time hypermedia support, utilizing dynamic regeneration, re-identification and re-location. One key difference is the fact that in our case the document temporal model plays a major role, as we focus on temporal operations that do not destroy the running timegraph of the presentation.

3.3 Mashups in Video Sharing Systems

In YouTube (and other commercial systems), dynamic mashups are not supported. End-users have to find suitable source material, cut it into shots, and assemble an encoded final video. While this solution does not impose hard requirements on delivery and rendering, it is limited in terms of adaptability and user interaction.

One solution might be the use of playlists in such environments, which are typically supported using Flash or HTML5. However, since the smallest granularity of a playlist is an entire video, mash-ups are only possible if, and only if, the videos are processed in such a way that the end point of the previous video matches the start point of the following one. Unfortunately, YouTube does not allow for seamless playback, since for each video of a playlist the Web page is reloaded. In other words, the application envisioned in this article is not possible to be implemented in existing commercial video sharing systems.

4. *MyVideos* CLIENT DESIGN

The design of the MyVideos application was driven by the three requirements sketched in section 2. The application is segregated into three major components: the MyVideos web interface, the Narrative Engine and the playback component. The Narrative Engine is implemented as a web server, where the other two components send their requests. There are basically three types of requests: *get-first-playlist*, *get-new-playlist* and *user-interaction*. The first two return a playlist that contains information on the media required within the following 20 seconds (approximately). The third one does not return any information, but is used to inform the Narrative Engine that some user interaction has happened, which the engine can then use to modify the playlist returned in the subsequent get-new-playlist call.

The playlist is explained in more detail in section 5, here it suffices to note that it does not contain absolute playout timing information, only an ordered list of media clips, in-points and out-points. Layout and presentation information is also not part of this playlist. This isolates the Narrative Engine from the details of multimedia composition, scheduling and playback, these are now the responsibility of the playback component.

The central aspect of this work is supporting the playback quality requirement in section 2: we need a playback engine that can seamlessly play back audio and video segments that come from different sources. Seamless switching from one video clip to the next is a difficult problem, especially if the clips come in over the network, and the in-point for the destination clip need not be on an I-frame. A complete description of the problem and solution for the case when the media items are known a priori can be found in [6, 7]. To summarize here, seamless switching requires:

- a mechanism to open, seek and prefetch clips before they are needed,
- scheduled control over switching from one clip to the next.

Taken together, these requirements point in the direction of a solution that uses a *timegraph*. Languages that treat media items as isolated timed islands in a sea of scripting, such as HTML5, do not allow the tight control from the second requirement.

From [7] we can learn that using SMIL as the multimedia format addresses the quality requirement, but for our dynamic use case this introduces a new problem: we now need to dynamically update the active SMIL document with information that is not known a priori. Moreover, we need to do these dynamic updates in such a way that we maintain the seamless playback. Please note that although we say here that this problem is introduced by our use of SMIL this does not mean that the choice of SMIL is a bad one: if we had chosen HTML5 as the basic format we would have faced a similar problem that was only different in the details, because in HTML5 the functionality of the timegraph will have to be encoded in a procedural scripting language.

When we modify the media items in the SMIL presentation, we need to make sure that our modifications do not affect the timegraph structure. In [10], the authors have presented a taxonomy of editing operations on active multimedia documents. We reproduce the table from that document here as Table 1. If we apply this taxonomy to our requirements it should be clear that operations from the *Selection* and *Adaptation* clusters are not sufficient for the problem at hand. Therefore, we need to come up with a design that uses operations from the *MediaItem* cluster only, and specifically operations from that cluster that do not lead to timegraph modifications. It turns out that we we cannot add (or remove) media nodes from the timegraph, we cannot modify `begin`, `end` or `dur` attributes of existing media nodes, we can only modify `src`, `clipBegin` and `clipEnd` of existing items.

These observations have led to a design with a carrousel-like structure in the SMIL presentation, with the individual media items in the carrousel being taken from SMIL State objects. The SMIL code now simply loops over the carrousel continuously. Now we only need to design one more bit of functionality: obtaining playlist data from the Narrative Engine and inserting it into the SMIL State objects, and communicating user interaction to the Narrative Engine. This is handled by the *Carousel Assistant*. It communicates user interactions to the Narrative

Table 1 - Taxonomy of Document Transformations ([10])

Selection cluster	Selection among predefined media items. It does not affect the time graph of the presentation.
Adaptation cluster	Modification of the style or layout composition. They do not affect the time graph of the presentation.
MediaItem cluster	Modification of the content of a media item. They might affect the time graph of the presentation.
Structural cluster	Modification of the temporal composition (add/remove item). They must recompute the temporal graph.

Figure 3. Flow of the presentation.

Engine as they occur, and periodically contacts the Narrative Engine to obtain new playlists. The data from these playlists is then inserted into the SMIL State variables.

The user-perceived temporal flow of the presentation is outlined in figure 3. The pre-concert section is a short set of clips meant to communicate the atmosphere of the concert: people greeting friends and finding seats, instruments being setup, etc. Not coincidentally, we also present the user with the initial set of interaction buttons during this pre-concert section. Close to the end of the pre-concert section we disable the interaction buttons and request a playlist from the narrative engine, which we then present as the first concert section. Again, close to the end of the concert section we disable the interaction (if any), and request the next playlist. This continues until the narrative engine decides to wrap things up in the conclusion section. This is played and the presentation ends.

The overall structure and the data flow is sketched in Figure 4. (1) shows how user interaction is communicated to the Narrative Engine. (2) shows the Narrative Engine selecting clips for playback. (3) and (4) show how media clip references pass from the Narrative Engine to rendering. (5) shows how the media data flows. Note that the Carousel Assistant is always the client (active agent) in the communication with the Narrative Engine. This is in line with the requirement that the Narrative Engine has no realtime requirements. In an earlier prototype we had the Narrative Engine responsible for actively delivering new playlists to the playback engine, which meant it did have limited realtime requirements. This led to problems when the playlist did not arrive in time.

5. IMPLEMENTATION

In this section we will examine the implementation of the client components of Figure 4. This includes an extension of the Ambulant Player[2] and a Carousel Assistant implemented in Python.

For the SMIL player we have selected the Ambulant Player. The player is an open source implementation of a SMIL 3.0 compliant player. The player includes a parser for the XML file, an scheduler for deciding when nodes become active and inactive, a layout manager for compositing different media items, and a DOM tree that stores the logical structure of the document. Moreover, Ambulant provides native media renderers for handling the media items and uses datasources for retrieving the actual data (e.g., video) included in the presentation. Ambulant is extensible,

allowing us to explore complex scenarios, like the one presented in this paper.

By extending Ambulant, a number of requirements for just-in-time multimedia mashups have been met. More specifically:

- *Sequential ordering*: SMIL has a temporal construct (in particular <seq>) for supporting playback of dynamically generated playlists.

- *Synchronization*: there is a need to synchronize different media elements (<par>). In particular, interaction components (such as buttons) need to be synchronized with active video elements

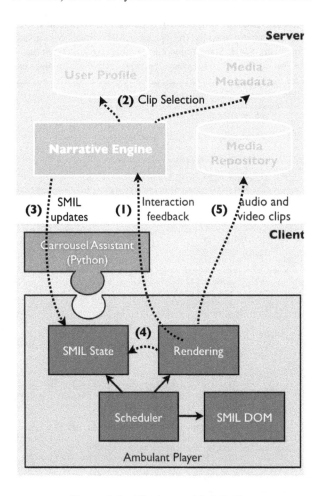

Figure 4. Architecture, with data flow.

---

[2] http://ambulantplayer.org/

during playback. By using SMIL, the narrative engine does not need to provide hard synchronization values (timestamps), but only relative synchronization structures (activate this interaction 2 seconds after such video has started).

- *Interaction*: the use case requires interaction capabilities, so users can interact in real time, while watching a story. In this case, XML interactive elements (`<submission>`) are supported by the rendering engine.
- *Seamless cuts*: there is a need to provide seamless playback of media items for offering an immersive experience to the user. In this case, the rendering engine supports elements such as `<prefetch>`, that have been extended for media fragments rendering.

In addition, a number of practical considerations are addressed:

- *Interfaces*: the presentations need to for interface to an external engine. In this case, the rendering engine needs to interface with the narrative engine (Carousel Assistant), which will dynamically provide the most adequate playlists for being rendered.
- *Dynamism*: the application depends on dynamic changes on presentations while they are active. In particular, the rendering engine supports SMIL State for managing changes without affecting the overall performance of the presentation, and without breaking the active timegraph.

The basic structure of the SMIL document is outlined in Figure 5. The document heavily relies on SMIL State for allowing dynamism. SMIL State allows for variable-like structures that will not be evaluated until they become active, allowing us to

```
<smil>
  <head>
    <state xmlns=''>
      <ta2>
        <videoplayed>0</videoplayed>
        ...
        <playlist>
          ...
          <videoItem>
            <url>http://.../clip1.mp4</url>
            <begin>5.2s</begin>
            <end>7.2s</end>
          </videoItem>
          ...
        </playlist>
        <prefetch>
          <prefetchItem>
            <url>http://.../clip4.mp4</url>
            <begin>22.0s</begin>
            <end>24.0s</end>
          </prefetchItem>
        </prefetch>
        ...
  <body>
    ...
    <seq repeatCount="indefinite">
      ...
      <par>
        <video src='{playlist/videoItem[4]/url}'
          clipBegin='{playlist/videoItem[4]/begin}'
          clipEnd='{playlist/videoItem[4]/end}'/>
        <prefetch
          src='{prefetch/prefetchItem[4]/url}'

clipBegin='{prefetch/prefetchItem[4]/begin}'
          clipEnd='{prefetch/prefetchItem[4]/end}'/>
      </par>
      <setvalue name="videoplayed" value="4"/>
```

Figure 5. Relevant sections of SMIL document

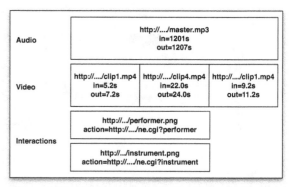

Figure 6. Playlist data as generated by Narrative Engine.

instantiate them as the Narrative Engine send subsequent playlists compilations.

The state of the document includes information about the current element that is played, links to which interactions at a given moment will make HTTP requests, and instantiations of the parameters of the videos (and audios) that compose the presentation. All these values (and the number of them) are not known at the time of creating the SMIL document, but will be filled in by the Carousel Assistant by interacting with the Narrative Engine.

The body of the document is a carousel: an infinite loop of video and audio structures. Since the number of videos that compose a compilation is unknown, we have created a list-like structure that will iteratively be repeated until the compilation is finished. In this structure, we include the video fragment to be played and a prefetch instruction for the next video fragment. The particular values are stored in the SMIL State section and being dynamically updated. This general structure is robust in terms of timing: (1) we assure that video fragments will be played sequentially and (2) we address the requirement of seamless playback (QoE). The body includes as well the audio elements (not shown in Figure 5), which use a similar structure as the video elements (item + prefetch next item). In the scenario, the audio to be be played is not the one embedded in the video file. Different cameras (and in different positions) will create perceptible audio changes, thus disturbing the quality of experience. In this case, SMIL allows for parallel constructs for synchronizing audio and video fragments. Moreover, interactions (not shown in the Figure) can be as well synchronized with specific video clips, thanks to the SMIL language.

Finally, `<setvalue>` allows the body of the document (rendering engine) to communicate with the Carousel Assistant. When a video structure has been played, a SMIL State variable (`videoplayed`) is updated, which triggers a function of the Carousel Assistant.

We have implemented the Carousel Assistant in Python. The Ambulant Player support extension modules in either C++ or Python, and for the task at hand Python seemed like the obvious choice. Ambulant extension modules have access to the complete internal API of the Ambulant Player, but because we have chosen to stick to the MediaItem cluster of operations (as per [10]) we only use the APIs to access the SMIL State portion of the document. This will guarantee that we do not modify the timegraph, which is one of the requirements for maintaining seamless playback.

The main entry points into the Carousel Assistant are SMIL State callbacks. The SMIL document is set up in such a way that it modifies SMIL State variables every time something interesting happens: (a) a video element has finished playback, (b) an audio element has finished playback, or (c) user has done an interaction.

The Carousel Assistant has requested callbacks for changes on any of these variables. However, as the operations that need to happen on the basis of these events may involve communicating to the Narrative Engine the operations are not executed inline, but instead a second thread is signaled, which will then implement the operation. The main thread immediately returns to the SMIL player so it can continue processing without further delay.

For video and audio elements finishing, the Carousel Assistant checks how many more elements are left in the currently playing playlist. Depending on this, it decides whether to contact the Narrative Engine for a new playlist (when the previous to last item has been played), otherwise it does nothing. The Narrative Engine returns the next playlist as a JSON data structure. The contents of this data structure are sketched in Figure 6. The data structure includes a complete new playlist with an audio fragment, a set of video fragments, and a number of interactions. Consecutive data structures (playlists) form the full interactive story the Narrative Engine generates.

The audio fragment and the video fragments provide the source (URL) together with the in and out points; the interactions include information about the representation (image), the synchronization parameters (relative to the videos), and the action (as HTTP requests to the Narrative Engine).

The Carousel Assistant implements an infinite buffer, in which all these data structures are stored. When a new playlist (as in Figure 6) is received, it calculates where the the elements should be updated in the SMIL State section (it knows the number of videos played so far, and the length of the playing playlist). The values included in the JSON data structure update the following video items, audio items, and interaction items ensuring a concatenation

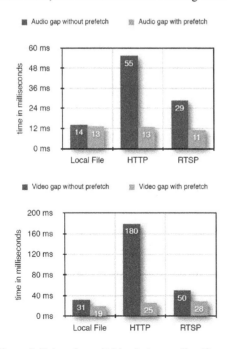

Figure 7. Delays for switching between clips (from [6])

of playlists, and that these are played seamlessly from the end-user perspective.

For interaction events the Carousel Assistant has to do very little: the Narrative Engine has earlier supplied all the data it wants in case of a user selection and this data has been recorded in the SMIL State (action of the interaction). When an interaction event happens the assistant simply communicates this data to the Narrative Engine through an HTTP request. Nothing is returned: the Narrative Engine will use this data to update its internal data structures, which will influence the next playlist it supplies to the Carousel Assistant.

The implementation presented in this section supports complex and rich media rendering (and interactions). The complexity, in comparison to previous work, is based on the high-level of dynamism enforced by our scenario. It supports synchronization of video fragments, interactive elements, and audio components. Moreover, the number of playlists that will be rendered (and their duration) is unknown in advance, so void media placeholders are of little use (we do not know how many of them we will need). Finally, each playlist is composed of an audio element, an interactive element, and an unknown number of video elements. As a result a highly flexible and dynamic implementation, as the one reported in this section, is needed.

6. RESULTS
The work described in this article is evaluated from three different perspectives: seamless playback performance, dynamic composition performance, and the user experience. First, we evaluate the playback aspects of the system, showing that at playback time the delays between consequent video items is minimal. From the document model angle, we provide a set of timegraphs that show how our decision of using a rich multimedia model provide a robust solution for complex multimedia applications, meeting the timing and synchronization constraints required for the use case. Finally, we explore the QoE of our implementation. User evaluations of our application indicate high user satisfaction.

6.1 Seamless Playback
In terms of performance, the use case described in this paper is highly demanding, since media transitions between fragments need to be seamless. First, audio files need to be lip-sync with incoming video clips (even more when dealing with a music concert). Second, video clips do not necessarily start from the beginning (`clipBegin`), which requires a seek operation within the videos. Third, the sequence of video clips need to be played seamless, as if it was a pre-compiled video.

Previous research, more fully described in [6], has investigated the behavior of our playback engine with predetermined media items. Figure 7 shows clip switching delays from [6], here we are interested in the case of delivery over HTTP: delays as low as 13 ms for audio and 25 ms for video,. These are almost non-perceptible.

6.2 Dynamic Composition
The timing and synchronization constraints of just-in-time multimedia mashups are relatively high, when compared to previous works in rich multimedia document models [15]. The complexity resides on the dynamic and non-predictive nature of the application. Typically, multimedia document models allow for compositing media items with variable duration coming from different sources. This allows the rendering of synchronized

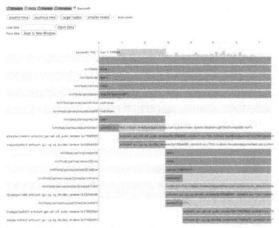

Figure 8. Visualisation of the runtime activity of a just-in-time multimedia mashup

media items (e.g., videos + extra material), which are reactive to user interaction. Nevertheless, the media items to be included in the application are known when packaging the presentation. More advanced research [4] explores the possibility of dynamically changing pre-existing media placeholders, thus allowing for live-editing of multimedia documents.

In our case, the constraints go one step further. The requirement here is to provide a robust solution that allows for dynamic changes in a running multimedia presentation. These changes are applied to active elements of the presentation (the video being played) and are not predictable. We cannot know in advance when the new playlists are to be inserted, we do not know their length, and we do not know the number of videos that they will contain. First, we have to composite media items from different sources in a synchronized manner (video + audio + interactions). Second, we need to provide as well support for lip-sync synchronization between these video clips and the audio track.

The results of the previous subsection are for statically known media items, so the next step is to show that our carrousel-based dynamic composition model does not introduce extra delays. In the process of determining these delays we realized that this is actually an instance of a much more general problem: if a multimedia presentation exhibits a different runtime scheduling pattern than what is expected, the author or maintainer needs to determine what causes this different behavior. This is because the

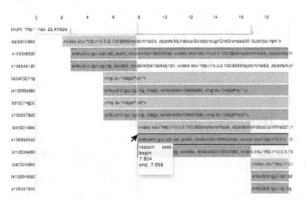

Figure 9. Visualising reason for presentation stall

reasons can be manyfold: mis-specified synchronization requirements, network overload, decoding overload, etc.

We decided to create a tool for multimedia playback that operates similar to what a multithreaded profiler does for programmers: show relevant execution data in a visual way to allow the author to quickly determine what the problem is. The tool is implemented as a plugin that is started the moment our multimedia player starts a presentation. The tool is reactive to dynamic modifications to the running presentation, as it shows the current internal state of the player. It visualizes various playback aspects at rendering time: bandwidth usage, timing and synchronization information, and current status of the XML elements (active, non-active).

To facilitate the visualizer, we instrumented the Ambulant Player to provide performance data. A raw performance data item consists of

- begin and end time,
- event type such as "element playing" or "element playback stalled",
- parameters such as bandwidth consumed, or reason for stall.

These raw events are sent, in realtime, to the visualizer running in a browser window. Figure 8 shows an overview of the visualization after a MyVideos document has been playing for eight seconds[3]. We can see all the information regarding playback, including scheduling, bandwidth use and SMIL State information. Note that we see actual behavior, including unintentional delays and such. We can see the behavior of the different elements in the presentation (darker color indicates that an element has been started). In addition, we can see peaks on bandwidth allocation due to just-in-time prefetching, and red bands denote unintentional stalls. The user can interact with the data, for example by selecting items to see why it stalls, to hide certain node types, etc.

As figure 8 shows the visualization of an actual MyVideos run that does not stall we have also created a MyVideos document without the prefetch elements to facilitate seamless playback. Playback of this document incurred a 0.2 second stall during the first transition. Figure 9 shows the user investigating this stall.

The use of the visualizer tool allows us to demonstrate that we can maintain seamless playback characteristics in documents that use dynamic composition.

6.3 User experience

In addition to evaluating the seamless playback capabilities offered by our prototype, we have evaluated the user experience in field trials with real users. In order to evaluate our prototype implementation, a set of parents from a high school in Woodbridge (UK) has actively collaborated with this research. Parents (together with some researchers) recorded a school concert of their kids in November 2011. The concert lasted around 1 hour and 20 minutes, in which 18 students performed in 14 songs. A total of twelve cameras were used to capture the concert. The master camera was placed in a fixed location, front and sideway to the stage, set to capture the entire scene (a 'wide' shot) with no camera movement and an external stereo microphone in a static location. Eight cameras were distributed among parents,

---

[3] The PDF version of the paper in the Digital Library allows zooming to see more detail in the image.

relatives, and friends of performers. Members of the research team used the other 3 cameras. In total about 331 raw video clips were captured, some of which were recorded before or after the event.

Between January and February 2012, a subset of parents was invited to evaluate our prototype application with the material recorded in that concert. Nine people (from five families) participated in the evaluation. The participants consisted of performers, parents and other relatives of the teenagers that performed in the Woodbridge school concert. All were English speakers and living in the UK. Five participant (~56%) were 40+ years old; the other four people were in the 11-20-age range, three of which performed in the concert. While the number of users might be considered as too small for drawing conclusive results, the set of users represents a realistic sample for our use case. Moreover, all the parents attended the school concert and recorded the video material that was used during the evaluation. We strongly believe that in this case realism balances group size, so results are valuable, significant, and representative.

We used multiple methods for data collection, including interaction with the prototype application, followed by questionnaires. Each session started with a brief description of the component, and participants were instructed to describe their experiences. Based on our observations, responses to the questionnaires, and analysis of the collected audio/video material from the interviews, we discuss the results and findings (see Figure 10).

Overall, participants liked the MyVideos application (Q01) and indicated it helps recalling memories of past social events (Q02). A majority of subjects (eight out of nine) also reported the system makes them feel more connected to the people featured in the videos (Q03). It is important to mention that even though all participants liked the system, this does not imply they would pay for MyVideos (Q04). Among the justifications users point out it would depend on the cost and frequency of use. These positive results, while valuable, could be due to the novelty of using a system that gives a better viewing experience that just playing a plain single video stream (which also would mean that we did a good job). The rest of the section is dedicated to analyze the subjective reactions and comments from the users, providing a more complete discussion on what users thought about the MyVideos application.

In particular, participants described the interaction with the Interactive Narrative component as relaxing and enjoyable.

It is more than just getting into that concert again. It was doing something completely different, almost like doing another activity. In itself, it was a fun thing to do... it is not just a utility software to give you the best impression of the concert, it allows you to have some fun as well. (Father of a performer)

In general, users mentioned the productions were visually compelling and had a good selection of cameras. Along these lines, one participant described the rich experience he had:

What I liked about that (Interactive Narrative) was that it started with a produced version and it almost felt we've gone up a level... it was more interesting somehow... .

and added

I liked the variety of cameras... when the shots came from there (another direction) it was really interesting because I

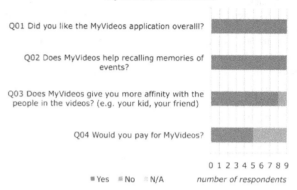

Figure 10. Results of the MyVideos evaluation.

was not even there (on that side of the audience). On TV they seem to switch every few seconds... and (with Interactive narrative) you are getting a similar experience to what you are used to... I felt this a little bit more immersive (than the Vault).

In addition, some users indicated this was a 'lazy' experience in which they would mainly sit and watch, and not interact often.

It is like the red button on TV... I've never clicked on it... but I would like (to use it).

Regarding the logical structure of narrative compilations, some users argued the playback of the pre concert material was disruptive and long. One participant suggested having a song selection interface before beginning the Interactive Narrative experience. Participants also complained about the lack of feedback in the user interface when they clicked on a button. This was a limitation of our implementation, which we plan to address in future work. In other occasions users mentioned that other forms of interaction also would be useful.

Some time ago the teacher said my daughter had problems with the (piano's) foot pedal... in a case like that it would be useful if we could say I am more interested on that specific part of the screen than any other shots of her. (Father of a performer)

Based on observations we also noticed that even though users understood their choices (e.g. give me more of this performer) would be realized later in the presentation, in some cases they were interested in immediate changes (e.g. switch camera angles). In future work we plan to further investigate how these different deadlines for interaction/updates impact the timegraph structure.

7. CONCLUSIONS AND IMPLICATIONS

Video sharing is a powerful mechanism for recording and documenting shared events. From our work it is clear, however, that simply providing access to a collection of content on-line is in and of itself not sufficient to support a personalized view of that event: such personalization required dynamic tailoring of content based on the context of view at the time the media is accessed.

As reported here, our attempts at just-in-time personalization provide a powerful model for content delivery. Support for this model requires careful engineering and adequate networking support. Both of these are technical issues that can be straightforwardly addressed. A more problematic aspect of this work is that -- from a practical perspective -- it requires a temporally-aware container document to host a skeleton incremental content document. In this respect, it is disappointing that recent trends in media deployment have favored a temporally-unaware model. Work with HTML5 [13] has demonstrated a desire to further compartmentalize (and thus marginalize) media content to become unstructured appendages to static document content.

In the future, lessons in including temporal synchronization will need to be integrated within the static models used by HTML. In this direction, INRIA has implemented Timesheets.js [3], a solution that takes advantage of HTML5 and CSS3, complementing them with a SMIL-based scheduler for handing timing and synchronization. Such implementation is based on a previous W3C working draft [21], aiming at compound XHTML documents, where different declarative languages could be used for the creation of complex multimedia applications. While we believe such work is in the right direction, research needs to be invested (as the exploration proposed in this article) for a solution that allows for dynamic modifications of running media items such as videos.

8. ACKNOWLEDGEMENTS

The work reported in this paper was funded in part by the European Community's Seventh Framework Programme under grant agreement No. ICT-2007-214793

9. REFERENCES

[1] Bocconi, S., Nack, F. and Hardman, L. 2008. Automatic generation of matter-of-opinion video documentaries. *Journal of Web Semantics*, 6(2): 139 – 150.

[2] Bulterman, D.C.A. et al. 2008. Synchronized Multimedia Integration Language (SMIL 3.0). W3C. URL=http://www.w3.org/TR/SMIL/

[3] Cazenave, F., Quint, V., and Roisin, C. 2011. Timesheets.js: when SMIL meets HTML5 and CSS3. In *Proceedings of the ACM Symposium on Document Engineering*, pp. 43-52.

[4] Costa, R., Moreno, M., Rodrigues, R., and Soares, L.F. 2006. Live editing of hypermedia documents. In *Proceedings of the ACM Symposium on Document Engineering*, pp. 165-172.

[5] Fraga, R., Motti, V.G., Cattelan, R.G., Teixeira, C.A.C., and Pimentel, M.G.C. 2010. A social approach to authoring media annotations. In *Proceedings of the ACM Symposium on Document Engineering*, pp. 17-26.

[6] Gao, B, Jansen, J, Cesar, P and Bulterman, D. 2010. Beyond the playlist: seamless playback of structured video clips. *IEEE Transactions on Consumer Electronics*, (53)3:1495-1501.

[7] Gao, B., Jansen, J., Cesar, P., and Bulterman, D.C.A. 2011. Accurate and low-delay seeking within and across mash-ups of highly-compressed videos. In *Proceedings of the International Workshop on Network and Operating Systems Support for Digital Audio and Video*, pp. 105-110.

[8] Guimaraes, R.L., Cesar, P., Bulterman, D.C.A., Zsombori, V., and Kegel, I. 2011. Creating personalized memories from social events: community-based support for multi-camera recordings of school concerts. In *Proceedings of the ACM International Conference on Multimedia*, pp. 303-312.

[9] Jansen, J., and Bulterman, D.C.A. 2008. Enabling adaptive time-based web applications with SMIL state. In *Proceedings of the ACM Symposium on Document Engineering*, pp. 18-27.

[10] Jansen, J., Cesar, P., and Bulterman, D.C.A. 2010. A model for editing operations on active temporal multimedia documents. In *Proceedings of the ACM Symposium on Document Engineering*, pp. 87-96.

[11] Kennedy L., and Naaman. M. 2009. Less talk, more rock: automated organization of community-contributed collections of concert videos. In *Proceedings of the Interactional Conference on WWW*, pp. 311-320.

[12] King, P., Schmitz, P. and Thompson, S. 2004. Behavioral reactivity and real time programming in XML: functional programming meets SMIL animation. In *Proceedings of the ACM Symposium on Document Engineering*, pp. 57-66.

[13] Pfeiffer, S. 2012. *The Definitive Guide to HTML5 Video*. Springer.

[14] Piacenza, A., Guerrini, F., Adami, N., Leonardi, R., Porteous, J., Teutenberg, J., and Cavazza, M. 2011. Generating story variants with constrained video recombination. In *Proceedings of the ACM International Conference on Multimedia*, pp. 223-232.

[15] Sadallah, M., Aubert, O., and Prie, Y. 2011. Component-based hypervideo model: high-level operational specification of hypervideos. In *Proceedings of the ACM Symposium on Document Engineering*, pp. 53-56.

[16] Shaw, R., and Schmitz, P. 2006. Community annotation and remix: a research platform and pilot deployment. In *Proceedings of the ACM International Workshop on Human-Centered Multimedia*, pp. 89-98.

[17] Shrestha, P., de With, P.H.N., Weda, H., Barbieri, M., and Aarts, E.H.L. 2010. Automatic mashup generation from multiple-camera concert recordings. In *Proceedings of the ACM International Conference on Multimedia*, pp. 541-550.

[18] Singh, V.K., Luo, J., Joshi, D., Lei, P., Das, M., and Stubler, P. 2011. Reliving on demand: a total viewer experience. In *Proceedings of the ACM International Conference on Multimedia*, pp. 333-342.

[19] Soares, L. F. G., Rodrigues, R. F. 2006. Nested Context Language 3.0 Part 8 – NCL Digital TV Profiles. Technical Report. Departamento de Informática da PUC-Rio, MCC 35/06. http://www.ncl.org.br/documentos/NCL3.0-DTV.pdf

[20] Soares, L. F. G., Moreno, M. F. and Sant'Anna, F. 2009. Relating Declarative Hypermedia Objects and Imperative Objects through the NCL Glue Language. In *Proceedings of the ACM Symposium on Document Engineering*, pp. 222-230.

[21] Vuorimaa, P., Bulterman, D.C.A., and Cesar. P. 2008. SMIL Timesheets 1.0. *W3C Working Draft*.

[22] Zhang, L., Bieber, M., Millard, D. and Oria, V. 2004. Supporting virtual documents in just-in-time hypermedia systems. In *Proceedings of the ACM Symposium on Document Engineering*, pp. 35-44.

[23] Zsombori, V., Frantzis, M., Guimaraes, R.L., Ursu, M.F., Cesar, P., Kegel, I., Craigie, R., and Bulterman, D.C.A. 2011. Automatic generation of video narratives from shared UGC. In *Proceedings of the ACM Conference on Hypertext and Hypermedia*, pp. 325-334.

TAL Processor for Hypermedia Applications

Carlos de Salles Soares Neto[1]
csalles@deinf.ufma.br

Hedvan Fernandes Pinto[1]
hedvan@laws.deinf.ufma.br

Luiz Fernando G. Soares[2]
lfgs@inf.puc-rio.br

[1] Departamento de Informática – UFMA
Av. dos Portugueses, Campus do Bacanga
São Luís/MA – 65080-040 – Brasil
0055-98-3301-8224

[2] Departamento de Informática – PUC-Rio
Rua Marquês de São Vicente, 225
Rio de Janeiro/RJ – 22453-900 – Brasil
0055-21-3527-1500 Ext:4330

ABSTRACT

TAL (Template Authoring Language) is a specification language for hypermedia document templates. Templates describe application families with structural and semantic similarities. In TAL, templates not only define design patterns that applications must follow, but also constraints on the use of these patterns. A template must be processed together with a padding document giving rise to a new document in some specification language, called target language. TAL supports the description of templates independently of the languages used to specify target and padding documents. Usually a specific processor is required for each target language and for each padding document used. This paper concerns TAL processors. However, we should note that the proposal can be easily extended to any other solution used to define templates. Any pattern language and any language used to define constraints could be used instead of TAL. The TAL processor architecture is general and it is discussed when presenting the processor framework. As an instantiation example, an implementation of a TAL Processor targeting NCL (the declarative language of Ginga DTV middleware) is examined, and also another one targeting HTML-based middleware. The use of wizards for defining padding documents is also discussed in the examples of the proposed architecture instantiation.

Categories and Subject Descriptors

D.3.3 [**Programming Languages**]: Processors - *Code generation, Interpreters, Parsing.*

General Terms

Documentation, Standardization, Languages, Verification.

Keywords

Digital TV Applications, iDTV, Nested Context Language, NCL, TAL, Ginga.

1. INTRODUCTION

Hypermedia documents usually share common design patterns[1]. To take profit of this characteristic, TAL (Template Authoring Language) [1] has been conceived to allow for developing common templates to be followed by applications. We call family of applications to the set of applications that follow the same specific set of templates.

However, it is not sufficient to define common design patterns that applications must follow. Sometimes we also need to set a series of constraints on the design pattern uses. In several situations, template authors are different from application authors, and the first want not only to be assured that their design patterns will be followed but also that some add-ons will not be allowed. For example, a particular application provider can require that every application it transmits must have its logo in the right upper corner of the screen. However, in addition, it can require that no other logo may be present in the application. Taking these scenarios into account, TAL extends the usual template concept to define not only common design patterns but also constraints on their uses.

Nevertheless, to guarantee that the template will be strictly followed, the final desired application must be checked against the template specification. This is one of the main roles of a *template processor*.

A *padding document* must fill at least the blanks (hot spots) of a template. Then the template must be processed together with the padding document giving rise to a new document in some specification language, called *target language*. Ideally, the padding document is written in any language understood by the template processor. Usually, a specific processor is required for each target language and for each padding document used.

We should stress that the final document is generated by the template processor. However, the process is completed only if the padding document does not deviate from the template specification. Figure 1 illustrates the process using TAL templates.

---

[1] We employ the term *design pattern* in this paper in its broad sense: a general reusable solution to a commonly occurring problem within a given context in software design. It is a description or template for how to solve a problem that can be used in many different situations.

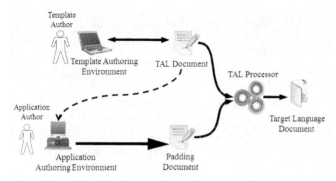

Figure 1. TAL Processing Flow.

In TAL, templates group a set of design patterns for hypermedia compositions. Hypermedia compositions include media objects and other hypermedia compositions, recursively, in addition to relationships (usually temporal relationships) among these elements. Media objects contain data to be processed and presented when their parent hypermedia compositions run. They also contain set of properties to control their presentations, as for example, the positioning of the exhibited content. Hypermedia compositions may implicitly define relationships among their child elements, as is the case of "par" and "seq" SMIL [2] containers with their embedded temporal semantics. But they can also have relationships explicitly defined, as is the case with NCL [3] links. In either case, hypermedia compositions encapsulate semantic relationships among objects. Note that even with languages that do not support composition abstraction, the whole body of the document denotes a composition. In other words, the concept of composition still prevails, although not allowing composition nesting.

Therefore TAL template is an open-composition that defines a family (a set) of compositions. TAL is independent of any authoring language used to specify hypermedia applications that can benefit from its templates to define a unique member of the composition family. TAL processors are in charge of generating this unique member, assuring that it is in agreement with the template.

This paper concerns TAL processors. However, we should note that the proposal can be easily extended to any other solution used to define templates. Any pattern language and any language used to define constraints could be used instead of TAL. The processor architecture proposed is general. It is also import to reiterate that the proposal is also independent of the target language used for the application specification.

As an instantiation case, a TAL processor implementation targeting NCL (the declarative language of Ginga DTV middleware [4]) is discussed, and also another one targeting HTML-based DTV middleware. The continuation of this paper briefly presents, in Section 2, some related work. In Section 3, TAL is overviewed. The TAL Processor architecture is discussed in Section 4. Section 5 presents two processor implementations having NCL as target language: one in which the padding document is obtained through a graphical wizard, and another one also using NCL as the padding document language. In addition, Section 5 discusses an implementation for HTML-based target languages. Finally, Section 6 presents some conclusions.

2. RELATED WORK

There are many good reasons for template-based development. First, templates promote coherent application *branding*, enabling content producers to define and follow the same hypermedia-application pattern. Second, as a consequence of having hypermedia presentations following the same interface patterns, thanks to a common source template, hypermedia applications can be more usable for those who view and interact with different documents of the same family. Third, template-based authoring promotes reuse, allowing authors to concentrate on filling out only the blanks that make a particular document unique within the family to which it belongs. Finally, templates can also encode domain concepts across related applications, creating a specific vocabulary and defining a set of constraints on this vocabulary, to be followed by all documents of a given family.

Some authoring tools are based on template approach. PageJokey [25] describes templates as classes of components to be embedded on target documents. It focuses mainly on application design and layout characteristics. Templates apply variables to denote what differ from one instance to another. GRiNS [26] is another tool that can use templates. It allows for using sample code as basis for a new document and provides graphical abstractions to help users to customize new document instances.

Several hypermedia applications embed common design patterns. However, to the best of our knowledge, all structure-based hypermedia languages (NCL, SMIL, SVG, etc.) fail to let authors create compositions with unspecified internal content or unspecified relationships. However, extension languages have been defined to increase the facilities of those languages in line with design patterns principles, like SMIL Timesheets [5] aiming at allowing any language to incorporate the XML elements and attributes of the SMIL temporal control modules. In this section we focus only on the process (and processor) used to define the resulting application when these extension languages are used.

Timesheet.js [6] is a Javascript library that incorporates SMIL Timesheets in HTML5 [7] or SVG [8] documents. This library processes the embedded SMIL Timesheets using the JavaScript engine present in browsers. After interpreting the temporal relationships, the library estimates each media duration and creates time containers to control each media execution time. The library architecture can be extended with new functions or Javascript libraries, if greater presentation control or if the inclusion of new temporal behavior is needed. Different of TAL, it is not possible to specify constraints on the application structure and behavior but only adding temporal relationships.

LimSee 3 [9] is a template-oriented authoring tool for multimedia documents. New markups are added to the document language, indicating where changes should be made when instantiating the final document. The instantiation may be incremental, and each time a document area is filled, the template markups are removed or altered to represent the new document configuration. In this approach there is not a clear separation between the template and the multimedia document, which reduces the possibility of reuse.

A model-driven approach for DTV application, called StoryToCode is presented in [10]. The tool makes use of template-based authoring concepts to standardize the structure of application requirements, to simplify the development process and to reduce the rework when coding interactive applications. The StoryToCode development process starts from an abstract template to which successive transformations are applied, in order to obtain the final hypermedia application. These successive transformations require processors at various abstraction levels, which can lead to a high cost development environment. However, the approach allows for having target document in different languages, simply by adapting the step-by-step processors.

XTemplate [11] is the predecessor language of TAL. However, unlike TAL, the XTemplate 3.0 version was developed to a specific target hypermedia language, the NCL. XTemplate requires specific knowledge about XPath [12] and XSLT [13]. This demands that the padding document author, who usually is a non-expert user, understands XSLT transformation, which is not easy and desirable. On the other hand, at the expense of greater complexity for its use, the development of XTemplate processors is simple, since a generic XSLT processor can be used to help generating NCL code.

It should be emphasized the correlation between TAL processors and the generic XSLT processors, since both have similar purposes. XSLT processors focus on generic XML transformations applied to a XML-based application in order to obtain new representations in different XML-based languages. On the other hand, TAL processors combine an incomplete document specification with a template to generate a complete target application. Usually, XSLT converters focus much more on performance issues [14] than in provided facilities to adapt these processors for creating new tools. In other words, the scope of XSLT transformations is generic and does not care about its processor specialization to specific uses.

3. TAL SPECIFICATION: AN OVERVIEW

In TAL, template content is given by:

- Vocabulary: defining the allowed classes of child-objects (the components) of the template; the allowed classes of interfaces for these child-objects and for the template itself; and the allowed relations to be used in relationships among child-objects;
- Constraints: defining rules on the classes defined in the vocabulary;
- Resources: defining common instantiated child object classes that shall be inherited by all compositions that use (follow) the template;
- Relationships: defining common instantiated relation classes, relating child-object classes and resources that shall also be inherited by all compositions that follow the template.

In defining the vocabulary we are also defining the basic hierarchy imputed to the child-objects, given by the composition nesting. Child-objects of templates can be media objects or other nested compositions, as anticipated. An interface can define part of the content of a media object, or can define a child-object property, like its positioning on the screen, etc. Child composite-

objects and the template itself may also have interfaces that externalize the interfaces of their internal child-objects.

Figure 2 shows two applications of the same family that we propose as examples. Both applications start presenting an invitation icon. If the icon is selected, a quiz starts presenting a series of questions. Each question is related with up to three incorrect answers and a right one, which can be selected by the color buttons of the remote control (red, green, yellow and blue). For each answer selected, a possible different message including the right solution is presented by a short period of time, followed by the next question of the quiz. Figures 2a. and 2b. show the first application (a talk show about health), in which each questions have three possible answers. Figures 2c. and 2d. show a documentary about a touristic state in Brazil; in it each question has four possible answers.

Although very simple, coding these applications is tedious, since there are many repetitive structures of relationships among their components: the selection of an option must be followed by the respective right answer message, and soon after by the new question with its possible answers. This repetitive code increases as the number of questions and options increase.

In TAL, applications are modeled based on component classes, besides component instances. Relationships applied on these classes reflect in every type instance, decreasing the authoring work load. Figure 3 shows the structural view of the template defined by the two applications of Figure 2, as modeled in TAL.

Indeed, we can have several models for the structure of this template of questions and answers. We have chosen the one in Figure 3 because it is simple and easy to be reused. The quiz family is represented by an open composition (the most external circle), containing another open composition, corresponding to each question of the quiz. So, we have here a case of a template that includes another template in its definition, as state in Listing 1. The root element is <tal> (line 1), which defines the template library. Note in line 4 how TAL specifies that a component (in the case id="subject") must follow a template (specified in the *template* attribute).

```
1.  <tal:tal id="set_of_templates">
2.    <tal:template id="quizTemplate">
      ...
4.      <tal:component id="subject"
                selects="context[class=subject]"
                template="questionTemplate"/>

19.   </tal:template>
20.   <tal:template id="questionTemplate">
      ...
81.   </tal:template>
82. </tal:tal>
```

Listing 1. TAL template including other TAL template.

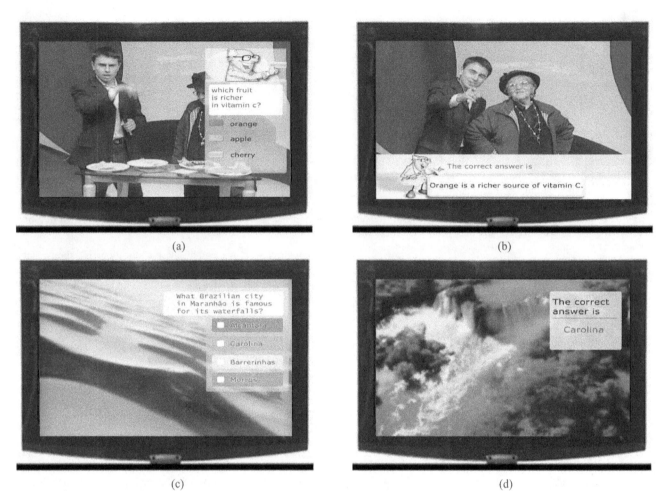

(a)

(b)

(c)

(d)

Figure 2. Application Examples.

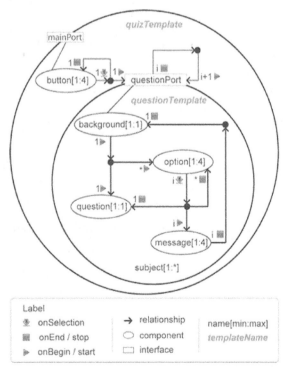

Figure 3. Template for the Applications in Figure 2.

In Figure 3, ellipses correspond to components of the templates; indeed, component classes. Every component class has a name followed by its cardinality: the minimum and maximum number of instances allowed for the class. For example, the quizTemplate must have one and only one "button" component (the invitation icon of the application quiz), and must have at least one "subject" component (the quiz's question), which follows the "questionTemplate". In Figure 3, the "background" component is associated to the background image over which the quiz question and its color button options (instances of the "option" component class) are placed. Depending on the selected option, a message, instance of the "message" component class, is presented. In TAL, <component> elements define component classes. Components can be media objects or nested compositions.

Constraints on the classes defined in the template vocabulary are specified using <assert>, <report> and <warning> elements. These elements establish constraint rules similarly to Schematron [15]. In all three elements the test attribute specifies the logical test to be evaluated. The error or warning message is defined in the content of these elements. The <assert> element requires the test evaluation returns "true", otherwise its error message should be presented. The <report> element is similar but requires that the test be evaluated as "false" to not exhibit its error message. The <warning> element requires that the test be evaluated as "false" to show its warning message. When an error message occurs, the template evaluation is aborted and no final document is generated by the template processor. On the other hand, a warning message does not stop the template processing.

Listing 2 adds components and constraints to the templates of Listing 1. Templates and classes defined in TAL may use selectors similar to CSS selectors [16]. The selector role is to identify which elements of the padding document must be processed in agreement with the class or template they are associated. Line 3 defines the component class (the media object class) that will be associated to the invitation icon of the application. The selector indicates that elements of the padding document that have their *class* attributes with value equal to "button" are instances of this class. Similarly, line 22, 23, 24 and 25 define the component classes for the template "questionTemplate": the set of questions, the set options, the background and the set of messages, respectively.

```
1.   <tal:tal id="template">
2.     <tal:template id="quizTemplate">
3.       <tal:component id="button"
            selects="media[class=button]"/>
4.       <tal:component id="subject"
                selects="context[class=subject]"
                template="questionTemplate"/>
     ...
13.      <tal:assert test="#button==1">
14.        It must have one BUTTON element.
15.      </tal:assert>
16.      <tal:assert test="#questionTemplate>=1">
17.        It must have at least one
           QUESTIONTEMPLATE element.
18.      </tal:assert>
19.  </tal:template>
20.  <tal:template id="questionTemplate">
     ...
22.      <tal:component             id="question"
                selects="media[class=question]"/>
23.      <tal:component              id="option"
                selects="media[class=option]"/>
24.      <tal:component          id="background"

    selects="media[class=background]"/>
25.      <tal:component id="message"
                selects="media[class=message]"/>
     ...
66.      <tal:assert test="#background==1">
67.        It must have only one BACKGROUND element.
68.      </tal:assert>
69.      <tal:assert test="#option==#solution">
70.        The number of OPTION elements must be the
           same of SOLUTION elements.
71.      </tal:assert>
72.      <tal:assert test="#option<=4">
73.        The number of OPTION elements must be at
           most four.
74.      </tal:assert>
75.      <tal:assert test="#option>=1">
76.        It must have at least one option element.
77.      </tal:assert>
     ...
81.  </tal:template>
82.  </tal:tal>
```

Listing 2. Components and constraints in TAL.

In lines 13 to 18 of Listing 2 we can see two <assert> elements, establishing constraints on the cardinality of the "button" and "questionTemplate" component classes, in this order. In lines 66 to 77 we can see the constraints on the cardinality of the components of the "questionTemplate".

Figure 3 shows several causal relationships among components. For example, the one linking the "button" establishes that when this component is selected, its presentation must be stopped and the first question must be presented. In TAL, relationships are defined by using <link> elements. As relationships can be established among classes, <forEach> child elements can be used to iterate on these class instances. In causal relationships, conditions defined on events must be satisfied in order to trigger action on events.

The current version of TAL has the following event types: presentation event, which is defined by the presentation of a subset of the information units (an interface) of a media object, or, in case of compositions, the presentation of the information units of any object inside it; selection event, which is defined by the selection of a subset of the information units of a media object being presented; attribution event, which is defined by the attribution of a value to a property (an interface) of an object.

As described in the previous paragraph, events are defined on interfaces of child components of a composition. Interface classes, both for the template itself and for its child components, are defined by <interface> elements. Every child component of a template and the template itself has an interface defined by default representing the whole content of the object. Except for the "questionTemplate", this is the case all other components in Listing2, which have only this implicitly defined interface class.

An <interface> element for a composition, in particular the template itself, can also define mappings to interfaces of child-objects of the composition. As mappings can be established among classes, <forEach> child elements can be used to iterate on these class instances. Listing 3 specifies the interface of "questionTemplate" template. Note that as the mapping is to the unique instance of the "background" component class, the mapping is established by using the *component* attribute of the <interface> element, without needing to define the <forEach> child element.

```
21.      <tal:interface id="questionPort"
            selects="port[class=questionPort]"
            component="background[1]"/>
```

Listing 3. Interface for the open-composition.

There are two relationships defined by the "quizTemplate", as shown in Listing 4. Lines 5 to 7 define the first relationship. It establishes that the selection of the invitation icon stops its presentation, and starts presenting the first "subject" instance, that is, the first question. The second relationship, in lines 8 to 12, establishes that when each "subject" instance finishes, the next instance of this component class must be started. Note in Listing 4 that the <forEach> in line 9 is responsible for the iteration on the set of "subject" instances.

Finally, there are six relationships defined by the "questionTemplate", as shown in Listing 5. The first, in lines 27 to 33 establishes that when the "background" component (the one that starts when the "questionTemplate" starts) begins, then the first question ("question[1]") must start, together with all its answering options. The <forEach> in line 29 is responsible for the iteration on the set of "option" instances. The second relationship defines that when the "option[1]" is selected with the RED remote control key, then the question presentation must be stopped, the "message[1]" must be presented (as specified in line 35), and that every "options" must be stopped (as specified in lines 36 and 37).

```
5.        <tal:link id="beginQuiz">
6.          onSelection button[1] then start subject
          [1]; stop button[1] end
7.        </tal:link>
8.        <tal:link id="nextQuestion">
9.          <tal:foreach
              instance="subject" iterator="i">
10.           onEnd subject[i] then start
                              subject[i+1] end
11.         </tal:forEach>
12.       </tal:link>
```

Listing 4. Relationships defined in the "quizTemplate".

The third, fourth and fifth relationships are similar to the second one, when "option[2]", "option[3]", and "option[4]" are selected, respectively with GREEN, YELLOW and BLUE remote control keys. The sixth relationship, in lines 62 to 65, establishes that when any "message" instance ends, the background" must be stopped, and, in consequence, the parent "subject" instance. In agreement with the link defined in line 8 to 12 of Listing 4, the next question must starts, until the last one is presented.

```
26.       <tal:relation id="link"    selects="link"/>

27.       <tal:link id="beginQuestion">
28.         onBegin background[1] then start
          question[1];
29.           <tal:forEach instance="option"
                              iterator="i">
30.             start option[i];
31.           <tal:foreach>
32.         end
33.       </tal:link>
34.       <tal:link id="option1Selection">
35.         onSelection option[1] with key = "RED"
          then start message[1]; stop question[1];
36.           <tal:forEach instance="option"
                              iterator="i">
37.             stop option[i];
38.           <tal:foreach>
39.         end
40.       </tal:link>
41.       <tal:link id="option2Selection">
42.         onSelection option[2] with key = "GREEN"
          then start message[2]; stop question[1];
43.           <tal:forEach instance="option"
                              iterator="i">
44.             stop option[i];
45.           <tal:foreach>
46.         end
47.       </tal:link>
48.       <tal:link id="option3Selection">
49.         onSelection option[3] with key = "YELLOW"
          then start message[3]; stop question[1];
50.           <tal:forEach instance="option"
                              iterator="i">
51.             stop option[i];
52.           <tal:foreach>
53.         end
54.       </tal:link>
55.       <tal:link id="option4Selection">
56.         onSelection option[4] with key = "GREEN"
          then start message[4]; stop question[1];
57.           <tal:forEach instance="option"
                              iterator="i">
58.             stop option[i];
59.           <tal:foreach>
60.         end
61.       </tal:link>
62.       <tal:link id="endQuestion">
63.         <tal:forEach instance="message"
                              iterator="i">
64.           onEnd message[i] then stop
                      background[1] end
65.         </tal:forEach>
66.       </tal:link>
```

Listing 5. Relationships defined in the "questionTemplate".

It is important to stress that TAL also allows for defining constraints on relations. Note that in line 26 of Listing 5 a relation class is defined for relationships defined by <link> elements. This allows for defining the constraint of Listing 6.

```
78.       <tal:assert test="#link==0">
79.         There cannot be any <link> element on the
          application apart from those defined by
          the template.
80.       </tal:assert>
```

Listing 6. Constraints on relations.

Listing 1 to 6 define our template example. Finishing this section, Listing 7 gives the padding document body for the application of Figure 2.a. and 2.b (just one question is shown). Note that the padding document is all that an application author must fulfill.

```
      ...
30.   <body template="template.tal#quizTemplate">
31.     <port id="pinit" component="initButton"
                          class="mainPort"/>
32.     <media id="initButton" … class="button"/>
33.     <context id="quizSubject1" class="subject">
34.     <!-- port to background at template -->
35.         <media id="backgroundS1"…
                  class="background"/>
36.         <media id="questionS1" …
                  class="option"/>
37.         <media id="option1S1" …
                  class="option"/>
38.         <media id="option2S1" …
                  class="option"/>
39.         <media id="option3S1" …
                  class="option"/>
40.         <media id="message1S1" …
                  class="message"/>
41.         <media id="message2S1" …
                  class="message"/>
42.         <media id="message3S1" …
                  class="message"/>
43.     </context>
      ...
85.   </body>
86. </ncl>
```

Listing 7. Padding document example.

4. TAL PROCESSOR ARCHITECTURE

As aforementioned, TAL specifies its templates independent of the target document language and independent of the language used in defining the padding document. This requires a template processor framework with hot spots to be specialized to each input and output language. In agreement with this principle, TAL Processor architecture is divided in three modules, as presented in Figure 4. These modules and their components follow the analysis-synthesis paradigm usually adopted in modern compilers [17]. In Figure 4, components in dark grey are the hot spots.

The first module is the Interpreter. The Padding Document Parser component initiates the whole process converting the padding document to an internal data structure, called Padding Document Model in Figure 4. This intermediate data structure is easier to be handled when generating the final coding, and it is completely independent of the padding document language.

The Padding Document Model is based on the NCL Raw profile [18]. This conceptual model has been chosen because it can represent the majority of hypermedia declarative language models. During the parser process, XML elements of the padding document that have *template* attributes are used to identify which templates TAL Parser component must use.

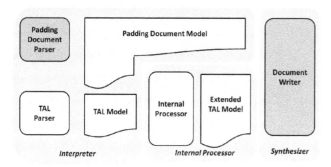

Figure 4. TAL Processor Architecture.

The TAL parser component interprets the templates referred by the padding document. The component is responsible for validating template syntaxes. Validation cannot be performed only using XML Schema [19, 20], since TAL presents the particularity of combining three additional distinct syntaxes within the same TAL document: CSS-like syntax to bind components to padding document entities; Schematron-like for constraint definitions; and TAL own syntax for relationship and interface mapping definitions. After checking if a document complies with the TAL Type Definition, TAL Parser generates an internal data structure, called TAL Model in Figure 4.

TAL Model is an intermediate data structure that reorganizes the different parts of TAL documents to make them easier to be handled in generating final coding. TAL Parser gets TAL *selects* attributes, TAL *Constraints* and TAL *Relationships*, processes them, and generates the corresponding internal structures for each one.

Selectors are converted into functions, responsible for searching the corresponding elements in the Padding Document Model that refers to the selectors. Constraints are converted to functions to evaluate the cardinality of components defined in the template vocabulary. Relationships are transformed into other data structures ready to be easily combined with information defined in the Padding Document Model.

Based on the Padding Document Model and the TAL Model, the Internal Processor component validates the template constraints, process all relationships and all interfaces defined in the template, and uses the functions created when processing the selectors to retrieve the corresponding structures from the Padding Document Model.

In validating the constraints, if any of them is not satisfied, the whole process is stopped. The message defined in the invalid constraint is then presented to the TAL Processor user. In case of "warnings", as defined in Section 3, the message is also presented to the user, but without stopping the processing.

As discussed in Section 3, <relation>, <link> and <forEach> TAL elements are used to define causal relationships. Some of these relationships are transformed in new ones by the Internal Processor component. New relationships are generated when <forEach> elements are found in relationships of the TAL Model that refer to elements in the TAL vocabulary. The example presented in Figure 5 can help in understanding the process.

The top of Figure 5, denoted by (1), represents the relationship as originally defined in TAL. Let us now assume that the padding document has three elements referring (using TAL selectors) to the "subject" component class. Based on the Padding Document Model and the description of the TAL relationship in the TAL Model, the Internal Processor component resolves the iteration creating three new relationships as depicted in part (2) of Figure 5.

Similar converting procedure is employed by the Internal Processor component in transforming TAL <interface> elements having <forEach> elements as children.

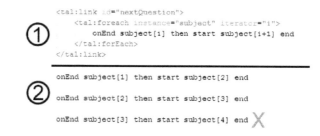

Figure 5. Converting TAL relationships.

If the Internal Processor component comes across an invalid index value when solving <forEach> expressions, it stops the generation of the relationship (or interface) and ignores the invalid relationship (or interface). Figure 5 shows a relationship generated by referencing an inexistent element (exemplified by subject [4]). In this case, the relationship is discarded.

In the Extended TAL Model generated by the Internal Processor, constraints are removed and selector functions are replaced by the set of elements of the Padding Document Model that they refer. New generated relationships and interfaces are added, replacing the old ones, and formatted according to the structure of the NCL Raw Profile.

The Synthesizer Module has just one component: the Document Writer. This component creates the target document in a given specification language based on the Padding Document Model and the Extended TAL Model.

Note in Figure 4 that components filled in dark grey are those that depend on the padding and target document languages. Note also that the architecture is loosely coupled, in the sense that it is possible to change the Padding Document Parser and the Document Writer components and reuse all other elements. Therefore, in order to incorporate new target languages to a TAL Processor, only hot spots of the Document Writer component must be filled. Likewise, in order to incorporate other input padding languages, or include communication with other tools for data entry (as for example wizards, IDEs, etc., as discussed in the next section), only hot spots of the Padding Document Parser component must be filled. Section 5 explores this feature instantiating the architecture for two target languages and using two ways of defining the padding document.

5. TAL PROCESSOR INSTANCES

Tal Processor has been designed to be smoothly integrated to other tools. This integration can be done either at the front-end (Padding Document Parser component in Figure 4) and the back-end (Document Writer component in Figure 4) of TAL Processor.

Regarding the front-end integration, TAL Processor can be added to a tool that assists the construction of padding documents, possible making use of graphical abstractions to simplify the data entry process.

As for the back-end integration, the target document generated can be directly sent to a second authoring tool as its input, for example, or to a playout station.

No matter if in the front-end or in the back-end, the integration can take place either directly or indirectly. Integration is said to be direct when the integrated tool acts as a component of the TAL Processor, replacing part of its tasks. Indirect integration is through using TAL processor without interfering with the integrated tool operation, thus using it as a black box. In this second case, the tool input or output is used as a means to establish the integration.

To clarify the integration with other tools, some examples are presented in the following subsections. In 3.1, the integration of TAL Processor with a wizard tool is presented. In 3.2 the generation of NCL and HTML documents is discussed. This paper does not present examples of indirect integration since this type of integration is straightforward and does not change any TAL Processor modules.

5.1 Front-End Integration: NCLWizard

Usually, the input information of a TAL processor is defined in a document specified using the same language used to specify the target document. Listing 7 in Section 3 illustrates a Padding Document written in NCL 3.0 [3] for the template presented in the same section, resulting in the NCL application shown in Figure 2.a and 2.b.

The specification of padding documents directly in NCL or other languages requires certain degree of experience and knowledge from the application author. As a consequence, the time needed for application development can increase. Generally, content producers and writers of TV programs do not have any experience with programming languages, even with declarative ones. To enable their participation in all stages of application developments, it is necessary to use tools possibly with graphical abstractions close to their daily live perceptions.

A simple and powerful abstraction is the interface pattern known as wizard. As an example, we have done the integration of TAL Processor with the NCLWizard [21] framework, combining the ease of using templates with the clarity of wizard interfaces. In complex and repetitive tasks it is recommended to use wizards to assist users [22]. They provide a step by step, clear and direct interface, highlighting and directing their users to points that deserve their attention.

In a direct integration with TAL Processor, wizards can take over the functions of the Padding Document Parser component of Figure 4. The result is graphical interfaces used to communicate with application authors rather than the direct textual authoring of documents. Figure 6 shows two screenshots coming from the integration of TAL Processor with the NCLWizard framework. They are gotten during the Padding Document Model generation for the TAL template defined in the Section 3.

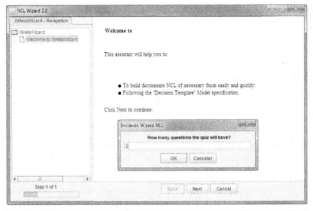

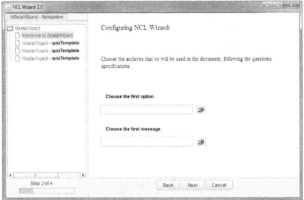

Figure 6. Wizard for the Template of Listing 1.

5.2 Creating NCL and HTML Applications

The key task performed by the Document Writer component of Figure 4 is translating the TAL Model relationships to the temporal presentation semantics of the target language conceptual model. NCL [3], for example, defines the temporal semantic by using NCL <link> elements. On the other hand, SMIL [2] use <seq> and <par> temporal containers, besides temporal attributes defined in SMIL media objects. In HTML, scripts will be necessary, and so on.

Relationships defined using TAL has a one-to-one translation to <link> entities used in NCL version 3.1. This contrast with the NCL language profile version 3.0 used in the standardized Ginga middleware [4], which requires the translation of TAL <links> to two NCL 3.0 entities: <connector> to define relations, and <link> to define relationships referring to <connector> pre-defined elements. Figure 7 shows an example: in 7 (1) we have the TAL relationship and in 7 (2) we have the generated NCL 3.0 elements.

```
onSelection button[1] then
stop video[1]; stop video[2]; stop video[3];
start video[1] end
```

```
<causalConnector id="onSelectionStartStop">
    <simpleCondition role="onSelection"/>
    <compoundAction operator="seq">
        <simpleAction role="stop" max="unbounded"/>
        <simpleAction role="start" max="unbounded"/>
    </compoundAction>
</causalConnector>

<link xconnector="conn#onSelectionStartStop">
    <bind role="onSelection" component="mthumb1"/>
    <bind role="stop" component="video1"/>
    <bind role="stop" component="video2"/>
    <bind role="stop" component="video3"/>
    <bind role="start" component="video1"/>
</link>
```

Figure 7. TAL Relationship Translated to NCL elements.

The structured organization of TAL, in which a component can contain other components, has a one-to-one correspondence to NCL <context> elements. Interfaces with mapping specifications in the Extended TAL Model have a one to one correspondence to <port> elements of NCL. The other interface types are translated to NCL <property> and <area> elements.

Indeed, TAL has been designed aiming at having NCL as its client target language. That is why it is so easy to translate the Extended TAL Model (referring to and using the Padding Document Model) into an NCL application. This makes the Document Writer component implementation very simple.

The translation from the Extended TAL Model to HTML documents is not straightforward as it is to NCL, but it is still easy to implement. The structured organization of TAL can be used by <span> and <div> HTML elements. However, some TAL relationships cannot be described by HTML declarative tags and may require the use of scripts. Figure 8 shows an example: in 8 (1) we have the same TAL relationship of Figure 7, and in 8 (3) we have the script generated.

```
onSelection button[1] then
stop video[1]; stop video[2]; stop video[3];
start video[1] end
```

```
document.getElementById("thumb1Link").click{
    function(e){
        e.preventDefault();
        stop("video1, video2, video3");
        start("video1");
    });
```

Figure 8. TAL Relationship Translated to ECMAScript.

Using ECMAScript library, the Document Writer component implementation becomes workable. Building this complete library is left to future work. Similar work has been done for SMIL Timesheet [5].

Table 1 shows how TAL conditions and actions are related to those of NCL and HTML. Note that there is a one-to-one correspondence between TAL and NCL, as previously mentioned. HTML relationships are based on events captured by its scripting language, especially when they handle attribution events.

Table 1. Mapping TAL conditions and actions.

	TAL	NCL	HTML
Actions	Start	start	play/show
	Stop	stop	stop/hide
	Pause	pause	pause
	Resume	resume	play/show
	Abort	abort	abort
	Set	set	Script hadling
Conditions	onEnd	onEnd	Ended
	onBegin	onBegin	Playing
	onAbort	onAbort	Abort
	onPause	onPause	Pause
	onResume	onResume	Playing
	onEndAttribution	onEndAttribution	Script hadling
	onBeginAttribution	onBeginAttribution	Script hadling

6. CONCLUSIONS

In this paper we have presented the TAL Processor architecture and how it can be easily specialized to be integrated with other application developing tools.

Currently we are working on the integration of TAL Processor with other tools that ease the specification of padding documents. In particular, we are integrating TAL as a plug-in of Composer [23]. Composer provides high-level abstractions by means of graphical views, making easier the authoring process of NCL applications in conformance with the language DTV Profile. Integration with Composer will allow a complete development cycle, in which Composer can be used to create NCL padding documents. In this case, TAL Processor will be used for the generation of NCL applications based on predefined templates. These NCL applications could then be enhanced using other Composer plug-ins. Moreover, since TAL allows template nesting, the final document generated by TAL Processor can feedback the whole process as a new padding document, and so on, until the DTV application is finally ready. In addition, as there are playout-station plug-ins for Composer, TAL processor could also take profit of this facility to transmit applications besides the automatic publication of produced applications in NCL specialized sites, like the one in www.club.ncl.org.br.

Several experts in NCL language have attested the usefulness of TAL in speeding the development of DTV applications, in special applications with dynamically generated content [24]. A usability study is planned as future work to validate the use of TAL by non-expert programmers and obtain further evidence on the perception of users about the ease and applicability of TAL.

TAL Processor has been implemented in Lua, the scripting language of NCL. Therefore, TAL Processor is able to be executed by Ginga middleware in the client side (viewer side). Another future work targets the creation of applications (indeed padding documents) by viewers at the client side, based on pre-defined templates. In this case, it will be possible for viewers to play the role of application authors even using the limited resources of set-top boxes. Today, some applications dynamically generated at the client side by TAL Processors have already been developed [24].

Finally, a template repository is being created for Ginga-NCL, with extensive semantic documentation (metadata) about families of applications addressed by each template. This can speed up the use of TAL and get faster the development of NCL DTV applications.

7. ACKNOWLEDGMENTS

This research has been partially supported by CNPq and MCT.

8. REFERENCES

[1] Soares Neto, C. S.; Soares, L. F. G.; and Souza, C. S.. TAL - Template Authoring Language. To be published in *Journal of Brazilian Computer Science*. 2012.

[2] W3C. *Synchronized Multimedia Integration Language (SMIL 3.0) W3C Recommendation*, 2007. Available at: http://www.w3.org/TR/SMIL

[3] NBR 15606-2. ABNT NBR 15606-2. *Digital terrestrial television – Data coding and transmission specification for digital broadcasting – Part 2: Ginga-NCL for fixed and mobile receivers – XML application language for application coding*. September, 2007.

[4] ITU-T Recommendation H.761. *Nested Context Language (NCL) and Ginga-NCL for IPTV Services*. Geneva, April, 2009.

[5] W3C. *SMIL Timesheets 1.0. W3C Working Draft*. Available at http://www.w3.org/TR/timesheets/. 2011.

[6] Cazenave, F.; Quint, V. and Roisin, C. Timesheets.js: When SMIL Meets HTML5 and CSS3. In: *Proceedings of the 11th ACM Symposium on Document Engineering*, DocEng, Mountain View: United States. 2011.

[7] W3C. *HTML5 A vocabulary and associated APIs for HTML and XHTML* W3C Working Draft. Available at: http://www.w3.org/TR/html5/. 2011.

[8] W3C. *Scalabe Vector Graphics*. W3C Recommendation. 2009. Available at: http://www.w3.org/TR/SVG11/.

[9] R. Deltour and C. Roisin. The limsee3 Multimedia Authoring Model. In: *Proceedings of the ACM Symposium on Document Engineering*, DocEng, p. 173-175, New York: United States. 2006.

[10] Kulesza, R., Meira, S. R. L., Ferreira, T. P., Lívio, Á., Filho, G. L. S., Marques Neto, M. C., Santos, C. A. S. Uma Abordagem Dirigida pòr Modelos para Integração de Aplicações Interativas e Serviços Web: Estudo de Caso na Plataforma de TV Digital (in Portuguese). In: *18th Simpósio Brasileiro de Sistemas Multimídia e Web*, Florianópolis, Brasil. 2011.

[11] Santos, J. A. F., Muchaluat-Saade, D. C. XTemplate 3.0: spatio-temporal semantics and structure. In: *Multimedia Tools and Applications*. 2011. DOI 10.1007/s11042-011-0732-2.

[12] W3C. *XML Path Language (XPath) 2.0 (Second Edition)*. W3C Recommendation. 2011. Avaliable at http://www.w3.org/TR/xpath20/

[13] W3C. *XSL Transformations (XSLT) Version 1.0* W3C Recommendation. 1999. Avaliable at http://www.w3.org/TR/xslt

[14] Bittner, T. *Performance Evaluation for XSLT Processing*. Tech. Report, University of Rostock. 2004.

[15] ISO/IEC 19757-3. *Information technology -- Document Schema Definition Language (DSDL) -- Part 3: Rule-based validation – Schematron*. 2006

[16] W3C. *Cascading Style Sheets Level 2 Revision 1 (CSS 2.1) Specification*. 2009. Available at: http://www.w3.org/TR/CSS2/.

[17] Grune, D., Bal, H., Jacobs, C., Langendoen, K. *Modern Compiler Design*. Wiley. 2000.

[18] Lima, G.; Soares, L.F.G.; Soares Neto, C.S.; Moreno, M. F.; Costa, R. R.; Moreno, M. F. Towards the NCL Raw Profile. In: *Simpósio Barsileiro de Sistemas Multimídia e Web*, WebMedia 2010, Belo Horizonte. 2010.

[19] W3C. *W3C XML Schema Definition Language (XSD) 1.1 Part 1: Structures*. W3C Recommendation. Available at: http://www.w3.org/TR/xmlschema11-2/. 2012.

[20] W3C. *W3C XML Schema Definition Language (XSD) 1.1 Part 2: Datatypes*. W3C Recommendation. Available at: http://www.w3.org/TR/xmlschema11-2/. 2012.

[21] Soares Neto, C. S.; Soares, L. F. G. Autoria orientada a arquétipos para TV digital: uma abordagem restritiva e direcionada (in Portuguese). In *Proceedings of the Conferencia Latino Americana de Informatica*, CLEI 2008, Santa Fe. 2008.

[22] Parvan, M., Maurer, M., Lindermann, U. Software Wizard Design for Complexity Management Application. In: *International Design Conference*, Design 2010, Dubrovnik, Croatia, May 2010.

[23] Lima, B. S., Soares L. F. G., Moreno, M. F. Considering Non-functional Aspects in the Design of Hypermedia Authoring Tools. In: *ACM Symposium on Applied Computing*, SAC 2011, Taiwan. 2011.

[24] Soares, L.F.G.; Soares Neto, C.S.; Sousa, J.G. *Architecture for DTV Dynamic Applications with Content and Behavior Constraints*. Technical Report. Informatics Department of PUC-Rio. Rio de Janeiro. January, 2012. ISSN 0103-974. Submitted to DocEng 2012.

[25] S. Fraïssé, J. Nanard, and M. Nanard. Generating hypermedia from speci cations by sketching multimedia templates. In *ACM Multimedia 96*, pages 353-364, Boston, MA, EUA, 1996.

[26] Bulterman, D. C. A., Rutledge, L., Hardman, L., Jansen, J. and Mullender, K. S., GRiNS: an authoring environment for web multimedia, *World Conference on Educational Multimedia, Hypermedia and Educational Telecommunications*, ED-MEDIA 99, Seattle, WA, USA, 1999.

Advene as a Tailorable Hypervideo Authoring Tool: a Case Study

Olivier Aubert
Université de Lyon, CNRS
Université Lyon 1, LIRIS,
UMR5205, France
olivier.aubert@liris.cnrs.fr

Yannick Prié
Université de Lyon, CNRS
Université Lyon 1, LIRIS,
UMR5205, France
yannick.prie@liris.cnrs.fr

Daniel Schmitt
Université de Strasbourg,
LISEC EA-2310, France
daniel.schmitt@etu.unistra.fr

ABSTRACT

Audiovisual documents provide a great primary material for analysis in multiple domains, such as sociology or interaction studies. Video annotation tools offer new ways of analysing these documents, beyond the conventional transcription. However, these tools are often dedicated to specific domains, putting constraints on the data model or interfaces that may not be convenient for alternative uses. Moreover, most tools serve as exploratory and analysis instruments only, not proposing export formats suitable for publication.

We describe in this paper a usage of the Advene software, a versatile video annotation tool that can be tailored for various kinds of analyses: users can define their own analysis structure and visualizations, and share their analyses either as structured annotations with visualization templates, or published on the Web as hypervideo documents. We explain how users can customize the software through the definition of their own data structures and visualizations. We illustrate this adaptability through an actual usage for interview analysis.

Categories and Subject Descriptors

H.5.4 [**Hypertext/Hypermedia**]: User Issues,Navigation; H.5.1 [**Multimedia Information Systems**]: Video

Keywords

Hypervideo, Annotation, Video Analysis, Mediafragments, Active Reading

1. INTRODUCTION

As described in [1], video analysis is often carried out through active reading, an iterative activity based on the creation of structured metadata and the usage of various visualizations for this metadata, in an intermediary stage for video navigation or as a final publishing stage. Documents produced by this activity can take the form of *hypervideos*.

Many video annotation tools are often strongly tied to a specific application domain. This allows them to offer a customized experience, with dedicated tools and interfaces, at the expense of some difficulty to be used outside of intended uses. For instance, a tool like ELAN [8] does not allow overlapping annotations, which may make sense in the linguistic context but may not be convenient for other practices. Moreover, most specialized tools being aimed at analysis, they do not particularly insist on the final phase of the process: publishing documents. Tools like Anvil [4] or Elan [8] propose multiple predefined structured export formats but do not allow users to define their own visualizations. On the other hand, rendering environments like [5] do not focus on the analysis side.

The Advene project and its main application Advene [2] are trying to reach a larger usability spectrum by offering a number of generic tools and interfaces, that can be user-customized to fit the application domain. Users can also define their own visualizations, in order to accommodate their specific needs and possibly to generate publishable documents. We claim that it is necessary that tools adapt to some extent to the user's needs, especially in such an exploratory activity. Furthermore, this flexibility must always be effective, in order to accompany the continous evolution of the user's ideas and needs.

In this article, we first present how Advene has been conceived to provide generic but customizable tools in order to accommodate a variety of usages. We briefly highlight the main features that provide this flexibility. Then we illustrate these capabilities by detailing a real use example and how Advene features were used to adapt to this particular situation.

2. ADVENE PRINCIPLES

The Advene software covers the whole range of active reading activities [1]: 1/ it allows to create annotations, either through dedicated interfaces, by importing data or through some feature extraction algorithms. Annotations can be structured through user-defined schemas. They also can be linked through n-ary relations, also user-defined, in order to express any kind of relationship. 2/ Once annotations are present, they can be used as a reference to navigate the audiovisual document, in order to investigate the material and possibly to update or extend the annotations. 3/ Annotations and possibly pieces from the video document can be used to generate various visualizations, as custom interfaces or as documents that may be published. The application offers a number of customizable interfaces for various actions (annotation edition, visualization or search). It integrates a template-based document generation system, allowing users to specify various renderings for their data. Eventually, the application can be extended by developers either through the use of plugins, for dedicated developments, or by contributions, Advene being free software.

The principles and architecture of Advene have been described with more details in previous articles [2]. We will focus here briefly on the main aspects of Advene that allow more specifically its flexibility.

2.1 Data model

As described in [2], the Advene/Cinelab[1] data model features explicitly structured annotation data, as well as the definition of queries and visualization templates. In our audiovisual context, we define an annotation as a piece of data of any kind associated with a video fragment, i.e. with two timecodes designating beginning and ending instants in a given video.

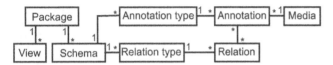

Figure 1: Global representation of the Advene/Cinelab data model

The annotation structure, summarized in figure 1, consists in user-defined annotation types and relation types that can themselves be grouped into schemas that represent a given point of view on the analysis. Views are used to transform annotations, along with the video, into visualizations appropriate for the user's task.

The model has been defined to be as expressive and flexible as possible. The definition of annotation types gives a way to categorize annotations, which is useful both for the user and for the computer. Relations, classified by relation types, may be used to express any graph structure, or more basically to link annotations according to the user's needs.

The annotation structure (annotation types and relation types) is defined by the user to fit his or her needs. It can be defined iteratively, and interactively, in order to foster experimentation with various analysis structures. New annotation types can be created on the fly, and annotations copied into this new type, seamlessly.

2.2 Visualization - hypervideo

Advene provides three main types of visualizations: ad-hoc views, dynamic views and static views.

Ad-hoc views are graphical components present in the software, such as a timeline or a tabular view. Such components provide great interactivity, and can be customized to some extent by users. For instance, users can define which annotation types are displayed in a timeline, and can save this configuration for future invocations.

Dynamic views use the annotation data to modify the rendering of the video while it is being played. Users can modify the display (caption textual or graphical data over the video, etc) or the time (automatically navigating from

one annotation to another one), or trigger different actions such as using text-to-speech or a Braille table [3] to render annotation data while the video is playing. Users can define dynamic views through rulesets, comparable to the filtering rules that can be found in e-mail client software.

Static views are visualizations specified by XML-based templates, combining information from the annotation structure and from the video. Using an XML-compatible template [9], users can define any kind of visualization according to their needs. The use of a template language is intended to lower the barrier to conceiving such visualizations. The Advene application embeds a webserver that dynamically serves the rendered templates to any web browser, or through an embedded HTML component. Links into the video control the Advene video player, offering the ability to directly play fragments related to annotations. This gives users the possibility to modify the underlying metadata (annotations) and get instant updates of the generated documents.

2.2.1 Hypervideo publishing

However, this approach implies that the Advene software has to be used to access visualizations and to fully experience their hypervideo nature by synchronizing with the Advene video player. In order to provide a publishing functionality, we integrated the possibility to statically export a set of defined visualizations.

The web export feature is basically a specialized version of a website copier, that walks through the defined visualizations (which are most often HTML documents with some specific links to control the Advene video player), captures the HTML content and injects javascript code to embed an HTML video player. Links to the Advene video player are converted into corresponding Media Fragment [7] URLs, to be able to address the embedded HTML video player.

Some features can be activated in the exported version, through the definition of HTML classes in the template. For instance, specifying the `transcriptHighlight` class will highlight elements of the class `transcript` synchronously with the video player.

We have seen that in addition to the annotation creation and navigation tools, user-definable visualizations allow Advene to cover the whole annotation lifecycle, from annotation creation to publishing. Besides, user-defined data structure and views offer a high level of tailorability. Their definitions represent the specialization of the tool, and they can be themselves shared and reused. We will now present how these features have been used through a real use case.

3. USE CASE

3.1 Context

Advene is used by Daniel Schmitt for his analysis of the visitors perception of museum exhibitions[2]. His experiment consists in fitting on visitors a small video camera mounted on glasses. The camera records a *subjective view* of the visit. At the exit of the exhibition, the subject and the researcher watch together the recorded video, and the researcher invites the subject to comment his or her behavior. For instance,

---

[1]The Advene data model has been refined and used in the context of the Cinelab project, see `http://www.advene.org/cinelab`.

[2]More explanations (in french) and public examples of interview analysis hypervideos are available on the `http://www.museographie.fr` website.

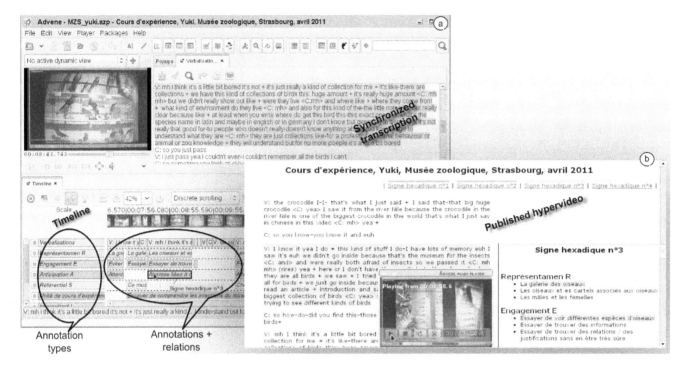

Figure 2: (a) Advene application GUI (b) Example of published hypervideo

he or she can be asked about his or her feelings when he or she stared for so long at a given piece of art, or sighed when arriving in front of another.

The interview process is itself recorded, and this recording constitutes the analyzed material: the audio track records the exchanges between the subject and the researcher, while the video track captures the video player that is used to replay the subjective view.

Once the interview is over, the researcher can later analyze the recorded material. He used the course-of-action [6] methodology, which is situated in the enaction paradigm. It involves recording a subject activity, and inviting the subject to verbalize explanations during a self-confrontation phase. The course-of-action methodology then distinguishes 6 kinds of components in the discourse, named *hexadic signs*: Involvement in the situation, Potential actuality, Referential, Representamen, Unit of course of experience and Interpretant. The researcher's aim is to identify in the discourse of the subject various *courses of experience*, in order to find out how the visitor builds up knowledge in the course of her or his action. For instance, from the following interview (extract):

Yuki and her friend, both students in biology (Master) are visiting the bird gallery in a zoological Museum. They look at different species and compare the size or the color of birds. This methodology shows that in fact, Yuki is disappointed not to find more indications.

Visitor: Before we came to this museum, I read an article... introduction and it said this museum has one of the biggest collection of birds [...] I think it's a little bit bored... we have this kind of collections of birds... this huge amount... it's really a huge amount but we didn't really show out like, where they live, where they come from, what kind of environment do they live and also for this kind of little notes, it's not really clear because [...] they are just collections for a professor of animal behavior or animal or zoo knowledge [...] I'm very

interested maybe just for the color... or maybe for... oh it's cute! [...] there are too many.

the researcher may identify the following hexadic signs:

Representamen The birds in the gallery
Involvement in the situation Try to find information
Potential actuality Would like to know where the birds live, where they come from and their environment
Referential This museum presents one of the biggest collection of birds / (I am student in biology)
Interpretant This gallery doesn't provide enough information
Unity of course of experience Try to understand what the museum intends to do without success

3.2 Methodology implementation

The implementation of this methodology in Advene was done in 4 steps, that include the definition of the annotation structure and of the visualization template that were done only once. After the structure and visualization were defined, the necessary steps were then reduced.

1. A transcription of the interview is carried out, using Advene dedicated interfaces – mainly the synchronized note-taking view. It appeared later that thanks to the interaction features of Advene, the exact transcription was not always strictly necessary for the analysis: some keywords used for navigation, accompanied with direct access to the audiovisual material could sometimes be enough to carry on the task of identifying the hexadic signs. However, transcription, though costly, is always useful for other uses such as publication.

2. The annotation structure is defined, based on the course-of-action [6] methodology. This consists in finding out how to best translate hexadic signs into data structures. The flexibility of Advene in the definition of data structures allowed rapid experimentation with different setups before finalizing an appropriate schema, which was then used for

all analyses. The final structure defines one annotation type for each hexadic sign, and uses relations to identify related hexadic sign occurrences that take part in a single course of experience.

3. Once the structure is stabilized, the video can be analyzed along the different hexadic signs. Fragments of the discourse are identified by the researcher as being instances of a given hexadic sign. A new annotation is then created in the type corresponding to the sign, with an explanation of the analysis. Advene ability to copy and move elements from one type to another was used. For instance, verbalization timecodes could be simply used as references for the creation of hexadic sign annotations.

The timeline view, shown in figure 2(a), proved to be an interesting and inspiring visualization for these hexadic signs, providing visual time indications and some kind of temporal grouping. The Advene transcription view, visible in figure 2(a), presents verbalizations as an interactive text document, usable to navigate the video. It was also used to provide contextual information and as a navigation interface.

4. In order to publish on the web, an Advene static view is defined as a template (that is reused for all analyses). It generates a transcription of the verbalizations synchronized with the video, and aligned with the hexadic signs in a second column, also synchronized with the video. This visualization brings another perspective on the same data, by visually grouping elements (verbalizations and hexadic signs) that may be dispersed in other views. It offers another anchor to allow the emergence of the meaning.

An example output is presented in figure 2(b). An embedded video player is synchronized with the transcription, which is sided with the hexadic signs. Highlighting is used to indicate the parts of the transcription and analysis that are related, and which ones concern the active video moment. The view can be visualized dynamically through the embedded web server, and an Advene-independent version can be extracted through the website export feature of Advene, in order to be put online on any website. The document presented here is publicly accessible on the `http://www.museographie.fr` website.

3.3 Evaluation results and lessons

More than 40 interviews have been carried out and analyzed using this setup. The availability of different visualizations for the annotations proved to be precious for the analysis, sometimes opening new perspectives on the data. For instance, the graphical timeline offers an overview of the temporal distribution of hexadic signs over the whole interview, that allows to distinguish temporal patterns in the discourse, while the specialized HTML visualization provides another perspective by grouping verbalizations and related hexadic signs.

The possibility to add on-the-fly new structures, new annotations or new visualizations, allows the researcher to build his own dedicated tools during the course of his research. Advene plasticity accompanies the researcher in the emergence of ideas.

Eventually, the possibility to share the analyses, either as published web documents like the one presented in figure 2(b) or as structured data (a package containing the definition of the annotations, of their structure and of the

defined views) makes it possible to subject the analysis to a critic, but also to constitute communities of experience.

4. CONCLUSION

Advene is a generic video annotation platform offering explicit means of customization (schemas for data structure, parameters for visualization customization, templates for document generation) in order to be adaptable to specific tasks. The definitions of the specialized data structure and visualizations express the adaptation of the tool, and can be shared and reused. After presenting these features, we illustrated this adaptability through a real-world example, where Advene proved to be an appropriate companion in the development of an exploratory research.

The intention of Advene is to lower the barrier to conceiving dedicated structures and visualizations. The collaboration of researchers and programmers was still needed to design some of the templates, but we intend to gather more examples to be able to build a library which could serve as inspiration, and also make directly available some of the most used visualizations.

Acknowledgements. This work has been partially funded by the French FUI (Fonds Unique Interministériel) - CineCast project.

5. REFERENCES

[1] O. Aubert, P.-A. Champin, Y. Prié, and B. Richard. Active reading and hypervideo production. *Multimedia Systems Journal, Special Issue on Canonical Processes of Media Production*, page 6 pp., 2008.

[2] O. Aubert and Y. Prié. Advene: active reading through hypervideo. In *ACM Hypertext'05*, pages 235–244, Salzburg, Austria, Sep 2005.

[3] B. Encelle, M. Ollagnier-Beldame, S. Pouchot, and Y. Prié. Annotation-based video enrichment for blind people: A pilot study on the use of earcons and speech synthesis. In *13th International ACM SIGACCESS Conference on Computers and Accessibility*, pages 123–130, Dundee, Scotland, Oct 2011.

[4] M. Kipp. ANVIL - A Generic Annotation Tool for Multimodal Dialogue. In *Proceedings of Eurospeech 2001*, pages 1367–1370, Aaborg, Sep 2001.

[5] Mozilla. *Popcorn.js The HTML5 Media Framework*, 2012. Website `http://www.popcornjs.org/` accessed 2012/01/30.

[6] J. Theureau. *Handbook of Cognitive Task Design*, chapter Course of action analysis and course of action centered design. Lawrence Erlbaum Ass., 2003.

[7] R. Troncy, E. Mannens, S. Pfeiffer, and D. V. Deursen. Media Fragments URI 1.0. Technical report, W3C, 2011.

[8] P. Wittenburg, H. Brugman, A. Russel, A. Klassmann, and H. Sloetjes. Elan: a professional framework for multimodality research. In *In Proceedings of Language Resources and Evaluation Conference (LREC*, 2006.

[9] Zope Corporation. *Zope Page Templates reference*, 2004. `http://www.zope.org/Documentation/Books/ZopeBook/2_6Edition/AppendixC.stx`.

Content and Document Based Approach for Digital Productivity Applications

Thierry Delprat
Nuxeo
18-20 rue Soleillet
75020 Paris

ABSTRACT

In today's world most of the data produced and consumed by employees is content. In this talk we will present our approach to create and deploy content and document based applications to improve business processes and user experience.

Categories and Subject Descriptors

H.4.0 [**Information Systems**]: Information Systems Applications – *General.*

General Terms

Design, Management.

Keywords

Enterprise Content Management, ECM.

A First Approach to the Automatic Recognition of Structural Patterns in XML Documents

Angelo Di Iorio, Silvio Peroni, Francesco Poggi, Fabio Vitali
Department of Computer Science
University of Bologna
Italy
{diiorio,essepuntato,fpoggi,fabio}@cs.unibo.it

ABSTRACT

XML is among the preferred formats for storing the structure of documents such as scientific articles, manuals, documentation, literary works, etc. Sometimes publishers adopt established and well-known vocabularies such as DocBook and TEI, other times they create partially or entirely new ones that better deal with the particular requirements of their documents. The (explicit and implicit) requirements of use in these vocabularies often follow well-established patterns, creating meta-structures (the block, the container, the inline element, etc.) that persist across vocabularies and authors and that describe a truer and more general conceptualization of the documents' building blocks. Addressing such meta-structures not only gives a better insight of what documents really are composed of, but provides abstract and more general mechanisms to work on documents regardless of the availability of specific schemas, tools and presentation stylesheets. In this paper we introduce a schema-independent theory based on eleven *structural patterns*. We provide a definition of such patterns and how they synthesize characteristics emerging from real markup documents. Additionally, we propose an algorithm that allows us to identify the pattern of each element in a set of homogeneous markup documents.

Categories and Subject Descriptors

I.7.2 [**Document And Text Processing**]: Document Preparation—*Markup languages*; I.7.2 [**Document And Text Processing**]: Document Capture— *Document analysis*

General Terms

Algorithms, Theory

Keywords

XML, descriptive markup, document visualisation, pattern recognition, structural patterns

1. INTRODUCTION

Publishing has been part of a revolution in the last twenty years. The proliferation of digital formats and tools for digital publishing is undeniable, and the same World Wide Web is constantly used for publishing content, even personal, even by inexpert users. XML still plays a crucial role in this evolving scenario: XML-encoded documents such as books, articles, legal acts, reports, specifications are ubiquitous, and XML-based languages are widely used as intermediate formats for conversion and communication, and as final formats for publication.

In many cases, communities use well-known vocabularies such as DocBook [15] and TEI [14], other times they use customized vocabularies tailored for their purposes, others they completely invent new languages. It is not surprising that in all these solutions designers have to deal with complex constraints within the language. They are required to cover heterogeneous situations and to foresee possible (validation) mistakes and misinterpretations by the final users. All these difficulties contribute to produce rich and complex schemas, that often require a lot of effort to be fully understood and applied.

This paper discusses an alternative approach for studying and designing XML documents and schemas. Instead of focusing on the compliance to schemas that capture **all** aspects of a domain - from those general and used in most of the documents up to the irregularities and specific cases that are actually useful in a few cases – we propose to shift the analysis to a **meta-level** and to study classes of elements, i.e. patterns, that persist across documents and that distil the conceptualization of the documents and their components.

We have been investigating patterns for XML documents for some time [3] [4]. In this paper, we give a full description of our theory about *structural patterns*, meta-structures that we consider sufficient to express what authors of documents and schemas mostly need. We also provide a formal definition of our patterns and their relations, and discuss how they synthesize characteristics emerging from real markup documents.

A pattern-based classification can be used for different purposes. For instance, it can be adopted as reference model to extract information from legacy documents: rather than trying to derive (a posteriori) constraints on those documents, users can look for those patterns and derive the structural role of each piece of information. Similarly, compliance to patterns can be checked retrospectively in order to verify how user really follow certain grammars, how they share design approaches, and to what extent their documents follow community guidelines.

The adoption of structural patterns is useful for creating new documents and schemas too. They reduce choices, thus reduce possibility of errors and misinterpretations. Yet, some specific cases and constraints are not covered by patterns but patterns still capture the most relevant information of documents. Our goal is to investigate which are the most important and shared features of well-engineered documents, which of them should (and can) be extracted, which can be neglected and under which circumstances.

Notice also that a simpler model eases documents' processing by future applications: even those applications not yet existing today will be more reliable and easy-to-build if dealing with simpler and less ambiguous structures. The reliability and re-usability of patterns make them good solutions even when creating new XML documents, besides bringing benefits to human readers in terms of readability and noise minimization.

In fact, our approach is minimalist. We believe that it is possible to derive from any schema a sub-schema that is fully pattern-based and that authors actually adhere to in most of their documents. Towards this goal, we present some preliminary studies that illustrate how a significative set of XML documents produced by different authors within a given community – DocBook documents written by the authors of the Balisage Conference Series – follows the same meta-structural organisation. The paper also introduces the algorithm used for the analysis, that is able to identify the pattern of each element in a set of homogeneous documents. We exploit such automatic patterns recognition for automatically generating reasonable CSS stylesheets for the visualisation of XML documents – or, better, for their pattern-based counterparts – without making any assumption on the implicit semantics defined by the vocabulary in consideration.

The rest of the paper is organised as follows. In Section 2 we give an overview of our theory of structural patterns, while details of our theory and a formal description are provided in Section 3. In Section 4 we illustrate our algorithm for the automatic recognition of structural patterns and its application for automatic visualization. In Section 5 we present the experiments on our algorithm and we discuss the outcome of these experiments. In Section 6 we discuss some relevant work about the recognition of structures and meta-structures in XML documents. Finally, we conclude in Section 7 presenting some development we plan for the near future.

2. STRUCTURAL PATTERNS

The idea of using patterns to produce reusable and high-quality assets is not new in the literature. Software engineers [5], architects and designers often use – or indeed *reuse* – patterns to handle problems that occur over and over again. Patterns have also been studied to modularize and customize web ontologies [12]. They guarantee the flexibility and maintainability of concepts and solutions in several heterogeneous scenarios.

We have been investigating patterns for XML documents (e.g., [3] [4]) to understand how the structure of digital documents can be segmented into atomic components, which can be addressed independently and manipulated for different purposes. Instead of defining a large number of complex

and diversified structures, a small number of *structural patterns* needs to be found that are sufficient to express what most users need.

The two main characterizing aspects of such set of patterns should be:

- *orthogonality* – each pattern needs to have a specific goal and to fit a specific context. The orthogonality between patterns makes it possible to associate a single pattern to each of the most common situations in document design. Then, whenever a designer has a particular need he/she has to only select the corresponding pattern and to apply it;

- *assemblability* – each pattern can be used only in some locations (within other patterns). Although this may seem a limitation, such strictness improves the expressiveness and non-ambiguity of patterns. By limiting the possible choices, patterns prevent the creation of uncontrolled and misleading content structures. This characteristic still allows the presence of overlapping items – for example, a block that contains two different inlines that overlap upon the same segment continues to be a valid structure in terms of patterns because its content model is not violated, even though the presence of overlapping descendants.

These patterns allow authors to create unambiguous, manageable and well-structured documents. The regularity of pattern-based documents makes it possible to perform easily complex operations even when knowing very little about the documents' vocabulary. Designers can implement more reliable and efficient tools, can make hypothesis regarding the meanings of document fragments, can identify singularities and can study global properties of sets of documents.

In particular, the automatic recognition of structural patterns can help in the visualization of XML documents. In particular, given a set of schema-homogeneous XML documents, our idea is to identify markup elements and their related compliant structural patterns knowing neither the implicit semantics of markup elements nor any presentational stylesheet associate with the schema.

In Section 3 we derive the structural patterns using description logic formulas[1] to provide their formal definitions from the abstract conceptualization provided by the abstract patterns of Fig. 1.

3. A THEORY OF PATTERNS

In this section we introduce general properties of markup elements and organize them in abstract classes from which we derive the actual patterns we describe in our model. The overall structure of our pattern theory is summarized in Fig. 1. Nine abstract patterns (in yellow) are used to generate eleven instanceable patterns (in blue) that constitute the core of our model, as detailed in Table 1.

3.1 Basic properties of markup content models

Each structural pattern is characterised by general properties that restrict their elements to be compliant with a

---

[1]A brief introduction to description logic can be found in [10] and [8].

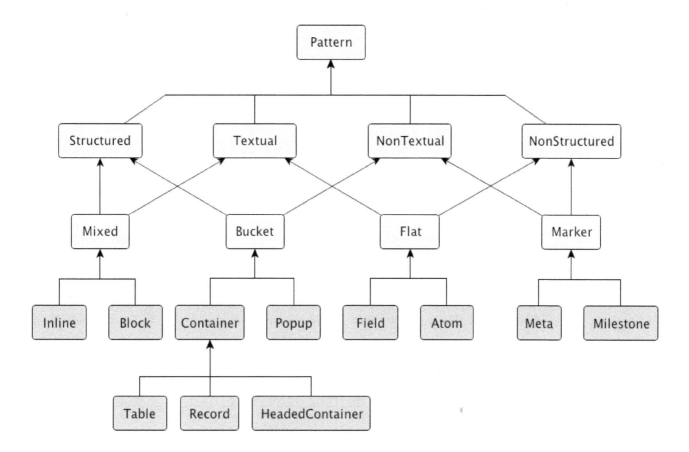

Figure 1: The classes defining the hierarchical structure of the structural patterns defined in our model. The arrows indicate sub-class relationships between patterns (e.g. Mixed is sub-class of Structured).

particular content model. Namely, we organize markup elements in four disjoint classes according to their ability to contain text and/or other elements.

We define *Textual* as the class of elements that *can have textual content* in their content models and *NonTextual* as the class of elements that cannot. These two classes are disjointed. We also define *Structured* as the class of elements that can *contain other elements*, and *NonStructured* as the class of elements that cannot. These two classes are disjoint.

```
Textual ⊑ ⊤
NonTextual ⊑ ⊤
NonTextual ≡ ¬ Textual
Textual ⊓ NonTextual ⊑ ⊥
Structured ⊑ ⊤
NonStructured ⊑ ⊤
NonStructured ≡ ¬ Structured
Structured ⊓ NonStructured ⊑ ⊥
```

We define the property *contains* (and its inverse *isContainedBy*) on *Structured* to indicate the markup elements its individuals contain:

```
∃contains.⊤ ⊑ Structured
isContainedBy ≡ contains-
```

While the content model of structured elements can contain any kind of optional and repeatable selection of elements, we need to be able to define some restrictions to their element repeatability. We thus define the boolean properties *canContainHomogeneousElements*, true if the element

can contain elements that share the same name[2] , and *canContainHeterogeneousElements*, true if an element can contain elements with different names. In addition, we define *containsAsHeader* as a sub-property of *contains* to specify when a structured-based element contains *header* elements.

```
∃canContainHomogeneousElements.⊤ ⊑ Structured
⊤ ⊑ ≤1canContainHomogeneousElements
∃canContainHeterogeneousElements.⊤ ⊑
    Structured
⊤ ⊑ ≤1canContainHeterogeneousElements
containsAsHeader ⊑ contains
```

By combining the four classes defined above we are able to generate four new classes:

- class *Mixed*. Individuals of this class can contain other elements and text nodes;

- class *Bucket*. Individual of this class can contain other elements but no text nodes;

- class *Flat*. Individual of this class can contain text nodes but no elements;

- class *Marker*. Individual of this class can contain neither text nodes nor elements.

---

[2]By *name* we mean the pair *(namespace, general identifier)* of XML elements.

Table 1: Eleven structural patterns for descriptive documents.

Pattern	Description	Example (DocBook)
Atom	Any simple box of text, without internal substructures (simple content) that is allowed in a mixed content structure but not in a container.	email, code
Block	Any container of text and other substructures except for (even recursively) other block elements. The pattern is meant to represent block-level elements such as paragraphs.	para, caption
Container	Any container of a sequence of other substructures and that does not directly contain text. The pattern is meant to represent higher document structures that give shape and organization to a text document, but do not directly include the content of the document.	bibliography, preface
Field	Any simple box of text, without internal substructures (simple content) that is allowed in a container but not in a mixed content structure.	pubdate, publishername
Headed Container	Any container starting with a head of one or more block elements. The pattern is usually meant to represent nested hierarchical elements (such as sections, subsections, etc., as well as their headings).	section, chapter
Inline	Any container of text and other substructures, including (even recursively) other inline elements. The pattern is meant to represent inline-level styles such as bold, italic, etc.	emphasis
Meta	Any content-less structure (but data could be specified in attributes) that is allowed in a container but not in a mixed content structure. The pattern is meant to represent metadata elements that assert things about the document, but are disconnected to its actual text content.	imagedata, colspec
Milestone	Any content-less structure (but data could be specified in attributes) that is allowed in a mixed content structure but not in a container. The pattern is meant to represent locations within the text content that are relevant for any reason.	xref, co
Popup	Any structure that, while still not allowing text content inside itself, is nonetheless found in a mixed content context. The pattern is meant to represent complex substructures that interrupt but do not break the main flow of the text, such as footnotes.	footnote, tip
Record	Any container that does not allow substructures to repeat themselves internally. The pattern is meant to represent database records with their variety of (non-repeatable) fields.	address, revision
Table	Any container that allows a repetition of homogeneous substructures. The pattern is meant to represent a table of a database with its content of multiple similarly structured records.	tr, keywordset

These classes are defined as follows:

```
Mixed  ⊑ Structured ⊓ Textual
Bucket ⊑ Structured ⊓ NonTextual
Flat   ⊑ Textual ⊓ NonStructured
Marker ⊑ NonTextual ⊓ NonStructured
```

Given these eight classes, we can now define our structural patterns which will be described in the next section with examples from DocBook [15].

3.2 Structural patterns

We define the class *Block* to organise the document content as a sequence of nestable elements and text nodes. In particular, elements following this pattern can contain text and other elements compliant with the patterns *Inline*, *Atom*, *Milestones* and *Popup*, which will be introduced in the following. Furthermore, it is a requirement that block elements are contained only by *container* and *popup* elements, as follows:

```
Block ≡
    Mixed ⊓
    ∀isContainedBy.(Container ⊔ Popup)
Block ⊑ ∀contains.(
    Inline ⊔ Atom ⊔ Milestone ⊔ Popup)
```

Examples of DocBook elements typically used as compliant with the *Block* pattern are *para* and *caption*.

We next define the class *Inline* with the same use and content model of the pattern *Block*, but differing primarily because:

- inline elements can contain other elements compliant with the same pattern while block elements cannot;

- inline elements must always be contained by other block or inline elements and by no other type of element.

These constraints also imply that inline elements cannot be used as root elements of documents and that the class *Block* is disjoint with the class *Inline* (i.e., a markup element cannot be a block and an inline at the same time), as specified by the following axioms:

```
Inline ≡
  Mixed ⊓
  ∀isContainedBy.(Inline ⊔ Block)
Inline ⊑
  ∀contains.(
    Inline ⊔ Atom ⊔ Milestone ⊔ Popup) ⊓
  ∃isContainedBy.(Inline ⊔ Block)
Block ⊓ Inline ⊑ ⊥
```

Examples of DocBook elements typically used as compliant with the *Inline* pattern are *link* and *emphasis*.

The class *Atom* is defined to describe literal text that is part of the document body. Moreover, similarly to *Inline*, elements following the *Atom* pattern can only be contained within block or inline elements (and consequently they also cannot be used as root elements of documents). It can contain textual content and no other elements, as shown in the following definition:

```
Atom ≡
  Flat ⊓
  ∀isContainedBy.(Inline ⊔ Block)
Atom ⊑ ∃isContainedBy.(Inline ⊔ Block)
```

Examples of DocBook elements typically used as compliant with the *Atom* pattern are *email* and *code*.

We next define the class *Milestone* to contain neither other elements nor textual content. Moreover, similarly to *Inline*, elements following the *Milestone* pattern can only be contained within block or inline elements (and consequently they also cannot be used as root elements of documents). The formal definition of this class is as follows:

```
Milestone ≡
  Marker ⊓
  ∀isContainedBy.(Inline ⊔ Block)
Milestone ⊑ ∃isContainedBy.(Inline ⊔ Block)
```

The distinctive characteristic of the pattern *Milestone* is the *location* it assumes within the document. Examples of DocBook elements typically used as compliant with the *Milestone* pattern are *xref* and *co*.

We next define the pattern *Popup* as that Bucket that is only present within block and inline elements. Moreover, similarly to *Inline*, elements following the *Popup* pattern can only be contained within block or inline elements (and consequently they also cannot be used as root elements of documents), as shown in the following excerpt:

```
Popup ≡
  Bucket ⊓
  ∀isContainedBy.(Inline ⊔ Block)
Popup ⊑
  ∀contains.(
    Container ⊔ Field ⊔ Meta ⊔ Block) ⊓
  ∃isContainedBy.(Inline ⊔ Block)
```

Popup elements are used whenever complex structures need to be placed within content elements such as paragraphs. Examples of DocBook elements typically used as compliant with the *Popup* pattern are *footnote* and *tip*.

We next define the class Meta also for elements that contain neither other elements nor textual content. Contrarily to the pattern *Milestone*, which was meant to describe

markup elements that impact the document because of their location, the main feature of its disjoint sibling is the mere *existence*, independently from the position it has within the document. *Meta* elements convey metadata information about the document or part of it, independently of where they are (e.g., the elements *imagedata* or *colspec* in DocBook). Thus, meta elements can be contained only within container or popup elements, as follows:

```
Meta ≡
  Marker ⊓
  ∀isContainedBy.(Container ⊔ Popup)
Meta ⊓ Milestone ⊑ ⊥
```

The class *Field* is defined to describe literal metadata or text that is not really part of the document body, contrarily to its disjointed sibling *Atom*. Its main difference with *Meta* is that *Field* can contain textual content, as shown by the following definition:

```
Field ≡
  Flat ⊓
  ∀isContainedBy.(Container ⊔ Popup)
Field ⊓ Atom ⊑ ⊥
```

Examples of DocBook elements typically used as compliant with the *Field* pattern are *pubdate* and *publishername*.

The next class to be defined is the pattern *Container*, which concerns the structural organization of a document. Elements following this pattern contain no textual content and contain only elements compliant with the patterns: *Meta*, *Field*, *Block* and any subtype of *Container*. It is disjointed with the pattern *Popup*, although they share the same content model. Its formalisation is as follows:

```
Container ≡
  Bucket ⊓
  ∀isContainedBy.(Container ⊔ Popup)
Container ⊑
  ∀contains.(Container ⊔ Field ⊔ Meta ⊔ Block)
Container ⊓ Popup ⊑ ⊥
```

Examples of DocBook elements typically used as compliant with the *Container* pattern are *bibliography* and *preface*.

Container has a very general definition. It is thus useful to define subclasses that describe situations all ascribable to the Container pattern, but that have a typicality worth of their own pattern. The first such pattern is *Table*. Elements compliant with *Table* must contain only homogeneous elements (but they can be repeated), as follows:

```
Table ≡
  Container ⊓
  canContainHomogeneousElements:true ⊓
  canContainHeterogeneousElements:false
```

Representative DocBook elements that are commonly used as compliant with the pattern *Table* are *tr* and *keywordset*.

The pattern *Record* has the opposite restriction than *Table*: its element can only contain heterogeneous and non repeatable elements, as in the following axioms:

```
Record ≡
  Container ⊓
  canContainHomogeneousElements:false ⊓
  canContainHeterogeneousElements:true
```

Examples of DocBook elements typically used as compliant with the *Record* pattern are *address* and *revision*.

Next, the pattern *HeadedContainer* is the subclass of *Container* whose content model need to begin with one or more block elements (the heading), specified through the property *containsAsHeader* as follows:

```
HeadedContainer ⊑
  Container ⊓
  ∀containsAsHeader.Block
```

Examples of DocBook elements typically used as compliant with the *HeadedContainer* pattern are *section* and *chapter*.

Finally, it is also important to point out that all these subclasses of *Container* are disjoint, as follows:

```
Table ⊓ Record ⊑ ⊥
HeadedContainer ⊓ Record ⊑ ⊥
HeadedContainer ⊓ Table ⊑ ⊥
```

In the following section we introduce an algorithm for determining the pattern that best describes each element of an XML document.

4. RETRIEVING STRUCTURAL PATTERNS IN DOCUMENTS

In order to verify whether the theory of patterns presented in the previous section is adequate and complete, we describe here an algorithm we have created to assign one of the patterns to the elements of one or more XML documents using the same vocabulary, relying on no background information about the vocabulary, its intended meaning and its schema.

During the first preliminary step the algorithm performs a visit of the whole input document in order to group the elements with the same pair *(namespace,name)*[3]. This task of associating a structural pattern to each element in the input document is performed in four different steps that will be described in the following.

Step 1. After this introductory phase the algorithm considers each group and assigns their elements to one of the following categories Section 3.1:

1. *Mixed* if the elements contain both non-empty text nodes and other elements. It is sufficient that one element of the group contains both non-empty text and other elements to add all the elements of the group to this category.

2. *Marker* if the elements contain neither other elements nor non-empty text nodes. It is necessary that all the elements of the group are empty to add all the elements to this category.

3. *Textual* if the elements contain text nodes but no elements.

4. *Structured* if the elements contain only elements but no text nodes.

These categories correspond to the first four abstract classes defined in the pattern ontology. The algorithm then proceeds to identify more properties of the elements, thereby moving the elements to more specific and eventually concrete pattern classes.

---

[3]We refer to this pair as its *general identifier* (as a nostalgic remembrance of the good old SGML days). In the rest of this discussion we will refer to these groups of element as "the element with general identifier *id*", or just "the element *id*", and we will talk simply of "elements" referring to all the elements with the same general identifier.

Step 2. In this step the definitions of the patterns are used to derive rules that identify even more specific characteristics of the element groups. Consider for instance the first rule:

- If a *Mixed* element (or of one of its subclasses) contains a *Textual* element, then the *Textual* element becomes *Inline*.

In fact, given the definitions of the patterns Section 2, elements classified as *Textual* can only belong to concrete classes *Inline*, *Block* or *Mixed*, but among these the only pattern that can be contained by *Mixed* elements is *Inline*. Using similar arguments we can derive the following rules:

- If an *Inline* element is contained within a *Structured* element, then the *Structured* element becomes *Mixed*.

- If a *Marker* element is contained within a *Mixed* element (or any of its subclasses), then the *Marker* element becomes *Milestone*.

- If a *Structured* element is contained within a *Mixed* element (or any of its subclasses), then the *Structured* element becomes *Popup*.

These rules are tested sequentially over the whole document. Since the effects of any rule may change the state of the either of the container and contained element, the premises of another rule could become true therefore triggering its execution, which could trigger yet another rule, and so on, the algorithm tests these rules over all the element groups of the document until no rule can be executed any more.

Step 3. After these steps the algorithm moves the elements that are still associated to abstract patterns into concrete ones. For example, since *Mixed* is an abstract class and has two concrete subclasses *Inline* or *Block*, and since in the previous steps we have identified all the *Inline* elements, the remaining *Mixed* elements can become *Block*. Similarly, *Textual* elements become either *Fields*[4], *Marker* elements become *Meta*, and *Structured* elements become plain *Containers*.

Step 4. The following step is to provide for the identification of the three *Container* subclasses, *Table*, *Record*, and *HeadedContainer*. The algorithm uses their basic properties to discern the Container elements. In particular the algorithm introduces the following shift rules:

- If each element in a group contains one or more elements with the same general identifier, then it becomes *Table*.

- If each element in a group contains many differently named elements with different general identifiers, then it becomes a *Record*.

- If each element in a group contains an initial list of *Block* elements with the given sequence of general identifiers, followed by a list of one or more elements whose identifier is not contained in the head, then it becomes a *HeadedContainer*.

---

[4]We decided not to consider the pattern *Atom* in the algorithm for simplicity, since in our experiments it was always captured by the pattern *Inline*.

5. TESTING THE THEORY

We finally performed a preliminary evaluation of the quality of the algorithm for the automatic recognition of structural patterns. To do so, we selected an XML vocabulary (i.e. DocBook), manually assigned each element of its schema to one of our patterns according to our understanding of the semantics of the element (as illustrated in Table 2), and compared it to the outcome of the algorithm over a number of documents. Since the schema gives less strict definitions of its element than those allowed in our patterns, and since we compared a human analysis of the schema against an algorithmic evaluation of actual documents, we aimed to prove two important points of our theory: first of all, that there is a reasonable sub-schema of the main schema that is pattern-compliant, and, secondly, that in most cases authors can and will adhere to such subschema for their expressive needs even if the grammar of the language does not require them to do so. The full results of the test and the generic CSS produced from the patterns we recognised are available online at http://fpoggi.web.cs.unibo.it/DOCENG2012/patterns.html.

Table 2: The assignments of each element of the DocBook schema in consideration to one of our patterns.

Pattern	DocBook elements
Inline	biblioid, citation, code, emphasis, link, quote, subscript, superscript, email, jobtitle
Block	bibliomixed, mathphrase, orgname, para, subtitle, term, title, programlisting, td, th
Container	affiliation, author, equation, figure, info, informaltable, listitem, mediaobject, note, table, variablelist, blockquote, td, th
Table	abstract, caption, itemizedlist, keywordset, legalnotice, orderedlist, personblurb, tbody, thead, tr
Record	confgroup, imageobject, personname, varlistentry
Headed-Container	appendix, article, bibliography, section
Popup	footnote, blockquote, programlisting
Field	confdates, conftitle, firstname, keyword, othername, surname, email,jobtitle
Meta	col, imagedata
Milestone	xref

Specifically, we have chosen a particular subset of the DocBook language used by the Balisage Markup Conference[5], and 118 papers published in the years by that conference. This was chosen as a first experiment for several reasons: first of all, all the papers of the conference are freely available online[6], then, we know the community and the publi-

---

[5]http://balisage.net/tagset.html

[6]http://balisage.net/Proceedings/index.html

cation process and are personally certain that the authors of the papers are the actual authors of the XML versions available online (i.e., only a very limited editorial process affected the actual ML vocabulary chosen) and, finally, we know that the authors belong to a community composed of markup experts.

We first run the algorithm on each paper independently: the outcome of each single execution assigned a pattern to each element present in each input document, thereby creating a scheme of patterns for each paper. We then compared each execution against each other to create a single scheme of patterns for all documents. As shown under the heading "algorithm's outcomes" of the results available online, this phase created a clear polarization of the outcomes in 2 homogeneous groups, composed of 68 and 50 documents respectively, each with really similar pattern schemes to each other. By analysing the results, the group of 68 papers are a good match to the the assignments in Table 2 created manually on the schema, while the second group did not provide a good set of patterns for a number of reasons, the more evident of which is that the pattern *Inline* heavily prevails over the others, being assigned to more than a half of the elements.

Table 3: All the admissible shifts among patterns.

Patterns	Pattern shift
Block,Field	Block
Milestone, Inline	Inline
Meta, Field	Field
Meta, Block	Block

Even in the first group of papers we had problems. For instance, the algorithm was not able to assign one pattern to each element: thirty elements (i.e., 50% of the total) received the same pattern in all the 68 documents, while the others had two or more patterns assigned. From our point of view this variability should be interpreted neither as a mistake of the authors of those documents nor as wrong outcome of our algorithm. Rather, it means that different authors use the same element in different ways, such as happened to the element *note*. In this case, all the authors of the first set of papers used this element as a container for one or more blocks (e.g. paragraphs) – and the algorithm correctly associated the pattern *Container* (or one of its subclasses) to it. However, in five of these documents the element *note* did not contain repeated elements and thus the algorithm recognised it as *Record*, while in other six documents it contained homogeneous and repeated elements (and thus it was recognised as *Table*). In addition, in one document *note* contained always a sort of header (i.e. an element *title*), and consequently it was recognised as *HeadedContainer*.

In order to reduce the multiplicity of assignments, we applied three specific reduction strategies to all the element groups, so as to select the most suitable pattern in case of disagreement (such as the aforementioned multiple assignment to the element *note*):

1. First, we applied a *pattern shift*. If element E is associated to both pattern $P1$ and $P2$ and $P1$ can be used in place of $P2$, then E has pattern $P1$. For instance, the element *para* has been recognised as both

Block (including both text and elements) and *Field* (including only text) by the algorithm. Since a *Block* element can happen to just contain text but Fields can never contain other elements, then *para* elements can be assigned to the pattern *Block* without problems. In Table 3 we illustrate all the possible pattern shifts.

2. We then applied a *discrimination rule for containers* , where we chose a specific kind of container whenever an element was associated to more that one subclass of containers. Namely, if an element ended up associated to two patterns (both subclasses of Container), then the element is associated to one of the subclasses if there was a clear disparity in the size of the two assignments (i.e., to the subclass that was selected more than 57% of the times), and to their superclass Container if no clear choice emerged (i.e., if both assignments ended up between 43% and 57% of the times).

3. Finally, we applied the *majority wins rule* to perform final discriminations in the remaining patterns, using a specific order for the comparisons and to solve equalities: first *Container* or any of its subclasses, then *Popup, Block, Inline, Milestone, Field*, and finally *Meta*. For instance, the element *orderedlist* was given pattern *Table* since it has been recognised twenty times as *Table* and only five times as *Popup*.

Table 4: The assignments returned by our process. The differences with the assignments illustrated in Table 2 are highlighted in italics.

Pattern	DocBook elements
Inline	biblioid, citation, code, emphasis, link, quote, subscript, superscript
Block	bibliomixed, mathphrase, orgname, para, subtitle, term, title, programlisting, td
Container	affiliation, *appendix*, figure, info, informaltable, mediaobject, note, table
Table	abstract, caption, *equation*, *imageobject*, itemizedlist, keywordset, legalnotice, orderedlist, personblurb, tbody, thead, tr, *variablelist*
Record	*author*, confgroup, *listitem*, personname, varlistentry
Headed-Container	article, bibliography, section
Popup	footnote, blockquote
Field	confdates, conftitle, firstname, keyword, othername, surname, email,jobtitle, *th*
Meta	col, imagedata
Milestone	xref

After disposing of all the ambiguous assignments, we obtained the list of pattern assignment shown in Table 4, where every element is associated with only one pattern. We then compared such assignments with the ones we illustrated in Table 2. Under the heading "Final discussion" of the results available at http://fpoggi.web.cs.unibo.it/DOCENG2012/ patterns.html it is possible to find a brief overview of all the stages of this process, together with the data related to the comparison with the assignments in Table 2. In addition, there are also links to download the code developed and to visualize these documents with the generic CSS produced from the recognised patterns.

In Table 5 we illustrate how many elements were assigned to the various patterns by our automatic process, highlighting also the amount of false-positive and false-negative assignments emerged from the comparison with the assignments in Table 2.

Table 5: The amount of elements assigned to each pattern by our automatic process, and the false positives and false negatives resulting from the comparison with the assignments in Table 2.

pattern	recognised	false positive	false negative
Inline	8	0	0
Block	9	0	1
Container	8	1	4
Table	12	3	0
Record	6	2	1
Headed-Container	3	0	1
Popup	2	0	0
Field	9	1	0
Meta	2	0	0
Milestone	1	0	0

The algorithm produced the same results as in Table 2 for 53 assignments over 60 (88%). We found the following issues on the other ones:

- some assignments (5 over 7) were *more specific*. In two ways: (i) the pattern assigned to an element was a subclass of the one we identified manually (for instance, the element *author* was recognized as *Record* instead of *Container*) or (ii) the recognized pattern could be shifted to the one identified manually (e.g., the element *th* has pattern *Field* instead of *Block*);

- one assignment detected a *more general* pattern. It is the case of the element *appendix* recognized as *Container* instead of *HeadedContainer*;

- one assignment was completely different from our interpretation, namely *imageobject* that was recognized as *Record* instead of *Table*. Notice that the patterns *Record* and *Table* are both (disjoint and not shiftable) subclasses of the same pattern *Container*.

Some "more specific" assignments may depend on this dataset. Some elements, in fact, are recognized as belonging to a class since the dataset does not contain examples of using that element in a different way. The algorithm does not found enough information to discriminate between patterns and to assign a more general characterization.

Overall, this preliminary results are very promising. In particular, they confirm that an incremental approach can be exploited to assign patterns to each element of a set of documents, even without knowing the schema that document is validated against. Moreover, experiments showed that the way authors actually use document elements, even if those elements do not follow patterns in the schema declaration, does not differ so much from their pattern-based counterpart.

Analysing in detail the remaining fifty documents we discarded in our experiments, we established that several elements assigned to the pattern *Inline* were the result of an ambiguous use (although allowed by the Balisage DTD) of particular elements. For instance, let us consider the element *figure*. Sometimes, some authors have been used that element within a paragraph (element *para*), thus implicitly assigning to it the role of *Popup*. Other times, *figure* has been used as direct child of *Containers* and, thus, it has been recognised as a proper *Container* by our algorithm (since a *Popup* cannot be contained by a *Container*). Of course, when these two conditions happen in the same document, the algorithmic computation tends to diverge to a "limit case", in which the root of the document is considered as a *Block* and all the other elements are *Inlines*. In order to avoid this issue, we are investigating strategies to calculate the most appropriate pattern scheme in such a scenario. In addition, we are investigating feasible approaches for the automatic suggestion of document changes (or *refactor operations*) so as to restructure these documents according to our pattern theory.

6. RELATED WORKS

In this section we provide an overview of some recent literature that is relevant to our work. For instance, Tannier et al. [13], starting from previous works by Lini et al. [11] and Colazzo et al. [2], describe an algorithm to assign each XML element in a document to one of three different categories: *hard tag*, *soft tag* and *jump tag*. *Hard tags* are all those elements that are commonly used to structure the document content in different blocks – they are the most frequent kind of elements and usually "interrupt the linearity of a text" and, in the DocBook vocabulary [15], correspond to, e.g., *para*, *section*, *table* etc. Next, all the elements that identify significant text fragments and are "transparent while reading the text" are *soft tags* – they are mostly inline elements with some presentation rule (e.g., in DocBook, *emphasis*, *link*, *xref*, etc. shown as bold, italic, in colour, etc.). Finally, the *jump tags* are elements that are logically "detached from the surrounding text" and that give access to related information – e.g., in DocBook, *footnote*, *comment*, *tip*, etc. Tannier et al. also introduce algorithms to assign XML elements to these categories by means of NLP tools. It is interesting to note that the "soft" category is very close to our *Inline* pattern, and that the group "hard" comprises *Block* and *Container* (and its subclasses), and "jump" includes our pattern *Popup*. This latter pattern, on the other hand, is a very good example of *reading context* as introduced by Tannier's work.

Zou et al. [16] categorise HTML elements as belonging to one of two classes: *inline* and *line-break* tags. Inline elements all those that do not introduce provide horizontal breaks in the visualisation of documents – e.g., *em*, *a*, *strong* and *q*, while line-break elements are those that do so – e.g., *p*, *div*, *ul*, *table* and *blockquote*. Based on this categorisation and a Hidden Markov Model the authors try to identify the structural role (e.g., title, author, affiliation, abstract, etc.) of textual fragments of medical journal articles expressed as HTML pages. Although this approach is tailored for HTML, and the algorithm exploits some features of the language, there are similarities with our work. In particular, the class *Inline* is very similar to ours. The class *line-break* is related to our idea of *Container*, that we further refined in subclasses (*Table*, *Record* and *headedContainer*)

The idea of distinguishing tags in two groups, those that do not interrupt the stream of flow and those that create nested structures, makes our approach also close to the work of Cardoso et al. [1]. The authors introduce an algorithm to segment news-oriented Web pages so as to recognise the title, publication date and the body of the story. They evaluate both the structure (the DOM hierarchy) and the presentation (the individual CSS styles) of a set of sample documents and train a machine-learning model to try to assess the role of HTML elements in other documents. Similar to us, Cardoso et al. point out that their approach is schema-independent and can thus be applied to other markup languages as well (although they tested only HTML documents).

Structural patterns have also been deeply studied by Koh et al. [9]. In particular, they identify text fragments and images that can work as surrogates of the whole document, where surrogates are "information elements selected from a specific document, which can be used in place of the original document". They address the issue of identifying *junk structures*, such as navigational elements of Web sites, advertisements, footers, etc., that usually do not carry the meaning of a document. Their approach is based on a pattern recognition algorithm that segments the XML elements of the document according to *tag patterns*, i.e., recurring hierarchies of nested elements that "contextualize the structured markup of text within a document". They find that junk structures are often described by similarly structured markup in different documents, and thus some tag patterns are crucial for their identification as junk within real HTML pages.

Finally it is worth mentioning Georg et al. [7], who introduce an NLP approach to the automatic processing of medical texts such as clinical guidelines, in order to identify linguistic patterns that support the identification of the markup structure of documents. This approach allowed the development of the system for the automatic visualisation and presentation of unstructured documents. In a more recent paper [6] Georg et al. illustrate an extension of such a work in which they introduce an improved version of their approach. This makes their work close to our idea of converting documents into pattern-based ones and using schema-independent visualization tools. Eventually this project exploits linguistic patterns - connected by precise containment and proximity rules - to create a pattern-based projection of the original document, on top of which they extract and visualize information through XSLT transformations.

7. CONCLUSIONS

The radical simplification of the documents (meta-)model is a key aspect of the theory presented in this paper: we believe that a small set of patterns is enough to express what users, authors and publishers need in most cases. In our vision, it is possible to find a reasonable pattern-based sub-schema from any schema and to use such a simplified version for validating most of the documents written by a community. The preliminary experiments on the Proceedings of Balisage Conference have confirmed such idea.

The application of automatic patterns' recognition and visualization to the DocBook galaxy is probably not so useful in practice, since a lot of powerful tools already exist for this language. The point is that the theory and algorithm discussed in this paper are schema-independent: patterns can be exploited to make sense of documents regardless of the availability of schemas, tools and presentation stylesheets. For instance, we plan to process the pattern-based conceptualization of documents to automatically generate table of contents (from *Containers* and *HeadedContainers*), to extract terms and glossaries (from *Inlines* and *Fields*), to extract structured data (from *Records* and *Tables*) and to automatically build editors and navigators.

In the future, we plan to test our theory taking into account documents written in other XML formats, such as TEI, and by alternative communities of document authors. For example, it will be interesting to use structural patterns for retrospective analysis, in order to investigate how the authors/communities actually use certain grammars, to what extent they share design rules, to what extent they use specific constructs and validation rules. Similarly, we plan to investigate automatic mechanisms to restrict existing grammars in order to be patterns-based and to isolate non-pattern-based examples in large document sets.

8. REFERENCES

[1] Cardoso, E., Jabour, I., Laber, E., Rodrigues, R., Cardoso, P. (2011). An efficient language-independent method to extract content from news webpages. In Proceedings of the 2011 ACM symposium on Document engineering (DocEng11). DOI: 10.1145/2034691.2034720.

[2] Colazzo, D., Sartiani, C., Albano, A., Manghi, P., Ghelli, G., Lini, L., Paoli, M. (2002). A typed text retrieval query language for XML documents. In Journal of the American Society for Information Science and Technology, 53 (6): 467-488. DOI: 10.1002/asi.10059.

[3] Dattolo, A., Di Iorio, A., Duca, S., Feliziani, A.A., Vitali, F. (2007). Structural patterns for descriptive documents. In Baresi, L., Fraternali, P., Houben, G. (Eds.), Proceedings of the 7th International Conference on Web Engineering 2007 (ICWE 2007). DOI: 10.1007/978-3-540-73597-7_35.

[4] Di Iorio, A., Gubellini, D., Vitali, F. (2005). Design patterns for document substructures. In Proceedings of the Extreme Markup Languages 2005. Rockville, MD, USA: Mulberry Technologies, Inc. http://conferences.idealliance.org/extreme/html/2005/Vitali01/EML2005Vitali01.html (last visited June 29, 2012).

[5] Gamma, E., Helm, R., Johnson, R., Vlissides, J. (1994). Design Patterns: Elements of Reusable Object-Oriented Software. Boston, Massachusetts, USA: Addison-Wesley. ISBN: 0201633610.

[6] Georg, G., Hernault, H., Cavazza, M., Prendinger, H., Ishizuka, M. (2009). From Rhetorical Structures to Document Structure: Shallow Pragmatic Analysis for Document Engineering. In Proceedings of the 2009 ACM symposium on Document engineering (DocEng09). DOI: 10.1145/1600193.1600235.

[7] Georg, G., Jaulent, M. (2007). A Document Engineering Environment for Clinical Guidelines. In Proceeding of the 2007 ACM symposium on Document engineering (DocEng07). DOI: 10.1145/1284420.1284440.

[8] Horrocks, I., Patel-Schneider, P. F., McGuinness, D. L., Welty, C. A. (2007). OWL: A Description Logic Based Ontology Language for the Semantic Web. In Baader, F., Calvanese, D., McGuinness, D. L., Nardi, D., Patel-Schneider, P. F. (Eds.), The Description Logic Handbook: Theory, Implementation and Applications (2nd edition): 458-486. Cambridge, UK: Cambridge University Press. ISBN: 9780521876254.

[9] Koh, E., Caruso, D., Kerne, A., Gutierrez-Osuna, R. (2007). Elimination of junk document surrogate candidates through pattern recognition. In Proceedings of the 2007 ACM symposium on Document engineering (DocEng07). DOI: 10.1145/1284420.1284466.

[10] Krotzsch, M., Simancik, F., Horrocks, I. (2011). A Description Logic Primer. Ithaca, New York, New York: Cornell University Library. http://arxiv.org/pdf/1201.4089v1 (last visited June 29, 2012).

[11] Lini, L., Lombardini, D., Paoli, M., Colazzo, D., Sartiani, C. (2001). XTReSy: A Text Retrieval System for XML documents. In Augmenting Comprehension: Digital Tools for the History of Ideas.

[12] Presutti, V., Gangemi, A. (2008). Content Ontology Design Patterns as practical building blocks for web ontologies. In Li, Q., Spaccapietra, S., Yu, E. S. K., Olivé, A. (Eds.), Proceedings of the 27th International Conference on Conceptual Modeling (ER 2008). DOI: 10.1007/978-3-540-87877-3_11.

[13] Tannier, X., Girardot, J.,Mathieu, M. (2005). Classifying XML tags through "reading contexts". In Proceedings of the 2005 ACM symposium on Document engineering (DocEng05). DOI: 10.1145/1096601.1096638.

[14] Text Encoding Initiative Consortium (2005). TEI P5: Guidelines for Electronic Text Encoding and Interchange. Charlottesville, Virginia, USA: TEI Consortium. http://www.tei-c.org/Guidelines/P5 (last visited June 29, 2012).

[15] Walsh, N. (2010). DocBook 5: The Definitive Guide. Sebastopol, CA, USA: O'Really Media. Version 1.0.3. ISBN: 0596805029.

[16] Zou, J., Le, D., Thoma, G. R. (2007). Structure and Content Analysis for HTML Medical Articles: A Hidden Markov Model Approach. In Proceedings of the 2007 ACM symposium on Document engineering (DocEng07). DOI: 10.1145/1284420.1284468.

XML Query-Update Independence Analysis Revisited

Muhammad Junedi
Inria/LIG
655 avenue de l'Europe,
38334 Saint Ismier, France
muhammad.junedi@inria.fr

Pierre Genevès
CNRS and Inria/LIG
655 avenue de l'Europe,
38334 Saint Ismier, France
pierre.geneves@inria.fr

Nabil Layaïda
Inria/LIG
655 avenue de l'Europe,
38334 Saint Ismier, France
nabil.layaida@inria.fr

ABSTRACT

XML transformations can be resource-costly in particular when applied to very large XML documents and document sets. Those transformations usually involve lots of XPath queries and may not need to be entirely re-executed following an update of the input document. In this context, a given query is said to be independent of a given update if, for any XML document, the results of the query are not affected by the update. We revisit Benedikt and Cheney's framework for query-update independence analysis and show that performance can be drastically enhanced, contradicting their initial claims. The essence of our approach and results resides in the use of an appropriate logic, to which queries and updates are both succinctly translated. Compared to previous approaches, ours is more expressive from a theoretical point of view, equally accurate, and more efficient in practice. We illustrate this through practical experiments and comparative figures.

Categories and Subject Descriptors

H.2.3 [**Database Management**]: Languages—*Query languages*

Keywords

XML, Query, Update, Independence

1. INTRODUCTION

XQuery is becoming increasingly popular as a transformation and query language for XML documents. XML Update Language extends the syntax and semantics of XQuery to provide update features, i.e. side effects on documents (for example insertion and deletion of nodes).

XML query-update independence analysis consists in statically checking whether the results of a given query are affected by an update. Determining independence has many important applications which makes it an important line of research: avoiding view re-materialization, concurrency control and transaction management optimization, access policy enforcement, query engine optimization, web page consistency and others. The fact that independence detection is undecidable in general for XQuery and XML Update Language raises the challenge of finding a compromise between the accuracy and efficiency of static analysis and trying to support the largest fragments of query and update languages.

The static detection of query-update independence usually follows a two-step approach. As a first step, a common representation of queries and updates should be established in order to analyze them jointly. This operation usually relies on the extraction of path expressions that model both queries and updates. As a second step, once the common representation is obtained, independence can be checked using some intersection testing techniques on these paths. Two aspects are key for the accuracy and efficiency of the whole process:

- the adopted common representation, as its expressiveness (e.g. being able to capture schemas) has a direct effect on the accuracy, and its succinctness has a direct impact on efficiency;

- the chosen intersection testing technique, as its theoretical complexity and algorithmic effectiveness directly affect the performance of the analyzer.

In [2], Benedikt and Cheney provide a generic framework for independence analysis based on destabilizers and compare different approaches for intersection analysis. The clear separation of concerns in [2] between the representation problem and the problem of intersection analysis provides a good environment for comparison between different independence analysis approaches in addition to the genericity of the framework that can handle any update and query language.

Contribution

In this paper, we revisit query-update independence analysis as proposed by Benedikt and Cheney [2] under the light of the latest developments in intersection testing through a satisfiability checker for an expressive logic, namely the μ-calculus.

We provide evidence that our approach is more expressive in theory, equally accurate, and provides better performance compared to the various alternatives suggested in [2]. We provide experimental results that back our claims and invalidates Benedikt and Cheney's claims that using such an approach is not competitive.

2. XML QUERY-UPDATE ANALYSIS

In this section we recall the XML query-update framework introduced by Benedikt and Cheney [2] that we have reimplemented as a prerequisite for developing our approach.

The framework of [2] relies on a common representation called selection queries for both updates and queries. Specifically, the query is represented as the set of updates that can change the result of that query, which is called the query *destabilizer* (i.e. the set of nodes that can destabilize the query if they are a target of some update).

Updates are represented by a description of the target nodes that are modified. Then, different intersection analysis techniques can be applied in order to check that none of the target nodes are in the query's destabilizer.

The XML query language supported by [2] is an XQuery subset called XQ and the supported update language is a part of snapshot semantics-based XQuery Update Facility [5]. XML documents are considered as tree structures. The reader is referred to [2] for full details on the syntax and semantics of XQ and XML Updates.

To illustrate destabilizers, we consider as an example the XPath query $Q1 = \$doc/C$, $\$doc$ refers to the document root. The result of $Q1$ can be affected in different manners:

- the subtree value of the result of $Q1$ is destabilized if update operations (i.e. insert, delete, replace and rename operations) have a target node in $\{\$doc, \$doc/C, \$doc/C/descendant\text{-}or\text{-}self::*\}$. This set is called the value destabilizer of $\$doc/C$ query, which is abbreviated as $\Delta_*^v(\$doc/C)$;

- the boolean result of $Q1$ can be changed from nonempty to empty if update operations have a target node in $\{\$doc, \$doc/C\}$. This set is called the negative boolean destabilizer and is abbreviated as $\Delta_*^{b-}(\$doc/C)$;

- the boolean result of $Q1$ can be changed from empty to nonempty if update operations have a target node in $\{\$doc, \$doc/child::*\}$. This set is called the positive boolean destabilizer and is abbreviated as $\Delta_*^{b+}(\$doc/C)$;

- the node structure of the result of $Q1$ is destabilized if update operations have a target node in $\{\$doc, \$doc/child::*\}$. This set is called a node destabilizer and is abbreviated as $\Delta_*^n(\$doc/C)$.

The previous example explains the four types of generic destabilizers. To improve accuracy, an update sensitive version of destabilizers is proposed which takes only the update in question into consideration. For example no insert operation can change the results of a query from nonempty to empty. Similarly, no delete operation can change the results of a query from empty to nonempty. Moreover, only a renaming operation on $\$doc/child::*$ can destabilize the node structure of $Q1$, which is an example of a rename sensitive node destabilizer: $\Delta_{rename}^n(\$doc/C) = \{\$doc/child::*\}$ which is more accurate than including $\$doc$ also in node destabilizer set.

These four types of generic and operation sensitive destabilizers are used in the query rewriting algorithm (from an XQ query to a destabilizer) as four mutually recursive functions on the structure of the query. The resulting query belongs to a subset of XQ called *SelXQ* (Selection Query) that excludes from XQ the rule for output generation. The rewriting algorithm for generic and operation sensitive destabilizers can be found in [2].

While queries are transformed into destabilizers, updates are transformed into the selection query which represents the targets of update operation. The transformation function *Targ* is defined in [2].

After representing the queries as destabilizers and updates as target queries, a function can translate this unified intermediate representation into a target logical language depending on the chosen intersection testing technique.

3. INTERSECTION TESTING

Intersection testing uses different static analysis techniques to find the intersection between two structured representations that correspond to a query and an update.

The simplest form of intersection testing for XPath sets is by using heuristics: suffix incompatibility, displacement tests and prefix incompatibility for downward paths [2]. These techniques have a polynomial time complexity but they work only for a very restricted fragment of downward XPaths.

For downward XPath fragments with child, descendant and wildcard fragments, intersection can be solved in polynomial time by building an automaton for XPath expressions and finding the intersection using product automata and emptiness check [14]. This solution is accurate but obviously of very limited expressiveness.

To handle more expressive fragments, [2] proposes to use the Satisfiability Modulo Theory (SMT) approach for intersection analysis using the theory of linear order $(N,<)$. This is done by first transforming selection queries to positive existential first order logic (over trees) formulas. Then these formulas are translated using interval encoding [6] and passed to an SMT solver such as Yices [7] to check for independence.

To handle all the fragments of SelXQ queries:

- Selection queries can be transformed into first-order formulas over trees for child, descendant and sibling relations [3] and intersection analysis reduces to satisfiability which has a non-elementary lower bound for time complexity [17]. These formulas can be checked for disjointness by monadic second order (MSO) satisfiability solvers, like MONA [15, 10];

- Selection queries can be transformed into a set of XPath expressions which in turn are translated into μ-calculus formulas. The conjunction of these formulas can be checked for satisfiability using a μ-calculus satisfiability solver [12, 11].

4. COMPARATIVE STUDY

We now compare the three mentioned approaches (SMT Solver, MSO Solver and μ-Solver) first from a theoretical perspective, and then from a practical point of view.

Theoretical aspects

Figure 1 illustrates the whole approach and each alternative for performing the intersection test. Vertical arrows correspond to translations which turn a given expression from a source language into an equivalent expression in another target language. The figure also summarizes the theoretical characteristics of each alternative regarding expressivity, accuracy, and complexity.

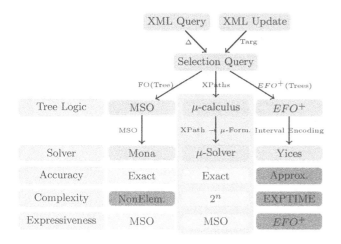

Figure 1: Independence Analysis Framework

The theoretical complexity of satisfiability on monadic second order formulas is known to be non-elementary whereas it is exponential for simplex based linear arithmetic satisfiability. The complexity of satisfiability on μ-formulas is simple exponential 2^n.

Reduction to Satisfiability modulo order theory requires positive existential first order formulas to be translated into constraints; which is not sufficient to represent negation in qualifiers for example. Mondaic second order logic is equal in expressiveness to μ-logic [9].

Practical aspects

We have implemented the destabilizer approach, in Java, to evaluate intersection analysis using the μ-solver. We compared our results with those obtained in [2]. The input to the analysis method consists in an XQuery expression and an XQuery Update Facility update.

The analyzer first transforms the update expression into its corresponding target selection query using $Targ$ method. Then, it transforms queries into query destabilizers using the function Δ_*^v which is called on the query expression in the case of a generic destabilizer (or $\cup_{op}(\Delta_{op}^v)$ in the case of an operation sensitive destabilizer where op is the set of update operations detected in the input update expression).

Then all XPath expressions are extracted from the query destabilizer and the update target query. Finally, they are passed to the μ-solver that checks the satisfiability of the formula $QueryXPaths \wedge UpdateXPaths$, where QueryXPaths is the disjunction of the members of the set of XPaths extracted from query destabilizer and UpdateXPaths is the disjunction of the members of the set of XPaths extracted from the update target query.

For example, the following query Q and update U:

$Q =$ **for** x **in** doc/C **return** $<A>$x/D</A>$
$U =$ **delete** $doc/A/B$

are independent because none of the extracted path expressions of value destabilizer of Q intersects with the target XPath expressions of U. The following steps denote the whole execution process:

1. The target query is executed on the update U: $Targ_*$ (**delete** $doc/A/B$) = ($doc/A/B$);

2. The Destabilizers rules are applied on the query Q:
$\Delta_*^v($**for** x **in** doc/C **return** $<A>$x/D</A>)=$
(doc, $doc/child::*$), **for** x **in** doc/C
return ($x/desc-or-self::*$, $x/child::*/desc-or-self::*$)

3. XPath expressions are extracted from the target query and the result is the set $\{$/child::A/child::B$\}$

4. XPath expressions are extracted from destabilizers and the result is $\{$ /self::*, /child::*, /child::C, /child::C/desc-or-self::*, /child::C/child::*/desc-or-self::* $\}$

5. The two sets are passed to the μ-solver that indicates the unsatisfiability.

On the opposite, Q and U'= **delete** $doc/C/D/E$ are not independent because the XPath expression /C/D/E will intersect with /C/D/descendant-or-self::*.

We used the exact same set of 20 Query examples of XMark benchmark [16] used by Benedikt and Cheney in their experiments, with the same necessary modifications to fit in the supported query fragments. We automatically generated 4 kinds of updates (rename, insert into, insert before, delete)[1] on the 16 XPath queries (A1-A8, B1-B8) of XPathMark [8].

We applied this analysis on all the combinations of queries and updates and we compared the mean execution time of the μ-solver with the results found in [2] for the Yices SMT solver.

We used the version of the μ-solver implemented in Java (using JavaBDDs) and shared with Benedikt and Cheney. Experiments are carried out on a laptop with an Intel Processor (3.0 GHz), with 2GB of memory.

Figure 2 compares the running times of the μ-Solver and the SMT-solver. The running times of the SMT-solver (Yices) are taken from [2]. The running times of the μ-solver carefully followed the method for calculating running times found in [2]. Specifically, each update is tested for independence using the generic analysis with the twenty queries of the XMark benchmark and then the mean time is taken and the results are grouped by the update.

Efficiency. Figures 2 and 3 show comparisons between the execution times obtained with the μ-solver with those obtained with the MONA solver and the Yices solver. [2] finds that Yices is the most efficient in practice, MONA follows and they do not give measurements for the μ-solver whose performance was judged not attractive. Our measurements prove that the μ-solver approach is far more efficient in practice compared to Yices (and obviously to MONA).

An interesting finding was revealed when looking carefully at the time decomposition of the resolution process. This process involves various aspects such as constructing destabilizers, parsing formulas, initializing the BDD library, and the actual resolution time within the solver. It turned out that if we concentrate on the μ-solver time (see Figure 4), leaving aside the other costs, we observe that time spent in the resolution procedure is negligible compared to the overall figures presented in [2]. This gives a clear evidence (somehow counter-intuitive compared to the conclusions of [2]) that the dominant cost do not necessarily reside in the resolution procedure. We believe that times spent in the resolution procedure better reflect the intrinsic difficulty of each problem instance.

---

[1]these four updates are sufficient to cover different destabilizer rules

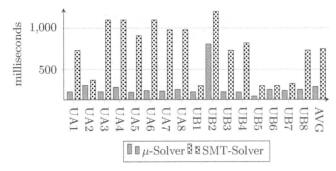

Figure 2: μ-solver vs. SMT-solver running times.

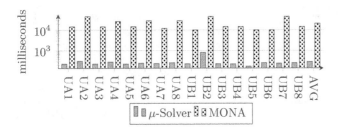

Figure 3: μ-solver vs. MONA running times [logarithmic scale].

Accuracy. Both MONA and the μ-solver approaches can determine exactly whether two selection queries overlap (because they both have the expressivity of MSO, notably encompassing First-Order logic, FO) whereas Positive Existential First-Order logic (EFO^+) can return false negatives (since EFO^+ is strictly less expressive than FO and thus obviously strictly less expressive than MSO).

Providing MSO expressivity is an unquestionable advantage as this allows capturing regular tree languages (XML schema languages) for which FO expressivity is insufficient.

5. RELATED WORK

The notion of destabilizers introduced by Benedikt and Cheney [2] was partly inspired by previous works on XML projection [4], where the goal is to identify nodes that can be deleted without modifying the result of a query (this corresponds to independence problems involving deletion only). As noticed in [2], prior techniques either required a schema [1, 4] or apply only to downward fragments of XPath. [13] proposes a conservative analysis for an XML update language and a theorem that can be used to identify commuting expressions. However a different update language proposal is considered and independence is not addressed.

6. CONCLUSION

We have revisited the XML query-update independence analysis problem by exploring in depth the approach based on the μ-solver. For that purpose, we have reimplemented a destabilizer's framework for evaluating the relevance of this approach which was neglected in previous studies. We show that performance can be drastically enhanced using the μ-solver based approach. Surprisingly, our results show that the best performing approach in practice does not require any loss of precision. This questions systematic search for trade-offs between expressivity and precision.

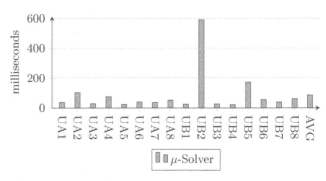

Figure 4: Actual resolution times for the μ-Solver.

7. REFERENCES

[1] Michael Benedikt and James Cheney. Schema-based independence analysis for XML updates. *Proc. VLDB Endow.*, 2(1):61–72, August 2009.

[2] Michael Benedikt and James Cheney. Destabilizers and independence of XML updates. *Proc. VLDB Endow.*, 3(1-2):906–917, September 2010.

[3] Michael Benedikt and Christoph Koch. From XQuery to relational logics. *TODS*, 34(4):25:1–25:48, 2009.

[4] Véronique Benzaken, Giuseppe Castagna, Dario Colazzo, and Kim Nguyên. Type-based XML projection. In *VLDB'06*, pages 271–282, 2006.

[5] Don Chamberlin, Daniela Florescu, and Jonathan Robie. XQuery Update Facility. W3C WD, 2006.

[6] David Dehaan, David Toman, Mariano P. Consens, and M. Tamer Özsu. A comprehensive XQuery to SQL translation using dynamic interval encoding, 2003.

[7] Bruno Dutertre and Leonardo De Moura. The Yices SMT solver. Technical report, 2006.

[8] Massimo Franceschet. XPathMark: an XPath benchmark for the XMark generated data. In *XSym'05*.

[9] Pierre Genevès. *Logics for XML*. PhD thesis, Institut National Polytechnique de Grenoble, December 2006.

[10] Pierre Genevès and Nabil Layaïda. Deciding XPath containment with MSO. *Data Knowl. Eng.*, 63(1):108–136, October 2007.

[11] Pierre Genevès and Nabil Layaïda. XML reasoning solver user manual. R. Report 6726, INRIA, 2008.

[12] Pierre Genevès, Nabil Layaïda, and Alan Schmitt. Efficient static analysis of XML paths and types. In *PLDI '07*, pages 342–351, 2007.

[13] Giorgio Ghelli, Kristoffer Rose, and Jérôme Siméon. Commutativity analysis for XML updates. *ACM TODS*, 33(4):29:1–29:47, December 2008.

[14] Beda Christoph Hammerschmidt, Martin Kempa, and Volker Linnemann. On the intersection of XPath expressions. In *IDEAS'05*, pages 49–57, 2005.

[15] Nils Klarlund and Anders Møller. *MONA Version 1.4 User Manual*. BRICS, January 2001.

[16] Albrecht Schmidt, Florian Waas, Martin Kersten, Michael J. Carey, Ioana Manolescu, and Ralph Busse. XMark: a benchmark for XML data management. In *VLDB'02*, pages 974–985, 2002.

[17] Sergei G. Vorobyov. An improved lower bound for the elementary theories of trees. In *CADE*, pages 275–287, 1996.

Structure–Conforming XML Document Transformation Based on Graph Homomorphism[*]

Tyng–Ruey Chuang
Institute of Information Science
Academia Sinica
Nangang 115, Taipei, Taiwan

Hui–Yin Wu[†]
Program in Digital Contents and Technologies
National Chengchi University
Wenshan 116, Taipei, Taiwan

ABSTRACT

We propose a principled method to specify XML document transformation so that the outcome of a transformation can be ensured to conform to certain structural constraints as required by the target XML document type. We view XML document types as graphs, and model transformations as relations between the two graphs. Starting from this abstraction, we use and extend graph homomorphism as a formalism for the specifications of transformations between XML document types. A specification can then be checked to ensure whether results from the transformation will always be structure–conforming.

Categories and Subject Descriptors

I.7.2 [**Document and Text Processing**]: Document Preparation—*Markup languages*; G.2.2 [**Discrete Mathematics**]: Graph Theory—*Graph labeling*; D.2.4 [**Software Engineering**]: Software/Program Verification—*Validation*

General Terms

Design, Theory, Verification

Keywords

Document Transformation, Graph Homomorphism, XML

1. INTRODUCTION

In XML document processing, one often faces the problem of ensuring the correctness of the structure of a program–generated document. As an example, Figure 1 shows the structural constraints of two XML document types (named DocBook Tiny and XHTML Tiny). Each of the two graphs

---

[*]An extended version of this paper is freely available from the authors' websites under a Creative Commons License.

[†]Hui–Yin Wu is also a research student at the Institute of Information Science, Academia Sinica.

show what kinds of elements can appear as the children of other kinds of elements. If an element of type `parent` can have elements of type `child` as its children, then there is an edge from node `parent` to `child` in the graph.

For the graphs in Figure 1, it is natural for us to find mappings between nodes that are semantically close. For example, we may transform `orderedlist` elements in DocBook Tiny into `ol` elements in XHTML Tiny, and `listitem` elements into `li` elements. It too seems fitting to map `para` elements into `p` elements. However, such a straightforward mapping could transform DocBook Tiny documents into ill–structured XHTML Basic documents. Take the following DocBook Tiny document fragment as an example.

```
<orderedlist>
 <orderedlist>
  <para>A preface here and ... </para>
 </orderedlist>
 <listitem><para>...A list item</para></listitem>
</orderedlist>
```

By the proposed straightforward mapping, this structure–conforming DocBook Tiny document fragment will be transformed into the following XHTML document fragment which is ill-structured.

```
<ol>
 <ol>
  <p>A preface here and ... </p>
 </ol>
 <li><p>...A list item</p></li>
</ol>
```

The output is ill–structured because according to the parent–child constraints for XHTML Tiny element types, `ol` element cannot have `ol` or `p` elements as children.

In this paper, we propose to use and extend graph homomorphism as a formalism for the specifications of mappings between XML document types, so that the results can be ensured to be always structure–conforming.

2. RELATED WORKS

There is a wealth of research on the modeling of XML document types, and on the techniques and languages for expressing XML document transformations. Since the late 1990s, there have been many works on using formal languages for modeling SGML/XML document editing and transformation [2, 4, 6, 7]. This paper continues these efforts by using graph homomorphisms, a formalism relatively new to the document engineering community.

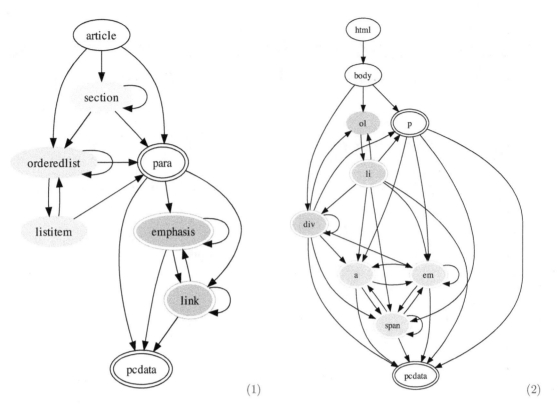

(1)

(2)

Figure 1: Parent-child constraints among DocBook Tiny (1) element types and among XHTML Tiny (2) element types. Double–circled nodes denote types whose elements may appear as leaves in document trees.

Programming languages have been designed and implemented to accommodate XML content models as native data types [1]. Many of these languages are high–level languages with expressive type systems to help detect type errors at compile–time. XML query and transformation languages such as XPath, XSLT, and XQuery have long been developed, standardized, and put into use; but these languages do not have a notion of document types for the input and output documents. Our method models XML document transformation before the transformation itself is programmed, and is not specific to particular programming languages.

Researchers in the database community have used graph homomorphism for matching data schema and for matching navigation paths [3]. These works focus on the similarity among graphs; ours is on expressing transformation using graphs. Some works analyze web applications in order to verify if they produce valid HTML/XML documents [9]. These works seem to concentrate on the target document types, but not the source document types.

3. GRAPH HOMOMORPHISM

This section provides a brief introduction to graph homomorphism and some basic graph theory [8]. We use the notations that $g, h, \ldots$ are graphs, V_g is the set of nodes in graph g, and E_g is the set of edges in graph g. The graphs are directed and, if not noted otherwise, without multiple edges. That is, $E_g \subseteq V_g \times V_g$ is a relation on V_g. We write $u \rightarrow v$ to denote an edge $(u, v) \in E_g$. An edge $u \rightarrow v$ is a loop if $u = v$. A function $f : V_g \rightarrow V_h$ is a *graph homomorphism* from graph g to graph h if $f(u) \rightarrow f(v)$ is an edge in E_h for all edges $u \rightarrow v$ in E_g. That is, a graph

homomorphism is a node–to–node function that preserves edge connectivity. A graph is strongly connected if there is a path from each node to each other node in the graph. The *strongly connected components* (*SCCs*) of a graph are its maximal strongly connected subgraphs.

We extend the notion of graph homomorphism by the following. A function $f : V_g \rightarrow V_h$ is an *extended graph homomorphism* from g to h if, for all edges $u \rightarrow v$ in E_g, there is a *path* $f(u) \rightsquigarrow f(v)$ connected by edges in E_h. That is, an extended graph homomorphism preserves path connectivity. One can see that a function $f : V_g \rightarrow V_h$ is an extended graph homomorphism from g to h if and only if f is a graph homomorphism from g to the transitive closure of h.

In the context of XML document transformation, often we are mapping documents from a particular document type (the *source*) to those of another document type (the *target*). In this paper, we focus on the parent–child constraints among element types as imposed by their content models, using graph homomorphism as a formalism to guide and specify document transformations. It leads to a general method for mapping elements types from the source document type to those in the target document as the following.

- Produce the source graph g and target graph h respectively from the source and target document types. Nodes in the graphs are element types. Edges are parent–child constraints.

- Decompose g and h, respectively, into their SCCs. Find a graph homomorphism from the condensation of g to the condensation of h. Note that,

    - Each SCC node in the condensation of g must be

100

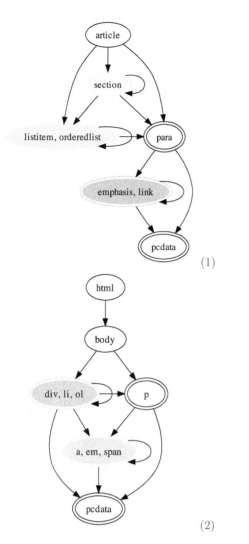

(1)

(2)

Figure 2: The condensations, and the related strongly connected components, of the two graphs.

use the following mapping f:

$$
\begin{aligned}
f(\texttt{article}) &= \texttt{body} \\
f(\textit{yellow}) &= \textit{orange} \\
f(\textit{green}) &= \textit{orange} \\
f(\texttt{para}) &= \texttt{p} \\
f(\textit{violet}) &= \textit{pink} \\
f(\texttt{pcdata}) &= \texttt{pcdata}
\end{aligned}
$$

It can be verified this is indeed a graph homomorphism. For the mapping from the yellow SCC to the orange SCC, one has no choice but to map `section` to `div` as node `section` forms a loop and `div` is the only looping node in the target SCC. The same goes for the mapping from `orderedlist` to `div`. From the above, `listitem` can only be mapped to `div` too. For the mapping from the violet SCC to the pink SCC, we map `emphasis` to `em`, and map `link` to `span` instead of `a` because both `link` and `span` are looping nodes but `a` is not.

Also, since all documents we are mapping from the Doc-Book Tiny document type to the XHTML Tiny document type are tree–shaped, we must make sure that whatever can appear as leaf elements in the input, will only be mapped to leaf elements in the output, and that the root element is mapped to the root element. That is, we will be transforming an XML document tree to a complete XML document tree, not just to some fragments of a tree.

For leaf nodes in the graph for DocBook Tiny (that is, `para`, `emphasis`, `link`, and `pcdata`), indeed they are mapped to leaf nodes in the graph for XHTML Tiny (that is, `p`, `em`, `span`, and `pcdata`). The root node `article` is mapped to `body`. But the root node in the target graph is `html`, not `body`. This is easy to fix in an extended graph homomorphism, as there is a path from `html` to `body`. That is, we map the node `article` to the subgraph consisting of the edge `html` → `body`.

4. INDUCTIVE TRANSFORMATION

The solution we arrive at in the previous section is not satisfactory as much information is lost. The element types `orderedlist` and `listitem` are mapped to the element type `div`. We also do not get to use element `a` in the target graph to express element `link` in the source. In an extended graph homomorphism, an edge is mapped to a path (as illustrated by mapping the edge `article` → `section` to the path `html` → `body` → `div`). In this section, we aim to develop refined mappings for element types in which paths in the target graph are used to connect the parent–and–child pairs of nodes mapped from the source graph.

In the following, we show we can still map `orderedlist` to `ol`, and `listitem` to `li`. Node `orderedlist` has children `listitem`, `orderedlist`, and `para` in the source graph. We map them respectively to `li`, `ol`, and `p` in the target graph. But in the target graph node `ol` only has `li` as its child. What do we do with `ol` and `p`? A solution is to connect node `ol` to `ol` by a path `ol` → `li` → `ol`, and to connect node `ol` to `p` by a path `ol` → `li` → `p`. Note that by insisting nodes in a SCC in the source graph are mapped to nodes in a SCC in the target, for any edge $u \rightarrow v$ in the source SCC, we are ensured there is a path $u \rightsquigarrow v$ in the target SCC.

We use the following notation to describe such a mapping:

`orderedlist{@li, @ol, @p} = ol{@li, li/@ol, li/@p}`

mapped to a SCC node in the condensation of h (to preserve cycles inside the source SCC);

– One–to–one function is preferred when mapping SCC nodes in the condensation of g to those in h (to preserve structural information).

• For each pair of source and target SCCs, find a graph homomorphism for nodes in the source SCC to those in the target SCC.

• A loop in the source SCC must be mapped to a loop in the target SCC.

Figure 2 shows the condensations of the two graphs in Figure 1. The SCCs in DocBook Tiny (1) are colored in $yellow = \{\texttt{section}\}$, $green = \{\texttt{listitem, orderedlist}\}$, and $violet = \{\texttt{emphasis, link}\}$. Those in the XHTML Tiny (2) are colored in $orange = \{\texttt{div, li, ol}\}$ and $pink = \{\texttt{a, em, span}\}$. For a graph homomorphism from the condensation of DocBook Tiny to the condensations of XHTML Tiny, we

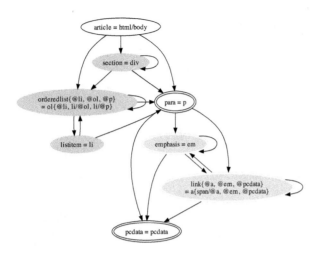

Figure 3: A structure–conforming mapping from DocBook Tiny to XHTML Tiny.

In the above, *@element* on the left hand side of the equation is a pattern that matches a node labeled with *element* (in the target); on the right hand side, it is the matched node. The pattern *element*{...} on the left hand side represents a mapping for the node labeled *element* (in the source) and for its transformed children (matched by using patterns inside the bracket). The expression *element*{...} on the right hand side represents the result in the target, which is a node labeled *element*. The node's children are inside the bracket. The notation p/q expresses a node p with a single child q. That is, p/q is a subgraph connecting two nodes p and q. This notation can be easily extended to express a subgraph consisting of a longer path, such as $u_1/u_2/\ldots/u_n$.

Figure 3 shows a mapping from DocBook Tiny element types to XHTML Tiny, based on an extended graph homomorphism. This mapping is more refined than the one given at the end of Section 3.

This mapping describes an inductive transformation on XML document trees. It leads naturally to a bottom–up transformation of DocBook Tiny documents: It maps leaf elements in DocBook Tiny to leaf elements in XHTML Tiny, and it specifies how to convert any (non–leaf) DocBook Tiny element to an XHTML Tiny element depending on the type of the element and its converted child elements. It is also a typed specification; the mappings are expressed in terms of element types (and their expressions) in the source and target document types. Further, the specification can be checked to see if it will always transform documents of the source type to documents of the target type.

The specifications are checked as the following. For each node u in the source graph, one first looks into the mapping equation

$$v_i\{ \ \ldots \ \} = y_i\{ \ \ldots \ \}$$

that is associated to each node v_i to which $u \to v_i$ is an edge. Nodes $y_1, y_2, \ldots, y_n$ are in the target graph, and they are u's children when u is being transformed. Then, one checks if each of the nodes $y_i, 1 \leq i \leq n$, appears as a pattern $@y_i$ in *pattern* in the mapping equation associated to node u:

$$u\{ \ pattern \ \} = x\{ \ expression \ \}$$

If so, the pattern–matching is exhaustive, and one proceeds to check if each of the corresponding expressions in *expression* leads to an edge or a path from x to y_i in the target graph. In cases where the mapping equation associated to node u is just $u = x$, one simply checks if $x \to y_i$ is an edge in the target graph.

This method of describing an inductive transformation based on an extended graph transformation can be further applied to cases where a node in the source graph is mapped to multiple nodes in the target graph. This is often necessary when one needs to break a SCC in the source graph into several subgraphs which are then mapped to different SCCs in the target graphs. In these scenarios, a node in the source SCC, depending on its already transformed child nodes, can be mapped to nodes in different SCC in the target graph.

5. CONCLUSIONS AND FUTURE WORK

In this paper we have proposed a method for transforming XML documents that takes into account both the source and target document types. We shall end this paper by mentioning that our method can be further generalized. Until now we use only paths in the target graphs as the results from inductive mappings. Actually we can use any subgraph in the target graph as an inductive outcome. That is, from the already transformed child elements, we can assemble any XML document fragment as the inductive result, as long as it is a subgraph in the target graph.

6. REFERENCES

[1] V. Benzaken, G. Castagna, and A. Frisch. CDuce: An XML–centric general-purpose language. In *Int'l Conf. on Functional Programming*, pp. 51–63, 2003.

[2] T.–R. Chuang and J.–L. Lin. On modular transformation of structural content. In *ACM Symp. on Document Engineering*, pp. 201–210, 2004.

[3] W. Fan, J. Li, S. Ma, H. Wang, and Y. Wu. Graph homomorphism revisited for graph matching. *Proc. of the VLDB Endowment*, 3:1161–1172, Sept. 2010.

[4] E. Kuikka, P. Leinonen, and M. Penttonen. Towards automating of document structure transformations. In *ACM Symp. on Document Engineering*, pp. 103–110, 2002.

[5] E. Meijer, M. Fokkinga, and R. Paterson. Functional programming with bananas, lenses, envelopes and bared wire. In *Functional Programming Languages and Computer Architecture*, pp. 124–144, Aug. 1991.

[6] M. Murata. Transformation of documents and schemas by patterns and contextual conditions. In *Principles of Document Processing*, pp. 153–169, 1996.

[7] E. Pietriga, J. Vion–Dury, and V. Quint. VXT: A visual approach to XML transformations. In *ACM Symp. on Document Engineering*, pp. 1–10, 2001.

[8] A. Shapira and N. Alon. Homomorphisms in graph property testing — a survey. *Electronic Colloquium on Computational Complexity*, 12(085), 2005.

[9] R. Stone. Validation of dynamic web pages generated by an embedded scripting language. *Software: Practice & Experience*, 35(13):1259–1274, 2005.

[10] M. Wallace and C. Runciman. Haskell and XML: Generic combinators or type-based translation? In *Int'l Conference on Functional Programming*, pp. 148–159, Sept. 1999.

Toward Automated Schema-Directed Code Revision

Raquel Oliveira
Inria/LIG
655 avenue de l'Europe,
38334 Saint Ismier, France
raraujo.oliveira@gmail.com

Pierre Genevès
CNRS and Inria/LIG
655 avenue de l'Europe,
38334 Saint Ismier, France
pierre.geneves@inria.fr

Nabil Layaïda
Inria/LIG
655 avenue de l'Europe,
38334 Saint Ismier, France
nabil.layaida@inria.fr

ABSTRACT

Updating XQuery programs in accordance with a change of the input XML schema is known to be a time-consuming and error-prone task. We propose an automatic method aimed at helping developers realign the XQuery program with the new schema. First, we introduce a taxonomy of possible problems induced by a schema change. This allows to differentiate problems according to their severity levels, e.g. errors that require code revision, and semantic changes that should be brought to the developer's attention. Second, we provide the necessary algorithms to detect such problems using a solver that checks satisfiability of XPath expressions.

Categories and Subject Descriptors

H.2.3 [**Database Management**]: Languages—*Query languages*; D.2.4 [**Software Engineering**]: Software/Program Verification—*Validation*

Keywords

XML, Schemas, XQuery, Schema evolution

1. INTRODUCTION

In document management systems, documents usually encoded in XML are often rendered into output formats (e.g. HTML, SVG, PDF) using transformations, typically written in XSLT or XQuery.[1] XML documents conform to constraints expressed with schemas that continuously change in order to cope with the natural evolution of the entities they describe. However, these changes may break transformations for documents whose structure was described by the original schema.

A frequent scenario consists in an XQuery transformation executed over an XML document (conforming to some schema S_{in}), generating an XML document that is valid against another schema S_{out}. For instance, consider a schema

---

[1]It is known that XSLT can be compiled into XQuery.

describing bibliographical data for a writer (as illustrated in Figure 1a). The schema allows zero or more books, each book having a title of type string and a year of publication of type integer, and some information about its sales.

Now consider that this schema S_{in} evolved into a newer version S'_{in} (as illustrated in Figure 1b), with three changes: (I) the type of the year is now a string (II) the book is distributed at most once and (III) the *city* element is removed. Figure 2 gives two document instances. Instance (a) is valid

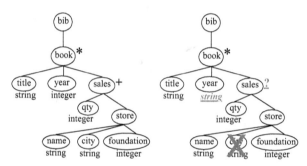

(a) S_{in}=bibliography data   (b) S'_{in}=evolved schema

Figure 1: Example of a schema evolution.

against S_{in}, but not valid against S'_{in} (because at most one sale is expected in S'_{in}). Instance (b) is allowed by S'_{in} whereas it was not allowed by S_{in}, since S_{in} prevented *book* elements to occur without a least one *sale* child.

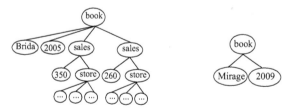

(a) instance valid againt S_{in} (b) instance valid against S'_{in}

Figure 2: Instances of documents

The XQuery transformation shown below extracts the sales information for book structures valid against S_{in}. If the book was published in 2012 and was sold in New York, it considers only "new" stores (founded in 2010 or later). For other cases, it considers "old" stores too. Finally it returns the sales only for books that were distributed at most once.

```
for $s in doc("bib.xml")//book
let $y as xs:integer := xs:integer($s/year)
where
   if (($s/sales/store/city = "New York")
         and ($y = 2012)) then
         $s/sales/store/foundation >= 2010
   else
         $s/sales/store/foundation >= 1960
return
         <book>{$s[count(sales)<=1]/sales}</book>
```

In our scenario, the output document is validated against the schema shown in Figure 3.

Figure 3: Output schema S$_{out}$

Contribution

Our goal is to propose a framework to detect impacts of schema changes on transformations automatically.

2. TAXONOMY OF ERRORS

We now introduce a taxonomy of impacts on transformations according to various changes brought to a given schema. The taxonomy is divided into two main groups. The first group gathers different errors that can be detected by a joint analysis of the transformations and the input schemas. The second group consists in extending the analysis by taking advantage of the availability of the output schema. Basically, the goal is to check whether the transformation results would still be valid against the output schema. The taxonomy categories are summarized in Table 1. In our setting, the transformation analysis results in one of the two following conclusions: either no problem was detected among the ones we cover in the taxonomy, or a problem is detected, in which case it is properly categorized.

Schema considered	Acronym	Category
Input Schemas	TYPECAST	Type casting
	DEADCODE	Dead code
	REDUNDCODE	Redundant code
	INVQUERY	Invalid query
	DIFFRES	Different results
Output Schema	INVRES	Invalid results

Table 1: Summary of the taxonomy

We detail each category in the following subsections.

2.1 Analysis w.r.t. input schema versions

Type casting problems. Type casting problems can occur in XQuery clauses that bind variables (e.g. *for* and *let* clauses). Specifically, a type casting error is detected whenever the schema change results in an assignment of an element with type t_1 to a variable with type $t_2 \neq t_1$. For instance, in our motivating example, this problem occurs in the binding between the XPath expression *//book/year* and the integer variable $y, since the *year* element is of type string in the new schema S$'_{in}$.

Dead code. A given code portion is dead whenever it is never reached by any execution of the program, for example, the *else* part of a condition when it is known that the *if* part always evaluates to true (or the *then* part whenever the *if* part is found unsatisfiable). In a XQuery program, there are several places where a dead code can potentially occur, as studied in [3]. We detect errors reported in [3] as well as other categories not covered in [3]. In the motivating example, dead code can be detected in the *if* expression. Once we detected that this condition always return an empty set (because the *city* element was removed from the schema), the *then* part will never be executed.

Redundant code. A code portion is redundant if its execution does not affect the result of the program. It can be safely removed from the program, like a condition that is always evaluated to true. The relevance of the detection of this problem resides on the possibility to propose query rewriting, with the purpose of optimization and/or size reduction of a program. In our motivating example, the XPath qualifier in the *return* clause becomes redundant following the schema change. In the new schema, the *sales* element can now occur at most once in the document. As a result, the condition of the qualifier is always true under this schema, making it removable.

Invalid query. We identify as invalid the XPath expressions that are unsatisfiable under the considered schema. Using the satisfiability algorithm proposed in [5], we check statically (at compile time) whether an XPath is satisfiable against schema S$'_{in}$. Otherwise, we deduce that the XPath (and subsequently the expression that uses it) is invalid. The XPath used in the *if* condition of the motivating example is invalid. It is never satisfied given that the *city* element was removed from the schema.

Different query results. In this category, we are interested in highlighting to the user at compile time the fact that, due to the schema evolution, the result of the query will change unexpectedly. The query will not raise type casting problems, does not contain neither dead nor redundant code, but it will select unexpectedly more (or less) nodes in the input XML document, due to, for example, insertion (or removal) of elements in the XML schema, or changes in the constraints of the elements, or in its content model. In our motivating example, once we remove the *city* element from the schema, the content model of the *store* element changes (it is somehow "decreased"). Since *store* is part of the content model of the element that will be returned, we can conclude that the result of this XQuery is affected by the schema change (knowing that the *return* clause creates a document consisting of the selected element of the XPath and its content model).

2.2 Analysis w.r.t. the output schema

Invalid query results. When the output schema is available (S$_{out}$), we can go further and detect at compile time that the changes in the input schema will produce an invalid document with respect to the output schema S$_{out}$. First, we review the validation process of the output document before considering the input schema changes. The XQuery of our example returns the sales information of books which were sold at most once. This XQuery is launched on instances of the schema S_{in} of Figure 1a. This schema allows instances of books with at least one sale ($< + >$ constraint at the element *sales*). When the transformation is executed, only books with **exactly** one sale will be returned, which is a valid result considering S_{out} ($< + >$ constraint at the element *sales*). Now consider the input schema change (II): the book will be distributed at most once (*sales?*). Now this schema allows instances of books with no sale. When we run the XQuery transformation, the condition of the *return* clause will also allow such kind of documents. When considering the output schema of Figure 3 we observe that each book should have at least one sale ($< + >$ constraint at the element *sales*). So, the XQuery transformation of our example may generate invalid results against S_{out}.

3. ERROR DETECTION

We present the analysis technique for detecting errors for each taxonomy category. For this purpose, we develop inference rules as a detection mechanism for a fragment of XQuery defined below.

Considered XQuery fragment

Specifically, we consider the fragment of XQuery whose syntax is defined in Table 2, that uses XPath expressions whose syntax is described in Table 3. In these grammars, n stands for any integer number, v for any variable's name, *tag* for any string corresponding to the name of a tag and *cst* for any constant value. For *FLWOR* expressions, we consider *for*, *let*, *where* and *return* clauses. The considered fragment captures the most important features for extracting and generating information.

$$
\begin{aligned}
e ::= \quad & () \\
& | \ \$v \\
& | \ xpath \\
& | \ \$v/xpath \\
& | \ e,e \\
& | \ <tag> \ e \ </tag> \\
& | \ \text{element}\{e\}\{e\} \\
& | \ \text{if } e \text{ then } e \text{ else } e \\
& | \ \text{let } \$v \text{ as } t := e \text{ (where } e\text{)? return } e \\
& | \ \text{for } \$v \text{ (as } t\text{)? in } e \text{ (where } e\text{)? return } e \\
t ::= \quad & \text{xs:integer} \ | \ \text{xs:string} \ | \ \text{xs:boolean}
\end{aligned}
$$

Table 2: Syntax of XQuery Programs

$$
\begin{aligned}
xpath \quad & ::= \ step \ | \ xpath/xpath \ | \ xpath[qualifier] \\
step \quad & ::= \ axis::nameTest \\
qualifier \quad & ::= \ xpath \ | \ xpath \ op \ cst \ | \ count(xpath) \ op \ n \\
op \quad & ::= \ < \ | \ > \ | \ \leq \ | \ \geq \ | \ = \ | \ ! = \ | \ \text{eq|ne|lt|le|gt|ge} \\
axis \quad & ::= \ \text{self} \ | \ \text{child} \ | \ \text{parent} \ | \ \text{descendant} \ | \ \text{ancestor} \\
& | \ \text{following} \ | \ \text{preceding} \ | \ \text{following-sibling} \\
& | \ \text{preceding-sibling} \\
nameTest \quad & ::= \ tag \ | \ *
\end{aligned}
$$

Table 3: Syntax of XPath Expressions

Inference Rules

For each category of the taxonomy, we develop a set of inference rules that are applied recursively. Specifically, we

design one inference rule per construct of our XQuery fragment shown on Table 2. A given rule tests for the presence of an error by invoking logical predicates in the premises. A logical predicate corresponds to a property involving XPath queries, schemas and more generally constraints over XML document trees. The truth status of these logical predicates is evaluated using calls to an external XML reasoner such as the one proposed in [5]. Depending on the truth status of the properties described in the premises, the conclusion of a rule attaches the detected error to the corresponding XQuery subexpression. We only detail rules for cases where an error is detected, other obvious cases are omitted.

Type casting problems. In order to detect type casting errors in variable bindings of the *for* and *let* clauses, we use an environment Γ' that keeps track of the **type** of variable $\$v$. The main rule is shown in the table below.

TYPECAST

for	$\dfrac{S_{in},S'_{in},\Gamma,\Gamma'\cup(t,\$v) \vdash has\_different\_type(xpath,S'_{in},t)}{S_{in},S'_{in},\Gamma,\Gamma' \vdash for \ \$v \ as \ t \ in \ xpath \ return \ e_3 \rightarrow TYPECAST}$

This rule invokes the predicate $has\_different\_type$, that checks if an element selected by an XPath is of type t in the considered schema. This predicate formulates the property that the type of an element returned by the XPath is different from the one expected by the schema.

Redundant code. For checking redundant code, we introduce the predicate $removable\_qualifier$. It successively removes qualifiers from the XPath expression one by one and checks for the equivalence with the original one (meaning that such a qualifier is redundant). To check for equivalence, we use the predicate $non\_equivalence(xpath1, xpath2)$ that is satisfiable iff there exists an element which is selected by one of the XPaths and not by the other one.

REDUNDCODE

$xpath$	$\dfrac{S_{in},S'_{in},\Gamma \vdash removable\_qualifier(xpath)}{S_{in},S'_{in},\Gamma \vdash xpath \rightarrow REDUNDCODE}$

Invalid query. The rules for detecting invalid queries are based on satisfiability tests for each XPath, directly available in any XML reasoner, that we denote here through the predicates *select* and *type*. The rule concludes that a given XQuery expression is invalid with respect to an input schema iff it contains XPath expressions that are unsatisfiable in the presence of the schema (i.e. always empty).

INVQUERY

$xpath$	$\dfrac{S_{in},S'_{in},\Gamma \vdash \neg select(xpath,type(S'_{in}))}{S_{in},S'_{in},\Gamma \vdash xpath \rightarrow INVQUERY}$

Different query results. For this category, the rules expressed in the table bellow focus on analyzing parts of XQuery expressions that, combined with elements and document constructors, generate content dynamically. For example, in a $< if \ e_1 \ then \ e_2 \ else \ e_3 >$ expression, only e_2 and e_3 are evaluated, since they can generate new content depending on the boolean condition. In the inference rules, we use the predicates $new\_regions$ and $new\_contents$ introduced in [4]. The first one returns true when an XPath selects nodes that were already present in the old schema, but that now appear in different regions of the document, due to the schema changes. The second predicate returns true when the XPath selects elements that already occurred in the old schema, but whose content model has changed. The main rules are shown in the table below.

DIFFRES

$xpath$	$\dfrac{S_{in},S'_{in},\Gamma \vdash new\_regions(xpath,S_{in},S'_{in})}{S_{in},S'_{in},\Gamma \vdash xpath \rightarrow DIFFRES}$
$xpath$	$\dfrac{S_{in},S'_{in},\Gamma \vdash new\_contents(xpath,S_{in},S'_{in})}{S_{in},S'_{in},\Gamma \vdash xpath \rightarrow DIFFRES}$
for	$\dfrac{S_{in},S'_{in},\Gamma\cup(\$v,e_1) \vdash e_3 \rightarrow DIFFRES}{S_{in},S'_{in},\Gamma \vdash for\ \$v\ in\ e_1\ where\ e_2\ return\ e_3 \rightarrow DIFFRES}$

Invalid query results. To detect invalid query results, it is necessary to statically analyze whether the document produced by the transformation validates against the output schema S_{out}. We know that the structure of the output document is influenced by changes brought to input schema. For example, assume that we launch our XQuery on some document that follows S_{in} of Figure 1a. In this case, the output document will follow the structure described by S_{out} of the Figure 3.

In order to check if the generated document remains valid against S_{out} whenever S_{in} changes, we proceed in two steps. First, we abstract over the structure generated by the XQuery transformation using a set of XPath expressions that describe the location of nodes created in the output document. Those XPath expressions are collected during the application of the inference rules. As a second step, we check whether these XPath expressions are unsatisfiable against the output schema (using the "select" predicate), in which case we raise the INVQUERY error.

INVRES

$xpath$	$\Gamma \vdash xpath \mapsto /selected\_node(xpath)$
seq	$\dfrac{\Gamma \vdash e_1 \mapsto p \quad \Gamma \vdash e_2 \mapsto p'}{\Gamma \vdash e_1,e_2 \mapsto p/following\_simbling::*[p']}$
tag	$\dfrac{\Gamma \vdash e \mapsto p}{\Gamma \vdash <tag>e</tag> \mapsto /tag/p}$
$elem$	$\dfrac{\Gamma \vdash e_1 \mapsto p \quad \Gamma \vdash e_2 \mapsto p'}{\Gamma \vdash element\{e_1\}\{e_2\} \mapsto /p/p'}$
if	$\dfrac{\Gamma \vdash e_2 \mapsto p \quad \Gamma \vdash e_3 \mapsto p'}{\Gamma \vdash if\ e_1\ then\ e_2\ else\ e_3 \mapsto (p|p')}$
for	$\dfrac{\Gamma\cup(\$v,e_1) \vdash e_3 \mapsto p}{\Gamma \vdash for\ \$v\ in\ e_1\ where\ e_2\ return\ e_3 \mapsto p}$
e	$\dfrac{S_{out},\Gamma \vdash e \mapsto p \quad S_{out},\Gamma \vdash \neg select(p,type(S_{out}))}{S_{out},\Gamma \vdash e \rightarrow INVRES}$

We introduce the predicate $selected\_node$ that takes an XPath as argument and returns the selected node name (for example, $selected\_node(/a/b/c)=c$). Consider the *return* clause of our motivating example:

return <book>{$s[count(sales)<=1]/sales}</book>

The XPath that abstracts over the generated structure for this *return* clause would be: */book/sales*. In the inference rules above, the construction of an XPath p from the XQuery expression e is denoted as $e \mapsto p$ (see table INVRES).

4. RELATED WORK

Impacts of schema evolutions have been recently investigated in the literature by several authors [8, 7, 1, 2, 6, 4].

In [8] the authors address the problem of schema evolution assuming that a mapping between schemas is provided. In [7] the authors propose a five-level framework (called XCase) to manage XML evolution, but they do not deal with propagation of schema changes at query level. [1] is concerned with a structural similarity measure as a step for the automatic inference of a transformation from one schema to another. However the approach is approximate and does not deal with XQuery. The work found in [2] addresses evolution in schemas but the process is not fully automatic in the sense that the user must indicate which queries are potentially affected by schema changes. The work found in [6] deals with revalidation of documents whenever their schema evolves but does not deal with queries. Finally, the present work extends our previous results on evolution restricted to XPath expressions and schemas analysis [4]. The extension consists in considering a transformation language such as XQuery that can not only select nodes in input documents but also generate output documents. In addition, we analyze the impact of input schema changes over the output generated by the transformation.

5. CONCLUSION

We highlighted various consequences that schema changes may have on transformations. We presented a new taxonomy of possible problems induced by schema changes. We proposed automated static analysis techniques to detect each category. The analyses are presented through inference rules that operate on a core fragment of XQuery. We believe this is a step toward automated schema-directed code revision techniques for modern document management systems.

6. REFERENCES

[1] A. Boukottaya and C. Vanoirbeek. Schema matching for transforming structured documents. In *Proceedings of the 2005 ACM symposium on Document engineering*, pages 101–110, 2005.

[2] C. A. Curino, H. J. Moon, and C. Zaniolo. Graceful database schema evolution: the PRISM workbench. *Proc. VLDB Endow.*, 1(1):761–772, Aug. 2008.

[3] P. Genevès and N. Layaïda. Eliminating dead-code from XQuery programs. In *Proceedings of the 32nd ACM/IEEE International Conference on Software Engineering - Volume 2*, pages 305–306, 2010.

[4] P. Genevès, N. Layaïda, and V. Quint. Impact of XML schema evolution. *ACM Transactions on Internet Technology*, 11(1):4:1–4:27, July 2011.

[5] P. Genevès, N. Layaïda, and A. Schmitt. Efficient static analysis of XML paths and types. *SIGPLAN Not.*, 42(6):342–351, June 2007.

[6] G. Guerrini, M. Mesiti, and D. Rossi. Impact of XML schema evolution on valid documents. In *Proceedings of the 7th annual ACM international workshop on Web information and data management*, pages 39–44, 2005.

[7] M. Necaský and I. Mlýnková. Five-level multi-application schema evolution. In *DATESO*, pages 90–104, 2009.

[8] Y. Velegrakis, R. J. Miller, and L. Popa. Mapping adaptation under evolving schemas. In *Proceedings of the 29th international conference on Very large data bases - Volume 29*, pages 584–595, 2003.

Effective Radical Segmentation of Offline Handwritten Chinese Characters towards Constructing Personal Handwritten Fonts

Zhanghui Chen
State Key Laboratory for Superlattices and
Microstructures,Institute of
Semiconductors,Chinese Academy of Sciences
No. A35, QingHua East Road
Haidian District, Beijing, China
zhanghuichen88@gmail.com

Baoyao Zhou
EMC Labs China
8F, Block D, SP Tower, Tsinghua Science Park
Zhongguancun Dong Road Beijing, China
baoyao.zhou@emc.com

ABSTRACT

Effective radical segmentation of handwritten Chinese characters can greatly facilitate the subsequent character processing tasks, such as Chinese handwriting recognition/identification and the generation of Chinese handwritten fonts. In this paper, a popular snake model is enhanced by considering the guided image force and optimized by Genetic Algorithm, such that it achieves a significant improvement in terms of both accuracy and efficiency when applied to segment the radicals in handwritten Chinese characters. The proposed radical segmentation approach consists of three stages: constructing guide information, Genetic Algorithm optimization and post-embellishment. Testing results show that the proposed approach can effectively decompose radicals with overlaps and connections from handwritten Chinese characters with various layout structures. The segmentation accuracy reaches 94.91% for complicated samples with overlapped and connected radicals and the segmentation speed is 0.05 second per character. For demonstrating the advantages of the approach, radicals extracted from the user input samples are reused to construct personal Chinese handwritten font library. Experiments show that the constructed characters well maintain the handwriting style of the user and have good enough performance. In this way, the user only needs to write a small number of samples for obtaining his/her own handwritten font library. This method greatly reduces the cost of existing solutions and makes it much easier for people to use computers to write letters/e-mails, diaries/blogs, even magazines/books in their own handwriting.

Categories and Subject Descriptors

I.4.6 [**Image Processing and Computer Vision**]: Segmentation

DocEng'12, September 4–7, 2012, Paris, France.
Copyright 2012 ACM 978-1-4503-1116-8/12/09 ...$15.00.

General Terms

Algorithms, Performance

Keywords

Radical segmentation, offline handwritten Chinese character recognition, snake model, Genetic Algorithm, personal handwritten fonts

1. INTRODUCTION

Chinese characters are structured symbols, each of which is composed of one or more basic structured components called *radical*. Although there are more than 20,000 characters in the computer-used Chinese character set GB13000.1, the number of radicals is only around 500 [15]. Moreover, the main radical composing patterns of Chinese characters, or Chinese character layout structures, are not many, in which the left-right structure and the top-bottom structure have covered about 90% of characters. The study of radicals can greatly benefit the processing of Chinese characters. For example, if handwritten Chinese characters could be decomposed into basic radicals, the difficulty of characters recognition will be decreased to that of the recognition of fewer types of radicals [11]. Radicals extracted can also be used in evaluating the representation of handwriting characters, which is useful in calligraphy assessment and verification. In addition, the radical extraction and assembling can facilitate the construction of personal Chinese handwritten font library by reusing radicals in a few of user input characters samples.

Although the radicals are very important, the research on those in offline handwritten Chinese characters is quite rare and limited [1, 2, 3, 5, 7, 8, 9, 11, 12, 13]. This may be due to the first step, radical segmentation, which is rather complicated. Radical segmentation of handwritten Chinese characters is similar to character segmentation of handwritten Chinese text. Because of various overlaps and connections between radicals and complicated radical composing patterns, radical segmentation is more difficult than character segmentation.

In this paper, a systemic strategy of radical segmentation of offline handwritten Chinese characters based on an enhanced snake model and Genetic Algorithm (GA) is proposed. The strategy contains three stages. First, the snake model with guided image force is constructed through strokes analysis. The parameters library pre-built through analyzing the FangSong font characters offers the search space of the snake curve and other guided information. In the second stage, GA is employed to search for the optimal snake curve. Finally, an embellishing method based on skeleton image and contour image is adopted to correct and refine the wrong segmentation curves of the characters. The three-stage strategy considers different radical composing patterns and various connections and overlaps between radicals. Results show this strategy can segment radicals with connections and overlaps effectively for main radical composing patterns.

In addition, considering the complexity of radical segmentation, radicals are not the prior option for fast character recognition. This paper uses radicals extracted from sample characters to construct personal Chinese handwritten font library to demonstrate the advantages of the segmentation strategy. The direct way to construct personal font library is to ask the user to write down all the necessary characters on paper sheets, which are then scanned into images and vectorized into font library file (TrueType or OpenType format). However, there are more than 20,000 characters in the computer-used Chinese character set. It is unacceptable burden for most people. Fortunately, Chinese characters are structured symbols. The same radical keeps relatively stable representation in different characters. We can reuse the segmented radicals in sample characters to construct other characters. In this way, the user only needs to write a few characters and others can be generated automatically, which greatly decreases the burden of the user. The experimental results verify the feasibility of the method.

The rest of the paper is organized as follows. Section 2 introduces the related work on radical segmentation and constructing personal Chinese handwritten font library. The composing patterns of radicals and the connections and overlaps between radicals in handwritten Chinese characters are summarized in Section 3. Section 4 presents the details of the three-stage radical segmentation method. Section 5 introduces how to construct personal font library by reusing radicals extracted from the sample characters. Section 6 illustrates the experimental results on radical segmentation and handwritten fonts construction. Finally, the concluding remarks are discussed in Section 7.

2. RELATED WORKS

Although there are many researches on radical segmentation for on-line handwritten Chinese characters [7, 8], the researches on offline characters is very few. The methods for on-line characters are often based on the sequenced data and thus are very different from the methods for offline ones. So the researches about on-line characters are not shown here.

Casey and Nagy [1] are the first to employ radicals to recognize Chinese characters. In their paper, 64 radical templates are used to sort characters globally, and then, fed to the fine classification and recognition stage. Wang et al. [13] used relaxation method to extract radicals, which are used in the partial matching and characters recognition. This method shows the good performance for the neat handwriting.

Cheng et al. proposed strokes analysis [2] and background thinning [3] to search for a curvilinear dividing path to segment the character. In the strokes analysis method, the

extracted strokes with the information of long strokes and projection are used to divide the characters into left-right or top-bottom type. The background thinning methods consists of three steps: dividing by projection; dividing by background thinning; dividing by window extraction. It can give cursive dividing path for characters with unconnected radicals or simple joining strokes between radicals. But the background thinning offers too many optional dividing paths and the extracted widow cannot handle the complicated joining strokes well.

Shi et al. [9] presented active shape models to recognize the radicals, which can well adapt to various radical deformations. But the landmark points have to be labeled in advance. The complicated connection among radicals will bring noise into matching.

Wang et al. [11, 12] presented a recursive hierarchical scheme, which used character pattern detection, straight cut line detection and stroke clustering to extract radicals. The straight cut line detection makes use of the gaps information among radicals. This method has good segmentation results for neat handwriting with non-connected radicals, and we will use it to help construct the guided information library. The disadvantage of this method is still its incapability to deal with the connected radicals and relative unconstrained handwriting.

Ip et al. [5] adopted deformable templates, i.e., snake model, to extract radicals, which can give non-linear segmentation path for various structures. But it can only discompose characters with unconnected radicals because there was no guided force for connected strokes, and its successful rate was only 85.8%. In addition, the energy minimization scheme of the snake curves employed a greedy strategy with exhaustive search, which had four-layer loops and was not efficient enough. Compared with it, we will use an enhanced snake model and GA to seek the non-linear segmentation path.

On the whole, most of existing work focused on printed characters or neat hand-printed characters, and cannot handle connected radicals effectively.

For the construction of personal Chinese handwritten font library, researches have proposed some models to facilitate the generation of Chinese characters. Xu et al. [17] presented a way to automatically generate personal Chinese handwriting by capturing the characteristics of personal handwriting. It first decomposed the sample Chinese handwriting characters into a hierarchy of reusable components. Then the target character was constructed by these components and some captured characteristics. However, the components used were too detailed and not stable in different characters, which made the newly generated characters lose the handwriting style of the user. Lai et al. [6] used radicals and heuristic search to generate Chinese glyph which was evaluated by some beauty function. It mainly made use of glyph beauty evaluation metrics to generate characters of different styles rather than the font library of the user style. In the work of [18, 10], each character was generated by strokes, which was, however, effective only for simple characters rather than those with multiple character components and many dragging-strokes. In our solution, radicals extracted from samples are reused to construct new characters. Because of the relative stability of the same radicals in different characters, the generated characters can well maintain the writing style of the user. Besides, our method works for arbitrarily complex components and can generate almost all of the characters commonly used.

3. RADICALS OF HANDWRITTEN CHINESE CHARACTERS

3.1 Structures of Chinese characters

Chinese characters have a total of 12 kinds of common layout structures according to the composing patterns of their radicals, as shown in Figure 1. These structures can be further classified into 4 classes in the view of segmentation.

- Single or frame: The characters with single radical have no need to be segmented, while characters of frame structure are difficult to be segmented. These two kinds of characters can be regarded as the single or frame class.

- Left-right: For the characters of left-right and left-middle-right structures, their segmentation curves are always in vertical direction. These two structures can be combined into the left-right class.

- Top-bottom: Similarly, the top-bottom and top-middle-bottom structures can be intergrated into the top-bottom class.

- Surrounding: The segmentation curves of characters of the other 7 structures can be viewed as circle shape, so they can be classified to the surrounding class.

Table 1 shows some examples of each class with the coverage rate in the Chinese character set GB13000.1. It can be found that the left-right and top-bottom structures cover more than 90% characters.

Characters with more than two radicals, such as '保' and '想', have a hierarchical radical combination structure with multiple layers, in which the radicals should be segmented from the top layer to the low layer.

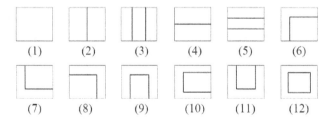

Figure 1: The common layout structures of Chinese characters: (1) Single/frame; (2) left-right; (3) left-middle-right; (4) top-bottom; (5) top-middle-bottom; (6) top-left; (7) left-bottom; (8) top-right; (9) left-top-right; (10); top-left-bottom; (11) left-bottom-right; (12) surrounding.

3.2 Radical Overlap and Connection

In practical handwritings, radicals within a character often have overlaps and connections between each other, which bring the difficulty for radical segmentation. In general, the overlaps between radicals appear in the nearest endpoints of strokes, while the connections between radicals are corner points or fork points. Figure 2 gives some examples of overlaps and connections. The first character '埯' has overlap

Table 1: Chinese characters' classes and their coverage rates in the Chinese characters set GB13000.1.

Class	Example							Percent (%)
Single or frame	中	车	大	九	乘	爽	巫	噩	1.87
Left-right	祆	行	保	朝	街	辩	衡	斑	69.80
Top-bottom	台	宋	贸	想	曼	衰	器	案	21.00
Surrounding	病	赵	式	周	匪	凶	国	图	7.33

between radicals; the second character '祆' has connected corner point between radicals; the third and the forth characters have connected fork point between radicals. These feature points can give many guide information for radical segmentation, thus it is important to detect them.

Figure 2: Handwritten Chinese characters with overlaps and connections.

In addition, the skeleton of the character image is also helpful for detecting these feature points. Figure 3 shows the process and result of the feature point detection. Figure 3 (a) is the skeleton image of character '祆' and Figure 3 (b) shows the pixel P and its 3×3 neighbors. Supposing the value of black pixel is set to 1 and the white one is 0, the neighborhood feature of black pixel P can be defined as follows [19]:

$$N(p) = \sum_{i=1}^{8} |x_{i+1} - x_i|$$

where $x_9 = x_1$. According to the neighbor feature, the endpoints and fork points can be determined by the following expression:

$$N(p) = \begin{cases} 2 & endpoint \\ 6 & three - fork\ point \\ 8 & four - fork\ point \end{cases}$$

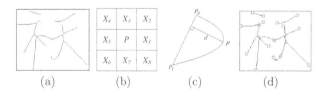

Figure 3: Feature points detection. (a) is the skeleton image of the character. (b) shows pixel P and its 3×3 neighbors. (c) shows how to find the corner point. (d) labels different kinds of feature points in the skeleton image, in which the square points are endpoint, the triangle points are three-fork point, the cross points are four-fork point and the circle points are corner point.

As shown in the skeleton image of character '祆', the four-fork point or multi-fork point may be mistaken as two or more three-fork points because of the thinning algorithm. It can be corrected by the following rule: If two connected three-fork points are too close, they will be revised to four-fork points. The corner point can be detected through the stroke between two feature points. Figure 3 (c) shows the stroke between P_0 and P_1, and the corner point P in the stroke. The distance d will be biggest and exceeds certain threshold or the angle $\angle P_0 P P_1$ will be smallest and lower than certain threshold for the corner point. The corresponding stroke is divided into two strokes at the found corner point. All these feature points and strokes are conserved for the latter segmentation. Figure 3 (d) labels different kinds of feature points in different symbols in the skeleton image. It can be found that the above method can well detect these feature points.

4. RADICAL SEGMENTATION

4.1 The snake model of radical segmentation

4.1.1 The snake model

Snakes, also known as *active contours*, are curves that can move and deform under the influence of internal force coming from the curve itself and external force coming from the image [16]. The internal and external forces are defined for guiding the snake to creep from the starting position to the objective position. Similar to other applications of snake model, the energy of the snake curve for radical segmentation is defined as follows:

$$E_{snake} = E_{\text{int}} + \lambda E_{image}$$

where E_{int} represents the internal energy from the curve shape, E_{image} represents the energy from the image and λ is the relative weight.

As the discrete formulation of the snake model, the internal energy can be expressed below:

$$E_{\text{int}} = \alpha E_{continuity} + \beta E_{smoothness}$$

$$E_{continuity} = \sum_{i=1}^{n} |v_i - v_{i-1}|^2$$

$$E_{smoothness} = \sum_{i=1}^{n} |v_{i+1} + v_{i-1} - 2v_i|^2$$

where $E_{continuity}$ and $E_{smoothness}$ denote the continuity and smoothness of the curve respectively. α and β is the corresponding weight. $v_i = (x_i, y_i)$ denotes the position of the point in the snake curve. n is the number of the points that form the snake curve.

4.1.2 The image force

The image energy can be intuitively defined as the number of the pixels where the snake curve intersects with the character image. Such method cannot deal with connected radicals because the snake cannot decide where to cross through the connected stroke. Besides, the region of overlaps has no gradual guide. As stated before, the feature points can give many guided information for segmentation. If let the force of the black pixel near feature points be lower than the common black pixel, then the snake will be attracted to the vicinity of features points, which is propitious to segmentation. Through strokes analysis and segmentation

simulation, the neighborhood N of feature points is set to be a circle region, as shown in Figure 4 (a). The pixel force and the image energy of snake curve are set as follows:

$$I(v) = \begin{cases} 0 & v \text{ is white pixel} \\ 0.2 & v \text{ is corner point or the black pixel in its } N \\ 0.3 & v \text{ is } 3-\text{fork point or the black pixel in its } N \\ 0.5 & v \text{ is endpoint or the black pixel in its } N \\ 0.8 & v \text{ is } 4-\text{fork point or the black pixel in its } N \\ 1 & v \text{ is other black pixel} \end{cases}$$

$$E_{image} = \sum_{i=1}^{n-1} \sum_{j=1}^{m_i} I_i(v_j)$$

where $v = (x, y)$ is the pixel in the position (x, y), and $I(v)$ is the image force of pixel v; n is the number of the points constituting the snake curve; m_i is the number of the pixels in the line formed between the ith point and the $(i+1)^{th}$ point, thus $\sum_{j=1}^{m_i} I_i(v_j)$ is the energy brought by this line.

The smaller force of the corner point and three-fork point can guide the snake to determine where to cross through the connected stroke. The value of endpoint can build buffer between strokes and background, thus bring gradual conduct for the snake. The four-fork point seldom exists in the connected strokes but is very common in the inner of radicals. Considering the noise of guide, the force of four-fork point is set to be 0.8. The last two images of Figure 4 label the image force of the character '祆' and '驰' by gray level. It can be forecast that the snake will be guided to reasonable position.

(a)   (b)   (c)

Figure 4: Image force. (a) shows pixel P and its circle neighborhood. (b) and (c) shows the image force of two characters respectively, in which the pixel with grayer level has larger force.

4.1.3 The search space of the snake curve

As mentioned earlier, Chinese characters can be classified into four classes according to the shape and direction of the segmentation curves. The search space of the snake curve for characters of the latter three classes can be defined as shown in Figure 5.

For characters of the left-right class, the snake's search space is a vertical region. This region is parameterized by a tuple of $(Xmid, Xd, Npoint, Nvary)$, in which $Xmid$ means the x-coordinate of the midnormal line of the region; Xd means the distance between the midnormal line and the left or right border; $Npoint$ means the number of the points constituting the snake curve, which is equal to the number of the horizontal lines with equidistance in Figure 5 (a); $Nvary$ means the number of the varying pixels in each horizontal line. Similarly, the search space for characters of the top-bottom class can be parameterized by a horizontal region, i. e. $(Ymid, Yd, Npoint, Nvary)$ accordingly.

110

For characters of the surrounding class, the snake's search space is a region between two rectangles, and the varying pixels for each point in the snake curve are not in the same vertical or horizontal line but in a narrow sector region. The search space can be parameterized by $(x_0, y_0, Xd_1, Xd_2, Yd_1, Yd_2, Npoint, Nvary)$, in which (x_0, y_0) is the overlapped center of the two rectangles; Xd_1 is the distance from the centre to the left border of the inner rectangle and Xd_2 is the distance from the centre to the left border of the outer rectangle; Yd_1 and Yd_2 are the distance from the centre to the upper border of the inner rectangle and the outer rectangle respectively; $Npoint$ is the number of the points forming the snake curve, which is equal to the number of the narrow sector regions with equidistance; $Nvary$ means the number of the varying pixels in each sector region.

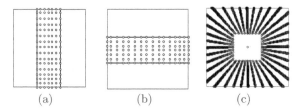

(a)   (b)   (c)

Figure 5: The search space of the snake curve. (a) is for characters of the class left-right; (b) is for the class top-bottom; (c) is for the class surrounding.

Usually, the search spaces of different characters may have big difference, while those of the same character with different printed and handwritten styles are often similar due to their same internal structure. Besides, there are some fixed patterns in the overlaps and connections between radicals for the same character. Therefore, the parameters of the search space for each character can be pre-computed through analyzing the characteristic of each corresponding printed Chinese character, and then be transformed into the radical segmentation of handwriting through relative rate. In this paper, we build such parameters library through analyzing the characters of FangSong font and their various possible deformations one by one. For each FangSong font character, this building process consists of three steps:

Step 1: Determine the hierarchy structure of the character and label the structure type of each layer manually.

Step 2: Obtain the "separator" of each layer. The "separator" is defined as a rectangle that segments the image in each layer into radicals. There are three types of separators. For the layer with left-right class, the separator is a vertical rectangle gap with the shorter width and longer height; for top-bottom class, it is a horizontal rectangle gap with the longer width and shorter height; for surrounding class, it is a rectangle which can divide the layer's image into an inner radical and an outer radical. Because FangSong font is a standard printed character set and almost has no connections between radicals, we adopt the following two schemes to obtain these separators. Firstly, the method of Wang et al. [2] is employed to automatically segment the radicals and calculate the separator between radicals. Secondly, if the separator offered by the automatic method is not satisfactory, then revise it manually to obtain a good search space. Figure 6 shows some examples of separators in some sample characters.

Step 3: Determine the snake's search space in each layer.

After obtaining the separator, the snake's search space in this layer can be defined as follows. Firstly, for left-right class, the parameter $Xmid$ is set to be the x-coordinate of the midnormal line of the corresponding separator; Xd is set to be 15% of the width of the image in this layer; $Npoint$ and $Nvary$ are assigned to be 25% of the number of the perpendicular and transverse pixels in the search area respectively. The parameters setting for top-bottom class is similar to the left-right class. For the surrounding class, the corresponding separator contracts in the length of 15% of the image perpendicularly and transversely to form the inner rectangle of the search space; similarly, the separator expands in the same proportion to form the outer rectangle. Secondly, the uniform parameters may not be better values for some characters and need to adjust manually. For example, the point ' ` ' in the radical '心' of the character '忌' is easy to be wrongly segmented into the upper radical. We can set Yd be larger in the upper direction and smaller in the bottom direction to avoid such wrong segmentation.

Through the above three steps, the parameters library of the search spaces for the segmentation curves in each character is built. These search space parameters with the threshold of corner point, the radius of circle neighborhood and the position information of radicals form the final guide information library of each character.

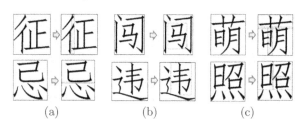

(a)   (b)   (c)

Figure 6: Detecting separators for FangSong font characters: (a) Left-right and top-bottom class; (b) Surrounding class; (c) Multi-layer structure.

4.2 The Genetic Algorithm for snake optimization

The searching of the optimal snake curve is a combinatorial optimization problem [4]. GA has great advantages in the global optimization of combinational problems. Some previous studies has used GA to optimize the snake curve and obtained better performance than the classical methods [4, 14]. Thus we adopt GA to optimize the segmentation curve.

4.2.1 Individual coding

The snake curve is comprised of a sequence of points, so individual coding of each segmentation curve can be defined as follows:

$$(p_1(x_1, y_1), p_2(x_2, y_2), \ldots, p_{Npoint}(x_{Npoint}, y_{Npoint}))$$

where p_i represents a point in the snake curve; x_i and y_i are its values on X and Y coordinates.

4.2.2 Initial population

Each point in an individual is randomly selected from the pixels in the corresponding search space, i.e., horizontal line, vertical line or narrow sector region. The initial population is then comprised of these randomly generated individuals.

4.2.3 Fitness function

The total energy of each snake curve can be expressed as below:

$$E_{snake} = \alpha \sum_{i=1}^{n} |v_i - v_{i-1}|^2 + \beta \sum_{i=1}^{n} |v_{i+1} + v_{i-1} - 2v_i|^2 + \lambda \sum_{i=1}^{n-1} \sum_{j=1}^{m_i} I_i(v_j)$$

The objective of GA is to minimize the total energy, thus the fitness function can be set as:

$$f = \text{rank}(E_{snake})$$

where the function rank() is the sorting of variables from low to high value and the higher ranking has larger fitness. This function can keep the fitness of different individuals in the same order of magnitude to avoid prematurity and local optimization.

4.2.4 Genetic operators

Genetic operators are defined as follows.

Selection operator: Adopt roulette wheel strategy and keep the best 10% individuals to the next generation.

Crossover operator: Adopt two-point crossover method, which exchanges the points betwixt the two randomly selected points between two individuals with a certain probability. Such strategy is more useful for the characters of left-right or top-bottom structure because the overlaps and connections in these two structures mostly appear in the middle region.

Mutation operator: Adopt multi-point mutation strategy, which randomly select some points in the individual and substitute the values of these points by values randomly selected from the corresponding pixels with a certain probability.

4.2.5 Termination criterion and genetic parameters

In this paper, the program is terminated when the evolution reaches 100 generations. The size of the population is twice as many as the number of the genes in the individual. The probability of crossover is 0.8. The number of probably mutated genes is 10 percents of the number of the genes and the probability of mutation is 0.1. The energy parameters α, β and λ is set to 1, 1 and 3000 respectively.

4.3 The embellishment of the segmentation curve

Because GA is a random searching algorithm and sometimes may not find the satisfactory solution, thus an embellishing strategy based on skeleton image and contour image is proposed to amend the segmentation curve output by GA.

The embellishment is implemented as follows:

Step 1: Determine whether there are cross points between the segmentation curve and the strokes. If not, end the program.

Step 2: Find the strokes that the segmentation curve crosses through in the skeleton image. The two feature points at the ends of each of these strokes will be optional embellishing positions. Two layers of criterions are designed to determine which feature point is selected as the embellishing position. (1) Select the prior point according to the following priority level: end point > corner point > three-fork point > four-fork point. (2) Select the point closer to the segmentation curve, if the two feature points have the same type.

Step 3: Determine whether it is necessary to embellish the segmentation through the distance between the segmen-

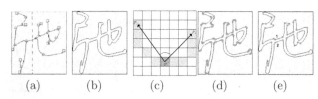

(a)   (b)   (c)   (d)   (e)

Figure 7: The process to find the required corner points in Step 4. (a) shows the skeleton image of the character and its feature points. The dotted line is a virtual segmentation curve that needs embellishment. (b) is the contour image of the character. (c) shows the pixel P and its neighborhood angle $\angle P_1 P P_2$. The gray pixels in the figure are the contour and the white ones are background. (d) and (e) shows the corner points found before and after reducing respectively.

tation curve and the feature point selected. If the distance is rather small, end the program.

Step 4: Find the accurate embellishing position according to the corner points of the contour image. Then revise the segmentation curve along the border of the contour.

Figure 7 shows the process to seek the required corner points in Step 4. Figure 7 (a) is the skeleton image of the character '驰' with feature points and a virtual segmentation curve that needs to embellish. Figure 7 (b) is the contour image. The pixels in the contour are sequenced through the neighborhood relationship. For each pixel in the sequence, the angle formed by the pixel and its two adjacent contour pixels, which both have an interval in the sequence with this pixel, is computed. This angle here is called neighborhood angle of the pixel. Figure 7 (c) shows the neighborhood angle $\angle P_1 P P_2$, in which P_1 and P_2 have an interval of 5 contour pixels with P. If the angle is smaller than a given threshold, the pixel can be regarded as a corner point. Figure 7 (d) labels such corner points when the threshold is set to 150°. It can be found that there appears a cluster of points in one corner or the end of strokes by measuring the neighborhood angles. However, these points in each cluster are close to each other and can be reduced to one representative point, which has the largest distance to the line formed by the two end points of the corresponding corner point cluster. Figure 7 (e) shows the results after reducing redundant corner points. Similar to the skeleton image, the strokes formed by these corner points can be found in the contour, and the corner points at the two ends of the strokes that the segmentation curve crosses through are taken as the optional accurate embellishing positions. Those points at the same side with the feature point given by Step 2 are selected as the final embellishing positions. In Figure 7 (e), the two points marked by 1 and 2 respectively are the selected points.

In summary, Step 1 and Step 3 are used to determine whether embellishment is needed or not; Step 2 is used to find the coarse embellishing positions by the skeleton image and Step 4 is used to find the accurate positions in the contour image. In addition, more heuristic embellishing strategies for each character can be constructed to obtain more accurate embellishment.

4.4 The complete procedure of radical segmentation

Figure 8 gives the complete procedure of the radical segmentation that integrates all the methods introduced in Section 3-6 and outlines the relationship among them. The procedure contains three stages, which are framed by different dashed rectangles respectively. Firstly, the snake model with guided image force is constructed through strokes analysis. In the same stage, the search space and other guided information are read from the parameters library prebuilt through analyzing the characters in the simplified Chinese FangSong font and their various possible deformations. Then, in the second stage, GA is employed to optimize the snake curve. Considering that GA is a probabilistic searching strategy, the algorithm need be rebooted certain times when necessary. Finally, the embellishing method is adopted to revise the segmentation curve of the characters whose radicals are not segmented correctly.

For characters with a multi-layer structure, the last two stages will be re-performed on the segmented radicals output by the higher layer until the character is decomposed completely.

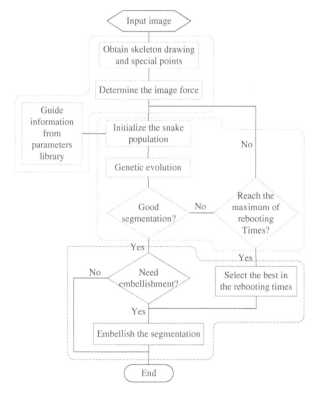

Figure 8: The complete procedure of the radical segmentation.

5. CONSTRUCTION OF PERSONAL CHINESE HANDWRITTEN FONT LIBRARY

Because of the relative stability of the same radical in different characters, radicals in sample characters can be reused to construct other characters. In this way, construction of personal Chinese handwritten font library can be decreased into the following two processes. Firstly, some characters are selected as the user input samples. These samples shall cover all the radicals appearing in the characters commonly used. Then the method in Figure 8 is adopted to extract the components, all of which form the candidate library of rad-

icals. Secondly, these radicals are used to construct all the other characters. The construction process can be guided by the structure information of the corresponding FangSong characters and shall consider the handwriting characteristics of the user. The following steps show the details of the program for generating a new character.

Step 1: Obtain the structure information of the character. It is generally acknowledged that characters written by different persons have different height-width ratio. Some persons' characters are tall and thin while others' might be short and fat. In addition, the height-width ratio of a character is affected by characters' content. Different character written by the same person has different height-width ratio. However, the character's relative height-width ratio of one person to other persons is stable and affected little by characters' content. Therefore, for maintaining the handwriting style of the user in new generated characters, we first calculate the mean relative height-width ratio of the user input characters to the corresponding FangSong ones, and then, resize the initial structure read from the guide library constructed before with the mean ratio. The structure after resizing is used in guiding the following process.

Step 2: Select radicals from the radical library. If there are more than one candidates, the one with more similar position and relative size will be selected.

Step 3: Organize these radicals together to form the handwritten character according to the position and relative size of radicals from Step 1.

Figure 9 shows the process for constructing a new character.

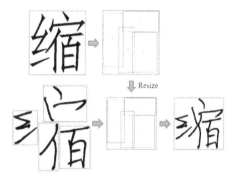

Figure 9: The construction process of a new handwritten character.

6. EXPERIMENTAL RESULTS AND DISCUSSIONS

In this part, we first analyze the performance of the segmentation method. Then the results of constructing personal handwritten font library are presented.

6.1 Experiments on radical segmentation

The samples used in the experiment come from the personal calligraphy font library of Ms. Jinglei Xu, a popular Chinese movie star and director. These samples have been well pre-processed and converted into the binary images. Thus, we can conduct the experiment of radical segmentation on these samples directly.

Figure 10 and Figure 11 show the searching process of the GA for the character '标'. In Figure 11, the optimal segmentation curve in the 1st generation is rather random and crosses strokes several times. But that in the 5th generation is much better and the 10th generation's has totally avoided cross points and reached a satisfactory result. From the 10th to 100th generation, the segmentation curve turns to be much smoother. It can be predicted that the curve will be slowly smoother with the population evolving. Figure 10 and Figure 11 indicate that GA has excellent global convergence to get the satisfactory result quickly despite its local convergent speed may not be fast enough. Furthermore, it can be found that the image force has greater impact on the evolution in the initial stage and the internal energy dominates the latter evolution.

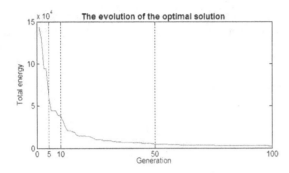

Figure 10: The relationship between the total energy of optimal solution and the generation in the process of searching the segmentation curve of the character.

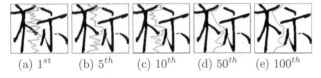

(a) 1st (b) 5th (c) 10th (d) 50th (e) 100th

Figure 11: The corresponding optimal segmentation curve of Figure 10 in different generation.

Figure 12 gives the segmentation results under various situations. (a1)-(a4) are segmentations of characters with overlaps but without connections between radicals. Presented by the four examples, the snake can well find the gap in the overlap for various structures even when the gap is quite narrow. (b1)-(b4) are characters with connections between radicals, in which the first one has one connected corner point between radicals and the other three ones have one or two connected fork points.. In order to directly illustrate how the snake is guided, the four results are shown by the image-force figure, in which grayer pixel represents larger force. It can be found that all of these connections are segmented correctly under the guide of image force. The results of (a1)-(a4) and (b1)-(b4) indicate the snake model with GA can well deal with overlaps and connections of radicals for characters with various structures. The eight characters are segmented correctly without embellishment. As mentioned earlier, the segmentation curve given by GA may not be satisfactory sometimes and need further embellishment. (c1)-(c4) shows such situation. (c1) is an accidental example, most of the time which will be segmented correctly under the guide of image force. (c3) is a case in which the connection is segmented successfully but the overlap doesn't get well handled. As presented in (c2) and (c4), both of the

Figure 12: Some results of radical segmentation. (a1)-(a4) are characters with overlaps but without connections between radicals. (b1)-(b4) are characters with connections between radicals, all of which are shown by the image-force figure. The eight characters are segmented correctly without embellishment. (c1)-(c4) present the situations where radical are not segmented correctly by GA. (c1) and (c3) are the results output by GA. (c2) and (c4) are the results after embellishment. All the four ones are shown by the contour image to illustrate the embellishing process clearly. (d1)-(d4) show the segmentation of characters with multi-layer structure.

two cases obtain satisfactory segmentation curve after embellishment. All the four results are shown by the contour image to illustrate the embellishing process clearly. (d1)-(d4) show the segmentation of characters with a multi-layer structure. Through decomposing from the top layer to the low layer, these characters also get satisfactory results. In conclusion, the results in Figure 12 indicate that through the three stages: constructing guide information, GA optimization and post-embellishment, radicals with overlaps and connections can be well segmented in various situations.

In order to further evaluate the segmentation method, 452 samples selected from the personal calligraphy font library of Ms. Jinglei Xu are tested. The samples consists of 248 characters with left-right structure, 113 with top-bottom structure and 91 with surrounding structure, most of which have complicated overlaps or connections between radicals. In addition, 60 sample characters have the multi-layer structure and each of them need decomposing more than two times from the top layer to the low layer.

Table 2 shows the testing results when the maximal rebooting times of GA is 10. Figure 13 displays the segmentation curves of some samples, in which 8 characters are wrongly segmented and labeled by the underlines. In Table 2, the whole successful rate reaches 94.91%, which outperforms that in the previous researches [11, 5] and thus verifies the validity of our method. Furthermore, in the top layer segmentation, the successful rate reaches 98.39%

Table 2: The segmentation results of the radicals with overlaps and connections for the selected 452 samples. Successful rate (*Srate*) is the rate of the characters segmented successfully.

	Top layer				The whole
	LR	TB	S	Total	
Srate (%)	98.39	90.27	94.51	95.58	94.91

Figure 13: The segmentation curves of some samples.

for the characters with the left-right structure, 90.27% for the top-bottom one, 94.51% for the surrounding one and 95.58% in total. Because the combination of the radicals is more complicated, the segmentation results of characters with top-bottom structures are a little worse than those with the other two structures. The method obtains the best performance in the characters with the left-right structure. The failed radical segmentations are mainly caused by the inaccurate thinning algorithm and the ambiguous information, which makes that the method cannot decide where to segment without more accurate recognition. Taking the characters '茛, 區' as examples, it is difficult for the method to determine which radical the stroke ' 丶' belongs to. Segmentation of such characters can be improved by increasing the recognition information to the embellishment stage. The segmentation of the characters '朝, 散, 鯢' is failed due to the inaccurate thinning algorithm, which brings in some noise points wrongly attracting the snake. For the characters '垦, 骶, 晋', there are interfering guiding information near the correct segmentation curves, but revising the searching area properly can increase the successful rate. Generally speaking, the segmentation given by the three-stage method is successful and satisfactory. Compared with the previous methods which cannot handle the radicals with overlaps or connections, our approach effectively solves these problems and improves the successful rate.

Besides, the average running time of radical segmentation is around 0.05 second per character for our implementation in C language, which is about 300 times faster than the greedy method in [5]. It indicates that GA indeed accelerates the optimization of the snake curve. Furthermore, in our testing experiments, the greedy method often falls into the local optimum and its mean successful rate with different parameters is lower than 60% for these samples. Therefore, our approach achieves a significant improvement in terms of both accuracy and efficiency.

6.2 Experiments on constructing personal handwritten fonts

In this experiment, 522 characters are selected as the user input samples [15, 20]. These samples cover all the radicals appearing in the 2500 characters commonly used. They consist of 158 characters with single radical, 196 characters with left-right structure, 90 characters with top-bottom structure and 78 characters with surrounding structure. Using the above segmentation method and samples of Jinglei font, the successful rate arrives at 95.88% for the 364 characters needing segmentation. Because most of radicals appear in multiple samples and the construction program tends to select the best ones, the successful rate is high enough for constructing personal font library.

For identifying the feasibility of the method, the newly generated characters are compared with the corresponding characters in the original Jinglei font library. Table 3 shows the comparison results, which include 20 characters with various structures. The first one is a single-radical character and generated directly from radical library without assembling. The 2th to 11th ones are with left-right top layer structure; the 12th to 15th are with top-bottom top layer structure; the 16th to 20th are with surrounding top layer structure. Besides, the 9th to 11th and the 14th to 15th ones have more than three radicals. The 9th and 15th ones have six radicals. Seen from the table, although the constructed characters are still more or less different from the original characters, their handwriting style is very close. All the constructed characters well maintain the handwriting style of the user. The results indicate that radicals reusing is an effective and quick way to construct personal handwritten font library. The user only needs to write a small number of samples for obtaining his/her own handwritten font library. This method significantly reduces the writing burden of the user.

Table 3: The comparison between the constructed characters and the original ones.

No.	1	2	3	4	5	6	7	8	9	10
Original Characters	失	娘	残	程	语	脚	酷	翻	罐	嚼
Constructed Characters	失	娘	残	程	语	脚	酷	翻	罐	嚼
No.	11	12	13	14	15	16	17	18	19	20
Original Characters	燃	悠	琴	蠢	攀	迷	赵	痛	围	戴
Constructed Characters	燃	悠	琴	蠢	攀	迷	赵	痛	围	戴

After constructing personal font library, the users then can use their own font to type documents, write articles in personal Blog, post messages in Twitter, write letters and do various other "writing" work in their own handwriting style. Figure 14 shows a letter typed by the constructed Jinglei font, in which the underlined characters are constructed. The letter is a part of an article from the famous book "Letter from Lei Fu". It can be found that most of constructed characters have good beauty representation and the same style as the other original ones.

7. CONCLUSIONS

In this paper, a snake model with guided image force is proposed to segment the radicals of offline handwritten Chinese characters. Testing results indicate that the three-stage

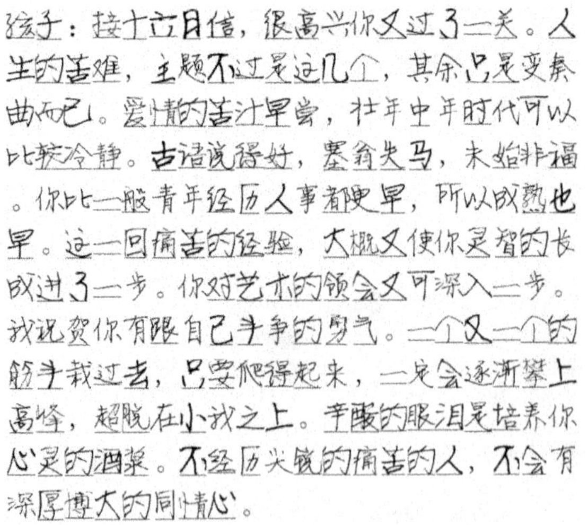

孩子：接十立月信，很高兴你又过了一关。人生的苦难，主题不过是这几个，其余只是变奏曲而已。爱情的苦汁虽苦，壮年中年时代可以比较冷静。古语说得好，塞翁失马，未始非福。你比一般青年经历人事都更早，所以成熟也早。这一回痛苦的经验，大概又使你灵智的长成进了一步。你对艺术的领会又可深入一步。我说贺你有跟自己斗争的勇气。一个又一个的够手我过去，只要爬得起来，一定会逐渐攀上高峰，超脱在小我之上。辛酸的眼泪是培养你心灵的酒浆。不经历尖锐的痛苦的人，不会有深厚博大的同情心。

Figure 14: A letter typed by the constructed Jinglei font. The underlined characters are constructed.

strategy can segment radicals with connections and overlaps effectively for characters with various radical composed patterns. The segmentation accuracy reaches 94.91% for complicated samples of the overlapped and connected radicals and the segmentation speed is 0.05 second per character. Compared with previous methods, our approach can handle radicals with various connections and overlaps, and achieves a significant improvement in terms of both segmentation accuracy and efficiency.

Experiments for constructing personal Chinese handwritten font library demonstrate the applicability of the proposed radical segmentation method. The constructed characters well maintain the handwriting style of the user and have good beauty representation. It indicates that reusing radicals in the user input samples is an effective way to construct personal handwritten font library. In this way, the user only needs to write a small number of samples for obtaining his/her own font library. This method greatly reduces the cost of existing solutions and makes it easier for people to use computers to write letters/e-mails, diaries/blogs, even magazines/books in their own handwriting.

8. REFERENCES

[1] R. Casey and G. Nagy. Recognition of printed chinese characters. *Electronic Computers, IEEE Transactions on*, (1):91–101, 1966.

[2] F. Cheng and W. Hsu. Partial pattern extraction and matching algorithm for chinese characters. 1985.

[3] F. GHENG and H. Wen-Hsing. Radical extraction from handwritten chinese characters by background thinning method. *IEICE TRANSACTIONS (1976-1990)*, 71(1):88–98, 1988.

[4] O. Ibáñez, N. Barreira, J. Santos, and M. Penedo. Genetic approaches for topological active nets optimization. *Pattern Recognition*, 42(5):907–917, 2009.

[5] W. Ip, K. Chung, and D. Yeung. Offline handwritten chinese character recognition via radical extraction and recognition. In *Document Analysis and Recognition, 1997., Proceedings of the Fourth International Conference on*, volume 1, pages 185–189. IEEE, 1997.

[6] P. Lai, D. Yeung, and M. Pong. A heuristic search approach to chinese glyph generation using hierarchical character composition. *Computer Processing of Oriental Languages*, 10(3):307–323, 1996.

[7] S. Lay, C. Lee, N. Cheng, C. Tseng, B. Jeng, P. Ting, Q. Wu, and M. Day. On-line chinese character recognition with effective candidate radical and candidate character selections. *Pattern recognition*, 29(10):1647–1659, 1996.

[8] P. Liu, L. Ma, and F. Soong. Radical based fine trajectory hmms of online handwritten characters. In *Pattern Recognition, 2008. ICPR 2008. 19th International Conference on*, pages 1–4. IEEE, 2008.

[9] D. Shi, R. Damper, and S. Gunn. Offline handwritten chinese character recognition by radical decomposition. *ACM Transactions on Asian Language Information Processing (TALIP)*, 2(1):27–48, 2003.

[10] J. Shin, K. Suzuki, and A. Hasegawa. Handwritten chinese character font generation based on stroke correspondence. *International Journal of Computer Processing of Oriental Languages (IJCPOL)*, 18(3), 2005.

[11] A. Wang and K. Fan. Optical recognition of handwritten chinese characters by hierarchical radical matching method. *Pattern Recognition*, 34(1):15–35, 2001.

[12] A. Wang, K. Fan, and W. Wu. Recursive hierarchical radical extraction for handwritten chinese characters. *Pattern recognition*, 30(7):1213–1227, 1997.

[13] A. Wang, J. Huang, and J. Fan. Optical recognition of handwritten chinese characters by partial matching. In *Document Analysis and Recognition, 1993., Proceedings of the Second International Conference on*, pages 822–823. IEEE, 1993.

[14] X. Wei, S. Ma, and Y. Jin. Segmentation of connected chinese characters based on genetic algorithm. In *Document Analysis and Recognition, 2005. Proceedings. Eighth International Conference on*, pages 645–649. IEEE, 2005.

[15] H. B. Xing. *Feature analysis and computing research of Modern Chinese characters*. The Commercial Press, Beijing, China, 2007.

[16] C. Xu and J. Prince. Snakes, shapes, and gradient vector flow. *Image Processing, IEEE Transactions on*, 7(3):359–369, 1998.

[17] S. Xu, T. Jin, H. Jiang, and F. Lau. Automatic generation of personal chinese handwriting by capturing the characteristics of personal handwriting. In *Twenty-First IAAI Conference*, 2009.

[18] S. Xu, F. Lau, W. Cheung, and Y. Pan. Automatic generation of artistic chinese calligraphy. *Intelligent Systems, IEEE*, 20(3):32–39, 2005.

[19] S. Zhao and P. Shi. Segmentation of connected handwritten chinese characters based on stroke analysis and background thinning. *PRICAI 2000 Topics in Artificial Intelligence*, pages 608–616, 2000.

[20] B. Zhou, W. Wang, and Z. Chen. Easy generation of personal chinese handwritten fonts. In *Multimedia and Expo (ICME), 2011 IEEE International Conference on*, pages 1–6. IEEE, 2011.

Structural and Visual Comparisons for Web Page Archiving

Marc Teva Law   Nicolas Thome   Stéphane Gançarski

Matthieu Cord

LIP6, UPMC - Sorbonne University, Paris, France
{Marc.Law, Nicolas.Thome, Stephane.Gancarski, Matthieu.Cord}@lip6.fr

ABSTRACT

In this paper, we propose a Web page archiving system that combines *state-of-the-art* comparison methods based on the source codes of Web pages, with computer vision techniques. To detect whether successive versions of a Web page are similar or not, our system is based on: (1) a combination of structural and visual comparison methods embedded in a statistical discriminative model, (2) a visual similarity measure designed for Web pages that improves change detection, (3) a supervised feature selection method adapted to Web archiving. We train a Support Vector Machine model with vectors of similarity scores between successive versions of pages. The trained model then determines whether two versions, defined by their vector of similarity scores, are similar or not. Experiments on real archives validate our approach.

Categories and Subject Descriptors

H.3.7 [**Information Storage and Retrieval**]: Digital Libraries

Keywords

Web archiving, Digital preservation, Change detection algorithms, Pattern recognition, Support vector machines

1. INTRODUCTION

With the explosion of available information on the World Wide Web, archiving the Web is a cultural necessity in preserving knowledge. Most of the time, Web archiving is performed by Web crawlers (bots) that capture Web pages and the associated media (images, videos...). To update archives, crawlers have to regularly revisit pages, but they generally do not know if or when changes appeared. The crawlers cannot constantly revisit a site and download a new version of a page because they usually have limited resources (such as bandwidth, space storage...) with respect to the huge amount of pages to archive. Hence, it is technically impossible to maintain a complete history of all the versions of Web

pages of the Web, or even an important part of it. The problem of archivists is then how to optimize crawling so that new versions are captured and/or kept only when changes are important while limiting the loss of useful information. A way to optimize crawling is to estimate the behavior of a site in order to guess when or with which frequency it must be visited, and thus to study the importance of changes between successive versions [1]. For instance, the change of an advertisement link, illustrated in Figures 1(a,b), is not related to the main information shared by the page. In contrast, changes in Figure 1(c) are significant. The crawling of the second version was thus necessary. In this paper, similarity functions for Web page comparison are investigated.

Most archivists only take into account the Web page source code (code string, DOM tree...) [2] and not the visual rendering [3, 4, 1]. However, the code may not be sufficient to describe the content of Web pages, e.g. images are usually defined only by their URL addresses, or scripts may be coded in many different languages that make them hard to compare. Ben Saad et al. [1] propose to use the tree obtained by running the VIPS [3] algorithm on the rendered page. They obtain a rich semantic segmentation into blocks and then estimate a function of the importance of changes between page versions by comparing the different blocks. The VIPS structure of a Web page is a segmentation tree based on its DOM tree. It detects visual structures in the rendering of a Web page (e.g. tables) and tries to keep nodes (blocks) as homogeneous as possible. Two successive paragraphs without html tags will tend to be kept in the same node, whereas table elements with different background colors will be separated in different nodes. Image processing methods have been proposed for Web page segmentation. Cao et al. [5] preprocess the rendering of Web pages by an edge detection algorithm, and iteratively divide zones until all blocks are indivisible. They do not take the source code of Web pages into account. In the context of phishing detection, Fu et al. [6] compute similarities between Web pages using color and spatial visual feature vectors. However, they are only interested in the detection of exact copies.

We propose to investigate in this paper structural and visual features to carry out an efficient page comparison system for Web archiving. We claim that both structural and visual informations are fundamental to get a powerful semantical similarity [7]: structural to catch the dissimilarity if different scripts have the same rendering or if the hyperlinks are changed, visual if the codes of the versions of a Web page are unchanged but a loaded image was updated. Methods combining structural and visual features have been proposed

(a) Similar versions   (b) zoom over the **only** difference   (c) Dissimilar versions
between the versions of (a)

Figure 1: Similar and dissimilar versions of Web pages. The versions of (a) share the same information, they are exactly similar except the links in (b), they do not need to be crawled twice. The versions of (c) have the same banner and menus but the main information of the page is changed, a second crawling is then necessary.

for content extraction [8], they use the relative positions between elements of pages but no visual appearance features. Additionally, we propose a machine learning framework to set all the similarity parameters and combination weights. We claim to get in this manner a semantic similarity close to archivists' attempts. Our contribution is three-fold: (1) a complete hybrid Web page comparison framework combining computer vision and structural comparison methods, (2) a new measure dedicated to Web archiving that only considers the visible part of pages without scrolling, (3) a machine learning based approach for supervised feature selection to increase prediction accuracy by eliminating noisy features.

2. WEB PAGE COMPARISON SCHEME

Two versions of a given Web page are considered similar if the changes that occurred between them are not important enough to archive both of them. They are dissimilar otherwise (see Figure 1). To compare versions of Web pages, we first extract features from them as described below.

2.1 Visual descriptors

Important changes between page versions will often produce differences between the visual rendering of those versions. We propose to quantify these differences by computing and comparing the visual features in each page version. Each version is described as an image of its rendering capture (snapshot). We compute a visual signature on this captured image for each page. Images are first described by color descriptors, because they seem appropriate for Web page changes and are already used in Phishing Web page detection [6]. We also incorporate powerful edge-based descriptors with SIFT descriptors [9] because they give state-of-the-art performances in real image classification tasks.

For image representation, we follow the well-known Bag of Words (BoW) representation [10, 11]. The vector representation of the rendered Web page is computed based on a sampling of local descriptors, coding and pooling over a visual dictionary. Recent comparisons for image classification point out the outstanding performances of a regular dense sampling [12, 13]. We apply a first strategy called *whole Web page* feature, that samples regularly the visual representation of the whole page. However, the most significant information is certainly not equally distributed over the whole captured Web page. As noted in [14], the most important information is generally located in the visible part of pages without scrolling. A second strategy called *Top of Web page* feature, provides a visual vector using only the features located in the visible part of the page without scrolling.

Since the visible part of a Web page without scrolling depends on the browser window size, we take a generic window height of 1000 pixels, greater than 90% of users' browser resolutions to ensure we do not miss information directly visible by most users. In the next sections, we will denote *the visible part of Web pages without scrolling* by *top of Web pages*.

2.2 Structural descriptors

We extract various features directly from the code of Web pages. For instance, we extract Jaccard indices [2], a similarity value that indicates the preservation between versions of hyperlinks and of URL addresses of images. We assume that similar pages tend to keep the same hyperlinks and images.

We also extract some features from the difference tree returned by the VI-DIFF algorithm [4] that detects some operations between the VIPS structures of versions, e.g. insertions, deletions or updates of VIPS blocks, or even a boolean value returning whether two versions have the same VIPS structure. The more operations are detected, the less similar versions are assumed to be. We denote the features extracted from the VI-DIFF algorithm by VI-DIFF features.

2.3 Similarity between versions

Let V^A be the last archived version of a Web page and V^N the new version of the same Web page. We extract several visual and structural descriptors (see sections 2.1 and 2.2), and use different metrics (Euclidian, χ^2 distances, *etc*) to compare them. Heuristics may be used to set them individually and to select the best similarity function with a manually-tuned threshold to discriminate dissimilar pairs of Web pages from the similar ones.

We propose here an alternate scheme embedding all the similarity functions into a learning framework. Let the M visual feature/metric associations and the N structural similarities be aggregated in a vector $\mathbf{x}$. We can write $\mathbf{x}^T$ as: $[s_v^1(V^A, V^N) \ldots s_v^M(V^A, V^N), s_s^1(V^A, V^N) \ldots s_s^N(V^A, V^N)]$.

We observed that none of the similarities we experimentally extracted presented a trivial individual decision boundary. However, all of them did seem to follow certain expected patterns, some of them working better than others. Instead of using them individually, we propose to combine those different similarities in a binary classification scheme that returns whether a couple of versions are similar or not by using $\mathbf{x}$, the vector of their similarity scores. Combining both approaches then seems appropriate to have a better understanding of the changes as perceived by human users. Learning combinations of complementary descriptors also makes the categorization task more efficient [15]. We investigate in the next section a statistical learning strategy based on a labeled dataset to classify the vectors $\mathbf{x}$.

3. CLASSIFICATION FRAMEWORK

We are interested in learning distances [16] between versions in a supervised framework to determine whether two versions are similar or not. However, it is not a version classification problem as in many distance learning problems [17]. Indeed, we do not want to classify samples (versions) but similarities. Moreover, our similarities are based on human judgement and allow subtilities as shown in Figure 1.

We then propose to express the learning of the combination of similarities as a binary classification in similarity space: for any couple of versions $(V^A, V^N)_i$, let their class $y_i = 1$ iff V^A and V^N are similar, -1 otherwise. Let $\mathbf{x}_i$ be a vector derived from heterogeneous similarities between V^A and V^N (as defined in subsection 2.3). We train a linear Support Vector Machine (SVM) to determine $\mathbf{w} = \sum_j \alpha_j y_j \mathbf{x}_j$ such that $\langle \mathbf{w}, \mathbf{x}_i \rangle = \sum_j \alpha_j y_j \langle \mathbf{x}_j, \mathbf{x}_i \rangle$ gives us the class of $(V^A, V^N)_i$. The similarity vectors $\mathbf{x}_j$ of training couples $(V^A, V^N)_j$ are used to train an SVM. For any test couple $(V^A, V^N)_i$, the trained SVM returns (1) whether $y_i = 1$ or $y_i = -1$, (2) whether V^A and V^N are similar or dissimilar, (3) whether V^N needs to be archived or not, with V^A already archived. Those three propositions are equivalent.

To study the contributions of the different types of features in the discrimination task, we first train a linear SVM with all the features. Each element w_k of $\mathbf{w}$ corresponds to the weight associated to the k-th similarity feature of $\mathbf{x}$. Therefore, if the learned w_k are close or equal to 0, the k-th similarity features of $\mathbf{x}$ are not determinant for categorization. Such similarities are considered noisy, irrelevant (not discriminant) in determining whether two versions are similar or not. To go one step further, we also propose a more explicit feature selection method based on the automatic *normal based feature selection* [18] that uses the fact that a feature k with the weight w_k close to 0 has a smaller effect on the prediction than features with large absolute values of w_k. Then features with small $|w_k|$ are good candidates for removal. The number of selected features may be set based on data storage and calculation constraints, or iteratively reduced using a validation set.

4. EXPERIMENT RESULTS

4.1 Dataset and settings

We work on a dataset of about 1000 pairs of Web pages manually annotated "similar" or "dissimilar" provided by *The Internet Memory Foundation*[1]. The pages are captured from many different governmental Web sites from the United Kingdom about education, health, sport, justice, industry, security... The identical couples of versions are removed and not taken into account in the evaluation. Finally, 202 pairs of Web pages were extracted: 147 and 55 (72.8% and 27.2%) couples of similar and dissimilar versions, respectively.

To compute visual similarities, we use SIFT and HSV (Hue Saturation Value) color descriptors with visual codebooks of sizes 100 and 200. These are relatively small compared to the sizes used on large image databases but consistent with the size of our base. Bigger codebook sizes did not improve our classification task. The BoWs of page versions are computed using the two strategies described in section 2.1: (1) over the rendering of whole Web pages

---
[1] http://internetmemory.org/

and (2) the top of Web pages. Euclidian and χ^2 distances are then computed between the BoWs of successive page versions normalized using L^2-norm and L^1-norm, respectively. We also compute for each couple of page versions, the VIPS structures [3] and the VI-DIFF difference trees [4] from which we extract structural similarity values, e.g. the (symmetrized) ratio of identical nodes, boolean values on some criteria such as an identical VIPS structure. In the end, we have 16 visual and 25 structural features.

4.2 Binary classification

We use leave-one-out cross-validation (on the 202 pairs) to evaluate our model. We compare our results to the random classifier which automatically predicts the most represented class in the dataset, yielding a baseline accuracy of 72.8%.

Evaluation of visual features.

Selected Visual Features		Accuracy (%)
Whole Web page	Top of Web page	
None	SIFT	84.2
None	color	82.7
None	SIFT + color	**87.1**
SIFT	None	79.7
color	None	80.7
SIFT + color	None	83.2
SIFT + color	SIFT + color	85.1

Table 1: Visual feature classification performances.

We first use only the visual information of pages. Structural similarities of $\mathbf{x}$ are ignored. The accuracies when selecting different subsets of local descriptors (SIFT and color) sampled on whole pages or top of pages are presented in Table 1. SIFT and color descriptors achieve good performances for Web page change detection. Using the top of pages (87.1%) is also a lot more discriminant than using whole pages (83.2%). Combining both of them gives even worse results (85.1%) than using only the top of pages (87.1%). Important changes are more likely to be directly observable whereas changes at the bottom of Web pages, often advertisements, are more likely to be less important and noisy. The accuracies obtained validate our approach.

Evaluation of structural features.

Selected Structural Features		Accuracy (%)
Jaccard Indices	VI-DIFF	
Yes	No	85.1
No	Yes	76.7
Yes	Yes	**87.6**

Table 2: Structural feature classif. performances.

We study in Table 2 the accuracies when different subsets of structural similarities only are used. Jaccard Indices of links are the most discriminant structural features (85.1%) but the other structural features extracted from VI-DIFF are still informative, 4% better than the random classifier.

Structural and visual feature combination evaluation.

We investigate the combination of structural and visual features in Table 3. The accuracy when combining all of them (90.1%) is better than when using only structural (87.6%) or visual (87.1%) features. Visual and structural features are then complementary.

Selected Feature similarities		Acc. (%)
Structural	Visual	
All	All	90.1
All	Top of Web page	92.1
Jaccard indices	All	91.6
Jaccard indices	**Top of Web page**	**93.1**

Table 3: Structural and visual feature classification performances.

Furthermore, we propose to combine in Table 3 the visual and structural features that gave the best accuracies in previous sections. An exhaustive manual selection among all the 41 structural and visual features to find the set that maximizes prediction would be too time-consuming. The accuracy is improved up to 93.1% when combining only Jaccard indices of links and the top of page visual representations.

Concerning misclassified examples, we observed that many dissimilar pairs of versions that were predicted as similar were news pages in which old news were shifted towards the bottom of the page by more recent news. The shifts of these news do not impact the BoW distances since we do not take the spatial information of image patches into account. Many similar pairs of versions predicted as dissimilar had a lot of new irrelevant hyperlinks (significantly more than in Figure 1 (b)). A better detection of important regions and their shifts in position could improve the decision by ignoring their related visual and structural comparisons.

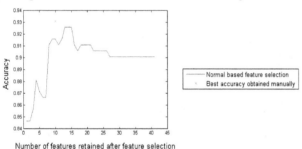

Figure 2: Feature selection performances.

We also investigate the automatic *normal based feature selection* method described in section 3 corresponding to the blue curve in Figure 2. The best accuracy obtained with that automatic method is 92.6% when the 13 to 15 features with the highest absolute values in **w** are selected. It is comparable to our best accuracy of 93.1% (Table 3 and red cross of Figure 2) with 10 features selected.

5. CONCLUSION

We have proposed a complete Web page comparison framework effective for Web archiving. We combine structural and visual features to understand the behavior of Web sites and estimate when or with which frequency they must be visited.

We confirm that both structural and visual informations are useful for change detection. We explore several features and similarities. One of the main results is that important changes generally appear at the visible part of Web pages without scrolling. Moreover, we propose a new scheme to learn an optimal similarity combination as a classification problem. Experiments on real Web pages are presented to validate our strategy. A large set of pages with associated labels performed by archivists has been used for a quality evaluation of our visual and structural similarity method.

Acknowledgments. This work was partially supported by the SCAPE Project. The SCAPE Project is co-funded by the European Union under FP7 ICT-2009.4.1.

6. REFERENCES

[1] M. Ben Saad, S. Gançarski, and Z. Pehlivan, "A novel web archiving approach based on visual pages analysis," in *IWAW 2009*.

[2] M. Oita and P. Senellart, "Deriving dynamics of web pages: A survey," in *TWAW*, March 2011.

[3] D. Cai, S. Yu, J. Wen, and W. Ma, "Vips: a vision-based page segmentation algorithm," *Microsoft Technical Report, MSR-TR-2003-79-2003*, 2003.

[4] Z. Pehlivan, M. Ben Saad, and S. Gançarski, "Vi-DIFF: Understanding Web Pages Changes," in *DEXA 2010*.

[5] J. Cao, B. Mao, and J. Luo, "A segmentation method for web page analysis using shrinking and dividing," *JPEDS*, vol. 25, 2010.

[6] A.Y. Fu, L. Wenyin, and X. Deng, "Detecting phishing web pages with visual similarity assessment based on earth mover's distance (emd)," *TDSC*, vol. 3, 2006.

[7] N. Thome, D. Merad, and S. Miguet, "Learning articulated appearance models for tracking humans: A spectral graph matching approach," *Signal Processing: Image Communication*, vol. 23, no. 10, 2008.

[8] A. Spengler and P. Gallinari, "Document structure meets page layout: Loopy random fields for web news content extraction," in *DocEng*, 2010.

[9] D. Lowe, "Distinctive image features from scale-invariant keypoints," *IJCV*, vol. 60, 2004.

[10] W.Y. Ma and B.S. Manjunath, "Netra: A toolbox for navigating large image databases," in *ICIP 1997*.

[11] J. Fournier, M. Cord, and S. Philipp-Foliguet, "Retin: A content-based image indexing and retrieval system," *PAA*, vol. 4, no. 2, pp. 153–173, 2001.

[12] S. Avila, N. Thome, M. Cord, E. Valle, and A. Araújo, "Bossa: Extended bow formalism for image classification," in *ICIP 2011*.

[13] K. Chatfield, V. Lempitsky, A. Vedaldi, and A. Zisserman, "The devil is in the details: an evaluation of recent feature encoding methods," *BMVC*, 2011.

[14] R. Song, H. Liu, J.R. Wen, and W.Y. Ma, "Learning block importance models for web pages," in *WWW 2004*.

[15] D. Picard, N. Thome, and M. Cord, "An efficient system for combining complementary kernels in complex visual categorization tasks," in *ICIP 2010*.

[16] L. Yang and R. Jin, "Distance metric learning: A comprehensive survey," *Michigan State University*, pp. 1–51, 2006.

[17] A. Frome, Y. Singer, and J. Malik, "Image retrieval and classification using local distance functions," in *NIPS 2006*.

[18] D. Mladenić, J. Brank, M. Grobelnik, and N. Milic-Frayling, "Feature selection using linear classifier weights: interaction with classification models," in *SIGIR 2004*.

Receipts2Go: The Big World of Small Documents

Bill Janssen
Palo Alto Research Center
3333 Coyote Hill Road
Palo Alto, California 94304
janssen@parc.com

Eric Saund
Palo Alto Research Center
3333 Coyote Hill Road
Palo Alto, California 94304
saund@parc.com

Eric Bier
Palo Alto Research Center
3333 Coyote Hill Road
Palo Alto, California 94304
bier@parc.com

Patricia Wall
Xerox Research Center
Webster
800 Phillips Road
Webster, New York 14580
Patricia.Swenton-Wall@Xerox.com

Mary Ann Sprague
Xerox Research Center
Webster
800 Phillips Road
Webster, New York 14580
MaryAnn.Sprague@Xerox.com

ABSTRACT

The Receipts2Go system is about the world of one-page documents: cash register receipts, book covers, cereal boxes, price tags, train tickets, fire extinguisher tags. In that world, we're exploring techniques for extracting accurate information from documents for which we have no layout descriptions – indeed no initial idea of what the document's genre is – using photos taken with cell phone cameras by users who aren't skilled document capture technicians. This paper outlines the system and reports on some initial results, including the algorithms we've found useful for cleaning up those document images, and the techniques used to extract and organize relevant information from thousands of similar-but-different page layouts.

Categories and Subject Descriptors

H.3.1 [**Information Storage And Retrieval**]: Content Analysis and Indexing—*abstracting methods*

General Terms

Algorithms, Design

Keywords

receipt analysis, image normalization, geometric information analysis

1. INTRODUCTION

Though many information transactions have moved to purely digital forms, various types of paper records persist. Items such as register-tape receipts, parking receipts, train tickets, fire-extinguisher inspection tags, and ATM receipts are all interesting oddities in the ever-more-digital world.

While all are different, they share the common form of a small typically single-page layout (some are printed on both sides of the paper) with small pieces of information such as dates and dollar amounts and check-marks arranged on the page.

In addition, while the information on any instance from one of the specific document genres is roughly the same as that on any other instance, that information is arranged in a creative profusion of document layouts. Any specific expected piece of information on the form might occur almost anywhere on the form. Consider, for instance, the problem of analyzing a subway ticket from any English-speaking region of the world. It will typically include a date, a purchase price, the name of the underground system, and a serial number of some sort. However, these items may be scattered almost anywhere on the ticket, and use assorted fonts, sizes, and spacings.

In this paper, we present a system that we are developing to handle documents of this type, and walk through an example using a very common document type, the "register-tape" receipt issued by conventional cash registers. Our system is based on a study using ethnographic methods to understand receipt management in small businesses. [10] Receipts are particularly problematic in the modern world because even though they were originally designed as ephemeral, to be quickly discarded, modern tax regulations have forced them to be kept and curated well beyond their original designed lifespans.

We report on some of our results for cleaning up photos of documents to the point where they can be successfully processed by an OCR system, and describe our three-stage follow-on workflow for successfully extracting the pertinent genre-specific information items from a document without a prior model of the document's layout and formatting. Finally, we conclude with some thoughts about where we plan to extend the system in the future.

2. EXISTING SYSTEMS

Production document processing has developed a number of standard technology approaches over the years [15]. The techniques in our system — image normalization, regular expression processing, and rule-based information distillation — are not unique, though the specific image-processing algorithms and rule sets used are.

There are a number of commercial products that advertise capabilities for working with small documents such receipts and/or business cards. NeatReceipts [2], which runs on your PC, extracts entities such as currency amounts and vendor names, and can export your database of receipts to a file in various formats, such as Intuit Interchange Format. Scan-Drop [4], lets you scan data to the cloud. ProOnGo [3] has apps for smart phones and can sync information across devices. JotNot Scanner [1] provides an app that captures a receipt and sync it to an application like EverNote for later viewing.

3. THE WORKFLOW

Our projected workflow consists of five parts: image normalization, text extraction, entity extraction, entity understanding, and information dispatch. We've made significant progress on two of these, which we discuss in more detail below.

3.1 Image Normalization

Our target image source is the cell-phone camera. However, these cameras vary widely in focus, resolution, and light-gathering ability. Some have flash capabilities of various kinds; some do well in certain lighting conditions and abysmally in others. Thus we need specialized image processing to convert a photo from such a camera (see Figure 1(a)) to a bitonal image suitable for text extraction. This processing includes orientation correction, deskewing, normalization of lighting differences across the surface of the document, and removal of background artifacts and noise elements, where possible.

We apply two improvements that depend on the sizes of the characters on the image. Since the resolution of input images can vary widely, we need to dynamically determine the likely characters on the page so that their sizes can be measured. We do this by applying a clustering algorithm to the connected components of a simple thresholded binary version of the image, which generates two or more clusters of decreasing size. The largest of these clusters is typically noise – speckles and dust on the image. The second largest is taken as the cluster of character images. We measure the average width and height of the components in this cluster and use that measurement as the average width and height of the characters on the image.

Most deskew algorithms work only on a small range of skew angles, so radical skew angles, like 90 degree rotations, must be handled separately; we refer to this process as "orientation correction". Our OCR system will accept either right-side-up or up-side-down images, so our orientation detection need only recognize "sideways" images and correct them. Our system takes advantage of the fact that typical frequently-occurring characters in English text tend to be taller than they are wide. It uses the extracted connected components which represent characters, and calculates the average aspect ratio of those components. If the average is "wider" than it is "tall", the image is taken to be "sideways", and rotated by 90 degrees.

Our system then measures the skew from horizontal of the document image, using a standard Hough transform approach [5]. We check to see if the average height of character connected components is less than some limit (currently we use 20 pixels), and if so, supersample the image by 2x to increase the average character size. We then deskew the possibly supersampled image, using the skew angle measured previously.

Once we have a properly oriented, deskewed, and possibly supersampled image, we remove the background and attempt to normalize the illumination across the foreground content of the image. This is done by an iterative technique that estimates and interpolates the color distribution of light background across the image, and then applies a combination of high-pass filtering and distance measures on the hue-saturation-brightness values of individual pixels. This algorithm is described in detail in [13] and [12].

This normalized image is then binarized using a simple thresholding technique, thus creating a version suitable for OCR input. We then crop the image to cover the area in which the "character-sized" connected components were found, giving us the image shown in Figure 1(b).

3.2 Entity Extraction

We then run our document image through a commercial OCR system to extract the text. We convert this information from the OCR system's proprietary format to the hOCR format standard for OCR output [8], which allows us to effectively separate the particular OCR system from the rest of our system. Bounding box information is present for each word, using the "bbox" hOCR tag. Character and word confidences are present in the hOCR, using the optional "x_confs" and "x_wconf" tags suggested in [8].

The standard workflow for production document processing starts with a classification step, to identify the correct information extraction techniques for a given document, followed by application of those techniques. However, we needed to have a system that would work with a wide variety of documents, and would function correctly even on instances from subgenres which hadn't been encountered before. In addition, we needed it to work without a model-building step which would require a trained technical operator. So we rely on a generic model of receipts and invoices which is based on text features and certain geometric relationships between those features.

We start by applying context-free regular-expression patterns to identify high-value information fragments, which we call "entities", in the OCR text. These are typically structured pieces of information, such as telephone numbers, dates, URLs, names and addresses, currency amounts, email addresses, and credit-card numbers. We also look for certain key phrases like "TOTAL AMOUNT" or "DATE PAID" which help to disambiguate other entities. These phrases are typed with the kind of related entity it would help to disambiguate; for instance, "DATE PAID" would be a "date" key phrase. These entities are shown in Figure 1(c). Note that we've found a number of amounts and amount keywords, as well as a date, a timestamp, a phone number, and an Internet domain.

To allow for OCR errors, we employ a regular expression engine which supports "fuzzy" matching [6] for finding these entities (and also supports very large regular expressions). This allows us to specify regular expressions which match sub-strings within a specified Levenshtein distance of the expression. In addition, the patterns are written to allow for certain typical OCR errors, such as confusing zero with capital or lowercase O.

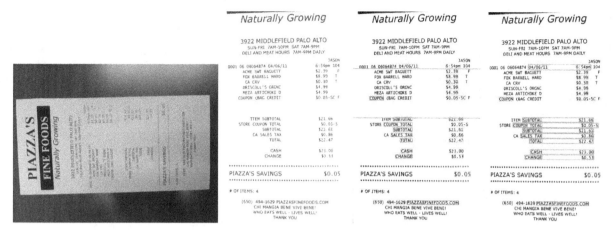

Figure 1: (a) A photo of a grocery store receipt captured by a cell phone. (b) The rotated, deskewed, binarized cropped receipt image ready for OCR. (c) The receipt image, showing the recognized entities and discovered limits of the line-items region. (d) The receipt image, showing various groupings of entity combinations.

We next group each key phrase entity with another entity of the proper type, if the key phrase occurs in a specified geometric relationship with the other entity, with no intervening text. The relationships currently used are "RightOf", "LeftOf", "Below", and "Above". For instance, we use a timestamp as a "date" key phrase entity, and require it to have a "RightOf" relationship with any date it applies to. This helps us to identify the actual date of the receipt, as opposed to an expiration date or special offer date that might also appear on the receipt. Similarly, "amount" key phrases that indicate a total are required to appear "Above" or "LeftOf" a currency amount entity in order to be associated with it. Figure 1(d) shows a number of groupings found in our receipt image.

These groupings, along with the other entities identified, are stored in a file, using an XML format. The bounding box on the image of each entity is stored along with its data and type, and a confidence value; in our current system, the confidence value is simply the minimum of the word OCR confidences for all of the words in the entity. This file is used as input to the rule application step.

To support line item table parsing, we also need to identify the region of the receipt containing the line items. We use a simple algorithm for this, which will work for cash register receipts, but is probably suboptimal for large-form receipts. We first identify the topmost currency amount entity, and use the top of its bounding box as the top of our list items region. We then look for the first currency amount entity below it that is also tagged with an amount keyword, such as "total" or "subtotal". The top of that entity is used as the bottom of the list items region. The left and right sides of the receipt form the left and right sides of the region. Figure 1(c) shows these bounds identified in our receipt image. This information is then stored in the XML file along with the other entity information.

3.3 Information Extraction and User Rule Application

The remainder of our system is rule-based. We use the expert system platform CLIPS [11], a mature, fast, forward-chaining system implemented in C. We apply two distinct stages of rule-based processing to our document. The first stage is designed to either extract or infer additional information about the document; the second is used to apply application-specific rules designed by the user to the extracted information.

Our first stage identifies instances of the two classes we currently support, receipts and invoices. It looks for features — textual keywords and entity patterns — present in a document class and absent in other classes. A classification rule integrates the evidence and comes up with a total score.

Once the document has been recognized as an instance of a particular genre, we apply a set of rules which attempt to extract a uniform set of data appropriate for that genre. For instance, we want to find the total amount a receipt is for, along with the date of the receipt and any tax charged. We do this by examining the entities; e.g., one "receipt" rule locates the currency amount tagged with a "amount" key phrase that contains the word "total" that is lowest on the receipt image, and identifies it as the total of the receipt.

The results of information extraction from our sample receipt are

```
Computed information:
    Date: 4/6/2011
   Total: 22.47
     Tax: 0.86
  Vendor: Piazza's Deli
Category: 581209 - Delicatessens
```

An important feature of a receipt is the vendor or supplier who provided it. We have rules which take any business names, telephone numbers, or URLs found on the receipt and consult a business directory. This directory contains a list of local businesses, drawn from a nationwide list, which the user can edit or extend. For each business listed, the directory contains its addresses, accounting categories such as "Grocery" or "Hardware", nicknames (often found on receipts), phone numbers, and URLs. If the phone number or URL on the receipt is found to match one of the businesses in the directory within a small edit distance (which varies depending on the length of the text string), that business is assigned as the "vendor" of the receipt. The accounting categories for that vendor are also assigned to the receipt.

In the above example, "Vendor" and "Category" are derived from the store's telephone number.

The "Date" was accepted as the receipt date because of the associated timestamp; receipts which include return information often have multiple dates, including both the date of the original purchase and the date of the return. It's important to distinguish between them, and we've found that the presence of a timestamp is a strong indicator of the correct date.

The second stage of rule-based processing deals with the user-defined rules. They consist of preconditions and resultant "service actions", which are drawn from system-provided application libraries. These rules are stored in an XML-format file which is automatically transformed into additional CLIPS rules, which are then added to the rule base for that user. These rules typically reason over the uniform set of data extracted in the first phase of rule processing, though the full set of extracted entities is also available to user rules.

When a document is detected which matches both a user rule's set of preconditions, and the preconditions for any service actions associated with that rule, the action specified is taken on that receipt. Note that this can be triggered by adding a receipt, but also by changing the preconditions or actions of an existing user rule to match receipts already in the database.

4. FUTURE WORK

There are a number of additional things which could be done here. The vicissitudes of data rates and data plans introduce issues not present in scanner-based systems. They make it desirable to "qualify" a photo before uploading it for further processing. Better image normalization, including image de-warping techniques such as those discussed in [9] and [14], would improve accuracy. Contextual post processing of OCR results to use results from receipts already processed, or from the user's PIM data, might be able to improve the extracted data.

Robust line item identification would enable more varied kinds of actions to be taken. We are currently experimenting with a line-item parser based on a table-parsing algorithm developed by Evgeniy Bart [7]. This uses a machine-learning approach which requires a small amount of explicit labelled data, but has the interesting property of generalizing well to previously unseen tables. Improvement of the feature set for this algorithm, and improvement of the objective function used, are among the things being investigated.

5. CONCLUSIONS

Our Receipts2Go system is capable of automatically extracting pertinent information from a large variety of samples of the receipt and invoice document genres, without having specific format layout models to work from, by using image normalization algorithms, generic entity extraction techniques, and genre-specific grouping rules and and group selection rules. Additionally, it uses the now common cell phone camera as an input device, instead of requiring a specialized scanner. We think these techniques could also be applied to other "small document" genres, such as train tickets or fire extinguisher tags, thus tying those currently isolated pieces of data into the digital world.

6. ACKNOWLEDGEMENTS

Evgeniy Bart contributed his experimental table-parsing framework for our line item identification, and altered his code to make it easier for us to use. Mic Campanelli was kind enough to tweak the FireWorX OCR support in XIPS to allow us to retrieve character and word confidences. MRAB (regex@mrabarnett.plus.com) altered his "regex" library to provide the fuzzy matching we needed. Peter Jarvis, Eric Saund, and Marshall Bern graciously serve as a review and advisory board for this project.

7. REFERENCES

[1] Jotnot scanner.
See http://itunes.apple.com/us/app/jotnot-scanner/id310789464?mt=8.

[2] Neatreceipts. See http://www.neat.com/.

[3] Proongo. See http://www.proongo.com/.

[4] Scandrop. See http://www.officedrop.com/scandrop-scanning-software/scan-google-docs/configure-neatreceipts-scanner.

[5] J. Anderson, 2008.
See https://github.com/horndude77/image-scripts/blob/master/pnm_java/src/is/image/FindSkew.java.

[6] M. A. Barnett, 2011.
See http://code.google.com/p/mrab-regex-hg/.

[7] E. Bart. Parsing tables by probabilistic modeling of perceptual cues. In *Proceedings of the IAPR International Workshop on Document Analysis Systems*, 2012.

[8] T. Breuel. The hOCR microformat for OCR workflow and results. *Document Analysis and Recognition, International Conference on*, 2:1063–1067, 2007.

[9] S. S. Bukhari, F. Shafait, and T. M. Breuel. Coupled snakelet model for curled textline segmentation of camera-captured document images. In *Proceedings of the 2009 10th International Conference on Document Analysis and Recognition*, ICDAR '09, pages 61–65, Washington, DC, USA, 2009. IEEE Computer Society.

[10] B. Janssen, E. Bier, E. Saund, P. Wall, and M. A. Sprague. Receipts2go: Cloud-based automated receipt processing. Technical Report IR_736, Palo Alto Research Center, Inc., December 2011.

[11] G. Riley. CLIPS: An expert system building tool. In *Technology 2001: Proceedings of the Second National Technology Transfer Conference and Exposition*, 1991.

[12] E. Saund. US Patent 7177483: System and method for enhancement of document images, February 2007.

[13] E. Saund, D. Fleet, D. Larner, and J. V. Mahoney. Perceptually-supported image editing of text and graphics. In *UIST 03: Proceedings of the 2003 ACM Symposium on User Interface Software and Technology*, pages 183–192, 2003.

[14] A. Ulges, C. H. Lampert, and T. M. Breuel. Document image dewarping using robust estimation of curled text lines. In *Proceedings of the Eighth International Conference on Document Analysis and Recognition*, ICDAR '05, pages 1001–1005, Washington, DC, USA, 2005. IEEE Computer Society.

[15] P. S. P. Wang and H. Bunke, editors. *Handbook of Character Recognition and Document Image Analysis*. World Scientific Publ. Comp., 1997.

Displaying Chemical Structural Formulae in ePub Format

Simone Marinai
Dipartimento di Sistemi e Informatica
Università di Firenze, Italy
simone.marinai@unifi.it

Stefano Quiriconi
Dipartimento di Sistemi e Informatica
Università di Firenze, Italy
stefano.quiriconi@stud.unifi.it

ABSTRACT

We describe one tool designed to enhance the visualization of chemical structural formulae in E-book readers. When dealing with small formulae, to avoid the pixelation effect with zoomed images, the formula is converted to a vectoral representation and then enlarged. On the opposite, large formulae are split in sub-images by cutting the image in suitable locations attempting to reduce the parts of the formula that are broken. In both cases the formulae are embedded in one ePub document that allows users to browse the chemical structure on most reading devices.

Categories and Subject Descriptors

I.7.4 [**Document and Text Processing**]: Electronic Publishing; H.3.1 [**Content Analysis and Indexing**]: Indexing Methods

Keywords Chemical Structural Formula, E-book Conversion, ePub, SVG, Vectorization

1. INTRODUCTION

Portable reading devices, such as Ebook readers and tablet computers, are becoming more and more popular. Including also general purpose devices such as laptops, netbooks, and cell phones, the dream of a paperless world is closer than before. While reading novels, newspapers, and magazines on dedicated devices is now possible with a satisfying reading experience, it is more difficult to effectively appreciate scientific and technical works that contain complex objects that are hard to fully understand on small screens. Typical examples include mathematical equations, tables, and illustrations. Also magazines usually contain a large amount of illustrations, however in most cases the user usually does not need to finely inspect the images and the visualization on the small colored screen of tablets is satisfactory.

On the opposite, the full understanding of large technical illustrations on small screens is still difficult. Chemical structural formula are one typical example of the latter problem whose solution is explored in this work.

Even if most structural formulae are nowadays produced with drawing tools, the illustrations in journals are usually raster images not stored in vectorial formats. Therefore, also when processing digital-born PDF documents, the information extraction task must process the images with Document Image Processing techniques. Examples of applications in the chemical domain include the development of tools for the recognition of chemical structure [5] [7]. However, when the user is mostly interested on browsing the formulae and one explicit indexing is not needed, the actual recognition can be avoided and the the visualization can be addressed with a format conversion.

In previous work we addressed the conversion of PDF books in ePub format. In particular, in [2] we described a method for the semi-automatic extraction of the Table of Contents (ToC) from *PDF* books that is subsequently used for a whole book conversion in [3]. Expanding this work on scientific and technical works we deal in this paper with the conversion of structural formulae in ePub format. The segmentation of formulae in the pages is not addressed in this paper.

In Section 2 we describe the technique used to obtain a vectorial representation of the formula, while Section 3 summarizes the approaches proposed to combine the formulae in an ePub file. Some conclusions are reported in Section 4.

2. VECTORIZATION

In the proposed system, the formula is initially vectorized with the Qgar library[1] that has been designed to develop document image analysis applications. The vectorized images are then improved with the techniques discussed in Section 2.1.

The Qgar project is composed by three main parts: `Qgar-Lib` is a C++ library that implements graphics recognition algorithms. `QgarApps` is one collection of application programs that can be executed as command line tools. `QgarGUI` is a graphical user interface that allows users to interact with the applications. The vectorization used in our system is obtained with the `QAvectorizationRW` application program that implements the polygonal approximation proposed by Rosin & West [6]. The input to the `QAvectorizationRW` tool is a raster image (in our case corresponding to a chemical structural formula) while the output is a vectorial representation of the formula stored in a DXF (Drawing Interchange Format) file. DXF files represent the drawings with a textual description by encoding all the objects and the settings required to reproduce the original drawing. The main

---

[1]The latest version can be downloaded from www.qgar.org

Figure 1: Protruding segments.

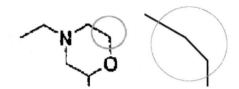

Figure 2: Split segments.

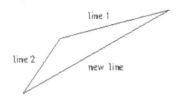

Figure 3: Fixing split segments.

types of objects in DXF files are lines and polygons, however, other information such as tables for colors and layers are included as well. One DXF file contains seven sections (header, classes, tables, blocks, entities, objects, thumbnail-image) but the unique mandatory section is the `entities` one that contains all the graphical objects that form the drawing (lines, polylines, arcs, circles, etc.). The output of the Qgar tool is a DXF file that contains only POLYLINE entities. One polyline is a sequence of segments where each segment has one end point in common with the next one. Separated segments are therefore represented by different polylines.

The most common file format for e-book readers is ePub. Similartly to other recent file formats, one ePub file is actually one `zip` file renamed with `.epub` extension that contains a pre-defined folder structure and file organization. Most files in ePub are based on XML and represent general information and book metadata. The main book content is described by one or more `XHTML` files and the page formatting is described with CSS files. Graphical objects can be represented both with bitmap images and with SVG files. In 2011 the new standard *ePub3* has been adopted by the International Digital Publishing Forum [1] consortium. *ePub3* incorporates HTML5 and CSS3 and allows documents to include multimedia elements, such as video and SVG objects. In ePub 2.0, that is supported by most devices, the vectorial graphics can be described with Scalable Vector Graphics (SVG) embedded in XHTML pages. SVG is an XML language designed to represent bidimensional vectorial graphics. An SVG file contains tags that define the image. The most important tags for our purpose are: `<rect>`, used to describe one rectangle; `<line>`, used to draw one segment; `<polyline>` used to describe a sequence of segments. Since the output of the Qgar vectorization tool is in DXF format, to insert the vectorial images of structural formulae in an ePub file it is required to convert the DXF file in an SVG one. The DXF drawing generated by QGar contains only polylines and therefore the conversion is straightforward: each polyline in the DXF file will be transformed in an equivalent SVG polyline. The details of this mapping are not described in this paper.

Even if the vectorization is made with a state of the art algorithm the results obtained on chemical formulae are not perfect and the visual effect is worst than expected. The main reason is the low resolution of the input images[2] that gives rise to some problems in the output SVG file. We address these problems by fixing the resulting vectorial representation by means of domain-specific information (e.g. taking into account the peculiarity of bonds in chemical formulae) in a post-processing stage described in the following section.

---

[2]The images used in our experiments are obtained from the Infty database of chemical structure images [4].

2.1 Correction of vectorization errors

We address in the following the main problems noticed on the vectorized images and some solutions adopted to solve them.

2.1.1 Protruding segments

One very common problem in the converted images is the presence of short segments protruding from the bonds in the structural formula (Fig. 1). These segments are due to the low resolution in the input raster image that influences the vectorization algorithm.

We address this problem both by choosing a suitable `prune` parameter in the `QAvectorizationRW` procedure, and by "cleaning" the vectorial image deleting the segments in polylines shorter than a given threshold.

2.1.2 Split segments

Another problem that frequently occurs is the split of bond segments in two or more connected segments with close, but different, slope (Fig. 2). In this case the solution is based first on the identification of potential split segments that are found by looking for adjacent segments with close slope. The two segments are then replaced with a new segment that connects the two end points that are not touching (Fig. 3). When a segment is split in more than two parts, the algorithm is called several times until no split segment is found and fixed.

2.1.3 Broken segments

The noise in the input image can give rise to broken segments, in particular when the bond lines are drawn with thin segments (Fig. 4).

To address this problem, all the segments are pairwise compared searching contiguous segments not touching each other.

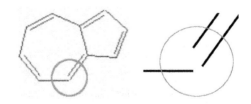

Figure 4: Broken segments.

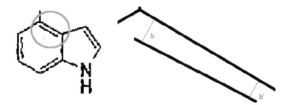

Figure 5: Nearly parallel bonds.

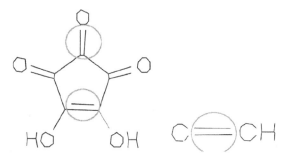

Figure 6: Three cases of nearly parallel bonds.

Figure 7: Non-horizontal bonds.

Figure 8: Horizontal alignment.

When the minimum distance between the segments is lower than a given threshold, the gap between the closest points in the two segments is "filled" with a new (short) segment that restores the contiguity of segments. In order to fix potential non-alignment of the new segment with existing ones the method defined to fix split segments (Section 2.1.2) is subsequently invoked again.

2.1.4 Nearly parallel bonds

Double bonds, represented by parallel segments, can give rise to non-parallel segments in the vectorial representation. The visualization of double bonds with non-parallel segments is particularly annoying and we fixed this problem as follows.

For each pair of segments the distances between all the end points are computed and the two lowest distances are found (h and h', see Fig. 5). When $h \simeq h' < Th_h$ we have a double bond and we therefore compare the slopes on the two segments to check whether we should make them parallel. Three cases of double bonds are handled by the algorithm (Fig. 6):

- When the two segments have one of the two ends touching other bonds (top-left of Fig. 6) then the opposite ends are moved to obtain two parallel segments of the same length.
- When one segment is linked to other bonds (the bond links two Carbon atoms, bottom-left of Fig. 6) we move one of the two ends of the other segment to make the two bonds parallel.
- When the two segments are isolated from other lines (and therefore represent a double bond between two named atoms, right of Fig. 6) one end is moved to align the two segments.

2.1.5 Wrong bond alignment

One problem related to the previous one occurs when segments that should be aligned with the sides of the image are not exactly horizontal or vertical. This case is handled similarly to the one described in Section 2.1.4 identifying which

end of the non-aligned segment must be moved. The vertical and horizontal alignments are similar and we describe here the horizontal one. There are three sub-cases to handle:

- If the segment has one and only one end not connected to other bonds we move this end as shown in Fig. 8.
- When the segment is free and has no touching segments we rotate the segment around the left-most end (x_l, y_l) by moving the right-most end vertically to obtain an horizontal bond (we fix $y_r = y_l$).
- When the segment is linked to other bonds on both ends we should move not only the right-most end point of the segment, but also the touching segments. Since the latter segments are moved we should also check possible double bonds that become non-parallel.

2.1.6 Additional problems

Some problems are still unsolved and we are currently working on their solution. The most critical is related to the bad vectorization of some atom names. To address this problem we will include an OCR tool in the whole system so as to recognize the names and replace them with a textual description (rather than a graphical one) in the SVG file.

3. EPUB BUILDING

After converting the bitmap image in an SVG vectorized image and fixing some visualization problems we embed the image in an ePub file that can be displayed on dedicated e-book readers. The description of the details of the structure of the ePub file are omitted in this paper, where we focus on the scaling of the formula image. The target image size that we adopted is 600×800 (a size common to most devices) and we designed two approaches to convert the chemical formula and allow a nice-looking visualization. The first approach is a linear scaling of the image. The second one attempts to split the image in sub-parts.

3.1 Image resize

The first solution is based on the linear scaling of the image of the chemical formula. This is particularly useful when the size of the input image is smaller than the desired output and therefore a scaling would result in a pixelated image. Since the image is vectorized, it is possible to scale the SVG file to the final size without visual distortions. In

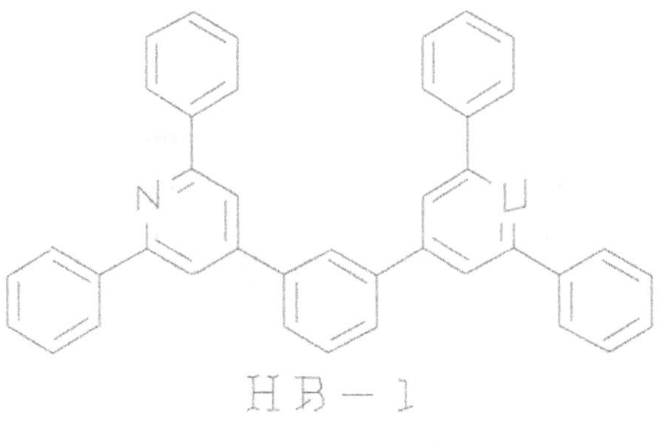

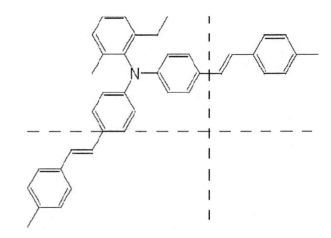

Figure 9: Scaling of one vectorized formula.

Fig. 9 we can see one vectorized and scaled formula. While the bonds look aligned there are still some problems in the vectorization of textual parts.

3.2 Image split

The previous approach is suitable when the chemical formula is small and needs to be expanded. When the original image is larger than the desired output it is in principle possible to scale-down it, but the readability can be difficult when the final image is too much compressed. In this case a better approach relies on the split of the original image in multiple frames that will then be navigated with horizontal and vertical movements.

The simplest approach would rely on the division of the image at fixed locations (e.g. multiples of 600 pixels). However, in this way it is unlikely that the final frames will be nice to observe since the formula will be broken in random places. We therefore define a *safe cut* as one split of the image that reduces the number broken bonds. There are three main types of safe cuts that are illustrated in the following for vertical splits:

1. The split location crosses one horizontal bond in the middle (first example in Fig. 10).

2. The split location is on the intersection point of more bonds (second example in Fig. 10).

3. The split location overlaps with one parallel bond without crossing other bonds. In this case both two sub-images will contain the bond segment (third example in Fig. 10).

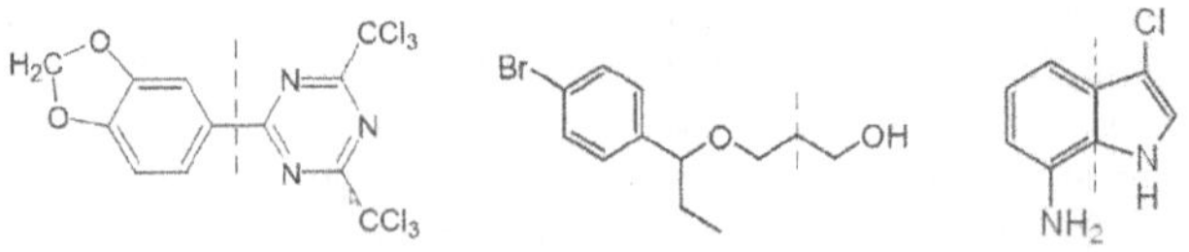

Figure 10: Safe vertical cuts.

The vertical split procedure explores in parallel the ranges $[400 - 600]$ and $[200 - 400]$ starting from the position 400 and looking for one safe cut. The first safe cut found is used to split the image and the same procedure is applied to the remaining right frame until all the frames have width < 600. At the end each frame is processed with an horizontal split procedure that looks for safe cuts among horizontal splits. One example of the resulting framing of one formula is shown in Fig. 11.

Figure 11: One large image split in three parts.

4. CONCLUSIONS

In this paper we described a tool developed for the conversion of chemical structural formulae represented as bitmap images in ePub format that can be displayed on most E-book readers. The proposed approach allows us to deal with both small and large formulae. Some problems are still to be solved for the processing of the text in the images.

5. ACKNOWLEDGMENTS

This work has been partially supported by the PRIN project *Statistical Relational Learning: Algorithms and Applications.*

6. REFERENCES

[1] IDPF. Epub3 International Digital Publishing Forum, May 2012. http://idpf.org/epub/30.

[2] S. Marinai, E. Marino, and G. Soda. Table of contents recognition for converting PDF documents in e-book formats. In *Proc. 10th ACM symposium on Document engineering*, DocEng '10, pages 73–76, New York, NY, USA, 2010.

[3] S. Marinai, E. Marino, and G. Soda. Conversion of PDF books in ePub format. In *ICDAR*, pages 478–482, 2011.

[4] K. Nakagawa, A. Fujiyoshi, and M. Suzuki. Ground-truthed dataset of chemical structure images in japanese published patent applications. In *9-th Int. Workshop on Document Analysis Systems*, pages 455–462, 2010.

[5] J. Park, G. R. Rosania, K. A. Shedden, M. Nguyen, N. Lyu, and K. Saitou. Automated extraction of chemical structure information from digital raster images. *Chemistry Central Journal*, 3(1):4, 2009.

[6] P. L. Rosin and G. A. W. West. Segmentation of edges into lines and arcs. *Image Vision Comput.*, 7(2):109–114, 1989.

[7] A. T. Valko and A. P. Johnson. Clide pro: The latest generation of clide, a tool for optical chemical structure recognition. *Journal of Chemical Information and Modeling*, 49(4):780–787, 2009.

Logical Segmentation for Article Extraction in Digitized Old Newspapers

Thomas Palfray, David Hébert, Stéphane Nicolas, Pierrick Tranouez, Thierry Paquet
LITIS, University of Rouen
UFR des Sciences et Techniques
F-76800 Saint Etienne du Rouvray

FirstName.Surname@univ-rouen.fr

ABSTRACT

Newspapers are documents made of news item and informative articles. They are not meant to be read iteratively: the reader can pick his items in any order he fancies. Ignoring this structural property, most digitized newspaper archives only offer access by issue or at best by page to their content.

We have built a digitization workflow that automatically extracts newspaper articles from images, which allows indexing and retrieval of information at the article level. Our back-end system extracts the logical structure of the page to produce the informative units: the articles. Each image is labelled at the pixel level, through a machine learning based method, then the page logical structure is constructed up from there by the detection of structuring entities such as horizontal and vertical separators, titles and text lines. This logical structure is stored in a METS wrapper associated to the ALTO file produced by the system including the OCRed text. Our front-end system provides a web high definition visualisation of images, textual indexing and retrieval facilities, searching and reading at the article level. Articles transcriptions can be collaboratively corrected, which as a consequence allows for better indexing.

We are currently testing our system on the archives of the Journal de Rouen, one of France eldest local newspaper. These 250 years of publication amount to 300 000 pages of very variable image quality and layout complexity. Test year 1808 can be consulted at plair.univ-rouen.fr.

Categories and Subject Descriptors

I.7.5 [**Document and Text Processing**]: Document Capture – *Document analysis*

Keywords

page layout analysis, information extraction from document images, logical structure, articles extraction in newspapers, document image labelling, conditional random field, structural analysis.

1. INTRODUCTION

During the last twenty years, the archives and national libraries of the whole world implemented many programmes of digitalization of their historical funds in order to preserve them while facilitating public access. The case of old newspapers is emblematic of this will of historical dissemination of information,

because of the wealth and diversity of these. Nevertheless, these documents require particular treatments to fully exploit their informational contents, because of their size, of their particularly complex page layout and its evolution with the technical innovations of printing, Moreover, the quality of conservation of this kind of document is often variable depending on the historical periods, resulting sometimes in a very degraded digitized copy, even unusable. In order to exploit these documents as well as possible, it is necessary to have a segmentation in articles making it possible to isolate the interesting parts of a newspaper for an easier consultation by the user, by the means of modern digital tools. Having in mind these difficulties, we developed a new method for logical labelling of old newspapers. This method is intended to extract metadata in the images of the digitized newspapers, thanks to the joint use of a method of classification of sequence of pixels based on Conditional Random Field modelling, associated with a set of rules defining the concept of article within a newspaper. We will first describe the previous work related to this task in the literature, then we fully describe the method we propose before presenting the results obtained on newspaper issues from "Journal de Rouen", a regional French newspaper. Finally we describe briefly the complete process in which this method is integrated, and then we conclude by a discussion about the potential of the method and future work.

2. Related work

Since 2001 is organised in the context of the ICDAR Conference, a document page segmentation competition [1] in which some of the proposed algorithms may have goals similar to the system we propose in this paper. Nevertheless, the document dataset used for this competition contains only modern documents; therefore the proposed methods may be inefficient for old newspapers. We can cite however the work described in [2] which exploits a method of labelling at pixel level adaptable to this type of documents. [3] describes an approach based on the determination of the maximal empty rectangles to delimit columns and text blocks. This method is integrated in the system OCROPUS. Although interesting, this method does not allow for difficulties inherent to old documents (skewing, deformations,...). A more interesting method taking into account these difficulties is described in [4]. The authors propose to use a multiscale approach to extract text blocks in old newspapers. This method seems to be efficient, but as the previous one, only the segmentation in text blocks is provided, but no logical reading order, what is important to determine the logical structure of articles. In [5] a full document digitization lifecycle for complex magazine collection is presented. The proposed workflow which provides according to the authors, all the tools and systems needed for the conversion of a large collection of complex documents, gives promising results on a database of the Time magazine covering 80 years. This complete system is interesting but it is dedicated to magazines and the requirements are quite different when dealing with old newspapers. For example it is no possible to exploit table of content (TOC) analysis because there is generally no TOC in old newspapers. Furthermore as it is said in [6], newspapers present a rich and complex variety of layouts. Some works deal specifically with newspapers analysis, but are focused generally on one aspect, such as layout segmentation as it is the case for the Fraunhofer Newspaper segmenter [1], or article segmentation [6], and do not propose a complete processing workflow. Furthermore the proposed solutions are generally much more adapted to modern layouts rather than old historical newspaper archives.

In this paper we propose a complete solution similar to the one proposed in [5] in some aspects, but adapted to this type of documents, and able to face the variety of layouts over the ages.

3. Proposed approach

Binary images of the digitized newspaper issues are considered at the input of the system, and files in METS format are produced at the output. The METS files contain the structuration of the newspaper issues in articles, and the ordering of the articles according to the reading order. To do that we want to identify the editorial model of the document using visual clues determined thanks to a Conditional Random Field (CRF) model associated to a structural analysis using a recursive algorithm. The distinctive steps of the proposed bottom-up method are:

- logical labelling at pixel level using conditional random field modelling

- logical labelling at connected component level using majority vote

- extraction of the text lines

- generation of a segmentation mask using identified rulers

- recursive analysis of the document page to extract articles and determine the reading order

3.1 Logical labelling at pixel level

The proposed method for article extraction in newspaper document images relies on a segmentation stage using an analysis of the document image by a particular CRF model with multi-scale quantization feature functions. This system provides a fine segmentation at pixel level, where each pixel is associated to a logical label specifying the logical function of the entity this pixel belongs to. See [7] for more details about this model. This bottom-up segmentation considers ten logical labels describing precisely the physical organisation of the textual content, and particularly the inter and intra character spacing. Each image is analysed line by line at the pixel level, and the labelling results of all the lines are concatenated to produce a labelled image noted $Icrf$, which is then exploited by the next analysis stages. An example of labelling obtained at this stage is shown on Figure 1b. These ten labels are finally grouped into six informative labels for the logical labelling into articles or article parts:

- vertical separator

- horizontal separator

- title (grouping the labels "title character", "title inter-character" and "title inter-word")

- text line (grouping the labels "character", "inter-character" and "inter-word")

- noise

- background

At the end of this stage we have an image whose pixels are labelled by these six categories.

3.2 Post processing for the logical extraction of the articles

3.2.1 logical labelling at connected component level

Starting from a pixel analysis we want to build our way back to the top level structure of the page. We will now label the connected components of the preceding image.

Algorithm 1: majority vote on connected components

---

input: $Icrf$, binary image with labelled pixels
output: Icc, binary image with labelled connected components

Extract from $Icrf$ the connected components of the pixels not labelled "background";
For each connected component CC **do**
  Begin
  For each label Ei **do**
  ⌊ $nEi \leftarrow$ the number of pixels of CC labelled Ei;
  label CC with the label $argmax_{Ei}(nEi)$
  Add CC and its convex hull to Icc
  End

3.2.2 Article extraction using a layout model

Icc is made of zones of the document image as described in 3.2.1. We will now assemble those zones to build a reading order and articles.

3.2.2.1 Article definition

Provided a reading order, we define an article as an entity starting with a *Title* zone, followed by at least one *Text* zone, and ending before another *Title*.

There are more complex exotic cases that we do handle (e.g. articles delimited by special *Separators* rather than *Titles*) but that we will leave aside for the clarity for the explanation.

3.2.3 Definition of the grid of separators

The horizontal and vertical separators of the newspaper pages constitute robust information to identify the structure of the pages and extract the articles. The vertical separators delimit the columns while the horizontal ones separate either the articles belonging to a column or the different sections of the page. Titles can have the same role.

Separators and *Titles* can therefore be used to build a grid that would delimitate blocks of the document.

Newspapers are divided in sections, these sections in subsections etc. down to articles. As a consequence, the delimitated blocks can contain other blocks (subsections) or empty spaces (articles).

We will therefore model our document as a tree of blocks,whose root is the whole page, its children the sections etc. (figure 1d).We call hierarchical position, the height of a block or of a separator in this tree.

3.2.3.1 Generation of the grid and text blocks extraction

The first step of our segmentation method consists in prolonging all the *Separators* and *Title* zones in order to generate a grid of separators. For that we apply the following algorithm:

- Create the vertical and horizontal separator mask

- Connect the closed vertical separator

- Prolong the vertical separators as long as they do not cross a horizontal separator or a title

- Connect the closed horizontal separator

- Prolong the horizontal separators and the titles as long as they do not cross a vertical separator

Thus we obtain a full grid covering the entire image and then we can use it to extract the articles. For that we generate the list of blocks which correspond to the boxes of our grid and we compare the coordinates of these blocks those of the *Test* zones . We extract also the "title" entities and we add to the blocks the text lines which are fully included. The blocks containing no text line are rejected from the list. Finally we obtain a list of boxes positioned on the separator grid, and we only have to use this list of boxes to obtain a list of articles ordered according to the reading order of the document defined by the editorial model. The figure 6 shows an example of reading order interpretation.

3.2.3.2 Article extraction and reading order determination

The boxes of the previously described grid may contain a full article or part of article. By part of article we mean two *Text* zones that follow each other in the reading order, but are separated by a *Horizontal separator*, an end of page or a much larger *Title*. To be able to regroup these parts of a same article, it is necessary to identify the reading order in the section including them.

As explained in the subsection 3.2.3.2, the separators divide the page in sections, the sections into subsections and so on up to the block level which corresponds to the leaves of the logical tree model. In the subsection 3.2.3.3 we explained how the boxes of the grid are determined, and we now explain how we determine the sections.

For each section s, we seek the nearest horizontal separator strictly longer than the considered section and situated just above it. This horizontal separator delimits two sections. Among them the one containing s is called the parent section. We repeat this process until having considered the entire tree model from the leaves to the root.

In each intermediate node of the tree, we order the contained children sections. We consider that a section precedes another if its top-left coordinate is strictly on the left or higher in the document image. For the children sections corresponding to the leaves of the tree model, this order relation implies the reading order of these sections. If a longer separator delimits a box which contains no title, it means that this box is the second part of a fragmented article. In this case this part of article is grouped with the box just before it.

Finally at this end of this stage we obtain the list of articles ordered by sections.

4. Results

This method was tested on a dataset containing 42 document images issued from a French regional newspaper called "Journal de Rouen". The results are determined visually because we do not have the ground-truth data to check them automatically. We determined the detection rate and the over-segmentation rate. These results are given in Table 1.

The analysis of the errors produced by our method allow us to see that a great number of them are due to the labelling errors at the output of segmentation stage performed by the CRF model. For example on our test dataset we have 14 text lines labelled by error as "title" causing the creation of a new article when the editorial rules described in subsection 3.2.3.1 are applied, and then we obtain 28 articles instead of the 14 we should find. Theses errors cause in general an over-segmentation.

Table 1. Results of the logical segmentation into articles

#articles	#detected	#correct	%correct
226	245	194	85.84

The results obtained at each stage of the system on a simple two-column layout are visually illustrated on figure 1. The system is also able to process different complex layouts with good results as we can see on figure 2. which illustrates the final article identification obtained on page layouts with several columns and advertisements in newspapers of the 19th century.

5. Full processing system

The method we present in this paper is integrated in a full system able to process a large amount of old newspaper document images. This system first applies on the images binarization and skew correction processing before applying the article extraction method described previously. Then the extracted text lines are used to feed on OCR engine to recognize the textual content. Our system provides as output XML files in METS/ALTO format. These files contain both the logical structure describing the reading order of the articles and the physical layout constituted by the detected text lines and the associated OCR results. They can be used to index the documents to improve the online access to the data they contain in digital archive applications. For that we propose a web newspaper browsing application, which exploits the data produced by the system presented in this paper. This front-end system, which will be presented in a further paper, provides a web high definition visualisation of images, textual indexing and retrieval facilities, searching and reading at the article level. Articles transcriptions can be collaboratively corrected, which as a consequence allows for better indexing. We are currently testing the system on the archives of the Journal de Rouen, one of France eldest local newspaper. These 250 years of publication amount to 300 000 pages of very variable image quality and layout complexity. Test year 1808 can be consulted at plair.univ-rouen.fr.

6. Conclusion and future work

We presented in this paper a logical segmentation method based on the analysis of low-level labeling results produced by a CRF model, using a set of grouping rules defined by a generic layout model. The proposed method is able to segment the textual content of old newspapers with complex Manhattan structure (multi columns), using a little set of simple rules. We obtain with this method an article segmentation rate of 85.84% on a test dataset containing 42 images of "Journal de Rouen", one of the oldest French regional newspapers.

These first results are promising, and allow us to identify the main improvement issues. In a future work we will improve further both the CRF model and the layout rules in order to be able to take into account some important other entities of the document structure, such as figures, pictures, captions and tables.

7. ACKNOWLEDGMENTS

The PlaiR project (Regional Indexing Platform, in French "Plateforme d'Indexation Regionale") is funded by the "Haute-Normandie" regional council and the European institutions by the FEDER program. This project is supported by the CHU and the University of Rouen.

8. REFERENCES

[1] Antonacopoulos A., Pletschacher S., Bridson D., Papadopoulos C., « ICDAR 2009 Page Segmentation Competition », *2009 10th International Conference on Document Analysis and Recognition*, IEEE, p. 1370-1374, 2009.

[2] An C., Yin D., Baird H., « Document Segmentation Using Pixel-Accurate Ground Truth », *2010 International Conference on Pattern Recognition*, IEEE, p. 245-248, 2010.

[3] Breuel T., « Two geometric algorithms for layout analysis », *Document Analysis Systems V*, vol. 2, p. 687-692, 2002.

[4] Lemaitre A., Camillerapp J., Couasnon B., « Approche perceptive pour la reconnaissance de filets bruités, Application à la structuration de pages de journaux », *in* , A. T. et Thierry Paquet (ed.), *Dixième Colloque International Francophone sur l'Ecrit et le Document*, Groupe de Recherche en Communication Ecrite, France, p. 61-66, 2008.

[5] Yacoub S., Burns J., Faraboschi P., Ortega D., Abad Peiro J., Saxena V. 2005. Document digitization lifecycle for complex magazine collection. In *Proceedings of the 2005 ACM symposium on Document engineering* (DocEng '05). ACM, New York, NY, USA, 197-206.

[6] Beretta R., Laura L. 2011. Performance Evaluation of Algorithms for Newspaper Article Identification. In *Proceedings of the 2011 International Conference on Document Analysis and Recognition* (ICDAR '11). IEEE Computer Society, Washington, DC, USA, 394-398.

[7] Hebert D., Paquet T., Nicolas S., « Continuous CRF with multi-scale quantization feature functions Application to structure extraction in old newspaper », *Document Analysis and Recognition (ICDAR), 2011 International Conference on*, IEEE, p. 493-497, 2011

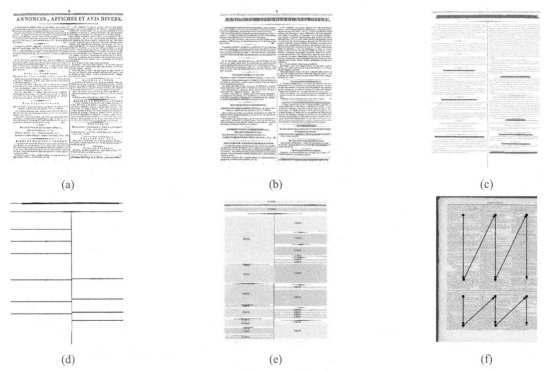

Figure 1. (a) original image (b) pixel level logical labeling result (c) labelling smoothing (d) grid of separators (e) result of the segmentation into articles (f) example of reading order

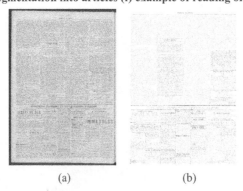

Figure 2. (a) original image of a page with complex layout, (b) result of the article identification

Scientific Table Type Classification in Digital Library

Seongchan Kim, Keejun Han
Dept. of Knowledge Service
Engineering
KAIST
Daejeon, Korea
sckim, keejun.han@kaist.ac.kr

Soon Young Kim
Dept. of Overseas Information
KISTI
Daejeon, Korea
maya@kisti.re.kr

Ying Liu
Dept. of Knowledge Service
Engineering
KAIST
Daejeon, Korea
yingliu@kaist.edu

ABSTRACT

Tables are ubiquitous in digital libraries and on the Web, utilized to satisfy various types of data delivery and document formatting goals. For example, tables are widely used to present experimental results or statistical data in a condensed fashion in scientific documents. Identifying and organizing tables of different types is an absolutely necessary task for better table understanding, and data sharing and reusing. This paper has a three-fold contribution: 1) We propose Introduction, Methods, Results, and Discussion (IMRAD)-based table functional classification for scientific documents; 2) A fine-grained table taxonomy is introduced based on an extensive observation and investigation of tables in digital libraries; and 3) We investigate table characteristics and classify tables automatically based on the defined taxonomy. The preliminary experimental results show that our table taxonomy with salient features can significantly improve scientific table classification performance.

Categories and Subject Descriptors

H.3.m [**Information Storage and Retrieval**]: Miscellaneous; I.2.6 [**Artificial Intelligence**]: Learning – knowledge acquisition.

General Terms

Algorithms, Measurement, Experimentation

Keywords

Scientific tables, IMRAD, fine-grained, taxonomy, classification

1. INTRODUCTION

Tables are ubiquitous in all types of documents such as scientific publications, web pages, financial reports, newspapers, magazine articles, etc. Understanding table type, function, and purpose is crucial for better table understanding and for more accurate table data sharing and reuse. Moreover, automatic identification of the functionality of each document table could be useful for many information-processing tasks, including advanced information retrieval, knowledge extraction [2], mobile access, and data integration.

Tables are differently used to present different types of information with various purposes. Scientists use various types of tables to display such things as experimental results or statistical data for multiple purposes. Scholars can easily obtain valuable insight by examining such type-specified tables. For example, a medical scientist may want to search for tables containing information about "cancer." He or she may want only tables that contain definitions, experimental results, or medical interview questions. However, none of the currently available table search engines (e.g., BioText Search Engine [5], *Tableseer* [7]) support table categorization by type. When issuing a query to these table-specialized search engines, end-users will get only a list of keyword-relevant tables, regardless of their types. The purpose of search by table type is, therefore, to help users to easily recognize the relevance of results by referring to the same type of tables.

Table type related research has recently been receiving considerable attention. Crestan and Pantel [2] report on a census of the types of HTML tables on the Web and propose a fine-grained classification taxonomy. However, their taxonomy is too limited to apply to scientific tables, since table types are heavily dependent on the nature of documents. Kim and Liu [6] first suggest functional-based table types for scientific tables; however, they do not provide fine-grained taxonomy but only two types of table: commentary and comparison. To the best of our knowledge, this is the first study of fine-grained table taxonomy for scientific tables in digital libraries.

In this paper, we observe tables in scientific papers, abstract the underlying table functional-based types, investigate the table characteristics, and demonstrate the distribution of different table types. We focus on scientific papers, since they are one of the most important media in digital libraries and contain many tables (1.28 tables per paper in our dataset), which are all genuine, unlike Web tables [2]. The preliminary experimental results show the effective performance of our system of automatic table type classification. The contributions of this paper are as follows: 1) We propose the finest (IMRAD-based) table functional classification system for scientific documents by considering the structural position of tables within a document; 2) A fine-grained table taxonomy is introduced first, based on an extensive period of table observation and investigation in digital libraries; 3) We investigate the scientific table characteristics and automatically classify tables based on the defined taxonomy; and 4) The whole system and methodology can be easily applied to tables in any fields and formats without much modification in order to achieve a fully automatic table classification and understanding.

The paper is organized as follows. In section 2 we present our table type taxonomy including definitions and descriptions for each category. Section 3 reports the design of our experiment and our results. Finally, we conclude in section 4.

2. Table Type Taxonomy

We propose a brand-new table type taxonomy that is the results of our extensive observation and investigation of 2,500 tables that were randomly collected from 25 randomly selected scientific journals [1] published by Springer from 2006 to 2010 in five

---

[1] All lists are available at http://issl.kaist.ac.kr/table

domains (Biomedical and Life Science, Chemistry and Materials Science, Computer Science, Electrical Engineering, and Medicine). We manually examined a large sample of tables and propose two table taxonomies in different perspectives: 1) IMRAD-based table taxonomy, which considers the structural position of tables within a document, and 2) fine-grained table taxonomy, which looks further and analyzes table content.

2.1 IMRAD-Based Table Taxonomy

The IMRAD[2] structure is currently the most prominent norm to represent the document structure of a scientific paper. Many scientific journals now prefer this structure and have adopted the IMRAD, which is an acronym for Introduction, Methods, Results, and Discussion, as an instructional device for their authors, recommending the usage of the four terms as main section headings. We define IMRAD-based table taxonomy by borrowing the IMRAD paper structure. In this taxonomy, table type is simply decided by the location of the table; in other words, in which section the table appears. For example, if a table is in the introduction part of the paper, the type of that table is introduction. Though this method is coarse-grained, it can help us to understand the basic purpose of the authors who designed each table.

Introduction Tables The introduction section of a paper is designed to inform readers of the background of the research. It usually includes a short preface or relevant background that leads to a statement of the problem that is being addressed. Tables in these sections are usually used to supplement the explanation of the background theory, to analyze the related studies, and to list statistical data.

Methods Tables The methods section of the paper usually addresses contents in various degrees of detail, methodologies, materials (or subjects), and procedures. Tables in these sections are mainly used to present the system details, itemize the theoretical steps, and explain the implementation procedures.

Results Tables The results section of the paper contains the major findings of the experiment, which were performed to approve the research question, topic, and hypothesis suggested in background part. Tables in the results section are widely used for describing results found and what has been learned in the study. Results tables are often accompanied by others in order to allow a comparing of results as well as a presentation of commentary about experimental results and an organization of findings.

Discussion Tables The discussion section of the paper usually offers interpretations and conclusions about the findings. Tables are used to support interpretation, conclusion, and discussion.

2.2 Fine-Grained Table Taxonomy

In this section, we present a fine-grained table taxonomy, organized according to what the tables contain and by the purposes for which they are used. Since there has been no previous comprehensive study that has attempted to identify and classify tables found in scientific articles in any detailed degree, we both define the table types and describe them. Our analysis yields seven functional types for tables[1].

Definition Tables These consist of defining terms and their explanations. It is very nice to provide readers with definitions of the terms that for the protocol of the study by using a compact table. This type of table usually appears before the experiment and

results sections. When the experiment section begins, the number of occurrences of this type of table becomes significantly smaller.

Statistics/distribution tables Statistics/distribution tables are often used to support the main topic of the paper by citing common statistical or distribution data that has been used in the other work or was presented by others. We define statistics/distribution tables as limited to tables whose contents are not related with the current experiment being carried out in the paper. Statistics/distribution tables are usually confused with experimental results tables because experimental results tables also frequently use statistical results to show the outcome of experiments. In this case, the classification between the two types of tables becomes clear when we consider the location of the table in the paper by again using the IMRAD approach.

Survey question/result tables Survey question/result tables contain questionnaires of the survey and the results of those questionnaires. They list a series of questions that have been used to find out information about interviewee's opinions or behavior, usually by asking the questions to the interviewees; or, these tables present detailed output of certain examinations.

Example tables Example tables show instances that introduce and emphasize something that needs to be explained clearly. These tables consist of a target and its examples and instances. They focus on one of the possible consequences of experiments rather than explaining all of the outcomes.

Procedure tables Procedure tables describe the sequence, step, flow, or schedule of the methods. This type of table describes steps, processes, or sequences of a task with a timeline. Sometimes, they are drawn in the form of a pseudo code. This type of table can be easily defined due to its clear contents, which are organized in a logical flow according to the introduced algorithms or methods in the paper.

Experimental setting tables Experimental setting tables can be described as having items required for the experiment including configurations, parameters, data, apparatus, etc. Such tables contain necessary arrangements for the experiment that was performed in the study.

Experimental result tables Experimental result tables are accompanied with a summary describing the output of the experiment. The results are usually shown using specific measures to evaluate the performance of the methods. Some are shown comparing the results with results from other well-known methods; others include statistics and distribution.

2.3 Table Type Distribution

In order to estimate the proportion of table types with our taxonomies, we manually annotated 2,500 tables according to these categories by hiring 15 domain specialists in five domains. Three annotators were assigned per domain; as a result, each table was judged by three annotators. Annotators were instructed to classify a given table according to the IMRAD-based and the fine-grained taxonomy. The inter-annotator agreement among the three annotators was $k = 0.64$ for IMRAD annotation, considered to indicate substantial agreement; the agreement was $k = 0.53$ for fine-grained annotation, considered to indicate moderate agreement according to Fleiss kappa [3]. Finally, we obtained only 2,380 and 2,324 tables that had agreed on labeling from more than two annotators in IMRAD and fine-grained annotation, respectively; we considered these tables to be our Gold Standard for IMRAD and fine-grained classification. We also obtain 2,293

---

[2] http://en.wikipedia.org/wiki/IMRAD

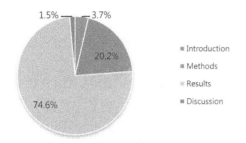

Figure 1. Distribution of Tables with IMRAD Taxonomy

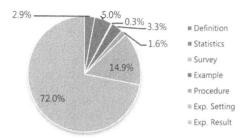

Figure 2. Distribution of Tables with Fine-grained Taxonomy

tables that were agreed on by more than two annotators using both IMRAD and fine-grained annotation at a same time.

Figures 1 and 2 show the distribution of the tables by each taxonomy with 2,293 tables. According to IMRAD classification, the dominant majority of tables were the results tables (74.6%); the second highest number of tables was methods tables (20.2%). As we expected, scientists use tables in the results and methods section, more than in other sections of their papers (94.8%). In fine-grained classification, 1,651 (72.0%) of the tables we analyzed dealt with experimental results, 342 (14.9%) dealt with experimental setting, and, surprisingly, only 6 (0.3%) were in the survey question/result. This last value is very small and different from what we had predicted. However, the percentage of this type of table is expected to heavily increase if we include other fields (such as the field of the humanities). We summarize that tables in scientific papers are highly skewed toward experimental results; further, we assert that scientists usually employ tables to describe their experiment, rather than for other purposes.

In Figure 3, we show a further estimation of the proportion of fine-grained type tables based on the IMRAD taxonomy. In other words, we can find scientific authors' table usage in papers with Figure 3. In the introduction, example, definition, and statistics/distribution tables (87%) were mainly found to appear. The methods section mainly consists of experimental setting tables (60%) and a small portion of other types of tables. In results and discussion, chiefly experimental result tables are found (92%, 83%). With the results, we discover that authors move from general discussion of the topic using various tables (example, definition, and statistics/distribution tables) and details settings in the methods section, to reporting on and discussing the topic with results tables in the latter part of the paper. This is parallel to the general IMRAD writing style.

3. EXPERIMENTS
We automatically conducted a preliminary classification for the IMRAD and the fine-grained taxonomy by using textual analysis of the tables. In this study, we only focus on table classification with complete tables which were extracted by *TableSeer*. Table extraction is not scope of this study.

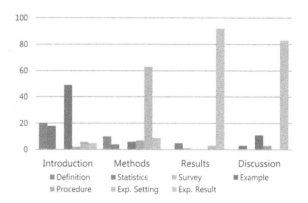

Figure 3 Fine-grained Types based on IMRAD taxonomy

3.1 Experimental Settings
We extracted 2,500 tables using *TableSeer* [7] and used 2,380 tables for IMRAD and 2,324 tables for fine-grained classification. First, we considered table captions and reference texts, which were obtained from table metadata extractor of *TableSeer*. Table captions are caption (sentence(s)) that appear along with the tables; table reference text is the text in the document body that refers to the table and discusses the content of the table. Only unigram tokens were extracted from the texts, tokens were converted to lowercase, and stemmed; however, stopwords were removed.

3.2 Textual Features
In this experiment, we present only the textual features necessary for our results to be discriminative enough to determine table type. Given a table caption and reference text T, we compute the following features and feed them into the classification algorithms. Feature selection was performed by chi-square to determine the correlation of each term with a desired class. The top 300 terms were used as features; all other terms were discarded. Once a decision was made about what to consider as a feature term, the meaning of the numerical feature had to be determined. Several different techniques can be used to generate feature values: binary, Term Frequency (TF), or Term Frequency-Inverse Document Frequency (TF-IDF). However, we designed an innovative term weighting scheme: Table Term Frequency-Inverse Category Frequency (TTF-ICF), which is a tailored Table Term Frequency-Inverse Table Term Frequency (TTF-ITTF) [7]. Because Liu et al. [7] showed the advantages of TTF-ITTF in table search by calculating the term frequency in the table metadata instead of in the whole document, and because Cho and Kim [1] showed the effectiveness of using TF-ICF over TF-IDF for text categorization, we combined these two ideas for our table classification work. Let's assume that category C_1 has tables T_1 and T_2, and that category C_2 has tables T_3 and T_4. A table term W_1, which is a word in the table metadata, appears in T_1 and T_2; W_2 appears in T_1 and T_3. In this case, W_1 is more powerful than W_2 to determine the category; however, two words have the same weight by TTF-ITTF while W_1 is given more weight than W_2 by TTF-ICF.

$$C_1: T_1, T_2 \qquad W_1: \text{appears } T_1 \text{ and } T_2$$
$$C_2: T_3, T_4 \qquad W_2: \text{appears } T_1 \text{ and } T_3$$

TTF-ICF estimates the term weighting as follows:

$$W_i = freq_i * \log(M) - \log(CF_i) + 1$$

where $freq_i$ is the term frequency of the table term in the table captions, reference text, or both, M is the total number of categories, and CF_i is the number of categories that contain the term W_i.

Table 1. Performance of IMRAD Classification by Features

Features	SVM			Decision Tree		
	P	R	F	P	R	F
Cap.(Baseline)	0.836	0.506	0.543	0.947	0.550	0.792
Ref.	0.875	0.705	0.761	0.930	0.639	0.73
Cap.+Ref.	**0.967**	**0.784**	**0.866**	0.938	0.746	0.831

Table 2. Performance of Fine-grained Classification by Features

Features	SVM			Decision Tree		
	P	R	F	P	R	F
Cap.(Baseline)	0.627	0.333	0.397	0.522	0.271	0.302
Ref.	0.707	0.615	0.649	**0.790**	**0.673**	**0.716**
Cap.+Ref.	0.701	0.657	0.668	0.764	0.62	0.671

Table 3. Performance of IMRAD Classification by Types

Type	SVM			Decision Tree		
	P	R	F	P	R	F
Introduction	0.968	0.6	0.741	0.907	0.68	0.777
Methods	0.901	0.996	0.943	0.912	0.992	0.95
Results	1	1	1	1	1	1
Discussion	1	0.543	0.704	0.933	0.314	0.44
Macro Avg.	**0.967**	**0.784**	**0.866**	0.938	0.746	0.831
Micro Avg.	**0.977**	**0.976**	**0.973**	0.973	0.975	0.972

Table 4. Performance of Fine-grained Classification by Types

Type	SVM			Decision Tree		
	P	R	F	P	R	F
Definition	0.689	0.609	0.646	0.837	0.522	0.643
Statistics	0.699	0.879	0.779	0.898	0.681	0.775
Survey	0	0	0	0	0	0
Example	0.716	0.725	0.72	0.875	0.525	0.656
Procedure	0.9	0.486	0.632	1	0.649	0.787
Exp. Setting	0.905	0.9	0.902	0.74	0.963	0.837
Exp. Result	1	1	1	1	1	1
Macro Avg.	0.701	0.657	0.668	**0.764**	**0.62**	**0.671**
Micro Avg.	0.947	0.947	0.946	**0.94**	**0.936**	**0.987**

3.3 Experimental Results

The classification was conducted with a 10-fold cross validation. We used *SVM* and *Decision Tree*, which have been widely adopted for classification, in Weka tookit [4]. We used default parameters in Weka for classifiers. We report 3 measures: *precision (P)*, *recall (R)*, and *F-measure (F)*. Tables 1 and 2 show the results (macro average of each table type class) of IMRAD and fine-grained classification using different features. The results clearly reveal the effectiveness of the lexical feature. SVM with both captions and reference text gives the best result in IMRAD while Decision Tree with only reference text does in fine-grained. Performance is increased by 59.5% (F-measure) in IMRAD and by 137% in fine-grained when comparing with only captions (baseline). Using both captions and reference text shows better performances without the case of Decision Tree in fine-grained.

In order to analyze the performance by table type, the IMRAD and fine-grained classification results using both captions and reference text for each table type with the macro and micro average are reported in Tables 3 and 4. Macro average of 0.866 (F-measure) with SVM in IMRAD and 0.671 with Decision Tree in fine-grained were best achieved. One of the remarkable things is the performance of fine-grained. In Figure 2, experimental result type is 72.0% of all 7 types in fine-grained. This implies that, hypothetically speaking, for any given table, if we declare it as experimental result type in fine-grained, then our expected accuracy would be 72.0%. However, the results reported in Table 4 do not assure that our classifier is really good. For example, the macro average F-measure of our fine-grained is low (0.67), because the performance of the survey question/result class is 0, whereas the experimental result class is 1. This discrepancy is thought to originate from our data set's being very skewed; the number of samples for the survey question/result type is definitely small (i.e. only 0.6% of the data is survey question/result while 74 % is experimental results). Though we have the results, we still propose these seven types based on a consideration of all the fields in scientific digital libraries. Since our experimental data were limitedly selected from only five domains, it is natural to have skewed results. Once we change the table source and enlarge the data scalability, the performance will be greatly improved.

4. CONCLUSIONS

In this paper, we introduce our study of table types and classifications in scientific papers; we report our experimental results, which not only delineate the underlying table types, but also demonstrate the distribution according to those types. With preliminary experiments, we show the effective performance of automatic type classification, which can be used to better understand table contents and author motivation. For future work, we will develop salient features from the table layout and content to improve the overall performance, not only in digital libraries, but also in any other fields with tables.

5. ACKNOWLEDGEMENTS

We thank Jinhyuk Choi and Jinsup Shin for helpful discussions. This research was supported by Basic Science Research Program through the National Research Foundation of Korea(NRF) funded by the Ministry of Education, Science and Technology(2012-0004316)

6. REFERENCES

[1] Cho, K. and Kim, J. 1997. Automatic Text Categorization on Hierarchical Category Structure by using ICF(Inverted Category Frequency) Weighting KOREA INFORMATION SCIENCE SOCIETY, 507-510.

[2] Crestan, E. and Pantel, P. 2011. Web-scale table census and classification. In *Proceedings of the fourth ACM international conference on Web search and data mining* (Hong Kong, China2011), ACM, 1935904, 545-554.

[3] Fleiss, J.L. 1971. Measuring nominal scale agreement among many raters. *Psychological Bulletin 76*, 5, 378-382.

[4] Hall, M., Frank, E., Holmes, G., Pfahringer, B., Reutemann, P., and Witten, I.H. 2009. The WEKA data mining software: an update. *SIGKDD Explor. Newsl. 11*, 1, 10-18.

[5] Hearst, M.A., Divoli, A., Guturu, H., Ksikes, A., Nakov, P., Wooldridge, M.A., and Ye, J. 2007. BioText Search Engine. *Bioinformatics 23*, 16, 2196-2197.

[6] Kim, S. and Liu, Y. 2011. Functional-Based Table Category Identification in Digital Library. In *Proceedings of the 11th International Conference on Document Analysis and Recognition* (Beijing, China2011), 1364-1368.

[7] Liu, Y., Bai, K., Mitra, P., and Giles, C.L. 2007. TableSeer: automatic table metadata extraction and searching in digital libraries. In *Proceedings of the 7th ACM/IEEE-CS joint conference on Digital libraries* (Vancouver, BC, Canada2007), ACM, 1255193, 91-100.

Document Understanding of Graphical Content in Natively Digital PDF Documents

Aysylu Gabdulkhakova
Department of Computing Mathematics and
Cybernetics
Ufa State Aviation Technical University
K. Marx str. 12, 450000, Ufa, Russia
aysylu.gab@gmail.com

Tamir Hassan
Pattern Recognition and Image Processing
Group
Technische Universität Wien
Favoritenstraße 9-11, 1040 Wien, Austria
tam@prip.tuwien.ac.at

ABSTRACT

This paper presents an object-based method for analysing the content drawn by graphical operators in natively digital PDF documents. We propose that graphical content in a document can be classified either as structural or non-structural and present an output model for our analysis result. Heuristic techniques are used to group the instructions into regions and determine their logical role in the document's structure. Experimental results demonstrate the effectiveness of the algorithm.

Categories and Subject Descriptors: I.7.5 [**Document and Text Processing**]: Document Capture—*document analysis*

Keywords: Document analysis, document understanding, PDF, PDF operator, natively digital, logical structure, structural, non-structural

1. INTRODUCTION

Graphic objects play an important role in documents. Figures, diagrams and images can concisely and intuitively represent information in such a way that no amount of text can. Lines and rectangles can also be used to visually separate different logical parts of the document. The increasing need to reuse or repurpose this information has led to the development of document analysis and understanding techniques to detect their logical structure.

In natively digital PDF documents (*PDF Normal* or *Formatted Text and Graphics*) embedded vector graphics and other graphical content are drawn on the page using low-level primitives such as lines, curves, rectangles and glyphs. For the goal of repurposing or indexing this content we need to group such primitives into higher-level logical entities. Therefore, the task of document understanding of graphical content in documents is of high importance.

Most techniques for document understanding, such as [6], focus on the textual content, detecting individual structural items such as headings, paragraphs, etc. Our goal is to determine the logical role of the graphical content and clas-

Figure 1: The desired output of our algorithm

sify each item as *structural* (e.g. ruling lines or rectangles that visually separate logical blocks from each other) or *non-structural* (illustrative content; the objects are grouped into regions) as shown in Figure 1. Here, the illustrative regions are highlighted in yellow, the structural elements are marked in green and the text regions in red.

This paper proposes an object-based method that considers the geometrical relations between the graphic objects that appear in predominantly textual documents such as newspapers. In Section 2 previous research work relating to this problem is presented. Section 3 describes the methods we have developed for document analysis and understanding of vector graphic elements. Section 4 presents our ground truthing and evaluation procedures, and experimental results obtained by using this methodology. Finally, Section 5 concludes the paper.

2. RELATED WORK

There are several papers that describe methods that work on natively digital PDF documents, i.e. use the individual operators or another low-level representation instead of a bitmap representation as the initial starting point. The majority of these approaches are focused on textual information, so that graphical regions are detected as non-textual rather than explicitly analysed.

Chao and Fan [1] propose a method that combines object-based and bitmap processing approaches for information extraction. Text and images are detected directly from the PDF content stream and form distinct logical components. For the vector graphics they first find the regions which are more likely to have path objects using a document image segmentation tool and heuristically compare these regions with the path objects taken from the PDF content stream to determine the grouping of the logical components.

In contrast, Déjean and Meunier [3] present a system which uses only the PDF operators and uses a combination

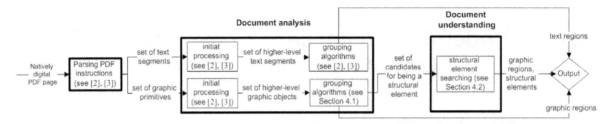

Figure 2: Stages of the whole algorithm for processing natively digital PDF page

of the X-Y cut algorithm and grouping heuristics to group textual and illustrative content into logical entities.

Hassan [4] also proposed an object-based method for the extraction of text and graphic objects directly from the PDF content stream. This method is included in the *PDF Extraction Toolkit (pdfXtk)*[1] which is built upon the *PDFBox* library and returns the graphical content as line, rectangle (filled and non-filled) and image objects, as well as text objects. Grouping algorithms are used to merge overlapping paths into regions for illustrative content.

In contrast to the above approaches, we determine the *logical role* of the vector graphic objects, i.e. we classify them as structural and non-structural. Using the output of pdfXtk as a starting point, our bottom-up approach uses geometrical properties and mutual arrangement of the given vector primitives to find illustrative regions and structural elements in the document.

3. METHODS

In order to represent a natively digital PDF document as a set of text regions, illustrative regions and structural elements, our system performs three processing phases. First, the page content is extracted from the PDF operators and transformed into Java object primitives. These primitives are defined by their rectangular bounding box coordinates in 2D Cartesian space. In pdfXtk the following types of primitive objects are returned: line segments, rectangles, bitmaps and text segments (corresponding to a single `Tj` or a partial `TJ` instruction).

Next, the grouping rules are applied in order to obtain higher-level graphic and text objects. In the final processing phase, we determine which of the graphical objects represent structural elements, as opposed to graphic regions. The diagram of the whole algorithm can be seen in Figure 2. The remainder of this section describes our grouping rules and our methods for determining whether a vector object is structural. The task of processing text blocks is not addressed in this paper (see [4, 5] for a description).

3.1 Grouping rules

The grouping rules that we have devised take into account geometrical properties of the graphic objects as well as their mutual spatial arrangement. We classify these rules into two categories: intersection-based and distance-based. When applied in combination with each other, they enable higher-level objects to be constructed, which usually correspond to distinct logical objects in the document's structure.

3.1.1 Intersection-based rules

Line and line. When the intersection between two lines is established, we group them together. For the next line,

[1]PDF Extraction Toolkit (pdfXtk):
http://pdfxtk.sourceforge.net

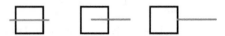

Figure 3: Three cases of intersection between line and rectangle objects

we check the intersection with each member of the group. The special case is when two lines construct a solid line, i.e. visually they are perceived as one. In this case we merge these line segments and no group is created.

Rectangle and rectangle. This method is applicable not only to rectangles, but also to bitmap objects and complex figures (in the latter case, the bounding box is used). It is based on the assumption that two *structural* rectangle objects on the page are unlikely to intersect. Specifically, when the topmost coordinate of one rectangle is less than the bottommost coordinate of the other or when the leftmost coordinate of one rectangle is greater than the rightmost coordinate of the other.

Often, advertisements or other separated content is enclosed in structural rectangles, which are very close to each other or even overlap. Hence, before merging such elements using the above rule, we check whether they enclose other objects. If yes, then the given pair of rectangles is not grouped.

Line and rectangle. In predominantly textual documents, two types of intersection between line and rectangle objects can occur:
1. structural line intersects the rectangular object;
2. line segment intersects the rectangular object, both are part of a graphic region.

In order to avoid overmerging, three actions are sequentially performed:
a) the width ratio or height ratio, whichever is the larger, is compared to the given threshold;
b) we determine the type of intersection or, more precisely, the mutual arrangement of the intersecting objects (see Figure 3);
c) the ratio between both parts of the line, split at the intersection point, is compared to a given threshold.

Line and text. There are a variety of ways in which line segments and text fragments can intersect each other. In our research we focused on four cases that commonly occur in newspapers:
a) line segment underscores textual content;
b) line segment crosses a word;
c) line segments form the axes and text blocks represent labels (as in a chart or similar diagram);
d) text block is surrounded by lines which separate it from other parts of a document.

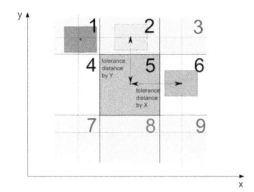

Figure 4: The grouping method for rectangles, based on the sizes and mutual arrangement of the given objects

Cases a) and b) can be distinguished from each other by the distance between their centres projected on the Y-axis: if the line is closer to the centre of the text bounding box than to its border, then case a) applies; otherwise case b). Cases c) and d) can also be distinguished by the distance between their centres, but projected on the X-axis: if the line is touching or intersecting the text bounding box, then case c) applies; otherwise case d).

Rectangle and text. As in the previous situation, there are several possibilities of intersection between the given objects. More precisely:

a) rectangle encloses the text fragment;
b) rectangle intersects the text fragment;
c) rectangle touches (or partially overlaps) the boundary of the text fragment.

The last case occurs in tight layouts, where the rectangular bounding boxes of neighboring components often slightly overlap each other.

3.1.2   Distance-based rules

Line and line. Here the distance-based rules consider the possibility of dashed lines. Line segments represent small objects with the distance between them less than or equal to the element size.

Rectangle and rectangle. Two rectangles are considered as a single object if the distance between their centres is less than a given threshold. This threshold depends on two parameters: a granularity-level coefficient and the widths or heights of the rectangles. It is calculated by multiplying the first parameter with the sum of the second.

The granularity-level coefficient depends on a size ratio of the given rectangles and is divided into 3 types: high (0.55), normal (0.6) and low (0.65). These numerical values were obtained experimentally.

Next, the algorithm continues by detecting one of nine cases of mutual arrangement between two rectangles (as illustrated in Figure 4).

If the current rectangle is located in area 4 or 6 towards the rectangle being considered (green and blue rectangles respectively), the threshold distance uses the sum of both widths. For cases 2 or 8 (yellow and blue rectangles), the threshold distance depends on their heights. For the remaining cases 1, 3, 7, 9 (red and blue rectangles), two threshold distances are counted using the widths and heights.

Finally, the threshold distance is compared to the distance

Figure 5: Newspaper heading representation in *pdfXtk*

between the centres of the given objects projected on the appropriate axis. In cases 1, 3, 7 and 9 the comparison is conducted on both axes with the corresponding thresholds.

It is worth noting that our system represents composite objects by their rectangular bounding box. In such a manner, graphic glyphs that form parts of logos, newspaper headings etc. are introduced as rectangular objects. A vivid example of the above glyphs is the heading of newspapers such as *The Sydney Morning Herald*, *International Herald Tribune*, etc. (Figure 5). Here, low-level primitives are positioned sequentially in one row/column. In order to detect this case, we refer to the golden ratio font rules [2].

Errors can occur with advertisements that have the same size and are close to each other (Section 3.1.1, *Rectangle and Rectangle*). These advertisements differ from glyphs as they also contain text. Moreover, the advertising boxes are usually filled with objects as large as at least one third of their size, whereas glyphs have a negligibly small filled area.

3.2   Finding structural elements

Lines. Generally a structural line occurs as a horizontal/vertical line or rectangle that looks like a line, which does not intersect other non-structural objects (strokes, lines, rectangles, merged graphic regions, text fragments) and is not enclosed in any graphic region.

In Section 3.1.1, paragraph *Line and Text* we considered four cases in which line and text objects can intersect each other. Case a) is a special case, where the line is neither structural nor illustrative, but rather an integral part of the formatting of the text. In case b) the line is likely to form part of an illustrative region.

In cases c) and d) there is a pair of identical groups of straight lines with different semantics: in case c) these lines form part of a chart, whereas in case d) the lines are used as a "barrier" and serve the purpose of separating the text paragraph from the remaining page content. Thereby we conclude that c) is an example of non-structural lines and d) is an example of structural lines. In order to detect the correct variant, the closeness of line segments and text fragments is taken into account.

Rectangles. Generally, a structural rectangle occurs does not intersect other graphic primitives and regions, but can enclose them. The special case is that of "stand-alone" rectangle objects, which often look like and serve the same logical function as lines. Therefore, in Section 3.1.1, paragraph

	Total	Retrieved	Correct detections	Incorrect detections	Partial detections	Over-segmentations	Under-segmentations	False positives	Missed objects
Structural lines	847	875	710 (86%)	93 (11%)	0	0	28 (3%)	122	30
Structural rectangles	464	377	291 (69%)	119 (28%)	1 (<1%)	11 (2%)	4 (<1%)	68	42
Graphic regions	364	670	291 (82%)	55 (15%)	2 (<1%)	105 (29%)	32 (9%)	228	11

Table 1: Evaluation results

Rectangle and Text, case a), the rectangle can represent the bounding box of textual content and thus is more likely to be structural than in cases b) and c).

4. EVALUATION

We have tested our approach against manually generated ground-truth on 100 pages from 10 different newspapers taken from 15-17 April 2012: *Bresciaoggi, Il Tirreno, L'Eco di Bergamo, Nuovo Quotidiano di Rimini, El Mundo del Siglo XXI, Äripäev, China Daily, Die Tageszeitung, International Herald Tribune* and *Le Monde*.

The evaluation was performed on the bitmap level using the methods in [7]. We developed a graphical tool to align the manually generated ground truth and resultant images, enabling pixel-by-pixel comparison. As our approach goes further than current related work in this field – we do not just group the objects but distinguish between structural and illustrative items – we chose not to compare our results with those of other approaches.

First, the given PDF document is rasterized to create a binary image at a given resolution – 72 dpi, which is sufficient for this purpose. The ground truth is generated manually by colouring the black pixels in one of three different colours, one for each type of region: structural lines, structural rectangles and illustrative regions. In the same way, we automatically generate a result image from the output of our algorithm.

As soon as the resultant and ground-truth images are generated, pixel-by-pixel comparison is applied to compare the color values of the corresponding pixels.

As in [7], we use the following measures to determine the nature of overlapping between the regions:

- *correct detection* – regions are mainly overlapping;
- *partial detection* – some overlapping detected, but not sufficient as in the first case;
- *incorrect detection* – the types of region in ground truth and result of the algorithm are different (structural rectangle, structural line or graphic region);
- *false positives* – the region is marked by the algorithm, but does not occur in the ground truth;
- *missed objects* – the region is marked in the ground truth, but has not been detected by the algorithm.

The results of our evaluation are given in Table 1. The algorithm demonstrates a high performance on predominantly textual, natively digital PDF pages. The following paragraph discusses the possible causes of the errors that were encountered.

Limitations. One of the causes of some of the errors that have occurred is that the implementation of certain PDF operators in pdfXtk and PDFBox is incomplete. This can lead to invisible lines and rectangles, which may have been used for alignment purposes in typesetting the page, being output as rectangular objects, which in turn can lead to the entire region being detected as a graphical region.

Further limitations include the less common situations of using bitmap images or text elements to draw structural content, and using graphical elements to draw text. In the former case, some analysis steps on the bitmap rendition of the page are necessary to correctly detect its structure, whereas the output of an OCR product could be combined with our methods in the latter case.

Finally, it is worth mentioning that PDF has its roots in the page description language PostScript. As such, there is an almost limitless number of ways that a given visual result can be achieved, with completely different underlying operator structures. It is therefore possible to purposely format a PDF in such a way that it looks normal to the reader, but confuses algorithms that work directly on the operator level.

5. CONCLUSION

In this paper we have introduced a new approach to document analysis and understanding of vector graphic content in natively digital PDF documents. Our method includes grouping algorithms that take into account intersections, enclosures, overlapping and mutual arrangement of several types of objects. Moreover, we use a set of heuristic rules in order to define the purpose of the content: whether it is structural or illustrative. The experimental evaluation shows that our methods achieve good performance, and the causes of some of the errors have been determined.

Acknowledgement: This work was funded in part by the Austrian Federal Ministry of Transport, Innovation and Technology (Grant No. 829602).

6. REFERENCES

[1] H. Chao and J. Fan. Layout and content extraction for PDF documents. *DAS 2004: Proceedings of the International Workshop on Document Analysis Systems*, 3163:213–224, 2004.

[2] Y. Chernihov and N. Sobolev. *Composing Scripts*. Architektura-S, 2007.

[3] H. Déjean and J.-L. Meunier. A system for converting PDF documents into structured XML format. In *DAS 2006: Proceedings of the International Workshop on Document Analysis Systems*, pages 129–140, 2006.

[4] T. Hassan. Object-level document analysis of PDF files. In *DocEng 2009: Proceedings of the 9th ACM Symposium on Document Engineering*, pages 47–55, 2009.

[5] T. Hassan. *User-Guided Information Extraction from Print-Oriented Documents*. PhD thesis, Technische Universität Wien, 2010.

[6] S. Klink, A. Dengel, and T. Kieninger. Document structure analysis based on layout and textual features. In *DAS 2000: Proceedings of the International Workshop of Document Analysis Systems*, 2000.

[7] A. Shahab, F. Shafait, T. Kieninger, and A. Dengel. An open approach towards the benchmarking of table structure recognition systems. In *DAS 2010: Proceedings of the International Workshop on Document Analysis Systems*, pages 113–120.

HP Relate – A Customer Communication System for the SMB Market

Steve Pruitt
HP Exstream R&D
810 Bull Lea Run
Lexington, KY 40511
011-859-422-6257
steve.pruitt@hp.com

Anthony Wiley
HP Exstream R&D
810 Bull Lea Run
Lexington, KY 40511
011-859-422-6210
anthony.wiley@hp.com

ABSTRACT

Enterprise businesses rely on variable data publishing solutions to produce customer communications, such as letters, statements, and financial reports, which are tailored to individual recipients. Until now, however, such customer communications systems were out of the reach of the small and medium business (SMB) market for several reasons. In order to produce enterprise-quality documents, businesses needed employees with advanced skills in document design and automated document composition. In addition, customized documents typically require scripted business logic and complicated data integration. To achieve this level of document composition and delivery would require the SMB user to have access to IT systems and staffing that would be prohibitively expensive.

HP Relate is an innovative document design system that delivers enterprise-quality documents for a next-generation customer communication system for the SMB market. HP Relate features easy-to-use document design tools that require no more than self-assisted training. Document business logic and data integration is accessible to SMB users through common office tools, such as dragging and dropping and spreadsheets. Instead of requiring software installed on the user's system, HP Relate is provisioned on a cloud-based platform using a software as a service (SaaS) subscription-based model. In addition, the HP Relate platform enables SMBs to deliver documents in the format of a customer's choosing, including traditional print forms, web-based deployment, and mobile devices.

Categories and Subject Descriptors

D.3.2 [**Programming Languages**]: Java, Flex; H.5.2 [**Information interfaces and presentation**]: User Interfaces – User-*centered design*; I.7.1 [**Document and Text Processing**]: Document and Text Editing

General Terms

Design, Economics, Human Factors, Interactive

Keywords

Interactive Document, Document Layout, Document behavior, Enterprise, Cloud-deployment, Mobile

1. PROBLEM STATEMENT

Today's services-based economy increasingly relies on direct customer communication to attain new customers, retain existing customers, and maximize the value of the customer base. On the other side of this equation, customers increasingly demand timely, tailored communications delivered through channels convenient to each customer. These prompt and personalized communications are typically produced interactively by customer-facing employees working from underlying systems of sophisticated document design tools, scripted business logic, and complicated data integration components. The entire range of skill sets required to maintain and use these systems is rarely found in individuals and requires a highly trained front-office staff working in parallel with a responsive IT organization.

In addition to the challenges of designing, creating, and deploying personalized documents, businesses must also strive to make these documents as effective as possible in attracting and retaining customers. To stay competitive, all enterprises, large and small, are increasingly motivated to adopt outcome-based metrics. Integrating with enterprise analytics frameworks adds to the set of complex skills needed in a SMB organization.

2. OUR SOLUTION

HP Relate is a full-featured business document system deployed on a public cloud. The cloud deployment allows the SMB enterprise to avoid retaining costly IT organizations to host and administer HP Relate. By using the cloud's inherent scalability and availability advantages, the SMB can concentrate on its core competency: customer service.

For the user, HP Relate offers a document design experience that is uncomplicated and within the capabilities of a typical, non-technical business user—a skill level roughly equivalent to the level required to use Microsoft Office[1].

Specifically, the HP Relate solution has the following innovative features tailored to the skill level of a typical SMB knowledge worker.

- **A "container-based" document design format**—HP Relate uses layout "containers" as the starting point for composing various types of documents. Document components, such as text boxes, buttons, and calendars are easily added to the document by dragging them from a palette into the layout containers. Each layout container has a built-in instruction set that determines how its constituent components are arranged.

- **A spreadsheet paradigm for easy implementation of business rules**—Customized documents require business rules to control variable content. In HP Relate, business rules are created and attached to components using the HP Relate design tool's spreadsheet editor: business rules are written as spreadsheet functions. Using a natural drag and drop gesture, spreadsheet cells can be associated with document components. In this manner, spreadsheet cells can set component values, and vice versa.

- **Plug-in components for external source integration**—Personalizing documents for individual customers requires access to external data sources containing the customer data, such as databases and web service-oriented sources such as SalesForce[2]. HP Relate features a plug-in architecture to install pre-composed external data components. Data from an external source is mapped to the document's spreadsheet data model.

- **Embedded document workflow**—HP Relate simplifies document processing by enabling workflow processes to be embedded within the document itself. Examples of business processes that can be supported include document design approval and document editing at the production phase. Workflow processes can be embedded automatically by administrative mandate, thus ensuring that a company's standard business practices are always followed.

- **Built-in document collaboration, including chat sessions**—Business processes are further simplified by the powerful document collaboration tools offered by HP Relate. Multiple users can view and edit the same document simultaneously across the network. Document changes are distributed to each client, so that a synchronized version of the document is maintained.

  Because each change is a discrete revision, users can then use the HP Relate timeline viewer to see the evolution of document changes. HP Relate also allows users to initiate chat sessions for specific document editing sessions. A chat transcript is keyed to specific document changes and can be reviewed in context with the document revisions.

- **Document analytics**—HP Relate provides a framework enabling the gathering of analytics across a document's lifecycle [3]. All data is collected in real time and is tracked to the document instance. The collected data can be imported to selected archiving or search appliances, such as Autonomy's IDOL [4] server.

3. PROBLEMS SOLVED

Developing the appropriate tools a business user can use for creating interactive documents based on custom data is the most important milestone in the SMB solution. An interactive document is the foundation upon which the rest of the HP Relate product rests. The remainder of this paper describes out interactive document solution to this critical problem.

The creation of an interactive document requires defining functional logic and specifying data binding for the variable content.

- *Functional logic* includes field calculations using formulas and data validation.

- *Data binding* involves using the cells of the spreadsheet for data population to and data capture from interactive controls. Examples of variable data fields are numeric and text fields, list boxes, dropdown lists, tables, paragraphs, and other form input controls

- *Data mapping* implies specifying data sources for the variable content to incorporate external data from xml files, database tables and web services into interactive web documents.

These three tasks are traditionally implemented using scripting or programming languages. The complexity and variability of these documents restrict potential designers to those who have advanced knowledge of programming languages. However, the primary users of these documents are business people. Not only they are not able to define functional logic and specify data binding when the document is first created, they cannot change these predefined values when the document is used, which is often required by the unstructured nature of the workflow process.

Thus a new approach is needed to allow business users to define functional logic and specify data binding and data mappings without using any programming or scripting language.

4. PRIOR SOLUTIONS

The majority variable data document design tools require use of scripting/programming languages to define functional logic and specify data binding. Thus, in web-based interactive document solutions, such as Adobe Lifecycle forms [5], Acrobat forms [5], and Microsoft Word Mail Merge [6], field calculations and validations of html forms are implemented with JavaScript, Visual Basic, and other scripting languages. Data binding is defined programmatically and is executed on the server side within .net or j2ee frameworks.

Drawbacks of current approach:

1. Advanced programming skill levels are required for users to be able to create and modify interactive documents.

2. Web documents have to be recompiled and redeployed if any changes are made to the functional logic or data binding.

3. Code maintenance issues: debugging tools are needed to support the scripting language environment.

An alternate cloud-based document solution offering is Google Docs [7] by Google. Google Docs is a cloud-based document word processor similar to the Microsoft Word product and has a very low price point. Google Docs enables the creation and editing of business documents. The documents can also be shared in real-time using a collaborative framework similar to HP Relate.

A close examination reveals the similarities end with the word processing features. Google Docs has no intrinsic business rule engine, nor the ability to query and embed user data from external data sources. These capabilities alone distinguish HP Relate as a complete business document system.

5. DESCRIPTION

We introduce a spreadsheet data model paradigm as a new approach to define functional logic and specify data binding in web interactive documents.

The primary users of interactive documents are business people, who have rich experience using spreadsheet logic to define formulas and calculate values of the variables. So using a spreadsheet interface and built-in functions, business users should be able to create interactive web documents quickly and define and modify functional logic on the fly.

The built in functions are provided for arithmetic, logical, date and time, financial and other miscellaneous operations.

A spreadsheet cell, or collection of cells, is bound to the content or properties of a visual interactive control on the document. This binding is bidirectional. Changes to the spreadsheet are reflected on the control, and user input captured by the control that modifies its bound content or properties will update the underlying spreadsheet cell(s).

The spreadsheet paradigm provides a simplified method to specify data mapping in the interactive document. HP Relate provides out-of-the box integration with commercially successful platforms.

In the future, HP Relate will provide more sophisticated data access tools, such as XPath [8] expressions, SQL [9] select statements, or URL functions to populate spreadsheet cells with external data. These special queries are entered into the spreadsheet cells similar to formulas. These are more complex data resources are targeted at satisfying more sophisticated users or large enterprise customers.

Scenario: At design time, a document designer defines functional logic by entering formulas into a spreadsheet cells using built-in functions and common spreadsheet syntax. These cells are bound to the visual controls on the document page. At runtime, the spreadsheet is not visible to the end user; values of the variables on the document page are calculated accordingly when data is entered by the end user.

Figure 1 is an example interface representing a generic data source mapping. The data values in Figure 1-A data can be mapped to the HP Relate interactive document by direct drag-and-drop operation to the document spreadsheet. Data can also be copied from the paste buffer or pre-existing Excel spreadsheets can be imported.

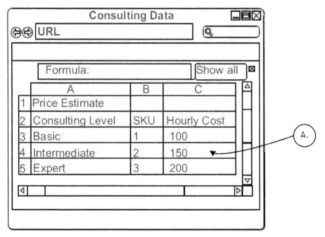

Figure 1. Generic Data Mapper.

Figure 2 illustrates the document spreadsheet interface. After the data has been mapped to the document's spreadsheet cells, a path representing the data's location within the data source is cached. When the data source is updated, each spreadsheet cell is updated with the new values. This is an important feature because the

binding is defined when the document's template is created, see Figure 2-A. When the document is instantiated with real customer data, the expected customer values are inserted into their appropriate cells and the cell's dependent document control is updated.

After data has been mapped to the document's spreadsheet, the document components controls (text boxes, label, lists, etc) are bound to the spreadsheet as demonstrated in Figure 2-B. The same drag-and-drop operations are used to bind controls to a cell or a set of cells. Once bound, data values in a cell are automatically visible in the control bound to the cell.

A document's spreadsheet cells can also contain functions which generate values dynamically. Document controls can be bound to cells with functions which makes the control's value completely derived data that may have been entered by a document editor.

Additionally, document control properties (visible, immutable, etc) can be bound to spreadsheet cells as shown in Figure 2-C. This adds the capability to completely drive an interactive document's look and feel through data and functions.

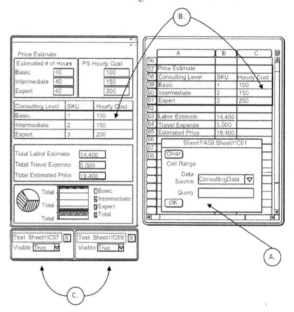

Figure 2. Document control and spreadsheet cell binding.

6. ADVANTAGES

Complexity of using scripting languages in interactive web document applications has forced a specialization of the interactive document designer, since the typical business user does have necessary programming language skills. Spreadsheet data model approach, on the contrary, uses a familiar functional logic paradigm, so it will significantly lower adoption barriers for business users. The suggested approach provides flexibility required in interactive document workflows, since business users can make necessary changes to the functional logic on the fly, with minimal IT or third party involvement. Another issue is the complexity in defining functional logic using a scripting programming language is the introduction of programming errors by business user. This approach eliminates code maintenance and deployment issues typical for programming environment.

In addition, spreadsheet model has proven to be an effective solution to perform calculations, validations, and data modeling for enterprise applications in many industries, including Finance, Insurance and Healthcare.

7. EVIDENCE THE SOLUTION WORKS

A pre-production of HP Relate was successfully deployed on the AWS cloud offering from Amazon. All HP Relate functionality is available and multiple client forms are available, including desktop, HP TouchPad, and Apple's iPad.

HP Relate is currently deployed and in Beta release.

8. NEXT STEPS

Active development is underway to build a SalesForce composite application for integrating with SalesForce customer data and additional Salesforce resources. The Beta is release is available for private download on the Salesforce App Exchange.

Development is actively researching Autonomy for leveraging IDOL and its ancillary functions to provide analytic services to HP Relate customers.

9. REFERENCES

[1] Microsoft Office, 2012. http://office.microsoft.com/en-us/

[2] Salesforce, 2012, http://www.salesforce.com/

[3] Kaushik, Avinash, 2010. Web Analytics 2.0. Wiley Publishing, Inc.

[4] Autonomy, 2012, IDOL10, http://idol.autonomy.com/

[5] Adobe, 2012, Lifecycle Forms, http://www.adobe.com/products/livecycle/forms/

[6] Mot, Bon; Mail Merge: Part I, October 2010, http://msdn.microsoft.com/en-us/library/aa140183(v=office.10).aspx

[7] Google, Google Docs, 2012, https://drive.google.com/start?authuser=0#home

[8] W3C, 1999, XML Path Language (XPath) Version 1.0, http://www.w3.org/TR/xpath/

[9] F IPS PUB 127-2, 1990, Database Language SQL

Structured and Fragmented Content in Collaborative XML Publishing Chains

Stéphane Crozat
Université de Technologie de Compiègne
Unité Ingénierie des Contenus et Savoirs

60200 Compiègne, France

stephane.crozat@utc.fr

ABSTRACT

In this paper, we present the main results of the C2M project through one of its operational deliverable: the Scenari4 collaborative editing and publishing system for XML content. The purpose of the C2M project was to design a system able to manage structured and fragmented contents - as XML *publishing chains* do - while providing collaborative possibilities - as Enterprise Content Management systems (*ECM*) do. The main issue is related to transclusion relationships which are massively used in XML publishing chains, in order to support repurposing without copying. This approach is not compatible with the classical way ECMs manage content, especially in terms of propagation of modifications, rights or transactions management. We propose two complementary solutions to manage two different levels of collaboration. The *workspace* is designed as a highly dynamic place able to deal with live fragments, linked together in a network, that can be easily updated at any time by any user. The *library* is a more static and more classical way to manage content, dedicated to *folder-documents*, which are XML frozen versions of sub-networks extracted from workspaces. While workspaces are dedicated to content elaboration and maintenance, libraries are places to store, to read, or to exchange stable documents. Scenari4 is released under FLOSS license and has been being used in several experimental and commercial contexts since the beginning of 2012.

Categories and Subject Descriptors

I.7.1 [**Document and Text Processing**]: Document and Text Editing – *Document Management, Version control*

General Terms

Design, Reliability, Experimentation.

Keywords

XML Publishing Chain, Structured Document, Fragmented Document, Transclusion, Repurposing, ECM.

1. INTRODUCTION

The C2M project (Multimedia Collaborative publishing Chains[1]) is a French research project funded by National Research Agency (ANR). It began in September 2009 and ended in March 2012. It was coordinated by the Université de Technologie de Compiègne (UTC) and gathered the companies Kelis and Amexio, the laboratories UMR-CNRS 7253 Heudiasyc and INRIA Rhône-Alpes, and the French National Audiovisual Institute (Ina). The C2M project addresses two important aspects of present mutations in the documentary field: the XML publishing chains and the Enterprise Content Management (ECM).

A *publishing chain* is a technology oriented toward the creation and publication of structured documents [1], *i.e.* documents described through their logical structure rather than their physical presentation. Early implementations in the 80s with LaTeX and SGML, addressed contexts with huge and strategic documentary issues (aeronautics, scientific publication...). Since 1998, XML and associated software progressively democratized the use of publishing chains in less specific areas. The interest of such an approach is to enhance automatic manipulation of digital document, in order to surpass the classical word processors, with writing control, polymorphic publication, reuse without copy (transclusion) or multimedia integration [3].

An *ECM* is a collaborative system dedicated to document management, born in the 80s as Document Management Systems (DMS), evolving in the 90s as Web CMS, and in the 2000s as ECM in companies, and "Web 2.0" in the mass market. The strength of these tools is to democratize digital content creation and circulation, anyone can now easily write and publish on line.

The aim of the C2M project is to articulate publishing chains and ECM in order to be able to produce highly qualitative documents, as expected by professional contexts (such as technical documentation, training...); along with collaborative practices organized though new cycles of information. The project is scientifically related to research in the field of document engineering, meaning systems designed to optimize technical manipulation and human interpretation of digital documents [2]. The project is based on the system Scenari[2], invented at UTC in 1999 and now edited by Kelis, and the main result of the project is the new version Scenari4, released in 2012.

---

[1] http://www.utc.fr/ics/c2m

[2] http://scenari-platform.org

2. REPURPOSING

2.1 Repurposing using transclusion

Repurposing is a documentary process consisting in building a new document with archives. Whereas in non digital approaches repurposing is more or less similar to an original creation, computer systems brought the possibility to *clone* a document fragment. Cloning helps in automating repurposing, and has become involved in most of document elaborations. But cloning engenders *redundancy* of information, and redundancy engenders lowering of information quality (by introducing inconsistencies). An alternative to cloning is *transclusion* [6], *i.e.* the multiple referencing of a single instance of a fragment via an address. This concept is poorly mobilized in ordinary writing tools and practices, whereas standards like XLink and Xpointer [9] exist and some technologies like HTML allow it in part (*iframe*). Transclusion is only used in some specific areas, such as technical documentation [4] where maintenance stakes are fundamental, or audiovisual where the cost of copy is high [5].

Transclusion and repurposing are one of the main basis of Scenari publishing chains : any content in the system is natively a network of fragments, some of these fragments being reused in several distinct documents.

2.2 Principles of transclusion

The document d1 contains an information i1 at the address &1, which is willing to be reused in a document d2 (see Figure 1). In the first case (cloning), i1 is copied in document d2 at the address &2, becoming a different instance i1' (even if identical to i1 at initialization, it will freely diverge from it in the future). In the second case (transclusion), d2' stores the address &1 of i1. A dedicated software will be able to resolve this reference, in order to integrate i1 in d2' when needed. So, logically d2 and d2' represent exactly the same content at the initialization. But the way information is stored is different, with deep impact on the *documentary nature* of the content. Cloning drives to two separate instances, which will follow their own separate evolutions: as traditional documents they can be separately transported, updated, destroyed... In the other hand, transclusion drives to a single digital instance acting as a network of dependent fragments. As a typical direct consequence, updating i1 in d1 will also modify d2'.

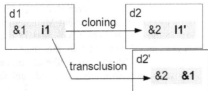

Figure 1. Example of repurposing by cloning or transclusion

2.3 Fragmented content and collaboration

Digitization intrinsically disturbs classical document definitions [7], since the document is a calculated reconstruction of a binary resource: what we read is *not* what is written on the support. Structured document reinforces this disruption by proposing several documentary forms from one single resource. We switch from a 1:1 to a 1:N relationship. Fragmented document reinforces it further more: document is now a reconstruction from a network of several resources, switching to a N:M relationship. The main problem is that the modification of a fragment in the network could be relevant for one document, but not for another sharing the same resource. The system has in charge to help the author in maintaining the consistency of the whole, with reasonable cognitive effort, so that not to handicap his writing process.

In a collaborative environment the management of the network can not be anymore held by one single person, each author is only aware of a part of the dependencies between fragments, it has to be the distributed responsibility of a group. The aim of the system is finally to be able to maintain the coherence of several documents represented by a single network of *live* fragments, in an environment in which several users are working at the same time. The difficulty of such a system is that it cannot be built on the classical solutions provided by ECM systems, since they were designed for non fragmented (and mainly not structured) documents.

3. MAIN ISSUES

3.1 Modification propagation

The first issue is related to the propagation of a modification one user does on one fragment at one moment. In Figure 2, Al changes fragment A in A'. But Bob uses also this fragment in B by transclusion, in a different context. The problem is that Al is not, in the general case, able to decide if A' is still consistent with B, moreover he may not be aware at all of the existence of this use of A by someone else. Only Bob can decide whether to use the live version A'; to remain linked to the dead version A (knowing he will not profit anymore from future updates); to copy A in A" in his context in order to manage it himself in the future; to merge A and A' in A" in order to use a part only of Al's modifications... Such a choice depends on the nature of the modification, a mistake correction is always to be propagated, a technical modification will always be context dependent. For instance if Al manages the technical documentation of a software and Bob the documentation of its installation in a specific company, the modification Al generates when the software evolves in a new version is to be propagated only when this version is installed.

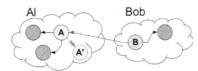

Figure 2. Example of modification propagation issue

3.2 Rights consistency

The second issue is related to the consistency of reading rights. There is no logical difference between a document composed with fragments integrated all together by copy, and fragments linked together by transclusion. In the example 1 of Figure 3, if B1 integrated B2 instead of referencing it, it would represent strictly the same content, the only difference being the future modification management, as seen before (in a totally static system, there would be no difference at all). Consequently it has no sense for Bob to give reading rights on B1 and not on B2. Similarly, in the example 2, if Al gives reading rights to Bob on his fragments, and Bob to Charlie on his owns, then Charlie's fragment C can reference B which can reference A, whereas Charlie has no right to read Al's fragments. These two cases show that classical document management can not directly apply to fragmented content for reading rights (there is no similar problem for writing rights management).

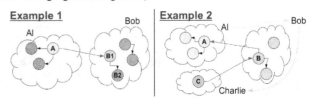

Figure 3. Example of reading rights consistency issues

3.3　Transactions management

A transaction is the way the system manages two (or more) concurrent accesses on one single peace of information. Inherited from databases management, we study here the main strategies exploited in ECM.

The *locking* makes unavailable (for writing and eventually for reading) a piece of information while it is under modification by a user. It can be either automatic or manual. It works well for short transactions on small pieces of information. In a fragmented network, the lock of a fragment should recursively lock every referenced fragment: the problem is that each modification in each fragment would potentially freeze the whole system, by propagation of locks.

A *working copy* is a temporary modifiable copy of a content destined to a single user, in order to isolate it and allow its modification independently of other user actions in the system. Once the modification is done, the working copy is released in the system, most of the time as a new version of the content it was originally copied from. If two users are allowed to ask for a working copy of the same content, a problem will occur when copies return to the system, since they will compete for replacing the original content. Solutions are mainly: *overwriting* of one version on the other, typically the first release is set as version x and the second as version x+1, eclipsing the previous; *merging* (automatic and/or manual) of the two copies in a single one representing changes of both; *forking*, each version is released as a distinct content. In fragmented context, we have to consider the working copies of networks rather than only isolated fragments.

The *check-in/check-out* process is a combination of both. It imposes one user to check-out a working copy, generally locking the original content at the same time, before being able to modify anything, and then check-in it when modifications are done, to make it available and unlock it.

4.　PROPOSITIONS

4.1　The workspace and the live network of fragments for intensive collaborative

To manage the issues raised by fragmentation, we define the concept of *workspace* as the only place in which transclusion is authorized. Its default behavior is: every modification is always propagated; every user of the workspace has reading rights on all the fragments of the workspace (not necessarily writing rights); and very permissive transactions are allowed, mainly based on forking and post managing of concurrent accesses. A workspace manages a single large *live network of fragments* created for multiple documents' publications. Collaboration and reuse outside the workspace will base on more classical approaches: management of consistent and isolated set of fragments, cloning and exchange of dead versions of content, traditional rights management (see extensive collaboration below).

So a workspace is *open* as everyone can see each others' work. In order to introduce privacy in the workspace, private fragments can be authorized, but they will *not* be allowed to be referenced until they are publicly opened to reading. The workspace is also *alive* since the network of fragments is constantly evolving thought each modification of each user. A workspace is to be considered as a highly collaborative space, dedicated to a team for a common project, only that way it is able to manage highly fragmented *and* dynamic content.

But even so, such a dynamic system must ensure the authors that, whatever happens, they will be able to find again a content in a state they had identified before, for instance in the state one had left it before other users modified it. Scenari4 propose two main

functions to protect content through dynamic modification: *automatic historization of each separate fragment*, and *manual versioning of network of fragments*. Every times a fragment is modified and saved, a new version is automatically created and the old one is kept as older version (as most wikis work). It ensures that any state of any fragment can be found again at any time by any user. Nevertheless, in highly fragmented context, finding back the state of a whole network looking for the right fragments one by one can be very difficult. The manual versioning of a network of fragments answers that: any user can at any moment ask the system to store a *snapshot* of a fragment along with all the fragments it references (recursively). The result is a dead (read only) sub-network (more precisely, a tree) of fragments, that can be consulted independently of the living network. On Figure 4, we visualize: on the left side some of the fragments that exist in the system; in the middle the current edition of the fragment "anomalies.chapter", which references the fragment "cfNoticesIndividuelles.chunk"; in the upper right frame the historization of changes that occur since the creation of fragment "anomalies.chapter", any previous state is so available for consultation; and in the lower right frame the versions "v1" and "v2" of the network composed with "anomalies.chapter" and its referenced fragments (for instance, "cfNoticesIndividuelles .chunk" will be available in the state it had when versions "v1" or "v2" of "anomalies.chapter" were set up).

Figure 4. Scenari4 structured and fragmented content editor

4.2　The library and the folder-document for extensive collaboration

The workspace is a place for a local and intensive collaboration, dedicated to a coherent team for a common project. Whereas the workspace is very dynamic, the *library* is on the contrary a place for exchanging stable versions of content. We propose the concept of *folder-document* (foldoc) as a frozen extract of the live network (a sub-network with a root fragment, *i.e.* a tree) packaged with some of its readable views. A foldoc is composed with (see Figure 5): a single generative form (GF), XML fragments linked together extracted from the workspace; the model (M), *i.e.* the formal code necessary for GF manipulation; eventually some pre-calculated transformed forms of the GF (TFi), for instance HTML, PDF, other XML format...; and metadata (MD) allowing standard identification of the foldoc (Dublin Core description for instance). Technically a foldoc is a ZIP package with an XML manifest file describing its content.

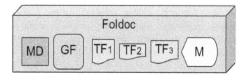

Figure 5. The folder-document (foldoc) structure

Libraries of foldocs are stable places to store and exchange content. GF and model make possible the future manipulation of the content by computers (to transform the content, to reintegrate it in a new workspace...), whereas metadata and TFs make the content searchable and readable by human beings. Foldocs are the mean to get back to a more classical grasp of documents, freezing and integrating parts of the networks that are living in workspaces. Libraries can so be implemented with classical ECMs (Alfreso, Documentum...), adding the function for introspecting foldoc packages. Integration of a native library in Scenari4 is also planned.

Figure 6. Workspaces and libraries

4.3 Other functions to manage transactions

Other functions have been designed and implemented to manage the issues related to transclusion, in order to maintain both the dynamism of the network and the consistency of each document represented in it. Their use is to be activated and parametrized depending on the context: Scenari4 is not a general ready-to-use system providing systematic functions, but mostly a generic framework to be specialized for specific organizational processes.

4.3.1 Automatic fragment locking

The system can automatically lock a fragment while it is edited in order to prevent concurrent modifications and unwilling overwriting or forking. Since it reduces dynamism, it is only available at the fragment level, to prevent from freezing huge parts of the network and locking many users' activities.

4.3.2 User information on system

The system can provide information on what other users do on fragments. It can help in monitoring what is occurring in the system. One simple example is an eye appearing in the XML editor when somebody else is reading the fragment, or a pen when he is editing it.

4.3.3 Diff and merge tools

Whereas it has not been integrated to the system yet, the C2M project permitted to research and prototype solutions to visualize differences between XML fragments and networks, and interactively merge them [8].

4.3.4 Planning and organizing of modifications

The system proposes the possibility to organize *a priori* the sequence of modifications by different users, and to program associated writing rights related to it. It is a more structured alternative, or complement, to permissive writing transaction processes.

4.3.5 The workspace derivation

To end with, the systems also provide a powerful mechanism of *derivation*. It is possible to create a virtual copy of a workspace, in order to be able to overwrite some fragments. The non modified fragments stay in the original workspace (and evolve synchronously with it), whereas overwritten ones (modified copies) are *informed* when their source has been modified (in order to be updated for instance). Derivation was originally used for content specialization in complex organizations (to complement transclusion, by re-introducing

"under control cloning"), and for language translation purposes. Associated with a committing possibility - the derivative fragment is allowed to replace the original one by a specific user commit action - workspace derivation can also be used to work on draft copies of the content (without locking).

5. CONCLUSION

The C2M project permits to achieve Scenari4 software, made available under FLOSS license. Scenari4 is a unique solution for collaborative edition of structured and fragmented documents, independently of any specific model. Scenari4 is already used by Kelis with his customers, and helped this company to win the project of re-factoring of the back office of *service-public.fr*.

R&D is also continued through several experiments running: with Ina for the republishing of radio archives; with Quick restaurants for managing a common base of documentation serving several services; with 2IE Burkina Faso water and environment institute for training contents; or with Costech, the human sciences laboratory of UTC, for a scientific journal. We also designed two demonstrators: Graphene for technical documentation, and Webradio2 for multimedia publication (conferences, documentaries...).

Theoretical research is also pursued through: formalization of collaborative processes and context adaptation of publishing chains; elaboration of philological tools to help authors of fragmented and structured content to take decisions while working in highly dynamic workspaces; and document conceptual and logical modeling formalisms, tools and patterns for publishing chains design.

6. ACKNOWLEDGMENTS

Our thanks to the ANR for funding C2M project, to C2M partners for their collaboration, and to Sylvain Spinelli for his great technical and conceptual work on Scenari4.

7. REFERENCES

[1] André J., Furuta R., Quint V. (1989). *Structured documents*. Cambridge University Press.

[2] Bachimont B. (2007). *Ingénierie des connaissances et des contenus : le numérique entre ontologies et documents*. Lavoisier. Hermès.

[3] Crozat S. (2007). *Scenari, la chaîne éditoriale libre*. Eyrolles.

[4] DITA (2010). *Darwin Information Typing Architecture (DITA) Version 1.2*. OASIS standard. DOI=http://docs.oasis-open.org/dita/v1.2/spec/DITA1.2-spec.html.

[5] Gaillard L. (2010). *Modélisation rhétorique pour la publication de discours multimédias : applications audiovisuelles*. Thèse de doctorat de l'UTC.

[6] Nelson, T. H. (1981). *Literary Machines*. Mindful Press.

[7] Pédauque R. T. (2005). *Le texte en jeu : Permanence et transformations du document*. DOI=http://archivesic.ccsd.cnrs.fr/docs/00/06/26/01/PDF/sic_00001401.pdf.

[8] Vu X. T., Morizet-Mahoudeaux P., Geurts J., Crozat S. (2011). Extension d'un algorithme Diff & Merge au Merge Interactif de documents structurés. *Proceedings of CIDE.14*, Rabat, Maroc.

[9] Wilde E., Lowe D. (2002). *XPath, XLink, XPointer, and XML: A practical guide to Web hyperlinking and transclusion*. Pearson Education.

Typesetting Multiple Interacting Streams

Blanca Mancilla
Computer Science Engineering
UNSW SYDNEY NSW 2052
Australia
mancilla@cse.unsw.edu.au

Jarryd P. Beck
Computer Science Engineering
UNSW SYDNEY NSW 2052
Australia
jarrydb@cse.unsw.edu.au

John Plaice
Computer Science Engineering
UNSW SYDNEY NSW 2052
Australia
plaice@cse.unsw.edu.au

ABSTRACT

We present a new means for specifying multiple interacting streams, as is needed for documents with multiple systems of notes, side-by-side translations, and critical editions. Each stream is treated as a sequence of components, and anchors are used in the concrete syntax to define reference points used by other streams. When these streams are loaded into memory, the anchors simply become iterators in a container. We present a set of algorithms for the typesetting of multiple streams of text, each with multiple streams of floats and footnotes.

Categories and Subject Descriptors

E.2 [**Data**]: Data Storage Representations—*Linked representations*; J.7 [**Computer Applications**]: Computers in Other Systems—*Publishing*

Keywords

Typesetting, Markup and markdown mechanisms, Critical editions, Parallel editions

1. INTRODUCTION

This paper proposes a simple model for the specification of documents composed of multiple interacting streams and illustrates the use of this model with a series of simple (typesetting) algorithms for segmenting these streams so that corresponding parts of the different streams can be placed on the same page. This model has been explicitly designed for the specification, manipulation and typesetting of parallel editions, in a manner that allows the layout of footnotes, critical apparatus, floats, running commentaries and parallel texts.

In this model, a document consists of a set of streams of "text", indexed by the natural numbers. For each kind of note or float, a new stream is used, and call-out links from the main text are placed for each note or float. Similarly, for each kind of commentary, a new stream is used, but this

time call-out links from the commentary stream are placed to the main text.

As an example application, consider a document with two texts, the second one a running commentary on the first, where the first text includes figures and two levels of footnotes and where the second text has its own footnotes. That document would then have six interacting streams:

1. Text 1, with call-outs to figures, level-1 footnotes and level-2 footnotes.

2. Figures for Text 1.

3. Level-1 footnotes for Text 1, with call-outs to level-2 footnotes.

4. Level-2 footnotes, called out from Text 1 and its level-1 footnotes.

5. Text 2, with call-outs to Text 1 and to its own level-1 footnotes.

6. Level-1 footnotes for Text 2.

In general, this document, if printed, would not fit on a single page. Printing onto several pages would then require that, for each page, it be decided how much of each of the six streams would appear. If we assume a single column is being used, then each page would look like this:

Text 1
Images for Text 1
Level-1 footnotes for Text 1
Level-2 footnotes for Text 1
Text 2
Level-1 footnotes for Text 2

(Note that in this paper, we do not concern ourselves for the details of the layout on a given page.)

This multi-stream segmentation must be undertaken by an algorithm which places called-out material on the same page, or as close as possible, to the corresponding calling-out material. The algorithms presented in this paper are all first-fit.

The paper consists of three parts. First, we present the model from the inside out, i.e., from the point of view of the data structures that would be used inside the programs manipulating the model. Second, we present how this internal model can be represented in text files edited with normal text editors. Third, we present a number of typesetting algorithms to do this parallel segmentation described above.

2. THE INTERNAL MODEL

The internal model, i.e., the data structures that would be seen inside a language such as C++, is what holds this paper together. In this model, a document is a set of named streams, one of them being considered the main stream. A stream is a triple (a, b, c), where

- a is a zero-based array of *units* representing the text: a unit is in most cases a Unicode character, but it can also be some complex hierarchical structure of its own, such as a JPEG image, a mathematical formula, or a stroke definition for a Chinese character not included in Unicode. In the algorithms presented below, the units are lines of typeset text.

- b is a mapping from *anchors* to *positions* in the array a: an anchor is a string designating a position. In turn, a position is an interval $[i_0, i_1)$, i.e., all of the indices i such that $i_0 \leq i < i_1$; if $i_0 = i_1$, the position corresponds to the specific point just prior to unit $a[i_0]$.

- c is an ordered sequence of *call-outs* to this or other streams: a call-out is a triple (p, q, r) where p is an anchor defined in b, q is the *call-out instruction* and r is a set of zero or more anchors, in this stream, in other streams, or in other documents. The set of call-out instructions is not bounded: it can include font settings, footnote call-outs, commentary call-ins, float call-outs, and so on.

This structure is incredibly flexible, and in no way forces a canonical representation for a given document. Even for a simple text, consisting just of a sequence of paragraphs with no embellishments, footnotes or floats, there are different possibilities for representing that document: the array of units could simply be the sequence of letters, spaces and punctuation, and the paragraphing structure would then be described using call-outs. On the other hand, the units could be the paragraphs themselves, where each paragraph is itself an array whose units are sentences, each of which is an array whose units are punctuation, spaces and words, each of the latter being an array with Unicode characters as units.

Since the positions correspond to intervals, this allows, for example, a footnote or a figure to be attached to an entire region of a text, rather than just to a specific point.

3. EMBEDDING THE MARKUP

The internal model of streams presented in the previous section leads to an obvious way of inputting a document: for each stream, there are three files, the first containing the text, the second specifying the anchors, and the third specifying the call-outs. This approach is suitable when the files are the output of an automatic process converting documents in other formats into this one. However, manually manipulating the text file would create inconsistencies in the anchor-specification file. Hence, attempting to simultaneously edit the three files would be a non-trivial operation for a typical user.

In this section, we first present the obvious model, then show how this model can be rewritten using markup embedded right in the text of a stream, reducing the number of streams needed for the purposes of typing. We then examine, without providing solutions, what needs to be done for more complicated document structures. The notation we use is LaTeX-like, but there is nothing preventing the use of another notation, such as XML.

3.1 The linearized internal model

A document is a file, containing a list of streams. The first one is considered the main one. Each stream is three files, so stream S corresponds to files S_text, S_anchors and S_callouts.

The S_text file contains the text of the stream. A "plain text" is simply a sequence of Unicode characters. The following characters must be escaped by a backslash (\): \, [,], { and }. Should there be more than simple text, then occurrences of

$$\texttt{\textbackslash unit}\{type\}\{string\}$$

can be used to insert units with their own structure, defined according to the *type*.

The S_anchors file is a sequence of lines, each of the form

$$\texttt{\textbackslash defanchor}[name]\{number\}\{number\}$$

This declaration states that this anchor corresponds to the position designated by the two numbers.

The S_callouts file is different because we do not know the full set of possible types of call-outs, whose structure is as follows

$$\texttt{\textbackslash callout}[name]\{type\}\{anchor, \ldots, anchor\}$$

Here *name* is the name of the anchor in the current stream that the call-out is referring to. As for the *anchor* arguments, these are anchors in this stream or in other streams, and their meaning depends on the *type* of the call-out.

Each *anchor* is a qualified name, where z means anchor z in the current stream, $y.z$ means anchor z in stream y, and $x.y.z$ means anchor z in stream y in document x.

3.2 The embedded model

The three files making up a stream can actually be combined into one. Below we describe how to embed the anchor file into the text file.

If we have an anchor *name* at a specific point (the beginning and end of the anchor coincide), then we simply need to insert

$$\texttt{\textbackslash anchor}[name]$$

at the right point in the text stream. If the start and end points of the anchor differ, then the start point is declared with

$$\texttt{\textbackslash beginanchor}[name]$$

and the end point is declared with

$$\texttt{\textbackslash endanchor}[name]$$

Note that this approach allows two anchors to overlap each other, with the start point of a second anchor preceding the end point of a first anchor, as the anchors in no way create any sort of nesting of the content of the text. Note that with no overlapping anchors, the [name] is not necessary for the \endanchor.

Embedding the call-out file into the text file can be done similarly. To add a call-out, introducing the anchor *name* at a specific spot, we write

$$\texttt{\textbackslash callout}[name]\{type\}\{anchor, \ldots, anchor\}$$

For a call-out whose anchor's start and end points differ, then we write

\begincallout[*name*]{*type*}{*anchor*, ..., *anchor*}

for the start point and

\endcallout[*name*]

for the end point. Once again, if there is no overlapping of anchors, the [*name*] is not necessary for the \endcallout.

3.3 Automatic generation of markup

It should be understood that the document model described above is probably not sufficient to cover the full complexity of the critical-edition workflow, including collating, editing and typesetting. Nevertheless, even documents taking advantage of the full power of TEI [1] need to be translated, either manually or automatically, to some structure that is typesettable. We believe that our model is both simple and general. Further research will determine how best to do this kind of automatic translation, so that the full typesetting process can be automated.

4. TYPESETTING

We consider in this section how to typeset a document with multiple text streams running in parallel to each other, each with multiple float and footnote streams, the latter arranged hierarchically. We will suppose for the purposes of this presentation that text has already been typeset and split into lines, that lines are all of a fixed width, that individual floats are a fixed size and are the width of the lines, and that the key algorithm to be developed is page breaking, i.e., the splitting of the different typeset streams to determine what part of which streams goes on which pages.

We consider that the proper resolution of this problem is the basis for even more complex typesetting. This algorithm could be combined with per-page layout algorithms, which once given a collection of material to be placed on a given page, could completely re-typeset it, and place it as appropriate.

4.1 The call-outs

For the purposes of this presentation, we have three kinds of call-out: the footnote, the float, and the commentary. Here are the constraints for these three kinds of call-out.

A footnote call-out connects a piece of text (here, a sequence of lines) in the main stream to a piece of text in a footnote stream. The constraint is that the last line in the piece of text from the main stream must appear on the same page as the first line of the piece of text appearing in the footnote stream.

A float call-out states that a text in the float stream must appear as a single block on a page (inclusively) between the page upon which the starting line of the piece of text in the main stream appears and the page upon which the ending line of the piece of text in the main stream appears.

A commentary call-out states that the starting line of the calling text from one stream and the starting line of the called text from another stream must appear on the same page, and the same holds true for the ending lines.

4.2 The algorithms

We will consider how to do the typesetting of these documents in an incremental manner, examining more and more call-outs, producing more and more sophisticated algorithms. We start with plain text, then add footnotes, then floats, then deal with parallel streams.

4.2.1 One stream, no call-outs

Our document consists of exactly one text stream, with text "by the kilometre". There are no footnotes, no floats, and no commentaries.

The typesetting algorithm is a standard greedy algorithm. The first line is placed onto the first page. Should the next line fit onto the same page, it is added. This process is repeated until no more lines can be added to this page. This page is then shipped out and the algorithm then continues with the next line becoming the first line, until there are no more lines to add to pages.

4.2.2 One main text stream, multiple footnote levels

Our document consists of exactly one text stream, in which call-outs appear to the first footnote stream. Both the text and the first footnote stream may have call-outs to the second footnote stream, and so on to the last footnote stream.

The typesetting algorithm is a variant of the one in §4.2.1. When a line from the main text stream is being considered for being added to a page, one must also consider the minimum vertical space from the footnote streams that must be added as well, should the line being added to the main stream have a call-out to a footnote.

Should a line have a call-out, then the first line of the called-out footnote must also appear. Should this called-out footnote also call out another footnote, then the first line of that other called-out footnote must also be added, and so on. If there is not sufficient room for all these lines, then they will all have to go on to the next page.

The currently called footnotes that have not yet been completely added to a page are called active footnotes. We then continue by adding lines from the deepest level of active footnote. Should there be no more, we move back up a level. Should a page break occur while there are active footnotes, we can consider the next page to be "being filled in from the bottom". Once there are no more footnotes, we continue to add the main text from the top.

4.2.3 One main text stream, multiple float streams

Our document consists of a main text stream with call-outs to multiple streams of floats (figures, tables, diagrams, etc.) All of the float streams are considered to be at the same level. A float call-out becomes active as soon as the starting point of the anchor in the main text stream has been reached on some page, and must be placed on a page prior to that anchor's end point being encountered.

Therefore, at any given moment there is a set of active floats to be placed as soon as possible. These floats are ordered in terms of importance, using the following 3-level order: the start point of the call-out, the end point of the call-out, the size of the floats.

The algorithm proceeds as follows. If any floats are active, an attempt is made to place the first—according to the order given above—on the current page. Should this float not fit, the test is repeated with the next float in the set of active floats, according to the aforementioned order; if that float is not smaller than the first float, it is ignored. As soon as a float is found to fit, it is added and removed from the set of active floats. Should none fit, the page is filled with text.

This algorithm can be adapted naturally to include multiple levels of footnotes, some of which might get called out from the floats themselves, as well as the forbidding of re-ordering floats within a stream.

4.2.4 Multiple main text streams

Our document consists of a set of text streams which are considered to be of equal importance from the typesetting point of view. One stream might be considered to be the main one, and so would go at the top of the page. However, this in no way influences the algorithm.

The problem here is to split every page vertically so that each stream gets a chance to have material placed on each page. The exact amount of material that a given stream will place on a given page can be quite variable, and is guided by the placement of the call-outs. Here a call-out can be to multiple streams simultaneously, stating that the text corresponding to the anchor in this stream is synchronized with the text in the corresponding anchors of the corresponding streams. We assume that there is no text in any stream which is not tied to the others through call-outs.

The algorithm begins on the first page, where the starting points of all of the texts are aligned. An estimate of the size of each of the streams up to the end point of the current anchor is made; from this estimate, a fraction of 1 is given to each of the streams. So now, each stream will attempt to place its material into its given fraction of successive pages. Should each of the streams finish on the same page, then the algorithm moves on to the next set of anchors. Should one stream take fewer or more pages than the others, then a recalibration algorithm is used to re-estimate the fractions for each stream, and the process is repeated. Should this algorithm not converge, the number of iterations could be bounded beforehand.

This algorithm can be extended to multiple streams of text, each with floats and footnotes. However, it does become more complicated because some floats might end up being bigger than the fraction of a page that is allocated to the text stream that calls out the float. In this situation, that stream would concede some of the space for that page to the other streams and would in turn be granted more space on the next page. Within the area allocated for a given stream on a given page, the placement of footnotes and floats is done as per the above algorithms.

4.2.5 Multiple-pass algorithms

It is common that footnotes, floats, lines, pages and so on are numbered when they are mentioned in a text. This numbering, and other forms of cross referencing, usually requires the generation of text that itself must be typeset; however, this generation can only take place during the typesetting process itself.

Therefore, all the algorithms given above can correspond to a single step in a multi-step iterative algorithm, where the exact streams of text used in one step are generated from both the source and the typeset material from the previous step. In the first step, of course, the typeset material from the previous step is empty.

5. CONCLUSION

The main contribution of this paper is a model for specifying complex documents, composed of multiple interacting streams. This model is very simple, yet sufficiently power-ful for a wide variety of parallel and critical editions. This model can be used directly, or could be the target of an (semi-)automatic translation from some more complex format, such as TEI.

In order to focus on the proposed model, for purposes of clarity, in this paper, we have dealt with only relatively simple final layouts. A perusal of older critical editions, such as Talmuds or parallel translations of ancient texts [2, 3], with complicated systems of footnotes and margin notes, would demonstrate the need for careful calculation of area per stream per page, in order to compute the exact shape of each stream's output for that page, and how these shapes fit together, forming one single beautiful page.

We believe that the algorithms presented in this paper, although simple, can be adapted to take into account much more complex phenomena. In particular, we think that the algorithms can be extended to involve text composed of sequences of characters, rather than lines, and that the float placement algorithms do not need to be first-fit. Most relevant in the literature is the work by Hurst, Marriott and Moulder [4, 5, 6].

The method for specifying a document with multiple interacting streams can be extended to a more general model of document with multiple components, each of which is indexable, but where the index is not necessarily a natural number. Possible uses of this general model include tables, musical staves, graphics, audio, video.

It should be noted that our model of multiple interacting streams is just a special case of a factory with multiple assembly lines, where, instead of pages, the synchronization points are time instants. If we extract out the document part, this describes a software engineering process with all of the complexities of workflow. This remark should not be surprising, given that the first modern industrial process with clear division of tasks was Gutenberg's printing press.

Finally, we believe that the concept of critical edition, so important for the revival of ancient Classical culture, is highly relevant to today's world of collaborative blogs with multiple levels of commenting and cross-referencing to other documents and blogs.

6. REFERENCES

[1] TEI, Text Encoding Initiative.
http://www.tei-c.org.

[2] John Lavagnino and Dominik Wujastyk. EDMAC, Critical Edition Typesetting.
http://www.tug.org/edmac.

[3] Yannis Haralambous. Unicode, XML, TEI, Ω and Scholarly Documents. In *16th International Unicode Conference, Amsterdam, The Netherlands*. Unicode Consortium, 2000.

[4] Nathan Hurst and Kim Marriott. Satisficing scrolls: a shortcut to satisfactory layout. In *8th ACM Symposium on Document Engineering*, pp.131-140, 2008.

[5] Nathan Hurst and Kim Marriott. Approximating text by its area. In *7th ACM Symposium on Document Engineering*, pp.147-150, 2007.

[6] Kim Marriott, Peter Moulder and Nathan Hurst. Automatic float placement in multi-colum documents. In *7th ACM Symposium on Document Engineering*, pp.125-134, 2007.

An Inheritance Model for Documents in Web Applications with Sydonie *

Jean-Marc Lecarpentier, Pierre-Yves Buard, Hervé Le Crosnier, Romain Brixtel
GREYC - CNRS UMR 6072
Université de Caen - Basse-Normandie
{firstname.lastname}@unicaen.fr

ABSTRACT

Each web site has to manage documents tailored for its specific needs. When building applications with a specific document model, web developers must make a choice: build from scratch or use existing tools with the need to accomodate the model. We propose an inheritance model for documents, implemented in the Sydonie open source web development framework. It offers a flexible environment to create classes of documents. Sydonie's document model uses entity nodes inspired by the Functional Requirements for Bibliographics Records (FRBR). Document content and metadata are modeled using a set of relations between entity nodes and attribute objects. Classes of documents or attribute types can be defined through a declarative XML file. Our inheritance model provides the possibility to define them at the framework level, application profile level or application level. This demonstration explains the document definition process and inheritance model implemented in the framework and gives several examples of its advantages.

Categories and Subject Descriptors

H.3.2 [**Information Systems**]: Information Storage; H.5.4 [**Information Systems**]: Hypertext/Hypermedia—*Architectures*; I.7.1 [**Document and Text Processing**]: Document and Text Editing—*Document Management*; J.7 [**Computers in Other Systems**]: Publishing

General Terms

Design, Documentation

Keywords

Document Management System, Document Model, Composite Documents, Web Development Framework

*Research work funded by the Conseil Régional de Basse-Normandie with the CPER program, the European Council with the FEDER program, and the TGE-Adonis.

1. INTRODUCTION

Content Management Systems (CMS) are widely used to manage web sites. They provide functionalities to easily create and publish content. Predefined document types and ready-to-use modules allow for customization of the web site or application. CMS usually focus on content creation and publication. With a different approach, Web development frameworks provide tools to help creating web sites or applications. Frameworks provide functionalities to avoid coding common tasks, such as database access, session management, templating, etc. While very useful, these tools do not provide a model for documents and their management. On the other hand, library systems focus on document management, in particular on document metadata. However, they do not manage the content of documents.

In this paper, we present Sydonie, an open source web application framework implemented in PHP. Sydonie takes its roots in the web development community and the library world. Sydonie provides a document model to manage multilingual composite documents. A document inheritance model provides web designers with a flexible development environment.

The remainder of this paper is structured as follows. The next section gives an overview of how some existing CMS or frameworks manage documents and the lessons learnt. Section 3 presents Sydonie's document model, its internal data model and how classes of documents are defined. Section 4 introduces the framework's inheritance model for the creation of custom classes of documents. Examples are given in Section 5. Finally, Section 6 concludes this article.

2. CMS, FRAMEWORKS AND DOCUMENTS

As the name indicates, Content Management Systems deal with *content*. With the Drupal CMS [2], the CCK module [1] allows web site administrators to customize the content of entities by associating field names to a type of content. The administrator builds new content types on top of the core system by adding new fields. In order to create a custom application, a developer will first make his application model fit into the CMS model.

On the other hand, frameworks provide more flexibility by letting the developer design the classes for the application, therefore reflecting the application model. For example, when using Symfony [4], a PHP web development framework, a document type corresponds to a class declaration, with formatted comments to define the relationships to other objects.

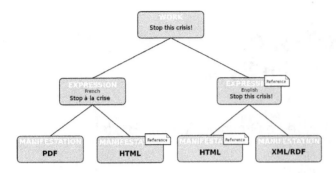

Figure 1: A Manifestation is an embodiment of an Expression of a Work

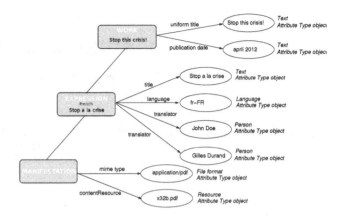

Figure 2: Branch of a document with its attributes

These systems are well designed to manage content, but are not made to manage *documents*. In the above cases, the system manages content components but does not consider the set of components as a document entity. The approach is to define a document as the rendition of some content [7], where a document is similar to the web page displayed to a user. Using an different approach, a library system considers a document to be a reference card including metadata and a pointer to the document itself through some kind of identifier. These systems manage document metadata but not their content.

We need an hybrid approach to define and manage digital documents. Documents on the web should not be treated as mere content, but as an information container where the information is both content and metadata. The next section presents how the Sydonie framework implements this concept.

3. SYDONIE

Sydonie, a Document Management System for Publishing on the Web[1], is a web development framework [3]. Sydonie is developed within the University of Caen Basse-Normandie, in conjunction with C&F_éditions[2], a publishing partner developing online services based on Sydonie. Sydonie[3] is open source software made available under a GPL license. Implemented in PHP and relying on a mySQL database, Sydonie can run on any basic LAMP server. This section introduces the core concepts of the framework.

3.1 Document model

From the CMS world, Sydonie's document model inherits the approach of using an online editing system to produce a web rendering document (i.e. the HTML version of a document). From the library world, it uses the metadata model and the Functional Requirements for Bibliographic Records (FRBR) [6]. The FRBR conceptual model introduces three groups of entities to capture bibliographic data. FRBR group 1 contains four hierarchical entity levels *Work*, *Expression*, *Manifestation* and *Item* which represent the different aspects of intellectual or artistic works.

Using the guidelines for group 1 entities from the FRBR report, Sydonie defines a document model with the entity

---

[1]In French: SYstème de gestion de Documents Numériques pour l'Internet et l'Édition
[2]http://cfeditions.com
[3]http://sydonie.net, under construction

levels Work, Expression and Manifestation to represent intellectual or physical aspects of a document. Sydonie's model considers a document as the complete tree, as shown in figure 1. A document is thus defined by a tree composed of Work, Expression and Manifestation entity nodes. The set of data attached to each node represents a document's data and metadata. Language negotiation and content negotiation are used to determine which Manifestation is to be served to a user. This process is also used within composite documents [5].

3.2 Document attributes

In order to manage any kind of application, a framework must be able to manage different kinds of documents. Using Sydonie's document model, a class of document is the definition of what information each entity level may contain. The kind of information associated to each node may vary depending on the class of document.

To provide a generic way to manage the information attached to a node, Sydonie uses an attribute-value based model. The framework provides a data structure that can adapt to any kind of information to be attached to a node. Each node has a list of attributes where the attribute points to an object that models the attached information. Within the framework, similarly to RDF, attributes are triples (subject, predicate, object) where:

- subject is an instance of a document entity node, i.e. a Work, Expression or Manifestation node;

- predicate is the name of the attribute, i.e. the name of the relation;

- object is the value. It is an object (in the OO sense). Its class models the information it represents. It can also be a list of objects when a predicate represents multiple values.

Figure 2 illustrates this model in the case of an article. The flexibility of the approach resides in the fact that entity nodes are generic objects used by all classes of documents. The `DocumentEntity` class represents a node of the document tree (i.e. either a Work, Expression or Manifestation node). The list of attributes is managed at the framework level and is composed of an array of attributes objects representing the named relations between a document entity and some data. The associated data are instances of objects

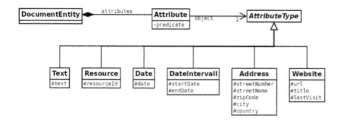

Figure 3: Relations between entity nodes (Work, Expression or Manifestation) and attribute types

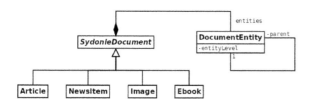

Figure 4: SydonieDocument abstract class and some document types

inheriting from an `AttributeType` abstract class. These children classes can model scalar data, such as text or integer, or more complex structures, such as a price or an address for example. Figure 3 shows the relations between entity nodes and `AttributeType` children classes. The framework provides predefined `AttributeType` classes. New types can be defined at the application level, allowing any document type to naturally "fit in" Sydonie's document model.

To create a class of documents, a developer needs to define what `AttributeType` objects each entity level may accept. The next section shows how to create classes of documents in a declarative manner.

3.3 Classes of documents

As explained in section 3.1, a document is a tree of entity nodes linked to `AttributeType` objects. The framework provides the model and routines for document reification through the abstract class `SydonieDocument`. The `SydonieDocument` class is the base class for all documents in Sydonie. It defines the tree structure of documents, the articulation between document entities (Work, Expression or Manifestation nodes), their attributes and the `AttributeType` objects that contain the document's data and metadata. Figure 4 shows the relation between the `SydonieDocument` and `DocumentEntity` classes. Any class of documents must inherit from `SydonieDocument`. Similarly to `AttributeType` objects, the framework provides some predefined classes of documents, as shown in figure 4.

A class of documents is the definition of what data each entity level nodes may contain. This information, the entity level and the type of data each attribute points to, must be defined in order for the framework to manage the document reification. An XML configuration file defines the needed information in a declarative way, therefore allowing a developer to learn and create a class of documents from existing examples. An example of configuration file is shown in figure 5. To declare a class of document, the configuration file specifies for each possible attribute: the predicate (name of the attribute); the entity level (Work, Expression or Manifestation); the multiplicity (the attribute can ap-

```
<configuration>
  <class>Article</class>
  <extends>SydonieDocument</extends>
  <attribute entityLevel="expression" minOccur="1"
                                      maxOccur="1" >
     <predicate>title</predicate>
     <objectClass>Text</objectClass>
  </attribute>
  <attribute entityLevel="work" minOccur="0"
                                maxOccur="1000" >
     <predicate>link</predicate>
     <objectClass>Website</objectClass>
     <!-- list mandatory information of
          the AttributeType object.
          Here, only the url property of a Website
          object will be mandatory   -->
     <mandatoryProp><prop>url</prop></mandatoryProp>
  </attribute>
</configuration>
```

Figure 5: Example of configuration file for an `Article` class of documents

pear 0, 1 or more times); the `AttributeType` class that contains the object value and the mandatory information the `AttributeType` will require.

Even though the XML file is simple to create, a developer must be able to reuse already defined classes of documents. Sydonie's architecture allows component reuse and customization. Existing classes of documents can be reused and finely tuned using Sydonie's inheritance model, introduced in the next section.

4. INHERITANCE MODEL

Sydonie uses its own inheritance model to determine, at the application level, the information a document may contain. A class of documents can be defined at the framework level or at the application level. Classic object oriented inheritance is not sufficient to manage document definition. For example, the framework's document layer defines a basic `Article` class of documents. Let us suppose that, when creating an application, a developer needs to use article documents with more information (i.e. more attributes). Using classic object oriented inheritance, one could create a `MyArticle` class of documents that inherits from the `Article` class. The `MyArticle` class would then define the changes made to the parent class. The trouble would appear when the developer wishes to reuse some already defined routines for `Article` documents: since `MyArticle` is a different document class, these routines may not work any more. A simple example is listing `Articles`: the framework would then list only the `Article` instances, but not `MyArticle` instances. This behavior would be fine if the application needs a *new* class of documents, but not if it only needs to *alter* an existing class.

In order to allow alteration as shown in the above example, Sydonie provides its own inheritance model. The classic object oriented inheritance model is used to allow the creation of new classes of documents. These classes inherit the properties of their parent class and add or alter properties. Sydonie's inheritance model adds new features to allow fine tuning of existing classes of documents. In our example, the `Article` class inherits the abstract base class `SydonieDocument` introduced in section 3.3. At the framework level, `SydonieDocument` declares common attributes to all classes of documents: `firstPublished` at the Work level, `title` and `language` at the Expression level and `content-`

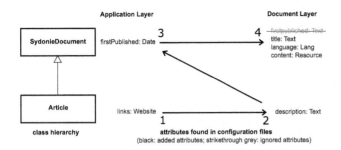

Figure 6: Sydonie's inheritance model

Resource at the Manifestation level. This information is specified in SydonieDocument's configuration file. At the framework level, the Article class adds the description attribute at the Expression level, using classic inheritance (i.e. by specifying that Article inherits SydonieDocument as illustrated by figure 4). Using the inheritance declaration, the framework compiles these two files to define the Article class.

Sydonie's inheritance model, shown in figure 6, named "cascading" inheritance, allows a web designer to enhance the already defined Article class. To alter the definition of Article in the application layer, the developer creates a configuration file for the Article class. The framework will process this file on top of the existing one. For example, the application needs Article documents to have the firstPublished attribute to be a Date attribute type object instead of Text, and to have a links attribute to add references to web sites (using the Website attribute type). The application will only need to specify the changes to firstPublished and the addition of a links attribute to the Article class of documents. Whenever the application uses an Article document, the framework will check the presence of a configuration file for each class and at each level, going from child to parent class and from application level to framework level. For each file, it will add the defined attributes that are not defined yet. It is important to note that, if firstPublished is specified as Date in the SydonieDocument configuration file in this application (instead of the Article configuration), then the firstPublished attribute type would be a Date for *all* classes of documents in the application built, as shown in figure 6.

5. CASE STUDY

The proposed model and architecture are implemented in the framework and have been tested with several applications. The Craham[4] is a historical and archaeological research unit at the University of Caen Basse-Normandie. It manages a collection of photographs of archaeological sites, and an application was built with Sydonie to manage the digital versions of the scanned slides[5]. It mostly relies on the framework's image class and uses Sydonie's metadata model and management within images using XMP. This application uses the framework's image class of documents, enhancing its default model with attributes to reflect on the specific data needed (e.g. archeological site, location, etc.).

C&Féditions created two applications using Sydonie. Polifile[6] is an application to create eBooks online using a WYSI-WYG editor. It relies on Sydonie to manage users, and uses Sydonie's document layer for eBooks and images. In the application layer, it interacts with an ePub library to create ePub files. *Mémoire des Catastrophes*[7] is an application to collect witness stories about disasters that occured in France. It uses Sydonie's document layer for images and articles. In the application layer, classes of documents were created to model disasters and witness stories. The next version of the site will use the application profile layer to provide a blog. A third application, companion website of the Net.Lang book[8], is currently under development.

6. CONCLUSIONS

In this paper, we present two main contributions. First, we propose a document model implemented in the Sydonie web development framework. Sydonie uses a tree model based on FRBR and a RDF-like structure to allow documents to contain any kind of information. Document content and metadata are stored at different entity levels to express their level of abstraction. Then, we propose an architecture and development model. The layered architecture and cascading inheritance model is applied for classes of documents, and also for templates, form bindings and interactions, as well as for actions on documents. Sydonie's model focuses on providing web designers with document and application models that they can easily adapt to their specific needs.

7. REFERENCES

[1] Drupal cck module, 2012.
[2] Drupal open source cms, 2012.
[3] Sydonie framework, 2012.
[4] Symfony framework, 2012.
[5] J.-M. Lecarpentier, C. Bazin, and H. Le Crosnier. Multilingual composite document management framework for the internet: an frbr approach. In *Proceedings of DocEng 2010*, page 13, Sept. 2010.
[6] O. Madison. *Functional Requirements for Bibliographic Records*. K. G. Saur, Munich, Germany, 1998.
[7] R. T. Pédauque. *Le document à la lumière du numérique*. C&F éditions, 2006.

---

[4]http://www.unicaen.fr/crahm/
[5]http://craham.info.unicaen.fr (under development)

---

[6]http://polifile.fr
[7]http://memoiredescatastrophes.org
[8]http://www.net-lang.net

500 Year Documentation

Francis T. Marchese
Pace University
Computer Science Department
New York, NY 10038
1 212 346 1803

fmarchese@pace.edu

Maninder Pal Kaur Shergill
Pace University
Computer Science Department
New York, NY 10038

ms34286n@pace.edu

ABSTRACT

Museum visitors today can regularly view 500 year old art by Renaissance masters. Will visitors to museums 500 years in the future be able to see the work of digital artists from the early 21st century? This paper considers the real problem of conserving interactive digital artwork for museum installation in the far distant future by exploring the requirements for creating documentation that will support an artwork's adaptation to future technology. In effect, this documentation must survive as long as the artwork itself – effectively, in perpetuity. A proposal is made for the use of software engineering methodologies as solutions for designing this documentation.

Categories and Subject Descriptors

D.2.7 [**Software Engineering**]: Distribution, Maintenance, and Enhancement - *documentation; restructuring, reverse engineering, and reengineering.*

General Terms

Documentation, Design, Management.

Keywords

Digital art, conservation, requirements engineering.

1. THE PROBLEM

Over the past decade cultural institutions have begun acquiring works by digital artists that have ranged in design from ephemeral performance to immersive installation. Conservators of digital media, whose job it is to preserve these works, are faced with the daunting task of managing a diversity of art so as to make any artwork displayable at any time in the future. The issues conservators face for maintaining a digital artwork's longevity are manifold. Digital artists employ a wide variety of contemporary computer languages, sometimes in combination, building upon a range of development libraries and environments, many of which may be either open source or of an artisanal nature. Software interfaces, formats, and protocols continue to evolve, and globally accessible resources either disappear or become redistributed. Finally, computer hardware is guaranteed to become obsolete.

In order to gain some sense of these issues consider the artwork *I Want You to Want Me* (2008), an interactive installation about online dating designed and built by Jonathan Harris and Sep

Kamvar [1], commissioned by the Museum of Modern Art (MoMA) in New York and installed on Valentine's Day 2008 as part of its *Design and the Elastic Mind* show [2]. Displayed on a vertically mounted high definition 56" touch screen monitor, the artwork portrays a sky filled with hundreds of pink (female) and blue (male) balloons, each representing an individual's online dating profile that has been harvested and coalesced from several dozen Internet dating websites. Viewers can touch individual balloons to reveal personal information about the dater found inside, and can rearrange the balloons in various ways to highlight different aspects of the world of online dating, including the most popular first dates, top desires, self-descriptions, and interests (Figure 1).

I Want You to Want Me is based on a client-server architecture in which the client locally controls a graphics display, with the application backend housed in a California server farm. An URL server provides addresses to a web crawler which sends dating site information to an information extractor, the responsibility of which is to fill a database with information about individuals, approximately one million elements in size. Data from this database is accessed and passed to the front-end application, using an API that configures search strategies and queries. The programming languages and components used to build the artwork include C++, Java, PHP, OpenGL, and SQL. The servers run the UNIX operating system and the client runs Windows XP.

I Want You to Want Me presents challenges for its future installation. Its processing and databases are distributed over multiple computing platforms and locations. It requires several programming languages for its construction and execution. The nature and structure of its database, and the information mining algorithms employed to extract data are unknown. And it is unclear how tightly coupled the display system is to the underlying computer graphics software. Thus, assuming this artwork's current technical state, it is uncertain whether it would be a good candidate for display in the distant future, given its scarcity of documentation and the current state of contemporary conservation practice.

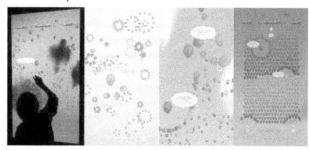

Figure 1: *I Want You to Want Me* **(2008) by Jonathan Harris and Sep Kamvar**

2. CONSERVATION STRATEGIES

Digital art conservators have taken two approaches to preserving digital art: technology preservation and document compilation. In technology preservation computer technology is stockpiled to support the artwork in the inevitable case that a component fails. In document compilation an extended set of documentation is assembled to help define and contextualize the artwork with the express purpose of making the artwork displayable at some future date. Artist interviews, questionnaires [3], artist-conservator-curator collaborative discussions, conservation workshops [4], and documentation of a program's source code are all approaches that have been taken [5].

We believe the technology preservation approach to a long term conservation strategy for digital artwork is problematic for all but the most historically significant works. Museums and cultural institutions neither have the resources to stockpile computer parts, nor routinely maintain computer-based artworks to extend their lifespans. It must be remembered that museums collect far more artwork than they can exhibit at any given time. With the exception of works that either define the museum's collection or are critical to the art canon, all remaining art may be expected to rotate from storage into galleries pursuant to curatorial discretion. In such environments it may be decades before artworks are reinstalled. As a result, routine maintenance of these works becomes managerially prohibitive because of time, staffing, and financial constraints; leaving open the prospect that when an artwork is finally scheduled for installation it may not be possible to do so, because either part or all of the artwork will have reached technical obsolescence.

We believe as well that the best long term preservation strategy should be based on document compilation. Our hypothesis is that if an artwork can be transformed into an appropriate set of representations, then it will be possible to reinstantiate the artwork within future technology. Documentation that underlies this strategy must:

- support both abstract and detailed descriptions of static artwork structure and its dynamic processes.

- provide a diversity of representations to satisfy all stakeholders (e.g. artists, curators, and conservators).

- be sufficiently extensible to support organization, categorization, and systemization of digital art collections.

- be sufficiently flexible to sustain both individual document and corpora evolution.

- be integratable into art conservation practice.

The last item in the list is important because art conservation is a formal scientific activity defined by the International Council of Museums Committee for Conservation as the "the technical examination, preservation, and conservation-restoration of cultural property."[6] As such, any methodology instituted to augment traditional conservation practice must be suitably formal, mature, and rigorous to meet this profession's requirements, as well as the preceding four criteria.

These criteria may be met by adapting software engineering processes and practice.

3. ENGINEERING DOCUMENTATION

Software engineering provides a systematic methodology for creating and maintaining documentation to support communication, preservation of system and institutional memory, and processes such as system auditing. Within this context a computer system's documentation should supply comprehensive information about its capabilities, architecture, design details, features, and limitations. It should encompass the following five components [7]:

1. *Requirements* – The artwork's conceptual foundation. What it is supposed to do.

2. *Architecture/Design* – An overview of software that includes the software's relationship to its environment, and construction principles used in design of the software components.

3. *Technical* – Source code, algorithms, and interface documentation.

4. *End User* – Technical, installation, and user documentation.

5. *Supplementary Materials* – Anything else related to the system.

Each component is important to the representation of digital art. Each may operate at a different level of abstraction or within a particular context. *Requirements* documentation presents the conceptual view of what the system is expected to do. It is written to be understood by all the stakeholders who comprise an art museum's business practice: directors, curators, conservators, artists, installers, and maintainers. *Architecture/Design*, *Technical*, and *End* User documentation are of importance to conservators, installers, and maintainers.

4. DOCUMENTATING DIGITAL ART

When a museum acquires an artwork, it is the conservator's responsibility to acquire sufficient documentation from the artist to ensure its proper installation. Other documentation may exist, including: examples of previous installations that have been approved by the artist, design histories, interviews, catalogues, scholarly works, alternative installation plans, drawings, models, documentary videos, websites, etc. Beyond that, conservators may resort to additional interviews, collaborative discussions, and questionnaires to flesh out the artwork's character.

As a whole, this documentation may exhibit varying degrees of incompleteness, inhomogeneity, and diversity in its content and format. In order to make this artwork maintainable, this documentation must be transformed into formats that clearly define the artwork's nature, allow individual document components to be assigned to one or more of the five document categories specified in Section 3, and make the documentation maintainable for the long term.

We have taken initial steps to this end by designing a checklist/questionnaire within a spreadsheet. Checklists [8][9], templates, and patterns [10] are integral to software engineering practice, facilitating timely solution of analysis and design problems, as well as providing for formal verification and validation of product and process. Integrating such methodologies into digital art conservation practice should facilitate the creation of a strategic maintenance strategy for digital artwork, as well as a means for assessing a digital artwork's installation requirements at some future time.

Our objectives in designing the checklist/questionnaire are threefold:

1. To define as completely as possible the exact technological state of a digital artwork upon its acquisition by a museum, along with the technological milieu from which it originated. This baselines the artwork.

2. To track and assess an artwork's increasing divergence from state-of-the-art technology at some future time. Here the documentation will help conservators determine which technologies need updating for a future installation. It should also support risk analysis for determining the degree of effort (e.g. costs) required for future installation.

3. To offer a means for comparing the technological underpinnings among artworks within a digital art genre and throughout digital art history. This latter point is important, because it will give the digital conservator a sense of the degree of technological heterogeneity within the museum's collection and provide information necessary for creating strategic plans for maintaining the digital art collection as a whole.

Our checklist/questionnaire's current version contains a large number of questions that we expect to expand with time. The questions shown herein have been condensed from the questions found in the spreadsheet and are provided to offer a sense of its breadth. It currently contains the following categories:

- **Algorithms Used**: What is the form of any special algorithm employed? What is its relationship to any standard algorithm?

- **Application Software Requirements**: What were the development languages, libraries, and interfaces used, and their versions? What development tools were employed? Is source code provided?

- **Authorship**: Who contributed to the design and building of the artwork and its parts? Who or what were the artistic or technical influences of the artwork?

- **General**: Questions related to administration of the artwork. What are the preservation priorities for this artwork? What are the preservation strategies to be used? How and where will the artwork be stored and accessed? What are the environmental constraints? May the artwork be reengineered?

- **Hardware Requirements**: Questions related to the complete description of the hardware substrate including: motherboard, CPU, RAM, video card, network adaptors, BIOS, system timings and interrupts, display devices and resolutions, etc.

- **Installation Requirements**: Questions related to the artwork's installation, including sources of materials, handling instructions, construction, etc.

- **Interview Questions**: What questions were asked of the artist and the answers?

- **Media Requirements (Audio / Video)**: What are the file formats, image and video resolutions, timings, codecs, and compression schemes used for various media?

- **Networking and Communication Requirements**: What is the network topology employed? What are the network protocols used by the artwork? What are the networking and communication services required?

- **Preservation Strategies**: What preservation strategies are expected to be used for this artwork?

- **Quality Assurance Procedures**: How will reliability issues be addressed? Does the artwork exhibit instability issues? Under what circumstances does the artwork fail? How is the faulty artwork to be maintained and tested?

- **References**: References related to the artwork itself, its artistic milieu, etc. This may include documents or links to resources from scholarly journals to videos.

- **Rights and Permissions**: What are the legal constrains placed on this artwork? What are the licensing terms for the use of media, software libraries, etc.?

- **Security Requirements**: Does the artwork have built-in security components? Is a firewall required? Does the artwork contain hidden files? Are encryption schemes uses for any files?

- **Supporting Documentation**: Technical, maintenance, and owner's manuals for hardware and software. Design histories, books and catalogs, alternative installation plans, drawings, models, documentary videos, websites, etc.

- **System Constraints:** What are the budgetary, architectural, technical, staffing, and scheduling constraints related to this artwork? What are the risks related to its installation and maintenance?

- **System Software Requirements**: What operating systems, systems libraries, etc. are required?

- **Web Requirements**: What web protocols are required (e.g. http, ftp, etc.). What web servers are required? What data formats (HTML, XML, style sheets) are required? What browsers and their version are required?

These questions should afford sufficient information to fulfill three documentation categories given in Section 3: *Requirements, End User,* and *Supplementary Materials.* If the artwork's software configuration contains source code, then the *Technical Documentation* category requirements would be fulfilled as well.

Architecture/Design documentation contributes significantly to a total understanding of the artwork system, making it possible in principle to recreate all or part of the artwork as required. Because these representations are intended to communicate what the artwork is supposed to do, as opposed to how it is supposed to do it, they are designed to articulate the system's high-level static and dynamical designs and interfaces, while suppressing the low-level implementation details. Three kinds of representations are considered here: UML use-case scenarios that define an artwork's functional requirements, class diagrams that fix an artwork's static structure, and sequence diagrams that convey an artwork's dynamics.

Most artists are not trained as software engineers, and thus cannot be expected to create UML representations of their works. However, it may be possible to extract use-case scenarios for an artwork from its "supporting documentation" where its temporal designs may have been elaborated as storyboards and alike. Otherwise, use-cases may be captured by observing and interrogating the artwork running within a gallery setting. Class and sequence diagrams are another matter. Given a complete set of use-cases, and utilizing the remaining documentation categories as the interpretive context, it should be possible to generate these UML representations – in effect, create a complete design document for the artwork from scratch [7]. Although this would be a time consuming process, and it may generate a design that does not represent the artist's original architecture, the design should fulfill the artwork's functional requirements. Alternatively, in circumstances where the artwork has been written in a popular programming language such as C, C++, or Java, UML class and sequence diagrams may be generated automatically from either source or executable code exploiting mainstream UML CASE tools [11]. The advantages of this transformation are that the resulting UML diagrams embody the artist's original software architecture, and the time required for creating these architectural designs becomes negligible.

Finally, *Architecture/Design* documentation offers a distinct advantage over source code. For example, if five hundred years from now the programming language employed by today's artist to create a digital artwork has disappeared into history, its source code upon which it is based becomes virtually useless. Although emulators [12] and virtualization technologies [13] may evolve to completely bypass source code issues by creating environments to allow an artwork's executable code to run as is, there is no way of predicting whether a future virtualized environment would be able to support part or all of an artwork from 500 years in the past. In contrast, *Architecture/Design* documentation provides a pathway for rebuilding part or all of the artwork, beginning from the artwork's high level requirements and designs, working down, refining implementation details in any language to suit.

5. SUMMARY
In this paper we have begun to consider issues involved in designing and maintaining documentation that will be expected to evolve in perpetuity, by analyzing the real problem of conserving digital artwork so that it may be installed in a museum in the far distant future. The approach we have taken is to employ a software engineering methodology to documentation that focuses on five classes of documents: *Requirements, Architecture/Design, Technical, End User,* and *Supplementary Materials* to set a systematic framework for capturing and organizing all materials related to a digital artwork. As part of this process we have created an extensive checklist/questionnaire, the objectives of which are to define the exact technological state of a digital artwork when it is acquired by a museum, and track the artwork's deviation from up-to-date technology over time. Finally, we have put forward a procedure for capturing the artwork's architectural design using software engineering's Unified Process model, and have proposed how this model could be applied to recreate the artwork in the distant future.

6. FINAL THOUGHTS
This research represents our initial foray into designing documentation for the long term preservation of digital artwork which, in essence, is a unique variation on a legacy system. Unlike a traditional legacy system, which is expected to be updated or overhauled at some point in time so as to capitalize on advances in state-of-the-art technology to improve its core attributes such as usability, speed, and performance; legacy digital artwork will become reliant on state-of-the-art technology to ensure that it functions identically to the first day it had been installed in a museum. To deal with this dichotomy of technological purpose, documentation will need to meet the objectives put forward in Section 4, as well as be able to characterize a digital artwork from its functional requirements through its technical details. In so doing, it will provide important information for adapting new technology to old art, by helping locate sources and kinds of incompatibilities that have evolved in technologies over time. To this end, we are exploring the expansion of our spreadsheet checklist into a database system, and categorizing a set of artworks with respect to their technological evolution.

7. ACKNOWLEDGMENTS
We thank those individuals who have contributed to the content of this checklist: Juan Amadiz, Eric Greene, Ingrid Grey, Samuel Martin, Jeffrey Pecan, Anthony Perrone, and Vishnu Sulapu.

F.T.M would like to thank the Helene & Grant Wilson Center for Social Entrepreneurship at Pace University for a fellowship supporting this work.

8. REFERENCES
[1] Harris, J. and Kamvar, S. 2008. *I Want You to Want Me*. Retrieved May 23, 2012 from http://iwantyoutowantme.org/

[2] *Design and the Elastic Mind*. 2008. Museum of Modern Art (MoMA). Retrieved May 23, 2012 from http://www.moma.org/interactives/exhibitions/2008/elasticmind/

[3] Ippolito, J. 2003. Accommodating the unpredictable: The variable media questionnaire. In *Permanence Through Change: The Variable Media Approach*, (Guggenheim Museum Publications and The Daniel Langlois Foundation for Art, Science, and Technology).

[4] ERPANET. 2004. The archiving and preservation of born-digital art workshop. *Briefing Paper for the ERPANET Workshop on Preservation of Digital Art*. Retrieved May 23, 2012 from http://www.erpanet.org/events/2004/glasgowart/briefingpaper.pdf.

[5] Yeung, T.A., Carpendale, S. and Greenberg, S. 2008. Preservation of art in the digital realm. *The Proceedings of iPRES2008: The Fifth International Conference on Digital Preservation*. British Library, London.

[6] International Council of Museums Committee for Conservation. The conservator-restorer: a definition of the profession, section 2.1. Retrieved May 23, 2012 from www.icom-cc.org/47/

[7] Larman, C. 2005. *Applying UML and Patterns: An Introduction to Object-Oriented Analysis and Design and Iterative Development*, 3rd Ed. Prentice-Hall, New Jersey.

[8] Pressman, R. S. 2001. Adaptable process model software engineering checklists: Reviewing OOA and OOD models. Retrieved May 23, 2012 from http://www.rspa.com/checklists/ooadmods.html

[9] Pressman, R. S. 2001. Adaptable process model software engineering checklists: conducting and reviewing the software design model. Retrieved May 23, 2012 from http://www.rspa.com/checklists/designmodel.html

[10] Riehle D. and Züllighoven, H. 1996. Understanding and using patterns in software development. In *Theory and Practice of Object Systems* 2, 1, 3-13.

[11] Khaled, L. 2009. A comparison between UML tools. In *Second International Conference on Environmental and Computer Science*, 111-114.

[12] van der Hoeven, J., Lohman, B. and Verdegem, R. 2007. Emulation for digital preservation in practice: the results. *The International Journal of Digital Curation* 2, 2, 123-132.

[13] Crosby, S. and Brown, D. 2006. The virtualization reality. *Queue* 4, 10 (December 2006), 34-41.

Personalized Document Clustering with Dual Supervision

Yeming Hu
Dalhousie University
Faculty of Computer Science
6050 University Avenue
Halifax, Canada
yeming@cs.dal.ca

Evangelos E. Milios
Dalhousie University
Faculty of Computer Science
6050 University Avenue
Halifax, Canada
eem@cs.dal.ca

James Blustein
Dalhousie University
Faculty of Computer Science
and School of Information
Management
Halifax, Canada
jamie@cs.dal.ca

Shali Liu
Dalhousie University
Faculty of Computer Science
6050 University Avenue
Halifax, Canada
shali@cs.dal.ca

ABSTRACT

The potential for semi-supervised techniques to produce personalized clusters has not been explored. This is due to the fact that semi-supervised clustering algorithms used to be evaluated using oracles based on underlying class labels. Although using oracles allows clustering algorithms to be evaluated quickly and without labor intensive labeling, it has the key disadvantage that oracles always give the same answer for an assignment of a document or a feature. However, different human users might give different assignments of the same document and/or feature because of different but equally valid points of view. In this paper, we conduct a user study in which we ask participants (users) to group the same document collection into clusters according to their own understanding, which are then used to evaluate semi-supervised clustering algorithms for user personalization. Through our user study, we observe that different users have their own personalized organizations of the same collection and a user's organization changes over time. Therefore, we propose that document clustering algorithms should be able to incorporate user input and produce personalized clusters based on the user input. We also confirm that semi-supervised algorithms with noisy user input can still produce better organizations matching user's expectation (personalization) than traditional unsupervised ones. Finally, we demonstrate that labeling keywords for clusters at the same time as labeling documents can improve clustering performance further compared to labeling only documents with respect to user personalization.

Categories and Subject Descriptors

H.3.3 [**Information Storage and Retrieval**]: Information Search and Retrieval—*Clustering*; H.1.2 [**User/Machine Systems**]: [Human Factors]; I.7.1 [**Computing Methodologies**]: Document and Text Processing—*Document Management*

General Terms

Algorithms, Human Factors, Design, Management

Keywords

User Supervision, Document Supervision, Feature Supervision, User Interface, Personalization

1. INTRODUCTION

Nowadays, academic researchers maintain a personal library of papers related to their research and courses, downloaded from digital libraries such as Association for Computing Machinery (ACM) digital library[1]. While those papers might be placed into different categories (folders) when they were downloaded, the categories are generally quite coarse. Even worse, papers with different topics might be put into the same folder only for temporary convenience. In fact, even if users categorize the papers appropriately at one time, they might change their mind later on and want to organize the papers in another manner. In addition, researchers might like one organization for their research but another one for preparing their courseware. Therefore, the organization of the personal library should be easily changed over time based on user's needs.

Clustering techniques are often employed to group a document collection into different topics. Unsupervised clustering does not require any user effort. However, the users may not be satisfied with the universal output since it does not reflect the individual user's point of view and completely ignores personalization. Semi-supervised clustering incorporates prior information, e.g., user input, into clustering algorithms and normally can produce better quality of clusters.

---

[1]http://dl.acm.org/

User input is generally provided through user supervision. With respect to document clustering, there are two types of supervision, i.e., document supervision and feature supervision. In document supervision, users provide document-level user input such as labeling a few representative documents for each cluster [2] or identifying relationship between two documents, i.e., "must-link" and "cannot-link" [21]. In feature supervision, users provide feature-level user input such as assigning a few keywords for each cluster [12] or identifying the features (words) which are useful for clustering [8, 9]. The semi-supervised clustering algorithms can also produce personalized clusters if combined with user inputs from individual users.

The previous semi-supervised clustering algorithms were all experimentally evaluated using oracles. Oracles are based on the underlying class labels of standard datasets. In the case of document supervision, two documents are put into the same cluster or identified as "must-link" by the oracle if they have the same class labels. Otherwise, they are identified as "cannot-link" and must end up in different clusters. With respect to feature supervision, a feature oracle is constructed using feature selection techniques such as χ^2 or information gain based on the underlying labels of documents. The constructed feature oracle determines whether a feature is useful for clustering and which cluster the feature should be assigned to. By using oracles, a new semi-supervised clustering algorithm can be evaluated and verified easily and quickly. However, there are two main disadvantages using oracles to evaluate semi-supervised algorithms. First, oracles always give the correct assignments of documents into clusters or "must-link" and "cannot-link". In real situation, human users can easily make mistakes in assigning documents. Therefore, the semi-supervised algorithms should be tested under noisy supervision, e.g., two documents are placed into the same cluster when they are not meant to. The same problem exists with feature supervision that a user can pick a useless feature or even assign one cluster's feature to another one especially when there are overlaps between clusters. Although one might claim that noise can be injected into oracle decisions [9], the probability method used to create the feature oracle may not be able to simulate a user's complicated decision process. Second, oracles constructed for one dataset always assign the same label for the same document or the same feature. Assume we have two papers and one talks about programming languages and the other is about software debugging. A document oracle based on underlying class labels will always give the same assignments on whether those two papers should be placed into the same cluster. However, one human user can assign them into the same cluster "software engineering" while another one would like to put them into two clusters, i.e., "languages" and "debugging". Clearly, the keywords (features) assigned for the two cases will be different too. Therefore, although semi-supervised algorithms have the potential to produce personalized clusters, they have not been explored for this purpose.

In this paper, we conduct a user study to verify whether semi-supervised clustering algorithms can still produce better quality of clusters when human users are asked to perform document supervision and feature supervision than unsupervised clustering without any supervision. At the same time, we explore the semi-supervised algorithms to produce personalized clusters for individual users when combined with their own user input. We develop an interactive interface to help users to group documents and assign keywords for clusters and documents. The interface helps users to create a new cluster, assign a document to an existing cluster, move a document from one cluster to another, merge two clusters, remove assigned documents and existing clusters. Thirty-two participants (users, used exchangeable) are recruited to label 80 out of the 580 documents (academic papers). The 80 papers are selected by an active recommender described in Section 2.3. The papers are generally assigned to three coarse categories assigned by their authors, i.e., software, information systems, and computing methodologies. However, the coarse labels are not used at all in this work, neither for user supervision nor for the evaluation of the algorithms. The participants do not know the actual number of clusters in the document collection and are asked to group the documents based on their own understanding during exploration. In fact, there are no gold-standard labels for this dataset because each user may create any number of sub-clusters within each coarse category. Therefore, we may obtain different sets of clusters of the same 80 documents from each participant, in terms of the number of clusters, the cluster membership of documents and the keywords assigned to clusters. At the same time, they are asked to select the cluster keywords while they are labeling documents. They can also assign keywords to each cluster directly. In order to demonstrate that semi-supervised clustering works with a small amount of user input, only the first few assigned documents (1 to 6) to each cluster are used as document supervision input (see details in Section 3.3). At the same time, only keywords associated with those documents or directly assigned to each cluster are used as feature supervision input. All 580 documents are clustered and the algorithms are evaluated based on the clusters of the 80 documents manually organized by each participant.

In summary, our contributions are: (1) We design and test useful operations and text visualization methods to help users to group documents, which should be included in supervision interface for document management software. We demonstrate that selecting keywords during assigning documents takes little time using the designed interface and operations. (2) We observe that different users group the same document collection differently, i.e., the number of clusters, the cluster memberships of documents, and the assigned keywords. In addition, we observe that a user's organization of a document collection changes over time. Therefore, clustering algorithms which accommodate personalization should be employed. (3) We show that semi-supervised clustering algorithms with a small amount of user input can produce personalized clusters and verify that semi-supervised clustering algorithms can still produce better quality of clusters with (noisy) user input than unsupervised clustering. (4) We demonstrate that assigning keywords for clusters can help clustering algorithms to organize documents better matching user's point of view than any single supervision, i.e., labeling only documents or only features.

The rest of this paper is organized as follows. In Section 2, we present the underlying clustering algorithms, propose an active learning framework to recommend documents for the user to label, and describe the design and components of the interactive user interface to collect user input. Details of the experiments and evaluations are given in Section 3. In this section, we present and discuss the results and observations from our user study. In section 4, we describe the related work. We conclude with a discussion of the implications of this work and the opportunities for further investigations in Section 5.

2. METHODOLOGY

In this section, we first introduce clustering algorithms we use to demonstrate and verify the usefulness of user input, i.e., the unsupervised clustering algorithm KMeans and semi-supervised clustering algorithm $DualSeededK$Means. Then, we briefly describe the active learning method we use to recommend documents for user supervision. Finally, we present the interactive user interface we use to collect user input through document supervision and feature supervision.

2.1 Unsupervised KMeans

KMeans is a clustering algorithm based on iterative assignments of data points to clusters and partitions a dataset into K clusters so that the average squared distance between the data points and the closest cluster centers are locally minimized. For a dataset with data points $\mathcal{X} = \{x_1, x_2, \ldots, x_N\}, x_i \in \mathbb{R}^d$, KMeans algorithm generates K clusters $\{\mathcal{X}_l\}_{l=1}^K$ of $\mathcal{X}$ so that the objective function

$$J = \sum_{l=1}^{K} \sum_{x_i \in \mathcal{X}_l} ||x_i - \mu_l||^2 \qquad (1)$$

is locally minimized based on the initial centers selected, where $\{\mu_1, \mu_2, \ldots, \mu_K\}$ represent the centers of the K clusters.

2.2 Semi-supervised $DualSeededK$Means

$DualSeededK$Means [10, 11] is a semi-supervised algorithm which can incorporate user input from both document supervision and feature supervision. It transforms user input from document supervision into document seeding [2, 10] using clusters derived from labeled documents and user input from feature supervision into feature seeding using a Feature-Vote-Model or Feature-Generative-Model [10]. Finally, it combines document seeding and feature seeding using the linear opinion pool [16]. $DualSeededK$Means is so general framework that it becomes $DocumentSeededK$-Means without feature supervision and $FeatureSeededK$-Means without feature supervision. In fact, $DualSeededK$-Means without any supervision is equivalent to unsupervised KMeans.

2.3 Active Document Recommendation for User Supervision

Since user supervision is labor-intensive, an active learning scheme is designed to recommend the most potentially informative documents for the user to label, i.e., assigning the documents to a cluster. Our algorithm is an adapted version of the explore-consolidate framework [3] to the situation when the number of clusters K is not predefined. In the original explore-consolidate framework described in [3], there are two steps to construct the cluster structure, i.e., "explore" and "consolidate". In addition, an oracle is used and the number of clusters K is assumed to be known. In each iteration of the "explore" step, a document farthest from the assigned documents is selected using a farthest-first traversal

scheme. Then, the document is either assigned to an existing cluster or a new cluster. This step stops after K clusters are created. In each iteration of the "consolidate" step, a document is randomly selected and assigned to one of the existing K clusters. The purpose of this step is to consolidate the cluster structure faster because all clusters exist and there is no need to search for the farthest document. However, it is not directly applicable to our work because human users create clusters according to their own understanding of the document collection and different users may create different numbers of clusters (unknown K). Therefore, we do not know when the "consolidate" step should start. In the adapted version, the "explore" and "consolidate" steps are interleaved. One iteration of the "consolidate" step is performed after every s (4 in this paper) iterations of the "explore" step. However, instead of random selection, a document closest to the smallest cluster is selected in the "consolidate" step. The main goal is to have balanced clusters and avoid having too many small clusters.

2.4 User Interface for User Supervision

As we mentioned in Section 1, we have two types of user supervision, namely, document supervision and feature supervision. Therefore, we need to provide operations in the user interface to support both types of supervision. We also have to provide visualizations of clusters and documents to aid user supervision. As shown in Fig 1, we have four panels in the user supervision interface:

(1) "Supervision Panel" $<1>^2$: This panel supports document supervision. The sectors of the outside circle denote the clusters and the inside circle represents the document that needs to be labeled (assigned to a cluster) by the user. The (yellow) slices inside a sector denote the documents assigned to the corresponding cluster. The number inside a circle, at the top left corner of a slice or sector is the document or cluster ID. There are always two auxiliary sectors, "New Cluster" and "Trash", which are used to create new clusters and remove clusters or documents respectively. The operations provided by this panel include: (a) Create a new cluster: Drag the inside circle or a slice to the "New Cluster" sector. (b) Move a document: Drag a slice from one sector to another. (c) Merge two clusters: Drag a sector to another. (d) Remove a cluster: Drag a sector to the "Trash" sector. (e) Remove (unlabel or unassign) a document: Drag the inside circle or a slice to the "Trash" sector.

(2) "Document To-Be-Labeled Panel" $<2>$: This panel displays the information of the document denoted by the inside circle in the "supervision panel" and the document ID matches the one in the inside circle. This panel includes two sub-panels to aid users in identifying the topic of the document, i.e., text cloud $<5>$ [13] and the whole content $<6>$ of the document. The user can select a keyword in either sub-panel, i.e., labeling a feature, by double-clicking on the word. After being chosen as a keyword, the word is highlighted in red. If a word is already being highlighted, double-clicking on it removes the highlighting and it is not a keyword any more (unlabeling a feature). The user can add and delete keywords by using the input field $<7>$ and using the corresponding add/delete buttons $<8,9>$ respectively. All

---

[2]Corresponding Identification number in Fig. 1

163

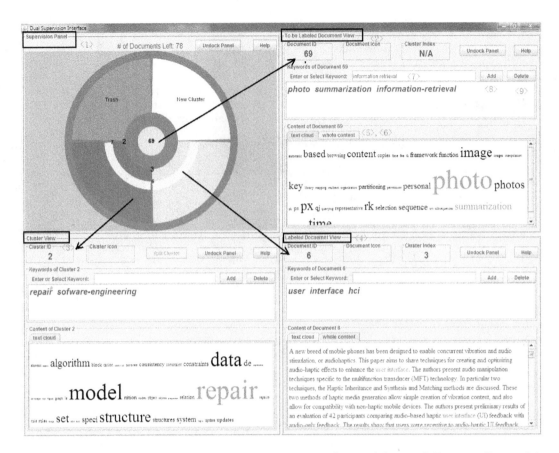

Figure 1: Interface for User Supervision: Document Supervision and Feature Supervision

keywords of this document will be shown in the keyword area of this panel.

(3) "Cluster View Panel" <3>: After the user single-clicks on a sector in the "supervision panel", this panel displays information about the corresponding cluster. This panel is similar to the "Document To-Be-Labeled Panel" except that there is no visualization of the whole content simple because a cluster does not have it. The user can assign keywords using the methods introduced previously. Note that keywords assigned to a document become keywords of its cluster while the keywords directly assigned to a cluster are not connected to any document assigned to it. Keywords assigned into a cluster should describe the topic of the cluster as they are used by $DualSeededK$ Means with Feature-Vote-Model or Feature-Generative-Model in Section 2.2.

(4) "Document Labeled Panel" <4>: This pane's layout is the same as the "Document To-Be-Labeled Panel". When the user single-clicks a slice in the "Supervision Panel", the information about the assigned document is shown here. The user can view the topic of the document and revise the keywords assigned to the document.

3. EXPERIMENTS

3.1 Datasets

The dataset we use for the user study is a collection of the 580 academic papers in full text from different areas of computer science. Those papers were manually collected by the authors from the ACM Digital Library. Based on the 1998 ACM Computing Classification System, those papers were assigned to one or more of the following areas by their authors: Software including Software Engineering and Programming Languages, Information Systems and Computing Methodologies. Generally speaking, the categories assigned by paper authors are very coarse and cannot reflect the accurate topics of the papers. In addition, it is not uncommon that one paper is related to multiple topics and can be assigned to multiple categories. Therefore, this dataset is well suited for us to verify whether different users have their own points of view of the same document collection. At the same time, we can demonstrate the usefulness of user supervision for producing personalized organization.

3.2 Evaluation Measures

We use Rand Distance based on Rand Index [18] to compare different users' clusterings (groupings) of the same document collection and determine whether different users have their own points of view, thereby motivating the inclusion of user personalization as a requirement for clustering algorithms. Based on Rand Index, we develop measures of cohesiveness and separation to evaluate the clusters produced by clustering algorithms in comparison with users' manual organizations. In addition, we use Jaccard distance [19] to measure the dissimilarity between the sets of features labeled by different users.

3.2.1 Rand Distance

We assume a document collection $\mathcal{D} = \{d_1, d_2, \ldots, d_n\}$ and two clusterings of $\mathcal{D}$, i.e., $\mathcal{X} = \{x_1, x_2, \ldots, x_r\}$ and $\mathcal{Y} = \{y_1, y_2, \ldots, y_s\}$, where x_i or y_j is a subset of $\mathcal{D}$. We also have $x_i \cap x_j = \emptyset$ and $\cup_{i=1,\ldots,r} x_i = \mathcal{D}$ where $i, j \in \{1, \ldots, r\}$ and $i \neq j$, and $y_i \cap y_j = \emptyset$ and $\cup_{i=1,\ldots,s} y_i = \mathcal{D}$ where $i, j \in \{1, \ldots, s\}$ and $i \neq j$. We define the following quantities:

- a, the number of pairs of documents that are in the same cluster in $\mathcal{X}$ and $\mathcal{Y}$.

- b, the number of pairs of documents that are in different clusters in $\mathcal{X}$ and $\mathcal{Y}$.

- c, the number of pairs of documents that are in the same cluster in $\mathcal{X}$ but in different clusters in $\mathcal{Y}$.

- d, the number of pairs of documents that are in different clusters in $\mathcal{X}$ but in the same cluster in $\mathcal{Y}$.

The Rand Index, $\mathcal{RI}$, is:

$$\mathcal{RI} = \frac{a+b}{a+b+c+d} \qquad (2)$$

and the Rand Distance, $\mathcal{RD}$, is:

$$\mathcal{RD} = 1 - \mathcal{RI} = \frac{c+d}{a+b+c+d} \qquad (3)$$

Rand Index and Rand Distance measure the similarity and the dissimilarity between two clusterings respectively.

3.2.2 Cohesiveness, Separation, and F-Measure

The clusters produced by clustering algorithms are evaluated against users' manual organizations of the document collection. Therefore, we do not use the Rand Index, which only computes the similarity between two clusterings. Instead, we develop measures *coh*, *sep*, and *F*-Measure to evaluate the clusters produced for this user with/without supervision. Those measures treat a user's manual organization as the gold standard. Assuming the gold standard partition $\mathcal{G} = \{g_1, g_2, \ldots, g_k\}$ and a clustering $\mathcal{C}$ produced by a clustering algorithm, we define the following quantities:

- a', the number of pairs of documents that are in the same cluster in $\mathcal{G}$.

- b', the number of pairs of documents that are in the same cluster in $\mathcal{G}$ and $\mathcal{C}$.

- c', the number of pairs of documents that are in different clusters in $\mathcal{G}$.

- d', the number of pairs of documents that are in different clusters in $\mathcal{G}$ and $\mathcal{C}$.

The cohesiveness of $\mathcal{C}$, *coh*, is:

$$coh = \frac{b'}{a'} \qquad (4)$$

The separation of $\mathcal{C}$, *sep*, is:

$$sep = \frac{d'}{c'} \qquad (5)$$

and finally *F*-Measure, F, is:

$$F = 2 \times \frac{coh \times sep}{coh + sep} \qquad (6)$$

where *coh* measures the cohesiveness of $\mathcal{C}$ while *sep* measures the separation of $\mathcal{C}$, based on a user's manual organization $\mathcal{G}$.

3.2.3 Jaccard Distance

Given two sets $\mathcal{A}$ and $\mathcal{B}$, the Jaccard Index, $\mathcal{JI}$, is:

$$\mathcal{JI} = \frac{|\mathcal{A} \cap \mathcal{B}|}{|\mathcal{A} \cup \mathcal{B}|} \qquad (7)$$

and the Jaccard Distance, $\mathcal{JD}$, is:

$$\mathcal{JD} = 1 - \mathcal{JI} = \frac{|\mathcal{A} \cup \mathcal{B}| - |\mathcal{A} \cap \mathcal{B}|}{|\mathcal{A} \cup \mathcal{B}|} \qquad (8)$$

Jaccard Index, $\mathcal{JI}$, measures similarity between two sets while Jaccard Distance, $\mathcal{JD}$, measures dissimilarity between two sets. Given two clusterings $\mathcal{X}$ and $\mathcal{Y}$ of a document collection $\mathcal{D}$ (Section 3.2.1), $\mathcal{X}_w = \{x_{w1}, x_{w2}, \ldots, x_{wr}\}$ and $\mathcal{Y}_w = \{y_{w1}, y_{w2}, \ldots, y_{ws}\}$ are the sets of keywords assigned to each cluster by users, i.e., x_{wi} and y_{wj} are the keywords assigned to cluster x_i and y_j respectively. We define two dissimilarity measures between $\mathcal{X}_w$ and $\mathcal{Y}_w$. One measure $\mathcal{JD}_a$ measures dissimilarity between $\mathcal{X}_w$ and $\mathcal{Y}_w$ without consideration of the cluster labels of the assigned keywords, i.e., $\mathcal{A} = \cup_{i=1,2,\ldots,r} x_{wi}$ and $\mathcal{B} = \cup_{j=1,2,\ldots,s} y_{wj}$ in Eq. 8. The other measure $\mathcal{JD}_b$ measures dissimilarity between $\mathcal{X}_w$ and $\mathcal{Y}_w$ with cluster labels considered. $\mathcal{JD}_b$ is defined as:

$$\mathcal{JD}_b = \frac{\sum_{i=1}^{r} \min_{j=1,\ldots,s} \mathcal{JD}(x_{wi}, y_{wj}) + \sum_{j=1}^{s} \min_{i=1,\ldots,r} \mathcal{JD}(y_{wj}, x_{wi})}{r+s} \qquad (9)$$

In this measure, we compute the average distance between a cluster and its closest match in the other clustering. A closest match is from the other clustering and has minimum distance from a cluster. In this way, cluster labels are considered when the measure is computed. Note that the closest match relationship is not symmetrical, i.e., with x_{wi}'s closest match being y_{wj}, the closest match of y_{wj} could be x_{wk}, where k might not be same as i.

3.3 Experimental Setup

We recruited thirty-two participants to group 80 of the 580 academic papers in our ACM dataset [3]. These 80 papers are selected by the active learning method presented in Section 2.3 and every participant groups the same 80 papers. The thirty-two participants include 5 female and 27 male graduate students from computer science. At the beginning, the task of the user study is introduced to all participant that there are not given predefined categories and they are asked to group papers based on their own understanding during the exploration of the collection. They are also aware that they need to assign keywords to a document and those keywords will become the cluster keywords automatically after the document is assigned to a cluster. They can also assign and remove keywords to and from clusters directly. Then, they are demonstrated how to group the documents and assign keywords using the software, whose interface is shown in Fig. 1 and then they are given 5 minutes to get familiar with the software. Finally, they are asked to use the software to group the 80 documents. At one time, there is only one document to be labeled (represented by the inside circle). The order of appearance of the

---

[3] The dataset and manual organizations from all participants will be available from the first author's homepage: http://www.cs.dal.ca/~yeming/. This will provide a dataset with multiple (noisy) organizations to evaluate future clustering algorithms.

80 documents depends on the active learning recommendation method. Although all participants group the same 80 documents, the order of documents appear for each user is different.

For all users, we experiment with document supervision consisting of fewer than the full 80 documents a user labels. We only use the first m documents assigned to each cluster, where m ranges from 1 to 6. Documents within each cluster are ordered based on the time they were assigned to the cluster, either when being labeled for the first time or when moved from another cluster. When a cluster B is merged into cluster A, documents in A precede documents in B. At the same time, only keywords associated with those documents selected for document supervision, or directly assigned to each cluster, are used as feature supervision input. Since the order the documents appear for labeling is distinct, the user input from each user for *DualSeededKMeans* includes different sets of documents and labeled features. All 580 papers are clustered and the clusterings produced from different algorithms are evaluated based on the 80 user labeled papers using *coh*, *sep*, and *F*-Measure.

3.4 Results

In this section, we present the user feedback and analyze results from our user study. We performed three kinds of analysis on the following aspects: user behaviors using the interface, personalization of the same document collection, and personalized document clustering with dual supervision.

3.4.1 User Satisfaction with the User Interface

Generally speaking, all participants think they know the topics of document collection well and it is easy to identify the topic of a document and identify the keywords that need to be assigned into a cluster after they manually organize the 80 documents recommended by the active recommender. They also indicate that the operations to assign and move a document, delete and merge clusters are easy to use. However, only one participant used the operation "split a cluster" since others did not realize its existence. They would like to use the software to organize their personal library of papers if the system is with proper documentation and agree that the system can help them to organize their papers better. A few interesting points we find out are:

- Twenty-nine participants think assigning keywords only takes a little time (less than 10 seconds) while only three of them indicate that it takes some time (more than 10 second but less than 1 minute). No one thinks it takes much time (more than 1 minute).

- All participants except one think that the whole content is more useful than text cloud in identifying the topic of a document. This point can also be verified by Table 5, which shows that about 70% keywords are labeled in the whole content. It is surprising since we expected that text cloud would be more helpful. One of the possible explanations is that we used single words for text cloud and multiple-word phrases could have made text cloud more useful.

- All participants review the topic of an existing cluster through keywords instead of reading a document assigned to this cluster. Therefore, it is very important to assign meaningful and correct keywords to a cluster from the beginning.

Table 1: Definitions of Operations

Name	Definition
Add	Assign a document into a cluster
Move	Move a document to another cluster
Delete	Remove a cluster
Merge	Merge two clusters
Label	Add a keyword by double-clicking
Unlabel	Remove a keyword by double-clicking
AddButton	Add a keyword through Add Button
DelButton	Remove a keyword through Delete Button

Table 2: Statistics of # of Clusters Created, Assigned Documents and Keywords

Name	Range	AVG	MED
# of Clusters	4–9	6.34	6
Assigned Documents	68–80	76.47	77
Assigned Keywords / Cluster	1–26	9.09	8

In addition, many participants suggest that they would like to have more functionality such as searching documents by words. They also suggest that we might add a spell checker for the keywords they enter. More specifically, some participants like to have all assigned documents with a keyword within a cluster highlighted when the keyword of that cluster is selected.

We present a few excerpts from users' feedback to support our claims:

- "The pie visualization [4] is very easy to use after practicing on it."

- "I really liked the drag and drop feature, which has made the system very easy to use."

- " 'Split A Cluster' helped me when I by mistake merged two clusters together."

- "I like the typing keywords feature because it allows me to generalize or be more specific about keywords without being constrained to a predefined list."

- "I found text clouds less useful than I expected."

- "It should be useful to have cluster or document keywords when the mouse hovers it in the supervision panel."

- "When a document or cluster is selected, I would expect this cluster or document was somehow highlighted in the supervision panel. Without it, it is not easy to move a document from one cluster to another."

- "I'd like to have the search (CTRL+F) function and a spell checker."

- ...

3.4.2 User Behaviors

We analyze operations defined in Table 1 which users use during grouping documents and assigning keywords so we can identify the most useful ones that should be included in

---

[4]The "Supervision Panel"

Table 3: Statistics of Operations Users Use

Operation	MIN	AVG	MED	MAX
Add	80	80.5	80	92
Move	0	4.31	3	22
Delete	0	3.03	2	10
Merge	0	1.84	1	10
Label	5	72.00	54	205
Unlabel	0	4.15	2	18
AddButton	0	12.53	9	80
DelButton	0	9.28	7	36

Table 4: Keywords Assigned through Documents or Directly

	Through Doc		Directly		Total
Label	68.03	91.13%	3.97	8.87%	72.00
AddButton	9.00		3.53		12.53
Unlabel	3.78	51.90%	0.37	48.10%	4.15
DelButton	3.19		6.09		9.28

Table 5: Keywords Assigned through Text Cloud or Whole Content

Name	Text Cloud		Whole Content		Total
Label	23.03	31.97%	48.97	68.01%	72.00
Unlabel	1.37	33.01%	2.78	66.99%	4.15

Table 6: Frequency of # of Clusters Created

#	4	5	6
Frequency	2	7	11
Percentage	6.25	21.88	34.38

7	8	9	Total
6	2	4	32
18.75	6.25	12.5	100

future interface design. We also present the analysis of the text visualization methods used in the user interface.

A document is considered as "assigned" after it is placed into an existing or a newly created cluster. Otherwise, it is considered as "unassigned", i.e., the document is placed into the "trash" cluster. The average of assigned documents out of the 80 documents is 76.47 (Table 2). Therefore, users know topics of most documents recommended by the active recommender. The most unassigned documents by a user is 12, which is 15% of all documents. However, most users only have less than 4 documents not assigned to any cluster. In fact, some users put a few documents into trash clusters at the beginning. Later on, those documents are retrieved and assigned into an existing cluster. Oracles in previous work could not simulate this behavior, in which not all recommended documents are assigned at the beginning and users can have chance to put some documents on hold and cluster them later. In addition, users are able to assign at least a few keywords for each cluster and generally assign about 9 distinct keywords for each cluster (Table 2).

In Table 3, we display the minimum, average, median, and maximum times users use each operation. The fact that we have 92 (more than 80) add operations indicates that some documents are moved from an existing cluster to create a new cluster. It is also not uncommon that a user move a document from one cluster to another, delete an existing cluster and merge two existing clusters. In addition, users also assign plenty of keywords for clusters. At the same time, many keywords are removed after they are assigned. On one hand, keywords are assigned through double-clicking more often than using add keywords buttons. That's mostly due to the fact users can assign the keywords during reading a document. However, some keywords have to be assigned or removed through add or delete keyword buttons because these keywords do not exist or are difficult to find in any document. On the other hand, users remove keywords mainly through the delete button. That's because users normally clean the keywords for a cluster using delete button at the end of the manual organization so that the keywords left can represent the topic of the cluster well. All frequent use of those operations verify that a user can change his perception

of the document collection while exploring the document collection. Therefore, clustering software should enable users to change the existing cluster structures.

Next, we analyze user behaviors on assigning keywords. A user can assign keywords to a document and the keywords associated with the document are assigned to a cluster automatically after the document is assigned into the cluster. A user can also assign keywords to a cluster directly. In addition, we are interested in which visualization method users use most often. From Table 4, we observe that most keywords are assigned through documents while a small percentage is assigned into clusters directly. Although most participants assigned keywords primarily by double-clicking and rarely by using "AddButton", one participant only used "AddButton" because he said the keywords that he came up with could best reflect his perception of the collection. With regards to keyword removals, users removed keywords equally often through documents and directly from clusters. It is observed that keyword removals through documents mostly take place when users read documents and try to learn its topic while users remove keywords from clusters directly after they finish the manual organizations and want to clean the keywords which represent the topics of clusters. From Table 5, we observe that more than two-thirds of the keywords assigned through double clicking are selected using whole content of document. This fact is consistent with the user feedback that the whole content is more helpful in discerning the topic of the document than the text cloud. However, text cloud is still useful for assigning keywords since it has fewer words than whole content and easier to find the word to be assigned. As some users indicated in the post-study questionnaires, text cloud is useful to have a general idea about the document but the whole content helps to find the exact topic of the document.

3.4.3 Personalization

We compare different groupings of the same 80 papers from all participants in terms of both documents and keywords assigned. We also compare the groupings of the same 80 papers from the same users at different times to see whether the same users have different views of the same collection over time.

First, users create different numbers of clusters based on their own understanding although all numbers are between

Table 7: Statistics of User Manual Organizations

	MIN	AVG	MED	MAX
$\mathcal{RD}$	0.1308	0.2483	0.2455	0.3817
$\mathcal{JD}_a$	0.6346	0.8632	0.8677	1.0
$\mathcal{JD}_b$	0.6483	0.9007	0.9082	1.0

Table 8: Manual Organizations by Five Users at Different Times

	P_1	P_2	P_3	P_4	P_5	AVG
$\mathcal{RD}$	0.2202	0.073	0.1652	0.1323	0.1647	0.1511
$\mathcal{JD}_a$	0.5574	0.4444	0.82	0.8684	0.6667	0.6714
$\mathcal{JD}_b$	0.6072	0.4348	0.8396	0.8269	0.7498	0.6917

Table 9: Rand Distances Between Clusterings Produced by Each Algorithm for Different Users

Name	No Supervision	Document	Feature	Dual
$\mathcal{RD}$	0.080	0.2540	0.1711	0.2226

4 and 9 (Table 2). More specifically, about 80% of the participants created 5, 6, or 7 clusters while others created 4, 8, 9 clusters (Table 6). The frequency of the cluster numbers are close to uniform distribution among 5, 6, 7 (the more frequent cluster numbers, about 74%) and among 4, 8, 9 (the less frequent ones, about 36%) respectively. Therefore, users tend to create different numbers of clusters. Later on, we will observe that different participants have distinct clusters regardless of whether the cluster numbers are the same or not.

We present the minimum, average, median and maximum Rand Distance and Jaccard Distance between organizations of all user pairs of clusterings in Table 7. The average Rand Distance between the user pair organizations is about 0.25. If different users create similar partitions of the same document collection, we would expect that the average Rand Distance is close to 0. Therefore, the Rand Distance 0.25 shows that there is substantial disagreement between different users and distinct clusters were created. In addition, the Jaccard Distances in terms of labeled keywords indicate even more disagreement between different users (average distance about 0.90). That is because there is normally a much bigger word vocabulary than the number of documents and many different keywords can be used to identify the same cluster topic, i.e., completely different keyword sets can be used for the same topic. $\mathcal{JD}_b$ shows a higher disagreement than $\mathcal{JD}_a$ because $\mathcal{JD}_b$ considers the cluster label of keywords while $\mathcal{JD}_a$ does not. Therefore, it confirms our conjecture that different users have different points of view of the same document collection.

Finally, we compare manual organizations by the same users but at different times. In our user study, we asked the same five users to organize the same document collection again one week after their first participation. Generally speaking, the two organizations are still distinct from one another although they are closer when compared to organizations from different users (Table 7 and Table 8). For example, the average Rand Distance between user pair's manual organizations is 0.25, while from the same user is 0.15.

3.4.4 Document Clustering with User Supervision

Semi-supervised clustering algorithms have been proved able to improve clustering performance over unsupervised peer algorithms using oracles [7, 8, 9, 10]. Since oracles used in previous work are assumed to give "correct" answer all the time, our purpose here is to verify that document clustering with human's noisy supervision can still produce more consistent clusters with user's manual organi-

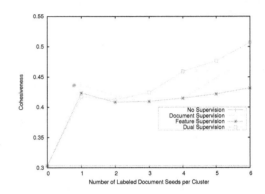

(a) Cohesiveness of Clusters: Measuring Similarity of Documents in one Cluster

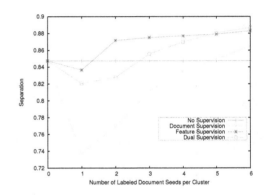

(b) Separation of Clusters: Measuring Dissimilarity between Clusters

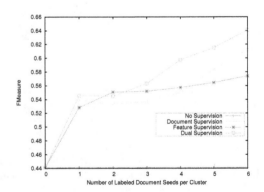

(c) F-Measure of Clusters: Measuring both Cohesiveness and Separation

Figure 2: Performance of clustering algorithms with no supervision, document supervision, feature supervision and dual supervision

zation than unsupervised clustering techniques. Instead of using a single universal ground truth as in previous work, each user has his own ground truth in our case. Therefore, we also explore whether document clustering with user supervision can produce personalize clusters. We present the results of clustering algorithms initialized by a few (1 to 6) documents and the keywords labeled in those documents or assigned directly into the clusters. We use *coh*, *sep*, and *F*-Measure to quantify the consistency of the computed clustering with the user's manual organization. From Fig. 2(a) and Fig. 2(b), we can tell that document supervision is able to group similar documents together while feature supervision is better at separating dissimilar documents. A small number of labeled documents appears to lead to unbalanced clusters with high cohesiveness (e.g. *coh* is 1 when all documents are place into the a single cluster), since the labeled documents can not represent the cluster structure well. We observe this behavior in Fig. 2(b). A small number of keywords assigned to clusters (through the labeled documents or directly by the user) appears to lead to more balanced clusters with a better representation of cluster structures, as seen in Fig. 2(b). Especially, document supervision can not separate dissimilar documents very well into different clusters when less than 4 labeled documents per cluster are provided (Fig. 2(b)). Since the keywords (features) assigned by users are representative of the clusters, feature supervision can provide good performance in terms of both cohesiveness and separation. Dual supervision, the combination of document supervision and feature supervision, can generally produce clusters better matching user's expectation (Fig. 2) [5]. Since assigning keywords is efficient for users, it is worth the effort to improve the clustering performance. In addition, the performance of the clustering algorithms improves with more labeled documents (and more assigned keywords) for initialization. It is easily understandable since more documents and/or keywords can represent the cluster structures better.

We also investigate how consistent the clusterings are between different participants. In Table 7, we compute and display the average Rand Distances between clusterings generated by the same algorithm for different users with same type and amount of supervision. Like the manual organizations from each user (Table 7), the clusterings produced with user's input are also distinct from each other (Table 9). In Table 9, the average Rand Distance between clusterings produced with document supervision and dual supervision with 4 documents and associated keywords is about 0.23, which is very close to the average Distance between different users' manual organization (about 0.25 in Table 7). On the other hand, the Rand Distance between clusterings produced without supervision is only 0.08. Therefore, clusterings obtained via semi-supervised clustering with user supervision are highly depended on user input, and therefore they can be viewed as personalized clusterings.

4. RELATED WORK

Traditional semi-supervised clustering techniques normally employ user supervision in the form of document-level constraints. The document constraints are generally used to modify the loss functions [4], initialize the cluster centers [2], learn adaptive distance metrics [22], and project high di-

mensional feature space to lower dimensional subspaces [20]. Recently, an alternative form of user supervision such as labeling features has been explored to aid semi-supervised clustering algorithms [8, 9, 10, 12]. Some work [8] uses only labeled words to guide clustering algorithms while others [9, 10, 12] integrate both labeled documents and words into a unified framework. However, these works are either evaluated based on oracles or no formal user study is performed. Drucker et al. [6] propose to use adaptive machine learning recommendations to help users group large numbers of documents faster. They did a formal user study by recruiting thirty-two participants to group the same document collection. Then, they asked a pool of 161 raters to rate the clusterings produced from the 32 participants. The user study demonstrates that clusters produced with the help of the adaptive machine learning method are significantly better than clusters automatically created. However, their work did not evaluate user's personalization of the same document collection since the generated clusters are not evaluated by users who provided the supervision. Feature supervision was also used to improve the performance of classification algorithms, such as using the labeled features for each class to constrain the probabilistic model estimation [5], making use of feature feedback with support vector machine [17], and creating pseudo-instances using the labeled features for each class [15], etc. However, classification methods assume there are pre-defined categories to which users can assign documents or keywords. In document clustering, users have to form their perception of the document collection during exploration. In addition, oracles were employed to evaluate the proposed algorithms and no formal user study is conducted in those works. Personalization has been explored in the clustering of search results [1] and search engine queries [14].

5. CONCLUSIONS AND FUTURE WORK

We recruited thirty-two participants to organize the same document collection. We analyzed users' behaviors during their manual organization. The analysis shows that users can easily find the keywords to assign to a cluster based on the whole content of the documents and it is efficient according to users' feedback. Instead of only assigning keywords existing in the documents, users also like to come up with phrases to describe the topics of clusters. By comparing all groupings from all participants, we find that each user has his own perception of the document collection and a clustering algorithm with user supervision is required to produce personalized clusters, which better reflect his point of view. At the same time, we confirm that previously proposed semi-supervised document clustering algorithms can produce personalized clusters with a small amount of user input even if it is noisy. It is also demonstrated that the same user can change his perception of the documents over time. Therefore, operations such as moving a document between clusters and merging two clusters should be available in software for document clustering. We also find that text cloud with single words is less useful than the full text for users to grasp the topic of a document.

Since text cloud with single words is not as helpful, it is worth to further investigate text cloud with multiple-word terms. According to users' feedback, functions such as searching documents by words, retrieving documents in a cluster with a specific keyword of that cluster, and a spell

---

[5]Two-tailed paired t-test with p = 0.05.

checker should be added to the user interface in the future. Since a user changes his perception of the document collection during exploration, the software should be able to interleave user supervision and clustering, i.e., the user should be able to make adjustments of documents and features after intermediate clusters are obtained, and then the clustering procedure is repeated with the updated user input. Other future work directions include enabling users to create hierarchical clusters with the user interface and allowing soft clustering, namely, a document to be assigned to multiple clusters.

References

[1] D.C. Anastasiu, B.J. Gao, and D. Buttler. Clusteringwiki: personalized and collaborative clustering of search results. In *Proceedings of the 34th International ACM SIGIR Conference on Research and Development in Information Retrieval*, pages 1263–1264, New York, NY, USA, 2011. ACM.

[2] S. Basu, A. Banerjee, and R. Mooney. Semi-supervised clustering by seeding. In *International Conference on Machine Learning*, pages 19–26, 2002.

[3] S. Basu, A. Banerjee, and R.J. Mooney. Active semi-supervision for pairwise constrained clustering. In *Proceedings of the SIAM International Conference on Data Mining*, pages 333–344, 2004.

[4] S. Basu, M. Bilenko, and R.J. Mooney. A probabilistic framework for semi-supervised clustering. In *Proceedings of the tenth ACM SIGKDD International Conference on Knowledge Discovery and Data Mining*, pages 59–68. ACM, 2004.

[5] G. Druck, G. Mann, and A. McCallum. Learning from labeled features using generalized expectation criteria. In *Proceedings of the 31st Annual International ACM SIGIR Conference on Research and Development in Information Retrieval*, pages 595–602. ACM, 2008.

[6] S.M. Drucker, D. Fisher, and S. Basu. Helping Users Sort Faster with Adaptive Machine Learning Recommendations. In *Proceedings of the 13th International conference on Human-Computer Interaction*, pages 187–203, 2011.

[7] Y. Hu, E.E. Milios, and J. Blustein. Interactive Document Clustering Using Iterative Class-Based Feature Selection. Technical report, CS-2010-04, Faculty of Computer Science, Dalhousie University, Canada, 2010.

[8] Y. Hu, E.E. Milios, and J. Blustein. Interactive feature selection for document clustering. In *Proceedings of the 26th Symposium On Applied Computing, On Track "Information Access and Retrieval"*, pages 1148–1155. ACM Special Interest Group on Applied Computing, 2011.

[9] Y. Hu, E.E. Milios, and J. Blustein. Enhancing Semi-supervised Document Clustering with Feature Supervision. In *Proceedings of the 27th ACM Symposium Applied Computing, On Track "Information Access and Retrieval"*, pages 950–957. ACM, 2012.

[10] Y. Hu, E.E. Milios, and J. Blustein. Semi-supervised Document Clustering with Dual Supervision through Seeding. In *Proceedings of the 27th ACM Symposium Applied Computing, On Track "Data Mining"*, pages 463–470. ACM, 2012.

[11] Y. Hu, E.E. Milios, and J. Blustein. A unified framework for document clustering with dual supervision. *ACM Applied Computing Review*, 12(2), 2012.

[12] Y. Huang and T.M. Mitchell. Text clustering with extended user feedback. In *Proceedings of the 29th Annual International ACM SIGIR Conference on Research and Development in Information Retrieval*, page 420. ACM, 2006.

[13] J. Lamantia. Text Clouds: A New Form of Tag Cloud? http://www.joelamantia.com/tag-clouds/text-clouds-a-new-form-of-tag-cloud, 2007. Accessed on April 12, 2012.

[14] K.W. Leung, W. Ng, and D. Lee. Personalized concept-based clustering of search engine queries. *IEEE Trans. on Knowl. and Data Eng.*, 20(11): 1505–1518, 2008.

[15] B. Liu, X. Li, W.S. Lee, and P.S. Yu. Text classification by labeling words. In *Proceedings of the National Conference on Artificial Intelligence*, pages 425–430, 2004.

[16] P. Melville, W. Gryc, and R.D. Lawrence. Sentiment analysis of blogs by combining lexical knowledge with text classification. In *Proceedings of the 15th ACM SIGKDD international conference on Knowledge discovery and data mining*, pages 1275–1284, 2009.

[17] H. Raghavan, O. Madani, and R. Jones. Interactive feature selection. In *Proceedings of IJCAI 05: The 19th International Joint Conference on Artificial Intelligence*, pages 841–846, 2005.

[18] W.M. Rand. Objective Criteria for the Evaluation of Clustering Methods. *Journal of the American Statistical Association*, pages 846–850, 1971.

[19] P. Tan, M. Steinbach, and V. Kumar. *Introduction to Data Mining*. Pearson Addison Wesley, 2005.

[20] W. Tang, H. Xiong, S. Zhong, and J. Wu. Enhancing semi-supervised clustering: a feature projection perspective. In *Proceedings of the 13th ACM SIGKDD International Conference on Knowledge Discovery and Data Mining*, pages 707–716. ACM, 2007.

[21] K. Wagstaff, C. Cardie, S. Rogers, and S. Schrödl. Constrained k-means clustering with background knowledge. In *Proceedings of the Eighteenth International Conference on Machine Learning*, pages 577–584, 2001.

[22] E.P. Xing, A.Y. Ng, M.I. Jordan, and S. Russell. Distance metric learning with application to clustering with side-information. *Advances in Neural Information Processing Systems*, pages 521–528, 2003.

The Glozz Platform: a Corpus Annotation and Mining Tool

Antoine Widlöcher[1,2,3]
antoine.widlocher@unicaen.fr

Yann Mathet[1,2,3]
yann.mathet@unicaen.fr

[1]Université de Caen Basse-Normandie, UMR 6072 GREYC, Caen, France
[2]ENSICAEN, UMR 6072 GREYC, Caen, France
[3]CNRS, UMR 6072 GREYC, Caen, France

ABSTRACT

Corpus linguistics and Natural Language Processing make it necessary to produce and share reference annotations to which linguistic and computational models can be compared. Creating such resources requires a formal framework supporting description of heterogeneous linguistic objects and structures, appropriate representation formats, and adequate manual annotation tools, making it possible to locate, identify and describe linguistic phenomena in textual documents.

The Glozz platform addresses all these needs, and provides a highly versatile corpus annotation tool with advanced visualization, querying and evaluation possibilities.

Categories and Subject Descriptors

H.5.2 [**Information Interfaces and Presentation**]: User Interfaces; I.2.7 [**Artificial Intelligence**]: Natural Language Processing; I.7.1 [**Document and Text Processing**]: Document and Text Editing; I.7.2 [**Document and Text Processing**]: Document Preparation—*Format and notation, Languages and systems, Markup languages, Standards*; J.5 [**Arts and Humanities**]: Linguistics

Keywords

Annotation formats and tools, Corpus Linguistics, Natural Language Processing

1. INTRODUCTION

More and more works in the linguistics, computational linguistics or Natural Language Processing (NLP) fields manifest an increasing interest for corpus studies. Through a wide range of approaches, the need for a systematic confrontation between models and corpora makes it necessary to have – and consequently, to produce – reference annotations to which linguistic models can be compared. Such reference corpora are also necessary for machine learning, to automatically learn models, and for evaluation tasks, to evaluate the results of NLP systems.

The elaboration of such annotations is a complex process which requires adequate formal grounds, encoding standards and dedicated applications. Despite the availability of several annotation tools, different requirements, especially in terms of abstraction, genericity and ergonomics, are overall not satisfied, as we will see in section 2.

The Glozz platform[1] [24], which will be presented in this paper, takes these constraints into account and provides a highly configurable environment, usable for corpus annotation and mining of various linguistic phenomena.

In order to satisfy the requirements of genericity and to support consequently the annotation of heterogeneous linguistic objects (in terms of structure, granularity...), Glozz relies on an abstract metamodel presented in section 3.

Given a specific linguistic model conforming to this metamodel, locating, identifying and describing linguistic objects in texts require adequate annotation tools. The incremental annotation process, Glozz GUI (presented in figure 5), as well as its main annotation features and tools, will be presented in section 4 and 5.

The annotation process, as well as the subsequent use of annotated data, require the ability to access information featured by the corpus. Glozz allows easy access to this information through different "navigation" tools and, in particular, by the mean of a powerfull query language called GlozzQL, which will be presented in section 6.

Building reference corpora makes it also necessary to align annotations and to measure agreement among annotators, in order to test the reliability of the annotated resources. Glozz features for alignment and agreement measure are presented in section 7.

Technologies, interoperability and availability will be discussed in section 8.

Presenting some recent research projets using Glozz, the last section will also mention its main strengths and weaknesses, and announce our roadmap.

2. STATE OF THE ART

2.1 A well-known problem

Several works and studies reveal the need for guidelines and tools to ensure production, long-term availability, inter-

---

[1]Glozz was initially developed within the Annodis project [20], supported by the french Agence Nationale de la Recherche (ANR). Glozz has also been supported by the french Contrat de Projet Etat-Région (CPER) and the Région Basse-Normandie. The URL address of its website is: http://www.glozz.org.

operability and efficient use of annotated corpora. Scientific events focus on these needs and reveal their importance for the NLP community. Let us just mention, for example, the LAW workshops [7] the LRT Standards workshop [3], the XBRAC workshop [25] or the ACL workshop on Discourse Annotation [22].

Among the works on linguistic annotation, three main topics may be identified : 1) annotation encoding, 2) annotation merging, mining and querying and 3) annotation process and tools.

Several works concern formats, standardisation and interoperability and aim to provide standards on which various annotation works could rely. From this point of view, guidelines developed by the Text Encoding Initiative (TEI)[2] are important contributions. Other works intend to provide unified means to represent heterogeneous linguistic annotations, and led to well-established formats. Works on LAF [8], GraF [9], annotation graph [2] and OLiA/PAULA [4] are, from this point of view, particularly important.

Other works mainly focus on annotation mining and querying. Due to dependencies between various linguistic phenomena, at different levels (word, syntagm, phrase, discourse unit, etc.) and from different points of view (morphological, syntactic, semantic, etc.), such mining and querying make it necessary to merge highly heterogeneous data, in order to explore them in a unified way. Frameworks such as CorpusReader [11] or Annis [4] enable integration of annotation data from different annotation tools and tag sets. As a consequence, integrated querying is possible, using unified query languages such as AnnisQL [4].

Other works aim to develop annotation tools and to make the annotation process as simple and reliable as possible. Some of these tools are embedded in more general purpose environments, made to deal with versatile linguistic data. They are consequently rather customizable. Widely used in the NLP community, the Gate platform [5] incorporates such a manual annotation tool, which can be configured by a user-defined annotation model. In the same way, the manual annotation tool available for the popular UIMA framework[3] has to be mentioned. Integrated to the well-known Protégé[4] environment, the annotation plugin Knowtator [18] takes advantage of ontologies to define rich annotation models.

Other standalone tools, on the contrary, are fully devoted to manual annotation. They provide more advanced features and enable annotation of more complex structures. Some of them, such as RSTTool [17], devoted to specific theories, are designed to deal with very specific annotation models, and may not be used for unrelated annotation campaigns, dedicated to other linguistic phenomena. In the same way, available tools for syntactic annotation, may not be used for annotation tasks devoted to other objects, in order to annotate, for example, argumentative structures. We deliberately focus here on more multipurpose tools.

Other works aim to provide more generic annotation tools. Nevertheless, their adaptability is often limited, not to linguistic categories, but to "structural types" : some of them mainly focus on text segmentation (annotation of textual segments); others focus on link-oriented annotation (annotation of relations between textual objects). Focusing on

segment annotation, UAM Corpus Tool[5] offers a flexible annotation environment for which complex and hierarchical annotation scheme can be defined. The integration of statistical tools makes it possible to mine available annotations. One of the noticeable features of Wordfreak [14] concerns the multiplicity of views it offers on text and annotations (*in situ* view, concordancers, representation as a tree...). Particularly used for anaphora/coreference annotation, MMAX [15] is nevertheless a customizable tool for creating and visualizing annotations on multiple levels. It pays particular attention to relations between segments, which can be graphically annotated, conforming to a user-defined annotation model. PALinkA [19] aims at providing a general purpose annotation tool. It allows segment or relation annotation, and user-defined annotation models. The importance it attaches to already available annotations, on which the annotation process may rely, has to be noted. The SLAT browser-based annotation tool [16] insists on the necessity of abstract and multipurpose environments, to take variety of annotation tasks into account. It allows segment and link-based annotation, relying on customizable tag sets. An other recent web-based annotation tool called BRAT [21] can be set up to support various collaborative annotation tasks involving segments and relations at quite low granularity levels. Some of its key strengths are its high-quality visualisation features, the embedded system for checking annotations, and the interoperability with NLP or machine learning systems to support manual annotation.

2.2 Yet another tool ?

Despite the availability of several annotation tools, and even if some of them are highly customizable, it must be noted that they do not meet the needs of all varieties of linguistic annotations. In a way, it is necessary to bridge the gap between broad enough formats (LAF, GraF, etc.) and too specialized tools. From this point of view, the following limits have to be emphasized:

1. Priority is globally given to the annotation of objects at quite local granularity levels, making it difficult to represent and then to explore, for example, structures at discourse level.

2. Available tools are often restricted to a particular theory or to a specific class of linguistic structures (segments, relations, chains...). Annotation tasks involving heterogeneous structures are then made difficult.

3. When a class of structure (segment, relation...) is available, ergonomic limits may nonetheless make its annotation process uneasy. For example, it is uneasy to express and visualise relations between textual segments, when annotation only consists in the attribution of a same ID to linked elements. A graphical artefact is necessary.

4. Strong constraints often restrict usage of the available classes of structures. For example, in the case of annotation of textual segments, embedded or overlapped structures are often not allowed or not adequately represented.

[2]http://www.tei-c.org.

[3]http://incubator.apache.org/uima/

[4]http://protege.stanford.edu.

[5]http://www.wagsoft.com/CorpusTool/.

5. It may be impossible to represent complex structures using only segments and relations (in particular if relations can only link segments). For example, annotation of enumerative structures [6] or complex discourse units [1] makes it necessary to link sub-structures and not only primary textual data. Moreover, linking non-adjacent elements in sub-structures is often needed, and can not be represented by embedding segments.

6. Annotations (segments or relations) are "labeled" to state the relevant information concerning identified objects. Simple tagsets are not expressive enough to meet requirements of rich annotation models, and it is necessary to implement richer labelling possibilities, using for example feature structure-based models.

Above mentioned limits mainly concern the expressive power of the data model. Other important limits concern the annotation process and the annotation environment:

1. Multiple views (*in situ*, concordancers, trees, graphs, etc.) on the same data are often required. And any of these views should notify any change to other views. However, available tools often give priority to one of these paradigms or feature multiple views which do not "observe" each others.

2. Querying/Mining of annotations should not be considered as a post annotation possibility. Indeed, at any stage of an annotation process, annotators need to rely on some specific existing configurations to which query languages can give access.

Most of these requirements, in terms of abstraction, genericity and ergonomics, have already been implemented in other tools, but not, to our knowledge, in a same tool. The general-purpose Glozz platform takes these constraints into account and provides a graphical and highly configurable annotation environment, usable for corpus annotation and exploration of various linguistic phenomena.

3. UNDERLYING MODEL

Due to the diversity of linguistic phenomena, corpus linguistics and NLP studies lead to a variety of models, theories and formalisms. This diversity often results in heterogenous description formats and annotation tools, each approach developing its own framework.

However, deep interactions between the different kinds of linguistic phenomena and paradigms make it necessary to define common frameworks and standards where most kinds of objects, resulting of heterogenous models or paradigms, can be described, in order to compare or combine various approaches.

3.1 The Unit-Relation-Schema metamodel

Glozz relies on an abstract metamodel, called URS (for Unit-Relation-Schema), originally coming from [23], which provides an adequate framework, unrestricted to a particular theory or to a specific class of objects, allowing description of existing or future linguistic models.

This metamodel, represented by the figure 1, relies on three abstract categories of *elements*: *units*, *relations* and *schemas* which will be described below.

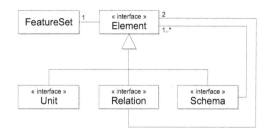

Figure 1: UML class diagram of URS

3.1.1 Metamodel and models

Within the general framework defined by the meta-model, specific models can be expressed, depending on the linguistic theory or approach. Each specific model declares available linguistic object types (identified by the theory) and explicits the way their instances have to be characterized (or labeled). The specialization of URS for a specific campaign will be presented in section 5.

3.1.2 Element

All available linguistic objects, called *elements*, may be *units*, *relations* or *schemas*. All of them are characterized by a *type name*, which explicits their linguistic category, and a *feature set*, representing their properties. Type names, expected features for a given type and possible values for these features depend on the specific user-defined model designed for a campaign.

3.1.3 Unit

Units, illustrated by figure 2, are textual segments, sequences or spans, of any size.

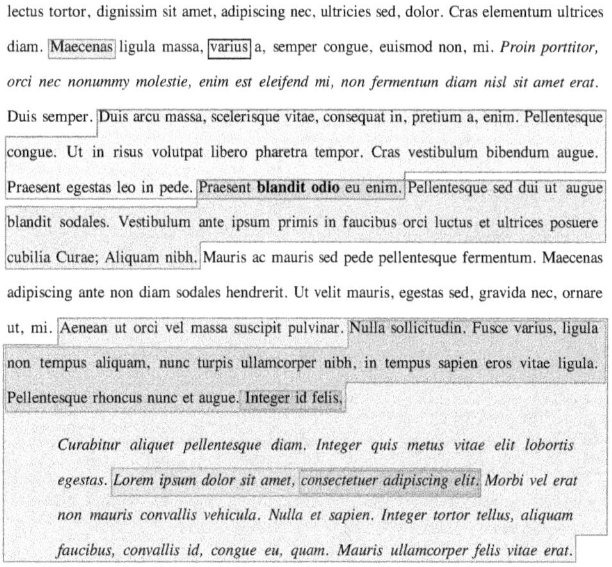

lectus tortor, dignissim sit amet, adipiscing nec, ultricies sed, dolor. Cras elementum ultrices diam. Maecenas ligula massa, varius a, semper congue, euismod non, mi. *Proin porttitor, orci nec nonummy molestie, enim est eleifend mi, non fermentun diam nisl sit amet erat.* Duis semper. Duis arcu massa, scelerisque vitae, consequat in, pretium a, enim. Pellentesque congue. Ut in risus volutpat libero pharetra tempor. Cras vestibulum bibendum augue. Praesent egestas leo in pede. Praesent **blandit odio** eu enim. Pellentesque sed dui ut augue blandit sodales. Vestibulum ante ipsum primis in faucibus orci luctus et ultrices posuere cubilia Curae; Aliquam nibh. Mauris ac mauris sed pede pellentesque fermentum. Maecenas adipiscing ante non diam sodales hendrerit. Ut velit mauris, egestas sed, gravida nec, ornare ut, mi. Aenean ut orci vel massa suscipit pulvinar. Nulla sollicitudin. Fusce varius, ligula non tempus aliquam, nunc turpis ullamcorper nibh, in tempus sapien eros vitae ligula. Pellentesque rhoncus nunc et augue. Integer id felis.

Curabitur aliquet pellentesque diam. Integer quis metus vitae elit lobortis egestas. Lorem ipsum dolor sit amet, consectetuer adipiscing elit. Morbi vel erat non mauris convallis vehicula. Nulla et sapien. Integer tortor tellus, aliquam faucibus, convallis id, congue eu, quam. Mauris ullamcorper felis vitae erat.

Figure 2: Units

A part of speech annotation task could for example define a unit type *word*, and two features to represent its morpho-syntactic tag and its lemma (the former having a predefined set of possible values). An annotator could then annotate all words of a text, each of them, instance of the type *word* (derived from the abstract meta-type *unit*), having its own tag and lemma values. Named entities, propositions, sentences, topical units, argumentative segments, sections or the whole document give other examples of possible units, at higher granularity levels.

3.1.4 Relation

Relations, illustrated by figure 3, designate links (directed or not) between two *elements*.

If relations between units are widely used, it must be noted that the possibility of relations linking whatever elements, including schemas or relations, significantly improves the expressive power of the metamodel.

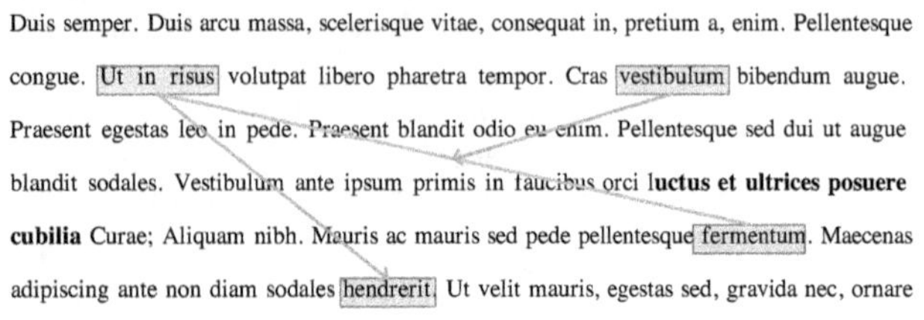

Duis semper. Duis arcu massa, scelerisque vitae, consequat in, pretium a, enim. Pellentesque congue. Ut in risus volutpat libero pharetra tempor. Cras vestibulum bibendum augue. Praesent egestas leo in pede. Praesent blandit odio eu enim. Pellentesque sed dui ut augue blandit sodales. Vestibulum ante ipsum primis in faucibus orci **luctus et ultrices posuere cubilia** Curae; Aliquam nibh. Mauris ac mauris sed pede pellentesque fermentum. Maecenas adipiscing ante non diam sodales hendrerit. Ut velit mauris, egestas sed, gravida nec, ornare

Figure 3: Relations

At a syntactic level, *dependancies* could, for example, be represented by directed relations. At a higher granularity level, a rhetorical annotation task would make use of directed relations to represent *causality* and benefit from symmetric relations to represent *contrast*, between propositions delimited as *units*, or between more complex patterns represented by *schemas*.

3.1.5 Schema

If both previous elements are quite common (even if designated otherwise), the schema category, illustrated by figure 4, is more original. Schemas are used to represent complex configurations or patterns involving any number of elements (units, relations or sub-schemas).

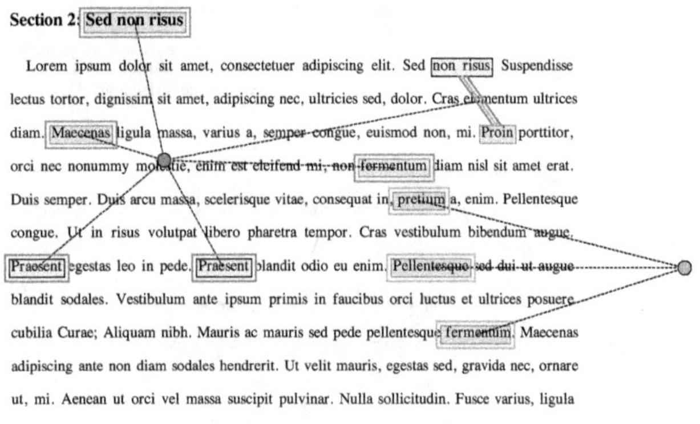

Section 2: Sed non risus

Lorem ipsum dolor sit amet, consectetuer adipiscing elit. Sed non risus Suspendisse lectus tortor, dignissim sit amet, adipiscing nec, ultricies sed, dolor. Cras elementum ultrices diam. Maecenas ligula massa, varius a, semper congue, euismod non, mi. Proin porttitor, orci nec nonummy molestie, enim est eleifend mi, non fermentum diam nisl sit amet erat. Duis semper. Duis arcu massa, scelerisque vitae, consequat in, pretium a, enim. Pellentesque congue. Ut in risus volutpat libero pharetra tempor. Cras vestibulum bibendum augue. Praesent egestas leo in pede. Praesent blandit odio eu enim. Pellentesque sed dui ut augue blandit sodales. Vestibulum ante ipsum primis in faucibus orci luctus et ultrices posuere cubilia Curae; Aliquam nibh. Mauris ac mauris sed pede pellentesque fermentum. Maecenas adipiscing ante non diam sodales hendrerit. Ut velit mauris, egestas sed, gravida nec, ornare ut, mi. Aenean ut orci vel massa suscipit pulvinar. Nulla sollicitudin. Fusce varius, ligula

Figure 4: Schemas

Coreference chains could, for example, be represented by a set (or a path) of binary relations, all grouped in a schema, whose features could describe the common reference. *Enumerative structures* provide a more complete example. Com-

posed of a set of consecutive *item* units, the enumeration is usually embedded in a larger structure (an *enumerative structure*), introduced by a *header* which is thereby in an *introduction relation* with items. In addition, *inheritance* relations between header and items, and *similarity* or *contrast relations* between items, often complete this quite frequent textual configuration.

3.2 Metamodel scope

This very abstract metamodel enables the representation of very many (if not all) configurations. If linguistic objects can then often be representend within the URS framework, it must be noted that "non-linguistic" information can also be encoded in this way.

For example, Glozz also uses the URS metamodel to represent document structure (titles, section titles...) and typographical information (ordered lists, emphasis...). Thus, with Glozz, everything but the raw text, is an annotation.

Represented in a unified way, all the available information can be used or mined in a unified way, as we will see in section 6.

3.3 Granularity and topology

The proposed meta-model makes no hypothesis on granularity level of elements or on distance between elements involved in relations or schemas. In particular, it meets the requirements of annotation at discourse level, which are overall not satisfied by multipurpose tools.

Furthermore, this data model accepts embedded and overlapping structures, as illustrated by the figure 2. More difficult to represent, the latter are often not well supported by annotation tools.

3.4 Standoff representation of annotations

Glozz uses standoff annotations. Units are linked to textual data using position offsets. Relations and schemas refers to objects they link or group.

3.5 URS and other data models

The URS metamodel is not "better" than established data models such as LAF/GrAF, and it shares a lot of features with them. Its expressivity is nevertheless slightly different. In particular, complex structure modeling using schemas differs from other representation strategies. They give a good framework to represent, for example, argumentative patterns, enumerative structures or coreference chains or for grouping several elements spread over a text, in particular when binary relations are not appropriate.

However, in most cases, translations between URS and other well-established data models are possible and achieving this interoperablity is a crucial point.

4. MAIN FEATURES

4.1 Polymorphism and heterogeneity of input

Annotated texts involve heterogenous data. In particular, in a same text, annotations may: come from different annotators; belong to various granularity levels (word, sentence, paragraph, text, etc.); be related to various linguistic paradigms (syntax, semantics, discourse, coreference, etc.).

An annotation environment should allow such an heterogeneity, and provide adequate ways to deal with it.

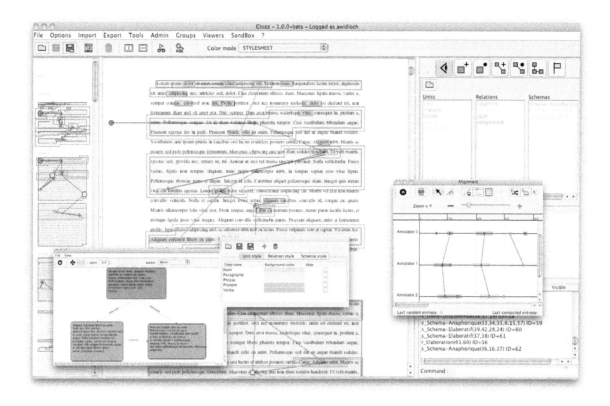

Figure 5: The Glozz main GUI

4.1.1 Several annotators

For a given annotation campaign, several annotators may add annotations to a same document. In Glozz, each annotator is authenticated, and each annotation is stamped with the identifier of its creator. This prevents collisions, and makes it possible to allow or disallow modifications by others, and to filter annotations by authors afterwards.

4.1.2 Granularity

Annotations attached to a same document may concern several levels of granularity. It may be a problem since each granularity level needs a specific modality to work with, particularly in terms of display.

Glozz proposes two simultaneous text views of the annotated document which are respectively set to "macro" and "micro" granularities. Thus, it is possible to have a global view of the document, where macro structures appear, and, at the same time, to have a focused local view, where micro structures can be well represented.

4.1.3 Several linguistic paradigms

It is necessary that several linguistic paradigms (syntax, semantics, etc.) can combine in a same document, because some paradigms may depend on others. However, too many structures at the same time make interpretation uneasy.

With Glozz it is possible to focus on one or several specific paradigms, and to hide annotations that do not belong to them. Indeed, annotation models can define groups of types, and each type can belong to one or several groups (see section 5). Users can hide as many groups as necessary.

4.1.4 Several linguistic types

Annotated items, instances of units, relations or schemas, are grouped in types (each type belonging to one or several paradigms). For example, in order to annotate the argumentative structure of scientific texts (this is an annotation paradigm), we could annotate unit objects having *types*: *introduction, background, state of the art, own work, experiment, evaluation, future works* or *conclusion*.

Annotation display, in Glozz, uses a stylesheet. This stylesheet makes it possible to define visual properties for each type, and, if necessary, to hide all instances of a given type.

4.2 Several representation paradigms

Different annotation paradigms (coreference chains, argumentative structures, rhetorical relations, etc.) often require different representation paradigms, called here *views*.

Nonetheless, we often need different paradigms at a same time, in a same campaign, hence in a same tool.

4.2.1 Annotations over the text, in situ annotation

Of course, the most usual way to annotate texts is to process directly upon them, in order to select and "highlight" identified objects. As shown in figure 6, it is possible to add or modify units, relations and schemas through a so-called WYSIWYG interface.

4.2.2 Annotations as a graph

If relations and schemas are integrated in complex constructions, or for specific annotation paradigms, a graph representation is obviously a good way to reveal what would be

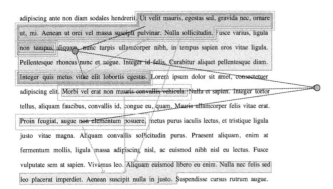

Figure 6: Annotations over the text

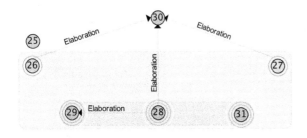

Figure 7: Annotations as a graph

confused on the flat view of the text. Hence, in figure 7, the annotations of figure 6 are represented by a graph, where the relations (of *elaboration*) and their interaction with schemas more clearly appear. In this configuration, units are represented by circled numbers and schemas by boxes.

4.2.3 Annotations as predicates

It may be convenient, as well, to read and create annotations directly as predicates, straight expressing, for example, that a relation should exist from annotation 1 to annotation 2, and so on. In Glozz, a module (illustrated by figure 8) permanently shows the list of all existing annotations in this way. A prompt may also be used to create new objects, with the help of auto-completion for element metatypes and type names, as well as for syntax checking.

```
...
u_Thesis(13260,13627) ID=25
u_Antithesis(13686,13731) ID=26
u_Synthesis(13858,13900) ID=27
s_Thesis/Antithesis/Synthesis(26,27,40) ID=39
u_Introduction(13260,13381) ID=28
u_Exemplification(13580,13627) ID=29
u_Exemplification(14157,14265) ID=30
r_Elaboration(28,29) ID=35
r_Elaboration(27,30) ID=36
s_Elaboration(28,29,44) ID=40
r_Elaboration(26,30) ID=41
r_Elaboration(28,30) ID=43
...
```

Figure 8: Annotations as predicates

4.2.4 Several simultaneous views

Moreover, a real strength of Glozz is its ability to make all its representation paradigms working at the same time, and together. Indeed, Glozz keeps central control of what is being selected through any view, and transmits the selection to all other views. This interaction is illustrated by figure 9, where the selection of an object in any of the 3 views selects it in the two other views.

This way, Glozz enhances the annotation process in two ways. Indeed, it makes it possible:

- to observe a same annotation from different points of view, in order to consider, for instance, its exact position in the text on the one hand, as well as its hierarchical position among other annotations, on the other hand;

- to select an annotation using a first view (the most adequate one to detect the searched object), and modify it using another one (more adequate to edit its properties).

5. CUSTOMIZING AND USING GLOZZ

For a given annotation task, it may be necessary to configure the annotation environment of Glozz.

5.1 Annotation campaign

An annotation platform should conform to the requirements of collaborative work. The concept of *annotation campaign* refers to an annotation task involving several annotators sharing resources.

Such resources, built by the *campaign managers*, and distributed to each annotator, include:

1. texts to be annotated;

2. one or several annotation models, to work with different paradigms;

3. one or several stylesheets to configure "points of view" on the data;

4. filters (see section 6.1), either to check reliability of the current annotation, or to bootstrap higher order annotations.

5.2 Annotation model

For a given annotation task, a specific annotation model is defined, conforming to the metamodel URS, which declares available types of units, relations and schemas. This *ad hoc* model also specifies the way of describing each instance of these types, by means of a feature set, and expresses constraints on the possible values for each feature. Available element types may also be grouped in categories or levels (see below and section 4). Relations may be declared directed or not.

Conforming to this specific model, annotators can locate instances of these types in corpora, and feed or select adequate feature values.

5.3 Customizing display

There are several ways in Glozz 1) to select annotations to be shown, and 2) to configure the way they are represented:

Filtering. Three options are given: 1) using style setting of types, since one of the style properties is visibility; 2) switching visibility of a whole group declared by the annotation model; 3) (temporary) switching visibility of individual annotation instances.

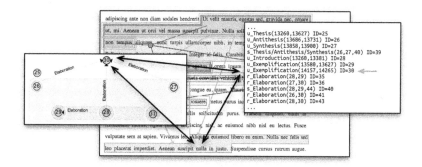

Figure 9: Several views on a same annotation

View settings. Type styling consists in choosing a color (for background or edge), and, for schemas, a shape. Several stylesheets can be defined for a same annotation model, in order to adopt successively different points of view on a same data.

6. ANNOTATION MINING

The annotation process, as well as the subsequent use of annotated data, requires the ability to access information featured by the corpus. This information concerns, of course, raw textual content, but it is also necessary to give a convenient access to linguistic (morphologic, syntactic, semantic, etc.) or infra-linguistic (document structure, typographical data, etc.) information, which may result from preliminary annotation (manual or computational) steps.

Annotating is an incremental process, which requires to take current annotations into account, to produce new ones. At a given stage of an annotation task, annotators need to find some specific configurations of annotations from previous steps (e.g. relations of a given type, units linked to other units by a relation of a given type, and so on).

Besides, it may be very helpful to check that all annotations conform to the annotation directives. Hence, the ability to locate non-valid configurations while annotating is a very convenient way to do so.

Glozz provides such facilities within annotation tasks by the means of some basic tools (not presented here), and a more advanced one named GlozzQL.

6.1 Introducing GlozzQL

6.1.1 Principles

GlozzQL (Glozz Query Language) is a language dedicated to Glozz annotations, and comes with an associated engine.

It is designed to select in a corpus each instance of element (unit, relation or schema) that satisfies expressed constraints. Requests are built piece after piece, in an incremental manner, using two interdependent concepts: *Constraint* and *Constrained-Annotation*.

Constraint: A constraint expresses one condition an annotation must satisfy in order to be selected. They are classified in 4 categories, depending on their domain, i.e. the kind(s) of element they concern (units, relations, schemas, any of them).

Constrained-Annotation: This simple concept refers to a set of annotations (of a given corpus) that all satisfy

a given constraint. For a given text, and depending on its associated constraint, a Constrained-Annotation contains 0 to n entities.

6.1.2 Examples

To get an idea of GlozzQL expressivity, let us mention some incremental possible queries:

- getting all Units of a given type (this set is called U1)

- getting all Units from U1, with a given value for a given feature (this set is called U2)

- getting all Relations whose target is an element of U2 (this set is called R1)

- getting all Schemas containing a relation among R1, with a maximum depth of 3 (this set is called S1)

- getting all Schemas belonging to S1 and from a given annotator

6.1.3 How it works

A more complete explanation of this system is provided in [12]. Let us only introduce here one real-world example coming from the Annodis project [20], in order to give an overview of the principles.

We need to find all schemas having *SE* type (acronym for Enumerative Structures, in french) embedding a unit having *amorce* type (french name of the header of an enumerative structure), as well as all the *SE* not embedding one.

To do so, we have first to define a Constrained-Unit which represents all *amorce* units. This is done by `Unit1`, in figure 11, which relies on `C1` Constraint, in figure 10.

ConstraintID	Content	Domain
C1	TypeName = amorce	Any
C2	Contains(Unit1), Level=1	Relation/Schema
C3	Not(C2)	Relation/Schema
C4	TypeName = SE	Any
C5	And(C2,C4)	Relation/Schema
C6	And(C3,C4)	Relation/Schema

Figure 10: Constraints

`C1` is a constraint which concerns the type name, which must be *amorce*. This constraint may be used with any kind of annotation (which is mentioned by its domain `Any`), hence with units. At this stage, having declared `Unit1` already

177

Annotation	Constraint	Matches
Unit1	C1 → TypeName = amorce	13
Schema1	C5 → And(C2,C4)	12
Schema2	C6 → And(C3,C4)	2

Figure 11: Constrained annotations

implies a mining process : as stated in figure 11, 13 units fitting C1 were found.

The second step consists in building Schema1, which represents all utterances of the first kind of searched schemas, that is to say schemas a) containing an utterance of Unit1, and b) having *SE* type. We express two preliminary constraints C2 and C4 respectively for a) and b). Then, a logical And constraint named C5 is built over C2 and C4. As a consequence, we get, with Schema1, 12 utterances of *SE* containing an *amorce*.

Then, we do the same to find all utterances of *SE* not containg any *amorce*, through C6 built over C3=not(C2) and C4. We get 2 utterances.

Hence, we have discovered that in the annotated text, 12 *amorce* units out of 13 are contained in a *SE* schema, and that 2 *SE* schemas out of 14 do not contain any *amorce*.

6.2 Annotating and querying simultaneously

As already mentioned, it is helpful to query what is currently being annotated, and to be able to go from query results to current annotations.

It's the reason why GlozzQL is integrated to Glozz, and interacts with it as shown in figure 12. On the right of the figure, is the list of all queries. We can click on any of them to make the list of its results appear, just below (arrow 1). Then, a click on one result will select it in Glozz main interface (arrow 2). We can immediately see this object in its context and are able to modify or delete it if needed.

7. ALIGNMENT AND AGREEMENT

In order to check the relevance of an annotation campaign, and to get reliable annotations, several annotators usually work on the same documents with the same task. Concurrent annotations may then be compared, and their agreement may be measured.

Glozz provides a dedicated view where each annotator is given a line representing the whole text. His annotations appear at their exact location (proportionaly to the line width), as shown in figure 13.

Moreover, we have developed a new approach to compute alignment and agreement measure, via a unified and holistic method described in [13]. This method is fully implemented in Glozz and we can get a visual representation of auto-alignment, as shown in figure 14, as well as an agreement score (from 0 to 1).

This method is generic enough to cope with complex unit configurations (with overlaps and so on), which are difficult to compare with other known methods.

8. REQUIREMENTS AND AVAILABILITY

8.1 Technologies

Fully implemented in Java, and representing annotation data, annotation models, styles and queries in XML formats,

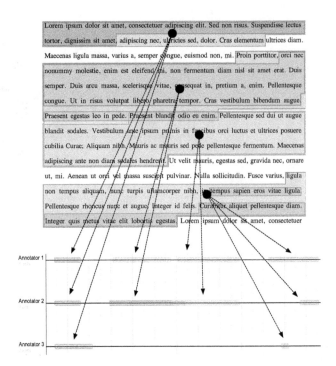

Figure 13: "One line per annotateur" view

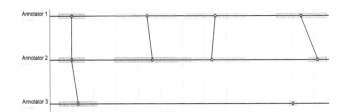

Figure 14: Alignment computation

Glozz may be used on several platforms, including Mac OSX, Linux or Windows on each of which it was tested.

8.2 Interoperability

Interoperability with other data formats (for corpora and annotations) relies on a set of import/export plugins. Raw text, and simple XML formats are already supported, as well as specific XML formats used in our NLP exprimental environment.

The import/export plugin set should grow in the future. In particular, well established formats, such as LAF/GrAF, should be supported soon. A work on a plugin dedicated to XML TEI is in progress.

It is also possible to export annotation data as an SQL file contaning structures and data. Loading this file in a RDBMS makes it possible to query annotations using SQL expressivity. It is also possible to export various annotation data as simple matrices, in order to explore them using for example a spreadsheet or any statistical tool.

8.3 Availability

Concerning availability and licence, this platform is already fully and freely available for academic research pur-

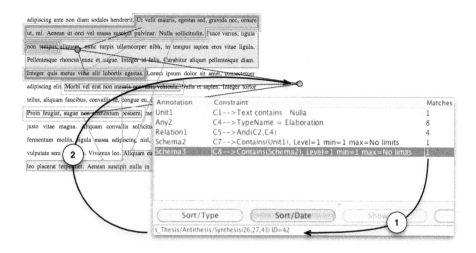

Figure 12: Querying while annotating

poses, and is widely used, even if mainly in France. Besides, its modular architecture relies on a core which is not open-source at this time (to keep control during the first years of development), and a plugin system allowing anyone to build additional tools (with whatever licence he chooses including open-source ones). XML formats are obviously open.

9. CONCLUSION AND FUTURE WORK

9.1 Recent works using Glozz

In conclusion, let us mention some recent research projects using the Glozz platform and proving its genericity and its usefulness for real-world annotation projects.

Within the Annodis project [20], it was used to create a corpus of discourse structures at several granularity levels.

Glozz is also used for the french Ontopitex ANR project, which is dedicated to opinion analysis. At low granularity levels, it allows annotation and fine description of linguistic structures. Post-annotation tools, were also used for alignment and evaluation purposes (agreement measure...).

Another recent work presented in [10], uses Glozz to study the combination of topical and rhetorical structures.

A french workgroup on coreference uses it to annotate complex (possibly imbricated) coreference chains, using expressive power of schemas.

9.2 Strengths and weaknesses

As far as we know, no other software provides such a range of capabilities for editing, viewing and mining annotations, in a same tool, at the same time. When an annotation campaign has to cope with various paradigms and scales, and has to edit and to explore data, it can rely on this comprehensive tool rather than using several tools at different stages and for different tasks. The versatility of Glozz is one of its main strengths.

But even when a campaign focuses on one phenomenon (e.g. coreference), and when dedicated tools do exist, some annotation campaign managers (well knowing other tools) switched to this one because of ergonomic and expressivity capabilities such as: direct view and "drag and drop" editing of relations, versatility of the meta-model (e.g. possibility

to represent coreference chains as schemas or as paths), multiple views (coreference chains *in situ* or as graphs).

Furthermore, its user-friendly interface makes it easy to use and learn without advanced computer skills. Users from linguistics domain successfully use it for annotation and annotation mining tasks.

The main limitation of Glozz is certainly the following: even if very versatile, its graphical interface is much more adequate for annotation tasks on discourse structure than for high density annotation at token level, for example for part-of-speech tagging or syntactic analysis. Indeed, in such a situation, the current visual environment may become somehow overloaded. Even if a workaround consists in setting the views to filter displayed annotations, a far better solution will be to provide a new dedicated visualization paradigm.

It must also be noted that the main interface can not be used to edit the content of the annotated text. However, an external tool makes it possible to correct a text, and then update annotations consequently.

9.3 Future works

At the moment, Glozz considers each text as an isolated entity, and annotators have to load individually each text they have to work with. A next step in the annotation campaign management will provide a "corpus" entity, composed of texts, which will make annotation and mining tasks on several texts easier, and will enable actions on the whole.

Currently, Glozz annotations are limited to the text scope. This scope will be extended to any text set, so that relations and schemas can apply to objects from different texts. Hence, it would be possible, for instance, to represent "alignment" relations between a text and its translations.

At last, it will be important to ensure interoperability of data produced (and imported) by Glozz, using standard such as LAF/GraF and TEI specifications for representing annotations and feature structures.

10. ACKNOWLEDGMENTS

The authors would like to warmly thank Jérôme Chauveau, who recently joined Glozz team and strongly contributes to its development.

11. REFERENCES

[1] N. Asher, A. Venant, P. Muller, and S. Afantenos. Complex discourse units and their semantics. In *Proceedings of Constraints in Discourse*, 2011.

[2] S. Bird and M. Liberman. A formal framework for linguistic annotation. *Speech Communication*, 33:23–60, 2000.

[3] G. Budin, L. Romary, T. Declerck, and P. Wittenburg, editors. *Workshop on Language Resource and Language Technology Standards – state of the art, emerging needs, and future developments*, La Valetta, Malta, 2010. Language Resources and Evaluation Conference (LREC 2010).

[4] C. Chiarcos, S. Dipper, M. Götze, U. Leser, A. Lüdeling, J. Ritz, and M. Stede. A Flexible Framework for Integrating Annotations from Different Tools and Tag Sets. *Revue Traitement Automatique des Langues (TAL)*, 49(2):189–215, 2008.

[5] H. Cunningham, D. Maynard, K. Bontcheva, and V. Tablan. GATE: A Framework and Graphical Development Environment for Robust NLP Tools and Applications. In *Proceedings of the 40th Meeting of the Association for Computational Linguistics*, pages 168–175, Philadelphia, USA, 2002.

[6] L.-M. Ho-Dac, M.-P. Péry-Woodley, and L. Tanguy. Anatomie des Structures Énumératives. In *Actes de la 17e Conférence Traitement Automatique des Langues Naturelles (TALN 2010)*, Montréal, Canada, 2010.

[7] N. Ide and A. Meyers, editors. *Linguistic Annotation Workshop*, Portland, Oregon, USA, 2011. Conference ACL/HLT 2011.

[8] N. Ide and L. Romary. Representing linguistic corpora and their annotations. In *Proceedings of the Fifth Language Resources and Evaluation Conference (LREC)*, 2006.

[9] N. Ide and K. Suderman. GrAF: A graph-based format for linguistic annotations. In *Proceedings of the Linguistic Annotation Workshop*, pages 1–8, Prague, Czech Republic, June 2007. Association for Computational Linguistics.

[10] A. Labadié, P. Enjalbert, Y. Mathet, and A. Widlöcher. Discourse structure annotation : Creating reference corpora. In Budin et al. [3].

[11] S. Loiseau. CorpusReader : construction et interrogation de corpus multiannotés. *Revue Traitement Automatique des Langues (TAL)*, 49(2):189–215, 2008.

[12] Y. Mathet and A. Widlöcher. Stratégie d'exploration de corpus multi-annotés avec GlozzQL. In M. Lafourcade and V. Prince, editors, *Actes de la 18e Conférence Traitement Automatique des Langues Naturelles (TALN'11), volume 2, papiers courts*, pages 143–148, Montpellier, France, juin 2011. LIRMM.

[13] Y. Mathet and A. Widlöcher. Une approche holiste et unifiée de l'alignement et de la mesure d'accord inter-annotateurs. In M. Lafourcade and V. Prince, editors, *Actes de la 18e Conférence Traitement Automatique des Langues Naturelles (TALN'11)*, pages 247–258, Montpellier, France, juin 2011. LIRMM.

[14] T. Morton and J. LaCivita. WordFreak: An Open Tool for Linguistic Annotation. In *Proceedings of Human Language Technology (HLT) and North American Chapter of the Association for Computational Linguistics (NAACL)*, pages 17–18, Edmonton, Canada, 2003.

[15] C. Müller and M. Strube. Multi-level annotation of linguistic data with MMAX2. In S. Braun, K. Kohn, and J. Mukherjee, editors, *Corpus Technology and Language Pedagogy: New Resources, New Tools, New Methods*, pages 197–214. Peter Lang, Frankfurt a.M., Germany, 2006.

[16] M. Noguchi, K. Miyoshi, T. Tokunaga, R. Iida, M. Komachi, and K. Inui. Multiple Purpose Annotation using SLAT - Segment and Link-based Annotation Tool. In *Proceedings of the 2nd Linguistic Annotation Workshop*, pages 61–64, may 2008.

[17] M. O'Donnell. RSTTool 2.4 – A Markup Tool for Rhetorical Structure Theory. In *Proceedings of the International Natural Language Generation Conference (INLG'2000)*, pages 253 – 256, Mitzpe Ramon, Israel, 13-16 June 2000.

[18] P. V. Ogren. Knowtator: A Protégé plug-in for annotated corpus construction. In *Proceedings of Human Language Technology (HLT) and North American Chapter of the Association for Computational Linguistics (NAACL)*, New-York, USA, 2006.

[19] C. Orăsan. PALinkA: a highly customizable tool for discourse annotation. In *Proceedings of the 4th SIGdial Workshop on Discourse and Dialog*, pages 39–43, Sapporo, Japan, July, 5-6 2003.

[20] M.-P. Péry-Woodley, N. Asher, P. Enjalbert, F. Benamara, M. Bras, C. Fabre, S. Ferrari, L.-M. Ho-Dac, A. Le Draoulec, Y. Mathet, P. Muller, L. Prévot, J. Rebeyrolle, L. Tanguy, M. Vergez-Couret, L. Vieu, and A. Widlöcher. ANNODIS: une approche outillée de l'annotation de structures discursives. In *Actes de la 16e Conférence Traitement Automatique des Langues Naturelles (TALN'09), session poster*, Senlis, France, 2009.

[21] P. Stenetorp, S. Pyysalo, G. Topic, T. Ohta1, S. Ananiadou, and J. Tsujii. BRAT: a Web-based Tool for NLP-Assisted Text Annotation. In *Proceeding of the 13th Conference of the European Chapter of the Association for Computational Linguistics*, Avignon, France, 2012.

[22] B. Webber and D. Bryon, editors. *Proc. of the ACL 2004 Workshop on Discourse Annotation.*, Barcelone, Espagne, 2004.

[23] A. Widlöcher. *Analyse macro-sémantique des structures rhétoriques du discours - Cadre théorique et modèle opératoire*. PhD thesis, Université de Caen Basse-Normandie, 17 octobre 2008.

[24] A. Widlöcher and Y. Mathet. La plate-forme Glozz: environnement d'annotation et d'exploration de corpus. In *Actes de la 16e Conférence Traitement Automatique des Langues Naturelles (TALN'09), session posters*, Senlis, France, juin 2009.

[25] A. Witt, U. Heid, H. S. Thompson, J. Carletta, and P. Wittenburg, editors. *Workshop on XML-based richly annotated corpora (XBRAC)*, Lisbonne, Portugal, 29 mai 2004. Language Resources and Evaluation Conference (LREC 2004).

Sift: An End-User Tool for Gathering Web Content on the Go

Matthias Geel, Timothy Church and Moira C. Norrie
Institute of Information Systems, ETH Zurich
CH-8092 Zurich, Switzerland
{geel|norrie}@inf.ethz.ch, tim.church@gmail.com

ABSTRACT

Although web sites have started to embed semantic meta-data within their documents, it remains a challenge for non-technical end-users to exploit that markup to extract and store information of interest. To address this challenge, we show how tools can be developed that allow users to identify extractable information while browsing and then control how that information should be extracted and stored in a personal library. The proposed approach is based on an extensible framework capable of using different kinds of markup to aid the extraction process and a unique fusion of several well-established techniques from areas such as the semantic web, data warehousing, web scraping and web feeds. We present the Sift tool which is a proof-of-concept implementation of the approach.

Categories and Subject Descriptors

H.3.m [**Information Storage and Retrieval**]: Miscellaneous—*Data Extraction, Semantic Markup, Web*

Keywords

information gathering, web content aggregation, information extraction

1. INTRODUCTION

The web is an abundant source of information about almost any topic, but information for single items of interest, such as movies, persons or events, is often dispersed across many different web sites and presented in a variety of formats. Over the years, a number of tools have therefore been developed to automatically locate and extract information published on the web using techniques commonly referred to as *web scraping*. In recent years, the Semantic Web community has worked hard to promote the widespread introduction of semantic markup to greatly simplify this process and the inclusion of some form of machine-readable seman-

tic metadata within web documents is certainly becoming more common.

However, it remains a challenge for end-users to exploit document markup to extract and store information of interest as they encounter it on the web. Although a number of research projects have investigated ways of allowing end-users to annotate data with semantic markup [5, 6, 9], surprisingly little research has gone into exploring the possibilities of making semantic metadata directly visible to end-users for extraction purposes.

We therefore decided to investigate how the increasing amount of hidden (from a user's perspective) semantic data could be leveraged to facilitate personal data collection on the web. Our goal was to support lightweight end-user extraction of web content by helping users identify extractable data and assist them in the extraction process by suggesting what and how data could be extracted. Importantly, we were not aiming for a fully automatic solution, but rather one where users participate in the process and can easily choose the data that they extract and customise how it is stored and organised.

As proof-of-concept, we have developed a system called Sift that fuses several well-established techniques from the Semantic Web, web scraping, web feeds and data warehousing in a unique manner in order to demonstrate our novel approach towards content aggregation. Users interact with Sift through two web tools—one offered as a browser extension for discovering extractable data and specifying how it should be extracted, and the other a web-based interface to the user's personal collection of extracted data referred to as the *topics dashboard*. At the core of the system is a content aggregation engine that is implemented as an extensible framework to cater for the variety of markup languages and vocabularies commonly found on the web today. In addition to the official standards from the W3C, there have also been several commercial and community efforts such as Schema.org, Facebook's Open Graph Protocol, Microformats and RDFa from the semantic web community. While most existing tools for processing data contained within web documents focus on a single format, it was important that we embraced rather than ignored the wealth of semantic markup available today in order that users can gather information freely across the web and are not limited by artificial boundaries of particular markup communities.

We first discuss related work in Sect. 2, before presenting an overview of our approach in Sect. 3. An overview of the proposed architecture is given in Sect. 4 with the content aggregation engine described in Sect. 5. Details of the implementation of the Sift system are given in Sect. 6. In Sect. 7, we highlight the advantages of our approach with the help of a scenario. Concluding remarks as well as some ideas for future work are given in Sect. 8.

2. RELATED WORK

A study by Schraefel and Zhu [15] found that users were interested in creating collections of information found within web pages. In other words, people want the ability to gather information at a finer level of granularity than a full web page. This led to the development of systems such as Hunter Gatherer [16], Internet Scrapbook [17], and myPortal [10] which allow users to save content blocks from various web pages and reassemble them into customised documents. By selecting components from within web pages, users capture only the desired information rather than the full document, which may contain additional, irrelevant material. These web page fragments, often referred to as 'web snippets', can then be arranged into collections to provide personalized access to the selected information. Although collecting only selected components of a web page is an improvement over saving the full document, the main shortcoming of these systems is that they still do not have any knowledge of the underlying semantics of these web page fragments. Without understanding the structure of the data, the use of the collected information is limited and sophisticated interaction with or repurposing of the data is not possible.

Web scraping, also referred to as web harvesting or information extraction, is a technique that uses software programs to extract information from within web pages so that the data may be reused in another context. Scraping emerged early in the history of the web as a mechanism for users to access and repurpose individual information items from websites. There are several possible ways that a web scraper can implement the extraction including rules based on the structure of the document, metadata attributes within the HTML, or the textual content of the web page. Since websites are dynamic in nature, much research [10, 11] has focused on creating robust extraction patterns that will continue to work even after a document has been updated. Methods that use relative paths within the Document Object Model (DOM) are generally more robust than those that use absolute paths. As stated in the survey by Laender et al. [11], popular methods for defining extraction rules include XPath, XQuery, and CSS selectors, while some systems utilize heuristics, ontologies, natural language processing, or machine learning techniques to identify which pieces of information to extract. Newer approaches propose algorithms to calculate the edit distance [14] between DOM trees or to partially align them [19], hereby exploiting the structural similarities of web pages to automatically extract data items from a large number of web sites.

In [1] and [2], Dontcheva et al. developed an information extraction system to collect, view, and organise personal web content. Users select and label web page elements using a browser-integrated toolbar. The interface allows users to define both structural and content-based extraction rules. These user-defined extraction patterns are applied to extract individual information items semi-automatically into a local database. Gathered content is presented through predefined summary layout templates. In [1] the authors extend the system to allow users to define their own custom templates for personalized presentation. The system created in [1, 2] does not leverage any existing semantic markup within the HTML but instead relies on users to manually define and label each individual data attribute. Also, extracted elements are limited to a small set of predefined labels within a single schema.

There have been a number of efforts by the Semantic Web community to address the problems of extraction and collection of structured web content. Thresher [7] is a tool that allows end-users to extract semantic structures from HTML documents on the web. Users label examples of semantic content on a web page to teach the browser how to find similar data items. Extraction is based on tree edit distance between the DOM sub-trees of the user-provided examples. For all matching objects, RDF data wrappers are created which allow for rich interactions inside the Haystack semantic web browser [1]. Thresher is integrated with the Haystack semantic browser and cannot be used with traditional web browsers. Also, this tool does not extract semantic data into a separate, user-controlled database, but rather automatically annotates web pages with semantic metadata as the user browses. Piggy Bank [8] is a browser extension that allows users to collect structured content from web pages while browsing and save them in semantic web format. For websites that do not publish information in RDF format, Piggy Bank relies on user-generated JavaScript screen scrapers to extract individual information items from within web pages. The goal of this work is to empower users to build the Semantic Web from the bottom up by creating and sharing custom screen scrapers as well as by sharing collected semantic information. A web interface is also provided which enables faceted browsing of the RDF data that has been harvested.

The idea of combining data warehousing and web technologies has been explored in previous research [18]. Web warehousing relaxes the view that input sources for a data warehouse are limited to operational databases and permits data resources to be located anywhere on the web. Various projects have attempted to find innovative, new methods to incorporate existing information from the web into a data warehouse. For example, Moya et al. [12] have investigated how to integrate web feeds into data warehouses. They use sentiment analysis on web feeds in order to include customer opinions in a corporate data warehouse for business intelligence purposes. Meanwhile, Nebot and Berlanga [13] have looked into ways to leverage the Semantic Web within the context of data warehousing. They propose a semi-automatic method for extracting and combining data in OWL format into a multi-dimensional star schema for OLAP analysis. Both of these research projects focus narrowly on a single data format, and both are only interested in converting web data into an OLAP-friendly format that is suitable for business analysis. These limitations make each solution unsuitable for general purpose information collection and less useful outside of the enterprise context.

3. GATHERING CONTENT ON THE GO

Our goal was to create a tool that would enable nontechnical users to quickly and easily gather data while browsing the web, allowing them to collect information directly from a web page without having to leave the browser. The user should be able to guide the extraction process, but the

---

[1] http://groups.csail.mit.edu/haystack/

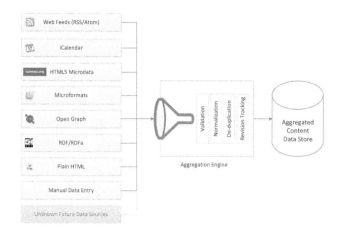

Figure 1: Conceptual overview of the content aggregation engine

bulk of the work should be done by a content aggregation engine with the user only having to confirm or correct the assumptions made by the best-effort predictions of the system. For more advanced and technically-inclined users, it should however be possible for them to specify custom extraction rules.

While each of the existing solutions discussed in Sect. 2 is useful for certain scenarios, each one on its own is limited in scope and insufficient for our needs. However, many of these diverse strategies and methods are not mutually exclusive. We therefore propose a hybrid approach that combines aspects from multiple, previously unrelated areas of research. In so doing, we provide the end-user with a larger toolkit from which to select the most appropriate means for collecting structured data from any given web page.

Data published on the web varies widely across many dimensions including file format, markup scheme, quality, consistency, completeness, and correctness. Some websites may embed semantic metadata in one or more different formats while others may only provide information items as unstructured text. We do not want to make any assumptions about the type or amount of details available for the data on any given web page. By utilising different techniques depending on the specifics of the information provided by a particular website, we are better able to cope with the diversity of the information found on the web.

Figure 1 shows a conceptual overview of our approach towards a content aggregation engine for the web. We aim to enable users to harvest information from any web page, regardless of the specifics of how that information happens to be presented to the user. For this reason, we propose an architecture that abstracts specific data formats and consolidates all incoming data before it is being processed by further components of the aggregation engine. To this end, all extracted individual data items are transformed to a hierarchical data structure, similar to a JSON document, and merged. This abstraction allows us to extend the system with custom extractors for new data formats and to add support for future semantic markup languages without having to adapt the data integration pipeline. Extractors are software modules that process a web page or web data source, if applicable, and may use any programming technique available to extract information. A number of built-in extractors

are described in Sect. 5. In addition, it is important that the extraction engine should not only be able to process numerous, diverse file formats and semantic markup specifications, but also allow user-generated content to be fed directly into the system. Manual data entry allows end-users to create new data items in order to capture information that may not yet be available online from existing websites.

Gathering web content is only one part of the aggregation pipeline. The web contains copious amounts of incomplete, inconsistent, invalid, and duplicate information. That is why we borrow well-established data integration and aggregation concepts from the data warehouse community, and this is another aspect that distinguishes our approach from most previous efforts. Data warehouses are traditionally found in an enterprise setting where they are used to integrate and aggregate data from heterogeneous sources. The data integration steps in our architecture are intended to clean up the data before it enters the local database and to ensure an acceptable level of quality and consistency within the data repository. This process includes validation, normalisation, duplicate entity detection, and revision history tracking. Only after data has successfully passed through all of the data integration stages will it be saved in the local data repository.

We now provide an overview of the approach by describing how users interact with the Sift system that was developed as a testbed for the proposed methods. Sift is the name of our content aggregation engine that runs as a service in the background. The users themselves are provided with the combination of a custom web browser extension that supports the gathering of data and a web interface for interacting with the saved information. This allows users to both collect and manipulate data items without ever leaving the web browser, thereby providing one integrated solution to harvest and organise web content.

Discovering.

The web browser extension provides a mechanism for alerting the user to web pages that might be good candidates for data extraction. When certain forms of structured, semantic metadata are detected on the current web page, the icon of the extension's toolbar button is updated to inform the user of this fact. As shown in Figure 2, the normal icon is a dull grey funnel, but when semantic metadata is detected, the icon is changed to a bright green funnel with a red plus sign overlay. By changing the colour and shape of the icon, we are able to notify the user of potential data sources without

Figure 2: Firefox toolbar button and notification icon

Figure 3: Inspecting extracted information

distracting from the web browsing experience. Other notification techniques, such as pop-up alerts, would be much more noticeable but would also disrupt and annoy the user. In contrast, our subtle icon notification method promotes awareness without user interference. Also, the use of toolbar icons to display additional information conforms to a commonly used design pattern for web browser extensions and should be familiar to most users.

Gathering.

In order to harvest the information discovered, the browser extension includes a graphical interface for configuring new data sources, called the extraction wizard. We utilise the software wizard paradigm to guide the user through the process in an easy to understand, step-by-step manner. In a first step, all extractable data is presented in a hierarchical tree structure organised by the extractor that can be expanded and collapsed. This interface, which can be seen in Figure 3, allows the user to easily browse and view all of the available metadata. That data is the result of the content aggregation engine exceecuting all applicable extractor components against the currently viewed web page and consolidating their output. To avoid users having to do any data modelling or design custom templates, we chose to adopt the single common data model defined by Schema.org[2] for the storage of extracted data. The second step triggers the execution of all default mappings to this model by the content aggregation engine. The extraction wizard uses these defaults to determine which schema type to pre-select by fol-

---

[2]http://schema.org

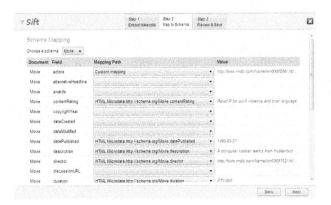

Figure 4: Defining mappings

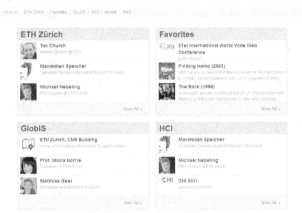

Figure 5: Topics Dashboard

lowing a simple heuristic approach: It chooses the schema type with the highest number of matching fields and also pre-populates all successfully mapped fields, see Figure 4. Furthermore, the user is able to select different extractors for certain fields or to define custom mappings. In the last step, the user is given the chance to revise the final rule set and to define a URL pattern to match similar related web pages. URL matching expressions relieve the user from creating the same set of custom mappings over and over again because many web sites that expose semantic markup follow a template-based approach, thereby facilitiating the re-use of extraction patterns.

Event Details

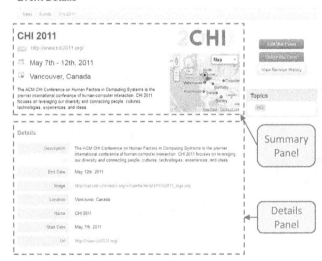

Figure 6: Dashboard Details View

Managing.

We provide the topics dashboard presented in Figure 5 as a default interface for interacting with the collected data. The user can *organise* saved records into custom collections, called topics. Next, the user can *browse* these collections of items in a unified way, regardless of the data type or original source location of the information. The user can also

184

view the details of individual data records as shown in Figure 6 and *edit* or *delete* any existing database entry. Finally, the user also has the ability to manually *create* new data items directly from the web interface. Before being saved to the local data repository, all information added through the web interface component is subjected to exactly the same data integration steps as information items extracted from web pages. Any violations of the validation rules will be displayed immediately to the user by highlighting the corresponding form elements.

It is important to note that our interface is just one possible way to interact with the collected data. Once the information has been harvested from the web and saved into the local data repository, it is under the complete control of the end-user. Technically-inclined users can develop their own custom interfaces on top of this data repository in order to meet their specific needs and requirements. Choosing a web-based application instead of a stand-alone desktop application has the advantage that users who are already experienced in web browsing and interacting with web applications will have a familiar and intuitive environment. Also, the web interface opens up the possibility to provide access to the data repository from remote locations. Further, it offers the potential for collaborative editing or group-based repositories.

In the following sections, we present the general architecture that we propose as well as details of the content aggregation engine. This is followed by a description of how the Sift system was implemented as proof-of-concept.

4. ARCHITECTURE

An overview of the proposed system architecture is shown in Fig. 7. In the upper part of the figure, we show the two web-based tools that the users interact with which were described in the previous section. On the left is the browser extension used to discover and extract data, while the web interface known as the *topics dashboard* used to interact with their personal database of extracted data is shown on the right.

The content aggregation engine is responsible for *extracting*, *mapping* and *integrating* the harvested data. The *extraction* process is initiated by the browser extension component and employs a variety of techniques to extract structured data from any supported format.

During the *mapping* step, individual data items are mapped from the consolidated extractor outputs to our internal data model. Schema.org was selected as the common data model because it is comprehensive, designed for the web, and based on the existing work of several previous semantic markup initiatives. For the purpose of demonstrating our approach, only a subset of the vocabulary has been implemented to date.

Our choice to use a single, common data model is not as flexible as allowing users to define their own custom data models, but has a number of benefits when considering the overall goal of our work to support non-technical end-users. By using Schema.org as a common model in conjunction with the extraction wizard, no data modelling is required and users can start extracting data immediately with little or no training. Also, users do not need to worry about designing any custom templates since the system already provides interfaces that are optimized for each of the predefined data types. As users become more familiar with the

system they can gradually progress to the level of customising the mappings which will allow them to extract more data and refine the ways in which it is stored in their personal database.

Another major benefit of using a common data model is the potential for sharing extraction rules between installations of the system. This enables the possibility of creating crowdsourced repositories for data sources and their related data mapping configurations. Finally, since the data schemas are reused by all instances of the system, collected data items themselves could be shared. Therefore, communal data repositories could be created to allow groups of people to contribute information extracted individually. Through this or other methods, users could exchange structured data and mutually benefit from the work of others in the community.

The data *integration* process is organised as a pipeline where incoming information items are required to pass through all integration phases in succession before finally being stored in the data repository. First, the extracted raw object is validated against the appropriate Schema.org type definition and transformed to the corresponding model classes. These steps clean the data by performing normalization, coercing information into the appropriate format, and ensuring certain required attributes are present. Second, it is also important to be able to detect duplicate records because the web contains several different datasets that often overlap. Information on various websites may differ slightly yet still refer to the same real world entity. These approximate duplicates exist for several reasons including differing amounts of information provided, slight differences in one or more attribute values due to user input errors (e.g. typos), or dissimilar formatting of the same data. We have included basic entity resolution logic to automatically detect and merge these duplicates to keep the data repository normalized. The final aspect of data integration is the ability to track changes over time, a pattern known as change data capture. Whether the source has updated its information, the extraction process produced incorrect results or the user has manually deleted some information by accident, there is always possibility that some existing data is overridden with new, possibly invalid values. To counter balance this, every update is logged in order to provide the user with the ability to view the full revision history for each item. With the help of the topics dashboard, the user is able to discover exactly what information was changed and when it was modified. Erroneous data updates can then be easily reverted back to a previous, valid state.

Since the original web data may be updated, the server will periodically re-execute the extraction and integration process so that the extracted data stored in the personal database is also updated automatically. Of course, the update process takes into account any custom mapping definitions created by the user for the original data source. The frequency of the updating process can be configured by the user.

Neither the browser extension nor the topics dashboard communicates directly with the data repository, but rather all database operations are mediated by the content aggregationengine. This enables the engine to manage all data updates in order to ensure proper data integration procedures are executed and all changes are appropriately tracked within the revision history. The content aggregation can ei-

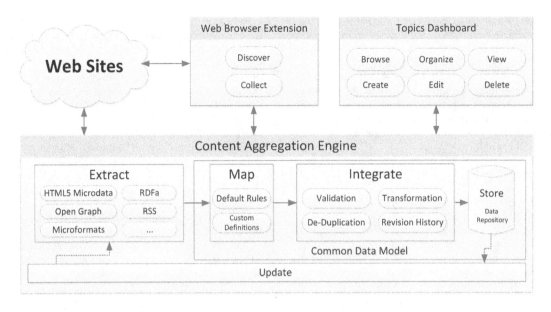

Figure 7: System architecture overview

ther be installed locally or on a dedicated web server. In the next section, we provide details of the components that make up the content aggregation engine, as well as the flow of data and communication between them.

5. CONTENT AGGREGATION ENGINE

A single data source is identified by its URL and might be represented by a character-based document, for example XHTML, HTML or XML. A fundamental requirement of our approach is the ability to combine multiple information harvesting techniques in order to support the multitude of possible data formats found on the web. Therefore, the extraction infrastructure was constructed in a flexible way that allows these diverse methods to coexist and work in harmony with one another. As a result, an extractor may add any kind and any amount of metadata to a gobally shared collection where each extractor is given its own namespace to prevent conflicts during the extraction step. Details about how to create custom extractors can be found in another paper [4]. The extraction step is designed as a chained execution of extractor components, where the content engine pre-parses the data source and calls each applicable extractor in turn.

Most notably, we include built-in support for the following widely used formats:

- *HTML* - The HTML extractor is intended to be used as a base class for creating any extractor that interacts directly with the HTML markup. This convention allows the HTML to be parsed only once and reused by all subsequent extractors that require access to this data.

- *HTML 5 Microdata* - HTML 5 introduced a mechanism, called Microdata, to allow machine-readable semantic metadata to be embedded within HTML documents. HTML elements can be annotated with name-value pairs from a Microdata vocabulary such as data-vocabulary.org or Schema.org. This extractor uses the

open-source *microdata*[3] library to extract HTML 5 Microdata from the underlying HTML. The output from this initial extraction is then reorganized in order to be grouped according to data type. Also, all relative URLs in the extracted data are automatically converted to absolute URLs.

- *Microformats* - Microformats[4] are a community-driven effort to create a set of open data format standards for annotating HTML and XHTML documents with machine-readable semantic metadata. This extractor utilizes the open-source *Microtron*[5] package to extract all Microformats metadata embedded within the given HTML. It supports the majority of current Microformats specifications and drafts including hCalendar, hCard, hAtom, hNews, hReview, hListing, hAudio, hProduct, hResume, adr, geo, Votelinks, xFolk, XFN, rel-tag, rel-license, and rel-principles. Note that this extractor intentionally excludes the no-follow specification as this is commonly used but not useful for our use case of extracting data objects. The Microformats extractor also converts all relative URLs to absolute URLs automatically.

- *Open Graph* - The Open Graph protocol[6] is a simplistic semantic markup initiative created by Facebook in 2010. The Open Graph protocol allows web pages to become objects in the social graph by embedding basic metadata in HTTP `<meta>` tags. This extractor parses all Open Graph information from the given web page using the open-source *PyOpenGraph*[7] library.

---

[3]https://github.com/edsu/microdata
[4]http://microformats.org/
[5]https://github.com/amccollum/microtron
[6]http://ogp.me/
[7]http://pypi.python.org/pypi/PyOpenGraph

- *RDFa* - RDFa is a W3C recommendation for adding semantic metadata to XHTML documents. Specifically, RDFa enables RDF subject-predicate-object triples to be embedded within XHTML markup. This specification provides a set of XHTML attributes to augment human-visible text with machine-readable hints without repeating content. The RDFa extractor employs the *RdfaDict*[8] package to parse and extract all RDFa annotations within the given document.

- *Web Feeds* - This extractor uses the open-source *Universal Feed Parser*[9] module for parsing syndicated web feeds. It can handle several different data formats including RSS 0.9x, RSS 1.0, RSS 2.0, CDF, Atom 0.3, and Atom 1.0, as well as several popular extension modules such as Dublin Core and Apple's iTunes extensions.

- *JSON* - This extractor attempts to read the input data as a JavaScript object. If successful, the entire JSON object is added to the output and made available for data mapping.

Which subset of the extracted data is actually forwarded to the data integration pipeline depends on a specific set of mapping rules, which in turn depends on the data source being processed. After the extractors have completed their work, we apply the corresponding mapping rules to map parts of the extracted attributes to the common data model defined by Schema.org.

Before an extracted entity is finally added to the data store, we check for duplicates based on exact and approximate matching of selected duplicate identification fields. These fields can be specified individually for each internal data type and serve as a composite key for entities of that type. In a first step, exact duplicates are detected by testing for equality of all duplicate identification fields. If that algorithm does not yield any results, the engine performs a second step where fuzzy matching techniques are being used to calculate approximate duplicates. The similarity comparisons for each field are type dependent. For strings, we based our matching algorithm on existing concepts from the database community [3]. The similarity metrics used are edit distance, partial string similarity, sorted token ratio and token set ratio. The latter two are variations of the edit distance that tokenize the strings first. In the case of temporal data, we developed our own date-time similarity metrics to perform fuzzy date comparison [4]. To perform the final classification, the computed scores of all fields are added according to their configurable weights and compared with a system-defined threshold.

Default mappings are defined in a YAML[10] configuration file which is organised on the first level by Schema.org data types and on the second level by their attributes. For each attribute, a list of mapping definitions can be defined which indicate the order of preference with the first mapping listed being the most preferred. Listing 1 shows a section of the default mapping definition illustrating how the information items from the extractor are mapped to our internal type *Event*. New Schema.org data types can be added to our

---

[8] http://pypi.python.org/pypi/rdfadict
[9] http://code.google.com/p/feedparser/
[10] http://www.yaml.org/

---

system by appending at least one corresponding mapping definition to the YAML configuration file.

```
...
Event:
    name:
        - [iCalendar, VEVENT, SUMMARY]
        - [Open Graph, title]
        - [Microformats, vevent, summary]
        - [HTML Microdata, event, summary]
    url:
        - [iCalendar, VEVENT, URL]
        - [Open Graph, url]
        - [Microformats, vevent, url]
        - [Microformats, vevent, url, href]
        - [HTML Microdata, event, url]
        ...
    image:
        - [Open Graph, image]
...
```

Listing 1: Snippet from default mappings

This flexible approach allows the system to automatically complement partial information provided by one semantic markup language with data from other extractors. For example, the name of an event may be provided by HTML Microdata whereas its URL is extracted from Open Graph markup. Furthermore, end-users are encouraged to create their own custom mapping rules to extend the system and capture a greater set of extracted attributes. For each data source, the set of effective mapping rules can be defined individually and may consist of built-in rules, custom rules or any mix between the two. The custom format for data mapping definitions, as a slightly simplified explanation, consists of a two-dimensional hash table. The keys of the hash table define the target schema type and attribute, while the value defines the mapping definition for that particular attribute. A sample data mapping definition is illustrated in Figure 8, which shows a mapping definition for the 'genre' attribute of the 'Movie' data type. The mapping definition is made up of a list of string values. The first item in the mapping definition list is the "extractor key". The extractor key uniquely identifies which extractor to use for this attribute. The remainder of the mapping definition consists of a list of string values which comprise the mapping path. The mapping path defines the traversal path through the output of the specified extractor to reach the desired value or values.

However, defining mapping rules for each data source individually is costly and laborious, even for expert users. In order to allow the re-use of mapping definitions, they can not only be associated with a single URL (representing a single data source) but with a set of URLs, described by a regular expression. Before any data source is processed, it is matched against all stored expressions and, if some mapping

Figure 8: Sample data mapping definition

187

definitions exist, they are executed directly, without the user having to perform the associated steps manually. For novice users, we provide an easy way of creating those expressions interactively.

6. IMPLEMENTATION

We implemented the Sift system to demonstrate the approach and to provide a testbed for the specific extraction methods proposed. The core of the system is a two-tier Python-based web application composed of three primary components. Two of these components, the browser extension and the topics dashboard, interact through web services with the backend server. Client-server communication between the tiers of the system is implemented via a REST interface over HTTP. In the case of the browser extension, these requests are made asynchronously via AJAX calls and return JSON objects, while the web interface uses traditional HTTP GET and POST requests for HTML documents.

Developing a custom extractor is designed to be quick and painless for developers by minimising the amount of work necessary. Extractors are Python modules that extend one of the base classes provided by the Sift framework and are required to implement a single method. Custom extractors are not limited to any specific techniques or methodologies but rather have the freedom to process data sources any way they choose. This means that, for example, one extractor can use XPath expressions, while another utilises semantic markup, while yet another relies on natural language processing.

All of the data is stored in MongoDB [11], a schema-less, document-oriented database. MongoDB stores JSON-style documents which are basically collections of key-value pairs. This unconventional choice was driven by several key advantages provided by MongoDB compared to SQL and object-oriented alternatives. MongoDB is schema free and does not impose any constraints on the structure of the documents it stores. This makes it particularly well-suited for storing schema.org types because they rely heavily on multiple inheritence, an intrinsic property that is hard to map to relational databases. By defining the data schema only in the application logic, we are still able to ensure data integrity when it is needed, while allowing the use of unstructured fields within our schemas as well. This technique also facilitates frequent schema modifications, such as the addition of new semantic types, because changes can be made in the code without requiring any updates to the database.

6.1 Browser Extension

The data collection process begins with the browser extension component, which is implemented as an add-on to the Mozilla Firefox web browser. The extension is written in a combination of XUL and JavaScript. To implement the notification mechanism, it uses client-side detection of selected structured data types to identify candidate sources. The extraction wizard is implemented as an XUL overlay panel attached to the bottom of the web browser which splits the viewing area of the browser horizontally. Through that interface, the user can specify which pieces of information to save. This interface communicates with the web server component via AJAX, and the server processes the web page in the background.

When a new data mapping is defined through the Firefox browser extension, it is stored internally in a separate MongoDB collection in a custom format. The Firefox extension sends the mapping definition to the server as a JSON object, which is then saved directly in the database. This takes advantage of the flexibility and schema-less nature of MongoDB which allows the storage of data objects of arbitrary size and structure.

6.2 Topics Dashboard

The topics dashboard is implemented as a reusable application for the popular Python Django web framework [12]. This application is capable of functioning as the primary user interface for the collected data, but it can also be used solely for data administration and allow other applications and interfaces to be built on top of the data repository. The design of the interface was built with the help of the Bootstrap toolkit [13] from Twitter, which includes a CSS framework as well as a number of JavaScript plug-ins.

7. SCENARIO

Although we acknowledge the fact that user acceptance of our system might be ultimately tied to the usability of the corresponding user interfaces, we argue that by choosing recognisable and widespread user interaction patterns such as the icon notification or the extraction wizard paradigm, we have already lowered the boundaries for end-users to a reasonable level. We now present a scenario to illustrate the immediate user benefits achievable with our system: Assume a researcher Bob wants to quickly assemble a list of his favourite movies and actors as well as gathering information about upcoming conferences.

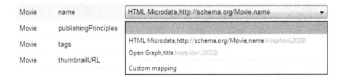

Figure 9: Choosing an appropriate extractor

Bob starts by visiting IMDb and navigates to the web page of a particular movie. He is immediately notified by the browser extension that extractable information is available, so he clicks on the toolbar icon. Since Bob has never extracted anything from IMDb before, the extraction wizard is launched and correctly identifies the web page as being about a movie and already fills in some fields. However, Bob is unhappy with the title extracted from the HTML Microdata markup because it lacks a whitespace between the name and the year and therefore decides to use the title provided by Open Graph instead (Figure 9).

This example also shows how data from multiple markup languages can be fused together, for instance the URL field being populated by the Open Graph extractor. In the last step, Bob can revisit the mapping rules, specify a URL pattern and finally save both the data and the mapping definitions. Luckily, the pattern is straightforward as URLs to

[11]http://www.mongodb.org/

[12]http://www.djangoproject.com/
[13]http://twitter.github.com/bootstrap/

movies on IMDb all share a common path. Afterwards, Bob continues to visit web pages of other movies and decides to gather some of them too. At this point, the information can be extracted right away and there is no need to re-create the mapping rules. Later, he visits a conference event calendar, and repeats the steps above for the individual web pages of upcoming conferences. Again, the pre-defined mappings for events help Bob specifying more comprehensive extraction rules.

Figure 10: Edit Form

The next day, Bob launches the topics dashboard web application to revise the data he has collected. All extracted data items can be browsed by type, so Bob navigates to the list of movies and opens the details view of a recently added movie. In order to add some details manually and classify the movie, he switches to the edit mode (Figure 10) and decides to add the movie to his list of favourite movies. Subsequently, he categorises the conference events according to their areas of interests (Figure 11). It is important to note that topics are not tied to a specific semantic type, but may be used to classify different types into the same category. This would allow Bob for example to group information about researchers, conference events and conference locations under the same topic. As a result, Bob only needs to bookmark the URL of the topic instead of having to bookmark all the web pages individually. In addition, the extracted and locally stored information provides him with a concise overview of all the relevant information and thus makes visiting the individual web pages obsolete. Missing information can be added in-place and does not need to be maintained separately. By gathering information only from user-selected web pages, our system allows Bob to create an individual, personal data repository with ease.

Figure 11: User-driven Classification

8. CONCLUSIONS AND FUTURE WORK

In this paper, we have presented a novel approach to leveraging semantic and hidden data for information harvesting in end-user scenarios. Our approach has led to the development of a set of end-user tools that allow them to discover, collect and organise web content on the go. We showed how end-users can participate in the extraction process and adapt the mapping rules in a straightforward way according to their preferences. Finally, we have presented an extensible content aggregation engine that showed how different well-established techniques from the Semantic Web and data warehousing can be combined to improve the overall quality of the collected data and to provide the user with features such as duplication elimination and revision tracking. We have motivated the choice of a common data model that allows us to abstract individual semantic markup languages from the data integration pipeline, hereby catering for the fact that the web is constantly evolving and several competing semantic markup standards exist nowadays. In addition, this decision facilies re-use and sharing of mapping rules.

We also note that the web content aggregation engine can be used independently of the user interface component and therefore serves as an extensible service to parse a diverse set of semantic markup languages. Since there exists a canonical mapping from the schema.org vocabulary used internally by our content aggregation engine to RDF, our system could be integrated with the Linked Data ecosphere. Another future direction of interest would be to investigate the potential of crowdsourcing to lower the entry barrier for and increase the acceptance of novice end-users. A crowdsourced repository of site-specific extraction mapping rules could be maintained by a small core of power users and shared with the larger crowd, thereby enabling users to start gathering information from popular websites without having to create mapping rules themselves.

9. REFERENCES

[1] M. Dontcheva, S. M. Drucker, D. Salesin, and M. F. Cohen. Relations, cards, and search templates: User-guided web data integration and layout. In *Proc. of the 20th ACM Symposium on User Interface Software and Technology (UIST 2007)*, 2007.

[2] M. Dontcheva, S. M. Drucker, G. Wade, D. Salesin, and M. F. Cohen. Summarizing personal web browsing sessions. In *Proc. of the 19th ACM Symposium on User Interface Software and Technology (UIST 2006)*, 2006.

[3] A. Elmagarmid, P. Ipeirotis, and V. Verykios. Duplicate record detection: A survey. *Knowledge and Data Engineering, IEEE Transactions on*, 19(1):1 –16, Jan 2007.

[4] M. Geel, T. Church, and M. C. Norrie. Mix-n-match: Building personal libraries from web content. In *Theory and Practice of Digital Libraries 2012 (TPDL 2012)*, 2012.

[5] W. Halb, Y. Raimond, and M. Hausenblas. Building Linked Data For Both Humans and Machines. In *WWW 2008 Workshop: Linked Data on the Web (LDOW2008)*, Beijing, China, 2008.

[6] S. Handschuh and S. Staab. Authoring and annotation of web pages in cream. In *Proceedings of the 11th*

international conference on World Wide Web (WWW 2002), pages 462–473, New York, NY, USA, 2002. ACM.

[7] A. Hogue and D. Karger. Thresher: Automating the unwrapping of semantic content from the world wide web. In *Proc. 14th Intl. Conf. on World Wide Web (WWW 2005)*, 2005.

[8] D. Huynh, S. Mazzocchi, and D. Karger. Piggy bank: Experience the semantic web inside your web browser. *Web Semantics: Science, Services and Agents on the World Wide Web*, 5(1), 2007.

[9] J. Kahan and M.-R. Koivunen. Annotea: An open rdf infrastructure for shared web annotations. In *Proceedings of the 10th international conference on World Wide Web (WWW 2001)*, pages 623–632, New York, NY, USA, 2001. ACM.

[10] M. Kowalkiewicz, T. Kaczmarek, and W. Abramowicz. Myportal: Robust extraction and aggregation of web content. In *Proc. 32nd Intl. Conf. on Very Large Data Bases (VLDB 2006)*, 2006.

[11] A. H. F. Laender, B. A. Ribeiro-Neto, A. S. da Silva, and J. S. Teixeira. A brief survey of web data extraction tools. *SIGMOD Rec.*, 31, June 2002.

[12] L. G. Moya, S. Kudama, M. J. A. Cabo, and R. B. Llavori. Integrating web feed opinions into a corporate data warehouse. In *Proc. 2nd Intl. Workshop on Business intelligence and the WEB (BEWEB 2011)*, 2011.

[13] V. Nebot and R. Berlanga. Building data warehouses with semantic data. In *Proc. of the 2010 EDBT/ICDT Workshops (EDBT 2010)*, 2010.

[14] D. C. Reis, P. B. Golgher, A. S. Silva, and A. F. Laender. Automatic web news extraction using tree edit distance. In *Proceedings of the 13th international conference on World Wide Web (WWW 2004)*, pages 502–511, New York, NY, USA, 2004. ACM.

[15] M. C. Schraefel and Y. Zhu. Interaction design for web-based, within-page collection making and management. In *Proc. 12th ACM Conf. on Hypertext and Hypermedia (HYPERTEXT 2001)*, 2001.

[16] M. C. Schraefel, Y. Zhu, D. Modjeska, D. Wigdor, and S. Zhao. Hunter gatherer: Interaction support for the creation and management of within-web-page collections. In *Proc. 11th Intl. Conf. on World Wide Web (WWW 2002)*, 2002.

[17] A. Sugiura and Y. Koseki. Internet scrapbook: Automating web browsing tasks by demonstration. In *Proc. 11th annual ACM symposium on User Interface Software and Technology (UIST 1998)*, 1998.

[18] X. Tan, D. C. Yen, and X. Fang. Web warehousing: Web technology meets data warehousing. *Technology in Society*, 25(1), 2003.

[19] Y. Zhai and B. Liu. Web data extraction based on partial tree alignment. In *Proceedings of the 14th international conference on World Wide Web (WWW 2005)*, pages 76–85, New York, NY, USA, 2005. ACM.

Faceted Documents: Describing Document Characteristics Using Semantic Lenses

Silvio Peroni
University of Bologna (Italy)
essepuntato@cs.unibo.it

David Shotton
University of Oxford (UK)
david.shotton@zoo.ox.ac.uk

Fabio Vitali
University of Bologna (Italy)
fabio@cs.unibo.it

ABSTRACT

The semantic enhancement of a traditional scientific paper is not a straightforward operation, since it involves many different aspects or facets. In this paper we propose eight different *semantic lenses* through which these facets may be viewed, and describe and exemplify the ontologies by which these lenses may be implemented.

Categories and Subject Descriptors

I.7.2 [**Document And Text Processing**]: Document Capture— *Document analysis*

Keywords

Semantic Web, document semantics, semantic publishing

1. INTRODUCTION

The enhancement of a traditional scientific paper with semantic annotations – one of the most important activities within the expanding field of *semantic publishing* [13] – is not a straightforward operation, since it involved much more that simply making semantically precise statements about named entities within the text. There are many additional aspects to a paper beyond the bare words it contains, that combine together to create an effective unit of scholarly communication. These include the context of the publication, contributing to the overall credibility and authoritativeness of the scientific activity, the structural components of the publication (e.g. author list, sections, tables, reference list, etc.) and in particular the rhetorically distinct sections of the publication (e.g. Introduction, Results, Discussion), the rhetorical devices used in the text, that contribute to its argumentative and persuasive power, and the citations that connect the publication with its wider context of scholarship.

These and other aspects coexist, and are usually so well integrated into the paper as a whole, and into the rhetorical flow of the natural language of the text, as to be scarcely discernible as separate entities by the reader. However, in order to create machine-readable semantic annotations over the paper, each of these aspects has to be clearly and separately identified and described, since each impacts and affects the semantic characterization of the content in different ways. Examining the semantic characterization of each of these aspects of a document can be envisaged as applying a set of *semantic lenses*, each of which magnifies or reveals one aspect or facet of the whole.

In this paper we propose a model for the semantic enhancement of scientific papers based on eight such *semantic lenses* that can be used to characterize its facets and in this way enhance its usefulness. These eight semantic lenses are:

- *Research context*: information about the background from which the paper emerged (the research reported, the institutions involved, the sources of funding, etc.).

- *Contributions and roles*: details about which individuals hold particular authorship roles for the paper and what specific contributions different people made.

- *Publication context*: information about related conferences, the journal in which the paper was published and the other papers with which it appeared.

- *Structure*: the explicit structural components (sections, paragraphs, etc.) into which the paper is organized.

- *Rhetoric*: the organization of the paper in terms of rhetorical sections having different purposes (Introduction, Results, Discussion, etc.).

- *Citation*: the purpose and target of each individual reference in the paper, and the manner in which the paper fits within the citation network.

- *Argumentation*: the structure and expression of each assertion within the paper, as a component of an argument to justify or invalidate a claim.

- *Semantics*: the actual meaning of each assertion, statement or named entity within the paper.

In what follows, we expand on these *semantic lenses*, and show how ontologies can be employed to describe each of the relevant facets of a paper, so that, when take together, these provide a complete semantic description of a scientific publication, its relationships with similar publications, and its role in the world of scholarship. The rest of this paper is structured as follows: in Section 2 we introduce our model in greater detail and present the various semantic technologies used to describe each facet of the paper; and in Section 3 we summarize and draw some conclusions.

2. SEMANTIC LENSES

The semantics of a scientific paper (or, more generally, of a document) is definable from different perspectives. Each perspective may be thought of as a *semantic lens* that can be *applied* to a document to reveal a particular semantic facet. In Section 1, we identified eight different semantic lenses that cover different perspectives. In the following sections we elaborate on the theories behind each of these semantic lenses, describe them, and discuss and exemplify the use of ontologies, developed either in previous works or specifically for this paper, that make possible the application of these lenses to documents by means of Semantic Web technologies.

2.1 The research context lens

Writing a scientific paper is usually the final stage of an often complex collaborative and multi-domain activity of undertaking the research investigation from which the paper arises. The organizations involved, the people affiliated to these organizations, the grants provided by funding agencies, the research projects funded by such grants: all these provide the research *context* that leads, directly or indirectly, to the genesis of the paper, and awareness of these may have a strong impact on the credibility and authoritativeness of its scientific content. A number of vocabularies for the description of research projects and related entities have been developed, e.g. the VIVO Ontology[1] – developed for describing the social networks of academics, their research and teaching activities, their expertise, and their relationships to information resources – and DOAP, the *Description Of A Project*[2] – an ontology with multi-lingual definitions that contains terms specific for software development projects.

To permit description of this research context, we have developed FRAPO, the *Funding, Research Administration and Projects Ontology*[3], that can be used for applying the *research context* lens to a paper, as illustrated as follows[4]:

```
:jisc a frapo:FundingAgency ;
  frapo:awards [ a frapo:Grant ;
    frapo:funds :open-citations-project ] .
:open-citations-project a foaf:Project ;
  foaf:homepage <http://opencitations.org> ;
  frapo:enables :spar .
:spar a frapo:Endeavour ;
  foaf:homepage <http://purl.org/spar> ;
  foaf:page :lenses-paper .
:lenses-paper a foaf:Document . # This paper
```

2.2 The contributions and roles lens

People can have a variety of *roles* in research projects and in the authorship of articles, and additionally can make different *contributions* to these activities with varying degrees of effort. This aspect of semantic description is made possible by our development of SCoRO, the *Scholarly Contributions and Roles Ontology*[5], as shown as follows:

```
:adventures a fabio:ResearchPaper . # Ref. [13]
:shotton a foaf:Person ;
```

[1] VIVO Ontology: http://vivoweb.org/ontology/core
[2] DOAP: http://usefulinc.com/ns/doap
[3] FRAPO: http://purl.org/cerif/frapo
[4] This and the following RDF examples are written in Turtle (http://www.w3.org/TeamSubmission/turtle/), with namespace definitions defined at http://www.essepuntato.it/lenses-paper/prefixes.
[5] SCoRO: http://purl.org/spar/scoro

```
  foaf:name "David Shotton" ;
  scoro:hasAuthorshipRole [ a pro:RoleInTime ;
    pro:withRole scoro:corresponding-author ;
    pro:relatesToDocument :adventures ] ;
  scoro:makesContribution [
    a scoro:ContributionSituation ;
    scoro:withContribution scoro:writes-paper ;
    scoro:withContributionEffort
      scoro:major-effort ;
    scoro:relatesToEntity :adventures ] .
```

2.3 The publication context lens

When analysing the social context in which a scientific paper is written, it is important to understand how it is *grouped* with other documents. For instance, it is relevant to know the book, journal and/or conference proceedings within which a paper appears, and separately to be able to describe groupings of bibliographic records and references, e.g. in tables of contents, reference lists, reference management systems and library catalogues. One of the most widely used ontology for describing bibliographic entities and their aggregations is BIBO, the *Bibliographic Ontology* [4]. FRBR, *Functional Requirements for Bibliographic Records* [8], is yet another more structured model for describing documents and their evolution in time. One of the most important aspects of FRBR is the fact that it is not tied to a particular metadata schema or implementation.

For this purpose we have developed two ontologies, FaBiO, the *FRBR-aligned Bibliographic Ontology*[6] [12] to describe bibliographic entities (e.g. books and journal articles) and their grouping (e.g. into book series and journal issues), and BiRO, the *Bibliographic Reference Ontology*[7], that permits the description of collections, for example of references in a reference list. Their use is exemplified as follows:

```
:version-of-record a fabio:JournalArticle ;
  frbr:realisationOf :adventures ;
  frbr:partOf [ a fabio:JournalIssue ;
    prism:issueIdentifier "4" ;
  frbr:partOf [ a fabio:JournalVolume ;
    prism:volume "5" ;
  frbr:partOf [ a fabio:Journal ;
    dcterms:title "PloS Computational Biology"
    ] ] ] ;
  frbr:part [ a biro:ReferenceList ;
    co:element [ biro:references
      <http://dx.doi.org/10.1371/journal.pcbi
        .0010034> ] ... ] .
```

2.4 The structure lens

The *structure* of a textual document is often expressed by means of markup languages such as XML and LaTeX, that have constructs for describing content hierarchically. We have been investigating patterns in XML vocabularies to understand how the structure of digital documents can be segmented into atomic components which can then be addressed and understood independently. Instead of defining a large number of complex and different structures, we identified eleven *structural patterns* [5] that have proved to be sufficient to express the structure of most documents, including scientific papers. This model, implemented in the *Pattern Ontology (PO)*[8], can be used in combination with

[6] FaBiO: http://purl.org/spar/fabio
[7] BiRO: http://purl.org/spar/biro
[8] PO: http://www.essepuntato.it/2008/12/pattern

EARMARK [6], an ontology[9] describing a markup metalanguage, to describe the structure of the document as a set of OWL assertions, and then to associate formal and explicit semantics with these descriptions. Thus we can associate a particular structural semantics to elements (e.g. an element *h1 expresses* the concept of being a block of text, while the element *div* containing it is a container). For instance, the first section of this paper[10] can be described as follows:

```
:div1 a earmark:Element # Sec. Introduction
  la:expresses pattern:HeadedContainer ;
  earmark:hasGeneralIdentifier "div" ;
  c:firstItem [ c:itemContent :h1 ... ] .
:h1 a earmark:Element # Title of the sec.
  la:expresses pattern:Block ;
  earmark:hasGeneralIdentifier "h1" ;
  c:firstItem [ c:itemContent :r1 ] .
:r1 a earmark:PointerRange ... # Text content
```

2.5 The rhetoric lens

Often, scientific communities require their papers to follow a particular rhetorical organization of sections, in order to identify meaningful aspects of the scientific discourse explicitly. These rhetorical components, for example Introduction, Methods, Results and Conclusions, give a defined rhetorical structure to the paper, which assists readers.

Previous works that introduced models to characterise such *rhetorical* aspect of a scientific publication included the rhetorical blocks within SALT, the *Semantical Annotated LaTeX Ontology* [7] and ORB, the *Ontology of Rhetorical Blocks* [2], as well as DEO, the *Discourse Elements Ontology*[11]. However, the rhetoric organization of a paper does not necessarily correspond neatly to its structural components (sections, paragraphs, etc.). Thus, in order to enable description both of the purely structural components of a document (introduced in Section 2.4) and its rhetorical components, we have developed DoCO, the *Document Components Ontology*[12]. This ontology provides the means to describe the organization of a document from both the structural and the rhetorical perspectives, as shown in the following brief example:

```
:div1 la:expresses doco:Section ,
  deo:Introduction .
:h1 la:expresses doco:SectionTitle . # etc.
```

2.6 The citation lens

Measuring how papers *cite* each other is often undertaken to generate metrics for the productivity of scientists and the impact of journals. Although citation metrics presently register the simple fact that one paper cites another, improved measures of the impact of the research and the productivity of authors might wish to take into account the *reasons* for particular citations, e.g. to express qualification of or disagreement with the ideas presented in the cited paper, which may significantly effect the evaluation of a citation network. In fact, it would seem sensible to weight differently citations that criticises a cited work from those used to acknowledge the benefit gained from its authoritative content.

---

[9]EARMARK: http://www.essepuntato.it/2008/12/earmark
[10]The XML version of this paper is available at http://www.essepuntato.it/lenses-paper/xml.
[11]DEO: http://purl.org/spar/deo
[12]DoCO: http://purl.org/spar/doco

CiTO, the *Citation Typing Ontology*[13] [12] allows one not only to assert in RDF that citations exists, but also to define the factual or rhetorical nature of the citations, as shown in the following example:

```
:lenses-paper cito:usesMethodIn
  <http://www.cambridge.org/0521092302> ;
  cito:citesForInformation :adventures .
```

2.7 The argumentation lens

The *argumentation* of the claims of the paper is crucial for scholarly and scientific publishing, in proposing hypotheses and advancing evidence in their support. Several works have been proposed in the past to model the argumentation of papers. For instance, the SALT application [7] permits someone such as the author "to enrich the document with formal descriptions of claims, supports and rhetorical relation as part of their writing process". There are other works, based on [14], that offer an application of Toulmin's model within specific scholarly domains, for instance the legal and legislative domain [9]. In [14], Toulmin proposed that arguments (including scientific arguments) are composed of statements having specific argumentative roles, of which three are essential:

- **The claim.** A fact that must be asserted – e.g. "This text is a scientific paper".

- **The evidence.** Another fact that represents a foundation for the claim – e.g. "This paper has been accepted to a scientific conference".

- **The warrant.** A statement bridging from the evidence to the claim – e.g. "A paper accepted to a scientific conference is a scientific paper".

In Toulmin's model, each instance that has a certain role in an argument (e.g. a warrant) may very well be the claim of another sub-argument. And, each statement of the sub-argument could be the claim of yet other sub-sub-arguments.

In order to use this argumentation theory, we have developed AMO, the *Argument Model Ontology*[14]. It allows one to express an argument using Toulmin's argumentation theory, as shown in the following excerpt:

```
:sentence1 dcterms:description "This is a
    scientific paper" .
:sentence2 dcterms:description "This paper has
    been accepted to a scientific conference" .
:sentence3 dcterms:description "A paper
    accepted to a scientific conference is a
    scientific paper" .
:argument1 a amo:Argument ;
  amo:hasClaim :sentence1 ;
  amo:hasEvidence :sentence2 ;
  amo:hasWarrant :sentence3 .
:argument2 a amo:Argument ;
  amo:hasClaim :sentence3 ; # etc.
```

2.8 The semantics lens

The main goal of a scientific paper is to express (and cite) findings that have specific scientific value. These finding are expressed through text, tables, and figures. Usually, they

---

[13]CiTO: http://purl.org/spar/cito
[14]AMO: http://www.essepuntato.it/2011/02/argumentmodel

are meant for human interpretation only and are not directly suitable for machines. This because the *semantics* of a piece of text, such as "EARMARK is more expressive than XML", is not explicitly defined in any formal way: it is just text that requires human interpretation. The *semantics lens* is employed to encode the meaning of the original scientific message contained in the paper using Semantic Web technologies such as RDF, as shown in the following statement:

```
<http://www.essepuntato.it/2008/12/earmark>
:isMoreExpressiveThan <http://www.w3.org/XML> .
```

2.9 An authorial activity

The application of a particular semantic lens to a paper involves adding information about the particular facet of semantics described by that lens, and constitutes an *authorial activity*, i.e. an action of a person (who may be the original author of the human-readable text, or someone else) who takes responsible for the specification of the semantic interpretations given to the document. Therefore, the tracking of semantic lens applications involves a requirement to record *data provenance*, i.e. the identification of the tools and processes that were involved in the creation of an artefact or resource, and the people involved in that creation. To encode provenance information, OPM, the *Open Provenance Model* [11], is a well-known model whose main requirements concerns the exchangeability of provenance data between systems, the digital representation of provenance for any resource, and the definition of a set of rules identifying the valid inferences that can be made on provenance graphs. Another implemented model for provenance is included in the SWAN ontology ecosystem [3], and aims to describe resources in terms of their accessing, authoring and versioning.

In our opinion, the *PROV Ontology* (*PROV-O*) [10] is one of the more appropriate ontologies for the definition of the authorial role of agents. Each set of RDF statements, produced as consequence of a lens application, should be enclosed within a *named graph* [1], in order to express all the provenance data as statements about the graph itself:

```
:citation-lens {
  :lenses-paper cito:citesForInformation
    :adventures ; ... }
:citation-lens a prov:Entity ,
  lens:CitationLensApplication ;
  prov:wasGeneratedBy [ a prov:Activity ;
    prov:wasAssociatedWith
      <http://www.essepuntato.it/me> ] . # etc.
```

3. CONCLUSIONS

In this paper we have sketched out a model for the enhancement of documents based on eight distinct *semantic lenses*, each of which can be used to identify a specific semantic facet of a document. Moreover, we have presented technologies, in the form of OWL ontologies, that can be used for the application of these lenses to actual documents, and for the specification of the authorial roles of the people responsible for these operations. Future works will mainly involve the improvement of the lens model, the development of automatic and semi-automatic tools for the application of the lenses to documents, the implementation of user interfaces for the dynamic interpretation and use of lens-related document semantics, and additional studies to analyse whether our model is enough generic or strictly depends on particular types of documents (e.g. scientific papers).

4. REFERENCES

[1] Carroll, J., Bizer, C., Hayes, P., Stickler, P. (2005). Named Graphs, Provenance and Trust. In Proceedings of the 14th International World Wide Web Conference: 613-622. DOI: 10.1145/1060745.1060835

[2] Ciccarese, P., Groza, T. (2011). Ontology of Rhetorical Blocks (ORB). W3C Editor's Draft. World Wide Web Consortium. http://www.w3.org/2001/sw/hcls/notes/orb/

[3] Ciccarese, P., Wu, E., Wong, G., Ocana, M., Kinoshita, J., Ruttenberg, A., Clark, T. (2008). The SWAN biomedical discourse ontology. In Journal of Biomedical Informatics, 41 (5): 739-751. DOI: 10.1016/j.jbi.2008.04.010

[4] D'Arcus, B., Giasson, F. (2009). Bibliographic Ontology Specification. Specification Document, 4 November 2009. http://bibliontology.com/specification

[5] Di Iorio, A., Peroni, S., Poggi, F., Vitali, F. (2012). A first approach to the automatic recognition of structural patterns in XML documents. To appear in the Proceedings of the 2012 ACM symposium on Document Engineering.

[6] Di Iorio, A., Peroni, S., Vitali, F. (2011). A Semantic Web Approach To Everyday Overlapping Markup. In Journal of the American Society for Information Science and Technology, 62 (9): 1696-1716. DOI: 10.1002/asi.21591

[7] Groza, T., Moller, K., Handschuh, S., Trif, D., Decker, S. (2007). SALT: Weaving the claim web. In Proceedings of the 6th International Semantic Web Conference: 197-210. DOI:10.1007/978-3-540-76298-0_15

[8] IFLA Study Group on the Functional Requirements for Bibliographic Records (1998). Functional Requirements for Bibliographic Records (FRBR). Final Report, http://archive.ifla.org/VII/s13/frbr/frbr_current_toc.htm

[9] Lauritsen, M., Gordon, T. F. (2009). Toward a general theory of document modeling. In Proceedings of the 12th International Conference on Artificial Intelligence and Law: 202-211. DOI:10.1145/1568234.1568257

[10] Lebo, T., Sahoo, S., McGuinness, D. (2012). PROV-O: The PROV Ontology. W3C Working Draft 03 May 2012. World Wide Web Consortium. http://www.w3.org/TR/prov-o

[11] Moreau, L., Freire, J., Futrelle, J., McGrath, R. E., Myers, J., Paulson, P. (2008). The Open Provenance Model: An Overview. In Proceedings of the 2nd International Provenance and Annotation Workshop: 323-326. DOI: 10.1007/978-3-540-89965-5_31

[12] Peroni, S., Shotton, D. (2012). FaBiO and CiTO: ontologies for describing bibliographic resources and citations. In press, Journal of Web Semantics. http://imageweb.zoo.ox.ac.uk/pub/2012/publications/Peroni&Shotton_fabiocito_ontology_paper_JWSaccepted.pdf

[13] Shotton, D., Portwin, K., Klyne, G., Miles, A. (2009). Adventures in Semantic Publishing: Exemplar Semantic Enhancements of a Research Article. PLoS Computational Biology, 5 (4): e1000361. DOI: 10.1371/journal.pcbi.1000361

[14] Toulmin, S. (1959). The uses of argument. Cambridge University Press. ISBN: 0521827485

A Framework for Retrieval and Annotation in Digital Humanities using XQuery Full Text and Update in BaseX

Cerstin Mahlow*   Christian Grün†   Alexander Holupirek†   Marc H. Scholl†

*Department of German
University of Basel
4051 Basel, Switzerland
cerstin.mahlow@unibas.ch

†Database & Information Systems Group
University of Konstanz
78457 Konstanz, Germany
[firstname.lastname]@uni-konstanz.de

ABSTRACT

A key difference between traditional humanities research and the emerging field of digital humanities is that the latter aims to complement qualitative methods with quantitative data. In linguistics, this means the use of large corpora of text, which are usually annotated automatically using natural language processing tools. However, these tools do not exist for historical texts, so scholars have to work with unannotated data. We have developed a system for systematic, iterative exploration and annotation of historical text corpora, which relies on an XML database (BaseX) and in particular on the Full Text and Update facilities of XQuery.

Categories and Subject Descriptors

J.5 [**Computer Applications**]: Arts and Humanities – Linguistics; H.2.4 [**Database Management**]: Systems – Textual databases; H.3.3 [**Information Storage and Retrieval**]: Information Search and Retrieval – Search process

Keywords

XML, TEI, database, XQuery Full Text, corpus linguistics, phraseology

1. INTRODUCTION

Traditional humanities are mainly concerned with the qualitative exploration of text to answer specific research questions. This includes investigating modern and historical texts: hand-written, printed, spoken, or in electronic form, probably mixed with images, etc. Digital humanities extend these traditional research methods and resources by applying quantitative methods to large amounts of electronically available texts. To answer linguistic questions, these methods rely on linguistically annotated texts. Usually, linguistic annotation is done automatically by applying natural language processing (NLP) tools to raw text.

However, research on historical texts in this paradigm is hampered by the fact that NLP tools are suitable for modern texts only.

Historical texts reflect different spelling conventions than today, inflection might have been different, and rules for word order or for syntax might have changed over time. Additionally, some centuries ago there was no fixed set of spelling rules writers were supposed to follow—we often find different spellings for a word within one text. For these reasons, using NLP for modern language on historical texts typically yields unsatisfying results [see for example 11, 30]. Therefore, when laborious manual annotation is no option, scholars prefer to apply methods from information retrieval to find relevant information in texts.

There are currently only limited resources to support scholars from the digital humanities in searching and enriching their data. Typically, project-specific or document-specific models, methods, and tools are developed, which is not an optimal situation, as Romary [28] argues. The result of a query in corpus linguistics tools might be exported to be later evaluated manually or statistically. However, to ensure reproducibility of linguistic research and to allow for comparing variants of queries considering slightly differing perspectives, it would be necessary to annotate the original data to make found information explicit and to enrich the data with information derived from interpretation of the query and the results. The result of a query should result in an annotation layer that might be extended by manually added information. These annotation layers might then serve as a resource for higher-level investigations.

In this paper, we propose a framework supporting at the same time retrieval and annotation of linguistic structures in diachronic corpora from the digital humanities. We present the architecture of BaseX, as an instantiation of an XML database as proposed by Salminen and Tompa [29], the W3C XQuery 3.0 language, its official Full Text and Update Facility extensions, and some specifics of the implementation in BaseX. As a case in point, we give details on exploring TEI document collections of German texts from 1650 until today; we discuss the tools and resources implemented so far and demonstrate how linguists investigating diachronic phenomena benefit from the application of state-of-the-art XML technologies.

2. A FRAMEWORK FOR RETRIEVAL AND ANNOTATION OF DIACHRONIC CORPORA

At various places, large amounts of hand-written or printed texts are currently being digitized and semi-automatically converted into XML data conforming to TEI P5 [34]. These TEI-annotated corpora are important sources in the growing field of digital humanities. A typical use of such data is the exploration of the XML structure to apply different display procedures depending on user preferences. Human users, e.g., scholars, can then inspect the data, which is tailored to their needs, or obtain a rendering that reflects the original rendering of the printed edition.

Research questions from the digital humanities may include investigations concerning the linguistic development of a certain language, exploring the ethical or legal development of societies, analyzing texts to learn about animals and plants existing at former times, getting evidence for historical events, etc. To answer these questions, researchers explore textual documents by applying queries which make use of the content and the existing annotation.

These queries typically search for concepts rather than specific words or phrases. Searching for a concept requires formulating various queries, taking into account possible variation of words to express a concept, involving variants of multi-word units like co-occurrences, collocations, or idioms. The hits are then interpreted by the researcher. In general, the automatic distinction between true and false positives is almost impossible. In most cases, corpus work involves both inspecting the text, considering already available annotation, and annotating specific aspects to be inspected in detail in a follow-up step. A corpus tool for the digital humanities thus has to support retrieval as well as annotation.

Researchers from digital humanities are linguists, historians, or jurists with limited experience in XML structures and techniques. Therefore, allowing users to query a corpus by writing XQuery expressions is no option. This also affects performance requirements. The display of results to be inspected—to decide whether to refine the query or to select certain hits for further exploration—cannot be limited to matched nodes or attributes. It involves the full rendering of hits including their context, e.g., highlighting the matched text and showing bibliographic data or preceding and following nodes. However, these additional requirements should have no considerable effect on the response times.

The corpora to be searched usually consist of various documents from different authors, written and published at different points in time, i.e., diachronic corpora consisting of heterogeneous texts. The TEI annotation of textual sources generally echoes the document structure only, there is no annotation with respect to language features. If there is linguistic annotation available—either done automatically for modern texts or manually for small document collections of historical texts—linguistic information usually is stored as separate layers to the basic data. These data can then be searched using dedicated tools; typically, special-purpose databases are used for retrieval, e.g., Corpus Workbench[1], making use of linguistic annotation like lemmatization, part-of-speech (POS) annotation, or syntactic annotation.

However, linguistically annotated corpora of a reasonable size exist for modern languages only. The use of corpus linguistic tools to explore large diachronic corpora is thus not possible and we can only make use of the TEI annotation.

2.1 State of the art and related work

Although corpus annotation is realized almost exlusively as XML annotation, there are only few NLP projects using standard XML tools or XQuery for exploration of linguistic data, see for example [12, 27, 31]. However, existing approaches have several drawbacks, due to the nature of the research objects as well as due to technical solutions chosen.

Researchers from digital humanities mainly care about the content of their textual resources. Creating a collection of relevant documents concerning a research question often results in a collection of heterogeneous documents: The documents are of different size ranging from a few kilobytes to hundreds of megabytes, eventually

[1]http://cwb.sourceforge.net/

resulting in large collections of dozens of gigabytes; the documents might be born digital or scanned and OCR-processed; the quality of the TEI annotation depends on the annotation process used; the character encoding might be inconsistent. Therefore most projects introduce a semi-automatic preprocessing step to either harmonize documents [see for example 27] or to even get rid of annotation, because actual processing is done on raw texts [see 25]. For example *brat*, a Web-based tool for NLP-assisted annotation [32], expects input data as plain text.

Baumann et al. [2] present a system suited to handle multi-layered data, intended to overcome performance issues of other systems. However, they do not report on the *creation* of the annotation. Similarly, Eckart and Teich [14] focus on querying and representation only.

Rehm et al. [27] report response times of up to 3 hours for typical queries. With their system they are not able to achieve performance desired for interactive use. When systematically *annotating* corpora, it might be possible to split the corpus into smaller portions to be able to inspect and annotate them with a reasonable performance. However, when *searching* for evidence of concepts that might occur only rarely, splitting the corpus is no option—the researcher will lose the overview.

Annotation tools support manual annotation of small portions of the corpus to be merged later. Adding information to existing XML data is usually done by systematically inspecting all information that has already been stored, introducing new tags for marking relevant parts, or adding attributes to existing elements.

Automatic annotation of linguistic information is done by applying NLP tools. These tools have been developed for and tuned to perform best on modern newspaper texts. Texts from the 17th, 18th or 19th century differ from modern texts—i.e., late 20th or early 21st century—with respect to spelling, vocabulary, inflection, word order, syntax, or any combination of the above. Applying modern tools to old texts is thus not easily possible, as Dipper [11] or Scheible et al. [30] have demonstrated. Annotating diachronic corpora, would therefore require manual annotation, which is usually not possible. Part of an alternative solution to overcome, for example, lack of lemmatization, would be to use query expansion, i.e., generating all inflected modern and historical forms in all possible spellings for a given lemma in a query. This would, however, require generation tools that take changes in inflection paradigms and spelling variation into account; tools that currently do not exist.

2.2 An integrated system for retrieval and annotation of large XML-annotated corpora

As most of today's corpus data comes in XML-annotated format, a framework for digital humanities should make use of this annotation rather than stripping it in a preprocessing step. Additional information should be added either directly into the corpus or as stand-off markup.

XML databases suited for diachronic corpora have to meet several demands, e.g., using standards, avoiding data-model transformation, supporting stand-off annotation, providing language-sensitive full-text search, performance issues [see 13]. When choosing an XML database, we also have to consider that looking for concepts or variants of multi-word units in texts is a different task than typical data-oriented XML search. The corpus is not a collection of highly structured records, but unstructured text with some metadata. We thus need a solution that allows fast and efficient search in the content of XML nodes supported by full text indexes while also considering information stored in attributes.

Exploring a corpus in the field of digital humanities is a recursive process of applying queries to a large heterogeneous corpus, inspecting results, annotating new information for some of the hits, and applying new queries making immediatly use of added annotation. A framework integrating high-performance search *and* annotation is needed. Accordingly, a separate retrieval engine such as Lucene is not the best option, while XQuery Full Text and XQuery Update [1] offer the desired facilities, as they additionally allow us to stick with the original XML format.

The integration of XQuery in a dedicated XML database like BaseX facilitates the implementation of applications that support non-technical users like linguists to query and annotate large collections of TEI documents in a comfortable environment and in real time. Using BaseX and the XQuery Full Text and Update implementation, we are able to overcome most of the deficiencies of other approaches. We can easily create corpora of heterogeneous documents; there is no need for semi-automatic preprocessing. Results of queries can be annotated immediately, this annotation can then be used in further queries without any need for additional processing steps. Retrieval and annotation can be nested, allowing scholars to refine queries and supporting interpretation of information.

3. ARCHITECTURE OF BASEX

BaseX[2] is a native XML database management system. In 2005, it was developed by the Database and Information Systems Group (DBIS) at the University of Konstanz as a research project on efficient storage layers for tree-structured data [19]. It soon turned out that the resulting storage system is suited especially well to provide visual access to large XML corpora [20]. A visual search application, which provided access to the complete catalog of the Library of the University of Konstanz, encoded as XML, has successfully spawned further research efforts during which the prototype evolved into stable software [18].

Since 2007, BaseX has been a publicly available, BSD-licensed open source project.[3] Today, the database system is actively used and developed by a growing community and a core team, which supervises the implementation efforts and introduces new features in the system. The core of BaseX is entirely written in the Java programming language. If the database is run as server, however, one of 15 client libraries for different programming languages (including C, Haskell, Perl, PHP, Ruby, and Scala) can be used to connect to the database and to process commands and queries with BaseX.

3.1 Working with BaseX

There are two main modes to operate BaseX: the standalone mode (with console or graphical user interface) and the client/server mode.

3.1.1 Standalone mode

The standalone mode is targeted at developers and XML architects who want to locally explore and work with XML data. BaseX is started as a conventional application (no configuration is needed). The standalone variant is feature complete and can be downloaded for Windows, Mac OS, and various Linux distributions from the project's website.

By default, the graphical user interface (GUI) is started, which is depicted in Figure 1. Visual access to XML data is provided by separate *views*. The figure shows the *Map View* in the bottom half. It is a space-filling representation of the opened database (`factbook.xml` in this case). The upper left pane shows the *Query Editor*, in which users can enter and evaluate XPath/XQuery expressions on the data

to get immediate feedback with each key click. The upper right pane gives information about compilation, optimization, evaluation steps, and timings of the executed query. Additional hierarchical visualizations are available to explore the stored XML data. All views are tightly coupled and provide instant result feedback.

In contrast to other XML tools and editors, BaseX GUI can both store and visualize very large XML documents (files up to 421 GiB have been successfully tested[4]). Databases in BaseX are very lightweight: When XML files are opened, they are converted to database instances on the fly. This allows for a fast exploration and analysis of large XML documents and collections, since all visualizations directly interact with the underlying storage layer [17, Chapter 2].

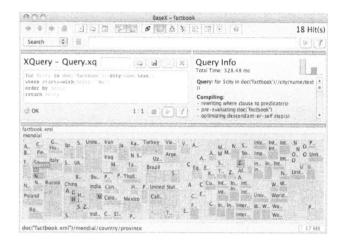

Figure 1: Standalone mode of BaseX.

3.1.2 Server mode

The server mode is the preferred solution if BaseX is expected to provide its services in a multi-user environment. BaseX Server offers a central storage for XML documents and binary files that can subsequently be accessed by remote clients in several programming languages.

XPath and XQuery are the default languages to access data stored in server database instances. This allows system architects to leverage low-level system internals in a high-level programming language. However, XQuery is far more than *just* a data query language (DQL), as described in more detail in Section 4.

In addition, BaseX offers two REST interfaces and an implementation of the WebDAV protocol for accessing and updating data. In a RESTful environment, for example, AJAX developers can send data of any format (e.g. XML, JSON, or binary data) to the server and take advantage of the XQuery language to process and retrieve relevant data.

Whatever mode is used, BaseX provides general features relevant for applications in the domain of digital humanities: (1) support for established W3C standards to operate on XML data: XQuery, XQuery Full Text, and XQuery Update, (2) a high compliance level regarding official test suites[5], (3) supporting infrastructure for large textual corpora: Text, Attribute, Full-text and Path indexes, and (4) facilities for tuning, optimizing, and accessing indexes.

---

[2]`http://basex.org`

[3]Source code can be retrieved for further development, adaptation, and improvements at `https://github.com/BaseXdb` and `http://basex.org/open-source/`

[4]`http://docs.basex.org/wiki/Statistics`

[5]`http://dev.w3.org/2006/xquery-test-suite/PublicPagesStagingArea/XQTSReportSimple_XQTS_1_0_2.html`

3.2 Building applications

At least three different ways exist to build higher-level applications with BaseX: (1) Since the database engine does not depend on other libraries and has a small memory footprint, BaseX can be a good choice for *embedded* systems. It can be used as an XML storage library and/or XQuery processor inside a Java application. (2) BaseX can be used as a classic *client/server* architecture, as described in Section 3.1. (3) The system can be deployed as a *web application* as central part of a pure *X-technology stack*.

XML, XQuery and XHTML are an ideal match to present and process information resources in a platform-neutral way. Whenever the underlying datasets are originally stored in XML, or can be easily represented as such, XQuery is the domain-specific processing language to *filter, select, search, join, sort, group, aggregate, transform, and restructure*, in short, analyze and process, stored data.

BaseX provides a service infrastructure to implement and deploy XQuery-based web applications. That way, XML technology can be applied on all layers of a classical three-tier-architecture [23]. The *persistence* layer is provided by a native XML database, *business logic* is implemented in XQuery, and the *presentation* layer is primarily driven by XHTML.

As such, a single data model is used throughout the architecture and no conversions have to be applied between the layers. If the "unified technology stack" is used, as shown in Figure 2, the full potential of the W3C language family can be leveraged, and benefits can be expected in terms of (1) a lean system architectures, with less components involved, and (2) a reduced amount of code, as no glue code is needed.

The architecture allows for the development of applications solely relying on the W3C technology family: Applications are provided with a uniform search and retrieval service, and can now be implemented on a more high-level and generic abstraction layer, while still being backed by a full-fledged database support.

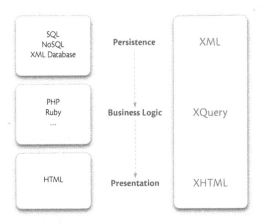

Figure 2: Uniform Application Stack: XML technology on all three tiers of a system architecture

4. XQUERY AND ITS FULL TEXT AND UPDATE EXTENSIONS

While XQuery is often labeled as query language for XML data, and put on a same level with SQL, it is actually a full, Turing-complete, functional programming language, which makes it perfectly suited for representing and processing full information workflows with XML data. It is continuously developed and enhanced

```
//library/title[content contains text
 ("apple" ftor "pear") ftand ("stem" ftor "tree")
 using diacritics insensitive
 using thesaurus default
 using case insensitive
 using language "en"
 using stemming
 ordered distance at most 5 words]
```

Listing 1: Example XQuery expression

with new extensions: currently, XQuery 3.0 is being standardized, and full-text, update and scripting extensions provide additional features for information retrieval, modifications, and batch jobs.

The XQuery core language makes use of XPath to navigate through XML nodes (elements, attributes, texts, etc.) in a single document or a collection of documents. So-called FLWOR expressions can be used to loop through, filter and order XQuery items. New XML nodes can be constructed on the fly, which can then be handled like existing XML nodes. The language provides support for user-defined functions and modules in different namespaces. Due to its functional nature, XQuery has only expressions and no statements: expressions within a function body are evaluated and returned as values. The data model of XQuery treats all values as sequences. Sequences are lists of items, and items can be nodes or atomic values. Atomic values may be for example strings, doubles, integers, booleans, or dates [4]. Nested sequences will be automatically flattened.

With XQuery 3.0, many important features have been added, which make the language more suitable for universal processing of XML encoded information: function items (also known as lambdas) can be used to write more modular code and use XQuery as a fully functional language. In line with the typed lambda calculus, higher-order functions can now be passed as arguments to or returned as results from functions. Next, the new language version introduces a try/catch expression to handle errors at runtime; serialization parameters can be specified within the query, the FLWOR expression has been extended with a `group by` clause, all its clauses can now be placed in an arbitrary order, and annotations can be used to change the visibility of functions or assign them special, implementation-specific properties.

In SQL, many vendor-specific extensions exist to process full-text requests. An alternative, unified approach has been taken in the XML domain: The XPath/XQuery Full Text Recommendation of the W3C [1] is fully composable and tightly coupled with the core language. Since its finalization, it is continuously attracting more and more users and developers from the information retrieval community. The recommendation offers a wide range of content-based query operations, classical retrieval tools such as stemming and thesaurus support, and an implementation-defined scoring model that allows core developers to adapt their database to a large variety of use-cases and scenarios. BaseX was the first implementation to fully support all features of the new specification; Qizx [16] and MXQuery [15] are two other implementations that are available at the time of writing.

The syntax of a simple full-text expression is similar to a "general comparison" in XQuery [5]. A `contains text` expression can get pretty verbose: the right hand side can be extended by numerous logical connectives, match options, and positional filters as shown in Listing 1.

BaseX provides an additional, implementation-specific match option `fuzzy`, which is based on an optimized variant of the Levenshtein algorithm [33]. Depending on the length of a string, a certain

```
declare namespace output =
  'http://www.w3.org/2010/xslt-xquery-serialization';
declare option output:method 'xhtml';
declare option output:omit-xml-declaration 'no';
declare option output:doctype-public
  '-//W3C//DTD HTML 4.01 Transitional//EN';
declare option output:doctype-system
  'http://www.w3.org/TR/html4/loose.dtd';
declare variable $words external := '-';
<html>
  <head>
    <title>Search: { $words }</title>
  </head>
  <body>{
    for $m in doc('library')//medium
    where $m/content contains text { $words }
    return (
      <h1>{ $m/title/data() }</h1>,
      <div>{ $m/content }</div>
    )
  }</body>
</html>
```

Listing 2: XQuery expression yielding an XHTML document

number of deviations from the search string will be ignored. A deviation may either be a missing, additional, wrong, or transposed character. The following query contains a single transposition and yields true:

```
'apple' contains text 'appel' using fuzzy
```

A further noteworthy enhancement, which is helpful for the discussed use case, and likely to be included in a future version of the Recommendation [6], is the possibility of highlighting found tokens in the query results with the `ft:mark()` function. With `ft:extract()`, longer texts can be shortened and limited to the regions that contain the relevant keywords. More details on the low-level implementation of XQuery Full Text in BaseX are described by Grün et al. [21].

Another essential requirement for query languages is the possibility of performing updates. The official XQuery Update Facility [8] fills this gap by introducing four new expressions to insert new data and modify or delete existing data (`insert`, `replace`, `rename`, and `delete`), thus offering a data manipulation language (DML). An additional `transform` expression allows developers to modify nodes in main memory. A special characteristic of XQuery Update is that all atomic update operations are first moved to a *pending update list*, which is processed in batch mode after the query itself has been evaluated. Next, similar to SQL, updating XQuery expressions may not return any results. Due to these two constraints, and numerous validity checks, any side effects are avoided: all updates are guaranteed to be atomic, and no data can be returned that has previously been deleted.

From the implementor's view, the batch processing allows for additional optimizations, as none of the reading data references need to be preserved at the final stage of database modification. An obvious drawback of this design approach is that subsequent read and write operations need to be encapsulated in multiple queries.

With XQuery 3.0 and its extensions, there is no need any more to mix different technologies and data models, e.g., MySQL, PHP, and HTML: complete web pages can be created without switching the language and platform. As a result, application development is getting simplified, and performance is improved as no abstraction layers need to be passed, as indicated in Section 3.2. Listing 2 is an example for an XQuery 3.0 expression that yields a valid XHTML document.

Especially XQuery's Full Text extension makes XML database systems like BaseX an interesting choice for building information retrieval systems in Digital Humanities, as we elaborate in Section 5. To offer high-performance throughput of XQuery Full Text queries, BaseX implements Text, Attribute, Full-Text and Path-Summary indexes to speed up the evaluation process. The index structures are designed to support more than 20 languages and incorporate features, as wildcards, stemming, case sensitivity, diacritics, TF/IDF scoring, and stop words. A point worth mentioning is the ability to programmatically access database internals, such as values stored in indexes from within XQuery.

5. USE CASE: RETRIEVING AND ANNO-TATING IDIOMATIC PHRASES

In the SNSF-funded project "German Proverbs and idioms in language change. Online dictionary for diachronic phraseology (OLdPhras)"[6], we are interested in finding historical evidence for phrasemes—in linguistics sometimes also referred to as phraseological units, idioms, or set phrases—in German texts from 1650 until today. A list derived from phraseme collections and general-purpose dictionaries from the 18th to the 21st century comprises the inventory of the intended dictionary.

More abstractly, phrasemes could be considered non-Fregian discontinuous multi-word expressions within sentence boundaries, where the meaning of the whole unit cannot be deduced from the meaning of the parts, see examples 1a and 2a below. Diachronic change of phrasemes might occur on various levels: lexical units, syntactic structure of the phraseme, meaning, syntactic role of the phraseme, etc., making searching for instances of phrasemes a complex task. Retrieving and annotating phrasemes is one step in the creation of the online dictionary.

Resources are a collection of diachronic TEI-annotated texts and a collection of printed dictionaries representing the knowledge about German phrasemes at different points in time from the 18th to the 21st century. The first step is the compilation of relevant data. Only some of the dictionaries are available in electronic form, i.e., have been digitized. Relevant information from dictionaries will be extracted semi-automatically or manually and stored using BaseX in XML format for further use. Relevant information from texts, i.e., evidence of phrasemes, will be collected and annotated within the database. Storing this information basically means storing annotation layers, not extracts from the texts.

In a further step, BaseX is used for the creation of single dictionary entries: all information concerning a particular phraseme—i.e., extracted parts of other dictionaries and annotated evidence— is merged. The phraseologist will arrange these elements and write comments concerning diachronic change. The resulting XML documents will then form the actual OLdPhras dictionary. Additionally, the annotation layers covering evidence of phrasemes can be merged with the TEI-annotated original texts, resulting in a corpus annotated with information on phrasemes. Figure 3 presents the overall architecture of the OLdPhras system. For more information about the project in general see [22, 24].

Phrasemes are relatively rare in corpora of written language; large corpora are thus required to obtain a significant amount of evidence [9, 10]. As diachronic corpora we use the *Deutsches Textarchiv* (DTA)[7], the *TextGrid Digitale Bibliothek* (DB125)[8], and *GerManC* [3], comprising digitized historical German texts up to the

---

[6] http://oldphras.net
[7] http://deutschestextarchiv.de
[8] http://www.textgrid.de/digitale-bibliothek.html

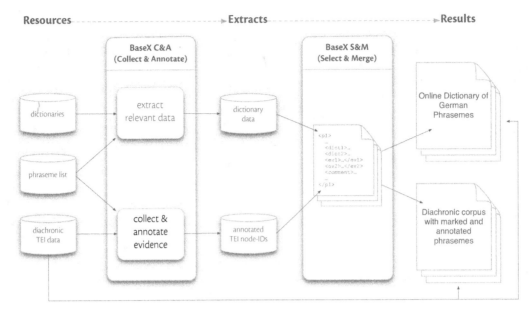

Figure 3: Overall architecture of the system.

early 20th century. All corpora include TEI-annotated documents, but the annotation and the organization of the documents differ.

In the rest of this section, we first outline general challenges for retrieving and annotating phrasemes and then present the principles of our solution based on XQuery 3.0 and its Full Text and Update extensions, and the implementation using BaseX.

5.1 Challenges

5.1.1 Linguistic challenges

Typically, multi-word units like co-occurrences, collocations, or phrasemes are searched for using dedicated tools from corpus linguistics, e.g., Corpus Workbench, making use of pre-existing linguistic annotation. Queries can then be constructed using the base forms of words, specifying syntactic relations, and allowing for instantiations of a particular POS. For example, query 1b would search for phrases consisting of a preposition, followed by a determiner, followed by any inflected form of *Strom* 'current', followed by any inflected form of the verbs *schwimmen* 'to swim' or *treiben* 'to drift'. Between the noun and the verb there might be other words, e.g., adverbs. With this query, we could look for evidence of variants of phraseme 1a.

(1) a. *gegen den Strom schwimmen*
      'to swim against the current'
      (today's meaning 'to act different than the majority')
    b. `PREP DET Strom * schwimmen|treiben`

In general, looking for phrasemes in texts with a focus on diachronic change concerning meaning, vocabulary, and structure, is a complex task. The starting point is a modern base form as listed in dedicated phraseme collections or general purpose dictionaries, like examples 1a and 2a: the verb is in infinitive form at the very last position as in 1a, valency fillers of the verb might be instantiated as in 2a or not mentioned at all as in 1a (a subject is needed, someone able to swim). From this base form, a linguist needs to construct a query that allows for variation on all elements, i.e., meaning, vocabulary, and structure, either one at a time or in combination.

For example, for phraseme 2a, on the lexical level we could expect variation with respect to the actual fruit—e.g., pears or plums

instead of apples— or with respect to the part of the tree—e.g., the tree as such, a branch, or a different plant. The best query would thus be query 2b, in which the first element—the valency filler of *to fall from*—is a fruit, and the second a plant or a part of a plant. Both valency fillers may be single nouns, complex noun phrases, or pronouns denoting real-world objects. And of course variation in word order is possible, too.

However, our corpus does not provide linguistic annotation. Even when using linguistically deeply annotated corpora and semantic resources like GermaNet[9], such queries would be hard to construct and it is almost impossible to find, for example, evidence 2c in a text from 1669 [26].

(2) a. *der Apfel fällt nicht weit vom Stamm*
      'like father like son'
      (literally 'the apple does not fall far from the stem')

    b. `something₁ fall from something₂`

    c. *die birn nit wey vom baum falt*
      (literally 'the pear not far from tree falls')

The best way to look for a variant of an idiomatic phrase is thus to look for some core elements, like *fall from*, and then to inspect the results manually to distinguish true from false positive hits. For this purpose, string-based queries are sufficient. Variation of a search string would include spelling variation and inflection. Therefore, XQuery Full Text with fuzzy search (for spelling variation) and stemming (for handling basic inflectional variation) is currently the most appropriate and flexible solution we are aware of.

5.1.2 Technical challenges

In principle, all XML documents represent scanned, OCR-processed, manually corrected, and semi-automatically TEI-annotated texts. However, documents are of different size, ranging from 30 KB to 90 MB. The collection of all XML documents is 2.9 GiB in size. The documents are organized differently; they may contain a single text or only part it written by a single author, a compilation of dozens of poems by a single author, or all books (which in turn can

---

[9]`http://www.sfs.uni-tuebingen.de/lsd/index.shtml`

```
teg an-<lb/>&#x201E;zeigen, damit ich zahlt werd.&#x201C;</p><lb/>&#x201E;Dem guten Gru&#x0364;nenwald war der Sp
ieß an Bauch<lb/>&#x201E;ge&#x017F;etzt, wußt nicht wo aus oder wo an, dann der Wirth<lb/>&#x201E;&#x017F;o auch mit
dem Teufel zur Schulen gangen, war ihm<lb/>&#x201E;zu &#x017F;charf. Er fing an die aller&#x017F;u&#x0364;ße&#x017F;
ten und glatte&#x017F;ten Wort zu geben, &#x017F;o er &#x017F;ein Tag je <lb/><pb
n="[5]" facs="#F0014" />
&#x201E;erdenken mocht, aber alles um&#x017F;on&#x017F;t war. Der Wirth <lb/>&#x201E;wollt aber keineswegs &#x017F;ch
weigen, und &#x017F;agt: ich mach<lb/>&#x201E;nicht viel Um&#x017F;ta&#x0364;nd, glattge&#x017F;chliffen i&#x017F;t t
bald gewetzt, du<lb/>&#x201E;ha&#x017F;t Tag und Nacht wollen voll &#x017F;ein, den be&#x017F;ten Wein, <lb/>&#x201E;
&#x017F;o ich in meinem Keller gehabt, hab ich dir mu&#x0364;&#x017F;en<lb/>&#x017F;&#x201E;auftragen, drum &#x017F;
uch nur nicht viel Ma&#x0364;us, ha&#x017F;t du<lb/>&#x201E;nicht Geld, &#x017F;o gib mir deinen Mantel, dann &#x017F;
F;o will ich<lb/>&#x201E;dir wohl eine Zeitlang borgen. Wo du aber in be&#x017F;timm-<lb/>&#x201E;ter Zeit nicht komm
m&#x017F;t, werd ich deinen Mantel auf der<lb/>&#x201E;Gant verkaufen la&#x017F;&#x017F;en, dieß i&#x017F;t der Be
&#x017F;cheid mit einander.<lb/>&#x201E;Wohlan &#x017F;agte Gru&#x0364;nenwald, ich will der Sache bald Rath<lb/>&#x20
1E;finden. Er &#x017F;aß nieder, nahm &#x017F;ein Schreibzeug, Papier,<lb/>&#x201E;Feder und Dinten, und dichtet nac
hfolgends Liedlein:</p><lb/><lg type="poem"><lg n="1"><l><l xml:id
01E;Und wollt gen Mu&#x0364;nchen gehn,</l><lb/><l>&#x201E;Und war in großen Sorgen,</l><lb/><l>&#x201E;Ach Gott wär i
&#x0364;r ich davon,</l><lb/><l>&#x201E;Mein Wirth, dem war ich &#x017F;chuldig viel,</l><lb/><l>&#x201E;Ich wollt ih
n gern bezahlen,</l><lb/><l>&#x201E;Doch auf ein ander Ziel.</l></lg><lb/><pb n="[6]" facs="#F0015" />
<lg n="2"><l>&#x201E;Herr Ca&#x017F;t ich hab vernommen</l><lb/>&#x201E;Du wo&#x0364;lle&#x017F;t von hinnen
u------XEmacs: arnim_wunderhorn01_1806.TEI-P5.xml     (XML PD XSLT Font)----L205--C1218--1%----------------------
                 <p rend="zenoPLm4n0" xml:id="tg228.2.5">Dem guten Grünenwald war der Spieß an
Bauch gesetzt, wußt nicht wo aus oder wo an, dann der Wirth so auch mit dem Teufel zur Schulen gangen, war ihm zu sc
harf. Er fing an die allersüßesten und glattesten Wort zu geben, so er sein Tag je studieren und erdenken mocht, abe
r alles umsonst war. Der Wirth wollt aber keinesweg schweigen, und sagt: ich mach nicht viel Umständ, glattgeschlif
fen ist bald gewetzt, du hast Tag und Nacht wollen voll sein, den besten Wein, so ich in meinem Keller gehabt, hab i
ch dir müssen auftragen, drum such nur nicht viel Mäus, hast du nicht Geld, so gib mir deinen Mantel, dann so will i
ch dir wohl eine Zeitlang borgen. Wo du aber in bestimmter Zeit nicht kommst, werd ich deinen Mantel auf die Gant ve
rkaufen lassen, dieß ist der Bescheid mit einander. Wohlan sagte Grünenwald, ich will der Sache bald Rath finden. Er
saß nieder, nahm sein Schreibzeug, Papier, Feder und Dinten, und dichtet nachfolgends Liedlein:</p>
                 <lb xml:id="tg228.2.6"/>
                 <lg>
                   <l xml:id="tg228.2.7">»Ich stund auf an eim Morgen,</l>
                   <l xml:id="tg228.2.8">Und wollt gen München gehn,</l>
                   <l xml:id="tg228.2.9">Und war in großen Sorgen,</l>
                   <l xml:id="tg228.2.10">Ach Gott wär ich davon,</l>
                   <l xml:id="tg228.2.11">Meim Wirth, dem war ich schuldig viel,</l>
                   <l xml:id="tg228.2.12">Ich wollt ihn gern bezahlen,</l>
                   <l xml:id="tg228.2.13">Doch auf ein ander Ziel.</l>
                 </lg>
u------XEmacs: Literatur-Arnim,-Ludwig-Achim-von.xml     (XML [teiCorpus] PD XSLT Font)----L39999--C0--16%-----------
```

Figure 4: Excerpt from XML representation of "Des Knaben Wunderhorn. Alte deutsche Lieder" by Achim von Arnim and Clemens Brentano

be compilations of poems or tales, single novels, etc.), of a single author. The texts themselves are also not alike, as the documents represent different literary genres, which differ from each other in style and syntax. In addition, they have often been printed by different publishers at different points in times, resulting in different layouts or document structures.

Moreover, the digitization guidelines differ as well: DTA and GerManC aim to digitize first editions, resulting in texts in the "original" language from the time of the writing or the first printing of a text. DB125 often used later editions, resulting in rather modern language even for texts originally written in the 17th century. The TEI annotation of DTA closely mirrors the original format and therefore includes page breaks and line breaks. The latter preserves hyphenation, which makes searching for words difficult. Applying appropriate rendering scripts to this data would easily allow displaying the text as lookalike to the printed source. The TEI annotation of DB125, on the other hand, does not preserve line breaks (except for poems) and thus no hyphenation occurs.

Figure 4 contains the same excerpt from "Des Knaben Wunderhorn. Alte deutsche Lieder" by Achim von Arnim and Clemens Brentano as found in DTA (top buffer) and in DB125 (lower buffer). It illustrates the characteristics of the two XML formats described above. Some texts have been included in both corpora: in this case, DB125 used an edition from 1979, whereas the source in DTA was printed in 1806. As BaseX allows the creation of collections with XML documents of different formats and different DTDs or XML Schemas, or no schemas at all, it is an optimal solution to store and query our heterogeneous corpus.

The smallest structural units are paragraphs (for prose) and lines (for poems or dramas). Within a paragraph or line, there might be rendering information (to preserve special formatting of the resource) and page breaks or line breaks. The text we hope to find phrasemes in is the content of these paragraph elements (<p>) and line elements (<l>).

A further challenge is the total amount of data to be processed. For phraseological research, the available data might be always too limited while, at the same time, it will be too large to be efficiently handled with common databases. Exploring texts for evidence of phrasemes means constructing the best query in a recursive process by querying the corpus, inspecting results, and refining the query. The phraseologists might also wish to save intermediate results as reference point for constructing optimized queries or to compile a result collection when no single best query is possible. Both scenarios require fast execution of the query and fast display of the result.

A pilot study revealed that for some phrasemes there is only little evidence, i.e., less than five relevant hits, but for others there are more than 800 relevant hits. On average, we have 90 relevant hits per phraseme and around 200 irrelevant hits. For a particular query there might be no hit at all or up to several thousand. Given the goal of investigating 1,000 phrasemes, this not only takes a lot of time for query formulation, result inspection, and further annotation, but it also creates a lot of data.

5.2 Applying XQuery expressions to the corpus

In our context, the main focus while searching the XML documents is not on the *structure*, but on the *contents*: The structure is used only to determine the bibliographic data needed to identify relevant excerpts and to be able to display context necessary for annotating linguistic aspects like meaning or register. Bibliographic information can be accessed by traveling up the document tree. The original page on which the text would be found in the printed version can be accessed by descending to the next page-break information. Context is defined as a certain number of preceding or following text nodes.

Index structures are mandatory if large databases are to be queried. For our purpose, we create a full-text index, including all stop words. Usually, stop words are conjunctions, prepositions, negation elements, pronouns, auxiliary verbs, etc. However, these are essential for retrieving phrasemes as they probably belong to the core of a phraseme. It might be better to search for combinations of prepositions and verbs without specifying nouns when looking for variation of nouns in a phraseme like 2a.

The creation of the full-text index results in a 4 GiB database. The index is applied if exact or fuzzy matches are performed. A second full-text index is created, in which all tokens are stemmed, and the resulting index is used to query inflected word forms. The German stemming algorithm is based on Caumanns [7].

A particular multi-word unit might be used literally or idiomatically—the latter constitutes a phraseme. However, we are interested in both occurrences in order to make statements about change: when did a multi-word unit become a phraseme and was less used literally or vice versa; was there a shift in meaning? Therefore, scoring or ranking of hits is not useful for this application; we are interested in all hits. As multi-word units might occur in various word order and be discontinuous, we cannot automatically distinguish correct and false positive hits, the latter defined as occurrence of all elements of the query but with no syntactic or semantic relation. The distinction has to be made by the phraseologist, i.e., manually.

With XQuery Full Text, queries can be created that specify (1) whether the elements of a search string have to occur as continuous string, i.e., as a "phrase", (2) as discontinuous string, i.e., all words have to occur or only some of them, (3) preserving or not the given order, or (4) within a given window. The latter allows for mimicking searching within sentence boundaries.

Listing 3 shows XQuery expressions from the query logs, which are related to find evidence of phraseme 2a. The first query contains no stemming option, but looks for exact matches of the search strings only. The other queries include the preposition *vom*, use different distances, and enforce the search strings to occur in the given order. All elements of the search string have to occur within a single paragraph or a line.

The results of a query, manually selected for annotation, are stored in a separate database, the *collect* database. The XQuery expression created by the phraseologist is stored as well. This serves documentation purposes, checking and approving procedures—this applies also to the information on who selected a specific hit—, and also allows for the creation of related or "better" queries by serving as inspiration. Listing 4 shows the structure of those entries.

The phraseologist will create various queries to find evidence for one phraseme as shown in Listing 3. After executing a query, she selects hits—i.e., paragraphs or lines where the search string was found in—to be annotated and saves the results. Hits not selected will be stored as well, having the value no for the element <selected> (also for documentation purposes and to be able to later automatically determine the "best" query with respect to recall and precision). The <node> element references the node-ID of the hit. When executing another query for the same phraseme, the results might include nodes that are already matched by a previous query and already stored as evidence for the particular phraseme. These nodes are no longer selectable, but the current query will be

```
//*[text() contains text
  ('Apfel' ftand 'Stamm' ftand 'fällt')
  distance at most 10 words][self::*:p or self::*:l]

//*[text() contains text
  ('vom' ftand 'stamm')
  using stemming using language "de"
  distance at most 10 words ordered]
  [self::*:p or self::*:l]

//*[text() contains text
('vom' ftand 'stamm')
  using stemming using language "de"
  distance at most 2 words ordered]
  [self::*:p or self::*:l]

//*[text() contains text
  ('vom' ftand 'stamm')
  using stemming using language "de"
  distance at most 1 words ordered]
  [self::*:p or self::*:l]
```

Listing 3: XQuery expressions intended to find evidence of the phraseme *Der Apfel fällt nicht weit vom Stamm*

```
<entry time = "2012-03-29T17:43:29" user = "..." >
  <node>3438425</node>
  <phraseme>Ad0018</phraseme>
  <query>[text() contains ...]</query>
  <secondquery>[text () contains ...]</secondquery>
  <selected>yes</selected>
</entry>
```

Listing 4: Pseudo entry in the *collect* **database**

stored in a <secondquery> element in the entry that represents this evidence.

We follow the paradigm of multiple layers to annotate the corpus. One layer contains information about which phraseme was found in a particular text node. The node-ID of this particular paragraph or line in the XML documents collection is used as reference point. The phraseme is also stored as a reference (<phraseme>) pointing to a list of given phrasemes and their prototypical meaning as found in dedicated collections or dictionaries. If an evidence is annotated, attributes containing information about linguistic aspects are created—i.e., register, modality, negation, voice, etc.—and stored in the *annotation* database, which contain entries like the ones shown in Listing 5. A particular paragraph or line may contain more than one phraseme.

As briefly described above, collecting and annotating evidence re-

```
<node id = "3438425" >
  <phraseme
    id = "Ad0018"
    mark = "Apfel fällt selten weit vom Stamme"
    voice = "active"
    negation = "no"
    meaning = "idiomatic"
    register = "..."
    time = "2012-04-19T16:04:33"
    user = "..."
  />
  <phraseme
    id = "Ad0048"
    mark ...
  />
</node>
```

Listing 5: Pseudo entry in the *annotation* **database**

sults in the creation of several sub-databases for intermediate results, to be later integrated into or merged with the original database. With XQuery Update, the original node can be replaced by the annotated one, in order to show evidence of phrasemes and their linguistic features within the original text.

5.3 Web interfaces for collecting and annotating evidence

The BaseX GUI is used for cleanup of annotation data whenever the phraseologists decide to no longer annotate specific features or to have additional annotation with default values. The GUI is also used on a local machine for developing efficient XQuery expressions to be used in the Web interface.

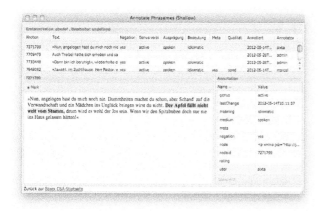

Figure 5: User interface for annotating phrasemes

For actual retrieval and annotation, the BaseX client/server architecture is used to allow remote and concurrent access for multiple users. The user interface for the phraseologists reflects the two-step process, consisting of collecting and annotating evidence: one interface allows retrieving evidence and storing relevant nodes, the other interface, as shown in Figure 5, supports annotation and is preferably used after collecting evidence for a particular phraseme is finished. The interfaces are implemented with Ext JS 4[10], and the communication with the BaseX server is based on the Perl API. Perl allows efficient and comfortable manipulation of the XQuery results in order to be displayed in a form convenient for phraseologists. The users of the web front-end do not have to write XQuery expressions, but they are provided with a simplified query language, in which most of the elements are added by choosing from fixed options. The input is then transformed into the final XQuery expression.

6. CONCLUSION

In this paper, we have given an insight into the current state of the art of XQuery, as implemented in the native XML database BaseX.

In contrast to Eckart [12, p. 187], who concluded that XML technologies are not appropriate to handle linguistic data, we could show that the capabilities of XQuery Full Text and Update now enable linguistically motivated exploration of heterogeneous documents. As a case in point, we presented the development of a framework for retrieval and annotation of phrasemes in diachronic texts.

This approach is transferable to other linguistic research questions investigating semi-structured data. An XML database like BaseX is more suitable than a relational database. XQuery 3.0 and

its Full Text and Update extensions are the basis for managing, retrieving, and annotating data consistently and efficiently in a single framework.

The search and annotation interface is put into productive use. The phraseologists in the OLdPhras project will create an evidence resource to serve as one source for the edition of dictionary entries. With our implementation, we proved that project or data specific development of XML dialects for storing, retrieving, and annotating as usual today [35] is not necessary. The capabilities of XQuery are, in our experience, powerful enough to effectively meet the requirements of corpus linguistics.

7. ACKNOWLEDGEMENTS

Alexander Holupirek is supported by the DFG Research Training Group GK-1042 *Explorative Analysis and Visualization of Large Information Spaces*. Research on phrasemes is funded by the SNSF under grant number 129577.

References

[1] S. Amer-Yahia et al. XQuery and XPath Full Text 1.0. W3C Candidate Recommendation. http://www.w3.org/TR/xpath-full-text-10, May 2008.

[2] S. Baumann, C. Brinckmann, S. Hansen-Schirra, G.-J. Kruijff, I. Kruijff-Korbayová, S. Neumann, and E. Teich. Multi-dimensional annotation of linguistic corpora for investigating information structure. In A. Meyers, editor, *HLT-NAACL 2004 Workshop: Frontiers in Corpus Annotation*, Stroudsburg, PA, USA, May 2004. Association for Computational Linguistics.

[3] P. Bennett, M. Durrell, S. Scheible, and R. J. Whitt. Annotating a historical corpus of German: A case study. In *Proceedings of the LREC 2010 Workshop on Language Resource and Language Technology: Standards - state of the art, emerging needs, and future developments*, pages 64–68, Paris, 2010. ELRA.

[4] A. Berglund et al. XQuery 1.0 and XPath 2.0 Data Model. http://www.w3.org/TR/xpath-datamodel/, December 2010.

[5] S. Boag et al. XQuery 1.0: An XML Query Language. W3C Recommendation. http://www.w3.org/TR/xquery, January 2007.

[6] P. Case. XQuery and XPath Full Text 3.0 Requirements and Use Cases. http://www.w3.org/TR/xpath-full-text-30-requirements-use-cases/, March 2012.

[7] J. Caumanns. A fast and simple stemming algorithm for german words. Technical report, Freie Universität Berlin, Fachbereich Mathematik und Informatik, 1999.

[8] D. Chamberlin, M. Dyck, D. Florescu, J. Melton, J. Robie, and J. Siméon. XQuery Update Facility. http://www.w3.org/TR/xquery-update-10/, March 2011.

[9] J.-P. Colson. The World Wide Web as a corpus for set phrases. In H. Burger, D. Dobrovol'skij, P. Kühn, and N. R. Norrick, editors, *Phraseology*, Handbooks of Linguistics and Communication Science, pages 1071–1077. Walter de Gruyter, Berlin/New York, 2007.

---

[10] http://www.sencha.com/products/extjs

[10] A. P. Cowie. Phraseology and corpora: some implications for dictionary-making. *Lexicography*, 12(4):307–323, 1999.

[11] S. Dipper. POS-tagging of historical language data: First experiments. In M. Pinkal, I. Rehbein, S. Schulte im Walde, and A. Storrer, editors, *Semantic Approaches in Natural Language Processing: Proceedings of the Conference on Natural Language Processing 2010 (KONVENS)*, pages 117–121, Saarbrücken, Germany, 2010. Universaar.

[12] R. Eckart. Towards a modular data model for multi-layer annotated corpora. In *Proceedings of the COLING/ACL on Main conference poster sessions*, COLING-ACL '06, pages 183–190, Stroudsburg, PA, USA, 2006. Association for Computational Linguistics.

[13] R. Eckart. Choosing an XML database for linguistically annotated corpora. *Sprache und Datenverarbeitung*, 32(1), 2008.

[14] R. Eckart and E. Teich. An XML-based data model for flexible representation and query of linguistically interpreted corpora. In *Data Structures for Linguistic Resources and Applications - Proceedings of the Biannual Conference of the Society for Computational Linguistics and Language Technology (GLDV)*, pages 327–336, 2007.

[15] P. Fischer et al. MXQuery – a low-footprint, extensible XQuery Engine. http://www.mxquery.org, 2009.

[16] X. Franc. Qizx/db. http://www.xmlmind.com/qizx/, 2012.

[17] C. Grün. *Storing and Querying Large XML Instances*. PhD thesis, Universität Konstanz, Konstanz, 2011.

[18] C. Grün, J. Gerken, H.-C. Jetter, W. A. König, and H. Reiterer. MedioVis – A User-Centred Library Metadata Browser. In A. Rauber, S. Christodoulakis, and A. M. Tjoa, editors, *ECDL*, volume 3652 of *Lecture Notes in Computer Science*, pages 174–185. Springer, 2005.

[19] C. Grün, A. Holupirek, M. Kramis, M. H. Scholl, and M. Waldvogel. Pushing XPath Accelerator to its Limits. In *ExpDB*, 2006.

[20] C. Grün, A. Holupirek, and M. H. Scholl. Visually exploring and querying XML with BaseX. In A. Kemper, H. Schöning, T. Rose, M. Jarke, T. Seidl, C. Quix, and C. Brochhaus, editors, *BTW*, volume 103 of *LNI*, pages 629–632. GI, 2007.

[21] C. Grün, S. Gath, A. Holupirek, and M. H. Scholl. XQuery full text implementation in BaseX. In *Proceedings of the 6th International XML Database Symposium on Database and XML Technologies*, pages 114–128, Berlin, Heidelberg, 2009. Springer.

[22] B. Juska-Bacher and C. Mahlow. Phraseological change – a book with seven seals? Tracing diachronic development of German proverbs and idioms. In P. Bennett, M. Durell, S. Scheible, and R. J. Whitt, editors, *New Methods in Historical Corpus Linguistics*, volume 3 of *Corpus linguistics and Interdisciplinary perspectives on language*. Gunter Narr, Tübingen, Germany, 2012.

[23] M. Kaufmann and D. Kossmann. Developing an Enterprise Web Application in XQuery. In *ICWE*, pages 465–468, 2009.

[24] C. Mahlow and B. Juska-Bacher. Exploring New High German texts for evidence of phrasemes. *Journal for Language Technology and Computational Linguistics*, 26(2): 117–128, 2011.

[25] M. Poesio, E. Barbu, E. Stemle, and C. Girardi. Structure-Preserving Pipelines for Digital Libraries. In *Proceedings of the 5th ACL-HLT Workshop on Language Technology for Cultural Heritage, Social Sciences, and Humanities (LaTeCH 2011)*, pages 54–62, Stroudsburg, PA, USA, 2011. Association for Computational Linguistics.

[26] Rechtsquellenstiftung des Schweizerischen Juristenverbandes, editor. *Appenzeller Landbücher*, volume SSRQ AR/AI 1 of *Sammlung Schweizerischer Rechtsquellen*. Schwabe, Basel, Switzerland, 2009.

[27] G. Rehm, R. Eckart, C. Chiarcos, and J. Dellert. Ontology-based XQuery'ing of XML-encoded language resources on multiple annotation layers. In N. Calzolari, K. Choukri, B. Maegaard, J. Mariani, J. Odijk, S. Piperidis, and D. Tapias, editors, *Proceedings of the Sixth International Conference on Language Resources and Evaluation (LREC'08)*, Paris, May 2008. ELRA.

[28] L. Romary. Stabilising knowledge through standards: A perspective for the humanities. In K. Grandin, editor, *Going Digital. Evolutionary and Revolutionary Aspects of Digitization*, volume 147 of *Nobel Symposium*, pages 188–218. Science History Publications, New York, NY, USA, 2011.

[29] A. Salminen and F. W. Tompa. Requirements for XML document database systems. In *Proceedings of the 2001 ACM Symposium on Document engineering*, DocEng '01, pages 85–94, New York, NY, USA, 2001. ACM.

[30] S. Scheible, R. J. Whitt, M. Durrell, and P. Bennett. Evaluating an 'off-the-shelf' POS-tagger on Early Modern German text. In *Proceedings of the 5th ACL-HLT Workshop on Language Technology for Cultural Heritage, Social Sciences, and Humanities (LaTeCH 2011)*, pages 19–23, Stroudsburg, PA, USA, 2011. Association for Computational Linguistics.

[31] S. H. Schirra, S. Neumann, and M. Vela. Multi-dimensional annotation and alignment in an English-German translation corpus. In *Proceedings of the 5th Workshop on NLP and XML: Multi-Dimensional Markup in Natural Language Processing*, NLPXML '06, pages 35–42, Stroudsburg, PA, USA, 2006. Association for Computational Linguistics.

[32] P. Stenetorp, S. Pyysalo, G. Topić, T. Ohta, S. Ananiadou, and J. Tsujii. brat: a web-based tool for NLP-assisted text annotation. In *Proceedings of the Demonstrations at the 13th Conference of the European Chapter of the Association for Computational Linguistics*, Stroudsburg, PA, USA, Apr. 2012. Association for Computational Linguistics.

[33] E. Ukkonen. Algorithms for Approximate String Matching. *Information and Control*, 64(1-3):100–118, 1985.

[34] C. Wittern, A. Ciula, and C. Tuohy. The making of TEI P5. *Literary and Linguistic Computing*, 24(3):281–296, May 2009.

[35] A. Zeldes, J. Ritz, A. Lüdeling, and C. Chiarcos. ANNIS: A search tool for multi-layer annotated corpora. In *Proceedings of Corpus Linguistics 2009, Liverpool, July 20-23*, 2009.

DocExplore: Overcoming Cultural and Physical Barriers to Access Ancient Documents

Pierrick Tranouez, Stéphane Nicolas, Vladislavs Dovgalecs, Alexandre Burnett, Laurent Heutte
University of Rouen, LITIS EA 4108
BP 12 – 76801 - Saint-Etienne du Rouvray – France
FirstName.SurName@univ-rouen.fr

Yiqing Liang, Richard Guest, Michael Fairhurst
School of Engineering and Digital Arts, University of Kent
Canterbury, CT2 7NT – UK
{Y.Liang, R.M.Guest, M.C.FairHurst}@kent.ac.uk

ABSTRACT

In this paper, we describe DocExplore, an integrated software suite centered on the handling of digitized documents with an emphasis on ancient manuscripts. This software suite allows the augmentation and exploration of ancient documents of cultural interest. Specialists can add textual and multimedia data and metadata to digitized documents through a graphical interface that does not require technical knowledge. They are helped in this endeavor by sophisticated document analysis tools that allows for instance to spot words or patterns in images of documents. The suite is intended to ease considerably the process of bringing locked away historical materials to the attention of the general public by covering all the steps from managing a digital collection to creating interactive presentations suited for cultural exhibitions. Its genesis and sustained development reside in a collaboration of archivists, historians and computer scientists, the latter being not only in charge of the development of the software, but also of creating and incorporating novel pattern recognition for document analysis techniques.

Categories and Subject Descriptors

H.3.7 [**Digital Libraries**]: Collection, Dissemination, Systems issues
J.5 [**Arts and Humanities**]

Keywords

cultural heritage, historical documents, manuscripts, document image analysis, document indexing, word spotting, authoring system, virtual book.

1. OBSTACLES AND SOLUTIONS

1.1 Obstacles

Many institutions hold within their depths unique artifacts of times past, concealed from the public's eye. For instance, the

Municipal Library in Rouen stores a document called the Ivory Book, an aggregation of manuscripts ranging from the 10th to 13th century, bound in a magnificent ivory plated cover. It is precious and fragile, therefore seldom accessed except by a few scholars and archivists. Another such document is a 20-meter long roll of scroll, which adds its cumbersomeness to the previously mentioned fragility. They would be worthy subjects of exhibition, as they are both beautiful and interesting, but are instead stored carefully for preservation.

Digitalization is a first step to breach this physical barrier preventing a general access, but it is not yet sufficient. Indeed, ancient documents, for example medieval manuscripts, can only be understood or appreciated if inserted into a coherent cultural context. The writing and the language are the first obvious obstacles, but a global understanding of the background of the document can be necessary to reach a culture so distant in time it may seem alien to a general contemporary observer.

1.2 Digitally overcoming these difficulties

Scientific and technological endeavors to help our written heritage enter the digital age are a field of rapidly growing importance. The number of conferences and workshops on digital humanities has exploded in the last couple of years. We can cite for example the HIP '11[1], ESF Digital Paleography[2], or DISH[3] conferences.

Some of these contributions aim at the scholar community: tools for transcribing or translating, annotations, simple text recognition (much more difficult in ancient documents than in modern productions) [1]. Others are supposed to be used by the archivists, helping them organize masses of digitized documents, often through the use of metadata and adapted indexable file formats [2]. Finally, others try to make the documents accessible to a more general public by developing software interfaces or simply viewers of digitized media [3].

The DocExplore project intends to overcome the obstacles of the previous section through the creation of augmented documents. As we will describe, we borrow from the three preceding fields, allowing scholars to pour their knowledge into textual and multimedia metadata that enhance the digitized document. We

---

[1] http://www.comp.nus.edu.sg/~hdocp/

[2] http:/www.zde.uni-
wuerzburg.de/veranstaltungen/digital_palaeography/

[3] http://www.dish2011.nl/

also provide tools for building exciting visualizations extracted from the augmented documents. Furthermore we capitalize on our past experience in handwriting recognition to try to provide tools for searching text in images of variable quality and from exotic handwriting. We want to spot words [4] without first segmenting the image into lines and words, thus letting us apply similar techniques to spot various kinds of patterns in the document image: details of illuminations, faces, crowns, colors etc.

2. OUR PROJECT

2.1 An Interreg IVa project

The DocExplore research project was funded by Interreg IVa France (Channel) England. It brought together on both sides of the Channel historians, archivists and computer scientists. The English side is centered on the University of Kent and the Canterbury Cathedral Archive, while the French side includes the University of Rouen and Rouen Municipal Library. It is headed by the LITIS laboratory.

Our project aims to investigate and implement an IT-based system for the exploration of historical documents, providing solutions that enhance the interaction with and understanding of documents and associated metadata.

The strong multi-discipline partnership ensures that DocExplore is not a pure theoretical project, but an effective effort aiming at satisfying at the same time computer science research scientist, historians, and archivists or librarian.

2.2 The DocExplore Software Suite

We are building a software suite that lets users build augmented documents, as well as multimedia presentations of these documents: 3D models of the codex, textured with high-resolution photographs of the digitized manuscript, as well as selected parts of the *augmentation* of the documents, relatively to the emphasis of the presentation. This suite is composed of three applications: (1) one application providing advanced computer-aided functionalities to manage and annotate collections of digitized manuscripts (the Manuscript Management Tool), (2) one application to easily build multimedia presentations of augmented documents (the Authoring Tool), and (3) one application to visualize and interact with multimedia presentations (the Viewer). The viewer is the front-end application for the general public, the authoring tool is more dedicated to the archivists and the professionals of cultural heritage preservation and promotion, and the manuscript management tool allows the scholars and researchers to study and enrich the digitized sources. Thus our software suite makes it possible to gather those, professional and general public, producers and consumers, who are concerned by cultural heritage discovery. The general architecture of our system is depicted on the Figure 1.

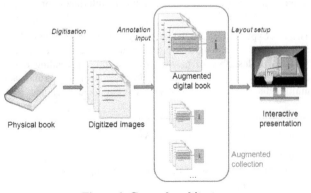

Figure 1. General architecture

2.2.1 A Manuscript Management Tool (MMT)

The MMT may be the most complex application of the three: it allows to aggregate pictures of manuscript in codices, it provides tools for text and pattern recognition or spotting, and allows historians or archivists to enhance the document with any knowledge they deem useful: transcriptions, annotations, comments, pictures, movies, hyperlinks (including inside the document). The user interface of the MMT is illustrated on figure 2.

2.2.1.1 Building virtual codices

The initial digitization leads to the creation of masses of document images. For other uses the images can then be embedded in a metadata containing file format (e.g. ALTO/METS), but in our suite we suppose we just have raw high-definition images (e.g. TIFF).

The first step of building an augmented document is aggregating a selection of these images into a virtual codex. It can be the same codex containing the original manuscripts, but it can also be a selection of some folios, a compilation etc.

Virtual libraries of such codices can be assembled.

Figure 2. The Manuscript Management Tool

2.2.1.2 Augmenting the document

Data and metadata can be added to the virtual codex. It can be related to the whole document, to one page or to a selection of this page called a Region Of Interest (ROI). ROIs can have any polygonal shape: they could delimit a face in a painting, a part of a text, an illumination etc.

Textual data linked to a ROI, a page or a book can be metadata such as keywords or tags, but also a transcription of text or any type of comment. The data can more generally be multimedia (movies, animations, pictures), or a mix of all these types.

The ROIs can have attributed hyperlinks indicating families of illuminations, variants on the scripting of a same word etc. The same links can point to other augmented documents of the same virtual library.

2.2.1.3 Indexing, Recognition or spotting: facilitating the navigation

One of the strengths of a digital document over a mundane one is its ability to be automatically indexed and searched. It is quite easy to provide this functionality to the added textual data.

We also try to address this difficulty in the actual text as depicted in the images of the manuscripts. On recent documents OCR allows a good automatic transcription that can be afterwards indexed. This is generally not the case on ancient documents: manuscripts are often hand written, as their name implies; they may have had an imperfect conservation trajectory, leading to degradations not fixable at the image manipulation level; they can have complicated scripts, with a very dense interweaving of ascenders and descenders. OCRs often fail spectacularly on this kind of document [5].

If full recognition is often not possible, word spotting may be more efficient [6].

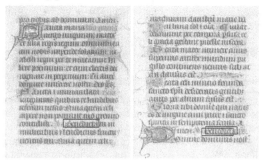

Figure 3. Query word (left) and retrieval result (right)

Completely new perspectives in digital document exploration are opened if word and general graphical pattern search capabilities are added to the existing system. Users are able to highlight a general object of interest such as a word (see Figure 3) or a pattern (see Figure 4) and the system returns the digitized pages containing the requested object and its location. Collection-wide search using this approach offers an efficient work tool for historians trying to discover regularities in the studied documents.

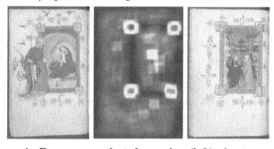

Figure 4. Four user selected queries (left), heat-map for pattern detection (middle) and four detected regions (right)

The challenge lies in the fact that digitized documents are of very complex structure and exhibit variable writing styles due to different authors or ages amongst other issues. This advanced search capability will naturally extend the software suite enabling exploration and search functionality. At the same time, historians can use the same approach for novel and unexplored manuscript annotation and study.

2.2.2 An authoring tool
The aim of the authoring tool is to allow building multimedia presentations, by defining a course through a selection of pages and annotations within a collection of augmented documents. This course can be linear like a book, but not necessarily - the presentation could also be like a graph of hyperlinked pages. The authoring tool interacts with the MMT, and allows the editor of the presentation to select the data and the associated metadata he wants to show in his presentation. This authoring tool is designed for use by anyone and requires no particular skills in programming, text encoding or data processing. The user has simply to provide a selection of the documents from a collection he wants to include in his multimedia presentation as well as supplementary metadata as attachment. The user can also define the order of the included data in the presentation easily by drag and drop operations, or the relationships between them in case of a non-linear presentation with links. The appearance of the user interface of the authoring tool is quite similar to that of the MMT in order to facilitate the user experience. The authoring tool is depicted on the Figure 5.

Figure 5. Multimedia presentation publishing using the authoring tool

The authoring tool bridges the gap between the knowledge database fed by the scholars through the MMT and the multimedia presentation restituted to the general public thanks to a multimedia viewer. This is the component that allows integration of the data and the metadata in a multimedia presentation, encompassing both the physical and cultural obstacles discussed in the introduction. Authoring tools available for the publishing of cultural heritage sources are few. Among the recent commercial solutions we can cite Apple's iBook Author software. However this solution is dedicated to the publishing on tablets, and not to the production of multimedia presentation for museums or libraries. Furthermore, the strength of our solution relies in the possibility to interact with the knowledge database provided by the MMT.

2.2.3 A viewer
The viewer is a front-end component of the system intended to present and allow interaction with the document presentations built in the authoring tool, for use by the general public in exhibition locations such as libraries or museums. This viewer exploits 3D modeling and textured rendering of the manuscripts (see Figure 6), in order to enhance the discovering experience of the users, and give them as much as possible the impression of handling a real book by proposing natural interactions, such as page flipping using touchscreen or gesture interactions.

Figure 6. 3D page rendering in the viewer

This viewer looks like some other digital book viewers, such as the Turning the Pages viewer[4] (a review of some viewing solutions dedicated to cultural heritage content is provided in [3]), and it enables the user to browse in a natural way the digitized content provided inside by flipping the pages. But it allows much more by offering access to supplementary material provided by the researchers, scholars, or any editor of the content. This material can be textual information such as transcriptions, translations, annotations, commentaries, as well as images, audio, video or hyperlinks to some other content. Therefore, the viewer is much more than a simple "page flipping app" for digitized

---

[4] http://www.turningthepages.com/

content: this is a viewer dedicated to the visualization of and interaction with augmented documents (see Figure 7).

Figure 7. Viewing the metadata attached to a ROI in the viewer

Furthermore, it works in a client-server mode, and is able to connect to a database to provide the user with access to several multimedia presentations available on the server. Thus the viewer is not dedicated to one particular digital book, but can be used to browse a large variety of multimedia presentations. For instance, it can be installed on multiple consulting stations in a library or a museum, allowing a centralized distribution and management of the diffused content. The inherent problems involved by the loading time of the data are obviously dealt with by the viewer.

From a technical point of view, our viewer is implemented using Java and OpenGL technologies. This choice is motivated by the fact that Java and OpenGL are supported by most platforms, including web browsers.

2.3 First uses of the DocExplore Software Suite

2.3.1 Manuscript Management Tool

Our historian partners have made use of the MMT to annotate and transcribe more than a thousand pages of medieval manuscripts. Hundreds of those transcriptions were aligned with the pictured words. They have thus built a learning base for our pattern recognition algorithms.

Our developers are currently addressing their bug reports and overall usability remarks.

2.3.2 Authoring and viewer tools

We joined our partner of Rouen Municipal Library at an ancient books trade fair called Salon du Livre Ancien in 2010, 2011 and 2012, where we demonstrated augmented documents created and presented with our suite. Attendant feedback was very positive[5].

This experience gave us a list of improvements needed for those tools, which we've implemented. A new version of the suite has been given to our partners in early January, so as to lead to a new cycle of improvements.

2.3.3 Advanced Search Tool

In our first part of preliminary experiments with word spotting in ancient documents we've obtained promising results by returning highly relevant and precise locations of the requested words. In the second part of our experiments we managed to obtain precise detection of requested objects in spite of natural visual variability, which is due to drawings performed by hand.

Our precision and recall need to be more formally evaluated and improved, but our first results are very encouraging.

3. DISCUSSION

The primary objective of the DocExplore Software Suite is to let archivists and scholars easily augment digital facsimiles of valuable and rare manuscripts, an application of this augmentation being the production of rich multimedia creations. The use of the suite does not imply advanced knowledge of data representation formats (SGML, XML, TEI schema), while allowing the definition of various rich annotations and interpretations.

The augmented multimedia creations can be used in cultural heritage exhibitions, by enhancing interactions with ancient documents, through natural user interfaces (currently touch and gestures) and multimedia content (images, audio, video, interlinks, hyperlinks). We are building an exhibition, scheduled for September 2013, on the theme of "Writings from the Middle Ages to Present Time in the Anglo-Norman Region". The DocExplore Software Suite will be an essential part of this setup.

We are currently working on the integration of pattern recognition functionalities, to complement full text search in annotations and transcriptions, at first in the form of *word spotting*: multiple occurrences of the requested word can be returned upon user's request. Finally, an extension of existing tools and approaches will allow searching for free form graphical patterns in a seamless manner.

4. ACKNOWLEDGMENTS

The authors would like to thank Interreg IVa for its funding of the DocExplore Project, as well as our partners, Catherine Richardson and Alixe Bovey from the University of Kent, Cressida Williams from Canterbury Cathedral Archives, Elisabeth Lalou, Alexis Grelois and Cécile Capot from GRHis laboratory of the University of Rouen, and Vincent Viallefond and Maïté Vanmarque from Rouen Municipal Library.

5. REFERENCES

[1] Romero, V, Serrano, N., Toselli, H. A., Sanchez, A. J., and Vidal, E. 2011. Handwritten Text Recognition for Historical Documents. In *Proceedings of the Workshop on Language Technologies for Digital Humanities and Cultural Heritage*.

[2] Constantopoulos, P., Doerr, M., Theodoridou, M., and Tzobanakis, M. 2002. Historical documents as monuments and as sources. In : *Proceedings of Computer Applications in Archaeology 2002*.

[3] Cauchard, J.R., Ainsworth, P.F., Romano, D.M., and Banks, B. 2006. *Virtual Manuscripts for an Enhanced Museum and Web Experience - "Living Manuscripts"*. 12th International Conference on Virtual Systems and Multimedia, 18-20 October 2006, Xi'an, China.

[4] Leydier, Y., Lebourgeois, F. and Emptoz, H. 2007. Text search for medieval manuscript images. *Pattern Recognition* no. 40, pp. 3552-3567.

[5] Govindaraju, V., Cao, H., and Bhardwaj, A. 2009. Handwritten document retrieval strategies. In *Proceedings of The Third Workshop on Analytics for Noisy Unstructured Text Data* (AND '09). ACM, New York, NY, USA, 3-7.

[6] T.M. Rath and R. Manmatha. Word spotting for historical documents. *International Journal on Document Analysis and Recognition*, vol. 9, no. 2, pp. 139-152, 2007

---

5   http://klog.hautetfort.com/archive/2012/04/01/un-feuilleteur-pour-valoriser-les-documents-patrimoniaux.html

Evaluation of BILBO Reference Parsing in Digital Humanities via a Comparison of Different Tools

Young-Min Kim
LIA, University of Avignon
339, chemin des Meinajaries
84911 Avignon, France
young-min.kim@univ-avignon.fr

Patrice Bellot
LSIS, Aix-Marseille University
Av. Escadrille Normandie Niemen
Marseille Cedex 20, France
patrice.bellot@lsis.org

Jade Tavernier
LIA, University of Avignon
339, chemin des Meinajaries
84911 Avignon, France
jade.tavernier@etd.univ-avignon.fr

Elodie Faath
LSIS, Aix-Marseille University
CLEO, Centre for Open
Electronic Publishing
3, place Victor Hugo
13331 Marseille, France
elodie.faath@openedition.org

Marin Dacos
CNRS / Aix-Marseille University
CLEO, Centre for Open
Electronic Publishing
3, place Victor Hugo
13331 Marseille, France
marin.dacos@openedition.org

ABSTRACT

Automatic bibliographic reference annotation involves the tokenization and identification of reference fields. Recent methods use machine learning techniques such as Conditional Random Fields to tackle this problem. On the other hand, the state of the art methods always learn and evaluate their systems with a well structured data having simple format such as bibliography at the end of scientific articles. And that is a reason why the parsing of new reference different from a regular format does not work well. In our previous work, we have established a standard for the tokenization and feature selection with a less formulaic data such as notes. In this paper, we evaluate our system BILBO with other popular online reference parsing tools on a new data from totally different source. BILBO is constructed with our own corpora extracted and annotated from real world data, digital humanities articles of Revues.org site (90% in French) of OpenEdition. The robustness of BILBO system allows a language independent tagging result. We expect that this first attempt of evaluation will motivate the development of other efficient techniques for the scattered and less formulaic bibliographic references.

Categories and Subject Descriptors

H.3.4 [**Information Storage and Retrieval**]: Systems and Software—*performance evaluation*

General Terms

Experimentation, Performance

1. INTRODUCTION

Automated bibliographic reference annotation aims to separately recognize different reference fields that consist of author, title, date, etc [8]. This is involved in citation analysis, which has already started several decades ago [2], intended for finding patterns among references such as bibliographical coupling and also for computing impacts of articles via citation frequency and patterns. A practical example is CiteSeer [3], a public search engine and also a digital library for scientific and academic papers that first realized the automatic citation indexing. Recent work concentrates in taking advantage of the extracted citation information, for example, for scientific paper summarization [6] and text retrieval [7]. The success of these applications depends especially on the extracted reference fields. The traditional machine learning techniques in sequence labeling such as Hidden Markov Models (HMMs) and Conditional Random Fields (CRFs) [4] are frequently applied to this problem and a recent work [5] shows a superiority of the latter approach. Since then CRF becomes a standard tool for reference parsing. A very recent work [1] proposes a universal information extraction algorithm, which can be applied to the task. They achieve good results but the used collections are homogeneous scientific research papers.

On the other hand, the real world data is not always well arranged or structured like scientific papers. Therefore we have no guarantee that the same technique will work for different areas, which have much less formulaic references. Our research project on this subject has been started from the necessity of an automatic structuring of references in the humanities and social sciences. The target data is the real world bibliographic reference data of Revues.org, an online publishing site of journals in this area. The primary interest of the project is testing the effectiveness of CRF model for this area, then defining a tokenization and a set of features and labels adapted to the various different reference formats in Revues.org site having more than 340 journals. For that we manually annotated three different levels of corpus that consist of more than 3000 references. We have finished this primary objective using for the first corpus with comparably regular format, then continued to improve our system with the second level of corpus including note data.

Since we seek to construct a robust system, which is independent of reference format and even of language, we focus on finding general rules of tokenization and of feature extraction. This paper aims to evaluate the current version of our system by a comparison of five different reference parsing tools. For the test, we use an external reference data, provided by our collaboration partner, University of Michigan (UMich) Library. As requested, we test four different areas, information technology, chemistry, biology, and finally the humanities. Even though our system is constructed with the humanities and social sciences data, this evaluation will allow us to see if our system works also for other areas.

2. AUTOMATIC REFERENCE ANNOTATION IN DIGITAL HUMANITIES

The automatic bibliographic reference annotation is a challenging task in digital humanities (DH) mostly because of various reference formats in this area. A brief introduction of our target data would allow a basic understanding of difference between DH reference data and traditional scientific reference data. An important thing in our evaluation is that we use a totally different set of references extracted from other digital library.

2.1 Learning with OpenEdition corpus

In BILBO project, we first construct three different training corpora according to the difficulty level of annotation: bibliography, footnotes, and implicit references integrated in the body of text. All these corpora are manually annotated with TEI guidelines and the first two corpora are our interest in this comparison. We have 715 references and 1147 notes manually annotated in OpenEdition corpus 1[1] and 2. These are extracted from the Revues.org site of OpenEdition platform, where the mostly used language is French, the original language of the platform. But it is originally designed for international electronic publishing such that the rate of articles written in a different language to French is 10%, of which more than half are in English. The articles have a diverse range of formats in their bibliographical references according not only to journal types, but also to authors in same journal. This is one of the general properties of the humanities and social sciences articles. Especially in the corpus level 2, we have a segmentation problem, caused by the property of note data that the data is in general a mix of bibliographic and non-bibliographic information. So we need to first exclude totally non-bibliographic notes and then well detect bibliographic zones only when tagging automatically new data. Figure 1 shows a simple note example, wrapped by <note> tags and including a reference with <bibl> tags. In our previous work, we evaluated our system on this data by keeping 30% of references as test data.

2.2 UMich Library Data for testing

In general, training and test data come from a closed set, and a constructed model is applied to new samples from the set. That is why we need to relearn or modify a model if new samples come from a different set. Here we try to check the capacity of our system with external dataset, UMich

```
«·socialisés en situation d'immigration·»<hi rend="sup"><note place="foot"
n="18">Définition donnée par <bibl><author><forename>Sayad</forename> <
surname>Abdelmalek</surname></author><c type="comma">,</c> <c type=
"guillemot_left">«</c>·<title level="a">Le mode de génération des générations
"immigrées"</title>·<c type="guillemot_right">»</c><c type="comma">,</c> <hi
rend="italic"><title level="j">L'Homme et la société</title></hi><c type=
"comma">,</c> <abbr>n°</abbr> <biblScope type="issue">11-112</biblScope><c
type="comma">,</c> <date>1994</date>.</bibl></note></hi>.</p>
```

Figure 1: Note including a bibliographic reference

Library data. It consists of four different xml files automatically extracted from their digital library database. Each file contains an article from different area that includes bibliography and(or) note part. We asked them to annotate the files with TEI guidelines as ours for ground-truth based evaluation. Table 1 shows a detailed information.

Table 1: UMich Library Data

file name	#elements bibl	note	area	heading
ark	6	0	chemistry	References
mbot	21	0	biology	Literature cited
basp	33	29	humanities	No heading
jep	34	37	technology, economics	Bibliography, Notes

2.3 Conditional Random Fields

We apply a linear-chain CRF to our reference annotation problem as in recent studies. By definition, a discriminative model maximizes the conditional distribution of output given input features. So, any factors dependent only on input are not considered as modeling factors, instead they are treated as constant factors to output [9]. This aspect derives a key characteristic of CRFs, the ability to include a lot of input features in modeling. It is essential for some specific sequence labeling problems such as ours, where input data has rich characteristics. The conditional distribution of a linear-chain CRF for a set of label $\mathbf{y}$ given an input $\mathbf{x}$ is written as follows :

$$p(\mathbf{y}|\mathbf{x}) = \frac{1}{Z(\mathbf{x})} \exp\{\sum_{k=1}^{K} \theta_k f_k(y_t, y_{t-1}, \mathbf{x}_t)\}, \qquad (1)$$

where $\theta = \{\theta_k\} \in R^K$ is a parameter vector, $\{f_k(y_t, y_{t-1}, \mathbf{x}_t)\}_{k=1}^{K}$ is a set of real-valued feature functions, and $Z(\mathbf{x})$ is a normalization function. Instead of the word identity x_t, a vector $\mathbf{x}_t$, which contains all necessary components of $\mathbf{x}$ for computing features at time t, is substituted.

3. EVALUATION AND COMPARISON

We compared five reference parsing tools, BILBO (ours), Grobid, Freecite, ParsCit and Biblio. The other tools are online services and provide downloadable codes.

3.1 Reference parsing tools

BILBO Our prototype reference parsing tool will be available online soon in two levels, bibliography and notes[2]. It provides 20 different reference fields over two levels. As the other tools have their own fields for annotation, we rearrange the other tools' fields to correctly match them with ours. We sometimes detail several fields more than the others such as separation of surname and forename, and sometimes less detail like annotating same tags on the edition information (volume, issue, number).

[1] It is available at http://bilbo.hypotheses.org/605

[2] http://bilbo.hypotheses.org/

ParsCit This is one of the oldest reference parsing services that provides general reference parsing[3]. It uses CRFs mainly with CORA dataset, a standard data for reference tagging, and other additional datasets as training data. It provides reference parsing from different data formats such as pdf, xml, plain text etc.

Biblio It is developed around the same time of ParsCit, and also designed for references at the end of articles[4].

Freecite Freecite[5] was inspired by ParsCit, and it also uses CRFs with CRF++ library implementation. Training dataset is CORA dataset, and it improves the system with lexical augmentation.

Grobid This tool provides both extraction and parsing of references from scientific articles[6] with CRF. An interesting point is it can enrich tagging result using external data. That is, based on their basic parsing result, it requests a more detailed information to Crossref site (an external service), then modifies the original reference string to enrich it. It is very effective but complicates the comparison process.

3.2 Difficulties

There are many difficulties for an exact comparison of experimental results. As mentioned before, we first need to find a reasonable correspondence between our reference fields and that of the others. Since only BILBO and Grobid separately find surname and forename, we consider them as a field, author. In the same way, we make several groups of similar fields then combine some detailed sub-groups if they are not provided by all tools. For the fields we cannot make a correspondence with this method, we eliminate it from the accuracy calculation. The punctuation and abbreviation fields in BILBO are excluded for both precision and recall.

A more difficult problem is the modification of tokens in the other tools. All the others modify the input string according to their rules, which are not explicitly described. In brief, there are elimination of tokens, modification of each token, and also change of token order. All tools eliminate some tokens when they found the tokens are not useful, especially in case of Biblio. Some method modify input token when printing result, for example when an initial expression of author is captured, eliminate punctuation in it. Very often they change the order of fields, even the order of surname and forename. It is not possible to count all these details from the beginning, so we re-run the evaluation process once we find a special case of token modification by manually verifying the parsing result of the other tools.

3.3 Experimental Result

The precision, recall and f-measure are used as the evaluation measures by comparing the real tag and the estimated tag of each token. We test the tools in two levels, bibliographic reference level and note level. For the first level (level 1), we take the references wrapped by <bibl> tags, and for the second level (level 2), the notes with <note> tags are selected. In notes, the tokens in non-bibliographic phrases are considered to be annotated by <nonbibl> tags. Our note parsing module is trained with OpenEdition corpus 2, containing these non-bibliographic fields. The other tools also have a special tag, intended to be assigned to

[3] http://aye.comp.nus.edu.sg/parsCit/
[4] http://paracite.eprints.org/developers/
[5] http://freecite.library.brown.edu/welcome
[6] http://grobid.svn.sourceforge.net/, grobid.no-ip.org/

the remaining tokens, which can not be classified among meaningful fields. Therefore we accept these special tags as <nonbibl> for the comparison. However, as the other tools are not designed to process notes, they often eliminate some of these tokens. Moreover the eliminated tokens are from various fields, so we cannot just consider them as <nonbibl> part neither. Therefore, we decide to show the evaluation result of note data in two ways, by including or excluding the non-bibliographic parts (Table 3).

On the other hand, Grobid adds some exact and more detailed information about references provided from Crossref site in case of finding DOI in the site, so we can not evaluate this tool for the enriched references. Therefore for Grobid, we necessarily abandon the most formulaic two files, 'ark' and mbot' that have some enriched references in parsing result. In the level 2 evaluation, the two files are naturally excluded because they do not have any notes.

Table 2: Evaluation on UMich Library level 1 data including all files (upper table) and excluding 'ark' and 'mbot' (lower table).

Tool	Precision			Recall			F-measure		
	total	author	title	total	author	title	total	author	title
BILBO	**0.68**	**0.86**	**0.84**	**0.69**	*0.86*	*0.73*	**0.68**	**0.86**	**0.78**
ParsCit	0.57	*0.79*	0.73	0.49	0.63	0.52	0.53	0.70	0.63
Biblio	0.57	0.72	0.62	0.55	0.57	**0.83**	0.56	0.64	0.71
Freecite	*0.65*	0.76	*0.76*	*0.62*	**0.94**	0.68	*0.63*	*0.83*	*0.72*
Grobid	-	-	-	-	-	-	-	-	-

Tool	Precision			Recall			F-measure		
	total	author	title	total	author	title	total	author	title
BILBO	*0.63*	**0.79**	**0.85**	**0.64**	*0.86*	*0.70*	**0.64**	**0.82**	**0.77**
ParsCit	0.51	0.69	0.71	0.41	0.53	0.51	0.45	0.60	0.59
Biblio	0.57	*0.72*	0.60	0.59	0.63	**0.88**	0.58	0.67	0.71
Freecite	0.59	0.71	0.75	0.57	**0.89**	0.68	0.58	*0.78*	*0.71*
Grobid	**0.64**	0.67	*0.79*	*0.62*	0.80	0.63	*0.63*	0.73	0.70

Table 2 shows the evaluation result on level 1 data. The upper table shows the result of four tools except Grobid on all test files. For notes including references, we extract the included references wrapped by <bibl>. It means that the non-bibliographic phrases are not considered for this level 1 evaluation. Total precision and recall are micro-averaged values over counted fields into evaluation that are essentially identical if we take all fields. But in our calculation, because of the exclusion of non-appropriate fields and the token elimination in the other tools, there are some differences between the micro-averaged precision and recall. Token elimination works to the advantage of the other tools in terms of precision because most of the eliminated ones are originally from a meaningful field but actually are not evaluated. The author and title fields are also selected to show the performance of individual field. The best result for each comparison (each column) is printed in bold and the second best is in italic. BILBO always outperforms three other tools in terms of f-measure as well as precision. The total f-measure of BILBO is 0.68 that is better than the second ranked tool, Freecite, which obtains 0.63 with the same measure. However, if we look inside of the result of each file, Freecite obtains a better result on the 'ark' file from chemistry that has less number of fields compared to the other files, because of the capacity of Freecite for the detection of author field (0.94 recall).

The lower table shows the result of all tools only on the 'basp' and 'jep' files including less formulaic references, which are extracted from the inside of the notes. So the performance naturally decreases compared to the upper table as we expect for almost all tools except Biblio. The reason is that Biblio distributes mostly author and title tags to the references in 'basp' file, but the micro-averaged values anyway increase because author and title are the most frequent fields. BILBO and Grobid outperform the others with a slight superiority for BILBO (0.64 vs. 0.63 with total f-measure) especially on both individual fields, author (0.82 vs. 0.73) and title (0.77 vs. 0.70). On the other hand, Freecite still has a best recall on author field like above.

Table 3: Evaluation with UMich Library level 2 data including (total) or excluding (in parenthesis) non-bibliographic fields in calculation.

Tool	Precision total(nbb)	ath.	tit.	Recall total(nbb)	ath.	tit.	F-measure total(nbb)	ath.	tit.
BILBO	.60(.34)	.69	.30	.64(.56)	.69	.62	.62(.42)	.67	.41
ParsCit	.15(.14)	.54	.12	.11(.32)	.46	.44	.12(.20)	.50	.19
Biblio	.21(.17)	.16	.19	.21(.48)	.42	.85	.21(.25)	.24	.31
Freecite	.19(.18)	.45	.14	.17(.51)	.67	.61	.18(.27)	.54	.22
Grobid	.23(.23)	.61	.15	.18(.55)	.64	.61	.20(.32)	.63	.25

Table 3 shows the evaluation result on the level 2 data. As mentioned above, we compute the performance on all meaningful fields in two ways, by including or excluding non-bibliographic fields. The total column presents the former case and the nbb in parenthesis column presents the latter case. The same notation to Table 2 is used to indicate the best and second best values.

Let us first look at the total f-measure including non-bibliographic part. BILBO (0.62) greatly outperforms all the other tools and even the second-ranked Biblio (0.21). This result had been predicted beforehand because the other tools do not deal with note data. Therefore the objective of the level 2 evaluation is verifying the difference between BIBLO and the others. We obtain the similar result for total precision and recall. Among four other tools, ParsCit is worse than the others especially because of its low recall of title. On the contrary, Biblio obtains a comparable result with Freecite and Grobid because it concentrates in author and title fields during its prediction. We have already witnessed this phenomenon in the level 1 evaluation.

Meanwhile, the performance without non-bibliographic part shows an interesting result. BILBO still outperforms the others but the gap declines quite much because the performance of the others get better while that of BILBO decreases. Grobid obtains particularly a similar total recall to BILBO (0.55 vs. 0.56) but still has about 0.1 of gap on total precision (0.23 vs. 0.34). It means that Grobid finds as much correct reference fields as ours, but annotates much more unnecessary tokens with one of the meaningful fields compared to ours. This is same for the remaining tools. Even though this second evaluation provides a comparison overview for meaningful fields, excluding non-bibliographic part is not reasonable because detecting bibliographic zone is an essential criterion for note processing.

4. CONCLUSION AND DISCUSSION

We have evaluated our reference parsing tool, BILBO by a comparison of different tools for the same objective that are accessible online. The evaluation is done on two different levels of data, reference level and note level and our system outperforms the other tools especially on the level 2 data. BILBO is originally developed for the automatic reference annotation in the humanities and social sciences, but gives a reasonable result in other areas. We also have another flexibility in language because our training data from the OpenEdition corpora contains mostly French references (more than 85 %), but the test data is in English. This language independency may come from the well defined local features in our model construction. During the comparison of differently structured outputs of different tools, we have found a lot of practical issues. And we expect they will contribute to improving BILBO system.

5. ACKNOWLEDGMENTS

This work was supported by the French Agency for Scientific Research (Agence Nationale de la Recherche) under CAAS project, and by Google with the Digital Humanities Research Awards that initiated the project. And we thank to University of Michigan Library for the test data.

6. REFERENCES

[1] E. Cortez, D. Oliveira, A. S. da Silva, E. S. de Moura, and A. H. Laender. Joint unsupervised structure discovery and information extraction. In *Proceedings of the 2011 ACM SIGMOD International Conference on Management of data*, pages 541–552, 2011.

[2] E. Garfield. Citation analysis as a tool in journal evaluation. *Science*, 178(60):471–479, November 1972.

[3] C. L. Giles, K. D. Bollacker, and S. Lawrence. Citeseer: an automatic citation indexing system. In *International Conference on Digital Libraries*, pages 89–98. ACM Press, 1998.

[4] J. D. Lafferty, A. McCallum, and F. C. N. Pereira. Conditional random fields: Probabilistic models for segmenting and labeling sequence data. In *Proceedings of the Eighteenth International Conference on Machine Learning*, ICML '01, pages 282–289, San Francisco, CA, USA, 2001. Morgan Kaufmann Publishers Inc.

[5] F. Peng and A. McCallum. Information extraction from research papers using conditional random fields. *Inf. Process. Manage.*, 42:963–979, July 2006.

[6] V. Qazvinian and D. R. Radev. Scientific paper summarization using citation summary networks. In *Proceedings of the 22nd International Conference on Computational Linguistics - Volume 1*, pages 689–696, Stroudsburg, PA, USA, 2008. Association for Computational Linguistics.

[7] A. Ritchie, S. Robertson, and S. Teufel. Comparing citation contexts for information retrieval. In *Proceeding of the 17th ACM conference on Information and knowledge management*, CIKM '08, pages 213–222, New York, NY, USA, 2008. ACM.

[8] K. Seymore, A. Mccallum, and R. Rosenfeld. Learning hidden markov model structure for information extraction. In *In AAAI 99 Workshop on Machine Learning for Information Extraction*, pages 37–42, 1999.

[9] C. Sutton and A. McCallum. An introduction to conditional random fields. *Foundations and Trends in Machine Learning*, 2011. To appear.

Glyph Spotting for Mediaeval Handwritings by Template Matching

Jan-Hendrik Worch
University of Bremen
Am Fallturm 1
D-28359 Bremen
jworch@tzi.de

Mathias Lawo
Berlin-Brandenburgische
Akademie der Wissenschaften
Jägerstrasse 22-23
D-10117 Berlin
lawo@bbaw.de

Björn Gottfried
University of Bremen
Am Fallturm 1
D-28359 Bremen
bg@tzi.de

ABSTRACT

This paper reports on the analysis of different approaches in order to search for glyphs within handwritten mediaeval documents. As layout analysis methods are difficult to apply to the documents at hand, template matching methods are employed. A number of different shape descriptions are used to filter out false positives, since the application of correlation coefficients alone results in too many matches. The overall goal consists in the interactive support of an editor who is transcribing a given handwriting. For this purpose, the automatic spotting of glyphs enables the editor to compare glyphs within different contexts.

Categories and Subject Descriptors

I.4.7 [**Image Processing and Computer Vision**]: [Feature Measurement - Size and shape]

General Terms

Algorithms

Keywords

mediaeval handwriting, transcription assistance, correlation coefficient, glyph spotting, shape descriptions

1. INTRODUCTION

The offline analysis of mediaeval handwritings is a challenging task due to the degradation of old documents which are yellowed, blotted, and distorted, let alone the difficulties arising in offline handwriting analysis, as for instance described in [9]. In this paper, we report on our first results regarding the spotting of single glyphs. The idea is to avoid the application of the standard pipeline in document image processing, since the aforementioned difficulties, in particular regarding the specific character of a single writer, are too

This work has been supported by the Deutsche Forschungsgemeinschaft, **DFG-Gz.: GO 2023/4-1, LA 3007/1-1**

complex for the given documents. Instead, we aim at an assistance function which supports the user who is interested in transcribing a given handwriting.

A glyph spotting function searches for specific glyphs in the text. While single glyphs are often difficult to recognise for the human user, the context within a whole word gives him additional information and supports the recognition process. However, some contexts are more helpful than others. Being uncertain in a particular word, it would be helpful to have a look at the same glyph at other places within the text.

The method we shall present below searches automatically for additional appearances of a selected character within the text and emphasises its occurrences visually by colour. This enables the user to get an idea of that character in different contexts. He can jump directly to those appearances, instead of searching for them by hand which would be a cumbersome task. In this sense, the resulting function is to support the user in the analysis of handwritings.

This paper is structured as follows. The methods which have been employed for glyph spotting are explained in the following section. Their application to two very different documents is shown in section 3. The discussion in section 4 identifies the most promising methods for glyph spotting. A summary closes this paper.

2. METHOD

2.1 Template Matching

The editor, whose first aim is the transcription of a handwritten text, can manually extract glyphs from the text which he intends to find within the document. The extracted glyphs are conceived of as templates for a matching method according to [3], as the underlying methodology for all of the following processing steps.

A template T is matched at position (x, y) of the image I using the correlation coefficient τ:

$$\tau_{x,y} = \frac{\sum\limits_{(i,j) \in T} \left(I(x+i, y+j) \cdot T(i,j) \right) - K\bar{T} \cdot \bar{I}(x,y)}{\sqrt{\sum\limits_{(i,j) \in T} \left(I(x+i, y+j) \right)^2 - K \left(\bar{I}(x,y) \right)^2} \, \sigma_T} \quad (1)$$

where

$$\sigma_T = \sqrt{\sum\limits_{(i,j) \in T} \left(T(i,j) - \bar{T} \right)^2} \quad (2)$$

is the variance of the template, $\bar{T}$ is the mean value of the template, $\bar{I}(x,y)$ is the mean value of the image region which coincides with the current location of the template and K is the number of pixels the template consists of. The range of the correlation coefficient is $[-1..1]$, but for the sake of implementation and visualisation it is normalised to $[0..255]$. A non-maximum suppression strategy takes only the highest value within a neighbourhood.

2.2 Postprocessing

The result of template matching depends on the chosen threshold. The threshold splits the results into possible and denied matches and lies, as the range of the correlation coefficient, between 0 and 255. If the threshold is 0, the number of possible matches m between the template T and the image I corresponds to the maximal possible matches for the given image:

$$m = (I_{Width} - T_{Width}) \cdot (I_{Height} - T_{Height}) \qquad (3)$$

By contrast a threshold of 255 will normally only find the template itself.

In the context of handwritten documents there will hardly be a single threshold that fits for every glyph. Hence, it is the aim to deploy a robust postprocessing method, which allows a low threshold that finds most instances, but avoids the problem of too many false positives. To analyse a wide variety of possibilities we compare three different kinds of postprocessing techniques that are based on the common categories in shape description: region-based, skeleton-based and contour-based.

2.2.1 Size Restriction (λ)

Before the above-mentioned postprocessing techniques are used, many false positives can already be rejected according to their size.

We try to find a glyph at every position in the image where template matching suggests a possible match, that is above a certain threshold. For this purpose, the height of the bounding box of the template is extended, its central point is placed at the point with the highest correlation coefficient within that locality, and the connected components within that region are taken as a probably disconnected glyph. Since the resulting glyph might not completely fill the according rectangular area, the region around the glyph needs to be cropped.

This finally results into a set of possible matches. For each glyph in that set the standard deviation in height is calculated and every glyph which has a size λ that fits the following range will be accepted for further processing:

$$\lambda \in [average_h + stdv_h, \ average_h - stdv_h] \qquad (4)$$

2.2.2 Moments (η)

In order to filter out false positives, we use the central, normalised moments as region-based, statistical features [5]. They are invariant w. r. t. scale and translation. The central, normalised moment η of order (p,q) is defined by

$$\eta_{pq} = \mu_{pq} \left(\frac{1}{\mu_{00}} \right)^{(p+q+2)/2} \qquad (5)$$

where μ_{pq} is the central moment of order (p,q).

The moments are calculated for order $(0,0)$ up to $(3,3)$. For two glyphs, which are to be compared, the sum of the pairwise absolute values of the differences are taken into account. If the resulting distance remains below a certain threshold, the tested glyph is accepted.

2.2.3 Skeleton Comparison (ζ)

Another common approach in the field of shape recognition is to compare skeletons [7]. In our approach the skeletons are extracted using the method of [8].

The resulting skeleton image is divided into four subimages. First the skeleton image is divided at half of the height, which leads to the first two subimages. Secondly, it is divided at half of the width. For all subimages the vertical and horizontal projections are computed along their direction of subdivision. In the projections the number of hills and valleys are counted, i. e. the sequences of rows with and without the occurrence of foreground pixels.

A second feature, which can be derived from the skeleton, counts the number of holes within the structure. Both features are concatenated and used to compare the skeletons.

$$\zeta = (num_{hills}, num_{valleys}, num_{holes}) \qquad (6)$$

If the values of the feature vector of the template and the corresponding values of the glyph at hand are equal, the skeletons are considered to be similar and the glyph is finally accepted.

2.2.4 Polyline Comparison (ρ)

The last approach to compare glyphs with each other is based on polylines [6].

Again, the image is divided into four subimages, the same way as described in section 2.2.3. In a first step, for each of the subimages the upper, the lower, the left, and the right contour profile is calculated. Connecting the single points within one profile leads to a polyline. This is done for every profile so that the result consists of four polylines.

To compare two different glyphs, the distance between corresponding polylines is taken into account. To reduce the effect of noise, the central point of one polyline is used as origin and the points of the other polyline are translated according to the origin of the first polyline. Now, one can calculate the distance between two polylines P_1 and P_2 by using

$$D(P_1, P_2) = \sum_{s_1 \in P_1} \min_{s_2} \{ d(s_1, s_2) | s_2 \in P_2 \} \qquad (7)$$

where $d(s_1, s_2)$ is the Euclidean distance between the middle points of the segments s_1 and s_2. If the distance of two polylines stays below a certain threshold, the glyph at hand is said to be similar to the template glyph.

In addition to this distance measure, a qualitative feature, which uses the positional contrast of each segment of a polyline, is taken into account: the so-called extent [4], which is a measure of complexity for polylines. The extent is calculated for each of the polylines and for two glyphs the corresponding values are compared. The absolute value of their distance must be below a certain threshold in order to accept a glyph.

3. EVALUATION

The first step within the transcription process is to mark manually a glyph to which similar glyphs are to be found. To mark a glyph the editor draws a rectangular area with the mouse around that glyph. In this area connected components are searched. Since there might be several connected components, the editor can choose which of them are part of the glyph, and additionally, he can edit the appearance of that glyph to get a proper template (e. g. removing or adding pixels, which were lost due to imperfections during binarisation).

To evaluate the different approaches, two different documents are compared: A mediaeval handwritten document with 1523 glyphs [1] (top of Fig. 1 shows a sample) and a printed one with 2233 glyphs [2] (bottom of Fig. 1). They have been chosen because of their different characteristics, in particular concerning irregular handwritten text as opposed to more regular printed text. Handwritten documents have a rather high variance within single character classes, whereas printed documents look much more regular.

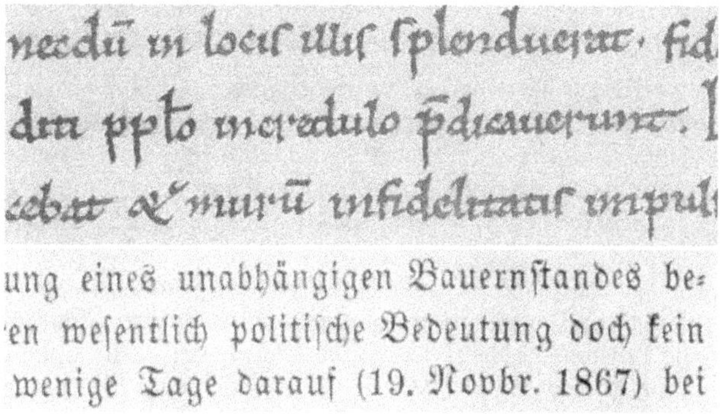

Figure 1: Subimages from [1] (top) and [2] (bottom)

Four experiments have been carried out. First of all, we evaluated template matching alone in order to learn how well the correlation coefficient works for these documents. For the other three experiments we combined template matching and size filtering with each of the three approaches described in sections 2.2.2 to 2.2.4. The glyphs were chosen according to their number of occurences, and additionally, specific glyphs were chosen because of their structure, i. e. some glyphs are substructures of other glyphs (e. g. 'r' is part of 'n' which is part of 'm'). They were taken into account in order to test the associated difficulties. Some examples are shown in Fig. 2.

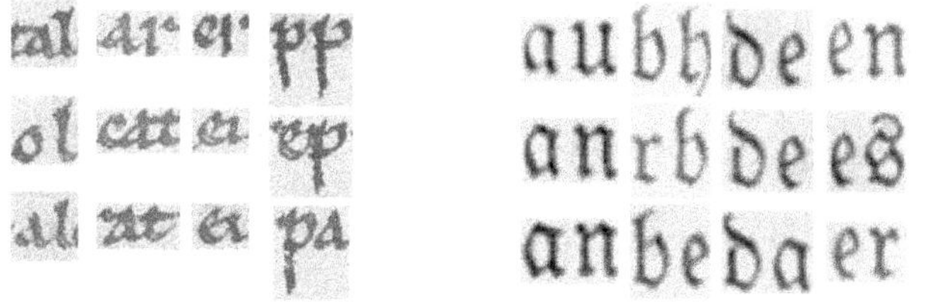

Figure 2: Some glyphs from [1] (left) and [2] (right) showing the intraclass differences.

The evaluation is testing different thresholds for template matching. The other thresholds have been determined experimentally and were not changed during the experiments. In the following sections, the mentioned threshold will always be the chosen one for template matching.

The results of the experiments can be seen in Table 1 and Table 2. The values are rounded average values over all runs of a single experiment. The values state how many matches were accepted at each threshold and how many of them were correct.

As expected, the template matching alone leads to the highest number of possible matches, but at the cost of accuracy. By contrast, the number of possible matches gets lower the higher the threshold of the correlation coefficient. But at the same time, a higher accuracy is achieved. The detailed conclusions from these experiments are drawn in the following discussion.

4. DISCUSSION

We started with the assumption that it would be easier to spot directly for glyphs on the document image than to analyse the layout first. It is in particular difficult to separate characters from each other in a single word, since handwritings do not clearly separate characters. Searching for specific glyphs on a document page calls for template matching methods, as by means of the correlation coefficient. It is our goal to analyse to what extent the correlation coefficient is able to make the physical layout analysis unnecessary, at least in connection with further filter methods.

4.1 The choice of a threshold

Employing the correlation coefficient, a threshold needs to be determined in order to separate accepted and rejected matches. We assume that too many false positives would be accepted with a low threshold. On the other hand, a rather high threshold could result into too many false negatives. However, aiming at the spotting of only a small number of example contexts of a specific glyph, a high threshold should serve for this application purpose: A high threshold might reject a number of true positives, but false positives will be avoided, or at least, small in number. This is what the results show in Table 1.

These results go with the observation that, in the case of a high threshold, there might be still false positives which are quite similar in their appearance. Conversely, true positives could be rejected with a high threshold if the variance of the handwriting is too large. In general, a high variability for the different instances of a class of glyphs results into many false negatives when taking a high threshold and a low threshold becomes necessary.

4.2 Template matching alone

The recall of true positives is quite large, employing the correlation coefficient alone. For instance, in [1] there are 11569 matches when looking for one of the characters as a template and when using a threshold of 25. One might wonder why there are so many matches, inasmuch as there are only 1523 characters on the document page. Omitting the layout analysis including the separation of characters, the correlation coefficient is determined for all conceivable positions on the entire document image, the latter having a resolution of 2469×1988 pixels. There are therefore 4,908,372 potential matches, which will be reduced by taking into account the size of the template, however, in the example this makes approximately 0.24%. Hence, this result is not particularly surprising. It shows the obvious necessity of adding a filter to the template matching method.

Table 1: Results when applying the presented methods to [1]

	possible matches at threshold					true positives at threshold					true positives [%] at threshold				
	25	175	200	225	240	25	175	200	225	240	25	175	200	225	240
τ	11569	351	54	2	1	52	44	30	2	1	0.45	12.47	55.73	100	100
$\tau+\lambda+\eta$	174	46	16	1	1	23	20	13	1	1	13.01	42.50	80.26	100	100
$\tau+\lambda+\zeta$	5	4	2	1	1	4	3	2	1	1	85.71	88.89	90.32	100	100
$\tau+\lambda+\rho$	13	11	8	1	1	9	8	7	1	1	65.43	69.68	87.62	100	100

Table 2: Results when applying the presented methods to [2]

	possible matches at threshold					true positives at threshold					true positives [%] at threshold				
	25	175	200	225	240	25	175	200	225	240	25	175	200	225	240
τ	15018	2103	753	222	86	112	112	112	108	82	0.74	5.31	14.84	48.41	95.55
$\tau+\lambda+\eta$	288	256	179	110	57	72	72	65	65	54	25.12	28.23	36.46	59.04	94.86
$\tau+\lambda+\zeta$	41	39	35	26	18	22	22	22	21	18	52.04	55.48	62.21	81.73	97.96
$\tau+\lambda+\rho$	63	60	52	46	34	39	39	39	39	33	61.71	64.99	74.02	83.72	98.13

4.3 The size constraint

The first filter considers the size of the matches. While the correlation coefficient finds too many matches, at least when taking lower thresholds, there are many false positives which mainly differ in their size. Sorting them out there is in fact a great reduction of the number of possible matches, which speeds up the postprocessing.

4.4 The choice of the threshold revisited

Irrespective of the filter method, a higher threshold means a higher fraction of true positives. For the application scenario, a high threshold seems to be the best choice. In this way, a small number of correct contexts can be found, which can be inspected by the human user who tries to determine the character class for a particular glyph.

4.5 The comparison with printed text

The comparison with a more regular style of glyphs is provided when referring to printed text, instead of finding another more regular handwriting style. As assumed, the recall of true positives is much larger in this case. The results show that this holds even for all methods.

An interesting difference is that, taking a threshold of at least 225, there only remain true positives in the case of the handwriting, while there are still some false positives regarding the printed text, even if for the latter a higher threshold is used. This seems to be related to similar glyphs which are neither sorted out by template matching, nor by the other filters. By contrast, different but similar glyphs are earlier sorted out in the case of the handwritten document.

For both document types, we learn that the filter based on normalised central moments leads to the best results. But moments are not the best filters in any case, if looking at the fraction of the results instead of the absolute values. Some of the other methods, as those based on skeletons, do have a rather small recall when using high thresholds for the correlation coefficient, but a superior fraction.

5. SUMMARY

We have proposed two new approaches to spot similar glyphs based on skeletons and polylines. The experiments point out that those approaches lead to a high accuracy at the cost of a low recall when applying them to mediaeval handwritings. In contrast, template matching alone and in combination with central normalised moments leads to a high recall at the cost of precision. Additionally, we found out that there is a clear impact of the variance in handwriting, which results in a low recall for all approaches, when applying them to [1].

Hence, the usage of one or the other approach depends on the desired application. In our case, the higher accuracy is the optimal choice: The human user can easily spot a few, but correct glyphs, which are considered to be similar. Based on them he can make a decision on the meaning of a glyph with the aid of different contexts, without searching for them by himself or looking at too many false positives.

6. REFERENCES

[1] Philipps 1870, fol. 11v. Staatsbibliothek zu Berlin Preußischer Kulturbesitz.

[2] Die Grenzboten, 28. Jahrgang, 2. Semester 1. Band, Leipzig 1869. Scan 27 von der Staats- und Universitätsbibliothek Bremen.

[3] R. C. Gonzalez and R. E. Woods. *Digital image processing*. Addison-Wesley, Reading, Mass., [3. ed.] reprint. with corr. edition, 1992.

[4] B. Gottfried. Qualitative similarity measures–the case of two-dimensional outlines. *Computer Vision and Image Understanding*, 110(1):117–133, 2008.

[5] M.-K. Hu. Visual pattern recognition by moment invariants. *Information Theory, IRE Transactions on*, 8(2):179 –187, February 1962.

[6] J.-C. Perez and E. Vidal. Optimum polygonal approximation of digital curves. *Pattern Recognition Letters*, 15:743–750, 1994.

[7] J. Stoppe and B. Gottfried. Skeleton comparisons: the junction neighbourhood histogram. In *Proc. of the 11th ACM symposium on Document engineering*, DocEng '11, pages 93–96, New York, NY, USA, 2011. ACM.

[8] T. Y. Zhang and C. Y. Suen. A fast parallel algorithm for thinning digital patterns. *Commun. ACM*, 27:236–239, March 1984.

[9] J. Zhou, Q. Gan, A. Krzyzak, and C. Y. Suen. Recognition of handwritten numerals by quantum neural network with fuzzy features. *Intl. J. on Document Analysis and Recognition*, 2:30–36, 1999.

Architecture for Hypermedia Dynamic Applications with Content and Behavior Constraints

Luiz Fernando G. Soares[1]
lfgs@inf.puc-rio.br

Carlos de Salles Soares Neto[2]
csalles@deinf.ufma.br

José Geraldo de Sousa[1]
jgeraldo@laws.deinf.ufma.br

[1] Depto. de Informática – PUC-Rio
Rua Marquês de São Vicente, 225
Rio de Janeiro– 22453-900 – Brasil
0055-21-3527-1500 Ext:4330

[2] Depto. de Informática – UFMA
Av. dos Portugueses, Bacanga
São Luís/MA – 65080-040 – Brasil
0055-98-3301-8224

ABSTRACT

This paper deals with the generation of dynamic hypermedia applications whose content and behavior their authors may not be able to predict a priori, but which must conform to a strict set of explicitly defined constraints. In the paper, we show that it is possible to establish an architecture configuration to be followed by this special kind of dynamic applications. In the proposed architecture, templates are responsible for specifying the design patterns and the constraints to be followed. Some alternatives for distributing (from the client side to the server side) the components that comprise the architecture are discussed, and one of them is used to exemplify an instantiation of the architecture. In the instantiation, TAL (Template Authoring Language) is used to define templates. In TAL, *templates* are open-compositions, that is, especial set of patterns for compositions, whose content must obey some explicitly defined constraints. The paper also shows how the architecture instantiation could be used to build dynamic digital TV applications.

Categories and Subject Descriptors

D.2.11 [**Software Architectures**]: Domain-specific architectures, languages, patterns.

Keywords

Dynamic DTV applications, Templates, TAL, NCL.

1. INTRODUCTION

Hypermedia applications comprise a set of media data to be presented and a specification document (their source code) relating these data in time and space. Dynamic hypermedia applications are those that can be modified (or created) on-the-fly, that is, while their data content is being presented on the client side, as a consequence of some internal or external event occurrences.

We call "modifier agent" the software module in charge of receiving the aforementioned events and accomplishing the

necessary tasks to make the desired changes (in the document specification or in data content).

The triggering events can be generated by human beings or automatically by the application itself. They can be generated at the client side (for example, a digital TV – DTV – receiver, in the case of DTV applications), or at the server side (the broadcaster, for example, also in the case of DTV applications). Events are sent to modifier agents that can be located in the server side, in the client side or in a proxy environment.

Dynamic applications are very important in digital TV domain. They allow for the personalization of application content, or the way application content is presented, depending on the viewer profile, the receiver profile, or even the viewer localization. Moreover, it is common in DTV applications having some media content that is only known at exhibition time. For example, during a soccer game, statistics about a goal can be shown in the moment the goal occurs (and if it occurs), and it depends on who makes the goal. It is also very common in DTV applications to have spatial and temporal relationships among media content that are not known a priori and that may depend on some live content. For example, in a talk show, depending on the matter under discussion, a link with other related matters can be established commanding their presentation when a viewer interacts. In addition, it is not unusual to have new content to be presented depending on viewers answers.

Modifier agents can be part of the language entities used to specify applications. For example, NCL (Nested Context Language) [1] and SMIL (Synchronized Multimedia Integration Language) [2] languages define the <switch> element to specify set of alternative media objects, and rules for their selection. In this paper we do not focus on this kind of dynamic application however. We are much more interested in dynamic applications whose alternatives cannot be predicted a priori.

Moreover, we are interested in dynamic hypermedia applications whose structure and content must observe some constraints that can be explicitly defined. There are many good reasons for establishing explicit constraints. First, they promote coherent application branding, enabling content producers to define and follow the same design pattern[1]. Second, thanks to a common source pattern, applications can be more usable for those who

---

[1] We are using the term *design pattern* in this paper in its broad sense: a general reusable solution to a commonly occurring problem within a given context in software design. It is a description or template for how to solve a problem that can be used in many different situations.

view and interact with different applications of the same family. Third, constraint-based authoring promotes reuse, allowing authors to concentrate on filling out only the blanks that make a particular application unique within the family of applications to which it belongs.

We must stress that it is not sufficient to define common design patterns (or templates) which dynamic applications must follow. Sometimes we also need to set a series of constraints on the design pattern uses. For example, a particular TV broadcaster can define that every application (dynamic or not) it transmits must have its logo in the right upper corner of the screen. However, in addition, it can require that no other logo may be present in the application. Therefore, the template concept must be extended to define not only common design patterns but also constraints on their uses. New content generated by modifier agents should be checked if it obeys the required template in all its extensions.

Thus, this paper is concerned with the generation of dynamic hypermedia applications whose content and behavior their authors may not be able to predict a priori, and whose content and behavior must be compliant to a set of constraints that can be explicitly defined. In this paper we show that it is possible to establish an architecture configuration to be followed by this special kind of dynamic applications.

The remainder of the paper is structured as follows. Section 2 presents some related work, calling attention for the different kinds of dynamic applications, and positioning this paper contribution. Section 3 details the architecture proposed for dynamic hypermedia application generation. Section 4 gives an example of implementation. Finally, Section 5 brings some conclusions.

2. RELATED WORK

As vaguely raised in Section 1, there are many types of dynamic applications. For the purpose of this paper, we can divide them in two subsets, discussed in Sections 2.1 and 2.2, respectively.

2.1 Applications without Explicit Constraints

The most prominent example of this set of applications comes from the inclusion in HTML-based applications of additional processing beyond pure interpretation of HTML tags; both in the client-side and the server-side.

In client-side Web browsers, plug-ins, scripts (in particular JavaScript/ECMAScript [3]) and applets are the usual technologies applied for modifier agent implementations. In HTML-based DTV middlewares, we usually find the ECMAScript approach [4] [5] [6] [7].

Scripts can have a series of constraints imposed by a system, for example, in DTV systems, for security reasons they do not have right to read or write files in the client receiver. Beyond these implicit system constraints, additional constraints cannot be imposed to application authors, for example, forcing them to follow some design patterns.

ECMAScript can be set to execute when some event happens, like when an object has finished loading or when a user clicks on an HTML element. Some events can also come from the server-side. For example, BML, the declarative language of the Japanese ISDB DTV system, allows for events (bevents [4]) coming from broadcasters to trigger the execution of ECMAScript functions. Live editing of DTV applications are possible by using bevents.

Similar functions are found in DVB-HTML [6] and HbbTV [7] middleware.

The server-side solution for dynamic content generation in the Web is very common and several technologies have been developed with this concern: CGI [8], PHP [9], ASP [10] and JSP [11] are examples. When a server receives requests for HTML pages embedding code in any of the previously mentioned technology, modifier agents are called, generating processed HTML code, with embedded dynamic content, ready to be exhibited in the client-side Web browsers.

Unlike client-side solutions, we can find frameworks for building Web applications in the server side using design patterns, similarly to what we propose in this paper for client-side solutions. ASP.NET MVC [12] is an example. However, our proposal also allows for defining constraints to be followed by family of applications, as is detailed in Section 3. Moreover and more important, content generated by modifier agents is checked if it obeys the constraints defined.

As aforementioned, in SMIL [2] and NCL [1] languages, <switch> element allows for specifying a set of alternative media objects and rules for their selections. SMIL is a W3C recommended XML markup language to describe multimedia presentations. NCL is the declarative language of the Japanese-Brazilian DTV middleware ISDB-T [13] [14], and also ITU-T Recommendation for IPTV services [15] [16]. Besides supporting alternative media objects, NCL allows for specifying presentation alternatives for the same media object. This kind of limited generation of dynamic content is resolved during runtime in the client-side receiver in the case of the Brazilian middleware implementation (Ginga-NCL), but could also be resolved at compile time in the server side.

NCL is a glue language that relates objects in time and space, independently from their types. As a glue language, NCL does not restrict or prescribe any media-object content type. The media objects supported depends on the media players embedded in an NCL engine (the Ginga-NCL). Therefore, Ginga can run any HTML application, depending only on its embedded XHTML player implementation, as for example, a BML application[2], or an HbbTV application. NCL does not substitute but embeds HTML-based objects. As a result, all support for dynamic application generation found in HTML solutions is inherited by NCL.

For particular procedural needs, as for example when more complex dynamic content generation is required, NCL provides the Lua scripting language [17] support. Lua is a powerful, fast, lightweight, embeddable scripting language. Scripts Lua are event oriented. Internal events can come from the NCL application execution, like the end of a clip in a video presentation, or when an object has any of its properties changed. Events can also come from external actions, like viewer interactions, etc. Like in HTML-based solutions, Lua scripts can have a series of implicit constraints imposed by the system.

NCL provides an API that allows for building and modifying applications on-the-fly through live editing commands. NCL editing commands are much more powerful than the events coming from the server-side in HTML-based solutions. NCL

---

[2] The current version of ISDB-T standard implements the XML markups, the stylesheet properties, the ECMAScript engine and the DOM API for the BML for basic services ("fixed terminal profile").

editing commands allow for dynamically changed applications by adding or removing any NCL element or attribute, without needing to trigger imperative scripts. Moreover, NCL editing commands can add and trigger Lua objects on-the-fly. That is, Lua scripts can not only act as static ECMAScripts does in HTML-based solutions, but can also be dynamically loaded. Moreover, NCL editing commands can come from the server side and can also be generated by embedded Lua scripts.

Despite having a richer model to generate dynamic content for hypermedia applications, NCL, by itself, does not allow incomplete application specifications that follow explicitly defined constraints, from which applications can be derived following some implicitly defined design pattern.

2.2 Applications with Explicit Constraints

Several hypermedia applications embed common design patterns. This is very usual in DTV domain. Design patterns have been intensively studied and proposed in the literature [18], including those targeting hypermedia applications [19] [20]. However, to the best of our knowledge, all structure-based hypermedia languages, including those used in DTV domain, fail to let authors create applications in which unspecified internal content or unspecified relationships have to follow some design patterns.

Some authoring environments for hypermedia applications use common patterns to guide and easy application authoring [21] [22]. However, they do not focus on dynamic application generation beyond those already mentioned in this Section 2.

In line with design patterns principles, SMIL Timesheets [23] [24] is an example of technology that allows for adding temporal behavior to hypermedia applications independently of the specification language used.

Dynamic DTV applications can be defined using design patterns, both in client and server sides. However, no DTV middleware offer this kind of support, although they can be roughly implemented using their scripting languages.

Unlike usual design pattern definitions, TAL (Template Authoring Language) [25] allows for defining not only common patterns but also a series of constraints on their uses. TAL can be considered as a specification language to a set of high level hypermedia design patterns expressed as a template. So, one of the main basis of TAL are templates for composition, proposed in previous versions of XTemplate language [26]. A *template* is formally described by means of a vocabulary of allowed child-object types, a set of relations allowed between those types, rules that constraint the instantiation of these child-object types and relations, and a set of fixed components of the composition (media objects, other composite objects and relationships). In this sense, a template is an incomplete hypermedia composition (an open-composition) that has certain blanks that must be filled out in accordance with rules that constrain the content and relationships that authors can insert.

TAL specifications can be used to generate hypermedia applications in declarative languages such as SMIL, HTML/ECMAScript, NCL/Lua, etc. Using TAL, dynamic hypermedia applications can be developed constrained to explicitly specified semantics.

Although any other language for designing pattern specifications could have been used in the architecture we propose in Section 3, TAL has been our starting point, as presented in Section 4.

3. TEMPLATE-BASED ARCHITECTURE

In order to have dynamic hypermedia applications following explicitly defined design patterns and whose modifier agents must follow explicitly defined constraints, the architecture depicted in Figure 1 is proposed. In the architecture, a template is responsible for specifying the design patterns and the constraints to be followed, as defined in the previous section.

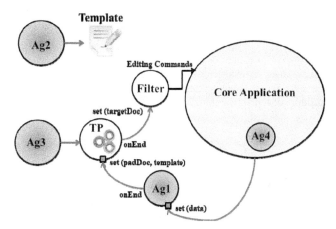

Figure 1. Template-based generation of dynamic applications.

It should be noted first that the template itself can be changed by a modifier agent (Ag2 in Figure 1). Therefore, even the design patterns that an application must follow and the explicitly defined constraints that other modifier agents must obey can be dynamically changed by the Ag2 component.

Second, the architecture also defines a processing flow, but it is agnostic to where (client side, server side, or both) any modifier agent runs, as discussed further on.

Third, as previously mentioned in Section 1, modifier agents are requested for changes by events that can be produced by human beings, that can be automatically generated by the applications themselves, or that can be caused by the modifiers agents themselves.

The Ag4 component is the usual modifier agent embedded in existing applications, which is responsible for creating dynamic content that has no explicitly defined constraint. They are the modifier agents discussed and exemplified in related work presented in Section 2.1: scripting objects, switch elements, etc.

The other components compound the core of our architecture. Some event coming from the hypermedia application starts the Ag1 processing. This event can be the result of user interactions; can come from the presentation of some application content (like its start, end, pause, etc.); can result from setting values to properties of some content (for example, establishing a new position for its presentation); can come from the processing of some object that contains imperative (probably scripting) code; etc.

The event triggering Ag1 can come with some input parameter. For example, the event can report a viewer interaction and which object was selected by the interaction. Based on the parameter received, Ag1 can start to reconstruct the application, which must follow a given Template, also present in Figure 1. The result of the Ag1 processing is a *padding document* (*padDock* in Figure 1).

The padding document is written in any language understood by the template processor (TP in Figure 1). This document must fill the blanks of the open-composition template (Template in the figure) with dynamic content that Ag1 generates based on the input parameter it has received.

After finishing its task, Ag1 calls the service of the template processor, passing the template to be used and the padding document as parameters. TP can then generate the completely new application.

A template must be processed together with a padding document giving rise to a new document in some specification language, called target language. Usually, specific processors are required for each target language and for each language used to specify padding documents. Figure 2 illustrates the process.

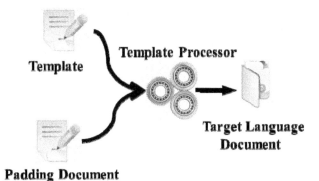

Figure 2. Target document generation.

On ending its processing, TP calls the service of the Filter component. The Filter can then compare the new generated Core Application with the old one, creating the necessary editing commands to change the old Core Application to the new one. Note that the Filter can be simple enough to only replace the old application with the new one. Our experience shows that this is not usually an efficient procedure and sometimes can led to undesired quality of experience (QoE) problems, like flicks, since the application does not change smoothly. However, the Filter can also change the application seamlessly, avoiding QoE problems.

Note that it is TP that generates the new application, and not the modifier agents Ag1 and Ag4, warranting that the new Core Application follows the template. It should also be noted that, although uncommon, TP can also be modified on-the-fly by an Ag3 modifier agent.

Authors of dynamic applications are usually only concerned with authoring applications with their Ag4 modifier agents, and authoring the Ag1 modifier agents. Ag2, Ag3, TP, and Filter components, besides the template document, are usually under the responsibility of another player: the one that requires

that applications follow the template. For example, in DTV domain, broadcasters can require that applications follow a given template. Therefore, they are responsible to implement the TP and Filter components to check if after each application change the Core Application remains in agreement with the template.

We must emphasize that the granularity of the components of the architecture were defined only to make clear the processing flow of the Core Application generation. An implementation of the architecture does not need to follow strictly the components defined, but only their functionalities. For example, it can be more efficient to have the TP template processor incorporating the functions of the Filter, creating editing commands directly.

Focusing on Figure 1, we can devise some alternative distributions for their components. Figure 3 shows some possibilities, no matter where the template document is stored.

The first alternative (Figure 3.a) builds all dynamic content at the client side. Indeed, in this alternative, the client-side can consider the Filter, TP, Ag1 and Ag4 as components (usually scripting objects) of the whole application. The dynamic content to be presented is the *Core Application*, also part of the whole application. The example given in Section 3.1 follows this alternative of distribution.

The second alternative (Figure 3.b) builds the dynamic content ruled by the template at the server side (usually a broadcaster station in DTV systems). In this case the event to trigger the Ag1 modifier agent must be sent from the client side to the server side. In terrestrial DTV systems, for example, this can be usually done using the return channel. In this case, the necessary editing commands to change the old application to the new one are usually sent in data carousels [27].

In the third alternative (Figure 3.c) the template processor and the Filter run at the server side. Ag1 and Ag4 run at the client side, which has to communicate with the template processor. Again, in terrestrial DTV systems the return channel can be used with this purpose. Note that in this alternative, as well as in the previous one, if the editing commands are sent by broadcasting, a client user can command an application change that will affect all other client users.

Of course other alternatives are possible including ones using a proxy provider to perform the dynamic content generation. This can be very interesting in social TV applications. For example, assume that in Figure 3.c, the server processing is now performed by a proxy server of some social network. Changes made by a member of this network, for example, the addition of a comment to a movie, will also reflect on the movie presentation in all other members of the same network. Note that all changes would still be controlled by who have implemented the template, the template processor, and the Filter.

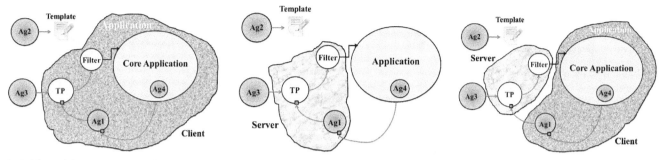

3.a) Client-side content generation   3.b) Server-side content generation   3.c) Client and Server side content generation

Figure 3. Alternative component distribution.

3.1 Architecture Instantiation Example

This section presents an implementation example of the proposed architecture. The architecture presented in Figure 1, with the component distribution presented in Figure 3.a, has been implemented targeting dynamic NCL applications running on Ginga middleware [14] [15] [16].

In the implementation, TAL [24] is used to define templates. TAL templates are generated and stored in some place accessible from client-side receivers. External modifier agents (Ag2) can change these templates, but are completely independent from the client-side implementation, as shown in Figure 3.a.

As aforementioned and illustrated in Figure 2, TAL templates are processed together with padding documents to generate applications in different target languages, depending only on the specific processor used. In this example case, the padding document is an NCL document and the target document is also an NCL application, named "CoreApplication" in Figure 3.a.

Any other pattern language and any other language used to define constraints could be used to define templates. We have chosen TAL because it has a template processor targeting NCL applications. In addition, this processor is implemented in Lua language. As presented in Section 2, Lua is the scripting language of NCL. This fact has an impact on the implementation, as discussed in what follows.

TAL Processor [28] for generic NCL applications is used in the implementation. The Ag1 modifier agent is also an NCL media object with Lua code, as well as the Filter component. Note thus that the Ag1 ,Filter, TP, and the "CoreApplication" are objects of an NCL encompassing application (as a glue language, NCL applications can embed objects with Lua code, and other NCL applications). Thus we have here a case of reflexive application: an application that adapts part of itself (the embedded "CoreApplication" NCL application), as presented in Listing 1.

As usual in declarative specification, we can understand how the encompassing NCL application works in performing its tasks, even without knowing the language syntax. So, let us browse the Listing 1 document, without worrying about the language details.

Lines 11 to 14 defines the Ag1 modifier agent (<media id="Ag1" src="../ag1.lua" type="application/x-ncl-NCLua" ...>), a media object whose content is a Lua code referred by the *src* attribute.

This media object contains two interfaces: an entry property ("Agentry") and an output property ("output").

Similarly, lines 15 to 18 define the TP (template processor) media object (<media id="TP" src="../tp.lua" type="application/x-ncl-NCLua" ...>), and lines 19 to 21 define the Filter media object (<media id="Filter" src="../filter.lua" type="application/x-ncl-NCLua" .../>). Note that the "Filter" does not have the "output" property since its output are NCL editing commands [16].

Lines 22 to 35 define the "CoreApplication". The initial "CoreApplication" is generic and has no content to be exhibited. It just starts the application building. The "CoreApplication" starts through its entry port ("appEntry") defined in line 23. The application has an output port, defined in line 24, externalizing the "shared.startChanging" property of its "globalVariables" object (defined in lines 25 to 27) to be used in the relationship with the "Ag1" media object.

Lines 7 to 9 define that "Ag1", "TP", and "Filter" must be started when the application begins. The starting of these event-oriented Lua objects call their initializer procedures that creates all code spans and data that may be used during the Lua-object execution and, in particular, registers one (or more) event handler.

Line 10 defines the "CoreApplication" as another opening component: the one that starts the whole dynamic process. The "CoreApplication" begins (line 23) with the exhibition of a fake component (represented by the "initializer" <media> element in line 28 without source content specified). The beginning of this fake content produces an event triggering the relationship specified in the NCL <link> element (lines 29 to 34), which sets the "initData" value to the "shared.startChanging" property (defined in line 26), starting the dynamic-changing process.

The end of the "initData" value attribution to the "shared.startChanging" property produces an event triggering the relationship specified in the NCL <link> element (lines 36 to 42), which sets the "Ag1entry" variable of Lua and calls the corresponding event handler.

Upon receiving the setting event, the "Ag1" lua object generates the NCL padding document, based on the "initData" information received. This padding document in then set by the Lua code to the "output" property (line 13) of "Ag1" together with the template location to be used: the "(padDoc, template)" pair value. The end of this attribution produces an event triggering the relationship specified in the NCL <link> element defined in lines 43 to 49, which sets the "TPentry" property (line 13) of the Lua template processor (`TP`) component, calling its corresponding event handler.

Using NCL editing commands [16] an external `Ag2` modifier agent can change (remove and add) "TP", as is usual with any other NCL application entity [1].

After creating the target document, the "TP" Lua code sets this document to its "output" property (line 17). The end of this attribution produces an event triggering the relationship specified in the NCL <link> element defined in lines 50 to 56, which sets the "Filterentry" property of the "Filter" element to "targetDoc", calling its corresponding event handler. The Lua code of "Filter" compares the new NCL Core Application ("targetDoc") with the old one. Based on this comparison, NCL editing commands are issued changing the previous "CoreApplication" to the new one.

The whole process restarts when a new Core Application calls `Ag1` to create a new dynamic application, by setting a "data" value to its "shared.startChanging" property. If the setting value is equal to "end", the Lua code of "Ag1" must generate the NCL editing command that finishes the whole reflexive application.

```
1.  <?xml version="1.0" encoding="ISO-8859-1"?>
2.  <ncl id="nclReflexiveApplication" xmlns=
       "http://www.ncl.org.br/NCL3.0/EDTVProfile">
3.  <head>
4.    ...
5.  </head>

6.  <body>
7.  <port id="startAg1" component="AG1"/>
8.  <port id="startTP" component="TP"/>
9.  <port id="startFilter" component="Filter"/>
10. <port id="startAppl"
                  component="CoreApplication"
                  interface="appEntry"/>
11. <media id="Ag1" src="../ag1.lua"
                  type="application/x-ncl-NCLua">
12.    <property name="Ag1entry"/>
13.    <property name="output"/>
14. </media>
15. <media id="TP" src="../tp.lua"
                  type="application/x-ncl-NCLua">
16.    <property name="TPentry"/>
17.    <property name="output"/>
18. </media>
19. <media id="Filter" src="../filter.lua"
                  type="application/x-ncl-NCLua">
20.    <property name="FilterEntry"/>
21. </media>
22. <context id="CoreApplication">
23.    <port id="appEntry"
                  component="initializer"/>
24.    <port id="startChanging"
                  component="globalVariables"
              interface="shared.startChanging"/>
25.    <media id="globalVariables"
                  type="application/x-ncl-settings">
26.      <property name="shared.startChanging"/>
27.    </media>
28.    <media id="initializer" type="video"/>
29.    <link xconnector="onBeginSet">
30.      <bind role="onBegin"
                  component="initializer"/>
31.      <bind role="set"
                  component="globalVariables"
              interface="shared.startChanging">
32.        <bindParam name="var" value="initData"/>
33.      </bind>
```

```
34.      </link>
35.    </context>
36.    <link xconnector="onEndAttSet">
37.      <bind role="onEndAttribution"
                  component="CoreApplication"
                  interface="startChanging"/>
38.      <bind role="getValue"
                  component="CoreApplication"
                  interface="startChanging"/>
39.      <bind role="set" component="Ag1"
                  interface="Ag1entry">
40.        <bindParam name="var" value="$getValue"/>
41.      </bind>
42.    </link>
43.    <link xconnector="onEndAttSet">
44.      <bind role="onEndAttribution"
              component="Ag1" interface="output"/>
45.      <bind role="getValue" component="Ag1"
                  interface="output"/>
46.      <bind role="set" component="TP"
                  interface="TPentry">
47.        <bindParam name="var" value="$getValue"/>
48.      </bind>
49.    </link>
50.    <link xconnector="onEndAttSet">
51.      <bind role="onEndAttribution"
                  component="TP" interface="output"/>
52.      <bind role="getValue" component="TP"
                  interface="output"/>
53.      <bind role="set" component="Filter"
                  interface="Filterentry">
54.        <bindParam name="var" value="$getValue"/>
55.      </bind>
56.    </link>
57.  </body>
58. </ncl>
```

Listing 1. Reflexive NCL application.

4. EXAMPLE OF DYNAMIC APPLICATION

Let us now use the architecture instantiation of Section 3.1, to create a dynamic application example.

The application is deliberately very simple, just to illustrate the concepts. Assume that an IPTV channel requires that every third-party movie it transmits must have its logo (TeleMídia) and also an image button (Zappiens) representing the channel's video repository, as shown in Figure 4.

Figure 4. Screenshot of the dynamic application example before selecting the repository.

222

Of course the IPTV channel, when tuned, also requires that only its logo can be exhibited and only its video repository is available to download movies.

The application also has a set (composition) of image buttons, each one associated with a video of the channel's repository that has some semantic relationship (same genre, same actors, etc.) with the movie being presented. This set of buttons is presented when the "Zappiens" button is selected, as shown in Figure 5.

Figure 5. Screenshot of the dynamic application example after selecting the repository.

If one of the semantically related video is chosen, the process of dynamic changes is started. The movie is substituted by the chosen one, and a new list of correlated videos is created. The new CoreApplication is then restarted: causing the presentation the new chosen movie, the "TeleMídia" logo, and the Zappiens" button, similar to Figure 4. The application must finish if the IPTV channel logo is selected.

Going on this section, we discuss in Section 4.1 the template used to create the application. Section 4.2 gives the padding document created by the modifier agent Ag1. Finally, Section 4.3 presents the application reconstruction.

4.1 The Template Example

Let us now move our attention to the TAL template, in which all the application complexity is defined.

In TAL, *template* is an open-composition (an incomplete composition). More precisely, in TAL template is an especial pattern for composition, whose content is given by:
• Vocabulary: defining the allowed *types of child-objects* (the components) of the template, the allowed *types of interfaces* for these child-objects and for the template itself, and the allowed *relations* to be used in relationships among child-objects;
• Constraints: defining *rules* on the types defined in the vocabulary;
• Resources: defining common instantiated child object types that shall be inherited by all compositions that use (follow) the template;
• Relationships: defining common instantiated relation types, relating child-object types and resources that shall also be inherited by all compositions that follow the template.

Our open-composition is the "CoreApplication", and its template is defined in lines 2 to 59 of Listing 2. As usual in declarative specifications, we can understand how TAL templates work, even without knowing the language syntax. So, let us superficially browse the Listing 2 document, without worrying about the language details. The structural view of the template, shown in Figure 6, also helps in its understanding.

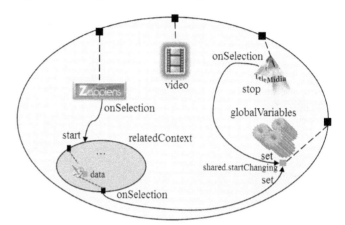

Figure 6. Structural view of the template.

The template has four <port> elements (lines 3 to 6), mapped to the video type component, to the two button resources ("Zappiens" and "TeleMidia"), and to the "shared.startChanging" interface of the "globalVariables" resource.

The video type component is defined in line 7. Its *selects* attribute establishes to which target padding language element the <component> type must be applied.

The two button resources ("Zappiens" and "TeleMidia") are specified in lines 9 and 10, respectively. They must follow the button type specified in line 8, as defined by their *class* attribute.

Another resource ("globalVariables") is specified in lines 11 to 13; its interface <property name="shared.startChanging"> is the one mapped to the "startChanging" port, defined in line 6.

Two other component types are defined. The first one is the composition ("relatedContext") defined in lines 14 to 28, which contains the button images representing the several videos semantically related with the video being presented. These button images follow the other component type ("relatedContent"), specified in lines to 25 to 27. The "relatedContext" component type has interfaces ("contentInterface") to each instantiated "relatedContent" type element, as defined in lines 15 to 19. The "relatedContext" component type has also interfaces ("dataInterface") to each "data" interface of instantiated "relatedContent" type elements, as defined in lines 20 to 24.

The CoreApplication behavior defined by the template is dictated by its links. The first one (lines 29 to 32) establishes that if the button corresponding to the Zappiens repository is selected, all buttons corresponding to the videos of the Zappiens site that are semantically related with the video in current exhibition have their exhibition started.

The second relationship ("videoSelection" in lines 33 to 37) is a TAL link relating child component types of the template. It will result in as many links as "relatedContent" type instances (children of the "relatedContext" instance) exists in the target document. For each one of these instances, it establishes that when the instance is selected, the "shared.startChanging" property of the "globalVariables" component is set to the corresponding "video-locator" value of the "data" property of the selected instance.

Finally, the third relationship (lines 38 to 43) determines that when the "TeleMidia" button is selected, the "shared.startChanging" property of the "globalVariables" component is set to the "end" value. As we have discussed in Section 3.1, this will end the application.

Constraints are defined on the components and relationships of the template by using TAL <assert> elements. The <assert> element requires that the test evaluation returns "true", otherwise an error message should be presented. All the constraints in Listing 3 can be understood by reading their corresponding error messages.

```
1.  <tal:tal id="template_repository">
2.  <tal:template id="coreApplication">
3.  <port id="pVideo" component="video[1]"/>
4.  <port id="pZappiens" component="Zappiens"/>
5.  <port id="pTeleMidia" component="TeleMidia"/>
6.  <port id="startChanging"
            component="globalVariables"
            interface="shared.startChanging"/>
7.  <tal:component id="video"
            selects="media[class=video]"/>
8.  <tal:component id="button"
            selects="media[class=botton]"/>
9.  <media id="Zappiens" src="ZappiensButton.png"
            class="button"/>
10. <media id="TeleMidia"
            src="TeleMidiaButton.png"
            class="button"/>
11. <media id="globalVariables"
            type="application/x-ncl-settings">
12.   <property name="shared.startChanging"/>
13. </media>
14. <tal:component id="relatedContext"
        selects="context[class=relatedContext]">
15.   <tal:interface id="contentInterface"
            selects="port[class=pContent]"/>
16.     <tal:forEach instanceOf="contentInterface"
                iterator="it">
17.         component=relatedContent[it]
18.     </tal:forEach>
19.   </tal:interface>
20.   <tal:interface id="dataInterface"
            selects="port[class=pContentData]"/>
21.     <tal:forEach instanceOf="dataInterface"
                iterator="it">
22.         component=relatedContent[it],
                interface=data[1]
23.     </tal:forEach>
24.   </tal:interface>
25.   <tal:component id="relatedContent"
            selects="media[class=relatedContent]">
26.     <tal:interface id="data"
                selects="property[name=data]"/>
27.   </tal:component>
28. </tal:component>
29. <link xconnector="onSelectionStart">
30.   <bind role="onSelection"
                component="Zappiens"/>
```

```
31.     <bind role="start"
                component="relatedContext"/>
32. </link>
33. <tal:link id="videoSelection">
34.   <tal:forEach instance="relatedContent"
                iterator="it">
35.     onSelection
          relatedContext.contentInterface[it]
        then
          set globalVariables.shared.startChanging
                = dataInterface[it]
        end
36.   </tal:forEach>
37. </tal:link>
38. <link xconnector="onSelectionSet">
39.   <bind role="onSelection"
                component="TeleMidia"/>
40.   <bind role="set"
                component="globalVariables"
            interface="shared.startChanging">
41.     <bindParam name="var" value="end"/>
42.   </bind>
43. </link>
44. <tal:assert test="#video==1">
45.   CoreApplication must have just one video.
46. </tal:assert>
47. <tal:assert test="#button==2">
48.   It must have only two button images.
49. </tal:assert>
50. <tal:assert test="#relatedContext==1">
51.   Coreapplication must have just one
                repository context.
52. </tal:assert>
53. <tal:assert test="#relatedContent > 0">
54.   It must have at least one related content
                in each related context.
55. </tal:assert>
56. <tal:assert test="#relatedContent == #data ">
57.   Each related content must have an
                associated data.
58. </tal:assert>
59. </tal:template>
60.</tal:tal>
```

Listing 2. TAL template example.

4.2 Padding Document Example

For generating new "CoreApplications", Ag1 is a Lua component that searches in the repositories the correlated videos (based on their metadata), creating the NCL padding document of Listing 3.

In Listing 3, the *template* attribute of the "padding_generatedByAg1" composition indicates to the TP template processor the template to be followed. Note in the listing how the media and composition objects are related with corresponding template types through their *class* attributes.

```
1.  <?xml version="1.0" encoding="ISO-8859-1"?>
2.  <!-- Generated by NCL Eclipse -->
3.  <ncl id="nclReflexiveApplication"
    xmlns="http://www.ncl.org.br/NCL3.0/EDTVProfi
    le">
4.  <head>
5.  ...
6.  </head>
7.
8.  <body>
9.  <context id="padding_generatedByAg1"
                  template="coreApplication">
10.   <media id="video" src="video.mpg"
                              class=video"/>
11.   <context id="relatedZappiens"
                  class="relatedContext">
12.     <media id="relatedZappiens1"
                  src="videoZappiens1.png"
                  class="relatedContent">
13.       <property name="data"/>
14.     </media>
15.     <media id="relatedZappiens2"
                  src="videoZappiens2.png"
                  class="relatedContent">
16.       <property name="data"/>
17.     </media>
18. <!-- Here all related videos are included -->
19. ...
20.   </context>
21. </context>
```

Listing 3. Padding Document Example.

4.3 Application Reconstruction

As aforementioned, TP is a template processor targeting NCL documents. Its open-source Lua code can be downloaded from [28].

Based on the new application generated by TP, the Filter Lua component just send several NCL editing commands [16] stopping the "CoreApplication" presentation, removing all child elements of <context id= "CoreApplication" .../> element, except the two image buttons and the context collecting the correlated videos (but without child elements). Then several NCL editing commands add new child elements to <context id= "CoreApplication" .../> element. Finally, this context is restarted using another NCL editing command.

5. CONCLUSIONS

The architecture instantiation presented in Section 3 has been intensively and successfully used for developing dynamic DTV application in the Brazilian SAGGA (Support to Automatic Generation of Ginga Applications) project [29]. Indeed, the application presented in Section 4 is the first application developed in SAGGA, with minor simplifications. In this application, the design of the Ag1 modifier agent encompassed the developing of a search machine which was not trivial, since there were very few metadata to be consulted in files of the Zappiens mentioned site.

All SAGGA dynamic applications have structure and content that must be in line with some explicitly defined constraints, usually established by TV broadcasters, to promote coherent application branding. The proposed architecture has supported quite well the design of these applications, enabling content producers to define and follow the same design pattern that, in addition, are more usable for those who view and interact with different applications using the same TAL template. Moreover, constraint-based

authoring reinforced by the architecture promotes reuse, making the modifier agents design much easier and structured then when they are built without any structured design, since the converter complexity is in the TAL processor, which is the same for all kind of target language application.

It should also be stressed that the architecture allows for event-based behavior change in applications, which has been very suited to live events and live content generation.

In SAGGA, the opening CoreApplication is the one that AG1 modifier agent must build when it receives the first "initData" value in its "Ag1entry" property, as discussed in Section 3.1. The "Ag1" Lua element of the reflexive NCL application of Listing1 is generic and specific wizards have been designed to help authors in defining the opening parameters, and to choose the template to be used by the TAL processor. For example, in the application of Section 4, the wizard only asks authors to enter the first video URI and the template URI to be used.

Given the similarities of these specific wizards, we have just started a work of developing a graphical authoring view (a plug-in) for Composer (an extendable NCL authoring environment) [30] to easy the design of general dynamic DTV applications that follows the architecture and distribution of Figure 3.a.

The next step in SAGGA is to use the architecture for creating health, educational and government applications. Templates will play a very important role in these application domains. The Brazilian public TV broadcaster has started its first steps in this direction.

Finally, until now we have concentrated our efforts in client-side dynamic content generation, following the distribution of modifier agents depicted in Figure 3.a. In a near future work we are planning to explore the server-side solution presented in Figure 3.b in developing social inclusive applications in cooperation with Brazilian public TV broadcasters. Of course the architecture presented in Figure 3.c. is the one that motivate us most, especially when the server processing is performed by a proxy server of some social network. We have already started a work in this direction using Ginga multiple device support [16].

6. ACKNOWLEDGMENTS

Our thanks to CNPq and MCT, Brazilian research grant organizations, for the financial support to this work. We would like also to thank the TeleMídia Lab team who provided a thoughtful discussion of this work. We would like also to thank the reviewers that help to clarify several issues.

7. REFERENCES

[1] Soares L.F.G., Rodrigues R.F. *Nested Context Language 3.0 Part 8 – NCL Digital TV Profiles*. MCC 35/06 Technical Report. Informatics Department of PUC-Rio. Rio de Janeiro. October, 2006. ISSN 0103-974. Available at: http://www.ncl.org.br/documentos/NCL3.0-DTV.pdf.

[2] Bulterman, Dick C.A., Rutledge, L. W. *SMIL 3.0 - Flexible Multimedia for Web, Mobile Devices and Daisy*. Talking Books. 2nd ed. Springer, 2009. ISBN: 978-3-540-78546-0.

[3] Flanagan, D. *JavaScript: The definitive guide*. O' Reilly Media Inc., 1056 p., 2011.

[4] ARIB STD-B24, Version 3.2, Volume 3: *Data Coding and Transmission Specification for Digital Broadcasting*, ARIB Standard, 2002.

[5] ITU-T Recommendation H.762. *Lightweight interactive multimedia environment*. Geneva, December, 2009.

[6] Digital Video Broadcasting (DVB*), Multimedia Home Platform (MHP) Specification 1.1.1*, ETSI TS 102 812, ETSI Standard, 2003.

[7] Merkel, K. *HbbTV— a hybrid broadcast-broadband system for the living room*. Published by the European Broadcasting Union, Geneva, Switzerland, Q1 2010. ISSN: 1609-1469.

[8] W3C. *CGI- Common Gateway Interface*. Available at: http://www.w3.org/CGI/ Accessed in 11/10/2012.

[9] Olson P. *PHP Manual*. Available at: http://php.net/manual/en/index.php. Accessed in 11/01/2012.

[10] Microsoft. *Official ASP site*: http://www.asp.net/ Accessed in 11/01/2012.

[11] Oracle – *JSP*. Available at: http://www.oracle.com/ technetwork/java/javaee/jsp/index.html Accessed in 11/01/2012.

[12] Microsoft *ASP-MVC*. Available at: http://www.asp.net/mvc Accessed in 11/01/2012.

[13] Soares, L.F.G.; Rodrigues, R.F.; Moreno, M.F. Ginga-NCL: the Declarative Environment of the Brazilian Digital TV System. *Journal of the Brazilian Computer Society*, vol. 12; No. 4, Março de 2007; pp. 37-46. ISSN: 0104-6500.

[14] Associação Brasileira de Normas Técnicas. NBR 15606-2. *Digital terrestrial television – Data coding and transmission specification for digital broadcasting – Part 2: Ginga-NCL for fixed and mobile receivers – XML application language for application coding*. 2nd Edition. May, 2011. Available at: http://www.dtv.org.br/download/en-en/ ABNTNBR15606_2D2_2007Ing_2008Vc2_2009.pdf

[15] Soares, L.F.G.; Moreno, M.F.; Soares Neto, C.S.; Moreno, M.F. Ginga-NCL: Declarative Middleware for Multimedia IPTV Services. *IEEE Communications Magazine*. Vol. 48, No. 6, pp. 74-81. Junho de 2010. ISSN: 0163-6804.

[16] ITU-T Recommendation H.761, 2009. *Nested Context Language (NCL) and Ginga-NCL for IPTV Services*. Geneva, April, 2009.

[17] Ierusalimschy, R. *Programming in Lua*, Second Edition, Copyrighted Material, 2006.

[18] Gamma, E. et al. *Design Patterns: Elements of Reusable Object-Oriented Software*. ISBN 978-0201633610. Addison Wesley Professional, November, 1994.

[19] Germán, D. M., Cowan, D. D. Towards a unified catalog of hypermedia design patterns. In: *33rd Hawaii International Conference on System Sciences*, 2000.

[20] Rossi, G.; Schwabe, D.; Garrido A. Design Reuse in Hypermedia Applications Development. In*: Proceedings of the Eighth ACM Conference on Hypertext, Hypertext Design*, pages 57–66, 1997.

[21] Cardinal Systems. *Cardinal Studio 4.0 User's Guide*, 2004.

[22] Chiao, H.; Hsu, K.; Chen, Y.; Yuan, S. A Template-Based MHP Authoring Tool. *In Proceedings of CIT. 2006.*

[23] Vuorimaa, P.; Bulterman, D.; and Cesar, P. W3C. *SMIL Timesheets 1.0*. W3C Working Draft. Available in: http://www.w3.org/TR/timesheets/.

[24] Cazenave, F.; Quint, V.; Roisin, C. Timesheets.js: When SMIL Meets HTML5 and CSS3. In Proceedings of the 11th ACM Symposium on Document Engineering. Mountain View, California, USA. September 19-22, 2011.

[25] Soares Neto, C.S.; Soares, L.F.G.; de Souza, C.S. TAL – Template Authoring Language. *Journal of the Brazilian Computer Society*. May, 2012. DOI: 10.1007/s13173-012-0073-7

[26] Muchaluat-Saade, D. C; Rodrigues, R. F.; Soares, L. F. G. XConnector: Extending XLink to Provide Multimedia Synchronization. In*: II ACM Symposium on Document Engineering 2002.*

[27] ISO/IEC 13818-6. Information technology - Generic coding of moving pictures and associated audio information - Part 6: Extensions for DSM-CC. ISO Standard, 1998.

[28] Available at: http://www.telemidia.puc-rio.br/TAL

[29] Available at: http://www.telemidia.puc-rio.br/?q=en/projetoSAGGA)

[30] Lima, B.S.; Soares, L.F.G.; Moreno, M.F. Considering Non-functional Aspects in the Design of Hypermedia Authoring Tools. In: Proceedings of the *2011 ACM Symposium on Applied Computing (SAC'11)*, pp. 1259-1266. TaiChung, Taiwan, 2011. ISBN: 978-1-4503-0113-8.

Full-Text Search on Multi-Byte Encoded Documents

Raymond K. Wong[*,†]   Fengming Shi[*]   Nicole Lam[*]
[*]School of Computer Science & Engineering
University of New South Wales
and
[†]National ICT Australia
Sydney, Australia
wong@cse.unsw.edu.au

ABSTRACT

The Burrows Wheeler transform (BWT) has become popular in text compression, full-text search, XML representation, and DNA sequence matching. It is very efficient to perform a full-text search on BWT encoded text using backward search. This paper aims to study different approaches for applying BWT on multi-byte encoded (e.g. UTF-16) text documents. While previous work has studied BWT on word-based models, and BWT can be applied directly on multi-byte encodings (by treating the document as single-byte coded), there has been no extensive study on how to utilize BWT on multi-byte encoded documents for efficient full-text search. Therefore, in this paper, we propose several ways to efficiently backward search multi-byte text documents. We demonstrate our findings using Chinese text documents. Our experiment results show that our extensions to the standard BWT method offer faster search performance and use less runtime memory.

Categories and Subject Descriptors

I.7 [**Document and Text Processing**]: Miscellaneous; H.3.3 [**Information Storage and Retrieval**]: Information Search and Retrieval—*search process*

General Terms

Performance

Keywords

Burrows Wheeler transform, multi-byte encodings, full-text search

1. INTRODUCTION

Large character sets (for example, Chinese, Vietnamese, Japanese and Korean) have several thousands of characters. Since an 8 bit byte can only represent 256 code points, we need more space to represent these large character sets.

Wide character encodings, which are fixed width, use correspondingly more bytes to hold the code points of the encoding being used. For example, 4 bytes can represent 4,294,967,296 unique code points. In fact, most Microsoft Windows application programming interfaces, as well as the Java and .Net Framework platforms, require that wide character variables be defined as 16-bit values, and that characters be encoded using UTF-16. Modern Unix-like systems generally require that 32 bit values are encoded using UTF-32. [1]

On the other hand, multi-byte encodings (usually variable length) use a sequence of bytes to represent a code point that cannot be represented in 8 bits. The first use of multi-byte encodings was in fact for the encoding of Chinese, Japanese and Korean, which have large character sets that are well in excess of 256 characters. Multi-byte encodings can be made more space efficient, but at the cost of increased complexity of processing. Furthermore, existing software that can handle 8 bit wide chunks can generally be ported to handle multi-byte encodings with relative ease, since each "chunk" in a multi-byte encoding is typically 8 bits in width.

As more and more information is encoded in these wider encodings, being able to search keywords from texts encoded in these encodings is vital. Recently, the Burrows Wheeler transform (BWT) [2] has become popular in text compression, full-text search [5], indexing and compressing XML documents [3], and DNA sequence matching [10]. In particular, full-text search on BWT encoded documents can be performed very efficiently using backward search [4].

However, to the best of our knowledge, the most recent study on BWT backward search was on ASCII encodings, with some proposals mentioning how they may be extended to multi-byte encoded texts.

In this paper we compare four methods of BWT and backward search for multi-byte encoded texts:

Approach A: This is a straightforward approach that most programmers would take, if space and runtime efficiency were not of concern. In this approach, characters in fixed width, m-byte encodings are treated as m-byte symbols during symbol comparisons and sortings in BWT and backward search. For example, instead of comparing and re-arranging byte by byte during BWT encoding, the texts will be compared and re-arranged in an m-bytes by m-bytes manner.

Approach B: In contrast to Approach A, this approach performs BWT and backward search on multi-byte

[1]From http://en.wikipedia.org/wiki/Wide_character

encoded text by treating every character as one byte long. This approach is ideal for UTF-8 encoded documents as UTF-8 is fully compatible with ASCII encodings. However, for most other encodings, an explicit check for word boundaries is needed to guarantee the matches returned from the backward search are correct. In this paper, we propose a concise bit array to mark the beginning byte of each character to resolve correct matches during backward search.

Approach C: BWT encoding and backward search performance is greatly affected by the length of text to be searched. Therefore, in this approach, we propose splitting the given text according to the byte location of each character, and then BWT encode each byte array separately. This will speed up the BWT encoding, and it will also enhance the performance of backward search (as shown in this paper). In this approach, an extra data structure and extra mappings need to be introduced in order to merge the matching bytes together to confirm the final matching characters. We will show that this approach outperforms Approach A and B in most situations.

Approach D: While Approach C is efficient in runtime, its extra data structure for mapping the bytes together can consume lots of memory. In Approach D, when the given character encoding is fixed width, we propose to maintain this mapping information only for every g bytes, so the extra data structure will be g times smaller. However, by doing so, we trade speed for space saving. Extra computations are needed to compute the mappings between the bytes from different byte arrays, since not every byte has its mapping information stored.

Finally, experiments to compare these approaches on different encodings (including UTF-8, UTF-16 and UTF-32) are included in this paper.

The rest of the paper is organized as follows. Section 2 presents the related work. Section 3 provides an overview of BWT and backward search, and Section 4 provides some background informaton on multi-byte encodings for Chinese characters. Section 5 describes our proposed approaches and our experiment results are shown and discussed in Section 6. Finally, Section 7 concludes the paper.

2. RELATED WORK

The most well known data structures used for full-text indexing are suffix trees [13] and suffix arrays [12]. They support efficient pattern search with a tradeoff of large space usage. Although there have been active improvements on this from the research community, the hidden constants in the space bound are usually very large in practice. Exploiting the relationship between the suffix array and the Burrows Wheeler transform (BWT) [2], Ferragina and Manzini proposed the FM-index [4] that encapsulates the input text and takes the same space used by traditional compressors that store the input text only. Given these parameters, the FM-index still performs full-text search using backward search in a very efficient manner.

Sadakane [15] proposed a modified, reversible transform, namely bwu, where the sorting of the rows of the cyclic shifts matrix is done by ignoring the case of alphabetic symbols.

He called this technique 'unification' and showed how to extend it to multi-byte character codes such as the Japanese EUC code [16].

Although word based indexes have been used widely in information retrieval [17] in the last 20 years (e.g., PAT trees and PAT arrays [6], word-based suffix trees have only been introduced recently [1]. The basic idea of word based indexes is to store just the text positions corresponding to word beginnings. Assume a document of size n with k words. [1] states that word suffix trees can be built with $O(k)$ working space in $O(n)$ expected running time. Recently, [7] improved this performance to $O(k)$ working space, in $O(n)$ running time, in the worst case.

Sparse string matching is similar to, but a more general problem than, word-based string matching. In sparse string matching, the set of points to be indexed is arbitrary, i.e., the indexed set of points are not necessarily the word boundaries. A special case where the indexed positions are evenly spaced was considered in [9]. In [9], algorithms on evenly spaced sparse suffix trees, i.e., representing every kth suffix of the text, were improved by using 'dual suffix trees'.

[18] stated that 16-bit Asian language texts are difficult to compress using conventional 8-bit sampling text compression schemes, and suggested a better scheme using lexicon dictionaries to first convert the input strings to 16-bit tokens. In this scheme, infrequent words that are not registered in the dictionary are encoded on a character by character basis. For similar reasons, most efficient word-based compression schemes either assume, employ or self-generate a dictionary for transforming the input strings into tokens before performing BWT [8]. This process uses the same concept as the unification technique in [15]. Most other efficient compression schemes for Chinese languages are mainly dictionary-based (e.g., [14])

The transformation of input strings into tokens that are more efficient for compression has proved to be very effective. However, these extra mappings increase the complexity and resource requirements (such as memory, CPU processing and possibly storage space), when our primary aim is for full-text search. Rather than proposing a new transform that may have different properties compared to the well-studied BWT, or utilizing word based indexes that may suffer from performance and space drawbacks as mentioned above, our proposal utilizes ordinary BWT. Hence, our proposal can be optimized by following any previous work or proposal on BWT optimization and its more efficient variants or auxiliary data structures (e.g. wavelet trees in RLFM [11]). Furthermore, we also study the use of byte-oriented BWT on multi-byte languages to avoid the word segmentation problem (which may be subject to the false positive problem as discussed later in this paper).

3. OVERVIEW OF BWT

3.1 BWT Basics

Let $T[1,n]$ be a text over a finite alphabet Σ. BWT permutes T, based on a reversible transformation, into a new string L that is easier to compress. Specifically, it consists of three steps:

1. append to the end of T a special character $\$$ smaller than any other character;

2. form a logical matrix M whose rows are the cyclic shifts of $T\$$ sorted in lexicographic order;

3. construct the transformed text L by taking the last column of M.

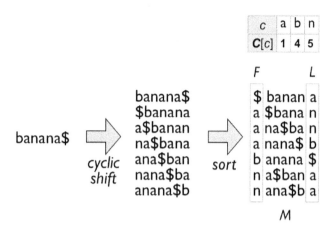

Figure 1: A BWT encoding process.

This BWT encoding process is illustrated in Figure 1 using the example string banana. Note that in particular, the first column of M, namely F, can be obtained by lexicographically sorting the characters of $T\$$ or L. The transformed text L usually contains long runs of identical characters, which can be compressed efficiently. For the scope of this paper, we will not go into detail on data compression using BWT. We will, however, focus on full-text search using BWT.

3.2 Backward Search

There is a bijective correspondence between the rows of M and the suffixes of T (and hence a strong relationship between L and the suffix array of T). This observation leads to the FM-index approach [4, 5]. For simplicity, FM-index focuses on two search operations, i.e., counting the number of matches in T and retrieving the positions of the matches. These operations are realised by the get_rows algorithm as shown in Algorithm 1. The algorithm exploits the properties of M: that all suffixes of T prefixed by a pattern $P[1, p]$ occupy a contiguous set of rows of M, and that this set of rows has start position $first$ and end position $last$, where $M[first]$ is the lexicographically smallest element of M that has prefix P. The value $(last - first + 1)$ is the total number of pattern occurrences.

Algorithm 1 Backward search algorithm for FM-index [4]

Algorithm get_rows($P[1, p]$)

```
1   i = p, c = P[p], first = C[c] + 1, last = C[c + 1];
2   while ((first ≤ last) and (i ≥ 2)) do
3       c = P[i − 1];
4       first = C[c] + Occ(c, first − 1) + 1;
5       last = C[c] + Occ(c, last);
6       i = i − 1;
7   if (last < first) then return "not found"
    else return (first, last).
```

In Algorithm 1, get_rows finds the set of rows prefixed by pattern $P[1, p]$. $C[1...|\Sigma|]$ is an array where $C[c]$ returns the number of occurrences in T of the characters $\{\$, 1, ..., c - 1\}$. Note that $C[c] + 1$ is the position of the first occurrence of c in F, if any. Function $Occ(c, k)$ counts the number of occurrences of character c in the string prefix $L[1, k]$. It can be implemented with constant runtime cost by an auxiliary data structure using the extra $O(\frac{n}{\log n} \log \log n)$ space, as shown in [4]. Hence, get_rows will take $O(p)$ time, in the worst case. However, for wide character encodings such as UTF-32, if we apply BWT using 32-bit as a unit, the auxiliary data structure to compute Occ can be very large (i.e., requires a lot of memory to run efficiently).

4. MULTI-BYTE CHARACTER ENCODINGS

Without loss of generality, we use Chinese characters as illustrating examples through out this paper to explain how our proposed methods work. Our proposal would work for other multi-byte languages, such as many Asian and European languages.

There are two kinds of Chinese characters: simplified and traditional. GB2312 is the registered internet name for a key official character set of the People's Republic of China, used for simplified Chinese characters. EUC-CN is often used as the character encoding (i.e. for external storage) in programs that deal with GB2312, thus maintaining compatibility with ASCII. Two bytes are used to represent every character not found in ASCII. The value of the first byte is from 0xA1-0xF7 (161-247), while the value of the second byte is from 0xA1-0xFE (161-254). Big5 is a Chinese character encoding method used in Taiwan, Hong Kong, and Macau for traditional Chinese characters. It is a double-byte character set with the first byte being a lead byte with a value from 0x81 to 0xfe (or 0xa1 to 0xf9 for non-user-defined characters), while the value of the second byte is within 0x40 to 0x7e or 0xa1 to 0xfe.

UTF (especially UTF-8, UTF-16 and UTF-32) encodings are also becoming popular in many Chinese websites and software applications. UTF-8 is a variable-width encoding that can represent every character in the Unicode character set and is backward compatibility with ASCII. The first 128 code points (used to represent US-ASCII) need one byte. The next 1,920 code points need two bytes to encode. This includes Latin letters with diacritics and characters from the Greek, Cyrillic, Coptic, Armenian, Hebrew, Arabic, and so on. Three bytes are needed for characters in the rest of the Basic Multilingual Plane (which contains virtually all characters in common use). Four bytes are needed for characters in the other planes of Unicode, which include less common CJK characters and various historic scripts and mathematical symbols. UTF-16 is capable of encoding 1,112,064 numbers (called code points) in the Unicode code space from 0 to 0x10FFFF. It produces a variable-length result of either two bytes or four bytes per code point. UTF-32 uses exactly 32 bits per Unicode code point while all other Unicode transformation formats use variable-length encodings. Therefore, compared to variable length encodings, UTF-32's Unicode code points are directly indexable.

Consider an example of the following five Chinese characters '上下左右中'. Their corresponding byte encodings for

Table 1: Example of some Chinese characters in different encodings

	上	下	左	右	中
GB2312	0xC9CF	0xCFC2	0xD7F3	0xD3D2	0xD6D0
BIG5	0xA457	0xA455	0xA5AA	0xA56B	0xA4A4
UTF-8	0xE4B88A	0xE4B88B	0xE5B7A6	0xE58FB3	0xE4B8AD
UTF-16	0x0A4E	0x0B4E	0xE65D	0xF353	0x2D4E
UTF-32	0x0A4E0000	0x0B4E0000	0xE65D0000	0xF3530000	0x2D4E0000

GB2312 (EUC-CN), BIG5, UTF-8, UTF-16 and UTF-32 are shown in Table 1.

5. BWT ON MULTI-BYTE ENCODED TEXTS

Before we discuss BWT on multi-byte text documents, we note that this application is straightforward when the encoding is UTF-8, since UTF-8 is fully compatible with ASCII encodings. However, characters 0x0800 through 0xFFFF use three bytes in UTF-8, but only two in UTF-16. As a result, text in Chinese (and Japanese or Hindi etc.) could take more space in UTF-8 than in UTF-16, as shown in the examples in 1 and later in the experiment section, i.e., Table 2. In addition, in the case of Chinese character sets, the most popular encodings to date are still GB2312 and BIG5, and neither of them can be handled correctly by software applications that are designed for ASCII encodings. Therefore, we believe that it is significant and important to consider different ways of processing multi-byte text documents that are not UTF-8.

5.1 Approach A: Multi-byte, fixed width approach

In the context of using BWT for full-text search on multi-byte encoded texts, we consider each multi-byte encoded character as a word of m bytes, i.e., a fixed width, m byte atomic unit. We then apply all the BWT and backward search data structures and algorithms from the literature without any extension, except that all the comparisons and sortings are done by assuming every symbol is m bytes long instead of one byte. This is the most straightforward approach if one wants to apply BWT backward search on multi-byte encodings (except for UTF-8 since it is ASCII compatible).

5.2 Approach B: Single-byte approach

Approach B treats a multi-byte text document as single-byte encoded document to apply BWT. This has many advantages. For example, all standard BWT and backward search algorithms can be applied without modifications or transformations (such as the unification process proposed in [15]). Hence the usual space and runtime costs / analysis apply. Furthermore, optimization techniques for BWT and backward search, e.g., wavelet trees [11], can also be used. This is especially the case for all files encoded using UTF-8.

However, for most multi-byte encodings, if they are treated as single-byte encoded for performing BWT, the results found by a backward search should be filtered (by discarding those results that do not occur at word boundaries). Otherwise the search results may contain false positives.

For example, consider the Chinese character '空' that has a UTF-16 value of 0x7A7A; and the Chinese character '中'

that has a BIG5 value of 0xA4A4. If we do not filter results that do not occur at word boundaries, searching the for character '空' using backward search on a single-byte based BWT of the UTF-16 encoded text '空空' will result in 3 matches instead of 2. Note that this problem may occur even for multi-byte characters with different byte values. For example, consider the text '的了牧' in GB2312 with byte values 0xB5C4 0xC1CB 0xC4C1, respectively. Backward search for '牧' (i.e., 0xC4C1) on this text will have 2 matches but in fact there is only one occurrence of '牧'.

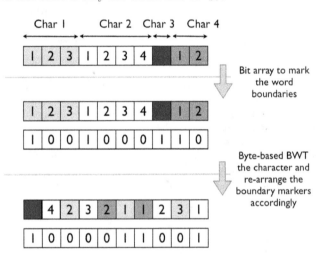

Figure 2: Byte based BWT encoding of multi-byte characters.

Discarding these false positives can be computationally costly. In addition, putting every byte into a single BWT index will result in unnecessary space occupancy of the index, waste cache / memory space and hence, slow down the backward search.

To minimize the space overhead of marking word boundaries, we use a bit array as illustrated in Figure 2. In Figure 2, we denote the byte position of each byte of a character by 1, 2, 3 and 4 respectively. After byte-based BWT transformation, these bytes will be relocated according to BWT. We will need to keep track of the relocations of all first bytes and relocate the boundary markers accordingly. Using the example above, two occurrences of 0xC4C1 on 0xB5C4 0xC1CB 0xC4C1 will be found by backward search. The byte 0xC4 of the first occurrence is not a boundary marker and hence will be discarded.

5.3 Approach C: Multi-byte characters split into byte arrays

To avoid explicit word boundary detection and to reject

false positives at an early stage during the search process, we propose Approach C – constructing byte arrays based on the byte location of each character in the text, and performing BWT on each byte array separately. For example, consider a multi-byte encoded text that encodes characters using one to four bytes as shown in Figure 3. In Figure 3, the bytes of

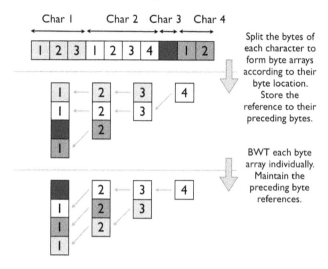

Figure 3: BWT encoding of byte arrays split from multi-byte characters.

characters: Char 1, Char 2, Char 3 and Char 4, in the given string are split according to the byte location of each character. i.e., all the first bytes of each character are grouped together in one array, and all the second bytes are grouped into another array, and so on. Same as Figure 2, in Figure 3, we denote the byte position of each byte of a character by 1, 2, 3 and 4 respectively (and we use different shading colors for different characters). Therefore, after the bytes are split according to their byte positions, all first bytes (all 1's) will be grouped into an array, ordered according to the order of their corresponding characters (i.e., the order of the shading colors are preserved). Similarly for all second, third and fourth bytes respectively. After that, when BWT is applied to each array, order of the shading colors will change.

When a byte (except the first byte) is being split from a character, reference to its preceding byte (represented as an array index to another array) is stored. The references between two arrays are stored as an array of preceding byte references, with its length equal to the shorter of the two arrays. Next, each byte array is BWT transformed separately, while references to the preceding bytes are maintained.

In practice, it is much faster to BWT encode several shorter single-byte arrays individually than to BWT encode all of them together as one array. Furthermore, the run-time memory requirement for efficient backward search is also lower for several smaller BWT transformed arrays than for the combined array, due to the larger data structure required for the Occ function when the BWT array is longer.

During backward search, bytes from the search string are split according to their byte locations (within each character) and are backward searched accordingly from their corresponding byte arrays. Next, matches from these arrays will be merged using their preceding byte references. This merging process is very efficient for fixed width character en-

codings. For example, for 32-bit fixed width encodings, we can use the matches from the array containing the fourth byte to construct the final match. This is done by starting each match from the fourth byte array and following its preceding byte reference to find all its preceding bytes (i.e. the third byte, followed by the second byte and finally the first byte). The byte array matches that are not included in any of these assembled characters will be discarded. For variable length encodings, the efficiency of this merging depends greatly on the distribution of the character lengths and query selectivity (i.e., number of matches).

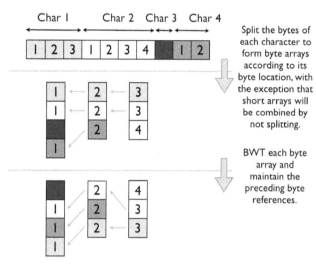

Figure 4: BWT encoding of byte arrays with short arrays merged.

To reduce the overhead of merging the matches from different byte arrays for variable length encodings, we propose not to split characters at byte location p, where most characters of a given document are encoded using less than p bytes. This proposal is shown in Figure 4. As shown in Figure 4, except for the first byte, a reference to the preceding byte will only be stored and maintained if the preceding byte is located in another array.

For example, suppose that most of the characters of a given UTF-8 document are English alphabets, with a small proportion of characters that are Chinese (and each of them is 3 bytes long). We can split the document into 2 arrays, with one of them containing all the first bytes and the other containing the rest of the bytes, and then BWT transform them separately.

Furthermore, many characters in documents encoded with wide character encodings (especially those larger than 16 bits) have trailing zeros (i.e., the last byte or last few bytes of these characters have the value zero). For example, in UTF-32, most characters can be encoded in two bytes and only extended character sets (and those characters are not very usually used) may need to use all four bytes to encode. Hence, we propose an extension to Figure 3 by trimming all trailing zeros, which would further reduce the space and runtime costs. This extension is illustrated in Figure 5. Note that different from the previous figures, the numbers in the byte arrays denote the actual byte values of the characters instead of byte positions, and 0s are used to represent the byte value 0s.

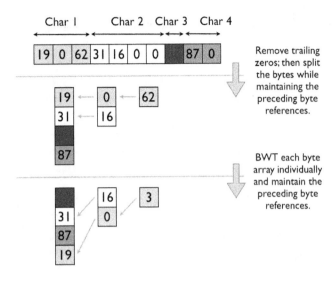

Figure 5: BWT encoding of byte arrays with trailing zeros trimmed.

5.4 Approach D: Location mappings with gaps

Given the string T, which contains n bytes and c characters. Each character is encoded by at most e bytes, and we use $T[i]$ to denote the i-th byte of T. Using Approach C (i.e. assuming that there are no trailing zeros and we split all the bytes), T will be split into $T_1, T_2, \ldots T_e$, where T_i contains the i-th byte of all characters in T. Note that $|T_1| \geq |T_2| \geq \ldots \geq |T_e|$. Since we need to maintain references to the preceding bytes, we will have the array $J_2, J_3, \ldots, J_e$ where J_j maps the bytes from T_j to T_{j-1}. Hence, $|J_2| = |T_2|, \ldots, |J_e| = |T_e|$. Therefore, the memory overhead for merging the matches is the worst when $|T_1| = |T_2| = \ldots = |T_e|$, i.e., for fixed width encodings.

To address this problem for fixed width encodings, we propose Approach D, which leaves a gap g between any two references such that each array J_j will be g times smaller. i.e., we only maintain the mapping to the preceding byte every g bytes in the T_j (same as every g character in T).

During backward search on each byte array L_j, where $L_j = \mathrm{BWT}(T_j)$, we continue to BWT decode L_j for each match, even after we complete the backward search process, until a byte that contains a mapping to its preceding character is found. Next, we merge the matches from different byte arrays using these mappings. In summary, although we need to spend (on average) an extra $g/2$ number of BWT decoding iterations for each match from each byte array, we save g times the amount of space to handling byte merging.

6. EXPERIMENTS

Experiments are performed in the machine with Core i5-430M (2.26GHz), 2GB memory and 7200rpm harddisk. It is running Ubuntu 11.10 and experiments are implemented in Java (1.6.0_31).

6.1 File size

All four approaches described in the previous section are considered in our experiments. For the purposes of this paper, we assume that the BWT encoding and byte location information (where appropriate) has already been written out to file, and hence are not included in our timings below. Table 2 shows the file sizes for each approach.

Approach A treats every symbol as fixed length (and therefore all symbols are treated as 2 bytes or 4 bytes at a time, for UTF-16 and UTF-32 respectively, in any sortings and comparisons for BWT), i.e., n is smaller (and $|\Sigma|$ is larger when compared to Approach B). Note that UTF-16 is either two bytes or four bytes per code point, but all the UTF-16 datasets used in our experiments are two byte encoded. Approach B treats every symbol as one byte so that all comparisons and sortings are done in a byte by byte manner, resulting in a relatively larger n and smaller $|\Sigma|$. In Approach C, we split the bytes of each symbol according to their positions and BWT them separately. References to the preceding bytes are stored and maintained to assemble the characters back during backward search. To reduce the size of these additional position mappings, we only keep the mappings of every g character in the file for Approach D. In Approach D, we vary the size of this 'gap' (g) from 10 to 30 as shown in Table 2 (labelled D_{10}, D_{20} and D_{30} respectively). For Approach C and D, the file size is calculated by adding up the size of all the files, i.e., the files for the BWT arrays and the files for the preceding byte references. We have tested our scheme using >10 popular Chinese ebooks in our experiments. For conciseness, we have selected three of them, ranging from 800KB to 10MB when in UTF-32, to present in this section. To easily identify these files in our discussion, we associate each file with an ID, for example, F1 for the ebook '地缘看世界.txt'.

In Table 2, Approach C is large due to the additional location mapping files, and as shown in Approach D, the size of these files decreases when we increase the gap (g) for the location mappings. To further optimize these numbers, traditional compression techniques such as differential compression could have been applied to the location mappings.

6.2 Memory usage and loading time

Table 3: Runtime memory required (in MB) for each approach.

ID	Encodings	A	B	C	D_{10}	D_{20}	D_{30}
F1	UTF-8	-	8	8	-	-	-
	UTF-16	68	15	11	13	11	11
	UTF-32	68	28	13	14	13	13
F2	UTF-8	-	38	23	-	-	-
	UTF-16	355	49	32	36	32	32
	UTF-32	360	94	42	48	44	43
F3	UTF-8	-	135	83	-	-	-
	UTF-16	>500	161	112	142	124	119
	UTF-32	>500	346	128	156	135	129

We recorded the memory usage (Table 3) and loading time (Table 4) required for each approach.

The loading time includes the time to read the files, allocate the runtime memory, time to construct data structures (e.g., the bucket structures for Occ [4]) and time to construct auxiliary data structures (if any). Therefore, without any surprise, the loading time is closely related to the runtime memory usage.

Overall, Approach D has the best loading time and memory usage, while Approach C is also very close. They are

Table 2: File size (in bytes) for each approach.

ID	Filename	Encodings	Original	A	B	C	D_{10}	D_{20}	D_{30}
F1	地缘看世界.txt	UTF-8	609,282	-	609,282	1,409,814	-	-	-
		UTF-16	418,676	418,676	471,011	1,256,028	586,148	502,412	474,500
		UTF-32	837,352	837,352	942,021	1,256,028	586,148	502,412	474,500
F2	刘亚洲文集.txt	UTF-8	1,862,281	-	1,862,281	4,282,681	-	-	-
		UTF-16	1,304,646	1,304,646	1,467,727	3,913,938	1,826,510	1,565,582	1,478,606
		UTF-32	2,609,292	2,609,292	2,935,454	3,913,938	1,826,510	1,565,582	1,478,606
F3	中国通史.txt	UTF-8	7,353,094	-	7,353,094	17,043,818	-	-	-
		UTF-16	5,018,258	5,018,258	5,645,541	15,054,726	7,025,546	6,021,898	5,687,346
		UTF-32	10,036,484	10,036,484	11,291,045	15,054,726	7,025,546	6,021,898	5,687,346

better than Approach A and Approach B because of their shorter BWT arrays (instead of combining these shorter arrays into one larger BWT encoded array). Hence the space and runtime costs for constructing the data structures for BWT backward search are relatively cheaper. Compared to Approach C, the location mappings for Approach D are much smaller due to the gaps. However, the performance of Approach C is still very close to Approach D, since both approaches do not need to build complicated auxiliary data structures in addition to the mapping arrays themselves.

Table 4: Loading time (in ms) for each approach.

ID	Encod.	A	B	C	D_{10}	D_{20}	D_{30}
F1	UTF-8	-	322	505	-	-	-
	UTF-16	3799	780	566	473	488	458
	UTF-32	3728	1449	700	593	492	507
F2	UTF-8	-	887	1216	-	-	-
	UTF-16	21871	2430	1567	1108	1042	1004
	UTF-32	30546	4430	1780	1326	1237	1154
F3	UTF-8	-	3112	3861	-	-	-
	UTF-16	>60000	4870	5173	3628	3330	3199
	UTF-32	>60000	17409	5557	4095	3651	3725

6.3 Full-text search performance

In order to test the full-text search performance for each approach, we have designed three groups of search queries by varying the length of the search pattern and query selectivity. For selectivity, we tested for queries with no matches, with exactly one match, and with many matches. These queries, labelled with ID Q1...Q9, are listed in Table 5.

The search performance (in microseconds) for Approach B and Approach C on UTF-8 encoded documents are shown in Figure 6. We did not perform these UTF-8 experiments using Approach A and Approach D, since these two approaches would not offer any substantial benefits (i.e., Approach A adds unnecessary space usage and Approach D adds unnecessary computation complexity) as UTF-8 is compatible to ASCII encodings.

The UTF-8 encoded files in our experiments contains characters with length ranging from one byte (e.g., punctuations, numerics) to three bytes (e.g., Chinese characters). Therefore, we use these UTF encoded files on our Approach C with the extension that all the second to fourth bytes (if any) of characters are not split.

With no surprise, Approach B performs really well overall and performs the best when the search pattern is short

and the selectivity is low. This is because UTF-8 is fully compatible with ASCII encodings, and hence the no frills BWT and backward search algorithms perform the most efficient without any additional data structures or operations such as checking for word boundaries. Approach C performs well too, due to the fact that all second, third and fourth bytes are BWT transformed and stored in one array. i.e., merging of matches happens between two BWT arrays (instead of three or four arrays). As a result, the extra cost of merging matches is minimized. Furthermore, Approach C performs better than Approach B for queries with long search patterns because the former breaks one long byte array into two. Hence, Approach C has a smaller Occ data structure footprint and better cache locality for the data in the array, i.e., faster backward searching for each byte. Long search patterns will amplify this effect and long search patterns usually result in high selectivity. Therefore, it will reduce the overhead of merging the matches between the two byte arrays. So, for long search patterns such as Q3, Q6 and Q9, Approach C outperforms Approach B. For the rest, Approach B performs better but Approach C is not far behind.

This has shown that our approach for splitting the multibyte encodings into byte arrays and then merging the matches is efficient and works well in practice. In fact, due to its relatively smaller Occ memory requirement as shown in Table 3, Approach C may be more preferable on devices with limited memory.

Figure 7 and Figure 8 show the backward search performance (also in microseconds) on UTF-16 and UTF-32 encodings, respectively. Approach A is always the worst performer. It assumes 2 bytes as a basic unit for UTF-16 and 4 bytes for UTF-32. So, it will have a large and relatively slower Occ and hence worse backward search performance. Approach C works the best overall as it has smaller and hence faster Occ than Approach A and B. This advantage is highlighted by the queries with long search pattern such as Q3, Q6 and Q9. Furthermore, the cost of merging the matches from byte arrays may be cancelled out by the cost of checking word boundaries needed by Approach B. Note that in order to eliminate the possibility of false positives for Approach B for UTF-16 and UTF-32, word boundary checking is unavoidable. Approach D (with gap size of 10, 20, 30) also performs better than Approach B for the same reasons. However, it performs far worse than Approach B and C due to its more complex computations for byte merging. However, it offers better loading time than Approach

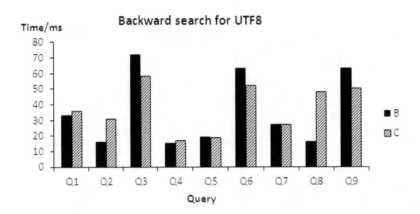

Figure 6: Search performance of different approaches for UTF-8 encodings.

Table 5: The list of search queries

ID	File	Query	#Results
Q1	F1	是中国挑战世界中心的路线图	0
Q2	F1	大中亚地区	22
Q3	F1	看了上面这张图大家就清楚了吧！中国沿海可以分为三个区域	1
Q4	F2	一九七人年参军	0
Q5	F2	金门战役	30
Q6	F2	这些商船是金门部队撤退用的。打平潭岛时，敌人不也派商船来撤兵嘛。	1
Q7	F3	他承史学工作者来信指教	0
Q8	F3	马克思	26
Q9	F3	长城外有一支细石器文化，它的特征是用燧石制成细小而锐利的锋刃	1

B and C, and a significantly smaller file size than Approach C. Note that the performance of Approach C is similar for both the UTF-16 and UTF-32 encodings, as trailing zeros are trimmed (cf. Section 5.3). Similarly for Approach D. As a result, UTF-32 will have a similar byte distribution to UTF-16. This is because, for most Chinese characters, the first two bytes of UTF-32 have the same values as UTF-16's, and the last two bytes of UTF-32 are zero (as demonstrated by the characters in Table 1).

7. CONCLUSIONS

We have discussed different approaches for applying BWT on multi-byte text documents. In particular, we have proposed techniques on efficiently backward search documents in multi-byte encodings. We use public domain Chinese ebooks to validate our findings, which are summarized as follows:

- Treating every character as a fixed width symbol and applying BWT directly on these wide symbols is straightforward but not computationally efficient, both in terms of space and runtime.

- If a document is in UTF-8, it is generally efficient to apply BWT and backward search on it, as if it is in ASCII. However, UTF-8 is not the most popular encoding for Chinese and Chinese characters encoded in UTF-8 consumes more space than in GB2312, BIG5 and UTF-16.

- Our proposed, new Approach C, which splits the bytes

of characters according to their byte locations and performing BWT on each byte array separately, out performs other approaches in most cases.

- Further extensions, such as the introduction of gaps (in Approach D) and trimming of trailing zeros, have been proposed to optimize Approach C.

Overall, we believe that our findings are useful and valuable for readers who want to perform search (especially full-text search) on texts with multi-byte encodings.

For those who are interested in improving our findings and extending the experiments to other languages or encodings, we have placed the source code at http://dbx.cse.unsw.edu.au under an open source license.

Our ongoing work includes applying compression techniques to the mapping structures between the BWT arrays in Approach C and Approach D. We are also interested in extending the concept of this paper into compressed BWT structures such as RLFM [11].

Acknowledgements

The authors would like to thank the reviewers for their very useful comments on improving the paper.

8. REFERENCES

[1] A. Andersson, N. Larsson, and K. Swanson. Suffix trees on words. *Algorithmica*, 23(3):246–260, 1999.

[2] M. Burrows and D. Wheeler. A block-sorting lossless data compression algorithm. Technical report, Digital Equipment Corporation, Palo Alto, CA, 1994.

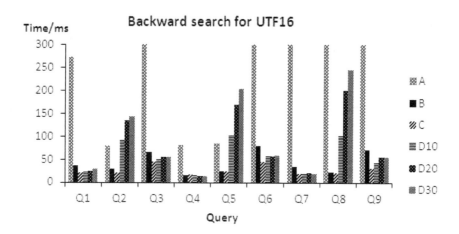

Figure 7: Search performance of different approaches for UTF-16 encodings.

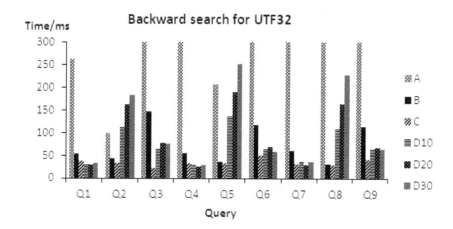

Figure 8: Search performance of different approaches for UTF-32 encodings.

[3] P. Ferragina, F. Luccio, G. Manzini, and S. Muthukrishnan. Compressing and searching XML data via two zips. In *WWW 2006*, Edinburgh, Scotland, 2006. ACM.

[4] P. Ferragina and G. Manzini. Opportunistic data structures with applications. In *Proceedings of the 41st Annual Symposium on Foundations of Computer Science*, FOCS '00, pages 390–398, Washington, DC, USA, 2000. IEEE Computer Society.

[5] P. Ferragina and G. Manzini. Indexing compressed text. *J. ACM*, 52(4):552–581, July 2005.

[6] W. B. Frakes and R. A. Baeza-Yates, editors. *Information Retrieval: Data Structures & Algorithms*. Prentice-Hall, 1992.

[7] S. Inenaga and M. Takeda. On-line linear-time construction of word suffix trees. In *in Proc. 17th Ann. Symp. on Combinatorial Pattern Matching (CPM'06*, pages 60–71. Springer-Verlag, 2006.

[8] R. Y. K. Isal, A. Moffat, and A. C. Ngai. Enhanced word-based block-sorting text compression. In *ACSC '02 Proceedings of the twenty-fifth Australasian conference on Computer Science*. ACS, 2002.

[9] J. Kärkkäinen and E. Ukkonen. Sparse suffix trees. In

J.-Y. Cai and C. Wong, editors, *Computing and Combinatorics*, volume 1090 of *Lecture Notes in Computer Science*, pages 219–230. Springer Berlin / Heidelberg, 1996.

[10] H. Li and R. Durbin. Fast and accurate long-read alignment with Burrows-Wheeler transform. *Bioinformatics*, 26(5):589–595, 2010.

[11] V. Mäkinen and G. Navarro. Succinct suffix arrays based on run-length encoding. *Nordic J. of Computing*, 12(1):40–66, Mar. 2005.

[12] U. Manber and G. Myers. Suffix arrays: a new method for on-line string searches. *SIAM J. Computing*, 22(5):935–948, 1993.

[13] E. McCreight. A space-economical suffix tree construction algorithm. *J. ACM*, 23(2):262–272, 1976.

[14] G. H. Ong and S. Y. Huang. A data compression scheme for Chinese text files using Huffman coding and a two-level dictionary. *Information Sciences*, 84(1-2):85–99, 1995.

[15] K. Sadakane. A modified Burrows-Wheeler transformation for case-insensitive search with application to suffix array compression. In *DCC: Data*

Compression Conference. IEEE Computer Society, 1999.

[16] K. Sadakane. *Unifying Text Search and Compression: Suffix Sorting, Block Sorting and Suffix Arrays*. PhD thesis, The University of Tokyo, 2000.

[17] I. Witten, A. Moffat, and T. Bell. *Managing Gigabytes: Compressing and Indexing Documents and Images*. Morgan Kaufmann, San Francisco, CA, 1999.

[18] S. Yoshida, T. Morihara, H. Yahagi, and N. Satoh. Application of a word-based text compression method to Japanese and Chinese texts. In *Data Compression Conference, DCC '99*. IEEE, 1999.

Deriving Document Workflows from Feature Models

Mª Carmen Penadés, Abel Gómez, José H. Canós
ISSI-DSIC
Universitat Politècnica de València
Cno. de Vera, s/n
46022 Valencia, Spain

{mpenades, agomez, jhcanos}@dsic.upv.es

ABSTRACT

Despite the increasing interest in the Document Engineering community, a formal definition of document workflow is still to come. Often, the term refers to an abstract process consisting in a set of tasks to contribute to some document contents, and some techniques are being developed to support parts of these tasks rather than how to generate the process itself. In most proposals, these tasks are implicit in the business processes running in an organization, lacking an explicit document workflow model that could be analysed and enacted as a coherent unit. In this paper, we propose a document-centric approach to document workflow generation. We have extended the feature-based document meta-model of the Document Product Lines approach with an organizational metamodel. For a given configuration of the feature model, we assign tasks to different members of the organization to contribute to the document contents. Moreover, the relationships between features define an ordering of the tasks, which may be refined to produce a specification of the document workflow model automatically. The generation of customized software manuals is used to illustrate the proposal.

Categories and Subject Descriptors

I.7.1 [**Computing Methodologies**]: Document and Text Editing – *document management.* I.7.2 [**Document Preparation**]: Languages and systems - Desktop publishing. D.2.13 [**Software Engineering**]: Reusable Software - *domain engineering*

General Terms

Management, Documentation, Design, Languages.

Keywords

Document Workflow, Document Generation, Document Product Lines, Variable Data Printing, Organizational Model.

1. INTRODUCTION

In recent years, the concept of document is changing fast; from a sequential, text-based vision, we have moved to a new model that sees a document as a composition of (linked) pieces of knowledge in different formats. As a consequence, new issues about how a document is created, managed, accessed, retrieved, shared and destroyed are emerging encompassed by the notion of document

lifecycle, which is realized in the form of a process known as *document workflow*. In general, document workflows are not explicit, that is, documents are composed along the execution of a business process, and parts of the documents are filled using the data flowing through the different tasks of the business process. Moreover, actors participating in the process are assigned to responsibilities to different document sections. The lack of an explicit document workflow model has led to the design of tools supporting specific aspects of the workflow. For instance, in the XFlow framework [5] the document flows are represented as XML documents. The PPCD proposal [2] provides a differential access control to documents by multiple actors in cross-organizational workflows. Adobe LifeCycle [1] provides interaction with processes and forms or PDF documents that can be saved and/or printed; administrators can set up more secure communications with access rights. All the above tools implement top-down approaches to document workflow: they focus on the business perspective and task analysis, being the documents generated as the result of the different tasks of the process.

However, in domains such as e-government or e-learning, among others, the document, is more relevant than the business processes. This is particularly true in cases where a process is created with the goal of producing a document (e.g. an emergency plan, or a learning object). In these cases, an explicit process model must be defined that includes tasks such as edit contents, read content before contributing to other contents, discuss contents or approve contents. Moreover, the document generation would be improved if we have methodological guidelines to analyze the documents and the data, design the document and its components to facilitate their reuse, provide mechanisms to generate variants of a document, provide access rights to multiple actors, etc.

In this paper, we introduce a document centric approach to the definition of document workflows. Specifically, we show the extension of a Document Engineering framework, called Document Product Lines (DPL) [8], to generate document workflows where multiple actors are involved in the document generation process with different access rights to the document content. The document workflow is obtained from two main sources: a document content specification in terms of features representing document components, and an organizational model describing the different actors involved. For each document component, different actors are assigned to specific tasks (e.g. edit, review, approve) according to their access rights. The specification of the workflow's control flow may be refined later by document engineers. As a result, an explicit document workflow is generated, which can be further analysed using traditional workflow analysis techniques, and enacted as document editors customized to each actor. The main contribution is the integrated bottom-up support to variable content document generation with multiple actors and variable data in an explicit document workflow specification.

The paper is organized as follow. Section 2, describes the organizational model which extends the DPL feature model and how to generate a document workflow model. Next, Section 3 illustrates the proposal with a case study, the generation of software manuals. Finally, the conclusions and our future work.

2. GENERATING DOCUMENT WORKFLOWS IN DPL

The Document Product Lines (DPL) approach [8, 4] provides a framework to variable content document generation following a bottom-up approach. DPL was created to support variable content document generation in contexts with high variability and high levels of reuse. With this aim, DPL follows the basic principles of Software Product Line Engineering (SPLE) [3].

DPL defines two main processes, namely Domain Engineering and Application Engineering. The goal of the former is to define a family of documents by means of document feature models, and to find or develop the different document components that will implement these features. The DPL Document Feature Metamodel allows the specification of the commonality and variability in a document family as a set of mandatory, optional and alternative features (see Figure 1). Two different types of features can be specified: on one hand, those related to the document content (ContentDocumentFeature or CDF), and, on the other hand, those related to the technology used to represent these contents (TechnologyDocumentFeature or TDF). TDFs were introduced to cope with the diversity of formats a CDF can be realized in. For instance, a business process can be described either by a textual description, a picture of a flow diagram or an executable Petri Net. The InfoElements are the pieces of knowledge that implement the CDFs. They are stored in the product line Repository as typed digital objects and accessed via Disseminators (e.g. text editors, image viewers, video players, or web services). The goal of the Application Engineering process is to generate a document as a specific instance of the product line. The process starts with the document configuration, that is, the selection of the specific features the document will include, followed by the retrieval of the InfoElements implementing the features. The set of InfoElements corresponding to an instance of the product line have to be put together to create the document.

The first version of DPL framework [4] had two limitations. On one hand, it only supported fully instantiated InfoElements. In practice, however, things are more complicated. Besides the case of non-editable document components, others can be only partially instantiated; this case corresponds to templates, or form-based parts that must be completed by the final users (the variable data). On the other hand, no support for multiple actors was provided. Real document generation is often the result of different users performing different tasks such as the editing, approval or publication of content. This is where the concept of document workflow arises from. Following classical workflow models, the different actors involved in the process are specified according to an organizational model, which describes an organization as a hierarchy of actors. Actors may be individuals (called users) or units (e.g. departments). Users may belong to one or more units, and units may be composed of other units. Every unit is managed by one user.

In order to link actors with document workflow tasks, we have merged this organizational model with the DPL document feature metamodel (see Figure 1). The connection between both models is done via three associations between the CDF and Actor classes. The instances of the actor class will contribute to complete the

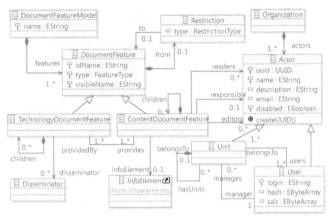

Figure 1. DPL Feature Metamodel extended with Actors

InfoElement associated to the CDF with different roles: as an editor, an actor has read/write permissions; as a reader, he/she has only read permission; and, as a responsible, he/she is the responsible for approving the content. Only actors granted with some of the above permissions can access the InfoElement associated to a CDF. The 0..n multiplicity in the "Actor" ends of the associations means that some CDF can be non-editable, non readable and/or not require approval.

2.1 Obtaining Document Workflow Models

For a given document configuration, a document workflow model is automatically generated from the relationships between the *CDFs*. The model is an instance of the workflow metamodel shown in Figure 2, which is based on BPMN [6]. The document workflow metamodel describes a process that has a beginning (*start* event), an end (*end* event), and a set of activities which are executed between these two events, according to a control flow. One activity may be a task, a subprocess, or a join or split gateway. A task is an atomic activity which cannot be broken down to a finer level of detail. A subprocess is an activity whose internal details are modeled using activities, gateways, and control flows. And, a gateway is used to control how the flows converge (join) and diverge (split) within a process. Finally, *FlowNode* is used to provide a single element as the source and the target that can appear in a process flow (tasks, subprocess, and gateways).

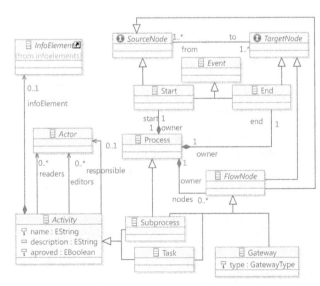

Figure 2. Document Workflow Metamodel

The generation of the document workflow model is as follows. For each CDF of the document configuration, an activity is added to the workflow model. In order to preserve the content of the InfoElement in the Repository, a copy of it is created and assigned to the activity; moreover, the assignment of actors to the CDF is propagated to the activity via the associations with the same names. Actors and permissions of the CDF are copied and assigned to the corresponding activity. If a CDF has not subfeatures, a task is created; otherwise, a subprocess is created instead, that is, the activity is decomposed in several subactivities.

The different activities are ordered according to some control flow specification, which may be derived from the relationships defined in the document feature model. For instance, if an activity needs the value of some data generated by another activity, the former cannot be performed before the completion of the latter. Additionally, different patterns may be applied to organize the activities of the process (or subprocess) generated. These patterns are depending on the TDF, that is, depending on the media of the final document. For example, for printed media, a sequence of activities is generated according to the order of the corresponding CDFs located at the same level in the document feature model. For multimedia, a set of parallel activities is generated. The automatically generated document workflow model may be modified using the workflow editor that has been added to the DPL framework, as the next section explains.

2.2 Extended DPL framework

The DPL framework presented in [4] has been extended to support the generation of document workflows (see Figure 3). The new components included are marked with a ⊕ symbol, and the elements modified are marked with a ⊗ symbol. The framework works as follows. The Feature Editor is used to characterize the variability of the domain as a document feature model. The Repository contains the InfoElements that will be reused latter to generate the product line instances. The Component Editor is used to create new InfoElements and add them to the Repository. The Organization Editor has been introduced to register the actors in a Credentials Manager (which provides the authentication mechanisms), according to the organizational model. By default, the DPL framework provides a credentials manager and organization editor, but any existing organization directory manager (for example, an LDAP directory) could be easily adapted instead. All of the above elements support the Domain Engineering subprocess.

The Application Engineering subprocess is supported by the remaining elements. The Configuration Editor supports the selection of variability points to define a specific document configuration; once a document configuration is defined, a first version of the document workflow is automatically generated. The Workflow editor visualizes this document workflow model automatically generated and allows the document engineer editing and refining it. The editor provides a tool palette to modify the control flow, the activities or the refinement of the actors. The document workflow model is reified as a set of Custom Documents Editors that are generated via their projection by actor. Therefore, each Custom Document Editor is the view of the document workflow that the corresponding actor has, which only contains the tasks which the actor is involved in. At the current version, these tasks only may be edit, read and approval task (according with the permissions defined), but we are working on identifying new types of tasks. Once the actors have executed their editors and completed their tasks, all the InfoElements are fully instantiated. Then, the Document Generator integrates them and obtains the final document, according to the control flow specified in the final document workflow model.

The current version of DPL framework has been developed on top of the Eclipse platform following the Model Driven Architecture (MDA) [7] paradigm, raising the level of abstraction and reducing development time by using code generators.

3. GENERATING SOFTWARE MANUALS

To illustrate the proposal, we use an easy case study: the generation of customized manuals for a software product. A software development organization produces customized manuals for its software products; in this case, we want to create a family of manuals for the DPL framework itself. First, the software development organization is registered using the organizational model editor (see Figure 4). The users are grouped into the following units: analysis & design, implementation, testing, deployment, which in turn includes a documentation unit, and project management. Each unit has one manager, marked with a checkbox.

Second, the domain engineer creates the feature model for the family of DPL manuals. In this case, the variability is defined by the type of manual. The document components change depending on whether a system administrator manual or a final user manual is generated. The former requires the following document components: installation information, including server installation steps, and information about all the product versions. The later, however, only requires information about the first steps to create a new project, and create and editing content components. Figure 5(a) shows a screenshot of the feature editor with all these document components modeled as CDFs and hierarchically organized; exclamation marks are used to denote mandatory features, whereas question marks for the optional ones; the double-head arrow

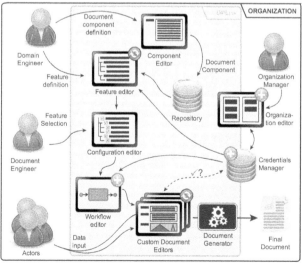

Figure 3. The extended DPL framework

Figure 4. Organization Editor

(a)   (b)

Figure 5. Manuals feature model (a) and configuration (b)

means alternative features, and the cross is used for denoting selection groups. Regarding TDFs, the manuals generated may be printed (as pdf files) or multimedia; these options are modeled as alternative TDF in Figure 5(a). Each CDF has associated a set of properties that include the InfoElement associated to it, whether is editable or not, and the actors assigned as editors, readers and responsible. If the actor is a unit, then every actor belonging to the same unit may contribute to the fulfillment of the InfoElement.

Third, a document engineer selects the optional and alternative features to generate a specific variant of manual. Figure 5(b) shows a screenshot of the document configuration of printed system administrator's manuals. The model restrictions (specifically, the *requires* relationship) make that, after selecting a feature, all the required by it are automatically checked by the configuration editor. Figure 6 shows a screenshot of the editor that shows the document workflow model generated from the document configuration. The document workflow shown has three sequential activities which correspond to the three first-level CDFs. In this case, these activities are subprocesses, and may be expanded to show their component activities. For instance, the Installation subprocess is composed of a task associated to the Requirements CDF, and a new subprocess called Installation Steps. The document engineer may modify the process using the tool palette provided by the editor. Finally, the enactment of the document workflow model generates the final document (see Figure 7). Previously, a projection of this model by actor is generated to obtain a set of Custom Document Editors. Each actor has their own Custom Document Editor which contains their worklist, that is, the tasks assigned to contribute to the InfoElements. For instance, the actor, Prog2, has a task to edit the InfoElement asso-

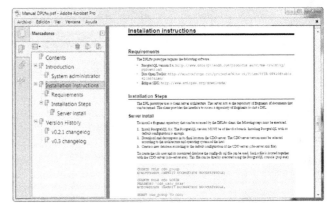

Figure 7. Generated manual for system administrators

ciated to Requirements CDF, whereas the actor, Prog1 (the Implementation Unit manager), is the responsible for its approval.

4. CONCLUSIONS

In this paper, we described how to obtain an explicit document workflow model from a document feature model extended with an organizational model. At its current status, the DPL framework supports a bottom-up approach to variable content document generation with multiple actors and variable data that produces Custom Document Editors. Such editors are task-based, and currently only classic tasks like edit read and approve content are implemented. We are working to incorporate other tasks, e.g. review, and to include a global view of the process for each actor that complements the current one, focused on the InfoElements. Furthermore, we are studying other control flow patterns to generate a more advanced version the document workflow model; so far, only the sequential and parallel patterns have been implemented, which are sufficient for most cases.

5. ACKNOWLEDGMENTS

This work is partially funded by the Spanish Government under grant TIPEx (TIN2010-19859-C03-03).

6. REFERENCES

[1] Adobe. LifeCycle Workflow Solution. 2012. http://www.ado be .com/ eeurope/products/server/workflowserver/

[2] Balinsky, H., Chen, L. and Simske, S. 2011. Publicly Posted Composite Documents in Variable Ordered Workflows. *In Proc. of IEEE TrustCom11*. IEEE ICESS. DOI= 10.1109/TrustCom.2011.81

[3] Clements, P., Northrop, L. 2002. *Software Product Lines: Practices and Patterns*. Addison-Wesley.

[4] Gómez, A., Penadés, M.C., Canós, J.H. and Borges, M. 2012. DPLfw: A Framework for Variable Content Document Generation. *In Proc. of SPLC2012*, Accepted.

[5] Marchetti, A., Tesconi, M. and Minutoli, S. 2005. XFlow: An XML-Based Document-Centric Workflow. *In Proc. of WISE*. LNCS 3806, pp. 290-303. Springer-Verlag.

[6] OMG. 2011. Business Process Model and Notation-BPMN v2.0. http://www.omg.org/spec/BPMN/ 2.0/PDF

[7] OMG. 2003. MDA Guide Version 1.0.1. Technical Report. OMG. http://www.omg.org/docs/ omg/03-06-01.pdf

[8] Penadés, M.C., Canós, J.H., Borges, M.R., Llavador, M. 2010. Document product lines: variability-driven document generation. *In Proc. of ACM DocEng '10*. pp. 203–206. DOI= 10.1145/1860559.1860

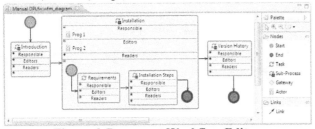

Figure 6. Document Workflow Editor.

Charactles: More than Characters

Blanca Mancilla
Computer Science Engineering
UNSW SYDNEY NSW 2052
Australia
mancilla@cse.unsw.edu.au

John Plaice
Computer Science Engineering
UNSW SYDNEY NSW 2052
Australia
plaice@cse.unsw.edu.au

ABSTRACT

In this paper, we propose a general notion of character which encompasses two concepts: points within a character set, such as Unicode, as well as arbitrary tuples defining structured objects. We call these general characters "charactles".

Using this model, text can be defined to be a linear sequence of charactles, not requiring the use of hierarchical structures to encode the text. As a result, all sorts of processing, such as searching and typesetting, are potentially simplified.

Categories and Subject Descriptors

J.5 [**Computer Applications**]: Arts and Humanities—*Literature*; J.7 [**Computer Applications**]: Computers in Other Systems—*Publishing*

Keywords

Multidimensional text, Character representation

1. INTRODUCTION

In this paper, we propose to generalize the concept of character to that of *charactle*, which is any entity that designates unambiguously an entry in a dictionary defined by a set of properties. A text then becomes a sequence of charactles, each of which may be versioned, i.e., tagged with further additional properties.

The proposed model has as goal a mechanism for extending the notion of character beyond Unicode, and is derived from several basic principles, conceived through an analysis of Unicode itself.

First, the concept of character used in the Unicode character set is deemed to be correct, and simply needs to be extended. In Unicode, a character is understood as a *logical* entity, not as a visual entity. For each code point—a number—in Unicode, there is an entry in the Unicode character data base, defining the set of properties for that char-

acter, the most important for identification purposes being the character's name.

Second, a linear text, i.e., a straight sequence of characters, is easier to search than a hierarchical structure. As a result, if we wish to create more and more complex texts, we would like to create them in a manner that allows them to be as *flat*—as untree-like—as possible.

Third, there are different notions of 'character' that cannot be included in Unicode. These include recently discovered Chinese characters that are *hapax legomena*, i.e., for which there is only one known occurrence in the corpus; individual 'glyphs' discovered in archaelogical digs which have not yet been identified as being instances of a known character; and glyphs in fonts that can be given meaning, such as thumbnails of images and corporate logos.

Fourth, the characters of Unicode do not all sit at the same level. Unicode encodes alphabets, such as Latin, Greek and Cyrillic; syllabaries, such as Devanagari (for Hindi and Sanskrit) and the Japanese Katakana and Hiragana; and Chinese characters, which, depending on the character, can be encoding different kinds of linguistic information. There is a need to be able to encode multiple languages in a text at the *same* level, for example at the *word* level, without having recourse to the widely differing scripts used on a daily basis.

Finally, even if a text is a sequence of Unicode characters, there are times when we wish to add certain information about these characters, without creating a hierarchical structure. For this to be possible, we need to be able to tag the individual characters with additional information in a standard manner.

We therefore propose that the notion of text be extended from sequences of Unicode characters to sequences of triples of the form (*dictionary*, *index*, *context*), where *dictionary* states what dictionary is being used, *index* designates the relevant entry in the dictionary, and *context* is a set of additional properties used to give information about the use and presentation of this particular entry. We assume that the individual entries in a dictionary are themselves sets of properties, i.e., (*attribute*, *value*) pairs.

When a text is linearized, i.e., when it sits on disk in a file, several different kinds of markup are possible. The exact linearization technique used, whether in LaTeX-style, XML-style, or another, is not important. What is important is that the positions of the characters are numbered in the text, starting from position 0.

As a result, whatever the linearization, the text, when live, in a data structure in a computer program, has a canonical form. Allowing several different kinds of linearization but one canonical internal form allows for the development of specialized syntaxes to enable searching through complex texts using multiple dictionaries.

The paper begins with the presentation of the Unicode model of character, as it is currently understood, and for the purposes of this paper. We then look at several examples of how this model of character can be extended using the above principles. Finally, we give a glimpse of how the model could be used in different document processing stages, including searching and typesetting.

2. THE UNICODE MODEL

Currently, the standard way to store a document is using XML and Unicode. In this combination, there is a division of labor: XML is used to encode the structure of the document, while Unicode is used to encode the characters. In this model, text appearing in the document is understood as a sequence of Unicode code points, numbers mapping to Unicode characters.

The simplest document we wish to encode is a sequence of Unicode characters, in a text file. For example, the sentence "*Once upon a time there was a family that lived happily ever after*" [8] becomes

$$C = \begin{array}{|c|c|c|c|c|c|c|c|c|c|c|} \hline \text{O} & \text{n} & \text{c} & \text{e} & & \text{u} & \text{p} & \text{o} & \text{n} & & \text{a} \\ \hline \end{array}$$

which is equivalent to the following equations:

$$C[0] = \text{`O'}; \quad C[1] = \text{`n'}; \quad C[2] = \text{`c'};$$
$$C[3] = \text{`e'}; \quad C[4] = \text{` '}; \quad C[5] = \text{`u'}; \quad \dots$$

which gives an idea of how to traverse this stream, or to extract elements from it.

This view gives the impression of simply putting characters in the cells. The correct view is that the box contains all the information necessary about its contents. So, the character 'O' is just an abbreviation for:

```
[
   Type: UnicodeChar
   CodePoint: U+004F
]
```

This information can then be used to look up this character in the Unicode Data database [3], where we will find the following entry:

`004F;LATIN CAPITAL LETTER O;Lu;0;L;;;;;N;;;;006F;`

If we ignore the default values, and use the explanations given in [4], the above line corresponds to the tuple:

```
[
   CodePoint : U+004F
   Name : "LATIN CAPITAL LETTER O"
   GeneralCategory : "Lu"
   CanonicalCombiningClass : 0
   BidiClass : "L"
   BidiMirrored : "N"
   SimpleLowecaseMapping : U+006F
]
```

i.e., the official Unicode Standard name of 'O' is 'LATIN CAPITAL LETTER O'; it is an uppercase letter; it is not reordered for combining purposes; it is a strong left-to-right character

and not mirrored for bidirectional text; and its lowercase mapping is code point U+006F (the letter 'o').

Although the Unicode book [5] gives substantial information about relationships and history of the characters, these are not part of the standard. The property set included in the standard is fixed: no additional information can be stored, since Unicode has frozen the characteristics of its elements.

Nevertheless, there are situations where one might add further properties to a specific Unicode character appearing in a text. For example, suppose we were encoding the above sentence in an illustrated manuscript, and we wished to note that the letter 'O' was to be a large initial letter. This could then be encoded as follows:

```
[
   Type: UnicodeChar
   CodePoint: U+004F
   Context : [ InitialLetter : True ]
]
```

The important thing is that for the purposes of searching, the additional context information can be simply ignored, and this character can be understood as the letter 'O'.

A similar example comes in the realm of the characters used for Chinese, Japanese and Korean. In Unicode, to reduce the size of the standard, a process called *Han unification* has been applied. If we look at the Unicode book [5, Table 12–6, p.421], we can see that the standard has unified visually distinct characters, with differences in writing sequence, overshoot at stroke termination, contact of strokes, and so on. Should an author insist on one of the visual forms, then the Context field could be used as above.

We now have the means for defining our model of character, which we call a *charactle*, i.e., a character-tuple. We assume that a character is a triple, where the field Type designates unambiguously a dictionary such as the Unicode database, and the field Context is a tuple encoding an arbitrary number of (*attribute*, *value*) pairs. The third field uniquely identifies the entry in the dictionary; for Unicode characters, it is called a CodePoint.

3. CHINESE STROKE SEQUENCES

With this approach, the set of characters can grow as needed, and is not limited to Unicode or some other established character set. For example, it is not possible to encode all of the Chinese characters, for one can always create new ones, and there are many cases of *hapax legomena*, i.e., characters only appearing once in the historical corpus which are not yet encoded. Our model allows the use of a character description language to register unencoded characters [9].

For example, suppose that the Chinese character for '*míng*', meaning *bright* or *clear*, were not encoded. Then we could break it down into its two radicals, '*rì*' (*sun*) and '*yuè*' (*moon*), as is shown in Figure 1. Suppose that we had a ChineseGlyph dictionary; then our charactle would be:

```
[
   Type: ChineseGlyph
   Entry: míng
]
```

and the dictionary entry for '*míng*', giving the full set of strokes, would be:

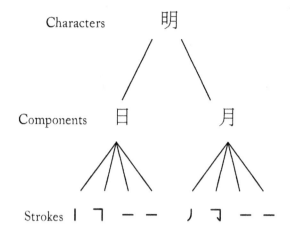

Figure 1: Decomposition of character '*míng*'

```
[
  Type: ChineseGlyph
  RadicalOrder: LeftRight
  RadicalOrder: LeftRight
  Left:  [
         0: "shù"
         1: "héng zhé"
         2: "héng"
         3: "héng"
        ]
  Right: [
         0: "piě"
         1: "héng zhé gōu"
         2: "héng"
         3: "héng"
        ]
]
```

4. ARCHAIC GLYPHS

When studying the early stages of development of the alphabet, there are a number of glyphs that are found around the Mediterranean basin and beyond, with a wide variety of presentation forms. Unicode includes the Italic scripts, which is the result of a long process by scholars of "Italic-unification", where it has been determined that several presentation forms actually correspond to a single character.

But suppose that the Italic writings were only just now being discovered. Then initially, all of the presentation forms would have to be considered to be separate characters, until such time as they could be brought together into equivalence classes. For example, Bernal [1, Table 5, p.39] gives a table of early Italian alphabets, with a number of presentation forms for each phonetic value. Our model would allow all of these to be considered separate charactles, and later as different versions of more abstract charactles.

Being able to do this kind of thing is important for the purposes of scholarly analysis. Over time, as a series of seemingly isolated glyphs are being studied, it becomes clear that these do fall in equivalence classes. Yet, at every stage of the analysis, one can write a document unambiguously, reflecting the current state of the analysis, and that document remains unchanged for posterity.

5. IMAGES

When studying steles in archæology: exact images are required for presentation, discussion and analysis, yet these still need to be treated as 'characters'. Figure 2 presents one such example, a cartouche at the bottom of the obelisk in the center of Paris's *Place de la Concorde* [2], originally from Luxor Temple in Egypt.

Figure 2: Cartouche from Luxor Obelisk in Paris

Then our charactle could be:

```
[
  Type: EgyptianCartouche
  Entry: "LuxorCartouche"
]
```

and the corresponding entry in the `EgyptianCartouche` dictionary could look like:

```
[
  CurrentLocation: "Place de la Concorde, Paris"
  CurrentDate: 1833
  OriginalLocation: "Temple, Luxor"
  OriginalDate: "3300BP"
  PNGfile: "LuxorCartouche.png"
]
```

6. LOGOS

Our last example is something that is becoming increasingly common. Consider the following:

Click 🔍 to launch ArcMap.

where an icon replaces a word or a phrase. Visually, this is similar to a Chinese character, except there is no encoding. However, with our model, we could have a dictionary of logos, hence logo charactles.

7. WORDS

The original use of a dictionary was to create a list of words from one or more languages, placed in some regular order, and to give meanings for these words.

If we are using dictionaries to define our characters, can words themselves be used as charactles? The answer is yes. Consider the Latin sentence:

"*Ille ut Histiæus mandavěrat fecit.*"

It can be consided to be composed of five charactles, one for each word:

```
[
  Type: LatinWord
  entry: "ille"
  context :
  [
    element: "demonstrative pronoun"
    declension: "nominative masculine singular"
  ]
]

[
  Type: LatinWord
  entry: "ut"
  context :
  [
    element: "preposition"
  ]
]

[
  Type: LatinWord
  entry: "Histiæ"
  context :
  [
    element: "proper noun"
    declension: "2nd nominative masculine singular"
  ]
]

[
  Type: LatinWord
  entry: "mandare"
  context :
  [
    element: "verb"
    tense: "pluperfect indicative active"
    person: "3rd singular"
  ]
]

[
  Type: LatinWord
  entry: "fecere"
  context :
  [
    element: "verb"
    tense: "perfect indicative active"
    person: "3rd singular"
  ]
]
```

Representing a text as a sequence of words is common practice for the purposes of search engines. It also allows all languages to be handled at an equal level, as was done by the late John DeFrancis in his pinyin-entried bilingual Chinese-English dictionary [6].

8. CONCLUSIONS

We have come up with a more general concept of character, which we call a *charactle*, i.e., a tuple representing a character. This notion of character is a generalization of the Unicode character, in which one has a brief means for designating a character (for Unicode, a number), and then a dictionary keeping track of the properties of the individual characters.

With charactles, we can encode all sort of different kinds of characters, including Unicode characters, font glyphs, historic glyphs, JPEG images, and even words or word-stems with grammatical analysis attached. This means that a text can be encoded at a number of different levels, and is not stuck with the linear sequence of Unicode characters that might be typed in directly by a user [7].

But it is not just the set of different charactles that can be encoded that is important. Because of the distinction of the callouts to the dictionary entries and the dictionary entries themselves, these new charactles can easily be entered into a text, using LaTeX or XML syntax, or into a search stream. Similarly, it should be easy to write rules for their visual presentation on different substrates.

We consider this work to be a first step towards developing the *Cartesian document*, in which every aspect of a document, from the highest component right down to the last byte, is indexed in a multidimensional space.

9. REFERENCES

[1] Martin Bernal. *Cadmean Letters: The Transmission of the Alphabet to the Aegean and Further West before 1400* B.C. Eisenbrauns, 1990.

[2] Wikipedia Commons. Image of Obelisk in Paris, 2006. upload.wikimedia.org/wikipedia/commons/3/31/Obeliskparis.jpg.

[3] The Unicode Consortium. www.unicode.org/Public/UNIDATA/UnicodeData.txt.

[4] The Unicode Consortium. www.unicode.org/reports/tr44/#UnicodeData.txt.

[5] The Unicode Consortium. *The Unicode Standard 5.0.* Addison-Wesley, 2007.

[6] John DeFrancis, editor. *ABC Chinese-English Comprehensive Dictionary.* University of Hawaii Press, 2003.

[7] John Plaice and Chris Rowley. Characters are not simply names, nor documents trees. In *Glyph and Typesetting Workshop*, East Asian Center for Informatics in Humanities, Kyoto University, 2003. coe21.zinbun.kyoto-u.ac.jp/papers/ws-type-2003/009-plaice.pdf.

[8] Charles M. Schulz. Peanuts comic strip.

[9] Wai Wong, Candy L. K. Yiu, and Kelvin C. F. Ng. Typesetting rare Chinese characters in LaTeX. *TUGboat*, 24(3):582–587, 2003. www.tug.org/TUGboat/Articles/tb24-3/wong.pdf.

Author Index

www.ingramcontent.com/pod-product-compliance
Lightning Source LLC
Chambersburg PA
CBHW080401060326
40689CB00019B/4095